**Books are to be returned on or before
the last date below**

LIBREX —

Documents of
European Economic History

VOLUME THREE

The End of the Old Europe 1914-1939

Sidney Pollard

Professor of Economic History, University of Sheffield

Colin Holmes

Senior Lecturer in Economic History, University of Sheffield

Edward Arnold

Printed in Great Britain by
Cox & Wyman Ltd, London, Fakenham and Reading

Table of Contents

v

Contents

Contents

Contents

Contents

Contents

Introduction

The Europe which went to war in 1914 was part of a single civilization, and in many senses it formed a single community. There were, to be sure, important differences in national characteristics, and these gave European cultural life its richness and variety, and there were also important clashes of national political interests, which ultimately led to the war. But the societies of Western and Central Europe, the societies around the Baltic and the northern shores of the Mediterranean, had a recognizably similar structure, similar ideals and similar aspirations. Even in Russia the Slavophils had made no headway, except as instruments of imperial expansion, and while the tsars' governments moved slowly in the direction of the West by the emancipation of the serfs, by railway building and by pressing the Stolypin reforms on the peasantry, the active opposition parties, Liberals and Marxists alike, had it even more clearly in mind to follow in the Western footsteps. This was also true, *a fortiori*, of the countries bordering on Russia, like Austria or Roumania.

The war itself did not, at first, change this sense of a common destiny. It kept the character, and the ferocity, of an internecine struggle, in spite of the participation in it of such countries as Turkey, Japan, the U.S.A. and the colonies of the main belligerents. Indeed, it was permissible to believe at its end that the transformation of imperial Germany into a liberal–democratic republic and the redrawing of her frontiers in line with the nationality of the populations concerned, together with the translation of the antiquated Austro–Hungarian monarchy into a set of constitutionally governed nation states, represented nothing more than a giant and overdue step forward in the inexorable march of progress. And progress, in turn, consisted of the conversion of Europe to the ideals of the British, the American and the French revolutions of the seventeenth and eighteenth centuries, the ideals of the liberal, bourgeois, capitalist nation state.

Yet such a view would have been superficial. The war interrupted, and often redirected, many streams of historical development at critical stages of their progress in a way which ensured that history did not take its expected course. Above all, it directed the development of the working-class movements away from the channel taken by the Anglo-Saxon model in which it had come about that, at the time that the proletariat was strong and self-confident enough to have some political power and to use it, it was also sufficiently well off not to wish to overturn the existing order. The war altered both sides of the equation in opposite directions. On the one hand, it lowered real standards of living, while on the other it removed the stability of existing governments with all their administrative apparatus and claims to loyalty, which have always been among the strongest barriers to revolution. Thus in Europe east of France, the war ended not only in political upheavals and revolutions, but these were accompanied by attempts at social revolution. Much of the accepted political and social map of Europe was changed before they were ultimately put down everywhere in the end – except in Russia.

Russia proved to be too large for the war-weary armies of the West to reconquer, and remained a symbol of the breakdown of European society and a challenge to its future. It was a tragedy that the attempted counter-revolutionary intervention served to confirm the belief of Russia's Marxist rulers that the 'liberal' West was liberal only as long as its bourgeois rule was not threatened, but would not shrink from using even the most violent means to prevent a genuine social revolution. Russia, as a result, went back to a siege economy and the rule of an obscurantist authoritarianism, albeit of a very different kind from the former one, and the Left in the rest of Europe was permanently split and fatally weakened.

Elsewhere, too, the hopes of liberal progress were to be disappointed. In country after country, electoral democracy, giving potential power to the masses of the poor, proved to be incompatible with a social system which was built up on inequality and propertyless labour, at least as long as there was no rapid absolute increase in national wealth to take the sting out of labour's demand for justice. Alas, the years of prosperity were too few for this increase to operate effectively. Instead, there was the post-war slump, there was inflation, and beginning in 1929 there was the worst economic depression in the history of Europe. As the poor began to doubt the value of the economic system, the rich began to doubt the value of democracy. One by one, beginning with Italy, governments turned authoritarian or Fascist rulers took over, even though in some of the Austrian successor states and in the Balkans, Fascist type governments had neither the excuse of having to settle social disorder, nor the saving grace of technical efficiency. Economic progress was stultified and social progress reversed.

In Germany, the economic crises were aggravated by the terms of the Peace settlement, including the vexed issue of reparations. Some of the tortuous turns and twists of the financial and economic policies imposed upon her between 1918 and 1933 are traced in Chapter 4: suffice it to say here that, in turn, they served to impoverish the middle classes, the agrarian classes, the workers and the lower middle classes, so that when mass unemployment and national bankruptcy faced the nation in 1932–1933, there was no one willing to oppose the organized madness of the Nazi party which took over the German state in 1933. The lights had indeed begun to go out in Europe when its most powerful government set out systematically to destroy its civilized heritage and plan aggressive war against its neighbours.

Much has been made, in Germany and elsewhere, of the responsibility of the Allies, and of the defeat of 1918 itself, for that disaster. But these circumstances, though they were real enough, merely served to sharpen a more universal tendency. For it was not only Germany and the countries mentioned above, but also others, like Portugal and Spain, that fell into the hands of the Fascist dictators, and even relatively privileged countries, like France and Belgium, had large and virulent Fascist parties in the late 1930s. There seemed to be no way of dealing rationally with an economic system that produced slumps, poverty and the hopelessness of unemployment – at a time when the victims had votes, and therefore promises of better things; and Europe seemed therefore on the way to turning increasingly to the irrational and the destruction of its own tradition.

No history can ignore those developments. But a truthful account must note also that in spite of slumps, restrictions, unemployment and distress, economic progress and the growth of national output was probably faster than ever before, over the period as a whole. After 1920, the increase in income was faster still owing to the relative price fall of European imports. Based on a rapidly developing technology, Europe began to enjoy new technical marvels, like mass-produced cars, aircraft, radios and the cinema, together with an undreamt-of expansion or improvement of older consumption goods and services, including housing, medical services, holidays, and mass-produced clothing, confectionery and preserved foods. In Russia, too, after the destructive storms of war, civil war and collectivization, output began to grow at unprecedented rates under the Five-Year Plans, though as yet mostly in the form of capital goods and armaments, with little to show for the consumer beyond minimum food and advanced medical and other social welfare provisions. Nazi Germany cured unemployment faster than any other Western nation after 1933, but all the increase, and according to some, more than the whole net increase, was swallowed up by rearmament and the stockpiling of war stores rather than being made available to the consumer, though even there, socially provided welfare, including holidays, became available to the mass of the population for the first time.

Looking back on this period after the lapse of more than thirty years, it is tempting to view much of it as an aberration, an interruption of the normal upward movement, particularly of material goods and economic services available to the people of Europe at large, and the parallel rise of their liberties and their culture. Since the Second World War, we have been incomparably more successful in banishing crises and depressions, in preventing mass unemployment, and in enjoying the increasing fruits of an improved productive apparatus, while combining political democracy with social peace. But can we be sure that economic prosperity will continue and permit all classes to share in the increment of output, as well as enjoying more leisure, more culture, and better working conditions? Can we be sure that, given a major economic failure, there will not be another plunge into the abyss of unreason?

One conclusion is clear. The economic power of the United States, which assumed critical importance on the Continent of Europe after the First World War, has come to overshadow Europe completely after the second. Beside the United States, there are the economic giants of Soviet Russia and Japan, and the awakening economies of China and the 'underdeveloped' world to challenge Europe's economic leadership, as they have successfully deprived her of her political privileges. If we had wanted to carry this story forward past 1939 into a fourth volume, we could not have made sense of the European economy in isolation from those other areas. The brief centuries, when Europe carried the banner of human progress, mainly because of her astonishing economic and industrial successes, are over. She must now find her place as one continent among the others in the emergent world economy.

The documents contained in Volume 3 have been selected and arranged on the same principles as in Volumes 1 and 2. Our main consideration has been one of space, and the need to fit in many themes from several countries into so limited a volume. We have, therefore, as before, tried to select documents which would each illustrate more than a single theme; we have attempted to favour documents which do so most succinctly; and, unlike some other collections, we have included very few complete documents, but have limited ourselves almost exclusively to extracts, so that by cutting out the formalities and inessentials, more of the real meat may be presented to the reader. It is for the same reason that we have reluctantly ignored the advice of some of the critics of Volume 1 who had urged us to introduce each document separately, showing its origins, its value and reliability, its consequences, and so on. Here too, we have considered that every paragraph by us would deprive the reader of a paragraph of contemporary material and we have therefore confined our comments, as in Volumes 1 and 2 to a general introduction to each chapter and have added only the briefest description and attribution for each document. As in the case of the earlier volumes, it is imperative that this collection shall be used together with, and not in substitution for, general books on the economic history of Europe.

In the matter of translation, also, we have held to our former principles. Wherever possible we have used documents in English, or existing English translations, amending the latter, in some cases substantially, or bringing them up to date, where necessary. Our own translations are marked as such. American documents have been anglicized throughout.

As before, we have to acknowledge a great deal of help from many quarters. In the first place, we wish to thank Mr Roger Munting of the University of East Anglia and Mr Everett M. Jacobs of the University of Sheffield for assistance in the translation of documents in the Russian language. The librarians and their staffs of the following institutions have borne with us with great patience and efficiency: Berkeley University Library, California, Birmingham University Library, British Museum, Hoover Library, Stanford, Institute of Historical Research, London, London School of Economics and Political Science Library, Nottingham Public Library and Sheffield University Library. We are particularly grateful to the many publishers who have permitted us to reprint extracts from their works: the list is too long to be included here and appears separately. Last, but not least, we are much indebted to Miss Helen Trippett, Miss J. A. Taylor and Mrs Helen Cox for their skill and patience in transforming scrawls and tapes into usable typescript and Mrs Rita Riddle and Mrs Joyce Holmes for their help with the proofs.

Editors.

Abbreviations

Ed.   = Editors, i.e. of the present volume. Editorial footnotes and comments in our sources, some of which originally carried a similar identifying label 'Ed.' have had these removed and appear without that attribution.

Ed. Tr.   = Translated by the editors of this volume.
E.M.J. Tr. = Translated by Everett M. Jacobs.
R.M. Tr.   = Translated by Roger Munting.

Acknowledgements

The Editors and Publisher wish gratefully to acknowledge permission given by the following to reproduce documents in this volume: Felix Alcan (Paris), 1/2, 1/6b; Allen & Unwin, 1/16; Alliance Nationale contre la Population, 7/2; American Academy of Political and Social Science, 5/28, 5/30; British Communist Party, 2/17; Cassell, 1/26b; Century Historical Series (N.Y.), 1/13; Chapman & Dodd, 7/24; Clarendon Press, 1/12; 1/15a, 1/15b, 7/7; Armand Colin (Paris), 3/22, 7/8; Columbia University Press, 6/22; Constable, 1/25a; Cresset, 7/14; Editions de Cygne, 7/23a, 7/23c; Imprimeries Delmas (Paris), 7/12b; John Day, 4/2e; Dietz (Berlin), 1/11a, 1/19, 1/21, 1/22, 1/27; *The Economist*, 4/23, 4/32b, 5/17b, 5/20, 5/21, 5/23a, 5/23b; Europa Publishing Co., 3/14; Fisher Unwin, 4/2a, 7/1; J. M. Dent, 1/17; Peter Hanstein (Bonn), 1/5b, 1/5c; Harcourt Brace Jovanovich, Inc. (renewed 1948 by Lydia Lopokova Keynes), 4/9a; Harrison (London), 1/33; Harvard University Press, 2/11; A. B. Hasse, W. Tullberg's Forläg, 7/27a; H.M.S.O., 1/24d, 1/25b, 1/25d, 1/25e, 1/26b, 1/26d, 3/1, 3/3, 3/4, 3/7, 3/8, 3/12, 3/13, 3/21, 4/11, 4/12a, 4/12b, 4/13, 4/15, 4/25a, 4/25b, 4/26, 4/27, 5/2, 5/11, 5/15, 5/26, 7/3, 7/4, 7/27b, 7/29a, 7/30; Hodder & Stoughton, 4/2d, 4/4a, 4/6a; Hoover Institute, Stanford, California, 1/24b, 1/24c, 1/25a, 1/25c, 1/26a, 1/26c; *L'Illustration*, 7/28; Institute of Economics, Washington, 4/17a; International Labour Office, 3/5, 5/31, 7/23b; International Military Tribunal, Nuremberg, 6/10; Jarrold's (London), 4/24, 4/29a, 4/29b, 4/31, 4/32a, 6/17, 6/19; Juncker & Dünnhaupt (Berlin), 6/5, 6/6, 6/7, 6/8, 6/9c; P. S. King, 3/19, 4/19, 7/32, 7/33; Alan Lane, 2/19; League of Nations, 3/2, 3/15, 3/18a, 3/18b, 4/8, 5/10, 5/12, 5/27, 7/16, 7/20; Macmillan, 1/4a, 1/8, 1/9, 1/24, 2/4, 2/18, 2/23, 4/5b, 4/10, 4/22, 4/29d, 5/13a, 5/13b, 5/14, 5/16, 5/29, 6/2a, 6/15, 6/21a, 6/23, 7/18, 7/34a; *Manchester Guardian*, 2/5; Methuen, 6/2c, 7/13a, 7/35b; Modern Books, 2/20; Musterschmidt (Göttingen), 1/29, 6/1; National Industrial Conference Board (N.Y.), 3/9; Oxford University Press, 1/6a, 1/20, 4/2c, 4/4c, 4/14, 4/16a, 4/34b, 5/1, 5/3, 5/5, 5/6, 5/7, 5/8, 5/9, 5/18a, 5/22, 6/14a, 6/14b, 6/21b, 7/5; Pitman, 3/16, 5/4; Rand McNally, 2/21; Reclam (Stuttgart), 1/1, 1/7a, 1/7b, 1/7c, 1/7d; *Revue des deux mondes*, 5/18b; Routledge and Kegan Paul, 2/26b, 2/27, 3/10, 7/6, 7/15, 7/31; John Scot, 2/22, 2/24; Sirey (Paris), 4/32e, 5/17a, 5/19, 5/25; *The Statist*, 1/24b; *Journal of the Royal Statistical Society*, 4/2b; Tandem Books, 4/16b, 6/3, 6/13; *The Times*, 4/34a, 7/29b, 7/34b; United States Government Printer, 1/23, 1/28, 1/31, 1/32, 7/19a, 7/19b; Van Nostrand, 2/26c; Otto Walter (Olten and Konstanz, Switzerland), 4/33; Weidenfeld, 7/35c; Dokumenten-Verlag Herbert Wendler (Berlin), 1/3, 1/5a, 1/5d, 1/11b, 1/30, 4/1b, 4/3, 4/18, 4/29a, 6/2b, 6/9b, 6/11a, 6/12, 6/16, 6/18, 6/20; Yale University Press, 1/10, 4/2c, 4/7a, 7/17.

Chapter 1   The War of 1914-1918 and its Aftermath

Introduction

At the outbreak of the war in August 1914, the leaders and planners on both sides thought in terms of a quick military victory. They had in their minds the kind of war represented by the Austro–Prussian War of 1866 and the Franco–Prussian War of 1870, or perhaps by the wars fought more recently by Japan, rather than the prolonged attrition of the American Civil War. The issue as they saw it, therefore, was to let their country's feature of strength come into play as rapidly as possible – the massive armies of Russia, German military skill and speed of mobilization, or the British navy – and meanwhile to expand the production of military supplies by traditional means, and prevent a panic in the only sphere in which previous experience would have led one to expect it, banking and finance. There was also some fear, in most countries, of unemployment in the early stages of the conflict.

These expectations proved wholly erroneous, except in one respect: in every country the banking and financial community turned out to have the weakest nerves, and to be the least patriotic, of all the sectors of society. As a result, payments moratoria were introduced in the major financial centres, and the gold standard was suspended at once by all the belligerents (1/1). This latter measure was generally passed in order to prevent the private hoarding of gold and thus the enforced suspension of gold payments with its attendant dislocations, but as in former wars, it also opened up the possibility of financing the war, at least in part, by inflation rather than by the taxation or the borrowing of genuine savings (1/33). Partly because of the false hope of an early end to the war, taxation was cranked up only slowly to meet the needs of governments and to withdraw purchasing power from the people, but excess profits taxes (1/4b) were enacted early in the war in order to reduce the gains and to minimize the evils of war profiteering (1/2, 1/3).

The degree of profiteering depended mainly on the speed and efficiency with which the different countries managed to control supplies, output and prices, or, in other words, on the success of the controlled war economy. For the central economic problem of the war turned out to be a very similar one in all the belligerent countries: how to deal with the enormous demands on manpower and resources, how to keep the armies in the field as well as the

1

civilian population at home supplied with their necessities, without permitting inflation, social unrest and social injustice to get out of hand because of failures in distribution, and how to carry all this through while productive powers were diminished and foreign trade was interrupted.

With import demand as high as ever and export capacity devoted to war production, one of the specific shortages was that of foreign exchange, to pay for supplies from the U.S.A. and the neutral world. France was not the only country to conscript holdings of foreign assets (**1/4a**) or to control the spending of foreign currency. But everywhere the most pervasive shortage was that of labour. Several belligerents, like Germany, attempted a form of direction of male labour (**1/5a, d**). To some extent, the labour shortage could be relieved by mobilizing female labour, for which some statistics are provided by the French experience (**1/6a, b**).

In all countries the labour shortage greatly improved the bargaining position of labour, to ensure at least that earnings, if not wages, rose in line with the cost of living. It also became necessary to expand welfare and protective legislation in order to keep the men at work and the munitions flowing. Despite the easy profits in many industries the war, by these economic-political effects of the labour shortage, greatly shifted power away from capital and to labour. Thus, in spite of the objections of some die-hard employers' associations who took time off to be troubled, *inter alia*, about the effects of a liberal attitude on the *next* war, official opinion had to support the strengthening of trade unions and the creation of Works Councils in Germany (**1/5b, c**).

German rent control became effective in 1917 and was strengthened in 1918 (**1/7e**). But it was food distribution and food prices which became the most sensitive areas of public social policy. Germany, hit by the blockade and not wholly self-sufficient in food, built up an expanding apparatus of control to minimize reductions of yield from the native soil, and that staple food was 'stretched' by the admixture of inferior and less palatable substitutes (**1/7a, b, c, d**). The country had been similarly vulnerable in the case of several strategic raw materials and, like Britain, built up step by step, in a halting, searching way and by necessity rather than by choice, a method of rationing raw materials in accordance with overall strategic demands (**1/8**). When countries with a weaker tradition of social discipline, and a less skilful administrative apparatus, like Austria–Hungary, Turkey or Russia (**1/9**) attempted similar methods of allocation and control, they were unable to match the economic demands of modern total war. As the war proceeded, both their war production and their social fabric slowly disintegrated behind the lines, almost in isolation from the military successes or reverses of their armies.

However, it proved impossible even for the best-organized military power on the Continent, Germany, to keep up the necessary consumer goods and food supplies in view of the withdrawal of so much of her male labour to the forces, and the general shortage of so many of the necessary raw material and capital inputs. The ill-effects of this, from the point of view of the successful prosecution of the war, was at least as much psychological as material, and, rather unexpectedly, the demoralization of the belligerent populations arose as much from failures of supplies at home and from the crass differences between the rich, including the war profiteers, and the poor, including the invalids, the widows and the orphans of war, as it did from military reverses. Germany, for example, never succeeded in dealing adequately with this threat (**1/10**), and it was ultimately the hunger as well as the American armies which sapped her power of resistance (**1/11a, b**). In Russia, too, starvation was one direct source of the Revolution (**1/12**).

The basic causes of the two Russian revolutions of February and October 1917 lay, of course, buried much more deeply in Russian society and Russian history. The peasants' hunger for land, and their common belief that they had been cheated out of a portion of it by the Emancipation Edict and by the policies which followed it, led to some forcible expropriation of land and the general assertion of peasants' rights as soon as law and order broke down in the chaos of war and of the February Revolution (**1/13**). It was on the basis of meeting these demands for land, for peace, and for some elementary civil rights for the great majority of the Russian population represented by the peasantry, that the Bolsheviks, whose original support base had been the numerically small industrial proletariat, rose to power in October 1917, and held on to that power despite the assaults by the other Socialist Party, the 'Mensheviks', and the Social Revolutionaries who claimed above all others to represent that peasantry (**1/14**). Thus among the first decrees of the new Soviet Government, controlled by Lenin's Bolshevik Party, was a decree nationalizing the land and awarding its use to those who were working it, but not to those who would employ others to work it (**1/15a**); and a decree establishing a primitive system of workers' control over industry (**1/15b**). Coupled with what in effect became a unilateral declaration of peace, these measures were symbolic of the workers'-soldiers'-peasants' alliance on which Soviet power was built, and on which it attempted to rescue the State from the administrative collapse and foreign invasions which it had suffered under the preceding regimes.

In the following years there was more than one occasion when that task seemed greater than the new Soviet State could bear, as former enemies, like the Germans, and former allies, like the British, the Poles, the Czechs and the Japanese, sent their armies into Russia, operating on their own or in support of remnants of Russian armies which were opposed to the Bolshevik Revolution. The savage civil war of those weary years destroyed most of what was left of industry, services and transport networks in Russia: some of the economic effects on the villages, on industry and on the food supply are illustrated in documents 1/16 and 1/17.

In Germany, hunger, war-weariness, mismanagement and the threatened military collapse after so much sacrifice in blood also created a revolutionary situation, but the German 'Revolution' of 1918 had only limited political implications, such as the proclamation of a Republic in place of the Empire, and ultimately a new constitution; it was not, like the Russian, a thorough-going social upheaval. For one thing, the army and state apparatus was not destroyed, but survived the war remarkably well; for another, in Germany, as in France, in Britain and in the other belligerents, the Socialist parties and the trade unions had become intensely patriotic during the war and had become totally identified with the Government and its war effort (1/18, 1/21b), so that the opposition had to work largely outside these bodies and was correspondingly slower to develop.

Yet in Germany, too, intolerable conditions gradually led to revolutionary sentiments among the workers (1/11a, 1/19). When the wage demands put forward in desperation went unheeded and strikes like those in the Berlin munitions industries in 1917 (1/21a, b) and the widespread January strikes of 1918 (1/22) broke out, the official bureaucracy of the Social-Democratic Unions was too compromised, and the leadership and political influence fell therefore to the revolutionary 'Spartacus' group. These strikes in the last few months of the war were later to be used by extremist nationalist propaganda to divert attention from the failure of German arms and to blame the defeat on the Socialists and Communists. In France, the strike movement was intensified in the same period, and for similar causes (1/20).

When the fighting ended in November 1918, at least in the West, the long-term economic damage of the war could begin to be assessed. Production had declined in most sectors, as in French agriculture (1/23). In some areas, like Belgium and Northern France, the damage was limited to the physical equipment (1/24a, b), while the local administration, and the link with the rest of the national economy, could quickly be restored. But elsewhere – and above all in the Austrian successor states – not only did the administration collapse together with its financial creditworthiness, (1/25a), but the new frontiers, maintained by rampant nationalism and inexperienced governments, paralysed whatever economic powers of recovery there might have been (1/25b, c, d). In Germany, the growing failure of the food supply, evident throughout the war years, turned rapidly into widespread starvation in the months following the armistice, in the midst of local revolutions, the breakdown in transport and the loss of certain provinces – though the Germans themselves were inclined to lay much greater blame on the actions of the Allies than on their own mismanagement in the war years (**1/26a, b, c, d, e**). In Austria, starvation was concentrated in Vienna, now without an accessible agrarian hinterland (**1/26f, g, h, j**).

Just as hunger and mismanagement, including inflation, (**1/33**), had brought great popular support to the revolutionary parties all over Europe, the relief of hunger, even of ex-enemies, was made palatable to the Western Allies as a counter-revolutionary weapon (**1/26c**). The massive Hoover Relief Administration itself operated on a mixture of humanitarian and political motives, and used its powers over life and death to prevent Soviet-style revolutions or to reverse them where they had actually occurred, as in Hungary.

In the early, confused days of the German 'Revolution', when those who had opposed the war all along, clearly had the upper hand in the working-class quarters, the employers were glad to make the kind of general agreement which was concluded with the official leadership a few days after the armistice (**1/27**) (though it contained demands they had always bitterly opposed), for fear of having to concede something worse to the militants. However, all sections of the labour movement, from the Spartacists, and soon the Communists, who worked for a Soviet-type revolution, to the moderates, who wished to maintain a liberal-bourgeois state (and the numerous groupings in between), were agreed on certain minimal reforms. These included the legal limitation of hours, the right to organize freely and bargain collectively, and a share in the management of firms, the right of co-determination by means of joint councils with parity of representation of workers and employers, as foreshadowed in the heads of agreement of 15 November. The Provisional Government supported these by formal decree in December 1918 (**1/28**). For a time the unions moved further to the left, and in the 'Guide Lines' laid down by the 1919 Trades Union Congress (**1/29**) even the official leadership subscribed to a programme which envisaged large-scale nationalization and the independent role of trade unions in socialized industry. But employers could count on the continued support of those union leaders who had collaborated with them during the war and who wanted a return to law and order (**1/30**). A reaction set in soon, and in the counter-revolutionary atmosphere of 1920 the works council which gave the workers some indirect say in the management of their firms became a symbol of the unions' post-war gains, a sticking point which they were unwilling to give up. The formal Act establishing works councils was passed in January 1920 and became law in February (**1/31**), but in the long run the typical German firm was able to absorb and contain the workers' representatives without allowing the balance of power to shift within the firm to any appreciable extent (**1/32**).

Thus, in one way and another, Europe west of Soviet Russia was preserved from social revolution; but the memory of hunger and administrative collapse, and the national rivalries and hatreds associated with the war and its aftermath could not so easily be eradicated from the mind of Europe.

1/1 Suspension of the Gold Standard in Germany

KARL PANNIER, *Kriegsgesetze des deutschen Reiches* (14 vols., Leipzig, 1915–1918), vol. I, pp. 53–55. (Ed. Tr.)

Act Amending the Coinage Act, of 4 August 1914

1. Until further notice, the provisions of the Coinage Act of 1 June 1909, paragraph 9, sections 2 and 3 are altered in this respect, that Reich Treasury Notes (*Reichskassenscheine*) and Reichsbank notes may be used in payment in place of gold coins. . . .

Act Regarding Reich Treasury Notes and Bank Notes, of 4 August 1914

1. Until further notice, Reich Treasury Notes are legal tender. . . .
2. Until further notice, the Reich Treasury shall not be obliged to cash its Reich Treasury Notes, and the Reichsbank shall not be obliged to cash its banknotes.
3. Until further notice, the private banks shall have the right to use Reichsbank notes in the encashment of their own notes. . . .

1/2 War Profiteering in France

G. RENARD, *Les répercussions économiques de la guerre actuelle sur la France* (Paris, 1917), pp. 59–62. (Ed. Tr.)

If many of the luxury hotels, 'palaces', as we call them, have become temporary hospitals or have been closed for lack of guests, the average and the small-sized hotels in many centres have done a roaring trade. This has happened wherever circumstances have led to an increase in the floating population. For example, Le Havre, which is the British army base and provisional capital of Belgium, has swarmed with officers, ministers and people with well-filled purses; a shower of gold has rained down on those who were in a position to provide the newcomers with accommodation and food. Exactly the same kind of situation prevailed in Boulogne, Marseilles and Bordeaux, during the period when Bordeaux was a miniature Paris.

Elsewhere, where workers have been called *en masse* to work in the war industries, at Bourges, Firminy and Châtel-lerault, they were charged at first large sums for board and lodging and even if they earned quite high wages, they were able to keep only a small amount in their own pockets. In the countryside and the suburbs, benefits such as unemployment relief have been an unexpected windfall for the working classes and the hard working and steady women have spent this money on home improvements and those less serious in outlook, on ribbons, fancy goods and high living. Travellers in cheap women's clothes have never done such business in the villages; and in the towns, the cinemas, small theatres, those selling choice foods, and sometimes, alas! the bars have benefited from an exceptional increase in purchasing power which stemmed from certain families of those who had been mobilized not having to pay their rents and also from the small daily sums of relief which they received. At, or near the front, the peasants have often sold wine and food to the *poilus** at more than profitable prices, and cheap-jacks have on more than one occasion abused the fact that they were the only ones to enter into the dangerous war zone, by increasing the prices of their shoddy goods and taking away the increases in pay earned by the soldiers.

It is also important not to forget the small workshops which the war has brought into being or made to prosper; those concerned with producing sleeping bags, woollen goods, sweaters, balaclavas, stoves for the trenches, bullet shields, first aid equipment, and those making mourning clothes and funeral wreaths; photographers, besieged by crowds of mothers, sisters, fiancées and friends eager to send their portrait to some absent loved one or even by soldiers wishing to perpetuate the memory of the fine figure they cut when in uniform; street hawkers who plastered their illustrated postcards on the windows of disused shops and whose gaily coloured displays will always remain one of the most picturesque aspects of Parisian life during the Great War; toy dealers offering peaceful cannons or multi-coloured lead soldiers; sellers of candles and ex-voto for novenas, through which people implored heaven for miracles, victory or the safety of a loved one; [and finally], sellers of hope. I refer to the increasing number of all kinds of clairvoyants who, in return for cash, you must understand, gave to all those who wanted them, prophecies, charms, and infallible secrets, guaranteed to prevent wounding or death.

One could easily give many more examples of cheap-jacks, whose business has found a favourable soil. But their profits are only trifles when compared with those amassed by the large-scale profiteers. I refer to those who have supplied the state, who have obtained contracts with the commissariat. There is a tradition according to our fathers that these suppliers never did badly for

* French soldiers. (Ed.)

7

themselves. In spite of a more active surveillance than has existed before, the practice has not been checked. Whether it is a question of meat, or fodder, horses or oats, explosives or vegetables, clothes or barbed-wire, the profits have been considerable, especially at first, when the urgency of the situation did not allow any discussion of the proposed conditions of sale. We have heard in the Chamber of the case when, either through the oversight or connivance of some civil servant, the price given for goods exceeded what was asked. Wheat offered at 18 francs 50 and 20 francs per hectolitre has been generously paid for at 23 francs. Alternative suppliers were ignored because an influential competitor already had an arrangement with the authorities. If only excessive payments by the Treasury went to the producers! But the latter were often unable to engage in such transactions; I have before me the letter of a proprietor who, wanting to sell several thousand hectolitres of wine direct to a military hospital, recoiled in fear before the Draconian demands of the *Cahier de Charges*, which it was attempted to impose on him. In such a case it was the middlemen, buying cheaply and selling at high prices, who benefited from the situation; sometimes even, a considerable commission business accrued to shady characters, who had done nothing except bring the two contracting parties together. And I have said nothing about certain supplies which were the subject of scandal; clogs with cardboard soles, bad cod, rotten potatoes, etc., nor of the hoarding attempted by some speculators in order to increase artificially the price of coal, oats, meat, etc.

There are then a number of traders who have profited from the war; they have become the *nouveaux riches*. But they are few. Most traders have suffered from the war. In some cases, dare I say it, it is a suffering which is, in part, also salutary. I have reserved until the last two of the most beneficial effects of the war; firstly, the temporary, but almost complete suppression of Austro-German competition, which allows French merchants to recover in France and elsewhere, the position they had lost and also to conquer new markets; then the shock imposed on their sleepy personalities, the conviction hence-forth implanted in their brains, that it is necessary for their well-being and that of the nation for them to offer a systematic and dogged resistance to the dangers which the war has brought to light. These two things may com-pensate for many of the losses.

1/3 War Profiteering in Germany

Memorandum dated 12 July 1917 by Capt. Richard Merton, an officer on the staff of the Head of the German War Bureau, together with a covering note by Lt. General Groener to Michaelis, the Reich Chancellor, dated 25 July 1917. Printed in HERBERT MICHAELIS and ERNST SCHRAEPLER, *Ursachen und Folgen. Vom deutschen*

Zusammenbruch 1918 und 1945 bis zur staatlichen Neuordnung Deutschlands in der Gegenwart. Eine Urkunden- und Dokumentensammlung zur Zeitgeschichte (16 vols., Berlin, 1958–1970), vol. I, pp. 216–220. (Ed. Tr.)

(*Covering Note*) . . . I hereby transmit to your Excellency a memorandum regarding the necessity for official intervention for the purpose of regulating profits and wages.

I am wholly in favour of the thoughts and the objectives on which the memorandum is based. Since the commencement of my work as Head of the War Bureau I have observed with growing anxiety how demoralizing the effect of the exploitation of the war prosperity carried on ruthlessly on all sides has been on our war economy and our total economy. . . .

(*Memorandum*) If we look back on the development of the war economy and ask ourselves what was the mainspring that ensured that German industry succeeded in such astonishing manner to meet the constantly growing requirements of the war, we have to conclude that such ethical motives as self sacrifice, patriotism, etc., have played only a minor part, and that in the creative urge which has emerged, and the incredible achievements evidenced in all spheres of the munitions industry, the profit motive has been almost exclusively the root of all good and evil, the cause of all successes and all failures. Moreover, it is a fact that the longer the war has gone on, the more widespread, and the more ruthless has become the urge on all sides to exploit the boom.

This exploitation of the boom was made easier for the munitions suppliers by the lack of economic preparation and expertise on the part of the purchasing agencies everywhere, evident particularly strikingly in the early days of the war. . . .

The longer the war has lasted, the clearer it has become that the development of our war economy by the sole motive of maximizing profits has, in addition to all other demoralizing and economically damaging effects, created one great danger which has begun to handicap increasingly the munitions industry, and which is growing rapidly. This danger arises from developments in the field of wages.

It is no doubt true that it was the question of poor food supplies which has in many cases given rise to labour unrest and to wage demands. But much more important in the whole field of labour unrest is the fact that the workers, for their part, are also increasingly concerned to exploit the boom for themselves by demanding the highest possible wages, which in part bear no relation to their productivity. This has been stated openly in several propaganda leaflets. Further, the growing shortage, first of skilled, and later of any

9

kind of labour, had led industry, which hardly feels any limitation in its pricing and thereby its profit opportunities, to attempt to secure its necessary labour force by mutual bidding up of its price. . . .

There appear to be several possibilities of solving this problem:

1. Revision of existing supply contracts;

2. Sharp increase in the excess profits tax, so that war profits become impossible in practice;

3. The passing of an Act akin to the British Munitions Act, by which the Reich Chancellor will be empowered to put industrial enterprises of all kinds under official control and to fix for them wages and profits according to circumstances. . . .

The best method appears to be an enabling Act on the model of the British Munitions Act. Together with a new war profits tax this may be expected to meet the need fully. The administration of this Act should most usefully be assigned to the War Bureau. . . .

It might also be put to industry that it might well voluntarily reduce its contract prices and thereby put its profit and loss account on a basis which might, in individual cases, make it unnecessary to apply the War Profits Act. Business must understand right now that the war is not an opportunity for profiteering, but on the contrary it demands and, if necessary, enforces sacrifices from everyone.

1/4 Conscription of Wealth in France and Germany

a French Decree on the Loan of Foreign Securities to the State, 1916. Printed in S. B. CLOUGH, T. MOODIE and C. G. MOODIE, *Economic History of Europe: twentieth century* (London, 1969), pp. 53–54.
b German War Taxation Act of 21 June 1916. Printed in ARTHUR NORDEN and MARTIN FRIEDLANDER (ed.), *Das Kriegssteuergesetz (Kriegsgewinnsteurer) vom 21 Juni 1916* (Berlin, 2nd ed., 1917), pp. 207–215. (Ed. Tr.)

a *Article 1.* The (foreign) securities of which a list is given below* can be made, under the conditions herein indicated, the object of a loan of securities to the state, which reserves to itself the right to appropriate them as a pledge on exchange operations to which it has given consent or on credits it has opened. . . .

Article 4. In the event the Treasury judges it necessary to sell any or all of the securities lent, it will pay their value at prices indicated in lists

---

* The list . . . contains, for the most part, long-term loan issues of neutral states. A few railroad stocks and bonds and Suez Canal stocks and bonds were included. The price offered was the market price. (Footnote in Clough.)

established by the Ministry of Finance, or, if the seller prefers, at the highest price quoted in the quarter preceding the announcement of sale.

Article 5. The lenders will have the right to the entire income from their securities under the normal conditions including profits from exchange, if there are any. In addition, they will receive each year a bonus equal to one-quarter (25 per cent) of the annual gross revenue without profits from exchange. This bonus is payable for the first year at the time the securities are delivered and for both the following years when the first coupons fall due in each of those years.

For stocks the bonus will be equal to one-quarter of the dividends of the previous year.

Article 6. The loan may be terminated before the end of the third year: (a) by a notice of termination of the contract by the Treasury, which has reserved the right to do so at any time, in whole or in part with one month's notice, the bonus paid remaining in full the property of the lender; (b) by the purchase by the Treasury of all or part of the securities lent, on condition of one month's notice, the price being fixed according to the provisions indicated above; (c) by the amortization or the redemption of the securities according to the terms of their issue; these securities or their equivalent will be returned to the lenders within three months. . . .

b (1) Private persons included in the Property Tax Act of 3 July 1913, whose property on 31 December 1916 has increased, or has suffered a loss of less than 10 per cent compared with the beginning of the tax period, are liable to an extraordinary war levy in favour of the Reich. . . .

(13) Inland joint-stock companies, commandite* companies having shares, mining associations in as far as they have standing in law as juridical persons, societies with limited liability and registered co-operative societies have to contribute an extraordinary war levy according to the excess profits as established in paras. 14 to 18. . . .

(19) For inland associations the levy shall be:

If annual average excess profits calculated on paid-up capital plus undistributed real reserve capital as proved in the first war year are	% of excess profits
no more than 2%	10
over 2%, but not more than 5%	15
over 5%, but not more than 10%	20
over 10%, but not more than 15%	25
over 15%	30

* See Glossary.

(21) In the case of foreign companies, the levy shall be:

If annual average excess profits are	% of excess profits
up to 20,000 Marks	10
20,000 up to 40,000 Marks	12
40,000 up to 60,000 Marks	14
60,000 up to 80,000 Marks	16
80,000 up to 100,000 Marks	18
100,000 up to 120,000 Marks	20
120,000 up to 140,000 Marks	22
140,000 up to 160,000 Marks	24
160,000 up to 180,000 Marks	26
180,000 up to 200,000 Marks	28
200,000 up to 250,000 Marks	30
250,000 up to 500,000 Marks	40
over 500,000 Marks	45

1/5 Conscription of Labour and Establishment of Works Councils in Germany

a Demand by the High Command for conscription of labour. Hindenburg to the Reich Chancellor, 2 November 1916. Printed in MICHAELIS AND SCHRAEPLER, *Ursachen und Folgen* (*see* Document **1/3**) vol. I, pp. 15–16. (Ed. Tr.)

b Memorandum of the Coal Owners' Association of Essen, 10 August 1915, opposing the recognition of trade unions. Printed in GERHARD ADELMANN, *Quellensammlung zur Geschichte der sozialen Betriebsverfassung: Ruhrindustrie* (2 vols., Bonn, 1960–1965), vol. I, pp. 431–433. (Ed. Tr.)

c Provincial President at Düsseldorf to Deputy Commander of VII Army Corps, Münster, 27 October 1916, in favour of Works Councils. Printed in *Ibid.*, p. 434. (Ed. Tr.)

d Act of 5 December 1916 on National Auxiliary Service (*vaterländischer Hilfsdienst*). Printed in MICHAELIS and SCHRAEPLER, *Ursachen und Folgen* [*see* Document **1/3**] vol. I, pp. 17–21. (Ed. Tr.)

a   Our opponents have at their disposal the factories and working force of the whole of the neutral world; Germany and her allies are limited to their own resources.

The mental superiority of the German soldier, his greater courage and his higher sense of duty and honour cannot outweigh this unbalance to the extent that our enemies are also greatly superior in numbers of population.

In the matter of food supplies the position is similar. This question could also become decisive for the outcome of the war, and in this area also the enemy disposes over more productive sources.

We can therefore win this war only if we provide sufficient supplies to the army so that it meets the enemy on a basis of equality, and if we secure the feeding of the whole population. In view of the vast resources available to our enemies, this will be possible only if everything that our industry and our soil can produce and if all the mineral riches of the country are used solely for waging war. But this maximum utilization can be reached only when the people as a whole enter the service of the fatherland. . . .

I am convinced that it is of the highest importance that an Act should be passed which explicitly extends conscription to the whole male population, covering the ages from the sixteenth to the sixtieth year, and covering employment in the whole of the war economy. . . .

Every man must be pressed into service according to his ability, at the lathe, in the office or in any other occupation in which he is most useful to the country. This will have to be covered by detailed provisions.

We need an Act, because the elected Parliament must bear part of the responsibility and because the population will submit to the new tasks with greater readiness if the Reichstag is drawn into the decision. . . .

b Reports have reached us that there tends to be a view held in military and civilian circles, that differences of opinion have arisen among the employers in the Rhenish-Westphalian mining industry regarding the trade unions and the attitude to the question how possible disagreements between them and their workers might be avoided or arbitrated, and that these differences would permit the conclusion that the employers are less hostile to such ideas as the setting up of a conciliation board than they have been hitherto.

We do not know the reasons for this view, but it is untrue, and we deem it necessary for the preservation of the trust which has been placed in us to deny publicly such speculations and rumours.

Strikingly misreading the facts and experiences which have passed before us in recent years, a view has been voiced in some quarters that the bearing of the workers in the course of this war should induce the employers and the legislature to change their former attitude in principle towards the trade unions. On the contrary: in our view, everyone who has kept an open mind for the lessons of reality must admit that the attitude which we have always had on this question has been the right one. In recent months it has been stated by non-employers a thousand times that German industry has proved itself, *vis-à-vis* the British, to be more efficiently organized, quicker off the mark, more adaptable and better managed, and that we owe it to this circumstance that the military demands on industry which have exceeded all

13

expectations have been met smoothly and that in spite of our great difficulties, our economic life has been preserved from disturbances and dislocations.

One of the main reasons for these facts is the circumstance that in spite of untold difficulties created by the Social Democrats and by public opinion, the German employer had hitherto kept any domination by the trade unions safely at bay. . . .

In Britain it has become necessary to organize, as it were, a revolution from above in order to cut out the crippling influence of the trade unions, at least temporarily for the duration of the war. The most gigantic efforts have to be made to get the industrial machine even tolerably well going and to deal with the strikes, the unrest and the interruptions of work which follow one another in quick succession.

Yet we have people in high places who declare, in the face of this world historic experience, that this British condition of 'constitutional rule' in the factory, the admission of the trade unions as factors of equal weight with the employer in negotiations on wages and management – which cannot be separated – is the goal towards which our development is also moving, and should represent a kind of reward for the German worker for his patriotic behaviour during the war.

To follow this advice would simply mean to denude ourselves of one of the most important weapons in our armoury for the next war and to deprive ourselves – in the way in which we see it today in Britain and which would be far more fatal for us than for Britain – of the industrial power of decision and adaptation, which must depend above all on the absolute rule of the employer in his concern, exactly as the readiness of the army depends on military obedience. . . .

c In my earlier report of 28 June 1915 I had already stated my views regarding works councils, and described works councils as the one institution from the general introduction and efficient development of which I anticipate the greatest success for the maintenance of good relations between employers and workers. From the point of view of social policy and since there is such widespread objection in wide circles of industry, especially heavy industry, against them, I would consider it highly desirable if you could use your influence with the large enterprises of at least fifty workers which are still without works councils, to create such institutions.

d 1. Every male German who is between the completed seventeenth and the completed sixtieth year of his life is obliged to enter the National Auxiliary Service for the duration of the war, unless he is serving with the armed forces.

2. All those persons shall be deemed to serve in the National Auxiliary Service who are employed by the public authorities, by official institutions, in war industries, in agriculture and forestry, in medical services, in war-important organizations of all kinds or in other occupations or firms which play a part in the waging of the war directly or indirectly or in food supply, as long as the number of these persons does not exceed the demand for them.

Those obliged to National Auxiliary Service who were engaged before 1 August 1916 in an agricultural or forestry enterprise, may not be removed from their employment for the purpose of transfer to any other employment in the National Auxiliary Service. . . .

4. The question whether, and to what extent, the figures employed by any authority exceeds the demand will be settled by the appropriate Land Central Government* in agreement with the War Bureau. . . .

7. Those obliged to National Auxiliary Service who were not employed in the manner laid down in para. 2 above may be conscripted at any time to National Auxiliary Service.

This conscription will be undertaken as a rule by a request to register voluntarily in the first instance, issued by the War Bureau or any other authority determined by the mediation of the Land Central Government. If this request does not meet with an adequate response, individuals liable to duty will be conscripted by written demand issued by an appropriate executive committee. . . .

Everyone receiving an individual written notice, must seek work in any of the employments enumerated in para. 2. If he is not in such employment within two weeks of receiving his notice, the executive committee will order him into such employment. . . .

11. All enterprises included in the National Auxiliary Service for which Chapter 7 of the Industrial Order is applicable and which employ as a rule at least fifty workers must have permanent works councils.

If any such concerns do not have permanent works councils according to para. 134h of the Industrial Order, they shall form them forthwith. The members of this works council shall be elected by the adult workers of the firm or the department from among their number in direct and secret ballot on the principle of proportional representation. Details shall be settled by the Land Central Government. . . .

12. It shall be the duty of the works council to further good relations within the work force of the enterprise and between the work force and the employer. It shall bring proposals, requests and complaints of the workers relating to works organization, wages and other working conditions in the

* See Glossary.

works and its welfare organizations to the attention of the employer and pronounce its views on them.

On the demand of at least one quarter of the works council a meeting shall be called and the proposed item shall be put on its agenda.

1/6 The Mobilization of Female Labour in France

a C. GIDE, *Effects of the War upon French Economic Life* (Oxford, 1923), pp. 156–158.

b RENARD, *Les répercussions* [*see* Document 1/2], pp. 291–294. (Ed. Tr.)

a At the same time that recourse was being had to military labour, the employment of women was also becoming general; and in the organization and regulation of female labour the State likewise intervened. It facilitated the recruiting of women workers chiefly by authorizing or tolerating certain deviations from the general principles of labour legislation as regards working hours, minimum age for factory work, interdiction of night work, etc. Its intervention extended also to the organizing of employment offices, to the hiring, discharging, and installing of women workers in newly industrialized cities, to the creating of refectories, dormitories, canteens, day nurseries, foundling hospitals, medical clinics, etc.

There is still lacking in France a general census indicating the total number of women engaged in industrial or agricultural war work and the number of women who abandoned domestic service and accessory occupations in order to take up a regular trade. On the other hand, a number of special investigations conducted by the Ministry of Labour, as well as by the ministries of the National Defence, furnish an abundance of sufficiently accurate information regarding the utilization and development of female labour, as also regarding its classification, productive power, and professional value, and the technical and economic consequences of its employment.

In July 1917, and July 1918, the Minister of Labour ordered a general investigation of private industries in France. The investigation took the form of inquiries, the first of which covered 52,278 establishments which had employed 487,474 women before the war. It showed that the number had fallen to 199,107 in August 1914, but had risen again to 418,579 in July 1915, and to 626,881 in July 1917 – an increase of 120 per cent. . . . The increase was especially pronounced in the industries of the National Defence, the personnel of which was recruited by levies made upon certain deserted branches. In July 1918, in seven of fifteen industrial groups the number of women employed was greater than it was in time of peace; thus for 100 women employed before the war, there were 677 employed in the iron and steel industries, 461 in transporting and handling merchandise, 150 in the wood industry, 141 in the chemical industry, 111 in the leather and hide industry, 301 in stone cutting and building, and 105 in various trades. On the other hand, there was a decrease in eight groups in which women are especially poorly paid; for 100 women employed before the war, there were only 69 in the food industry, 92 in the textile industry, 91 in the clothing industry, 85 in the fine-metal industry, 79 in the precious and non-precious stone industry, and 73 in the book industry. All told, the industries which gained in numbers did so to the extent of 118,614 additional workers (211,894 as against 93,280), whereas the industries which lost in numbers did so to the extent of 39,733 workers (321,629 as against 361,362). The net gain, therefore, was 78,881 (17·34 per cent). Finally, in the total personnel of the establishments embraced in the inquiry the proportion of female workers, which before the war had amounted to 33 per cent, increased to 38 per cent in August 1914, primarily in consequence of the departure of the men called into the army, and thereafter remained constant at approximately 40 per cent. In July 1918, there were 533,523 women to 785,380 men, as compared with 454,642 women to 929,407 men in July 1914.

In the above-mentioned industries of the National Defence analogous data were derived from a number of private investigations. For the powder mills and artillery factories alone are there figures for the entire duration of the war. On the eve of the mobilization, women were employed only in the State establishments, and to the very low number of 4,800; but immediately after the mobilization the employment of 8,400 women raised the total to approximately 13,000. Private industry followed suit. In January 1916 the war industries were employing 110,000 women; this number increased to 402,000 in August 1917; to 417,000 in January 1918; and to 445,000 in September 1918 – or approximately 24·5 per cent of the total working personnel. If we consider all the establishments working for the National Defence (armament, mines, commissariat, aviation service, sanitation service, navy, American army, great railway systems), with respect to which the general data run only to October 1917, we find that the number of women workers increased as follows: October 1917, 446,212; January 1918, 552,389; July 1918, 582,785; September 1918, 600,733. Finally, the number of women employed in various bureaus and services of the army as secretaries, stenographers, bookkeepers, &c., and not included in the above figures, amounted to 132,468 on 1 January 1918, whereas before the war not a single woman had been engaged in work of this kind.

b Once the war is over and life returns to normal, women will give up some of the jobs which are too heavy for them. It is neither useful nor desirable that they should continue to produce shells, drive trams and unload railway trucks. It is certain that most of them, of their own accord, will give up these masculine tasks, that many of them will return to the home, newly restored through the return of the father or the husband, and will find again great pleasure in performing their traditional household roles. There will no longer be a need to defend the mother country; it will be necessary to re-populate it. They will be asked to produce children rather than munitions. Motherhood will become a national duty; for young women it will be the equivalent of military service for the young men. Nevertheless, there will be some cruel gaps in the French population, some alas! which can never be replaced. For some time we must expect a shortage of labour. On the other hand, there will also be many widows, many spinsters condemned to remain spinsters, because husbands will be scarce and expensive on the morrow of the blood-bath France has undergone. In order to live, then, women will have to continue in several of the occupations which they had assumed were temporary In many branches of industry they will be in demand, welcomed and preferred because they are regarded as being more pliable, more docile, more inclined to accept a low wage. But it is possible that they will have some surprizes in store for those accustomed to exploit them. As a result of their more adventurous and testing experience, they will have learnt to look after themselves, to look after their collective interests, to frustrate the actions of those who in the past abused their isolation.

At the same time they will be given access to all kinds of knowledge. I saw established during the war an *Institut agricole pour les orphelines*, and an *École de hautes études commerciales pour les jeunes filles de la bourgeoisie*, another more modest body under the patronage of the Paris Chamber of Commerce, an *École de gouvernantes*, aimed at providing us with our own 'guardian angels' who formerly came to us from Germany, an *École technique* for producing women engineers and architects. Women will no longer be restricted to the role of... 'secondary employees', occupied in the lower ranks of commerce; the door will be opened which will lead to the top positions in which [already a number of French women] have brilliantly shown proof of the abilities with which women are endowed.

Then, by the nature of things, having become more educated, more expert, more closely involved with large concerns, having obtained a deliberative voice in the *Commissions agricoles* in the *Commissions mixtes departementales*, having shown in the management of benevolent societies, hospitals and all kinds of work, that they possess organizational qualities, they will be admitted without any problem to a share in the administration of public affairs. Already a proposal before the Chamber grants them a seat in the *Conseils municipaux*. There, they will receive their civic education. That will probably be a step towards the vote; and I hold the opinion that in their attitude towards problems such as alcoholism, poverty and war they may bring useful support and sometimes a necessary corrective action to the activity of the male politicians. How unwise and how defeatist would be the statesman who, in the years after the war, would confine them to the narrowness of domestic life! As for those good people who are anxious that women should not lose their charm and attraction, one may reply to them by quoting Stendhal: 'it is as if one were afraid to teach nightingales no longer to sing in springtime.'

All told, the war appears to me to have brought the women of France (and also to those of other countries) two essential advantages; firstly the opening of new careers where they will keep part of the gains they have achieved; then, an undoubted and well-earned improvement in their social importance and condition.

1/7 Food and Rent Control Legislation in Germany

a Ordinance (Bekanntmachung) on the Milling of Bread Grains, of 5 January 1915. Printed in PANNIER, *Kriegsgesetze* [*see* Document 1/1], vol. I, pp. 138–141. (Ed. Tr.)

b Ordinance (Bekanntmachung) on Ensuring Tillage, of 31 March 1915. *Ibid.*, vol. II, pp.–87 88. (Ed. Tr.)

c Ordinance (Bekanntmachung) on the Supply of Potatoes, of 26 June 1916. *Ibid.*, vol. V, pp. 248–251. (Ed. Tr.)

d Ordinance (Bekanntmachung) on the Use of Turnips in the Preparation of Rye Bread, of 5 February 1917. *Ibid.*, vol. VIII, p. 20. (Ed. Tr.)

e Ordinance (Bekanntmachung) on the Protection of Tenants, of 23 September 1918. *Ibid.*, vol. XIV, pp. 124–128. (Ed. Tr.)

a 1. In the milling of rye the extraction rate shall be at least 82 per cent. . . .

2. In the milling of wheat the extraction rate shall be at least 80 per cent. . . .

5. Wheat flour may be issued, particularly from the mills, only in a mixture containing at least 30 per cent of rye flour by weight. . . .

6. Police officers and experts appointed by the police authorities are entitled to enter rooms in which flour is manufactured at all times, and rooms in which flour is stored, offered for sale or packaged, at times of business, and to undertake inspections, examine the books and select samples for investigation to be taken away on issue of a receipt. They are to leave a part of the

sample taken in an officially sealed package and to make appropriate payment for the sample, on demand.

7. The owners of enterprises in which flour is manufactured, as well as the managers and supervisors appointed by them, are obliged to give on demand information to police officers and authorized experts on the method of production, the extent of the enterprise and the materials worked up, and particularly their quantities and point of origin.

8. The experts must preserve confidentiality about the organization and business relations which may come to their notice in the course of their inspection, and must refrain from transmitting to others or using for their own benefit any business or works secrets, with the exception of making appropriate official reports or giving evidence in cases of breaches of the law.

b 1. Local authorities are authorized, on detailed instruction from the Central Land Authority, to demand a statement from all those having the management of landed estates and agricultural holdings, on whether they intend to work all their acreage, or which areas are to remain unworked. On further demand, the ability to perform the planned tillage must also be proved to be credible. These demands may be made by public notice.

2. To the extent that those having the management of land do not work it, or fail to make their ability to perform the tillage credible, or fail to answer the demand notice, or cannot be contacted, the local authorities are authorized to withdraw their right to use the whole or part of their acreage, together with appurtenances, by the end of 1915 at the latest, and to transfer it to the local district authority (Kommunalverband).

3. In the working of the land, the local district authority is obliged to observe the rules of orderly husbandry, as far as this is advisable in the special conditions created by the war. The local authority shall determine, on transfer, how far the former occupant shall be paid compensation. The owner or other occupier is not responsible for the outlays of the local district authority....

c 1. District authorities (Kommunalverbände) are obliged to provide the quantities of eating potatoes as well as potatoes, dried potato and potato starch products for mixing with bread, necessary for feeding their population from 16 August 1916 to 15 August 1917 according to the regulations of this ordinance, to the extent that their needs cannot be met from supplies available in their own district....

3. The parish unions, the army commands, the naval commands, the Reich Distillery Office and the dried potato manufacturing association are obliged to register their needs for potatoes with the Reich Potato Office by the dates laid down by the latter.

4. .... The Reich Potato Office or the authorities delegated by it may determine the quantities and dates by which potatoes must be delivered up from the parish unions to the Potato Office, or to depots nominated by it....

10. The Reich Chancellor determines the extent and conditions under which potatoes, and dried potato and potato starch products may be used for industrial production.

d 1. In the preparation of rye bread, turnips and other roots (except sugar beet) may be used in place of potatoes. One hundred parts by weight of dried turnips shall be deemed equal to one hundred parts by weight of dried potatoes, and one hundred parts of fresh turnips equal to fifty parts by weight of squeezed or ground potatoes. ....

e 1. If any district contains an Arbitration Tribunal (according to the ordinance of 15 December 1914) the Central Land Authorities may empower this Tribunal to make decisions relating to paras. 2–4 below.

2. The Arbitration Tribunal may:

(i) on demand by the tenant

(a) decide on the effectiveness of any notice given by the lessor and on the continuance of the lease on which notice has been given, for a period of one year

(b) prolong a lease run out without notice, for a period of one year. ....
If the Arbitration Tribunal decides, according to (i) above to continue or prolong an existing lease, it may put new obligations on the tenant, and in particular raise his rent. ....

5. If in view of the Central Land Authorities, a particularly severe housing shortage exists in a district in which an Arbitration Tribunal is functioning, the Central Land Authorities may:

(i) empower or compel the local authority to make an ordinance that the lessor of any dwelling must report to it at once if a dwelling leased permanently or temporarily since 1 June 1915 is leased to a new tenant at a higher rent than to the last; and this report had to include the old and the new rent

(ii) empower the Arbitration Tribunal to lower, on request by the local authority, the rent agreed with the new tenant. This request must be made at once on receiving the information from the tenant.

Subsidiary payments and services rendered by the tenant shall be counted as part of the rent.

6. The Central Land Authorities may order for any district in which, in their view, a particularly severe housing shortage exists,

(i) that the lessor of dwellings may give legal notice only with the previous agreement of the Arbitration Tribunal, especially if the notice has the object of raising the rent

(ii) that a lease which has run out shall be deemed to have been prolonged indefinitely, unless the lessor has been granted permission of the Arbitration Tribunal prior to its ending.

The Arbitration Tribunal can make its decisions on continuation or prolongation of the lease in each case for the duration of one year . . . .

7. The Arbitration Tribunal decides by fair judgment. Before its decision it may make temporary orders. Its decisions may not be challenged in the courts.

If a continuance or prolongation of the lease is ordered (2(i) (ii) and 6) above, or if the rent is lowered (5(i)), the conditions laid down by the Arbitration Tribunal become the conditions of the lease.

8. The Tribunal's decisions are made by one chairman and at least two assessors. The chairman must be qualified to occupy the position of a judge or of a higher administrative civil servant; the assessors must belong to the extent of one half to the class of house owners, and one half to the class of tenants. . . .

9. The application of this ordinance cannot be superseded or restricted by agreement of the parties. . . .

1/8 Raw Material Control in Germany

Speech by Walther Rathenau, 20 December 1915. Printed in CLOUGH, *et al.*, *Economic History* [*see* Document 1/4a], pp. 31–39.

The object of my paper is to report to you a new departure in our economic warfare which has no precedent in history, which will have a decided influence on the war, and which in all probability is destined to affect future times. In its methods it is closely akin to communism and yet it departs essentially from the prophecies and demands resulting from radical theories. It is not my purpose to give an account of a rigid system based on theories, but I shall relate how this system grew out of our actual life, first taking concrete form in a small group, then affecting ever-widening circles, and finally bringing about a complete change in our economic life. Its visible result is a new department attached to the War Office which places our whole economic life in the service of the war. . . .

When on 4 August of last year England declared war our country became a beleaguered fortress. Cut off by land and cut off by sea it was made wholly self-dependent; we were facing a war the duration, cost, danger, and sacrifices of which no one could foresee. . . .

The first problem was the question of available supplies. It was necessary to ascertain the period of months for which the country was provided with the indispensable materials. Few of the materials needed for the army were available in quantities sufficient for a year (and since that time the yearly demands of the army have substantially increased); in most cases they were considerably less. . . .

Four measures appeared feasible and worth trying out for reconstructing our economic policies so as to afford proper protection for the country.

First: Coercive measures had to be adopted regarding the use of all raw materials in the country. No material must be used arbitrarily, or for luxury, of for anything that is not absolutely needed. The needs of the army are of paramount importance and everything must be directed towards that ultimate end. That was our first and most difficult task. . . .

And now the fourth measure. Materials difficult to obtain must be replaced by others more easily procurable. It is not ordained that this or that object must be made of copper or of aluminium; it may be made of some other material. Substitutes must be found. Instead of using the time-honoured materials for our household goods, etc., we must use new substances, and articles must be manufactured that do not require so much raw material. . . .

The very fact that the problem was not understood caused many difficulties. Up to the present the German people believe that the supply of raw materials takes care of itself. The food question is being discussed all day long; the question of raw materials is hardly mentioned. Even now it is hard for us to realize what the situation was at the beginning of the war. For the first six months no one had any idea what we were trying to do. In industrial circles our inquiries were sometimes considered to be offensive and unpleasant interference with the industrial situation. We were accused of injuring certain peace industries. . . .

We now come to the solution.

The first question was to establish a legal basis. . . .

'Sequestration' does not mean that merchandise or material is seized by the state but only that it is restricted, i.e., that it no longer can be disposed of by the owner at will but must be reserved for a more important purpose (or, that it must be put at the disposal of a higher authority). The merchandise must be used for war purposes only: it may be sold, manufactured, shipped, transformed; but no matter what is done to it, it always remains subject to the law that it must be used for war purposes only. . . .

The system of war boards is based upon self-administration; yet that does not signify unrestricted freedom. The War Raw Materials Department was established under strict government supervision. The boards serve the interests of the public at large; they neither distribute dividends nor apportion profits; in addition to the usual organs of stock companies, a board of governors and a supervising committee, they have another independent organ, a committee of appraisement and distribution, made up of members selected from various chambers of commerce, or of government officials. This committee serves as intermediary between the stock companies, representing capitalism, and the Government – an economic innovation which may be destined to become generally accepted in future times.

Their duty is to amass raw materials and to direct the flow of supply in such a way that each manufacturing concern is furnished the needed materials in quantities corresponding to the orders it receives from the Government and at prices fixed for such materials. . . .

. . . [Finally,] the question of obtaining and introducing substitutes and surrogates was taken up.

The materials used for the Prussian uniforms had to be changed. Worsted and other goods were added. Rare materials no longer could be used for helmets, buttons, and other accessories. In manufacturing ammunition zinc and steel were employed, replacing rare materials. Metals heretofore not used for such purposes were now introduced for the making of electrical apparatus. Many products thus became cheaper. New and large chemical works were constructed for the manufacture of known or hitherto unknown substitutes. Even the textile industries adopted the system of utilizing used materials. Today there are but few branches of industry using exclusively the same materials as before the war. Many have profited by the reorganization. . . .

When His Excellency von Falkenhayn came to Berlin this spring and asked after the state of our supplies, I was in a position to tell him: As far as the essentials are concerned our supplies are sufficient; the outcome of the war is not threatened by a lack of raw materials. . . .

I/9 Shortage of Metals in Russia

Report by A. G. KRUSHCHOV, 1916, Printed in CLOUGH, *et al.*, *Economic History* [*see* Document I/4a], pp. 41–45.

The purpose of this report is to draw the attention of the representatives of the Unions of Zemstvos* and of Towns to two pressing problems: on the one hand, the danger of a shortage of metals in Russia; on the other, an ever-increasing rise in the price of metals that has now reached bacchanalian proportions. These problems require the representatives of civic organizations to work actively to intensify the production of metals and to protect the consumer interest in their distribution.

A most alarming symptom is the decline in the amount of iron produced in the country, despite an expanding need for iron for defence requirements. Compared with the [pre-war] average annual iron production of 292 million puds,* the amount of iron smelted was, in 1913, 286·6 million puds; in 1914, 268·4 million puds; in 1915, 226·0 million puds. Consequently, in 1915, in comparison with 1913, output declined by 61 million puds, or by 21 per cent. In the foundries of [Russian] Poland, 1913 production was 25·5 million puds, while in 1914 it was 13·9 million . . .

We will not dwell on the causes of the fall in the production of iron. They are generally known and can be reduced to three factors: 1. Shortage of raw materials (coke, ore, flux, coal); 2. Disruption of transport; 3. Lack of labour – the great decline in the number of Russian workers. . . . An attempt to calculate supply and demand of iron for the current year of 1916 was made by the Metallurgical Committee. . . . Its calculations show that this year, after meeting the requirements of the military departments and the postal and telegraphic services, only an insignificant amount of iron will reach the private market, an amount far less than the demand. Thus, the civilian economy must get along on already exhausted stocks of iron from previous years and scrap from finished metal left over at the foundries after defence needs have been met. . . .

As in the case of supplying the population with bread in a year of famine, there is a known minimum impossible to reduce. The necessary minimum of civilian iron consumption must be determined and supplies of iron must not be permitted to fall below it, for the success of the army depends upon the well-being of the home front. We suggest that it would be reasonable to set as the minimum norm the consumption level of iron on the private market in the second half of 1915. . . . Thus, we have set the famine minimum to which the requirements of the private market can be reduced at 26 million puds [annually]. We must point out that any reduction of supply below this minimum threatens the country with great dislocation. . . .

. . . We present a price table for ordinary metal products, comparing prices before the war, in June 1914, and wholesale prices at present:

* See Glossary.

Product	Wholesale Prices, 1914 (pre-war)	Wholesale Prices, 1916	Increase over 1944 (%)
Copper in bars	12 rubles	32 rubles	167
Horseshoe nails	5 rubles 80 kopeks	15 rubles	158
Wire nails	2 rubles 50 kopeks	6 rubles 50 kopeks	160
Wire	1 ruble 80 kopeks	3 rubles 75 kopeks	170
Sheet iron	1 ruble 80 kopeks	4 rubles	120
Cast iron	1 ruble 55 kopeks	2 rubles 50 kopeks	61

. . . The information in the table on the increase in the price of metal products during the war (from 61 to 170 per cent) forces us to confront squarely the question of the necessity of regulating the prices of metals, setting fixed prices for them. . . .

. . . One the basis of the foregoing, the following resolution is suggested to the congress of representatives of the Zemstvos and Towns to be submitted to the State Duma* and the Special Conference for the Defence of the State:

1. It is necessary to adopt without delay the most energetic measures for increasing the smelting of iron, including restoring the factories that are not working. . . .

2. It is necessary for the Government to establish fixed prices for metals immediately.

3. It is necessary to eliminate the duties on copper temporarily because they are a factor in the increase in domestic copper prices.

4. It is necessary to assure the civilian population of a supply of iron in a quantity not less than 26 million puds, because without this minimum amount the country's economic life is threatened with complete dislocation. The distribution of this metal must involve the participation of and control by the civic organizations, the Unions of Zemstvos and Towns.

1/10 Shortages in Germany

Waldemar Zimmermann, 'Die Veränderung der Einkommens–und Lebensverhältnisse der deutschen Arbeiter durch den Krieg', in RUDOLF MEERWARTH, ADOLF GÜNTHER and WALDEMAR ZIMMERMANN, *Die Einwirkung des Krieges auf Bevölkerungsbewegung, Einkommen und Lebenshaltung in Deutschland.* Carnegie Foundation for International Peace. Department for Economics and History: Economic and Social History of the War, German Series (Stuttgart, Berlin, Leipzig, New Haven, 1932), pp. 416–423. (Ed. Tr.)

In addition to food and drink it was cleaning materials, fuel and clothing

* See Glossary.

which were available in any quantity without difficulty in the first two years of the war for those who were prepared to use their wealth ruthlessly, while the less well off already had to stand in long queues to obtain their necessities at reasonable prices. Indeed, it was precisely the fact that the rich could obtain almost anything without restriction thanks to their money-bags which . . . threatened ultimately to conjure up a class division of far more dangerous acuteness than in peacetime between those who had plenty and those who had to go short. These observations were the main causes which led progressively to requisitions, to compulsory deliveries or economic controls* and to the rationing of necessary foodstuffs, clothing and fuel except for items in the luxury class. . . . Luxury articles, particularly those of foreign origin, remained available to the wealthy with few restrictions, even in the second half of the war.

But conditions were very different with regard to basic foodstuffs – in part also with regard to fuel, clothing, linen and soap – as soon as these articles of mass consumption were subjected to control in the interest of the community because of their general indispensability for the broad mass of the people. By means of rationing which was extended very quickly from the spring of 1916 onwards from the items controlled earlier, bread and flour, to all other items, it came about that potatoes, fats, meat, sugar, sometimes also home-grown vegetables, eggs, milk, etc., were withdrawn from the easy access of the rich, and the latter could enlarge their 'rations' only 'by the back door', illegally at 'usurious prices' in the black market and by undertaking foraging journeys into the countryside at great expense in time and money. These difficulties greatly contributed to the fact that the supplies even for the rich had become, in the main, much less favourable in the second half of the war than they had been before, including in this category also the well-paid munitions workers who were able to meet their needs quite well right up to the 'turnip winter' of 1916. . . .

The difficulties of fuel and lighting in the second half of the war became sometimes as great as those of food supplies. Rich and poor were hit equally in many towns by the shortage when coal supplies stopped altogether and substitute fuel and lighting materials were not easily obtainable. . . .

The shortage of textile materials affected above all the mass consumption of cheap qualities, since it was here that supply and demand got into everworsening disproportion because of the shortage of new or substitute products. Welfare collections and re-use of second-hand materials could cover the needs only spasmodically. Among the poor working-class families there were no reserve stocks of clothing or underwear on which they could have

* *Zwangsbewirtschaftung*, or *Zwangswirtschaft*, the word used to describe the controlled war economy. (Ed.)

drawn as did the rich. As a result, there was a shabbiness about in the last year of the war which struck every neutral foreigner who visited Germany in 1918 even more sharply perhaps than the pale, lean appearance of the German urban population. Do-it-yourself repairs, particularly of footwear by the owner, e.g. of shoes with scraps of leather, rubber or cardboard or with wooden soles occasionally took on grotesque forms. Similarly, the involuntary absence of body and bed linen often exceeded the limits of the tolerable, especially when the shortage of soap, which was obtainable only in its war (clay) soap form, is taken into account. . . . Such clothing and manufactures as were available at all, were, apart from shoes, obtainable only at six to ten times the pre-war prices, compared with an overall increase in the cost of living of perhaps only two to threefold. . . . If the change in quality compared with the pre-war years is taken into account – and this meant either a drop in quality or else the sale of old, well-made but dead stock which could not be sold before the war because of tastelessness or unfashionable appearance and which achieved its belated, but all the greater triumph only in the war – the price differentials were no doubt even greater. Pure cotton or woollen goods hardly existed at all in Germany in the last year of the war, at any rate not in a form accessible to the ordinary consumer. Nearly everywhere substitute fabrics, paper fibre, artificial wool – which because of its impregnation, covered the wearer with a characteristic 'odour' – were mixed in.

1/11 Failure of the German Food Supply

a JULIAN MARKHLEVSKI ('Karski') in the *Spartacus Letter* No. 4 of April 1917. Printed in Institut für Marxismus-Leninismus beim Zentral Komite der S.E.D., *Geschichte der deutschen Arbeiterbewegung, Dokumente und Materialien* (Berlin, 1958–), Series 2, vol. 1, pp. 606–607. (Ed. Tr.)

b Official Notice of the War Food Office, 16 May 1918. Printed in MICHAELIS and SCHRAEPLER, *Ursachen und Folgen* [*see* Document 1/3], vol. I, pp. 278–279. (Ed. Tr.)

a On 5 February (1917) members of the Prussian Diet were assembled for a conference on the question of food supplies, at which Herr Batocki, President of the War Food Office and Herr Michaelis unfolded a picture of the supply position which deserves the widest publicity. Herr Batocki stated 'that the broad masses of the population, those of the cities naturally far more than those of the countryside, are on the brink of starvation until the harvest'.

Herr Michaelis, who also holds the position of chairman of the Reich Grain Office, added some statistical details: the estimate of the harvest produced a shortfall of over one million tons of grain. Even if the food supply from the middle of August until the middle of September is met from the current harvest, which is hardly feasible in practice since the harvest will not yet be ready for grinding at that time, Herr Michaelis had estimated as early as the beginning of February that there would be a deficit of 150,000 tons. This shortfall will be enlarged because flour had to be delivered in place of the potatoes which failed to materialize and because there are no other materials available to mix with flour for baking. Naturally, next to nothing came from Roumania – as explained explicitly by Herr Michaelis. The Roumanian grain is being sent wholly to Austria and Turkey, which are suffering worse deprivations than Germany. Austria and Hungary are so badly off that they demanded grain from Germany for their large cities, and received some from us. Herr Michaelis assumes that there will have to be further deliveries of grain to the allies of Germany in the future in order to meet the needs of the armies. Altogether, Herr Michaelis considers the position to be 'terribly grave', and 'the frightful moment may come when I (i.e. Michaelis) shall not be in a position to provide the necessary flour in time for the working class districts in the West'.

This picture was completed by the Assistant Director of the Reich Potato Office, Councillor Kutscher, in similar manner as far as the supplies of potatoes were concerned. While the pre-harvest estimates counted on about 46 million tons of potatoes, the check in October 1916 showed, after deducting seed potatoes, a stock of about 18 million tons. Herr Batocki drew these conclusions from the figures: 'It may even happen that we shall not have enough to live on altogether, and that we shall have to suffer hunger unless we consume a part of our seed potatoes. First we have to survive one period, then the next. Of course, no one is in any doubt about the danger for the future which this holds for us. If after all this there turns out to be another bad harvest, we shall have to put our trust in God to help us out.'

b Unfortunately, the condition of the grain imports from the Ukraine does not permit us to base our bread supplies for the last months of the current harvest year on these uncertain deliveries. If we want some certainty, we shall have to rely in the main on German home stocks for the rest of the husbandry year. The limited supplies now available make it necessary to restrict consumption. Accordingly, the Board of the Reich Grain Office at its meeting of 11th instant, in agreement with the directorate, resolved as follows with effect from 16 June of this year:

The daily flour ration is reduced for those entitled to it, from 200 grammes to 160 grammes.

The current supplements for heavy and heaviest workers will continue.

The quantities to be used by self-suppliers, which have already been reduced with effect from 1 April, also remain as they are.

As soon as sufficient supplies reach the Reich Grain Office from the Ukraine the former rations will be restored, and in any case no later than the restocking of the granaries arising from the early threshing of the home harvest of 1918.

This year it will not be possible to issue more meat in lieu of the shortfall of flour as was done last year. After the large reduction in our stock of pigs, the current meat ration is already making such inroads into our cattle stocks, that any increase would endanger most seriously the supply of milk and feeding stuffs. There will be some compensation by an increase in the sugar ration; and the issue of other nutriments will also be increased during the weeks of reduction in the bread supply.

1/12 Failure of the Russian Food Supply

K. LEITES, *Recent Economic Developments in Russia* (Carnegie Endowment for International Peace, Oxford, 1922), pp. 46–49.

The beginning of the war found Russia on the eve of the harvest of 1914. This harvest yielded 3,657,000,000 *poods** of cereals; but fell considerably below that of 1913, which yielded 4,594,000,000 *poods* – a decline of nearly 25 per cent. After the stoppage of the exports the deficit in the harvest would scarcely have been noticed, if the enormous requirements of the army had not greatly increased the national consumption. Besides, the diversion of the equipment of the railways to the transportation of troops, munitions and other war materials exerted a prejudicial influence on the food supply of the towns.

Very soon after the commencement of the war, accordingly, a scarcity began to be felt, first in Moscow and Petrograd, and afterwards also in other large towns; and this scarcity became more and more serious with the increase in transport difficulties, with the rise in wages and with the development of other conditions that produced similar effects in other countries, both belligerent and neutral.

Unfortunately, the Imperial Government merely made matters worse by measures which it took to ward off scarcity. . . . Not only villages and towns, but even whole districts, were evacuated, and during the evacuation the Government officials through their stupid orders caused so much confusion as seriously to compromise the food supply in places where the fugitives were assembled on the way to their destination, and even at the very points of destination. . . .

* See Glossary.

One of the measures which aggravated the situation was an order issued by the supreme central power giving the local administrative authorities complete discretion in the adoption of measures designed to relieve the food scarcity. But the establishment of fixed prices on articles of food was especially recommended, and the result was a great confusion of discrepant and frequently contradictory measures. . . . All Russia seemed to be broken up in independent districts, in which each governor, or each governor-general, was left free to carry out his own food policy. It happened not infrequently that, as soon as a price was fixed on an article in one place, that article disappeared from the market because the dealers and producers preferred to send it to other places, or else to conceal it in the hope that the fixed price would be raised or that fixed prices would be abolished altogether.

The enforcement of a general policy of price-fixing proposed . . . was not practicable for the reason that the Government itself constantly violated its own rules. The authorized agents of the Ministry of War bought up supplies for the army at prices much higher than those officially fixed. This unfair competition had serious consequences for the civil population, because the army was growing larger every day and its consumption of food articles increasing proportionately. During the campaign of 1914–1915, for instance, the army demand for grain was 230,000,000 *poods*; in 1915–1916, about 500,000,000 *poods*; and in 1916–1917, 700,000,000 *poods*. If one takes into account the fact that about one-half of this quantity was bought, not directly from the producers, but in the open market, one can easily imagine to what extent the interests of the civil population must have suffered. At the same time, moreover, it must be borne in mind that the amount of land placed under cultivation was steadily decreasing because of the drawing away of many of the most efficient food producers, first the landowners themselves, and second the most vigorous and experienced labourers. A no less unfavourable influence on agriculture was exerted by the repeated mobilizations of horses. Lastly, the gravest consequences were occasioned by the stoppage of the imports of agricultural implements and machines. . . . As early as the beginning of 1917 it was very difficult to get such products as meat, butter, sugar, eggs, etc., even at prices tremendously inflated by speculation. The introduction of the card system with fixed rations in so badly organized a country as Russia served only to increase the general confusion and to strengthen the position of the speculators.

The immediate cause of the overthrow of the Imperial Government was famine. Hungry women were the advance-guard of the revolutionary army, which was completed by the workmen and soldiers who followed close behind. . . .

1/13 The Russian Revolution: Peasant Seizure of Land between the February and October Revolutions

Report of Landowners in May 1917. Printed in F. A. GOLDER, *Documents of Russian History, 1914–1917* (New York, 1927), pp. 380–381.

Delegates, representing landowners in the gubernias* of Simbirsk, Nizhni-Novgorod, Samara, Saratov, Tver, Kharkov, Poltava, Kursk, Kherson, and Ekaterinoslav, submitted the following report to the Provisional Government and the Soviet of Workers' and Soldiers' Deputies:

In the full consciousness of the great moral responsibility before the country, imposed upon us by the Provisional Government, namely, the duty to produce food and fodder for the army and the population, we proceeded to carry out the obligation imposed upon us, totally oblivious to our own interests. However, at the very first steps in this direction, we met with the strongest opposition from village committees and commissars, who are acting illegally and carrying out undisguised propaganda for the abolition by every possible means of private landownership in these gubernias. A situation has thus been created which will compel the above-named guberniias, which serve the needs of the largest sugar factories and are for this reason engaged in intensive farming, to cease producing cereals, vegetables, and sugar. The general situation in these guberniias at the present time is as follows:

1. Public organizations and their representatives, contrary to the law, fix the rent on land so low that it does not even cover the necessary payments due on the land.

2. Land is forcibly taken from its owners and handed over to the peasants. In some cases, the land thus seized either remained fallow or was speculated with by being leased to a third party at a higher rate.

3. Wages for labour are arbitrarily set, interfering with freedom of labour and freedom of contract.

4. The sanctity of the home is being violated by searches and by confiscation of movable property. Landowners and their managers are deprived of liberty, without due process of law, for refusing to obey the unlawful demands of the committees and commissars.

5. The committees and their agents usurp the functions of courts, and, contrary to the express provisions of Article I of the Civil Statutes, examine conflicts relating to land and labour.

If the above situation continues, Russia, notwithstanding its rich black

* See Glossary.

earth, will in the very near future become a wilderness covered with weeds, a country with a population poverty-stricken, both morally and materially, with an insignificant amount of low-grade grain, insufficient even for the needs of the cultivators. Her highly efficient agriculture will be ruined, and there will be a total destruction of the starch, syrup, and sugar-beet production, and pure-bred stock.

Russia's economic ruin is unavoidable. We, the representatives of the guberniias named above, consider it our moral obligation to call this condition to the attention of the Provisional Government and the Soviet of Soldiers' and Workers' Deputies.

1/14 The Debate on the Decree on Land, 1917

JOHN REED, *Ten Days that shook the World* (London, 1961 ed.), pp. 110–113.

The lands of peasants and of Cossacks serving in the army shall not be confiscated.

'This [Decree on the Land] is not,' explained Lenin, 'the project of former Minister Tchernov,* who spoke of "erecting a framework" and tried to realize reforms from above. From below, on the spot will be decided the questions of division of the land. The amount of land received by each peasant will vary according to the locality. . . .'

The representative of the Left Socialist Revolutionaries† spoke on the Land Decree. While agreeing in principle his faction could not vote on the question until after discussion. The Peasants' Soviets should be consulted. . . .

The Mensheviki Internationalists,† too, insisted on a party caucus.

Then the leader of the Maximalists, the Anarchist wing of the peasants: 'We must do honour to a political party which puts such an act into effect the first day, without jawing about it!'

A typical peasant was in the tribune, long hair, boots and sheep-skin coat, bowing to all corners of the hall. 'I wish you well, comrades and citizens,' he said. 'There are some Cadets walking around outside. You arrested our Socialist peasants – why not arrest them?'

This was the signal for a debate of excited peasants. It was precisely like the debate of soldiers of the night before. Here were the real proletarians of the land. . . .

The left Socialist Revolutionaries proposed a half-hour intermission. As the delegates streamed out, Lenin stood up in his place.

'We must not lose time, comrades! News all-important to Russia must be on the press tomorrow morning. No delay!'

* Minister of Agriculture in the re-organised provisional government. (Ed.)
† See Glossary.

And above the hot discussion, argument, shuffling of feet could be heard the voice of an emissary of the Military Revolutionary Committee, crying, 'Fifteen agitators wanted in Room 17 at once! To go to the Front!' ...

It was almost two and a half hours later that the delegates came straggling back, the presidium mounted the platform, and the session commenced by the reading of telegrams from regiment after regiment, announcing their adhesion to the Military Revolutionary Committee.

In leisurely manner the meeting gathered momentum. A delegate from the Russian troops on the Macedonian front spoke bitterly of their situation. 'We suffer there more from the friendship of our "Allies" than from the enemy,' he said. Representatives of the Tenth and Twelfth Armies, just arrived in hot haste, reported, 'We support you with all our strength!' A peasant soldier protested against the release of [traitor Socialists]; as for the Executive Committee of the Peasants' Soviets, it should be arrested *en masse*! Here was real revolutionary talk. . . . A deputy from the Russian Army in Persia declared he was instructed to demand all power to the Soviets. . . . A Ukrainean officer, speaking in his native tongue: 'There is no nationalism in this crisis. . . . *Da zdravstvuyet* [i.e. long live (Ed.)] the proletarian dictatorship of all lands!' Such a deluge of high and hot thoughts that surely Russia would never again be dumb!

At two o'clock the Land Decree was put to vote, with only one against and the peasant delegates wild with joy. . . . So plunged the Bolsheviki ahead, irresistible, overriding hesitation and opposition – the only people in Russia who had a definite programme of action while the others talked for eight long months.

1/15 The Revolutionary Decrees on Land and on Workers' Control

a The Land Decree, 26 October 1917 (old style), 8 November 1917 (new style). Printed in G. A. KERTESZ, *Documents on the Political History of the European Continent, 1815–1939* (Oxford, 1968), pp. 378–379.

b The Decree onWorkers' Control, 14 November 1917 (old style, 27 November 1917 (new style). *Ibid.*, pp. 379–380.

a 1. The Landlord's right to the land is hereby abolished without compensation.

2. ... All lands ... are transferred to the *volost** land committees and the *uezd** Soviet of Peasants' Deputies until the Constituent Assembly meets. . . .

4. The following Land Mandate drawn up by the editorial board of the *Izvestiia*† of the All-Russian Soviet of Peasants' Deputies on the basis of two

* See Glossary.
† The official organ of the Soviets. (Ed.)

hundred and forty-two peasant petitions . . . shall everywhere regulate the realization of the great land reforms until their final solution by the Constituent Assembly.

CONCERNING THE LAND

1. The right of private ownership of land is abolished for ever. Land cannot be sold, bought, leased, mortgaged, or alienated in any manner whatsoever. All lands . . . are alienated without compensation, become the property of the people, and are turned over for the use of those who till them. . . .

2. All the underground resources, minerals [etc.] as well as forests and water of national importance, are transferred to the state for its exclusive use. . . .

3. Intensively cultivated holdings . . . are to be not divided but turned into model farms. . . .

6. All Russian citizens (irrespective of sex) who are willing to till the land, either by themselves or with the assistance of their families or in collective groups, are entitled to the use of the land, as long as they are able to cultivate it. Hired labour is not permitted. . . .

8. All the alienated land goes into one national land fund. Its distribution among the toilers is in charge of the local and central self-governing bodies. . . .

The lands of peasants and Cossacks of average means shall not be confiscated.

b 1. In the interests of a systematic regulation of national economy, Workers' Control is introduced in all industrial, commercial, agricultural [and similar] enterprises which are hiring people to work for them in their shops or which are giving them work to take home. This control is to extend over the production, storing, buying and selling of raw materials and finished products as well as over the finances of the enterprise.

2. The workers will exercise this control through their elected organizations, such as factory and shop committees, Soviet of elders, etc. . . .

3. Every large city, gubernia,* and industrial area is to have its own Soviet of Workers' Control. . . .

4. Until the meeting of the Congress of the Soviets of Workers' Control an All-Russian Soviet of Workers' Control will be organized in Petrograd.

5. Commissions of trained inspectors . . . will be established in connection with the higher organs of Workers' Control and will be sent out . . . to investigate the financial and technical side of enterprises.

6. The organs of Workers' Control have the right to supervise production, fix the minimum of output, and determine the cost of production . . .

* See Glossary.

8. The rulings of the organs of Workers' Control are binding on the owners of enterprises and can be annulled only by decisions of the higher organs....

10. In all enterprises the owners and the representatives of the workers and employees elected to the Committee on Workers' Control are responsible to the State for the order, discipline, and safety of the property. Persons guilty of hiding raw materials or products, of falsifying accounts, and of other similar abuses are criminally liable....

1/16 Civil War and the Land in Russia, 1918

M. PHILLIPS PRICE, *My Reminiscences of the Russian Revolution* (London, 1921), pp. 306–311.

The serious straits in which the urban proletariat of North Russia found itself, as a result of the counter-revolutionary offensive of the summer of 1918, led to an internal crisis of the first magnitude in the Soviet Republic. A storm, which had long been threatening, now burst. Certain elements of the villages, generally known as kulaks,* had from the first gone with the revolutionary elements of the towns, only because they saw a personal advantage for themselves in the division of the landlords' estates. They dreamed of becoming large proprietors themselves and of growing rich out of the needs of the towns . . . and they at once saw a chance of enriching themselves at the expense of the Revolution, when the Soviet Commissars turned their eyes on those 51 million pouds.* But part of this corn reserve was also in the hands of the 'middle peasantry'. This element had remained for the most part loyal to the land commune 'mir', had redistributed their allotments every five or six years with the rest of the community, and had never shown very strong leanings towards becoming land proprietors. They supplemented their scanty income from the land by working in little guilds of hand industry, such as basketmaking, woodwork and bootmaking. During the war they had shown a certain communist instinct by entering the consumers' co-operative societies, of which they were now the chief support. But they, too, could not resist the temptation of holding up the starving town populations to ransom. As the hunger of the towns increased, the communistic instincts of these peasants weakened, and their individualist instincts grew. When the local representative of the Commissar of Food proposed that they should deliver their small corn surplus through their co-operative societies on credit, after receiving a part payment in manufactured goods from the public stores, they held back. They feared that the Soviets could not live through this crisis,

* See Glossary.

and in that case they would be losers in the bargain, for the counter-revolution would not recognize their contract. . . .

But the towns had allies in the villages. These were the half-proletariat, who supplemented their income from the land by wage-earning for a part of the year in the towns or in the factories scattered about in the rural districts of North Russia. They had acquired the urban workers' psychology without losing touch with the village. Forming for the most part the recruits for the ranks of unskilled labour, they had become a floating population, drifting from one place to another. During their absence from the villages their land was cared for by their womenfolk. They rarely possessed more than one horse, and when they wanted to plough or reap, they had to borrow from the kulaks, to whom they were not infrequently in debt. They thus experienced the hunger of the towns with few of the advantages of the rural population, and the urban proletariat found in them hopeful auxiliaries for revolutionizing the villages and securing some of that 51 million pouds. . . .

Round these issues the struggle in the summer of 1918 in the villages raged. The agrarian revolution of the summer and autumn of 1917 had been made by a peasantry united against the landlords for the abolition of the right to hold more land than the owner could cultivate himself. It had ended in complete victory for the peasants. But the agrarian revolution which began a year later, and is not ended at the time of writing, was and is being fought out between two elements within the ranks of the peasantry on the question of the right of a section of the community to withhold the necessities of life from the remainder in times of dearth. The principle involved here is between the rights of unlimited proprietorship in the products of labour on the soil and the rights of the consuming community.

The first signs of the coming struggle on the land were to be observed on 11 June, when the food problem in the towns came up to be discussed in a joint sitting of the Central Soviet Executive, the Moscow Soviet and the Central Committee of the All-Russian Trade Unions. The food conditions in Petrograd and Moscow had been gradually becoming more and more critical. Living in private rooms on the Arbat, I used to receive during May one quarter of a pound of bread a day. I supplemented this with occasional purchases at the free price on the Sucharess market. But the quarter of a pound soon decreased to one-eighth, and after the Czechoslovak revolt, vanished altogether. And the Sucharess free market prices were only for those with long purses. Complaints in the working-class quarters of Moscow began to be loud. The Bolshevik regime must get food or go, one used to hear. Symptomatic of the state of feeling in these quarters was the remark which I heard of one of the doorkeepers at the Moscow Great Theatre, while waiting for the joint sitting of the Soviets and Trade Unions to begin. 'Something is wrong,' he said, 'if hunger increases like this. They must get it out of the villages, or we shall go and take it ourselves.' This indeed was the problem: how to get at that 51 million pouds in the hands of the kulaks and of the 'middle peasantry'.

The proceedings commenced with a report of a representative of the Food Commissariat. It was proposed to deal drastically with the situation. The Revolution was in danger if the 51 million pouds of corn could not be obtained for the towns, for then the urban workers would be unable to organize to defeat the White Guard bandits, who had seized the Don and Volga provinces. The Council of the People's Commissars proposed that measures should be taken to 'cleanse' the local peasants' Soviets in certain provinces, for many of them had got into the hands of kulaks and 'middle peasants', who were refusing to carry out the orders of the Central Soviet and were sabotaging the preparation of food for the towns. It was therefore proposed that in every village and rural district 'Committees of the Poorer Peasantry' should be formed. . . .

The decree for the formation of 'Committees of the Poorer Peasantry' was passed. Soon after this the expeditions began to go out into the villages. Armed parties of factory workers scoured the provinces of Voronesch, Tamboff and Pensa. Communist workmen, who were unemployed on account of the food and raw material shortage in Petrograd and Moscow, went to the villages, where their families were, and got to work in forming little groups of poor peasants and workmen. These became the new Soviets or 'Committees of the Poorer Peasants'. The kulaks resisted and got arms together. Some of the 'middle peasantry' joined them. They declined to deliver the corn. The 'Committees' replied by dissolving the old Soviets and the co-operative societies of the 'middle peasants'. Some excesses were perpetrated. In Tver, Tula and Ryazan pitched battles were fought and parts of villages wrecked. Spurred on by hunger and by desperation, caused by the oncoming counter-revolution, the urban workmen and the 'Committees' regarded the 'middle peasants' as traitors, who were stabbing them in the back. In return the 'middle peasants', unable to see the terrible straits which the urban population had been landed by the Germans and the Allies, and imagining that the Revolution had come to an end when they acquired their share of the landlords' estates, regarded the Bolsheviks and the 'Committees' as the agents of a neo-Tsarism interfering with the sacred liberty of the individual. . . .

The 'Committees of the Poorer Peasants' won through. Though a minority, they possessed a central apparatus and controlled the railway system. They were able to reduce piecemeal the backward masses of the distant villages. The corn began to come in. True, I never tasted any of the fruits of the requisitions. I lived during these days almost exclusively on potato skins and dried fish. But those who were organized in trade unions and who were members of factory committees began to receive again their quarter of a pound of bread a day, and with that they had to be satisfied till the Red Army had driven the Czechoslovaks from the Volga.

1/17 Industry and the Russian Revolution

J. W. WARDELL, *In the Kirghiz Steppes* (London, 1961), pp. 143–145.

It is now time to note the effects of the Revolution, which I will now describe up to 20 May 1918, on Sary Soo and the other camps of the Company. Because of the remoteness of the Kirghiz Steppes from the centre of these activities, it was some time before the new influences manifested themselves and they were often toned down. The news of the March Revolution and the establishment of the Provisional Government was joyfully received by all and there was much talk of the proposed Constitutional Assembly. Gradually, however, the Soviet system spread throughout the country, and turned public feeling against all forms of Western constitutional government and democracy as we knew it. It was not until June that workmen's and peasants' committees were formed in the villages in the area and in the Company's camps, and for two months after their foundation they remained innocuous. In August, however, the workmen felt that they had sufficient power to be aggressive, and efforts had to be made to keep them in check. This was done by making concessions from time to time, but by the end of 1917, two months after the November Revolution, the situation had become absolutely impossible. By then the workmen had obtained the eight-hour day, where it did not already apply, and then the six-day week. They had also secured 200 per cent rise in wages by gradual increases. These things were more or less reasonable, when conditions in other countries and the increased cost of living were considered, but the real trouble lay in the interference by the Soviets in the administration and operation of the works. They had become virtually the managers of the properties and practically nothing could be done without their sanction. A workman could not be engaged, dismissed, fined, promoted or degraded without the approval of the local Soviet, and discipline suffered because the committee invariably upheld the workman against the administration. The Soviets were in perpetual session and whenever questions arose which the members thought necessary to put to the whole community, a general assembly was called, which meant serious interruption to the operation of the mines, smelter or mill. For these and similar reasons the production of the works and the efficiency of the labour became rapidly lower.

Another difficulty now presented itself. Labour troubles throughout the country resulted in the stoppage of most factories and nearly every form of transportation, and, because of the consequent shortage of all sorts of supplies, there was nothing to induce the carters to continue working about the Company's properties. Towards the end of the year there was very little coal at the copper mine and the reduction mill, and it became evident, even to the committees, that operations at Oospensky and Sary Soo would have to be suspended at the end of 1917. Coal was still being produced at Karaganda, and as this was taken by the Company's railway to Spassky, the smelting plant was kept going after the other places closed down, but things continued to deteriorate. Finally, on 27 March 1918, the Spassky properties were nationalized by decree from Moscow and the local workmen's committee took over the mines and works; but I will deal with the banishment of the British staff later.

From the beginning of 1917 the Company had found it necessary to ration all commodities in the stores, because supplies from outside sources were falling off. By the summer, when strikes and general disorganization throughout the country prevented the obtaining of further stocks, this rationing became necessarily stricter, and luckily the committees had sufficient foresight to raise no objections. The essentials of life could be procured in the neighbourhood, but the prices of all local supplies were increased to balance the growing depreciation of the rouble.

1/18 The Role of the Trade Unions in the German War Economy

PAUL UMBREIT, *Soziale Arbeiterpolitik und Gewerkschaften* (Berlin, 1916), pp. 126–133. (Ed. Tr.)

The war temporarily removed one of the main tasks of the trade unions. While the arms were clashing at the frontier, there was no room in the economic life at home for a civil war between owners and workers. Domestic peace was not only a national, but also an economic necessity, for economic life threatened to collapse under the onslaught of the war. . . .

In the war the trade unions were also faced with important new tasks, above all the provision of work, unemployment relief and food supplies. In these tasks the well-understood interests of the German people coincided with the interests of the working class represented by the trade unions during the war. The trade unions were excellently capable of participating in social welfare activities since they possessed the largest mass organizations and controlled an extensive administrative apparatus with socially trained personnel as well as substantial resources. . . .

Even the Reich Government had to recognize this, though it had followed a shortsighted, anti-trade union policy solely in favour of the capitalist, right up to the outbreak of war, and it not only guaranteed the trade unions protection against attacks, but also drew them in most willingly to all tasks of war welfare schemes at home, as well as proclaiming a totally new orientation in its domestic policies.

Thus the German trade unions entered the war economy of the German people as the recognized representatives of the workers. They agreed with the employers' associations on the maintenance of the current wage settlements for the duration of the war, set up, together with them, committees for finding work for the unemployed, collaborated in the systematic distribution of war orders and in new wage agreements for the latter, including war bonuses as well as arbitration tribunals for the peaceful settlement of any differences. They collaborated with the Reich Centre for Job Registration for the purpose of channelling workers into harvest, fortress construction and moor and heathland reclamation jobs. They suspended all their other relief schemes in favour of unemployment benefits and family allowances for those in uniform, and levied additional sums among their members in order to extend these benefits. Their own staffs submitted in part to voluntary salary cuts in order to facilitate the survival of the unions during the war. . . .

Food supplies met increasing difficulties because of the British blockade of Germany against food imports from overseas which was clearly aimed at starving out the German population, and it became necessary to regulate home consumption and home production as well as price formation in the food market in such a way that even the poorest would be able to feed themselves adequately during the war. As early as August 1914 the General Council of the trade unions together with the Executive of the Social Democratic Party had submitted a programme to the Bundesrat for far-reaching regulation of the German food supplies. . . .

The rise in food prices naturally led to a reduction in the value of money wages which could not have been foreseen in the wage agreements made before the war. Therefore there arose wage demands for cost of living increases, in which the trade unions acted as negotiators for those groups of workers who failed to get an equivalent in war work for the rising costs of living, and achieved successes in numerous cases. . . .

The trade unions also have to take part in the preparations for the coming peace designed to lead to a conversion of the war economy to peace with the minimum of disturbance. First place is here occupied by an adequate register of work, able to meet the need of the demand for work after the war. The inadequacy of the existing registers caused the unions to demand from the Government in March 1915 a legal regulation of the work registers on a basis of parity, undertaken in collaboration with the offices of the Reich Bureau of Labour. The Reichstag agreed to these demands; however, the Government failed to institute any legal regulation, and went no further than introducing compulsory reports of the larger job registers to the Reich Office of Statistics.

1/19 Food Shortages and Anti-War Agitation in Germany

Spartacus broadsheet of June 1916. Printed in *Dokumente und Materialien* [*see* Document 1/11a], series 2, vol. I, pp. 403–405. (Ed. Tr.)

The inevitable has struck: *hunger!* hunger!

In Leipsig, in Berlin, in Essen, in Brunswick, in Magdeburg, in Munich and Kiel, and in many other places there are riots of the starving masses in front of the foodshops. In Kiel, as in Brunswick, the workers of the Germania shipyard have come out on strike in protest about the food mismanagement. And the Government of the emergency decrees has only one reply to the cry of hunger of the masses: an aggravated state of siege, police swords and military patrols.

Herr von Bethmann Hollweg accuses England of the crime of having caused the hunger in Germany, and the 'war at any price' brigade and the Government pimps parrot his cry. However, the German Government ought to have known that this was bound to happen, war against Russia, France and England was bound to lead to a blockade of Germany. . . .

They lied to us: German U-boats would cut off supplies to Britain, Britain would have to whine for peace, and the war would end. These are fairy tales for children. The U-boat warfare is setting new enemies on Germany's throat, but there can be no thought of cutting off supplies to Britain, even if Germany had ten times as many U-boats.

Then they said: the advance in the Balkans will give Germany room to manoeuvre; food in plenty would flow from Turkey. These were deliberate lies, because all those in the know are aware that Turkey cannot deliver anything, that there are shortages in Constantinople and the coastal towns of Asia Minor, and the Turkish Government can no longer feed its army.*

Now they are promising us the coming harvest: all shortages will disappear as soon as the new harvest arrives. This, too, is a deliberate swindle. A simple calculation shows that in twenty-two months of war two complete harvests had been eaten up, beside the large stocks of feeding stuffs, sugar and

* *See* Documents 1/11 a. and b. (Ed.)

other products that were available at the outbreak of war; besides all that could be 'requisitioned' in the occupied territories in Belgium, in northern France, Poland, Lithuania, Courland, and Serbia; finally all that could be imported from Holland and the Scandinavian countries. Now there is nothing left. The occupied territories have been eaten bare, men are already dying of hunger in Poland and Serbia. The neutral countries are prohibiting exports because they themselves are going short. The harvest at home cannot make up for this, for the fields have been badly tilled because of shortage of labour, of manure and of seed corn. The stocks of animals are down.

A 'food dictator' is to look after the distribution; too late! The food usurers have done their work. . . .

There is no choice. Only action counts. Arise, you men and women! Express your will, let your voice be heard:

Down with the war!

Long live the international solidarity of the proletariat!

1/20 Wartime Strikes in France

GIDE, *Effects* [*see* Document 1/6a], pp. 178–181.

1. *The number of strikes.* In paralysing the economic life of the country the war at first completely put an end to strike movements. The sense of danger aroused by the German invasion, together with the thought of defending the national territory, also helped to bring this about. Gradually, however, these movements began to increase again at the end of the year 1916, reaching a crisis in the spring of 1917, to be followed by relative quiet until the end of the war. In July 1914 there had been 109 strikes affecting 15 industries. In the first nine months of the war, that is, from 2 August 1914 to 30 April 1915, there were reported but 32 strikes involving only 1,723 workers; and the longest of these did not last more than three days. After the latter date, however, they became more and more frequent. In 1915 there were 98 strikes, 71 of which were due to wage demands. Moreover, their duration also increased, one of them lasting two weeks. They involved 9,361 workers, and resulted in 16 successes, 44 failures, and 38 compromises. In 1916 the number was still greater – 394 strikes involving 41,409 workers. Thus for the first two and a half years of the war there were altogether 430 strikes involving 51,830 workers. They were especially frequent in the textile industry (89), in the transportation business (80), in the metal trades (56), in the leather and hides industry (41), in the building trades (36), and in the chemical industry (25). The majority (348) were caused by wage questions. Of the total 430 strikes, 102 (involving 30 per cent of the strikers) were

successful, 178 (21 per cent of the strikers) were unsuccessful, and 150 (49 per cent of the strikers) resulted in compromise. The year 1916, however, was not comparable in this respect with the pre-war years, since in 1913, for example, there had been reported no less than 10,073 strikes involving 220,000 workers, and resulting in a loss of 2,223,000 days of work.

The year 1917, on the other hand, opened in an atmosphere of strikes. At first they attacked the munitions factories, where they were due to the new schedule of wages and to a system of bonuses to which the workers were opposed. In order to put an end to this, the Minister of Munitions ordered the establishment of a minimum wage and compulsory arbitration of wage questions – a matter to which we shall refer further on. The immediate result was not favourable. The order even had the effect of causing strikes, due to the impatience of workers to see the new rates put into force. In the months of May and June strikes became most numerous, especially among women workers. They began with the cloth-cutting branch as affecting luxury articles, and gradually involved the entire clothing and fine wear industry, finally spreading even to the munitions factories. In the cutting and clothing branches, as a matter of fact, wages not only remained low, but were even lower than in time of peace. The first struggle that took place in Paris tended to place them on the pre-war level. Dressmakers were found to be earning 3 francs per diem, excluding Sundays – that is to say, scarcely 80 francs a month in the height of the season. Another demand was that of the 'English week' – that is, a half-day's rest on Saturday with pay. The strike lasted 12 days and resulted in: (1) a rise of wages and the granting of the high-cost-of-living bonus; (2) the voting and enactment of the law of 11 June 1917, providing for the introduction of the English week.

At the same time, 171 strikes involving 58,571 workers (40,775 men and 17,796 women) took place in the munitions factories. They caused the loss of 142,339 days of work, and were due to wage demands (131) and the question of working-men's solidarity (35). Altogether, however, despite the fears to which they gave rise, they involved only 3·38 per cent of the men and 12·06 per cent of the women employed in the manufacture of munitions. Later on, towards the end of 1917, a number of strikes occurred in the steel and iron industry of the Loire, but they were quickly checked.

2. *The causes of strikes.* The causes of these strikes have been much discussed. Some people saw in them the hand of the enemy, and to this argument the arrest of a few foreign workers among the strikers lent colour. In reality, however, these strikes were due both to economic and to psychological causes. The misunderstanding of certain workshop regulations by workers new to the industry; unjust dismissals of workers; the state of lassitude brought about by the prolongation of the war and the difficulties to

which it gave rise; excessive profits of employers; demands of the retail trade; the rising cost of living; the increased demand for distractions and luxuries; the dissatisfaction of certain workers who considered themselves misplaced, or who were jealous of newcomers in the trade better paid than themselves; the question of the regulation of work; the demand for shorter hours; and finally, imitation and contagion – all these were elements in the problem.

The truth is, however, that it was especially economic considerations, rooted in the increasing disproportion between the reward of labour and the cost of living, that caused and sustained the discontent. Proof of this lies in the fact that the principal demand was for the so-called 'high-cost-of-living bonus'. The female workers in the clothing industry could not see why their former companions, who had entered the munitions factories, were earning from 12 to 15 francs a day, while they were forced to content themselves with 4 or 5 francs a day. Many workers, moreover, felt themselves wronged by the continual changing and refixing of wages. Their fears were sometimes imaginary, but often real. As regards piece-workers, an increased production was often followed by a reduction of the price per piece. The Minister of Munitions was forced to insist on greater fairness on the part of manufacturers. The substitution of time-work for piece-work at first led to a diminution of remuneration. Taking advantage of their authority and of the workers' fear of being sent back to the army, certain employers did not hesitate to reduce the wages of skilled military workers, who were jealous of the higher earnings of the newly arrived civil and female workers. The docking of wages and the imposition of fines increased, and the workers were deprived of certain advantages which they had enjoyed for a long time. The rates of compensation were obscure, secret, imperfect, or indefinite. All this accounts for the recrudescence of strikes in 1917, the total of which was 697 for the year, with 190 to 270 in May and June, respectively, against an average of not more than 40 a month in 1918.

1/21 The Berlin Munitions Strikes, February and April 1917

a Secret Agent's report of 19 February 1917, together with covering letter by von Oppen, President of Police in Berlin, to the War Office and the Army Command of the Marches, of 23 February 1917. Printed in *Dokumente und Materialien* [*see* Document 1/11a], Series 2, vol. I, pp. 554–556. (Ed. Tr.)

b Letter from the Army Command of the Marches (i.e. the Berlin Region) to the Prussian Ministry of War, 19 April 1917. Printed in *Ibid.* Series 2, vol. I, p. 611. (Ed. Tr.

a (*Covering letter*) I am enclosing a copy of a report of my agents on the causes of the recently increasing stoppages in the munitions works. . . . If it puts the blame for the existing dissatisfaction of the workers on the conditions of life, the latest reports suggest that these do not wholly account for the stoppages. Political causes also appear to play a not insignificant part in these movements. The working class of Greater Berlin supports politically the radical wing of Social Democracy. A large proportion supports the Spartacus Group. . . . In view of the salutary results of the call-up of rebellious workers into the army after the passing of the Auxiliary Service Act,* I leave it to you to decide whether in order to suppress the working class movements which are so damaging to the public welfare that method may not be used again. . . .

(*Report*) In the course of the war the attitude of the organized metal workers in the munitions factories of Greater Berlin has reached a dangerous level as a result of the subversive activities of unscrupulous elements. In view of the numerous stoppages of work recently, and in view of the fact that agitation is going on in nearly all large firms with predominantly radical work forces to shorten progressively the hours of labour, there is a danger that the munitions works here will in future not be able to deliver war materials in sufficient quantities and in time.

The undersigned has collected the following information in confidential intercourse with various organized munitions workers and in official contacts with several managers of large firms:

At present almost all officials of the German Metal Workers' Union (secretaries and shop stewards) who set the tone in the factories for the whole of the work force, are in political terms supporters of the opposition, and in large proportion support the so-called Spartacus Group, which has as its motto the end of the war by a refusal to work. In the course of the past year, a large number of factory meetings have taken place in Greater Berlin as a result of the activities of these officials in which demands after demands were made in the most impudent manner and these have since been met in part as a result of work stoppages. Wages have already risen into infinity in this way. Skilled workers like fitters, turners, moulders, engineers, etc., already obtain daily earnings of 15 to 22 marks for an average working day of 9 hours. But the demands continue. Thus there is currently pending a wage demand for around 700 fitters and turners of the Berlin Engineering Co., formerly L. Schwartzkopff, 13–28 Scheringstr. They are asking for an increase of 30 pf. an hour, even though they already get 18 to 22 marks for a day of 9 hours. As the company has rejected this impudent demand, the 700 workers have been out on strike since Saturday, 10th instant, and the torpedo manufacture of this important factory is now totally crippled. In the same works, as a result of activity by the radical elements, some 2,900 workers came out on

* *See* Document No. **1/5d**. (Ed.)

a protest strike on 3rd instant allegedly because of the food supply breakdown, in demonstration against the appropriate departments of State, and this cost the production of three torpedoes. As far as this radical subversive activity is concerned, conditions are similar in the German Arms and Ammunition Works, Charlottenburg and Wittenau. These actions are being imitated in other larger factories producing war material.

It is established that all these demands are totally unjustified at present, since, as shown above, the workers are making good money and in addition they get preferential food supplies provided by nearly all these firms, so that they are much better fed than the rest of the population of Greater Berlin. . . .

In the face of the power wielded by the 'radical union officials', the official secretaries of the Berlin branch of the German Metal Workers' Union, Cohen and Siering, are helpless and are forced to submit to this power, since their position depends on re-election by the same officials. The second-in-command, Siering, is therefore acting fully in accord with these radical officials by helping to agitate at the various works meetings for reductions of hours and increasing wages and thus gaining the sympathy of the radical elements. There is no doubt that war production is being adversely affected by these unscrupulous activities, and there will be no peace in the munitions factories until the radical elements have been made harmless, in the first place perhaps by the call-up of the chief agitators who have been in reserved occupations.

b Police inquiries about the extent of the stoppages of work on 16th instant have shown that a total of 148,903 workers in the works in Greater Berlin and surrounding districts came out, of whom 15,532 returned on 17th instant and the rest, except for about 25,000, returned on 18th instant. According to the 'Vorwarts',★ work stopped in 300 munitions concerns and included 210,000 strikers.

About 9,700 workers of the 'German Arms and Ammunition Co.' in Berlin–Moabit and Wittenau, 3,400 workers in the Otto Jachmann factory in Tegel–Wittenau, 1,200 workers of the Knorr-Bremse Co. in Lichtenberg, 5,000 workers in the factories of the A.E.G.† in Hennigsdorf and around 5,000 workers each in the Bergmann Electricity Works in Berlin–Rosenau and A. Borsig in Tegel remained out on 18th instant. Of these, 20,000 are still out today in the first-named concerns. To these have to be added workers of the Spandau factories who joined the strike only on 18th instant.

The strike has remained peaceful in form. The right-wing Social-Democratic Party as such and the trade union leadership officially dissociated themselves from it; it was led in the main by the trade union shop stewards.

★ The Social-Democratic Journal. (Ed.)   † The German electrica lcombine. (Ed.)

1/22 The German Strikes of January 1918

Reports by the Ministry of War to the Reich Ministry of the Interior, 29 January 1918.
Printed in *Dokumente und Materialien* [*see* Document 1/11a], Series 2, vol. II, pp. 84–86.
(Ed. Tr.)

WORKERS' MOVEMENT (AS AT 12.00 NOON)

1. Bavarian War Ministry reports on 28 January:
Southern Bavaria – Munich and Augsburg – are quiet.
In Northern Bavaria there are on strike in Nuremberg at least 50,000, in Furth at least 3,000. An extension of the movement is possible.
2. Baltic Command, Station Kiel reports on 28.1:
The meeting authorized for the torpedo factory in Friedrichsort had no success, since the workers declared in favour of continuing their political general strike.
There are now out – as reported previously in part:

Torpedo works Friedrichsort	4,700 workers
Imperial Yard	8,900
Germania Shipyard	6,350
Howald Works	1,400
Bohn & Kaehler	800
Neufeld & Kuhnke	500
In smaller works	600

There have been no disturbances.
Deputy G.O.C. VII Army Corps reports on 28.1:
In 9 pits in the district of the Command in Munster and in the copper works Kaiser & Co. in Lünen, 4,915 men are out.
The previously reported Hamburg mine in Annen has resumed work, similarly the Hansa mine in Dortmund with the exception of 157 men.
4. Command Altona reports on 28.1:
The strike which began in the Vulkan yard in Hamburg is being extended in the afternoon of 28.1 to Blohm & Voss.
5. Wumba (The Munitions Supply Department) reports on 29.1:
In the rifle factory in Spandau the workers of the day shift left off work after the first breakfast break at 9 a.m.
In the gun workshops in Spandau, 700 workers did not turn up for the night shift of 28 to 29 January, being turned back by strike pickets on the railway stations of Greater Berlin and Spandau.
In the gun workshops of North Spandau, 370 workers are out.
In the rocket laboratory in Spandau all is quiet.

6. The Command of the Marches reports on 29.1:
The strike position in Greater Berlin is at present totally confused, since the numbers out on strike have increased in some works and diminished in others. A survey will therefore only be possible in the afternoon.

WORKERS' MOVEMENT (AS AT 4.00 P.M.)

1. Command Breslau reports on 29.1:
All is quiet in the command district, but there are some signs that Polish agitators are stirring up the work force.

2. Command Altona reports on 29.1:
All is quiet in Bremen, but a strike is expected on 30.1. In the Vulkan Yard in Hamburg the numbers out on strike have grown to 7,900.
The extension of the strike reported earlier to Blohm & Voss has now spread further to the shipyards Stuelcken & Son, Reihersteig and a number of smaller firms. The above works have been placed under military management.
The Deputy G.O.C. has suspended Article 7 of the Prussian Constitution for Hamburg, Altona, Wandsbek, Bremen and Hemelingen, and the appropriate regulations of the constitution of Hamburg and Bremen, and has set up special Courts Martial. In the steel foundry Hermann Michaelson in Altona 300 workers stopped work in the morning of 29.1.

3. Deputy G.O.C. IV Army Corps reports on 29.1:
About 500 men in various industrial enterprises in Halle and Ammendorf have stopped work on 28.1. apparently because of wage disagreements.

4. Command Magdeburg reports on 29.1.:
In Halle the number of striking metal workers has increased to about 1,200. In Magdeburg about 10,000 workers are out on 29 January. The peace has not been disturbed. Preparations are being made for calling up those of military age and for militarizing the factories.

5. The Command of the Marches reports on 29.1:
The number of workers on strike in Greater Berlin has increased to about 150,000.

1/23 The Effects of the War on French Agriculture

L. G. MICHAEL, *Agricultural Survey of France*. Technical Bulletin No. 37. February 1928. U.S. Dept. of Agriculture. (Washington D.C. 1928) pp. 5–6.

The immediate effect of the [First] World War was primarily an enormous depletion of the nation's manpower and secondarily the devastation of a large area, including some of the richest agricultural sections in the country.

The general effect of the war upon French agriculture was to intensify each of those four trends which had characterized the farming of the country at the outbreak of hostilities.* These effects influenced in a similar manner, though to a different degree, the 77 Departments† outside the war zone, the 10 Departments occupied in whole or in part by war operations and the 3 Departments of Alsace-Lorraine restored to France at the end of the war.

During the war France lost 1,636,000 of those engaged in war activities. In addition, deaths among civilians exceeded births by 944,000. In 1919, there were 233,000 excess civilian deaths in France, including Alsace-Lorraine. Thus, France entered upon reconstruction at the beginning of 1920 with a loss of population approximating at least 2,813,000.

Probably two-thirds of this number represented effective manpower. Farm labour was depleted through these losses of manpower. The country districts of France lost nearly 2,000,000 inhabitants, for the most part men, between 1911 and 1921. During this decade the cities lost only 300,000. This great discrepancy between rural and urban losses is not accounted for by war losses alone, for city populations have been recouped through large migrations from country districts to the cities and industrial centres since 1919. . . .

The depletion of farm labour is not indicated alone by the actual numerical decrease in farm population. The effectiveness of males still actually residing in rural communities is lessened because of disease and mutilations incident to the war.

Various estimates have been made of the devastation in the war zone. The limits of the zone involved in war operations varied from time to time. The maximum area invaded is estimated at 10,514,325 acres, about one-thirteenth part of the country, of which 8,242,989 acres were 'occupied for a long time.'

The Department (county) of Ardennes (1,293,783 acres) was wholly occupied during the war and no data from this Department appear in French statistics between 1914 and 1918. In the Departments of Aisne, Marne, Meuse, Meurthe-et-Moselle, Nord, Oise, Pas-de-Calais, Somme, and Vosges, 6,948,251 acres were occupied the greater part of the war period.

It has been estimated that the devastation of ploughlands in the war zone exceeded 4,750,000 acreas and that losses of livestock in the 10 occupied Departments exceeded 50 per cent of the 1909–13 average.

Outside the war zone, lack of manpower forced millions of acres out of civilization and the requisitions of the Government reduced French herds by millions of animals.

* Change from cereals: o forage crops; expansion of grasslands; intensification of animal husbandry; increasing use of female labour. (Ed.)
† See Glossary.

1/24 War Devastation in Northern France

a Report by George B. Ford of the American Red Cross. December 1918. Printed in CLOUGH, *et al., Economic History* [*see* Document 1/4a], pp. 58–62.

b Report of Special Commissioner, *The Statist*, vol. XLV, 8 May 1920, pp. 857–858.

a The devastated area in France covers approximately 6,000 square miles in all, about 2 per cent of France, with a total population of nearly 2,000,000 people. This is about equal to the area of Connecticut and Rhode Island....

The hasty investigation since the signing of the armistice shows that [compared with the estimates of earlier reports] the total destruction in France has been quintupled, with something like 500,000 buildings damaged, and at least 250,000 completely destroyed.

The average cost of these buildings before the war was nearly $5,000. As the present cost of a building is about two and a half times greater than it was then, we can say that the total destruction in France of the buildings alone is today over $6,000,000,000, as estimated by the Government engineers, and $4,000,000,000 as estimated by the architects and constructors' associations....

According to a report made by the Office de Reconstitution Agricole to the Minister of Liberated Regions in May 1918, it was reckoned that at that time about 8,000 square miles of French land was in the hands of the Germans. About three-quarters of that area is tillable, and a large proportion of the rest is good for hay or pasturage. This is some of the very best and richest agricultural land in Europe. The ten invaded and liberated departments* produced in 1913 nearly $400,000,000 worth of crops. ... These regions constitute about 15 per cent of the total tillable area of France, and the crops constitute about 20 per cent of the total for France. The agricultural population here is about 807,000, or about 10 per cent of the working agricultural population of France. It is estimated that 250,000 acres are now rendered uncultivable by the war....

... In all something over 70 per cent of the total coal supply of France came from the invaded regions, and very much the best quality of coal at that. About 140,000 men were employed in these mines in the invaded regions out of 203,208 coal-miners for all of France. This means, with their families, three-quarters of a million people were largely dependent on the coal mines. Over $200,000,000 of machinery has probably been destroyed.

Before the war the total production of iron ore in France was about 21,918,000 tons, of which 19,629,000 tons came from the Briey and Longwy basins in the Meurthe-et-Moselle; that is, 90 per cent of the total, of which 16,500,000 tons were in the hands of the Germans. The miners who were employed in these invaded mines, with their families, represented at least

* See Glossary.

150,000 people out of employment. . . . More than $500,000,000 worth of machinery has been destroyed, including that of steel and iron mills.

Before the war 3,000,000 tons of steel were manufactured in the region invaded by Germany out of 4,686,000 tons for all of France, or nearly 65 per cent. The same percentage holds for cast iron. . . .

Before the war there were about 750,000 men in the various building trades, of whom about 75,000 were in the invaded departments. The total building done throughout France before the war in any one year was less than 7 per cent of the building that would have to be done to replace what has been destroyed in the invaded departments. Therefore if no building were to be done elsewhere in France after the war, and reckoning that 500,000 of the building tradesmen of France would be available to work in the devastated regions, it would take over twenty years to rebuild.

The total damage in the north of France, including buildings, agriculture, industry, furniture, and public works, is estimated at 64,500,000,000 francs, or about $13,000,000,000. These were the figures reported by M. Dubois for the Committee on Budget in the Chamber of Deputies, December 1918. We have checked most of these figures from various official and private sources and believe they are somewhat high. . . .

b Paris: 6 May 1920

A budget commission that reported last year to the Chamber of Deputies estimated the damage directly sustained in the invaded Departments of France as 96,000 million francs, and, allowing for indirect damage, calculated the total loss at approximately 120,000 million francs. The Departments which suffered from the enemy were 11 in number, and comprise the Nord, Aisne, Ardennes, Meurthe et Moselle, Vosges, Somme, Marne, Meuse, Aube, Haute-Marne and Belfort. Of these the first four, which were on the border, were almost completely devastated. The calculations of the Commission err, if at all, on the side of modesty, and the main difficulty before France is to make good in a year or two the work of many generations, and, moreover, to undertake the task with a population of whom 1,400,000 have been killed and 3,000,000 have been wounded. Of the wounded men 700,000 are permanently crippled or maimed and require support. Thus more than two millions of the male population have been rendered ineffective for economic purposes, and, in addition, the country is burdened with a most oppressive weight of internal and external debt. Besides the reduction in the labour force, the machinery of production has also suffered, and the supply of primary materials, such as coal, has been grievously curtailed. True, the onus of reimbursing France for part at least of the losses occasioned by the War has been laid on Germany; but Germany's ability to pay, no less than her willingness, has been called in question. She will not, at any rate, be in a position to discharge her obligations in full for quite a long period.

The problem of reconstruction in the devastated region is social as well as material. It is impossible for an outsider to picture the conditions that obtain in the desolated towns and villages to which the former inhabitants have returned. In many cases their old homes have been destroyed, and the newcomers are herded together in uncomfortable and insanitary dwellings, often open to every wind of heaven. They even lack, to some extent, the very instruments of production, and, as they are thus denied hopes of an immediate betterment in their lot, there is over a widespread area little of the animation and none of the gaiety that formerly marked French rural life. Villages and towns remain more or less isolated, because communications by rail, road and telegraph have not yet been fully restored. . . .

That area which now lies incapacitated was to France what Lancashire and Yorkshire are to England. It may readily be imagined how effectually England would be crippled by the loss of the two northern counties, and if, in addition, we had suffered equally in manpower, and were laden with a crushing weight of internal and external debt, our position would remotely resemble that of present-day France; remotely because nearly 40 per cent of Frenchmen between the ages of 30 and 50 have fallen in battle. . . .

. . . the growth of national barriers has checked the free interchange of food and other commodities. Moreover, the railways formerly controlled by large unit states are now divided up amongst a number of Governments, each of which is desirous to assert its authority and its importance in the eyes of its neighbour and of the world. This obstructionist policy, combined as it is with an exaggerated chauvinism, deprived France of some of its natural sources of food supply and its natural outlets for manufactured goods, and forces it into unhealthy borrowing in countries where it already owes considerable sums of money. Thus the Paris Municipal Council recently borrowed 20 million dollars at 6 per cent from a Canadian banking syndicate. The issue price was fixed at the low figure of 88, and the loan is redeemable after ten years. One of the conditions attaching to it is that the funds are to be spent exclusively in Canada for the purchase of foodstuffs, which will be used to feed the population of Paris. Food must, indeed, be provided from whatever source and at whatever cost, but French agriculture, if its reconstruction were aided by the Allies, could furnish the necessary supplies in a marvellously short time, as the country was to a large extent self-supporting before the war. This is the tragedy of the devastated area that money which is at present leaving France could be spent at home once the initial difficulties in the way of reconstruction were overcome. If the Allies co-operated for destructive purposes, it is all the less reasonable of them to refuse co-operation in repairing the damage they helped to cause.

1/25 Post-war Economic Dislocation in the Austrian Successor States

a ANNA EISENMENGER, *Blockade. The Diary of an Austrian Middle-Class Woman 1914–1924* (London 1932), pp. 115–118, entry for 15 December 1918.

b Report by W. H. Beveridge, of the Inter-Allied Commission on Relief of German–Austria, 17 January 1919. Hoover Institute, Stanford University, Archives, Paris files, Box 16.

c Alonzo E. Taylor, *Report on the Countries that have arisen from Austria–Hungary,* 28 January 1919. *Ibid.*, Box 16, pp. 9–10, 23–24.

d William Goode, *Economic Conditions in Central Europe* (Parl. Papers, 1920, LI, Cmd. 521), p. 8.

a In the large banking hall a great deal of business was being done and I had to wait some time before I was attended to. All around me animated discussions were in progress concerning the stamping of currency, the issue of new notes, the purchase of foreign money and so on. There were always some who knew exactly what was now the best thing to do! After my money had been stamped, I went to see the bank official who always advised me. 'Well, wasn't I right?' he said. 'If you had bought Swiss francs when I suggested, you would not now have lost three-fourths of your fortune.'

'Lost!' I exclaimed in horror. 'Why, don't you think the krone will recover again?'

'Recover!' he said with a laugh. 'Recover!' he repeated, leaning across the oak counter, behind which stood his writing-table. 'Our krone will go to the devil, that's certain.' He had spoken the last sentence very low, so that the people standing near me could not hear.

'Good heavens!' I said, and I must have looked very dismayed.

'Will you follow my advice this time. . . . At the present time it is well to possess a house or ground or shares in an industry or a mine or something else of the sort, but not to possess any money, or at least no Austrian or German money. Do you understand what I mean?'

'Yes, but mine are Government securities; surely there can't be anything safer than that?' I answered.

'But, my dear lady, where is the State which guaranteed these securities to you? It is dead, and do you imagine that its successor will or can take over all the liabilities of its predecessor? That is absolutely out of the question.'

My head was in a whirl, but as my adviser had been right on the previous occasion, and as, moreover, he was looked upon as an extremely clever businessman, I decided to do what he advised me.

He gave me an introduction to a friend who had a private banking business and whom he recommended as particularly trustworthy and experienced. This man would exchange my Government securities for corresponding industrial securities. I should, of course, lose money by this transaction, but I should at least have something safe.

b . . . The problem of unemployment, particularly in Vienna and Buda-Pest, is reaching portentious proportions. It only escapes notice at the moment through pre-occupation with more urgent questions and through the extravagant (sic) provision of relief. It represents, however, a source of immense danger for the near future.

The manpower of German Austria and Hungary has been engaged for four years in the production of war: it is now in the towns producing practically nothing at all. The armies are demobilized; the munitions works are stopped. The shortage of coal and transport and the maintenance of the blockade make the resumption of ordinary industrial activity on any large scale impossible. The workmen are being maintained in idleness by unemployment relief. In Vienna all unemployed workmen are receiving 60 per cent of their previous pay plus an allowance for dependents. In Buda-Pest men are receiving 14 Kronen and women 10 Kronen a day, figures which even at the reduced value of the krone are very high in relation to previous earnings. The Government finds the means to make these payments by continual recourse to the printing of more paper money.

It is unnecessary to elaborate the evils of such a situation; and the certainty of demoralization, disorder and bankruptcy involved in its continuance for any considerable period . . . the development of rioting, if nothing is done to provide real employment as well as food, is only a question of time. . . .

Wherever the Commission went – but particularly in Prague and Buda-Pest – they found a constantly repeated expression of fear of Bolshevism arising, both out of the hardship to which the workmen were being subjected and as a result of agitation fostered from Russia.

The expression of the fear was generally followed by a request for the presence of allied troops. . . . (He goes on to suggest a force of 5–10,000 Entente troops for Czechoslovakia to over-ween also the surrounding countries.) . . . Any permanent safeguard against disorder must clearly be sought, not in military occupation, but in the restoration of economic security: that is to say in the immediate provision of the minimum of food, clothing and fuel and in the resumption at as early a date as possible of ordinary industrial activity....

(*Summary*) . . . The cessation of war without the restoration of peace in Austria Hungary, combined with its political dismemberment has produced a state of general economic paralysis. It seems difficult to avoid the conclusion that in order to prevent a collapse of the social order comparable to what has occurred in Russia, the Allies must practically if not formally treat the war with all parts of Austria as finished, and must give positive help in reconstruction there.... The grounds are twofold:

(i) the war is in fact so completely finished, as far as these countries are concerned, and they are so completely smashed, that wartime standards of inhumanity are no longer applicable.

(ii) The further spread of disorder in Europe is a danger to the Allied countries themselves....

(*Proposals for action*) . . .

9. *Coal.* The increase in the coal supply of all the districts in question must be regarded as the most urgent of all the problems to be solved.

The means available are:

(a) Supply of materials and machinery to the mines.

(b) Supply of food and clothing to the miners.

(c) Suppression of disorder, if necessary by a display of military force.

(d) Supply of additional labour, if necessary that of prisoners....

c Had Austro-Hungary remained intact, she would have had indeed a hard time during the period of reconstruction, but having split into fractions that are formed rather on ethnological than on industrial or agricultural grounds, the difficulties have been enormously multiplied. The railways suffer not merely from lack of coal, friction metal, deterioration of equipment and inability to renew the stock, they suffer also from the sub-division of territory, whereby the railways of the separate states cannot be effectively operated. The same holds good in regard to the waterways. Salt is a monopoly of Austro-Hungary (sic), but Austro-Hungary possesses no coal. Sugar is a practical monopoly of Bohemia as against German Austria. The coal in Hungary is but a portion of their needs and their transportation system is helpless without the co-operation of the transportation system of Czechoslovakia and German Austria. An equitable sub-division of the foodstuffs is impossible. There is no consistent financial policy. The wealthy men living in Vienna and holding property in Czechoslovakia and Hungary do not know what these states will do with their property and are unable to utilize their resources. Under these circumstances no one can borrow money and an independent policy of retrenchment is as impossible as a policy of expansion.

Coal production varies somewhere between 40 and 60 per cent of the normal output and is, of course, inequitably divided. In Czechoslovakia, there is, for example, a considerable relative excess of coking coal, in Hungary there is no coking coal and no possibility of exchange in order that the gas works of Buda-Pest may be continued in operation. . . .

This lack of co-operation extends even to sanitary conditions. The Hungarians have withdrawn their sanitary control from their eastern frontier in the face of the advancing Roumanian army. The Roumanians have instituted no sanitary control, with the result that typhus has appeared in both Buda-Pest and Vienna. Even the operations of the post and telegraph, the circulation of newspapers, the payment of private debts, the transmission of moneys of insurance, have all been more or less interfered with by arbitrary acts, under the common impulse that the separate states will conserve their own interests by reckless disregard of the interests of others. This has led to a deplorable reduction in the efficiency of all operations of life. Let us assume, as a mere figure, that the total resources of Austro-Hungary at the signing of the armistice, were reduced to 60 per cent of the pre-war figure. Certainly the utilization of this remaining 60 per cent has been reduced one-third potentially and actually as the result of the sub-division of the dual monarchy into six parts. . . .

One of the worst features of the situation, from a commercial point of view, lies in the fact that the distribution of agricultural products from the producers to the non-producing classes was never correctly organized during the war. The authorities contented themselves with requisitioning for the army and with such demands of agricultural products from the producers as would enable them to offer a card ration of from 700 to 1,000 calories, leaving the supply of the remainder to trade. In other words, the authorities never pretended to supply over one-third of the diet. This worked well enough for two years. But when the production fell greatly, the system was not only intolerable to the consumer, but led to speculation and illicit handling on the part of the producer and his distributive agents that resulted in the total ruination of the civic consciousness of the producer. The people of Austria did not realize during the war that Austria had ceased to be a food-exporting state and had practically become a food-importing state, certainly under no conditions more than a self-sustaining state. . . .

Of the 55 per cent of a normal crop supposed to have been raised [?1918? Ed.], we may be sure that the producers, apart from their diminished count of stock, retained per capita, as much as before the war, leaving of course to the inhabitants of the cities and the industrial classes in general a greatly reduced ration. This has been covered in fact by the transfer of maize from animal food to human food.

d In all the economic welter of Europe there is no more perplexing vicious circle than that of coal and railways. In countries where I found wagons I found, almost invariably, a shortage of locomotives; where there were locomotives there was a shortage of wagons; where coal lay at the pithead awaiting transport there were no wagons; and where wagons waited, men were not available to work the coal. For want of coal in Austria whole trains of wagons stood idle on the tracks. There were locomotives, but you cannot get up steam without fuel. In Yugoslavia and Hungary the lines were congested with empty wagons for want of locomotives. In Poland, where efforts were made to stimulate the production of oil fuel, there were not enough tank wagons to carry the increased quantity of oil. . . . Up to December 1919 over 1,800 'armistice' wagons and 285 locomotives were provided to alleviate the situation, and efforts are being made to obtain raw materials with which to repair locomotives and rolling-stock worn out by the war. . . .

There is another regrettable feature of this transport tangle. It is epitomized in the following sentence from a report I have recently received from a British officer in one of the new states:

> Before one single truck can be moved from one station to another, various officials from the highest government official to the meanest railway employee expect monetary gifts.

That, I am sorry to say, is true not only of the country of which it was written.

The latest reports show a tendency to increased coal production throughout Europe – it is now about 80 per cent of the 1913 production – but the natural tendency of the coal-producing countries to retain the pre-war quantities for their own consumption, will result for some time to come in a continued under-supply to non-coal-producing countries.

1/26 Post-War Hunger in Germany and Austria

a The Rubner Report, of the Free Scientific Commission for the Study of the Present Food Condition in Germany, compiled 16–27 December 1918. In Hoover Institute Archives, Paris File, Box 64, p. 5.

b Report by Brig.-Gen. H. C. Rees on Germany, 12–15 December 1918, in *Reports by British Officers on the Conditions prevailing in Germany* (Parl. Papers, 1919, LIII, Cmd. 52), pp. 10–11.

c Letter by Lt.-Col. Jesse B. Roote, C.O., U.S. troops Bautzen, to Commanding General, U.S. Military Mission, Berlin, 26 March 1919, with enclosure. Hoover Institute Archives, Paris File, Box 64.

d Report on Silesia, *Reports by British Officers* [*see* Document **1/26b**] Cmd. 208, p. 11.

e Letter from Sir H. Stuart (Coblenz) to Mr. Waterlow at the Foreign Office, 26 April 1920. Printed in *Documents on British Foreign Policy, 1919–1939* (First Series, vol. X, 1960), pp. 214–215.

f Report by the Medical Officer of the City of Vienna on its state of health. Hoover Institute Archives, Paris File, Box 16. (Ed. Tr.)

g Report August–September 1919, Mrs. PHILIP SNOWDEN, *A Political Pilgrim in Europe* (London, 1921), pp. 113–114.

h Report on Distress in Vienna, by Lieut. John M. Oskison, Hoover Institute Archives, Paris File, Box 14, pp. 14–16.

i *Economic Conditions in Central Europe* (Parl. Papers, 1920, LI, Cmd. 641), pp. 6–7.

a (*Summary*)
I. It results from the statistical data that with regard to the health of human beings the blockade has in the main had the following effects:

(a) increase in mortality especially among children and among those in the later stages of life, caused above all by the lessened power of resistance against infectious diseases, especially tuberculosis (the general increase in the deaths amounting during the period of war to 763,000 persons).

(b) This increase in mortality corresponds according to the observations of the medical profession to a considerable increase in illnesses (tuberculosis, diseases of the intestines, diseases brought about by the loss of fat like hernia, oedema, etc.), although a computation of figures of this increase can naturally not be made with the same exactness as the number of deaths.

II. At the present moment at least 800 persons more die daily than was the case during the last few years before the war so that since the conclusion of the armistice 36,000 persons have already died. . . .

b 1. In Saxony, the situation as regards food is undoubtedly serious. Except perhaps for Berlin, the food situation in Saxony is worse than any-where else in Germany, for the following reasons:

(a) Saxony is an industrial state with a large mining and manufacturing population, while its agricultural resources are not sufficient to make it self-supporting as regards food.

(b) The main food supplies, such as corn and potatoes, are normally drawn from Posen, Silesia and Bohemia, which are now cut off owing to the political and international situation. . . .

2. The system of food control appeared to me to be very efficient, and the distribution is very scrupulously supervised. Every single article of food, except vegetables, is rationed, including potatoes, and the rations are very

much reduced, with the prospect of still further reductions owing to the cutting-off of supplies from Posen and Silesia, and also as a result of the restrictions in the train service (amounting to 90 per cent) by the handing over of rolling-stock imposed by the Armistice Commission.

3. It is true that one can still live fairly comfortably at the more expensive hotels. . . . In the country districts and smaller towns, life is still tolerable, but in a large industrial city like Leipzig, with 650,000 inhabitants, the situation is serious and getting worse. The people have a distinctly sallow and pinched appearance. . . .

6. Although the people on the whole are very dissatisfied with the quantity of their rations, they abide by the distribution system, because they know that without it the limited stocks would soon fail completely. On the other hand, the element of disorder is growing apace, owing to the unsettled political conditions and the great increase in unemployment. Before the Armistice, there were less than 700 men out of work in Leipzig. On 12 January there were 22,000 unemployed in the city. This enormous increase in unemployment is due to:

(a) The lack of materials, mainly due to the transport difficulties, caused by the Armistice terms.

(b) The demobilization of the army before the absorption of the men into civilian life can be organized.

7. The *weekly* ration per head of the civilian population in Leipzig during the first week of January, 1919, was:

	Adult	Child
Meat	200 *grammes*	100 *grammes*
Butter	50 *grammes*	50 *grammes*
Potatoes	2,500 *grammes*	2,500 *grammes*
Fish	—	—
Jam	—	—
Dried vegetables	100 *grammes*	250 *grammes*
Eggs	1 egg	1 egg
Cheese	40 *grammes*	40 *grammes*
Bread	2,500 *grammes*	1,500–2,000 *grammes*

A very limited supply of milk (one-fifth of the peace supply) is available, and only allows of a ration for very young children and hospitals. The principal reason for the shortage of milk is the low productivity of the cows, owing to the scarcity of fodder. A cow that in peace gave 6–8 *litres* of milk now only gives about 2 *litres*.

8. I had a conversation with the medical officer of the town of Leipzig, who gave me statistics testifying to the effects of malnutrition on the

population. The weekly birth-rate, which was 1,100 per week in 1913, has fallen to an average of 550 per week in 1918, while the mortality has increased from 700 to 900 in the same period. That is to say, the births, which previously exceeded the deaths by 400 a week, are now inferior to them by 350 a week. I was also given graphs showing the effect of malnutrition on the physical development of children during the war.

c 1. Major General Baron Oldershausen, Commanding General of the 32nd (Sachsen) Infantry Division of the German Army, has asked me to bring to the notice of the military representative of the Allied Governments the enclosed data concerning the state of nutrition and the shortage of food in Saxony. This data was prepared by officers of the Saxon Government.

2. I am convinced that the statements in the memoranda enclosed are substantially true. The people in this part of Saxony are literally starving to death.

3. I venture to offer the opinion that the receipt by the Germans of an adequate food supply in the immediate future would do much to check the spread of Bolshevism. . . .

(Enclosure*): *State of food supplies in Saxony.*

Saxony being a country with a very dense industrial population and with but few agricultural districts, depends largely on the supplies furnished by other parts of Germany. This dependency has during the war been the reason that the alimentation of the inhabitants has been poorer than in any other part of Germany.

At present the state is as follows:

Potatoes: According to the plan of distribution set up by the imperial authorities in 1918 the province of Posen in Prussia still has to supply Saxony with $1\frac{1}{2}$ million cwt. The delivery of this quantity is impossible on account of the Polish invasion.

The province of Silesia in Prussia still has to supply $\frac{1}{2}$ million cwt., the province of East-Prussia 125,000 cwt. Both provinces are also menaced by the Poles, the delivery is very doubtful.

The province of Saxony in Prussia is still in arrears with 670,000 cwt., it is incapable of delivering this quantity.

Of all the potatoes still due only about 100,000 cwt. can be expected from the province of Brandenburg.

Bread-cereals: According to the calculation of the authorities the rations for 76 days are lacking (sic). From the beginning of June 1918 (sic) cereals can no more be distributed.

Fats: The supplies reach till the middle of April only.

* There were altogether 9 enclosures. (Ed.)

The ration per week is 62½ grams, this quantity has not by any means been distributed everywhere in Saxony.

The meat-ration of half a pound per week can no further be distributed, but must be reduced to 140 grams per head and week.

Fish is so scarce, that a general distribution is impossible.

d The situation as regards food is serious. Silesia is a large agricultural and industrial district, and in peace-time was practically self-supporting. But now, owing to the general situation all over Germany, it has to export large stocks of potatoes, and is very little, if at all, better off than any other part of Germany.

Owing to lack of manures, artificial and others, the potato harvests have decreased steadily year by year, and at present the stock held is only expected to last to the end of April. This year's harvest is expected to be about half that of last year.

In Breslau itself, a town of about 600,000 inhabitants, the rich man can still obtain a good meal at a price – costing him approximately 40 *mk.* to 60 *mk.*, without wine – and one could live in the better hotels without realizing that there was any serious shortage.

But, directly one visited the poorer quarters, the real situation became apparent.

A large gas works had been turned into a soup kitchen, where 100,000 meals a day are cooked and issued.

Three forms of so-called food are prepared, all of which we tasted:

1. A brew of spinach for children from birth to 3–4 years of age.
2. A watery soup from mangolds, potatoes and a few carrots. (When tasted it took all one's courage to swallow.)
3. A thin stew of potatoes, turnips, carrots (sometimes), thickened with a little meal. (This also was most unpalatable.)

Thus the most unappetizing and unnourishing foods form the staple daily diet of approximately one-fifth of population (sic).

Also the local infants' home was visited, where children from birth to 3–4 years old were seen. The sight of children from 3 weeks to 3 years sucking spinach soup from a bottle instead of milk was very upsetting.

We were informed that the average weight of a normal new-born child was 4 lbs.

Each child had a chart showing its weight from birth. For the first year, the weight gains more or less normally, but the child, at the end of its third year, is really very little heavier or larger than at the end of its first.

e On the 24 April, Mr. Heatley, the British member of the Essen Coal Committee of the Reparation Commission, came to see me and gave me some interesting information regarding the state of affairs in the Ruhr Basin. His information lent strong support to the view I have frequently expressed that food is at present the key to the situation in the Ruhr. He told me, and what he said is corroborated by reports from other sources, that the ration of miners in Essen is 2 lbs of bread and 2 lbs of potatoes per head per week, with some lard and a few odds and ends of miscellaneous foods. There is no meat and the miners say they have forgotten how to eat meat. The meal that they take down into the mines is bread smeared with a little lard. At a mine which the Committee inspected the other day, 23 per cent of the miners were absent, looking for food. The Committee received a deputation of 30 miners a short time ago and these men said: 'We are neither Red nor White nor Black nor Blue: all we want is food.'

The Dutch recently proposed to lend 60 million gulden, to be earmarked for food for miners, on condition that a certain percentage of the output of the mines close to the Dutch frontier was reserved, on payment, for Holland, but the Reparation Commission turned down this proposal. The Dutch argued that if the miners got more food more coal would be produced, and the Essen Committee are unanimous in agreeing that this would be the case, and, I think, in recommending the acceptance of the Dutch proposal; but the French members of the Reparation Commission are apparently too strong for their colleagues. The French are unable to transport much more coal than they are receiving now owing to the difficulties in handling it at the junction points in France at which it is received from Germany. They fear therefore that an increased output of coal from the German mines would benefit not French but German industry and they are determined that this shall not be brought about.

f A large part of the population was inadequately fed even during the war. One of our leading physiologists, Professor Durig, calculated that the number of calories available to the population of Vienna according to the ration cards, which were not certain to be honoured, was 746 per head per day. But it has been ascertained scientifically that a man of average weight requires 2,500–5,500 calories a day, according to the exertions undergone.

Thus it came about that very many people lost up to 40 kilos (88 lbs) of weight during the war years, since they were obliged to live off their fat accumulated during the years of peace.

But now even those strata of the population which enjoyed a high standard of nutrition before the war have used up all their reserves. The exhausted body is no longer able to use up its own stored-up calories.

It is understandable that these conditions were bound to have an adverse influence on the health of the population. Because of it, mortality increased enormously. While in the last years before the war there were 15·5 deaths per 1,000 inhabitants per annum, this figure rose to 20·4 in 1917 and 19·6 for the first nine months of 1918. . . . This increase in general mortality was in the main influenced by the rise in the incidence of tuberculosis caused by under-nourishment. While there were 6,223 deaths due to tuberculosis in 1914, the number of those deaths rose to 11,741 in 1917 and to 8,867 in the first nine months of 1918, so that it almost doubled during the war years. . . .

Undernourishment had frightening results among the children. The infants' lives could be preserved with some success, since the number of births fell rapidly during the war (from 36,378 in 1914 to 20,688 in 1917 and 14,035 in the first nine months of 1918) and these infants were being breast-fed by their mothers in the first year of their lives. But now lactation is badly diminished among the women because of the food shortage; and neither cow's milk as a substitute for mother's milk, nor dietary flour is available instead.

The children below school age show massive signs of having fallen prey to rachitis, Barlow's disease and scurvy, attributable to insufficient and unbalanced diet.

But it is the condition of the children between the tenth and sixteenth year of their lives which give the greatest grounds for concern. For they were in the years of war at that stage of their development in which the need for nutrition is greatest, and in which the lack of adequate diet will have an adverse effect on the whole of their future lives. In many cases these children have remained at the same stage of their physical development at the end of four years of war as they were at its beginning. Of 58,849 children in Viennese schools examined in the summer of 1918 for the purpose of a recreational programme, only 4,637 were in a satisfactory state of health. The weight measurements undertaken on that occasion showed particularly among the boys a substantial retardation of the body weight compared with the normal average.

g   What sad sights were there for the observant in the streets and cafés of the once gay city of Vienna! The postman who delivered the letters at the hotel was dressed in rags. The porters at the railway stations were in worn cotton uniforms, and were glad of tips in the form of hard-boiled eggs and cigarettes. Uniformed officers sold roses in the cafés. Delicate women in faded finery begged with their children at street corners. Grass was growing in the principal streets. The shops were empty of customers. There was no roar and rush of traffic. The one-time beautiful horses of the Ringstrasse looked thin and limp. Frequently they dropped dead in the streets, of hunger.

I climbed a hill outside the city, and from the many hundreds of chimneys of mill and factory no smoke was rising. At the Labour Exchanges many thousands of men and women stood in long lines to receive their out-of-work pay. . . . In every one of the hundred one-roomed dwellings I visited were pitiful babes, small, misshapen or idiotic through the lack of proper food. Consumptive mothers dragged themselves about the rooms tearful about the lack of milk, which their plentiful paper money could not buy because there was none to sell. Gallant doctors struggled in clinic and hospital with puny children covered with running sores, with practically no medicines, no soap, no disinfectants. . . . As it is tens of thousands of child lives and old lives have been ended by famine and the diseases of famine; whilst over a long period the number of suicides from hunger and despair amounted to scores in every week.

h During the afternoon, a businessman of the city came to talk over a trade he wanted us to help him make – it was to secure certain quantities of specially nourishing food for tuberculous children. He asked me to go with him and see where the food was most needed – in the homes of the poor.

'Pick out any house, and we'll go in and talk to the family,' he bade me, as we left his taxicab, in a long street of two-storied houses. I indicated one across the way, and we entered. We penetrated to a small courtyard, about which the two-room apartments opened. Beside the door of the nearest stood a pale, bow-legged child – a boy of nine, who was about the size of a normal boy of four! My guide spoke to him, but he would not answer. His mother came, and we followed her inside. We passed through a room so dark that I could hardly distinguish its furnishings – on one side a bed and on the other a bench with a wash-tub on it. There was a window in the other room, which looked upon the street – a narrow, dingy window. It let in light enough to reveal the principal furnishings. Another bed took up half the space, a small table was at the foot of the bed, a baby's crib stood near the window, and two chairs seemed to crowd the room.

My guide began his questioning. How many in the family? Five: the woman, her husband, and three children, ages one, three, and nine. We were invited to look at the baby in the crib near the window – 'She says it is not well,' translated my guide, who had explained as we came in that I was connected with the Food Relief Commission. The bar of language was between the woman and me, but what she said in the long look she gave me as I stood beside her baby's crib was plain: 'What can you do to save my latest born?'

The woman's husband had been demobilized two months before, and was at work in a railroad warehouse for 7 kronen a day – enough to buy nearly 20 cents of American money! His wage for one day would buy just over two pounds of potatoes, and about one-half pound of flour. They had not bought meat for months, but the family's allowance of fat for one week (figured out on the basis of available supplies by the Food Controller of German Austria) had just been purchased, and was being tried out as we entered. The woman took the small stewpan off the top of the tiny stove to show me what 60 grams per week per person actually amounted to. I believe the supply could have been contained in two ordinary tea-cups. This fat is essential in preparing vegetables – the only articles of foodstuffs that are within the reach of the people's purses, and the only articles which are not strictly rationed by the State. . . .

Throughout this visit and during another long morning I spent in another poor quarter of Vienna, I received two impressions I shall never lose – languid, blue-lipped, blond young children, and the smell of stale cooked cabbage. I visited an apartment house, where 78 families lived, eating in a gloomy cellar, where a big country woman with three children stood amongst tattered remnants of clothes and bed furnishings. She had come to Vienna five years before with her husband. They had brought with them good house furnishings; he had taken a well-paid job. Then the war came, and he was killed early in the struggle. Little by little, she had sold her home furnishings in order to buy food. At last she had come down to this cellar – a common storage cellar lighted by one tiny window just above the level of the sidewalk. She was paying 25 kronen a month for two rooms down here, and was renting one of them to another family for 10 kronen a month! There was in that room one rickety, cheap little iron bed frame, and one battered iron crib. It was there the four slept. There were no bedclothes. It did not seem humanly possible to live here in this way; but to every specific question, the woman had an answer. Then her self-control broke. She began to weep. There was nothing more for her to sell in order to supplement the six kronen a day she was receiving, and she believed a process of slow starvation for her children must begin.

i The daily rations issued in Vienna in the period between January and August 1919 increased from 165 grammes to 233 grammes of flour, and from 6 grammes to 17 grammes of fat, with an additional ration of 18 grammes of bacon, although the meat ration had fallen from 18 grammes to 14 grammes. In December, the Austrian Chancellor informed the Supreme Council that it had not been possible to maintain even these rations after August, and that only 100 to 170 grammes of flour and bread could be issued per head per day, whilst other foodstuffs were equally short.* The distribu-

* *Note.* – The official rations of food per head per week in Vienna at the end of December were: bread, 2¾ lb.; flour, 9 oz.; fats, 4 oz.; meat, 4 oz. Sugar and potatoes were also rationed, but owing to lack of supplies regular distribution could not be made. (Footnote in original.)

tion of meat had frequently to be suspended, and at best could only be supplied in small quantities. Similar shortages occurred in fats and sugar. Milk was only given to children between two and five years old who received one tin of condensed milk per week. At this period a very short stock of cereals remained in the whole country, whilst in Vienna only three days' supply was left. The difficulties of maintaining distribution attendant on this position, and the frequent reduction in rations, produced an acute state of tension, and in some cases, where transport delays occurred, actual rioting resulted.

Even the provinces are not self-supporting in the matter of food, but the prevalence of illicit trading makes it difficult to determine their resources. The breadstuff crops gathered last harvest are according to official estimates only about half the quantity grown on the same area before the war. The official prices, which are still nominally maintained, are so low that the peasant producer will not look at them, and the provincial governments are not strong enough to compel him to sell. He therefore sells what he chooses at six or eight or ten times the official price to the well-to-do classes in the town as a smuggling transaction. What he cannot sell, or does not choose to sell, he allows to rot or gives to his pigs. The callousness of the peasant as to the fate of the towns, and especially of Vienna, must be seen to be believed. The extent of this so-called 'smuggling', which is more or less open and in which the provincial food administrations themselves on occasions engage, is impossible to estimate. For example, the official price offered by the Government to the peasant for wheat is 1 30 kronen per kilog., whereas the smuggler's price in Carinthia is something like 13 kronen.

In Vienna the situation was even worse than in the provinces, and the Food Controller estimated that the existing daily rations could only supply 1,271 calories, instead of the necessary minimum of 2,300 calories. Moreover, prices of all foodstuffs and essential commodities have risen beyond the reach of large numbers of the population in spite of state subsidies. Even between August and December 1919 the average cost of the rations of a normal family had risen a further 76 per cent, whilst the cessation of the Government subsidy on bread and flour would entail a 100 per cent increase in the price of these commodities.

1/27 Labour Demands in the German Revolution – the Agreement of November 1918

Agreement of the Working Party of the Associations of Employers and the Trade Unions, 15 November 1918. Printed in *Dokumente und Materialien* [*see* Document 1/11a], series 2, vol. II, pp. 393–394. (Ed. Tr.)

The major associations of employers agree with the trade unions as follows:

1. The trade unions shall be recognized as the official representatives of the labour force.

2. There shall be no limitation on the freedom of association of workers.

3. The employers and associations of employers shall in future leave the works associations (the so-called industrial peace associations*) wholly to themselves and shall not support them directly or indirectly.

4. All employees returning from the forces have a right to resume their pre-war place of work at once on demobilization. The employers and their associations shall see to it that this obligation can be met by appropriate provision of raw materials and orders.

5. Common regulation and parity of administration of workers' labour card.

6. Working conditions for all workers are to be fixed according to the needs of each industry by collective agreements with the associations of employees. Negotiations to this end are to be begin without delay and to be concluded as fast as possible.

7. Every enterprise employing at least 50 people has to form a workers' council which shall represent them and which shall, together with the employer, ensure that the conditions of employment are regulated according to the collective agreement.

8. The collective agreements shall make provision for arbitration committees and conciliation offices, consisting of employers' and employees' representatives in equal numbers.

9. The maximum daily hours of labour shall be fixed at 8. There shall be no reductions in earnings on the occasion of this shortening of the working day.

10. For the purpose of carrying out this agreement, as well as for further measures for the regulation of the demobilization, for the maintenance of economic life and for the safeguarding of the livelihood of the working force, especially the war invalids, the employers' and employees' organizations represented here shall form a central executive committee on a basis of parity and organized on an industrial basis. . . .

1/28 German Decree on Collective Agreements, Joint Councils and Arbitration, December 1918

Decree of 23 December 1918, published in the *Reichsanzeiger* of 28 December 1918. Printed in *Monthly Labour Review*, VIII, 4 (April 1919), pp. 160–166.

* i.e. 'yellow' unions. (Ed.)

In view of the steadily growing importance in Germany of collective agreements between employers and workers' and salaried employees' organizations as to working and wage conditions, the Council of People's Commissioners on 23 December 1918, promulgated a decree giving such collective agreements legally binding force. The decree also regulates the election and functions of workers' and salaried employees' committees and the arbitration of labour disputes. The full text of the decree as published in the *Reichsanzeiger** is as follows:

PART I – COLLECTIVE AGREEMENTS

Article 1. . . . Interested parties, within the meaning of paragraph 1, are employers and workers who are parties to the collective agreement or members of the signatory organizations, or on the conclusion of the labour contract have been members of these organizations, or who have concluded a labour contract which refers to the collective agreement.

Article 2. Collective agreements that have become of predominant importance in the development of working conditions in an occupation within the territory covered by the agreement may be declared generally binding by the Federal Labour Department (*Reichsarbeitsamt*). In such a case they shall, within the territory in which they are binding, also be binding, within the meaning of article 1, where the employer or worker or both of them are not interested parties in the collective agreement. . . .

Article 3. A declaration of the Federal labour department in pursuance of article 2 shall be made only on request. Each signatory party to the collective agreement, as well as organizations of employers or workers who would be affected by the declaration of the Federal labour department, is entitled to make such a request. . . .

PART II – WORKERS' AND SALARIED EMPLOYEES' COMMITTEES

Article 7. In all establishments in which, under article 11 of the law on the national auxiliary service, permanent workers' or salaried employees' committees are in existence, a new election of the members of these committees and their alternates shall take place. . . . The present members and their alternates shall remain in office until these elections have taken place.

Article 8. In all establishments, administrations, and bureaus in which as a rule at least 20 workers are being employed and in which permanent workers' committees are not already in existence in accordance with article 7 of this decree or in pursuance of the mining laws, such committees shall be

---

* *Deutscher Reichsanzeiger*, Berlin, 28 Dec., 1918.

created. . . . This is also applicable to establishments in which hitherto permanent workers' or salaried employees' committees have existed under article 134h of the Industrial Code and in consequence workers' committees under article 11 of the national auxiliary service law were not constituted. . . .

Article 9. In all establishments, administrations, and bureaus in which as a rule at least 20 salaried employees are being employed and permanent salaried employees' committees in accordance with article 7 of this decree do not exist such committees shall be formed. . . .

Article 10. Without prejudice to the provisions of paragraphs 2 and 3 of this article, the provisions of articles 7 to 9 of this decree shall also be applicable to establishments, administrations and bureaus of the National Government, the Federal States, communes, and communal unions, as well as to the administrations of the carriers of the legal workmen's and salaried employees' insurance. . . .

Article 11. The members of workers' and salaried employees' committees to be formed under articles 7 to 9 and article 10, paragraph 1, of this decree shall be elected by the workers or salaried employees of the establishment, administration, or bureau, or of the division of the establishment, administration, or bureau, for which the committee is to be formed, from among themselves by direct and secret ballot on the principle of proportional representation. . . .

Article 13. The workers' and salaried employees' committees . . . shall safeguard the economic interests of the workers and salaried employees against the employer in the establishments, administrations, or bureaus. In co-operation with the employer they shall supervise the enforcement in the establishment of the collective agreements affecting it. In so far as the working conditions are not regulated by collective agreements the committees shall, in agreement with the interested economic organizations of the workers and salaried employees take part in the regulation of wages and other working conditions. It shall be their duty to see to it that friendly relations are maintained within the working force or the staff of salaried employees and between them and the employer. They shall give special attention to the combating in the establishment, administration, or bureau of dangers to health and life. . . .

Article 14. Employers and their representatives are prohibited from restricting their workers or salaried employees in the exercise of their right of voting at the elections of workers' or salaried employees' committees or in the acceptance or exercise of the duties of membership of such a committee or to discriminate against them on account of such acceptance or mode of exercise. A reduction of earnings shall not be incurred because of absence from work owing to election of or membership on a committee. Agreements running counter to these provisions shall be invalid.

PART III – ADJUSTMENT OF LABOUR DISPUTES

Article 15. For the time being and until the adjustment of labour disputes has been otherwise legally regulated, new arbitration boards shall, without prejudice to article 19 of this decree, be established.... The arbitration boards shall consist of two permanent and one nonpermanent representative of the employers and a like number of representatives of the employees of their district. In addition, a nonpartisan chairman of the board may be appointed in accordance with paragraph 4 of this article.

The permanent representatives of the employers and employees in the old arbitration boards and their alternates shall in the same character enter the new boards....

Article 17. In their negotiations and voting the arbitration boards shall always be constituted as provided in article 15, paragraph 2, of this decree, and if a nonpartisan chairman has been appointed he shall preside at the sessions.

The chairman shall represent the committee in all dealings with outside parties, conduct current affairs, fix the date of sessions, and direct the proceedings.

A nonpartisan chairman's vote counts the same as the vote of an employers' or employees' representative; a chairman elected from among these representatives has only a vote as a representative of his group....

Article 20. The arbitration boards may be appealed to by the employer, the workers' and salaried employees' committees, and representative committees formed in accordance with article 12 of this decree, or, where such a committee does not exist, by the workers or salaried employees of an establishment, whenever in case of a dispute between the two parties as to wages or other working conditions an agreement has not been effected and both parties do not call on an industrial court, a mining industrial court, an arbitration board of a guild, or a commercial court to arbitrate the dispute in question. With the consent of the affected employers and employees economic organizations of employers or employees may also appeal to arbitration boards for adjustment of disputes, in so far as the enforcement of collective agreements is in question they may do so independently.

In disputes which come under the jurisdiction of special conciliation or arbitration boards in pursuance of a collective or other agreement between employers and employees, these special boards shall be appealed to, and

71

only when these do not take action shall the arbitration boards established by the present decree or other conciliation boards be called in to settle disputes.

Article 21. The arbitration board shall also take the initiative in having arbitration proceedings brought before it whenever both parties to the dispute have not invoked another conciliation board or a special conciliation or arbitration board does not have to be invoked in pursuance of a collective or other agreement. If the latter is the case and the special conciliation or arbitration board has not been invoked by one of the parties, the arbitration board shall point out this neglect to the interested parties, and if they fail even then to invoke this special board the arbitration board shall itself initiate conciliation proceedings. . . .

Article 26. If an agreement has been effected it shall be put in writing, signed by all the members of the arbitration board and the representatives of both parties, and be published unless both parties have previously agreed not to publish it. If an economic employers' or employees' organization has invoked the arbitration board in accordance with article 20, paragraph 1, sentence 2, of this decree, its authorized representatives are entitled to sign the publication of the agreement. The same holds good if such an organization, in agreement with a workers' or salaried employees' committee or as its representative, has taken part in the common discussions and in the attempt at conciliation.

Article 27. If an agreement has not been effected the arbitration board shall render an award which shall cover all questions in dispute between the parties.

1/29 The Role of the Trade Unions in Post-War Germany

Action Programme of the trade unions, adopted by the 10th Trade Union Congress held at Nuremberg on 30 June to 5 July 1919, and published under the title: *Guide Lines for the Future Role of the Trade Unions* (1919). Printed in ERNST SCHRAEPLER, *Quellen zur Geschichte der sozialen Frage in Deutschland* (2 vols., Göttingen, 1957) vol. II, pp. 143–146. (Ed. Tr.)

1. The trade unions have educated the worker to the class struggle in the period of private capitalist commodity production. They have united large masses of workers in strong associations against the employers, trained them in wage struggles and educated them economically to a recognition of their position and to an understanding of social relationships. The trade unions

have in systematic battles not only wrested from the employers reductions in working hours and increases in wages, but have also freed the worker from the whim of the employer in all firms under the influence of trade unions. They have won for the working class the recognition of their organization as an equal contractual partner, and have to a considerable extent safeguarded their trade union successes by collective labour agreements. Further, they have pioneered and fostered the transformation of the labour law, formerly a one-sided law of masters, into an equitable law, and have exerted a growing influence on social welfare policies and on legislation.

2. On the eve of the political revolution the trade unions had already forced the employers to fulfil the most important demands of the workers and driven them along the road to economic democracy by the creation of works councils, in which all questions of economic life and social welfare policy were to be solved by equal representation of employers and workers. All these successes of the trade unions are valuable achievements, but have so far met only in part the legitimate demands of the working population and thus the tasks of the trade unions. The fight of the trade unions must therefore go on.

3. The revolution has strengthened the political power of the working class and thereby at the same time enlarged its influence on the shaping of the economy. The reconstruction of the economic life shattered by the war must be undertaken in the direction of the collective economy and with the progressive dismantling of the private economy. This transformation must be undertaken in a planned way and is supported by the trade unions.

4. The trade unions look upon Socialism as a higher form of economic organization than the capitalist economy. Industrial democracy and the transformation of individual labour contracts desired by them, are important stages on the road to socialization. The further collaboration of the trade unions in this field is indispensable.

5. The trade unions have the duty to represent the workers within the collective economy also, and even in wholly socialized undertakings, against the management, the local authorities and the State. They are therefore necessary even in the age of Socialism. Social welfare provisions of society do not supersede the need for the mutual help of workers in their own organizations. . . .

6. Even in the collective economy, conflicts of interest between management and workers will not entirely disappear. Even if labour stoppages are much diminished in consequence of a social system of labour laws and the democratic co-determination by the workers, and even though they should be prevented by arbitration in the interest of the Socialist economic system as far as possible, the workers cannot give up their right to strike.

7. The right of co-determination by the workers must be put into practice over the whole field of production, from the single firm into the highest level of the central economic organizations. Within the firms, freely elected workers' representatives (workers' councils) must be created which, in agreement with the unions and supported by their power, have to bring about a state of industrial democracy in association with the management. The basis of industrial democracy is the legally valid collective labour contract. The tasks of the works councils, their rights and duties, will have to be laid down in the collective contracts on the basis of legal minimum provisions.

8. The fulfilment of the demands included in these guide lines will be the task of the central trade union organizations in the individual industries and occupations, united in the *Allgemeiner Deutscher Gewerkschaftsbund* (ADG). Every male and female worker is entitled to join the trade unions belonging to the ADG. Political and religious convictions shall be no obstacles to joining this organization. . . .

11. It is the character of the trade unions to be representative purely of the workers' interests and they cannot therefore themselves become agents of production, which is the task of the Chambers of Industry. It is their task to conduct a purposeful labour policy within the Chambers of Industry. They have to lay down guide lines for the workers' representatives in principle and practice and to see to it that these representatives maintain contact among themselves and with the trade unions. They have to take general measures to spread knowledge about economic affairs and on conditions of work, on technology and on business administration among the working population and thereby release the forces necessary for the introduction of the Socialist economic system.

1/30 Collaboration between Unions and Employers

Joint appeal by the Working Party (*Arbeitsgemeinschaft*) of industrial employers and employees of 10 February 1919, signed by C. Legien for the employees [*see* Document 5/25 in volume 2) and E. v. Borsig for the employers. Printed in MICHAELIS and SCHRAEPLER, *Ursachen und Folgen* [*see* Document 1/3], vol. III, pp. 72-74. (Ed. Tr.)

To the mine workers!
The almost hopeless position in which German economic life finds itself is to be attributed, beside the uncertain political conditions and the food shortage, to the coal shortage which is having increasingly serious consequences. From last November on, there has been one coal strike after another. Although the demands of the miners have been substantially met, there are ever new demands. The most recent demand is that the coal owners should pay to

every worker a large sum of money for work done in the past, irrespective of whether each of the recipients has in fact performed such work, but above all irrespective of whether the companies are able to pay out such extraordinarily large sums. It is clear that such demands have the sole object of reducing the output of coal and creating a coal shortage. As the shortfall of coal increases the source of our power, heat and light dries up, and there is a total lack of raw materials in all industries based on coal, coke and the distillation of by-products as the sole raw materials. Thus the unimaginable is happening: the German economy is being destroyed because the coal-miners are refusing to work, while millions of hands have to be idle because their opportunity of work has disappeared. The local authorities and the trade unions are spending huge sums to allow the unemployed to be fed, while unemployment is being increased by the prevention or limitation of coal-mining.

This must lead to a collapse of our economy and of subsistence of our people. In this hour of danger, the Working Party of industrial employers and employees considers it to be its duty to urge the workers concerned to save our country and its economic power from ruin. Our country has not been devastated during the war – it must not be devastated now by its own population, which has meanwhile received the most extensive political freedom.

Therefore *coups d'état* and strikes are not the way to lead to our goal! Your interests can be properly represented, and an appropriate income to meet your needs can be secured, only through the existing organizations.

We ask the employers to regulate conditions of work in accordance with the agreement of employers and workers of 15 November 1918.[*]

We demand of the Government to show the sternest resolution in taking all measures necessary to secure an adequate output of coal and the survival of these concerns which are vital for our economic life.

Only the united and combined action by these three factors can save us from the most dreadful catastrophe which ever threatened a nation. Let the appeal in this last hour remaining for a change of course, not remain unheard. German labour has to prove, not only to its own country, but to the world at large, that it is capable of reconstructing the economy. It must be conscious of its responsibility and do its duty to its families, and to its own people and its future. He who shirks his duty in these difficult days, will bear the responsibility for the misery which in the end will affect him and the members of his family too.

[*] *See* Document 1/27. (Ed.)

1/31 The German Works Council Act of 1920

Act on Works Councils, of 4 February 1920. Summarized in *Monthly Labour Review* (U.S. Dept. of Labour), X 5 (May 1920), pp. 175–181.

Establishment, election, and composition of works councils. – Works councils (*Betriebsräte*) are to be elected in all establishments employing 20 or more persons, whether manual workers or salaried employees. In establishments employing less than 20 but at least 5 persons a single shop steward (*Betriebsobmann*) is to be elected in place of a works council. The law is applicable also to agriculture and to home workers. A special law is to regulate the establishment of workers' representation in ocean and inland navigation. . . .

The manual workers (*Arbeiter*) and the salaried employees (*Angestellte*) – this careful distinction between manual and non-manual workers runs through the entire law – elect separately members of the works council by secret ballot and from their own midst. The works council is to safeguard the common economic interests of both manual workers and salaried employees as against the employer. In addition to the works council, there are to be formed in each establishment a workers' council (*Arbeiterrat*) and a salaried employees' council (*Angestelltenrat*) to represent the special interest of each of these two groups of employees. The members of the works council elected by the manual workers form the workers' council and the members elected by the salaried employees form the salaried employees' council.

All manual and non-manual workers, without distinction of sex, who are over 18 years of age and in possession of their civic rights have the right to vote at the election of works councils. Eligible to the works councils are all persons entitled to vote who are German citizens over 24 years of age, have finished their vocational training, and on election day have worked at least six months in the establishment and at least three years in the trade or occupation in which they are engaged. Members of the works council are elected for a term of one year. Their re-election is permissible.

Meetings of the council. – The works council, if composed of less than 9 members, elects from among its members a chairman and a vice chairman. If composed of more than 9 members, it elects from among its members an executive committee of 5 members. The chairman of the works council represents the council before the employer and before the arbitration board; he also calls the meetings of the council and determines the agenda. On request of at least one-fourth of the members of the council or on request of the employer a meeting must be called by the chairman. . . . Members of the works council and their alternates are to exercise their office without compensation. Necessary loss of time due to attendance of meetings of the council shall not entail reduction in wages or salary. The necessary costs of management of the works' council are to be borne by the employer, unless otherwise provided by collective agreement. He must put at the disposal of the council the rooms and equipment necessary for the holding of its meetings and the transaction of its business.

Termination of membership. – Membership in a works council comes to an end when any member resigns, ceases to be employed in the establishment for which the council has been formed, or loses his qualification for election. . . .

The Works assembly. – The law also provides for a works assembly (*Betriebsversammlung*) composed of all the manual and non-manual workers of the establishment. This assembly really stands in authority above the works council, for on demand of the employer or of at least one-fourth of the workers entitled to vote the chairman of the works council must convene the works assembly, and, as has been said above, a minority of only one-fourth of the workers entitled to vote may bring in a motion that the district economic council dissolve the works council. The works assembly can make demands and proposals to the works council. Separate works assemblies may be held by the manual workers and by the non-manual workers. . . .

Trade-Union representation. – In the preceding pages it has been stated that the movement towards works councils proceeded particularly from those who were opposed to the conservatism of the trade unions. Is it the endeavour of the present law to make the trade unions superfluous and to have their tasks taken over by the new system of works councils? The provisions of the law make it evident that this is in no sense the case. Article 8 seems to permit no misundertanding on this point; it says: 'The right of the economic organizations of manual workers and salaried employees to represent the interests of their members is in no way prejudiced by the provisions of this law.' The law, however, does not stop at this declaration; it is evident from a number of its provisions that there is no intention of driving the trade unions from their chosen field of activity. Article 31, for instance, provides that on motion of one-fourth of the members of a works council one representative each of the economic organizations represented in the council shall be admitted to the meetings in an advisory capacity. The same right, to be sure, is granted to the employer, who may demand that representatives of the economic organizations to which he belongs shall be admitted to the meetings of the council in an advisory capacity. Articles 66 and 78, prescribing the duties of works councils and of the group councils of manual workers and salaried employees, provide that they shall see to the fulfilment of the collective agreements concluded by the trade unions, and that if such agreements do not exist they shall co-operate in the establishment of wage and work-conditions in deliberation with the economic organizations of employees that may be concerned therein. Finally – and this is the farthest step of all – article 62

77

provides that if in a collective agreement declared by the Government to be binding on a whole industry, a method of representation for the employees is adopted different from that introduced by the present law, the works councils provided by the law shall not be introduced in that industry; and if they already function in that industry, they are to be dissolved.

It is evident from all these quotations that the Government has desired workmen's councils only in addition to and co-operating with the trade unions, and this is no wonder, for the socialistic members of the Government are recruited, for the most important part, from the leaders of the modern German trade-union movement.

Duties of the works councils. – The law assigns to the works councils the following duties:

1. In establishments with economic (commercial or industrial) aims to support the management with advice in order to assist it to bring the establishment to the highest possible state of efficiency.

2. To co-operate in the introduction of new labour methods.

3. To safeguard the establishment from violent disturbances, and, without prejudice to the rights of economic organizations of manual workers and salaried employees, to invoke the conciliation committee or some other conciliation or arbitration board agreed upon in case of disputes between the works council, the workers, or a part of the workers, and the employer which can not be settled by agreement.

4. To see to it that awards made by a conciliation or arbitration board in matters concerning the entire establishment and accepted by the interested parties be carried out.

5. To fix, in agreement with the employer, general shop regulations and any modifications of the same within the terms of collective agreements then in force.

6. To promote harmony among the workers and between them and the employer and to safeguard the workers' right of combination.

7. To receive complaints of the workers' and salaried employees' council and to dispose of them in agreement with the employer.

8. To take measures to combat danger to health and accidents in the establishment; support the factory inspectors and other officials in the task of combating these dangers by information, advice, and calling them in when necessary, and by supervising the carrying out of the orders of the industrial authorities and of the provisions for the prevention of accidents.

9. To take part in the administration of pension funds, company-owned workmen's dwellings, and other welfare institutions of the establishment. . . .

Control by the workers. – The most disputed provisions of the bill concerned the participation of the works councils in the management of the establishment and their right to interfere in the hiring and discharging of employees. These provisions were the crux of the law.

As has already been stated here, the works council has the right to 'support the management with advice', with the object of increasing output, and to 'co-operate in the introduction of new labour methods'.

In undertakings in which there is a board of directors the works council has the right to delegate one or two of its members to that board who shall represent the interests and demands of the employees as well as their views and wishes concerning the organization of the establishment. These delegates of the works council have a seat and vote in the board of directors but do not draw directors' fees. They are under obligation to maintain secrecy with respect to confidential information given to them.

In an undertaking which is obliged to keep books and which employs as a rule at least 300 workers or 50 salaried employees the works council may request that, beginning with 1 January 1921, a balance sheet and profit and loss account for the past financial year be submitted to the executive committee of the council, or, in the absence of such a committee, to the council itself six months after the close of the financial year, at the latest. In this case also the council must maintain secrecy with respect to information of a confidential character.

The rights of the works councils described in the two preceding paragraphs are somewhat limited by the provision of the law that establishments of the two classes specified may on their request be exempted by the National Government from granting these rights if important State interests require it.

In order that the works council may fulfil its duties it has in all establishments with economic aims the right to request the employer to give to the executive committee, or, where such a committee does not exist, to the council itself, information as to all the transactions of the establishment which affect the labour contract and the work of the employees. In particular the employer shall on request show the wage sheets and make a quarterly report as to the condition and output of the establishment and the expected demand for labour. This information is to be considered confidential.

The employers' associations strongly opposed granting to the works councils an insight into the financial affairs of industrial establishments. But the concessions made by the law to the workers are not of great value. It is true the works councils are given representation on the board of directors of stock companies, and in other concerns they are entitled to receive an annual balance sheet and a copy of the profit and loss account, but, as secrecy must be maintained on all information obtained in this manner, the councils cannot report back to the workers. This provision of secrecy was attacked by both socialist groups, but they were unsuccessful in the National Assembly. The council may inspect wage sheets but none of the books, or, in other words, it cannot get a real grip on the finances of the establishment. . . .

Protective and penal provisions. – The law prohibits the employer and his representatives from interfering with their workers in their right of electing members to the works councils or in the acceptance of membership on such a council and exercise of its functions or from discriminating against them for this reason. Before giving notice of discharge to a member of a works council or before transferring him to another establishment the employer must obtain the consent of the works council. . . .

1/32 German Works Councils in Operation

Factory Inspector's Reports on their operation in 1920. Printed in *Monthly Labour Review*, XIV, 2 (February 1922), pp. 1–12.

Since the introduction of works councils in Germany, in February 1920, this institution has been the subject of many articles. . . .

In the annual report of the [German] factory inspection service for the year 1920 each chief inspector of a district reports his observations on the operation of works councils. A selection has been made of the most important industrial districts and extracts from the reports of the chief inspectors for these districts are reproduced below.

DISTRICT OF POTSDAM

For the present the councils' activities aim more at safeguarding the interests of the workers than at promoting the productivity of the establishment. The views of employers and workers as to their mutual rights under the works councils law have diverged frequently. While the employers have generally shown a tendency to keep strictly to the letter of the law and to recognize only rights guaranteed by it, the councils have often attempted to interpret the law in such a way as to extend their rights. Differences in this respect have, however, in most instances been settled amicably. . . .

In a machinery works the workers refused to elect a works council in accordance with the legal provisions for such election. They made election rules of their own and voted into office a special 'revolutionary' council. Representations of the factory inspector induced them later on to hold a legal election. . . .

While the employers were at first reluctant to collaborate with the works councils, fearing the undermining of their authority, this reluctance disappeared gradually after they had had occasion to observe the amicable relations between factory inspectors and works councils. . . .

In small and medium-sized establishments there is often a lack of workers fitted to represent their fellow workers. The older workers frequently decline the office and the extra work it involves because they often get small thanks for their trouble, and the younger workers see in the works council more a political organization for carrying on the class struggle than a peaceful economic institution, and thus create discontent and strife.

CITY OF BERLIN

. . . Refusals of the employers to permit the election of councils or shop stewards or to have dealings with them after they were elected were very rare and such refusals were without exception withdrawn after proper explanation of matters by the factory inspector. In several establishments, however, especially those in which the great majority of the workers were women, the workers consistently refused to elect a council, saying that in view of the amicable relations so far maintained with the employer a works council was not needed. . . .

That numerous disputes as to the application of the works council law arose in the beginning between employers and workers has its chief reason in the fact that the provisions of the law were unsatisfactory to both parties. Many employers believed that the rights granted to the councils were too far reaching and therefore opposed firmly anything that seemed likely to extend these rights still further. Many workers, on the other hand, considered the rights granted to them by the law insufficient and consequently endeavoured to obtain more rights than the law gave them. This fighting spirit seems, however, gradually to have abated and given way to recognition of the fact that an operation of the councils beneficial to both parties can be achieved only by readiness on the part of each to meet the other half-way. Because of this recognition the employers are now more willing to negotiate with the councils, and the radicals originally elected to the councils are in many instances being replaced by more conservative members.

DISTRICT OF BRESLAU

. . . The majority of the employers have so far assumed a hostile attitude towards the works councils; some of them have expressed outright their belief that these institutions have an injurious and disorganizing effect. It must be admitted that many a council has made unjustifiable demands and meddled in matters that did not come within its legally regulated duties. Investigations made in a considerable number of large establishments have therefore shown that the relations of employers and works councils are very strained and that one cannot speak of any beneficial collaboration. On the other hand, and this is especially important in the case of so young an institution, there have developed frequently very favourable conditions, particularly in establishments in which the employer or manager has accepted the council as an accomplished fact entered into relations with it without prejudice, and has undertaken to interest the members of the council in their duties and to train them in their proper exercise.

DISTRICT OF OPPELN (UPPER SILESIA)

. . . The preponderance of the younger age classes among the members was one of the chief characteristics of the newly elected councils. The older workers who had seen long service were generally thought to be not radical enough to represent firmly the interests of the working forces. Resignations of council members were frequent. . . .

Little has become known as to activity of works councils in the economic field. In one instance, however, it was largely due to the efforts of the council of a large chemical works that a strike in another works was settled. The council of the chemical works intervened because the strike at the other works would have caused a shut-down of the former, it being dependent on the latter for raw materials.

The collaboration of the workers' and salaried employees' councils with the employers left much to be desired. Only in a few instances was such collaboration effected without friction and followed by results. The mutual distrust is in many instances due to widely diverse views caused by unfamiliarity with the provisions of the works council law or by a lack of willingness to compromise. . . .

It must be admitted that when works council law came into operation, great prejudice and strong opposition to the law prevailed among employers. During the course of months these have given way to a more dispassionate view. The moderating influence of reasonable works councils upon the easily excitable masses of workers has frequently saved the works managements from disturbances and disputes of long duration. On the other hand, instances – by no means rare – have become known in which works councils have harangued their electors into strikes, riots, and even violence. In one of these instances the works management demanded of the authorized conciliation board the removal of the entire council, whereupon the latter, conscious of being in the wrong, resigned voluntarily. In another instance the firm in question without further ado dismissed three leading council members. . . .

DISTRICT OF DÜSSELDORF

In a considerable number of establishments the workers refused to elect a council, either because they were satisfied with the existing workers' committees or because they set no value on being represented: sometimes the refusal was based on political reasons. Without exception workers hostile to trade unionism refrained from voting. In an iron and steel works with a working force of about 10,000 men of pronounced radical tendencies, only 55 per cent of the workers entitled to vote took part in the first election of a council, and at the second election, made necessary by the resignation of the entire council, only 35 per cent voted. In some instances the council members resigned soon after their election because they felt that they did not command the confidence of their fellow workers, or were tired of attacks by the latter, or felt it burdensome to attend the numerous party meetings of works council members. In establishments in which nomination lists had been submitted the candidates nominated by the free (socialistic) trade unions were generally elected and unorganized workers as well as those belonging to rival organizations were forced to join the free trade unions. Councils thus elected, which in addition assumed a very overbearing attitude and in some instances attempted to usurp the management of the establishment, were as a rule not recognized by the employers, and measures were taken by them for the election of a new council according to the prescribed procedure. . . .

Owing to the relatively short period of their operation it cannot be judged conclusively whether the works councils are doing justice to all the duties assigned to them by the law. It is in the nature of things that they consider it their principal duty to represent and safeguard the economic interests of their fellow workers. They are forced into this attitude by the entire economic situation as well as by the endeavour to be able to show to their electors some material success. In the steadily recurring movements for wage increases, in the negotiation and application of collective agreements, and in the determination of principles governing the hiring and dismissal of workers they have found a suitable field for their activities. Another principal duty of the councils, namely, the promoting of amicable relations between employers and workers has suffered seriously under the tendency of the councils to consider solely the interests of the workers. When the councils have had to act in a conciliatory capacity they have frequently proved to be ineffective. . . .

In justice to the workers it must be stated that some of the employers have not yet acquiesced in the extension of the rights of the workers through the works council law. These employers have only after serious struggles made concessions that could easily have been granted voluntarily. . . .

DISTRICT OF COLOGNE

. . . In spite of the resistance offered at first by some employers who felt that the works' council law restricted them in the free conduct of their business, relations between employers and works' council members have in general been satisfactory. Many employers have stated that they prefer dealing with a works council to having to listen to the grievances of each individual worker. The councils take part in the general regulation of wages and working conditions only in those establishments in which these matters are not in the hands of the trade unions. If need of changes in the hours of labour arises, the works council is as a rule given an opportunity to express its opinion before changes are ordered. So far, only in rare instances have rules governing the employment and dismissal of workers been agreed upon by employers and councils.

DISTRICT OF MUNICH

Membership on a works council is little sought after, because the position of mediator between the employer and the working force is very difficult. It must be acknowledged that the workers are becoming aware of this fact and are now endeavouring to choose as council members the persons most suited for this office. . . . While in several establishments the employers have expressed their appreciation of the co-operation of the councils in maintaining order in the establishment, in others complaints have been voiced as to the biased radicalism of the councils.

STATE OF SAXONY

. . . It can be stated that employers and councils are now generally co-operating in a satisfactory manner, and that, contrary to expectations, everyone is becoming accustomed to the new institution with surprising rapidity. This is especially true of the large and medium-sized establishments. In small establishments expressions of regret are sometimes heard that the direct intercourse of workers with their employer has been greatly limited through the interference of shop stewards and works councils. In such small establishments, especially in those employing predominantly woman labour, the workers have often refused to elect a council. . . .

Quite frequently it has happened that agreements arrived at by councils and the management of establishments have been disapproved by the workers of the establishments. Owing to such occurrences a good many council members have soon tired of their office and resigned. It has repeatedly been reported that the most efficient skilled workmen absolutely decline election to a council. Thus it happened that in an establishment employing a large number of highly skilled workers a porter was elected chairman of the workers' council. . . .

SUMMARY

As noted in several of the inspectors' reports quoted above, the period

84

during which works councils have been in operation in Germany at the end of 1920 is far too short to allow of general definite conclusions as to the efficiency of this new institution. A perusal of these reports reveals, however, a few outstanding facts. Briefly summarized, these facts are:

1. The works council law came into being in its present form against the will of the majority of all organized workers and that of the ultra-conservative employers. It was a compromise product of the coalition parties of that time. The principle of the right of co-management was almost entirely surrendered by this compromise. . . .

2. The comparatively large number of disputes that have arisen out of the operation of the works council law have nearly always been settled amicably through the intervention of the factory inspectors. Instances in which these disputes led to violence, strikes, or lockouts were rare. . . .

3. The most outstanding fact revealed by experiences from the first year's operation of the councils is that in disputes between the employers and councils both sides, as a rule, do not act on their own initiative but are generally guided by their respective organizations. This accounts for the fact that many disputes were initiated as mere test cases and were fought out through both tribunals of appeal permitted under the law.

4. The works councils, and still more the workers' councils, are entirely controlled by the trade unions. . . .

5. The councils so far elected are mostly composed of younger workers with pronounced radical tendencies. The older and more conservative workers either are not being considered in the nominations or refuse election. . . .

6. So far the councils have failed to take seriously one of their principal duties, that of 'supporting the management with advice in order to assist it in bringing the establishment to the highest possible state of efficiency'. The great majority of the councils have devoted their activities exclusively to matters of interest to the workers, such as wage increases, hours of labour, conclusion of collective agreements, etc.

7. All reports agree in one point, namely, that the smooth operation of works councils depends largely on their make-up. In districts in which the more radical elements among the workers have the upper hand and radical councils have been elected, friction between employers and councils is much more frequent than in districts where workers with more moderate tendencies predominate. A great deal depends also upon the intellectual and technical fitness of the council members for their office. . . .

8. . . . In establishments in which the employer was prejudiced against the new institution or the council has attempted to dictate to the employer there has been friction without end.

9. There seems to be little need for works councils in small establishments. Many of these failed even to elect a council, the workers stating that they preferred direct relations with the employer.

10. The majority of the employers are adapting themselves to the new institution, and facilitate the operation of the councils by providing them with office rooms, clerical help, telephones, etc., and by exempting a reasonable number of the council members from productive work. . . .

11. Women workers show scant interest in works councils. . . .

12. All works councils are supporting the factory inspection service to the best of their ability in combating health and accident hazards.

1/33 Inflation in Italy, 1914–1919

League of Nations, *Currencies After the War. A Survey of Conditions in Various Countries, compiled under the Auspices of the International Secretqriat of the League of Nations* (London, 1919), pp. 77–82.

Expansion of currency and credit in Italy during the war has very seriously diminished the purchasing power of the lira both at home and abroad. Attempts are being made to check inflation by the reduction of floating debt and by a capital levy: but in her efforts at reconstruction Italy is hampered by special disabilities which render the present currency and exchange situation particularly serious. Her dependence on foreign countries for raw materials accentuates the adverse balance of trade, and her reliance on foreign travellers and on remittances from emigrants exposed her to additional difficulties when these sources of supply were cut off. The general result of these and other factors has been that the public debt of Italy is greater in proportion to the estimated pre-war wealth than in other victorious countries. In spite of a strict control of exchange operations, the gold value of Italian currency continues to depreciate, and the need of foreign material is so great that the premium on dollars and sterling has not of itself produced the desired reaction towards equilibrium in the exchange of goods and services. . . .

Since the outbreak of war the following among other emergency measures have been taken:

(i) The maximum normal circulation of the banks of issue was doubled.

(ii) The maximum limit on the amount of Currency Notes to be issued by the State was increased from 500 million lire to 2,300 million.

(iii) Bank Notes of a denomination of 25 lire were issued after the outbreak of war, the smallest Bank Note until then having been for 50 lire.

(iv) The proportion of metallic cover to be held by banks of issue against their sight obligations (other than Bank Notes) was reduced from 40 per cent to 20 per cent.

(v) Silver was withdrawn into the coffers of the State and ceased to be legal tender. Buoni di Cassa (Notes for 1 and 2 lire) were issued by the Treasury, within a maximum of 310 million lire, against the deposit of an equivalent amount of silver coin of 1 and 2 lire withdrawn from circulation.

(vi) The regulation requiring a reduction of the normal limit of note circulation in case of an excess of deposits was abrogated.

All these measures had the effect of expanding the currency issues for the sake of meeting the financial needs of the Government.

The expansion of credit – and a consequent further expansion of the currency – was also resorted to in the following ways:

(1) The Government borrowed 485 million lire at $1\frac{1}{2}$ per cent from the banks under the heading of 'Ordinary Advances', one-third of which is guaranteed by a metallic reserve.

(2) The Government borrowed 5,651 million lire at $\frac{1}{4}$ per cent under the heading 'Extraordinary Advances', not covered by a reserve but guaranteed by Treasury Bills bearing interest of $\frac{1}{4}$ per cent per annum.

(3) About 1,800 million lire were lent by the Government at a rate of 0·15 per cent through public institutions, chiefly for food supplies, but partly for reconstruction.

(4) 700 million lire were borrowed for the reorganization of the currency in occupied districts.

(5) 700 million lire were lent against security to the Cassa dei Depositi e Prestiti, a Government institution for granting credit to municipalities and provincial authorities.

3. STATISTICS

(a) Gold and Silver Holdings

	(In Millions of Lire)	
	30.6.1914	30.6.1919
(i) Of the Treasury:		
Gold, in hand	136·7	17·6
Gold, abroad	–	158·7
Silver	18·4	200·4
(ii) Of the Banks of Issue:		
Gold, in hand	1,373·7	1,037·0
Gold, abroad	–	439·6
Silver	115·7	113·8
Total	1,644·5	1,967·1

87

(b) Notes in Circulation

	(In Millions of Lire)	
	30.6.1914	30.6.1919
(i) Banks of Issue:		
Notes issued for banking operations	2,198·9	4,254·9
Notes issued for advances to the Treasury	–	8,026·0
(ii) State Circulation:		
Currency Notes	499·1	2,271·3
Buoni di Cassa	–	251·4
Total	2,698·0	14,803·6

The amount of foreign bank notes held by the banks of issue amounted on:

Lire

30 June 1914 to   549,149·97
30 June 1919 to 67,864,081·49

Foreign bank notes do not circulate in Italy.

(c) *Estimate of the amount of gold and silver coin in the hands of the public.*

Little gold or silver coin remains in the hands of the public. Gold did not circulate widely before the war and silver has now been withdrawn. The amount remaining with the public is, therefore, limited to hoards of one kind or another. A collection of gold coins was organized by decree during the war, but it yielded to the Banca d'Italia little more than 2 million lire.

(d) Bank Deposits

	(In Millions of Lire)	
	30.6.1914	30.6.1919
Banks of Issue	1,044·6	2,510·4
Other banks	100·0	774·6
Total	1,144·6	3,285·0

To this total must, however, be added the estimated deposits in the hands of Popular and Co-operative Credit Institutions, Rural Banks, Savings Banks and Monti di Pietá, viz.:

1/33 *Inflation in Italy 1914–1919*

Million Lire

| On 30 June 1914 | 6,450·8 |
| On 30 June 1919 | 9,339·7 |

(e) *Exchange Rates*

	Par.	31.12.14	31.12.15	31.12.18	31.12.19
On New York	5·18	5·30	6·57	6·34	10·82
On London	25·22	25·87	30·99	30·31	44·87

Chapter 2   The Soviet Economy 1917–1939

Introduction

In treating the history of post-revolutionary Russia, it is important to bear in mind that 'The economic history of Russia since the Revolution* falls into distinct phases and much confusion is caused by thinking of Communism as a simple, well-defined economic organization. . . . The single objective of the Russian Government has been to make Russia a strong, economically developed country, without private ownership of the means of production, and the economic forms have been changed whenever circumstances seemed to require it.'†

During the initial post-revolutionary period, the economy came under the aegis of the Supreme Economic Council, consisting of representatives of government departments and trade unions, as well as technical experts, with the function of co-ordinating workers' control organizations and 'systematizing the process of nationalization' (2/1). In the same initial period, the nationalization of the banks, large-scale industry and land was embodied in legal form (2/2 also 1/15, 1/17). These first stages of policy have been described as 'State capitalism, characterized by control over private trade and industry rather than by extreme socialization'.‡ Two forces necessitated a change in policy in 1918. First of all, sections of the membership of local Soviets and sections of the party (the Left Communists), regarded many aspects of official economic policy as a continuation of the methods of bourgeois capitalism and were anxious for greater socialization. The second, more decisive factor, was the outbreak of the Civil War in the summer of 1918.

'The formation of White armies with foreign support and the beginning of the Civil War threw the country into total chaos. (See 1/16.) Whatever effort had been channelled into the restoration of normal life in the country was now disrupted; the valuable economic areas were cut off from the centre, depriving the Government of both foodstuffs and of individual resources.'§ It

---

* The Revolution, of course, is closely connected with the events of the First World War and some indication of early activity and difficulties is provided in 1/13, 1/14, 1/15, 1/16. (Ed.)

† W. A. Lewis, *Economic Survey 1919–1939* (London, 1965), p. 29.

‡ M. Dobb, *Soviet Economic Development Since 1917* (London, 1966), p. 88.

§ A. G. Mazour, *Soviet Economic Development. Operation Outstrip: 1921–1965*, (Princeton, N.J. 1967), p. 17.

was in this situation that the country embarked upon a policy of War Communism. In Lenin's view, it was a policy forced upon the Government as a temporary measure through the exigencies of war. The result was a more thorough-going type of Communism than had been attempted before, or to be tried afterwards. The regime decreed the temporary abolition of money values, the adoption of equality of earnings and an extension of nationalization, but was still faced with the crucial task of securing an adequate supply of grain. Urban starvation and the collapse of the army were likely results of any failure to deal with the situation. In this threatened position, the Government began the compulsory requisitioning of grain and made arrangements for its collection and distribution (2/3).

The policy of War Communism was abandoned after the end of the Civil War in late 1920, by which time the economy had virtually collapsed. During the period of War Communism many town workers became estranged from the State and the Party, reacting against growing bureaucratic methods and the shortage of basic necessities. However, the major opposition to the policy of the authorities during the period of War Communism was the peasantry. With its policy of forced requisitioning of grain and control over its collection and distribution, the regime had determined that the feeding of the urban population was a greater priority than peasants being allowed to sell their produce through the normal processes of the market. The result was that the peasant, as a producer, was unable to take advantage of the rampant inflation which raged during the period of War Communism (2/4), while the Government's policy of containing agricultural prices during a period of general inflation also guaranteed that he was adversely effected as a consumer of industrial goods. In these circumstances the Government's policy ran into problems. Peasants faced with requisitioning, reduced their sowings. Agricultural output decreased. Famine appeared. Workers left the towns for the countryside. Industrial production, faced with the general shortage of manpower and materials went into decline. In addition, the policy of War Communism drove a wedge between the workers and the peasants thereby destroying Lenin's conception of a revolution based on an alliance of these two groups. By the end of 1920, with a stagnant economy and deep divisions within society, 'a new beginning' was needed. In particular, the organization of agriculture called for long overdue reform (2/5): a major question was how to attempt this reform.

The answer was seen in the emergence of the New Economic Policy. The requisitioning of grain ceased. Private trading was permitted. The peasants were allowed to sell on the open market and a tax in kind replaced grain requisitioning (2/6). The proposed tax was to be assessed as a proportion of the net produce above the minimum subsistence needs of the family. It would be a definite rather than an arbitrary amount and, since it took only a fixed quantity of any surplus, the peasant would have an incentive to make his surplus as large as possible so as to enlarge the share which he had at his own disposal. It was openly admitted that the change in policy was related to the 'crisis of peasant farming' which affected 'the restoration of [the] transport system and of our industry' (2/7). The growth of the economy demanded the restoration of the peasantry as allies. At the same time, an attempt was made to restore confidence in private trading and to check inflation through the introduction of a new rouble, the Chervonetz. Such changes, it was emphasized, did not imply any fundamental change in long-term economic aims; the N.E.P. was claimed by Lenin as a 'strategic retreat' and was accepted as such by Stalin (2/8).

The N.E.P. did not achieve a solution of the agrarian problem, on which the economy demanded. A good harvest year, 1925–1926 was noticeable for the fact that the marketed surplus of agriculture was less than the 1913 level, even though the cultivated agricultural area and gross agricultural production surpassed these pre-war equivalents. The problem facing the Bolsheviks has been succinctly expressed by Dobb: 'so long as industry remained underdeveloped, it could supply neither the means of industrial construction nor finished commodities for village or foreign markets in adequate amount; and until the flow of agricultural products on to the market was increased, there was no possibility (short of starving the towns) of finding the exports with which the means for the expansion of industry could be purchased from abroad.'* The new attempt to deal with the problem issued from the Fifteenth Party Congress in 1927, where the decision was reached 'to embark on the first Five-Year Plan', aiming at a great expansion of state manufacturing industry and simultaneously at the collectivization of agriculture, which would involve 'the complete industrial and agrarian reorganization of the sprawling Soviet Union'.† In particular, 'this transformation of the age-old basis of agriculture was adopted as the "missing answer" for which the country was seeking.'‡

Stalin was at the centre of this debate over the transformation of Russia and was ultimately responsible for the new approach adopted towards the problem. In 1928 Stalin regarded the agricultural deficiencies mainly as a marketing problem, i.e. the refusal of peasants to release grain on to the official market. 'The basis of our grain difficulty,' he contended, 'lies in the fact that the increase in the production of marketable grain is not keeping pace with the increase in the demand for grain' (2/9). This was related to the structure of agriculture. The revolution had increased the number of small and the middle-sized peasant holdings at the expense of the large landlords and

* Dobb, *op. cit.*, p. 215. † Mazour, *op. cit.*, p. 34. ‡ Dobb, *op. cit.*, p. 222.

the kulaks yet the answer to the agrarian problem, Stalin believed, did not lie in private ownership. 'The way out lies in the transition from individual peasant farming to collective, socially conducted economy in agriculture' (2/9). From 1928/9 agriculture, therefore, began to be collectivized. It was regarded that a fast rate of development of industry in general, and the production of the means of production in particular' was 'the underlying principle of, and key to, the industrialization of the country and the transformation of our national economy along the lines of socialist development' (2/10). Such developments, however, could not be achieved without agricultural change and consequently the first major task was to 'raise the rate of development of grain farming' to a level that would 'guarantee rapid progress of the entire national economy' (2/10).

The agrarian problem and the approaches adopted towards it had wide repercussions for the Russian Communist Party and World Communism. Kamenev and Zinoviev had condemned what they regarded as the pampering of the kulaks under N.E.P. while Bukharin, at least initially, favoured peasant appeasement, a continuation of the New Economic Policy and consequently a slow rate of industrial advance (2/11). Stalin at first adopted a middle of the road position. Only after the victory of the Stalinist faction at the 1927 Party Congress did the final policy emerge. It was at this time, when a reaction was developing against the New Economic Policy – when there was 'a desire to prevent the complete defeat of the revolution by the forces of the N.E.P.'* – and when the Soviet Union was also in need of long-term credit but faced with isolation and international hostility, that the decision was taken to repudiate Western patterns of development.

By 1929 the tempo of the collectivization movement was raised, in the drive for 'the extensive socialist construction in the countryside' (2/12). Such a consideration overrode the fact that it was a process which had to face kulak opposition and resistance (2/13), as well as endure the inefficiency and mistakes of those who had to carry out the programme at a local level (2/14).

The whole movement towards collectivization, with the liquidation of the kulak opposition, was, of course, an issue which captured the attention of those innumerable contemporary foreign observers who entered Russia during these years and who were fully appreciative of the demand which existed in their respective countries for information on the far-reaching socio-economic changes in the Soviet Union. From among the many foreign opinions, it might be observed that the Webbs believed it was 'not so much the policy of removal' that was open to criticism, but 'the manner in which it appears to have been carried out' and 'the unsatisfactory conditions of life' into which the victims seemed to have been 'arbitrarily deported' (2/15).

* Mazour, op. cit., p. 34.

The collectivization movement brought havoc to the countryside. As part of their resistance peasants slaughtered their cattle and reduced their sowings. When this was accompanied by poor harvests, as it was between 1931–1933, widespread famine was inevitable. But collectivization was not halted. On 1 June 1929 only 4 per cent of farmers were in collectives; by 1936 the figure was 90 per cent. Indeed, as early as 1930, Stalin's famous letter to Pravda emphasized that 'a radical turn of the countryside towards socialism may now be considered as already achieved' (2/16), and a slowing down in the pace was indicated. It was easy to become 'dizzy with success' and attempt to dash 'to the full working of socialism'. What was needed, however, was 'a determined struggle against these sentiments', the consolidation of success and the systematic utilization of this success for 'a further advancement' (2/16).

With this successful socialist transformation of the agrarian sector, what had happened to industrial growth? We have already referred to the objective of the Russian Government, which was the achievement of a strong, economically developed country. It was a theme taken up by Bukharin and Preobrazhensky shortly after the revolution (2/17), and, as we have seen, was echoed by Stalin (2/10). In the 1920's planning was carried out for specific industries and from 1925 the State Planning Commission (*Gosplan*) published 'control figures' which set economic goals for the forthcoming economic year. In 1927, as already mentioned, the Fifteenth Congress committed the country to a great expansion of industry and the transformation of agriculture and Gosplan was formally instructed at the Congress to formulate five-year economic plans. It was intended that the plans should contain a degree of flexibility, to allow room for economic manœuvre.* The initial plan was to be based on the control figures of 1927–1928 (2/19).

By 1931 Molotov could claim that many of the output projections of the First Plan had been fulfilled within two years, together with the virtual abolition of unemployment, 'the solution of the grain problem', the final turn of the masses towards collectivization and the liquidation of the kulaks as a class (2/20). Even with these achievements, however, Stalin told the First All Union Conference of Managers of Socialist Industry that the threat of capitalist encirclement allowed no slowing down of the tempo of industrialization (2/21). The whole of the Soviet Union, in fact, was becoming 'a single enormous firm', a nation in which 'the management of the economy merged with the government of the country' accepting as its slogan 'Accumulate, Accumulate: that is Moses and all the Prophets'.†

This drive towards increased industrial productivity was encouraged by a

* The optimal variants of the first plan were soon raised. *See* Documents 2/20, 2/21. (Ed.)

† J. P. Nettl, *The Soviet Achievement* (London, 1967), p. 126.

version of Taylorism, known as Stakhanovism, which it was attempted to turn into a mass movement in 1937. The basic idea behind the Stakhanovite movement was simple. It was expected that 'reserves of new productivity, would emerge through what Stalin called 'the expression of a new wave of socialist emulation' (2/22). Another important development was that while workers were being urged to increase their output, managers endowed with power, responsibility and privileges became increasingly entrenched in industry (2/23). Notions of industry being managed by Soviets had disappeared. Both these developments were associated with the drive towards an industrialized Russia and the progress made towards this 'new order' was symbolized by centres such as Magnitogorsk, on the eastern slopes of the Urals, which was essentially a city of the Plans (2/24). By 1934 the degree of progress both in industry and agriculture was such that Stalin could claim at the Seventeenth Party Congress (the 'Congress of the Victors of Socialism') that the country had been effectively transformed (2/25).

Contemporary foreign observers reacted variously to these developments. For some, they signified Utopia: others were less sure (2/26). What could not be argued away, even though its huge cost could be stressed, was that enormous progress had been achieved by the Soviet Union in increasing its gross national product. On this criterion, Communism and the leaders of the Soviet Union could show a considerable measure of solid and substantial success (2/27), which was also accompanied by important, though frequently ignored, social and cultural benefits (7/9, 7/10, 7/11, 7/12a, 7/26). Such developments are one side of the picture, the other of which is filled with such important dark issues as the sensational purges and the human agonies of collectivization.

2/1 The Supreme Economic Council

Decree of the All-Russian Central Executive Committee and the Council of People's Commissars, 2 December 1917 (old style), 15 December 1917 (new style). Printed in *Reshenia partii i pravitelstva po khozyaistvennym voprosam* (7 vols. Moscow, 1967–1970), vol. I, pp. 27–28. (E.M.J. Tr.)

1. The Supreme Council of the National Economy [VSNKh] is established under the Council of People's Commissars.

2. The task of the VSNKh is the organization of the national economy and state finances. For that purpose, the VSNKh shall draw up general standards and a plan for the regulation of the economic life of the country, and co-ordinate and unify the activity of central and local regulating institutions (fuel board, metal board, transport board, central food supplies committee, etc., of the appropriate People's Commissariats of commerce and industry,

food supplies, agriculture, finances, war-navy, etc.), the All-Russian Council of Workers' Control, and also ... factory and trade union organizations of the working class.

3. The VSNKh is given the right of confiscation, requisition, sequestration, and compulsory syndication of various branches of industry and commerce, and other measures in the sphere of production, distribution, and state finances.

4. All existing institutions for the regulation of the economy are subordinated to the VSNKh, which is given the right to reform them.

5. The VSNKh is formed: (a) of the All-Russian Council of Workers' Control, the composition of which is determined by the decree of 14 November 1917;[*] (b) of representatives of all People's Commissariats, (c) of learned persons, who ... have a consulting vote.

6. The VSNKh shall be divided into sections and departments (for fuel, metal, demobilization, finance, etc.); the number and the sphere of activity of these sections and departments shall be determined by a general meeting of the VSNKh.

7. The departments of the VSNKh shall conduct the work of regulating the separate branches of national economic life, and also prepare measures for the appropriate People's Commissariats.

8. The VSNKh shall form out of its membership a bureau of fifteen persons to co-ordinate the current work of the sections and departments and to perform tasks demanding immediate attention.

9. All draft laws and major measures having reference to the regulation of the national economy as a whole shall be submitted to the Council of People's Commissars through the VSNKh.

10. The VSNKh shall unify and direct the work of the local economic departments of the Soviets of Workers', Soldiers' and Peasants' Deputies which include the local organs of workers' control, and also the work of the local commissars of labour, commerce and industry, food supplies, etc. In the absence of the appropriate economic departments, the VSNKh shall form its own local organs. All decisions of the VSNKh are binding upon the economic departments of the local Soviets, which constitute the local organs of the VSNKh.

2/2 Nationalization Decrees

a The Decree on the Nationalization of the Banks. Adopted by the Central Executive Committee of the Soviets of Workers', Soldiers' and Peasants' Deputies, 14 December 1917 (old style), 27 December 1917 (new style). Printed in, *Reshenia* [*see* Document 2/1], vol. I, p. 28. (E. M. J. Tr.)

[*] Old style; 27 November 1917, new style. (E.M.J.)

b The Decree on the Socialization of the Land. Adopted by the All-Russian Central Executive Committee of the Soviets of Workers', Soldiers' and Peasants' Deputies, 27 January 1918 (old style), 9 February 1918 (new style).* *Ibid*, pp. 33–45. (E. M. J. Tr.)

a In the interests of the proper organization of the national economy, of the thorough eradication of bank speculation and the complete emancipation of the workers, peasants, and the whole labouring population from the exploitation of banking capital, and with a view to the establishment of a single national bank of the Russian Republic which shall serve the real interests of the people and the poorer classes, the Central Executive Committee decrees that:

1. The banking business is declared a state monopoly.
2. All existing private joint-stock banks and banking offices shall be merged with the State Bank.
3. The assets and liabilities of establishments being liquidated shall be taken over by the State Bank.
4. The procedure for the merger of private banks with the State Bank will be determined by a special decree.
5. The temporary administration of the affairs of the private banks is entrusted to the Council of the State Bank.
6. The interests of the small depositors will be fully safeguarded.

b PART I: GENERAL PROVISIONS

Article 1. All private ownership of land, minerals, waters, forests, and natural resources within the boundaries of the Russian Federated Soviet Republic is abolished for ever.

Article 2. Henceforth, the land is handed over without compensation (open or secret) to the entire toiling population for their use.

Article 3. The right to use the land belongs to those who cultivate it with their own labour, except in cases specially stipulated in the present law.

Article 4. The right to use the land cannot be limited on account of sex, religion, nationality, or citizenship.

Article 5. Minerals, forests, waters, and natural resources, depending on their

* Publication of this decree was delayed until 6/19 February 1918 to coincide with the anniversary of the emancipation of the serfs under Tsar Alexander II in 1861. Russian sources usually cite the date of adoption, while Western sources usually cite the date of promulgation. (E.M.J.)

importance, are placed at the disposition of the uezd,* gubernia,* regional and federal soviets, under the control of the latter.† The method of use and disposition of the minerals, forests, waters, and natural resources will be determined by a special law.

Article 6. All privately owned livestock and agricultural implements of estates that are worked by hired labour shall be handed over, depending on their importance, to the disposition of the land departments of the uezd, gubernia, regional and federal soviets without compensation.

Article 7. All buildings of estates referred to in Article 6, together with agricultural enterprises attached to them, shall be handed over, depending on their importance, to the uezd, gubernia, regional and federal soviets without compensation.

Article 8. Pending the promulgation of a general law on the insurance of citizens unable to work, all such persons who are completely deprived of a means of livelihood because of the present law on the alienation of lands and forests and also of livestock and so forth found on these pieces of property, can, upon certification of the local courts and land departments of the soviets, enjoy the right of receiving a pension (until death or the coming of age) equivalent to the existing soldier's pension.

Article 9. The distribution of lands of agricultural value among the toilers shall be in the hands of the village, volost,* uezd, gubernia, regional, main and federal land departments of soviets, depending on the importance of these lands.

Article 10. The reserve land fund in each republic shall be in the hands of the main land departments [of the republics] and the federal soviet.

Article 11. Besides effecting a just distribution of lands of agricultural value among the toiling agricultural population and effecting the most productive use of national resources, the land departments of the local and central soviet authority have the following tasks in the distribution of the land: (a) creating conditions favourable to the development of the productive forces of the country by increasing the productivity of the land, improving agricultural techniques, and finally, raising the level of agricultural knowledge in the toiling masses of the agricultural population; (b) creating a reserve fund of agricultural land; (c) developing agricultural enterprises such as horticulture, apiculture, market-gardening, stock raising, dairying, etc.; (d) hastening in

* See Glossary.
† i.e., the importance of the resource determines which Soviet has responsibility for its disposition; the federal Soviet is responsible for overall supervision. (E.M.J.)

certain regions the transition from a less productive to a more productive system of land cultivation through an even settling of toiling farmers in new places; (e) developing the collective farm in agriculture at the expense of individual homesteads, the former being more profitable in saving labour and materials, with a view to passing on to a socialist economy.

Article 12. The distribution of land between toilers should proceed on labour-equalizing bases, so that the consumption–labour norm,* adapted in a given area to the historically established system of land tenure, should not exceed the labour capacity of the available work force of each individual household, but should, at the same time, provide the family of the farmer with the opportunity of a comfortable existence.

Article 13. The general and basic source of the right to use agricultural land is personal labour. In addition, in order to raise agricultural standards (through the organization of model farms or experimental and demonstration fields), the organs of the Soviet Government are permitted to secure certain portions of land from the reserve land fund (formerly belonging to monasteries, the State, the Imperial family, the Tsar, and pomeshchiks)† and to work them with labour paid by the State. Such labour is subject to the general regulations of workers' control.

Article 14. All citizens engaged in agriculture are to be insured at the expense of the State against loss of life and incapacitating old age, sickness or injuries.

Article 15. All incapacitated farmers and members of their families who are unable to work are to be supported at the expense of the organs of the Soviet Government.

Article 16. Every toiler's farm is to be insured against fire, livestock epidemics, poor crops, drought, hail and other natural calamities through mutual soviet insurance.

Article 17. Surplus income derived from the natural fertility of the best pieces of land or from nearness to markets is to be turned over to the organs of the Soviet Government for the benefit of social needs.

Article 18. The organs of the Soviet Government have a monopoly of trade in agricultural machinery and seeds.

Article 19. The grain trade, both foreign and domestic, is to be a State monopoly.

   [Part II defines who has the right to use the land for educational and

* i.e. a standard for distributing land, calculated on the basis of a household's consumption needs and the size of its work force. (E.M.J.)
   † The Russian equivalent to country squires. (Ed.)

cultural purposes, for building, for road construction, and for agriculture. For the latter, agricultural communes, agricultural associations, village societies, and separate families and individuals have the right to use the land.]

PART III: PROCEDURE FOR ALLOCATING LAND

Article 21. Land will be allocated in the first instance to those who wish to farm it not for personal gain, but for the public benefit.

Article 22. The distribution of land to those farming for their own benefit will proceed as follows:

In the first place, land will be given to the local agricultural population holding little or no land, and to local agricultural workers (*batraks*) on equal terms. In the second place, land will be given to the newly arrived agricultural population, i.e., those arriving in a given locality after the publication of the law on the socialization of the land. In the third place, it will be given to the non-agricultural population in the order of their registration at the land department of the local soviet.

Note: In allocating land, preference will be given to agricultural associations of toilers over individual farmers.

[Article 23 concerns the allocation of land for gardening, fishing, cattle-breeding, and forestry; 24, for construction purposes.]

PART IV: DETERMINING THE AGRICULTURAL CONSUMPTION–
LABOUR NORM

Article 25. The amount of land for agricultural purposes allotted to individual farms to provide the means of existence must not exceed a given zone's consumption–labour norm, which is calculated on the basis of the following Instructions:

Instructions for Determining the Consumption–Labour Norm for the Use of Land of Agricultural Value

1. Agricultural Russia is to be divided into as many zones as there are different systems of land cultivation (fallow land, three-field, eight-field, many-field, rotation of crops, etc.) in use at the present time.

2. Each such zone shall have its own special consumption–labour norm. Within the zone, the norm may vary depending on the climate and natural fertility of the soil and also depending on the proximity to a market (a city, or a railway) or other conditions having great local importance.

3. In order to determine the norm in each zone precisely, an All-Russian agricultural census will be conducted in the near future. . . .

4. [Distribution of land will proceed gradually.]

5. The basis of the consumption–labour norm for a given zone shall be the average size farm of the least densely populated uezd of the zone. . . . The uezd must have a ratio of different types of agricultural land . . . judged to be most normal, i.e. most favourable, for carrying on the type of agriculture dominant in this zone.

6. In determining the average size peasant farm as it exists today, only those lands will be taken into account which were in actual use by peasant-toilers before 1917, i.e. the lands bought, allocated, or rented by peasant societies, associations, and individual persons.

7. Forests, minerals, and waters shall not be included in this calculation.

[Point 8 excludes certain lands formerly under capitalist cultivation (e.g. church, Imperial, and pomeshchik lands) from the calculation; such properties to constitute a reserve land fund, from which allotments are to be made to peasants with no land or whose allotments fall below the existing consumption–labour standard. Points 9 through 13 concern the procedure for calculating the amount of land available for distribution.]

14. The numbers of worker units and mouths to feed shall be determined in the population census; the population shall be classified according to age as follows:

Incapable of work: girls and boys up to 12 years old; men from 60 years old; women from 50 years old. Those unable to work because of physical or mental illness shall be recorded separately.

Capable of work: men from 18 to 60 years old, 1 worker unit; women from 18 to 50, 0·8 worker units; boys and girls from 12 to 16, 0·5 worker units; boys from 16 to 18, 0·75 worker units; girls from 16 to 18, 0·6 worker units.

Note: Departure from these figures is permissible in accordance with climatic conditions and local customs by decision of the appropriate organs of the Soviet Government.

15. The amount of land per worker unit shall be determined by dividing the total desyatins available by the total number of worker units.

16. The number of dependants per worker unit shall be determined by dividing the number of persons in the farming population incapable of work by the number of worker units.

17. It is also necessary to calculate the quantity of cattle and other livestock which can be fed on one desyatin and by one worker unit.

18. In determining the average size of a now existing peasant farm in the uezd taken as a starting point for the whole zone, the average quality and fertility of a desyatin* must be established. . . .

* See Glossary.

19. The average found by the above means shall serve as the basis for determining the consumption–labour norm, in accordance with which the reserve land fund shall be used to equalize individual farms throughout the entire zone.

Note: If the above average proves inadequate for a comfortable existence (cf. Part I, Art. 12), it may be increased out of the reserve land fund.

20. [On determining the amount of additional land necessary for distribution from the reserve fund in uezds where peasant-owned land was insufficient to provide all peasants with allotments of the established size.]

21. Then, calculating the number of desyatins in the reserve land fund . . . and comparing these figures with the amount of land necessary for additional allocations to peasant farms below the average, it must be ascertained whether migration can be confined to the boundaries of the given zone. . . . If this is impossible, it is necessary to determine how many families must be moved to another zone. . . .

23. In the additional allotment of land to individual farms in conformity with the consumption–labour norm, the allocation must be increased depending on (1) an excessive overburdening of the work force by members of the family incapable of work; (2) the poor quality of the land already part of the farm; and (3) the quality of the land from the reserve fund which must be allotted to the given farmer (also in relation to meadow land).

[The rest of the decree includes articles on criteria for selecting farmers eligible to migrate at state expense; the preference given to socialist-type farms over private farms in receiving aid from the State; the non-transferability of the right to use a given plot of land; and the cessation of the right to use land.]

Translator's Note: Equal distribution of land within a village was universal as a result of the above decree, but equalization between areas in a given zone was not achieved in practice. Nor was the policy of peasant migration from places of land scarcity to places of land abundance pursued with any great success. According to the official figures published in *Izvestia* on 7 November 1920, as a result of this decree 20 million desyatins were distributed in 32 gubernias of European Russia in 1917–1918. The increase of land *per capita* varied between 0·007 desyatins in Olonetsk Gubernia to 0·77 desyatins in Petrograd Gubernia. The average figure, however, was between 0·09 and 0·39.†

† Cited by James Bunyan and H. H. Fisher, *The Bolshevik Revolution, 1917–1918: Documents and Materials* (Stanford, 1934), p. 679.

2/3 Decree on Grain Control under War Communism

Decree of the All-Russian, Central Executive Committee of the Soviets of Workers', Soldiers', Peasants' and Cossacks' Deputies. Adopted 9 May 1918 Printed in *Reshenia* [*see* Document 2/1], vol. I, pp. 55–57. (E.M.J. Tr.)

'On Assigning The People's Commissar of Food Emergency Powers In the Struggle Against The Rural Bourgeoisie Concealing Grain Reserves and Engaging In Grain Speculation.'

The disastrous process of disorganization affecting the country's food supplies, the grave heritage of four years of war, continues to become increasingly widespread and increasingly acute. While the food-consuming gubernias* are starving, in the food-producing gubernias there are right now, as before, large reserves of grain, not yet even threshed, from the 1916 and 1917 harvests. This grain is in the hands of the village kulaks* and profiteers, in the hands of the rural bourgeoisie. Well fed and well provided for, having put aside huge sums of money obtained during the war years, the rural bourgeoisie remains stubbornly deaf and indifferent to the wailings of starving workers and the peasant poor. They do not bring their grain to the collecting points, reckoning on compelling the State to raise grain prices again and again while they themselves sell grain in the localities at fabulous prices to speculators and bagmen.†

An end must be put to this obstinacy of the greedy village kulaks and profiteers. The practice of previous years for food has shown that the breaking of fixed prices for grain and the rejection of a grain monopoly would make it easier for our small band of capitalists to feast, but would make bread completely inaccessible to the many millions of toilers, subjecting them to inevitable death from starvation.

The answer to the violence of the grain owners towards the starving poor must be violence towards the bourgeoisie.

Not a single pood* should be left in the hands of those holding grain except for the amount needed for sowing their fields and for feeding their familes until the new harvest.

This policy must be implemented immediately, especially since the German occupation of the Ukraine compels us to get along with grain resources which are barely sufficient for sowing and reduced rations.

Having considered the situation created, and having taken into account

* See Glossary.

† Bagmen were black marketeers. This trade in grain violated the State monopoly established in February 1918 in the Decree on the Socialization of Land (Article 19). (E.M.J.)

that only through the strictest stock-taking and even distribution of grain reserves will Russia get out of the food crisis, the All-Russian Central Executive Committee of Soviets has resolved:

1. To reassert the firmness of the grain monopoly and fixed prices, and also the necessity of a ruthless struggle against grain speculators and bagmen; to compel each grain owner to declare the surplus above the quantity needed for sowing the fields and personal use, according to the established norms, until the new harvest, and to surrender the same within a week of the publication of this decree in each volost. The procedure for these declarations is to be determined by the People's Commissariat of Food through the local food organs.

2. To call upon all workers and poor peasants to unite at once for a merciless struggle against the kulaks.

3. To declare all those having surplus grain and not bringing it to the collection points, and also all those squandering grain reserves on illegal distilleries, enemies of the people; to turn them over to the Revolutionary Court with a view to sending the culprits to prison for a term of not less than 10 years; to expel them from the farm community for ever, all their property being subject to confiscation; to sentence illegal distillers, moreover, to socially-useful hard labour.

4. That in the event of discovering that someone has not declared his surplus grain for surrender in compliance with point 1, the grain shall be taken away from him without payment; after the actual receipt of the undeclared surpluses at the collection point, half their value, calculated at fixed prices, is to be paid to the person who pointed out the concealed surpluses, and the other half to the village commune. Declarations concerning concealed surpluses are to be made to local food organizations.

Further, taking into consideration that the fight against the food crisis demands the application of quick and decisive measures, that the most fruitful execution of these measures demands in its turn the centralization of all orders dealing with the food problem in a single body, and that such a body is the People's Commissariat of Food, the All-Russian Central Executive Committee of Soviets resolves to grant the People's Commissar of Food the following powers for a more successful fight against the food crisis:

1. To publish compulsory regulations, exceeding the usual limits of competence of the People's Commissar of Food, regarding the food situation.

2. To countermand regulations of local food organs and other organizations and bodies which contravene the plans and actions of the People's Commissar of Food.

3. To demand from institutions and organizations of all departments the unconditional and immediate execution of directives of the People's Commissar of Food in connection with the food situation.

4. To use armed force in the event of opposition being rendered to the removal of grain or other food products.

5. To disband or reorganize food organs in local areas in the event of their opposition to the directives of the People's Commissar of Food.

6. To dismiss, transfer, turn over to the Revolutionary Court, or subject to arrest officials and employees of all departments and public organizations in the event of their disorganizing interference with the directives of the People's Commissar of Food.

7. To transfer the present powers (except the right to subject to arrest, point 6) to other persons and bodies in the localities with the approval of the Council of People's Commissars.

8. All enactments of the People's Commissar of Food which are associated by their nature with departments of the People's Commissariat of the Means of Communication and the Supreme Council of the National Economy are to be carried out upon consultation with the corresponding departments.

9. Regulations and directives of the People's Commissar of Food issued under the present powers are to be verified by the College of the People's Commissariat of Food, which has the right, without suspending their execution, to appeal against them to the Council of People's Commissars.

The present decree takes force from the day of its signing and is to be put into operation by telegraph.

2/4 Inflation, 1919

Extract from LEAGUE OF NATIONS, *Currencies After the War*, etc. Printed in CLOUGH, *et al. Economic History* [*see* Document 1/4a], pp. 111–114.

Owing to the well-known but exceptional violence of the political changes which have taken and are taking place in what before the war was the Russian Empire, a summary of the financial measures taken on behalf of the Government cannot be scientific. From August 1914 to March 1917, the political condition of the country was, broadly, unaltered. But the empire had lost by invasion the industrially advanced province of Poland, and by the decision to suspend the sale of vodka the State lost a valuable source of revenue from this monopoly, which in 1911, produced nearly 28 per cent of the Budget receipts. During the war, there were some attempts to raise internal loans, and large sums were borrowed from abroad. Thus the State debt had risen from 9·3 billions of roubles in 1914 to 16·7 billions in January 1916, and to 33·6 billions by the beginning of 1917. At the latter date the gold reserve had fallen to 1,175 million roubles, while the note circulation (always the stand-by of Russian finance during a war) had increased to 9,103 millions; i.e. it had roughly been multiplied by five; further, the balance of trade had become unfavourable to Russia to the extent, in 1916, of 75 millions sterling. The rate of exchange had, however, not depreciated proportionately at this date, thanks in part to the pre-existent Chancery of Credit system (under which Russians selling goods abroad had to accept payment in roubles from the Russian Government, to which they handed the foreign monies they had received in the first instance). Other factors which helped to sustain the exchange value of the rouble were the credits given to the Russian Government abroad by the Allied Governments (including £568 millions by England) and some private credits arranged by bankers abroad for the Russian banks, including about £8 millions drawn on London accepting houses and banks. These factors had largely neutralized the effect of the inflation of the rouble circulation and the closing of the Dardanelles to Russia's principal export, wheat from the south. Thus the price paid for £1 sterling had in this time only risen from about 10 to 20 roubles.

In March 1917, came the first revolution, which was marked, financially, by more rapid inflation of the currency and a great deal of domestic speculation. In November 1917, the Bolsheviks obtained supreme power. Various portions of the old Russian Empire, representing, with Siberia, about one-quarter of the whole population, broke away from the centre (now, after many years, once more Moscow), and round the White and Black Seas, as well as in Siberia, governments hostile to Moscow were established. The Bolshevik rulers, first from weakness and finally out of set purpose, pursued a policy of rapid inflation of the currency, and all connection with a gold standard was completely abolished – part of what gold remained having been removed by the Germans after [the Treaty of] Brest-Litovsk.* By the terms of the Armistice of 1918, Germany was compelled to hand over this stolen gold, which had already figured in the Reichsbank's weekly returns, to the Allies for safe custody on behalf of a reconstituted Russia. The present position in regard to this gold, the remains of the Russian State Bank's own gold reserve, a small amount of Roumanian gold, and the foreign balances claimed by the Russian State Bank from pre-Bolshevik times, is a legal question of some obscurity.

* Treaty of Brest-Litovsk, imposed by Imperial Germany on the new Soviet Government in March 1918. By it Russia gained peace at the expense of substantial territorial cessions (including the Ukraine, Russian Poland, the Baltic provinces and Finland) which represented the most economically advanced and productive areas of the former Russian Empire. (Footnote in Clough.)

The circulation of Russian roubles, which at 9 billions at the beginning of 1917 had caused alarm, was largely increased during the Kerensky regime,* so that the rate of exchange fell from 20 to 35, and the circulation had risen to 18 billions. On 31 October 1918, it was 50 billions, and on 1 January 1919, the Bolsheviks officially gave the figure as 55 billions. On 30 June 1919, it was officially given as 70 billions, and unofficially but competently estimated at 85 to 100 billions, including forgeries. It is now increasing at the rate of 40 billions a year. Nor does this give a full account of what has taken place. For, according to the Bolshevik organ *Pravda*, economy of notes has been rendered necessary by the perpetual absorption of the output of notes by the peasant sellers of foodstuffs, who can buy hardly any of the tools which they need owing to the breakdown of importation, transport and domestic production, and this economy has been obtained by the 'partial abolition of money payments between government departments, and the partial payment of state employees in kind'.

Further, there are numerous issues of local currency in addition to those made by the various anti-Bolshevik governments at Omsk, Tiflis, Archangel and elsewhere. Coupons of War Loans are also legal tender, and even the scrip of these loans may be used to make settlements between governmental and semi-governmental institutions. . . .

For a short time after the Bolsheviks came into power scarcity of actual rouble notes in foreign centres and certain operations, political in origin, by foreign governments in Russia itself, maintained the rate of exchange at about 40 to £1, though the real value was not half that. Thereafter, economic laws asserted themselves, and, though in certain places a buyer of Tsar notes (on which sentiment has placed a premium) will only be able to get 120 such roubles for £1, transactions have taken place in Kerensky 'beer labels' [as the notes issued by the Provisional Government were called] at 1,600 to the pound.

As was indicated above, this depreciation of the currency is now regarded with favour by the Bolshevik Government, which in June 1919 decided to introduce a new note issue of its own (having hitherto relied on the reproduction of old types of notes). According to the latest available reports, these notes are regarded by the populace as even more worthless than their predecessors, which are in consequence being driven out of active circulation to some extent. These notes are apparently little different from food tickets, and it is the policy of the Government to educate the proletariat to dispense with money, the symbol of capitalism, altogether. Meanwhile, budgets are intro-

* That is, the Provisional Government, which governed Russia between the March and November Revolutions of 1917. Alexander Kerensky was Premier of the Provisional Government from July. (Footnote in Clough.)

duced half-yearly which are admittedly unreliable, and each of which is about double its predecessor. That for the first half of 1919 showed estimates of expenditure amounting to 50 billions of roubles and revenue amounting to 20 billions including about 4 billions from taxes. The balance was to be met by the printing of notes. . . .

The foreign trade of Soviet Russia can hardly be considered here, owing to the political anomalies of the relationship of that country to the rest of the world; broadly speaking, barter is the only basis. Within the Soviet area barter fails, because the towns have nothing to offer the peasants. The latter no longer come into the towns looking for work and offering goods, but remain at home and grow what food they need themselves. Their stockings are filled with unprecedented quantities of notes, received as compensation for their property expropriated in the earlier days of the Revolution. Examples of barter need not be given; it is sufficient to refer to the appeals officially issued by Lenin to the industrialists of the 'Centro-Textile' and other state trusts to increase production in order to provide a stock of manufactured goods to barter against the peasants' wheat. The experience of the Allied troops in North Russia in regard to the uselessness of ordinary currency and the value of cigarettes, etc., only confirms what is admitted by the Bolshevik Government. . . .

2/5 The Agrarian Problem in Russia

L. LEVINE, 'The Agrarian Problem in Russia' in *Manchester Guardian Commercial*, 17 August 1922, pp. 377–380.

Summing up the results of the redistribution of land among the peasants of Russia, Scheffler, one of the leading Soviet agricultural experts, is forced to conclude that 'it has not solved the agrarian crisis'. One more of the century-old illusions shared by all brands of revolutionists shattered by the experience of the last three years! . . .

Had the agrarian movement been less radical it might have been said that the new situation was the result of half measures. But as a matter of fact, the peasants have appropriated, as a result of the seizures in 1917–1918, practically all the private lands and estates. In the thirty-six provinces for which informations is available the peasants have divided among themselves 21,407,000 dessiatins* out of a total of 22,848,000 dessiatins which had belonged to noble landlords or non-peasant private owners. Before the Revolution, the peasants in these provinces had held 94,721,000 dessiatins. As a result of the Revolution their holdings have increased to 116,128,000 dessiatins. It is considered that throughout Russia 86 per cent of the land fund and 80 per cent of the farm

* See Glossary.

equipment of the former private and demesne lands passed into the hands of the peasants. In the thirty-six provinces referred to above the peasants have increased the area of usable land in their possession from 80 to 96·8 per cent of the total available. In other words, the peasants have realized their long-cherished desire of driving the landlord from the land. At last they are in sole possession of practically all the available land under cultivation.

But the age-old hunger for land was only momentarily gratified. It has not been appeased. As the agrarian excitement subsides it becomes clear that, to paraphrase a Russian proverb, hungry eyes see things large. The striking fact is that the amount of additional land *per capita* which the peasant population received as a result of the Revolution is very small indeed. In twenty-nine provinces for which figures are available the *per capita* amount of land in the hands of the peasants has increased from 1·87 dessiatin before the Revolution to 2·26 dessiatins after. But this average conceals the variety which is one of the characteristic features of the situation. At the agricultural conference held in Moscow in February 1922, it was pointed out that the *per capita* increase of land ranges from 17·8 square sazhens (a sazhen is seven English feet) to three-fourths of a dessiatin. In four provinces – Olonetsk, Viatka, Moscow, Novgorod – the additional amount of land received by the peasant averages less than one-tenth of a dessiatin. In some provinces – Vologda, Nijni, Novgorod Kostroma, Cherepovets, Gomel – the increase ranges from one-tenth to one-fifth of a dessiatin. In eight provinces – Vladimir, Riasan, Tula, Smolensk, Orel, Penza, Simbirsk, Voronezh – from one-fifth to two-fifths of a dessiatin. In two provinces – Kaluga, Saratov – from half a dessiatin to three-fourths.

The peasant who has dreamed for years of expanding his economy by increasing his landholdings will naturally be disappointed, though for the time being the old-time feeling that there is too little land is in abeyance. As a result of the disintegration which has come in the wake of war and revolution there is, at the present moment, enough idle land for anyone who has the means and the desire to sow and plant it. But this is temporary. As soon as agriculture is restored to a more normal condition the inadequacy of the quantitative gains will become evident. The old problems of 'landlessness' and 'over-population' will reappear in a new form.

In another respect also the agrarian movement has not led to any definite results. The violent seizures of land and the subsequent redistributions were made not in accordance with any specific conception as to the needs of a higher agricultural economy, but in accordance with local ideas and conditions....

As a result of these conflicting attitudes and efforts the village has come out of the Revolution in a state of confusion as to forms of landholdings. The tendencies which were inaugurated in the decade before the Revolution by the reforms of Stolypin* continue in unregulated form. In some villages the peasants are trying to get their strips of land allotted to them all in one place. In other villages homesteads are in favour. Still elsewhere the majority of the peasants hold tenaciously to the 'village-commune', with its accompanying features of periodic redistributions and compulsory three-field system. In addition to this, the division of the meadows and pastures has not been carried out, and there is much misunderstanding as to their use.

Not having solved the question of landholding, the Revolution could not overcome the technical evils which were always a part of the Russian village. On the contrary, these evils have been accentuated. The strips of land held by the peasants as a result of the desire to equalize have become narrower than before. They are more widely scattered, making the distance between the peasant's home and his land greater. The configuration of the peasant holdings have become uglier in their irregularity and the frontiers more indefinite. The land departments are swamped with complaints about the land, and the villages are in continuous excitement as a result of quarrels as to proper delimitation of landholdings and fields.

All these difficulties were admitted by Ossinski, the Commissar of Agriculture, in his report to the ninth All-Russian Congress of Soviets held in 1921. . . . There are few who do not realize now that the old agrarian problems were not washed away but have been carried by the tide of revolution to the shores of post-revolutionary Russia.

II

Every profound economic and social change – whether by reform or revolution – is generally accompanied by a setback in production and by much suffering. The Emancipation Act of 1861 in Russia resulted for many years in a decrease of the planted area and in a fall of the factory output of the country. The Civil War in America, which was in its essence an economic and social revolution, laid the south waste for decades, and was followed by the painful period of reconstruction.

Still the opinion prevailed in Russia for a while – and is held by some even today – that the Russian peasant gained in wealth and comforts as a result of the Revolution. . . .

The large masses of the peasants are suffering today from an agricultural crisis which is the price paid by Russia for the Revolution. Though the

* Russian statesman, whose land reforms, which followed the 1905 Revolution were designed to accelerate the decline of the village *mir* and 'to develop in the village a thriving class of capitalist farmers, producing for the market with the aid of hired labour'. *See* Pollard and Holmes, vol. 2, Documents 1/19, 1/20. (Ed.)

Revolution has not fulfilled the promise it had held out and has deviated from the goals which had been mapped out for it, the costs have been great and terrible. For the sweep and scope of the revolutionary changes contemplated determined the extent of the sacrifices exacted. Without exaggeration the present agricultural crisis in Russia has no parallel in modern history.

The most striking evidence of this crisis for the world is the terrible famine of 1921–2, the horrors of which have been depicted enough. I visited the famine districts of the Volga in August and September 1921, just when the bony hand of hunger was seen outstretched towards its victims. I spent two weeks in the famine-stricken districts of South Odessa, Cherson – in February 1922, – when the grip of that bony hand had tightened fast on the miserable population and was strewing the land with the dead. Nothing that can be said about it will ever convey the horrors of the scene. For the greatest horror of famine is the slow and passive shrinking of human beings into lifeless strips of flesh and bone.

But the extent of the agricultural crisis in Russia is not fully measured even by the famine. For in addition to the 8,000,000 starving, who are fed by various relief organizations, many more millions are barely managing to keep body and soul together, and practically the entire nation is underfed. In the days before the war there were differences of opinion whether Russia was exporting her 600,000,000 poods* of grain as a surplus or at the expense of her peasants who had to go hungry. It was questioned by some whether Russia really should export grain until it had raised her productivity to a much higher level. But I do not think it ever occurred to anyone that even under the worst circumstances Russia could ever become a grain-importing country. This is exactly what has happened in the last few years, and is the most striking illustration of the extent of the crisis.

To measure this crisis more concretely one must resort to comparative figures. Before the war Russia had an average production of 4,500,000,000 poods of grain. In 1921 the whole country, including the Ukraine, Siberia, and Turkestan, gathered in 2,170,000,000 poods, or less than 50 per cent of the pre-war amount. The drought, which struck the Volga region, the Northern Caucasus, and other parts of the country, was responsible for the loss of 400,000,000 poods. The far greater loss of 2,000,000,000 poods is due to the disintegration of the agricultural industry in Russia.

The immediate causes of this extraordinary fall in output are the decrease in the area of sowed land and the fall in the yield per dessiatin. In the provinces of European Russia, exclusive of the Ukraine, the area of sowed land fell from 49,442,400 dessiatins in 1913 to 45,922,900 dessiatins in 1916, and to

* See Glossary.

33,108,500 dessiatins in 1920. In all of Russia – including Siberia, Caucasus, and Turkestan, but excluding Ukrania – the area of sowed land dropped from 70,812,700 dessiatins in 1913 to 64,898,300 dessiatins in 1916, and to 47,122,300 dessiatins in 1920. In other words, the reduction in the area of sowed land between 1916 and 1920 equalled 40 per cent for Russia, exclusive of Ukrania, and 34 per cent for the entire country, including Ukrania. In 1921 the area of sowed land decreased still further. The figures of this decrease, as reported by various departments, differ somewhat, but according to the Central Statistical Department the area sowed in 1921 in European Russia, exclusive of Ukrania, was 28,748,000 dessiatins, or 13 per cent less than in 1920. Conservatively estimated, the area of sowed land in Russia between 1913 and 1921 decreased on an average by about 40 per cent, varying from 17 per cent in the south-west to 50 per cent and more in the south-east. The decrease became accentuated during the Revolution. Between 1914 and 1916 it was only 6 per cent, from 1916 to 1917 it equalled 2·5 per cent, and between 1917 and 1920 it was 27 per cent.

The decrease in the area of sowed land has been accompanied by a steady fall in the yield per dessiatin. Russia has always stood low in productivity, but the war and revolution have aggravated the situation. The average yield per dessiatin for all sorts of grain during 1909–1913 and 1915–1919 was respectively as follows: In the black-earth belt, 52·5 and 42 poods; in the less fertile northern and central zone, 48·6 and 44·8 poods; in the south-east, 51·9 and 44·2 poods. Only in Siberia is the situation reversed, showing an increase from 38·1 to 48·5 poods. In 1921 the yield fell more strikingly as a result of drought, locusts, etc., being less than 10 poods per dessiatin in 17 provinces and between 10 and 20 poods in 10 provinces.

The decline of productivity as illustrated by the above figures has been determined by several conditions. Russia has suffered a terrible loss in working and farm animals. Of the 31,415,000 horses in Russia in 1916 (considering the same frontiers as of 1921) only 23,670,000 could be counted in 1921. During the same period from 1916 to 1921 the number of cattle fell from 33,925,000 to 28,668,000, of goats and sheep from 83,000,000 to 47,157,000, of hogs from 18,931,000 to 13,502,000. The loss is especially great in the famine-stricken regions, where the population slaughtered their farm animals for food. From many parts of Russia come reports that peasants had to harness themselves bodily to pull a plough, and the population in some districts is so exhausted by famine and continued underfeeding that it takes a dozen and more to pull one plough.

The loss in animals resulted in a great decrease of manure, which is estimated from 25 to 50 per cent, and which was in no way compensated for by any increase in artificial fertilizers. On the contrary, while Russia consumed over 42,000,000 poods of mineral fertilizers in 1913, the Supreme Council of Economy distributed in 1921 only 1,200,000 poods of phosphorites at a time when the needs of the State farm and experimental stations alone were estimated at over 12,000,000 poods.

The exhaustion of the soil was aggravated by the lack and deterioration of seeds, by the destructive effects of locusts, grasshoppers, and other insects, and by the deterioration of and reduction in the number of farm implements and machinery. Between 1917 and 1920 the loss in ploughs was 18 per cent, in sowers 31 per cent, in mowers 15 per cent, in thrashers 21 per cent. Before the war the annual demand in Russia averaged about a million ploughs, a hundred and fifty thousand harvesting machines, five million scythes, two and a half million sickles, and so on. The Russian industry during the Revolution could supply only a small part of the demand it filled before the war, and the cessation of imports from abroad left a deep gap in the economy of the peasants. It was estimated in 1921 that the minimum need in the Russian villages was for three million new ploughs and for the repair of as many more, for over a million sowers, and for hundreds of thousands of harrows, rakes, and other implements. Regardless of all the efforts of the Commissariat of Agriculture to fit up special repair shops to serve the needs of the villages, the maximum achieved has not met over 20 per cent of the need. The implements used all over Russia are in a frightful condition as a result of wear and tear, and it is quite common to see a return to the most primitive methods of sowing by hand, of using a stick instead of a plough, and so on.

In this picture of Russian agriculture another feature must be noted. That is the decline of specialized cultures and of the industries closely allied with agriculture and animal husbandry. For instance, the area planted under cotton in Turkestan fell from about 900,000 dessiatins before the war to 110,000 dessiatins in 1920, and the harvest from 12,000,000 to 1,500,000 poods. The area planted under flax dropped from the pre-war figure of 1,100,000 dessiatins to 400,000 dessiatins in 1920, and the harvest from 25,000,000 to 4,000,000 poods. The area under hemp decreased for the same period from 485,000 dessiatins to 238,000 dessiatins and the harvest from 63,000,000 to 4,500,000 poods. The area under sugar beets in 1914–1915 in Great Russia alone was about 130,000 dessiatins; in 1920 this area had decreased to 47,000 dessiatins. In Ukrainia the area under sugar beets in 1915 was over 520,000 dessiatins; in 1920 it was only 135,000 dessiatins. A similar decline took place in the area planted and in the yield per dessiatin of potatoes, clover, alfalfa, and other crops. In addition to this, the decline in animal husbandry has resulted in a decreased production of hides, bristles, and what is just as important, if not more so, in the deterioration of the dairy industry. . . .

III

. . . What struck me most as I went through the villages was the fact that the young generation – the boys and girls under 16 and even up to 18 – were mostly illiterate. I could not quite believe that the Revolution had not given the people what was their most elementary demand. But the more I questioned the people the more I realized that it was so. As a result of revolution, civil war, famine, and all the other evils a generation was growing up in these villages that had not seen the inside of a school.

It was only gradually by studying the situation, visiting schools and talking to teachers that I realized that the situation was not confined to the famine-stricken districts. Throughout the entire country – in the cities as well as in the villages, but especially in the latter – the schools have, perhaps, suffered most from the turmoil of the last few years. Millions of children of school age are without schooling. Thousands of teachers have either deserted from the villages or turned to other occupations in order to keep alive. This is not the place to go into an explanation of the situation. All that I wish to call attention to is that the Russian village has not come out of the years of revolution improved in education and enlightenment.

A clear picture of the condition in which the Russian village finds itself today is given in the letters which are regularly published in the Soviet papers. As these papers are all official or semi-official and published under the auspices of the Government there can be no question as to bias. They are the sad outbursts of the more intelligent people who for one reason or another are living in the village and who cannot help seeing things as they are.

A writer in the *Pravda** of 27 January 1922, whose style betrays a peasant and who signs himself 'Nonpartisan', complains of the ignorance still prevailing in the village. 'Only the young people,' he writes, 'who have gone through the university of the Red Army are more or less imbued with the new spirit. But the remaining million-headed mass of peasants are as dark as before and as ignorant. No wonder in many provinces the peasants are bathing roosters as a means to fight the drought.' The writer continues: 'Is it not remarkable that in the course of four years of revolution you urban people could not realize that 95 per cent of the villages did not see a single newspaper in the course of the year?'

From the province of Ivanovo-Voznesensk a correspondent of the *Poverty* writes on 23 February 1922: 'Our province is considered one of the most revolutionary – a Red province. This is all true. . . . But it is also true that it is one of the most backward culturally, one of the poorest in spiritual life. This is why in our villages there is widespread hooliganism, drunkenness, card-

* Chief organ of the C.P.S.U. (Ed.)

playing, and thievery.' The writer goes on to cite instances, and then calls attention to one of the causes – illiteracy. 'In one of the largest factories out of every 100 women 75 can neither write nor read and out of every 100 men, 43 are illiterate. The union of leather workers reports that 60 per cent of the members are illiterate; in the union of paper workers 60 per cent are illiterate; in the union of land and forest workers 50 per cent; in the union of miners 40 per cent. 'This condition,' continues the writer, 'exists in the city, in the heart of the Red province. What, then, is the condition in the village? There one finds profound, impenetrable, hopeless darkness. . . .'

Writing in the same issue of the *Izvestia*,* one of the staff correspondents, Neradov, complains that 'since the new economic policy not a book nor a newspaper find their way into the village. People read absolutely nothing. At first they felt as if something was missing, but now they have become used to it and want nothing. Only some of the older peasants regret that the reading-rooms have been closed and that there is no way of getting paper for cigarettes.'

The situation is summed up by a writer in the *Izvestia* (4 February 1922) in the following words: 'The old, pre-war, pre-revolutionary village is coming back. Once more the youth is drinking. Once again there is wild hooliganism, quarrels, fights, kniving, broken heads, sides ripped open, murders. As if all the cultural work done in the village by the Revolution had been wiped out.'

IV

'Everything in the village is as before. Nothing changed.' Such is the pessimistic refrain of Communists and other revolutionists, who are not only discouraged by the conditions described above, but who are especially disheartened by the trend which has set in since the inauguration of the new policy. But this pessimism which today denies all gain from the Revolution is as unfounded as the optimism of yesterday which expected to revolutionize the entire life of the village from top to bottom.

The fact is that the Russian Revolution has achieved as much as any revolution ever can. It has let all the combustible and inflammable social material accumulated in the course of centuries burn itself out in a blinding blaze of fury and glory. . . .

Applying this idea more concretely to what has happened in the Russian village, one of the most important results of the Revolution is the elimination of the last vestiges of feudalism. The noble landlord – the creature of autocracy and the heir of an outgrown system of privilege – is gone. It is true that in the general mêlée punishment has beeen inflicted on a number of landlords who in the course of the last generation had transformed themselves into

* The Government newspaper. (Ed.)

efficient large-scale agriculturists and who relied for their superior economic position not on their inherited title and privilege, but on their acquired technical knowledge and higher methods of production. But their number was small. The Russian landlord had lost all economic *raison d'être* long before the Revolution. Not only immediately after the Act of 1861, but to the very last days, regardless of all the aid and credit advanced by the Tsarist Government, the Russian noble landowners displayed no capacity for assuming the direction of agricultural industry. They either let the land slip out of their hands or contrived in subtle ways to perpetuate the old feudal relations in new forms. In some parts of Russia the former process prevailed and the land passed rapidly into the hands of the peasants and other classes. But in the more fertile sections of the country a disguised feudalism developed which was very profitable to the landlords and exceedingly irksome to the peasant. In either case the landlord could not but appear to the peasant as an heir of unjustified privilege and as an exploiter. As long as this condition lasted the peasants, as a class, could not think of improving their economy except in one way – that is, to drive out the hated landlord and take his land.

In sweeping away this condition the Revolution transferred to the peasant class a considerable amount of actual and potential wealth. It has been estimated that perhaps 5,000 million gold roubles would have been required to buy out the land which the peasants have seized in a revolutionary way. The estimate is based on the fact that at the beginning of the twentieth century about 97,000 estates, with an area of about 45,000,000 dessiatins, which were under mortgage, were valued at 2,600,000,000 gold roubles. The land in private hands which was not mortgaged was valued at over 3,000,000,000 gold roubles. The peasants as a class have, as a result of the Revolution, wiped out the interest charges and the rents which the private ownership of this land imposed on them. For the time being the actual value of the transfer to the peasants is counterbalanced by the losses which have been caused by revolution, as described above. But the potentialities of the acquired wealth are there, and in time cannot but serve as a basis for a more prosperous peasant economy.

But the most important result is the change in psychology which all this implies. Having expelled the landlord, the peasant can no longer blame him for his own economic troubles. Having appropriated practically all the land, the peasant can no longer look longingly at the private estate of the landlord as the solution of all his difficulties. Having discovered that the division of the estates can add only a few dessiatins to his allotment, the peasant cannot but begin to reconsider the whole question of 'landlessness', in which his thoughts have run for centuries.

In other words, the Revolution has swept away the foundations on which rested the economic backwardess of Russian agriculture. As a result of historic conditions which cannot be entered into here the Russian peasant could think of his economy only in terms of extension. More land, land in new places – expropriation or migration – were his only remedies for a situation the seriousness of which he could not but fully realize. The Revolution has given him a chance to expropriate and also to roam about and seek new lands. But it has shown him that salvation does not lie entirely that way. A new line of thought and action must be sought. Not more land, but better cultivation of the land already in his hands. In short, not extension, but intensification of his economy.

Of course, the meaning of this change is only beginning to dawn upon the peasant. But it must become the central point of his economic thinking as the implications of the revolutionary change become explicit. Even though this generation may have to die in ignorance and squalor, the minds of the younger generation have been thoroughly shaken up. When the wave of rowdyism and unsettlement subsides – as it must – there will be found a new mental attitude which will reap the fruits of the Revolution and will put to good use all that has been learnt in pain and upheaval.

2/6 A Tax in Kind replaces Grain Requisitioning

V. I. LENIN, *Collected Works* (45 vols., London, 1960–1970), vol. 32, pp. 214–221.

REPORT ON THE SUBSTITUTION OF A TAX IN KIND FOR THE
SURPLUS-GRAIN APPROPRIATION SYSTEM, 15 MARCH*

Comrades, the question of substituting a tax for surplus-grain appropriation is primarily and mainly a political question, for it is essentially a question of the attitude of the working class to the peasantry. We are raising it because we must subject the relations of these two main classes, whose struggle or agreement determines the fate of our revolution as a whole, to a new or, I should perhaps say, a more careful and correct re-examination and some revision. There is no need for me to dwell in detail on the reasons for it. You all know very well of course what totality of causes, especially those due to the extreme want arising out of the war, ruin, demobilization, and the disastrous crop failure – you know about the totality of circumstances that has made the condition of the peasantry especially precarious and critical and was bound to increase its swing from the proletariat to the bourgeoisie.

A word or two on the theoretical significance of, or the theoretical approach to, this issue. There is no doubt that in a country where the overwhelming majority of the population consists of small agricultural producers, a socialist revolution can be carried out only through the implementation of

* 1921. (Ed.)

a whole series of special transitional measures which would be superfluous in highly developed capitalist countries where wage-workers in industry and agriculture make up the vast majority. Highly developed capitalist countries have a class of agricultural wage-workers that has taken shape over many decades. Only such a class can socially, economically, and politically support a direct transition to socialism. Only in countries where this class is sufficiently developed is it possible to pass directly from capitalism to socialism, without any special country-wide transitional measures. We have stressed . . . that this is not the case in Russia, for here industrial workers are a minority and petty farmers are the vast majority. In such a country, the socialist revolution can triumph only on two conditions. First, if it is given timely support by a socialist revolution in one or several advanced countries. As you know, we have done very much indeed in comparison with the past to bring about this condition, but far from enough to make it a reality.

The second condition is agreement between the proletariat, which is exercising its dictatorship, that is, holds state power, and the majority of the peasant population. Agreement is a very broad concept which includes a whole series of measures and transitions. I must say at this point that our propaganda and agitation must be open and above-board. We must condemn most resolutely those who regard politics as a series of cheap little tricks, frequently bordering on deception. Their mistakes have to be corrected. You can't fool a class. We have done very much in the past three years to raise the political consciousness of the masses. They have been learning most from the sharp struggles. In keeping with our world outlook, the revolutionary experience we have accumulated over the decades, and the lessons of our revolution, we must state the issues plainly – the interests of these two classes differ, the small farmer does not want the same thing as the worker.

We know that so long as there is no revolution in other countries, only agreement with the peasantry can save the socialist revolution in Russia. And that is how it must be stated, frankly, at all meetings and in the entire press. We know that this agreement between the working class and the peasantry is not solid – to put it mildly, without entering the word 'mildly' in the minutes – but, speaking plainly, it is very much worse. Under no circumstances must we try to hide anything; we must plainly state that the peasantry is dissatisfied with the form of our relations, that it does not want relations of this type and will not continue to live as it has hitherto. This is unquestionable. The peasantry has expressed its will in this respect definitely enough. It is the will of the vast masses of the working population. We must reckon with this, and we are sober enough politicians to say frankly: let us re-examine our policy in regard to the peasantry. The state of affairs that has prevailed so far cannot be continued any longer.

We must say to the peasants: 'If you want to turn back, if you want to restore private property and unrestricted trade in their entirety, it will certainly and inevitably mean falling under the rule of the landowners and the capitalists. This has been proved by a number of examples from history and examples of revolutions. The briefest examination of the ABC of communism* and political economy will prove that this is inevitable. Let us then look into the matter. Is it or is it not in the interest of the peasantry to part ways with the proletariat only to slip back – and let the country slip back – to the rule of the capitalists and landowners? Consider this, and let us consider it together.'

We believe that if the matter is given proper consideration, the conclusion will be in our favour, in spite of the admittedly deep gulf between the economic interests of the proletariat and the small farmer.

Difficult as our position is in regard to resources, the needs of the middle peasantry must be satisfied. There are far more middle peasants now than before, the antagonisms have been smoothed out, the land has been distributed for use far more equally, the kulak's† position has been undermined and he has been in considerable measure expropriated – in Russia more than in the Ukraine, and less in Siberia. On the whole, however, statistics show quite definitely that there has been a levelling out, an equalization, in the village, that is, the old sharp division into kulaks and cropless peasants has disappeared. Everything has become more equable, the peasantry in general has acquired the status of the middle peasant.

Can we satisfy this middle peasantry as such, with its economic peculiarities and economic roots? Any Communist who thought the economic basis, the economic roots, of small farming could be reshaped in three years was, of course, a dreamer. We need not conceal the fact that there were a good many such dreamers among us. Nor is there anything particularly bad in this. How could one start a socialist revolution in a country like ours without dreamers? Practice has, of course, shown the tremendous role all kinds of experiments and undertakings can play in the sphere of collective agriculture. But it has also afforded instances of these experiments as such playing a negative role, when people, with the best of intentions and desires, went to the countryside to set up communes but did not know how to run them because they had no experience in collective endeavour. The experience of these collective farms merely provided examples of how not to run farms: the peasants around either laughed or jeered.

You know perfectly well how many cases there have been of this kind. I

* Presumably a reference to the version of the Communist Utopia, published by N. Bukharin and E. Preobrazhensky. *See* Document **2/17**. (Ed.)

† See Glossary.

repeat that this is not surprising, for it will take generations to remould the small farmer, and recast his mentality and habits. The only way to solve this problem of the small farmer – to improve, so to speak, his mentality – is through the material basis, technical equipment, the extensive use of tractors and other farm machinery and electrification on a mass scale. This would remake the small farmer fundamentally and with tremendous speed. If I say this will take generations, it does not mean centuries. But you know perfectly well that to obtain tractors and other machinery and to electrify this vast country is a matter that may take decades in any case. Such is the objective situation.

We must try to satisfy the demands of the peasants who are dissatisfied and disgruntled, and legitimately so, and who cannot be otherwise. We must say to them: 'Yes, this cannot go on any longer.' How is the peasant to be satisfied and what does satisfying him mean? Where is the answer? Naturally it lies in the demands of the peasantry. We know these demands. But we must verify them and examine all that we know of the farmer's economic demands from the standpoint of economic science. If we go into this, we shall see at once that it will take essentially two things to satisfy the small farmer. The first is a certain freedom of exchange, freedom for the small private proprietor, and the second is the need to obtain commodities and products. What indeed would free exchange amount to if there was nothing to exchange, and freedom of trade, if there was nothing to trade with! It would all remain on paper, and classes cannot be satisfied with scraps of paper, they want the goods. These two conditions must be clearly understood. The second – how to get commodities and whether we shall be able to obtain them – we shall discuss later. It is the first condition – free exchange – that we must deal with now.

What is free exchange? It is unrestricted trade, and that means turning back towards capitalism. Free exchange and freedom of trade mean circulation of commodities between petty proprietors. All of us who have studied at least the elements of Marxism know that this exchange and freedom of trade inevitably lead to a division of commodity producers into owners of capital and owners of labour-power, a division into capitalists and wage-workers, i.e. a revival of capitalist wage-slavery, which does not fall from the sky but springs the world over precisely from the agricultural commodity economy. This we know perfectly well in theory, and anyone in Russia who has observed the small farmer's life and the conditions under which he farms must have seen this.

How then can the Communist Party recognize freedom to trade and accept it? Does not the proposition contain irreconcilable contradictions? The answer is that the practical solution of the problem naturally presents exceedingly great difficulties. I can foresee, and I know from the talks I have had with some comrades, that the preliminary draft on replacing surplus-grain appropriation by a tax – it has been handed out to you – gives rise to legitimate and inevitable questions, mostly as regards permitting exchange of goods within the framework of local economic turnover. . . .What does it mean, what limits are there to this exchange, how is it all to be implemented? Anyone who expects to get the answer at this Congress will be disappointed. We shall find the answer in our legislation; it is our task to lay down the principle to be followed and provide the slogan. Our Party is the government party and the decision the Party Congress passes will be obligatory for the entire Republic: it is now up to us to decide the question in principle. We must do this and inform the peasantry of our decision, for the sowing season is almost at hand. Further we must muster our whole administrative apparatus, all our theoretical forces and all our practical experience, in order to see how it can be done. Can it be done at all, theoretically speaking: can freedom of trade, freedom of capitalist enterprise for the small farmer, be restored to a certain extent without undermining the political power of the proletariat? Can it be done? Yes, it can, for everything hinges on the extent. If we were able to obtain even a small quantity of goods and hold them in the hands of the State – the proletariat exercising political power – and if we could release these goods into circulation, we, as the State, would add economic power to our political power. Release of these goods into circulation would stimulate small farming, which is in a terrible state and cannot develop owing to the grievous war conditions and the economic chaos. The small farmer, so long as he remains small, needs a spur, an incentive that accords with his economic basis, i.e. the individual small farm. Here you cannot avoid local free exchange. If this turnover gives the State, in exchange for manufactured goods, a certain minimum amount of grain to cover urban and industrial requirements, economic circulation will be revived, with state power remaining in the hands of the proletariat and growing stronger. The peasants want to be shown in practice that the worker who controls the mills and factories – industry – is capable of organizing exchange with the peasantry. And, on the other hand, the vastness of our agricultural country with its poor transport system, boundless expanses, varying climate, diverse farming conditions, etc., makes a certain freedom of exchange between local agriculture and local industry, on a local scale, inevitable. In this respect, we are very much to blame for having gone too far; we overdid the nationalization of industry and trade, clamping down on local exchange of commodities. Was that a mistake? It certainly was.

In this respect we have made many patent mistakes, and it would be a great crime not to see it, and not to realize that we have failed to keep within bounds, and have not known where to stop. There has, of course, also been the factor of necessity – until now we have been living in the conditions of a savage war that imposed an unprecedented burden on us and left us no choice but to take wartime measures in the economic sphere as well. It was a miracle that the ruined country withstood this war, yet the miracle did not come from heaven, but grew out of the economic interests of the working class and the peasantry, whose mass enthusiasm created the miracle that defeated the landowners and capitalists. But at the same time it is an unquestionable fact that we went further than was theoretically and politically necessary, and this should not be concealed in our agitation and propaganda. We can allow free local exchange to an appreciable extent, without destroying, but actually strengthening the political power of the proletariat. How this is to be done, practice will show. I only wish to prove to you that theoretically it is conceivable. The proletariat, wielding state power, can, if it has any reserves at all, put them into circulation and thereby satisfy the middle peasant to a certain extent – on the basis of local economic exchange.

Now a few words about local economic exchange. First of all, the co-operatives. They are now in an extreme state of decline, but we naturally need them as a vehicle of local economic exchange. Our programme stresses that the co-operatives left over from capitalism are the best distribution network and must be preserved. That is what the programme says. Have we lived up to this? To a very slight extent, if at all, again partly because we have made mistakes, partly because of the wartime necessity. The co-operatives brought to the fore the more business-like, economically more advanced elements, thereby bringing out the Mensheviks and Socialist-Revolutionaries in the political sphere. This is a law of chemistry – you can't do anything about it! (*Laughter.*) The Mensheviks* and Socialist-Revolutionaries* are people who either consciously or unconsciously work to restore capitalism and help the Yudeniches.† This too is a law. We must fight them. And if there is to be a fight, it must be done the military way; we had to defend ourselves, and we did. But do we have to perpetuate the present situation? No, we do not. It would be a mistake to tie our hands in this way. Because of this I submit a resolution on the question of the co-operatives; it is very brief and I shall read it to you:

'Whereas the resolution of the Ninth Congress of the R.C.P. on the co-operatives is based entirely on the principle of surplus-grain appropriation, which is now superseded by a tax in kind, the Tenth Congress of the R.C.P. resolves:

* See Glossary.

† A reference to the supporters of the 'White' General Yudenich. In October 1919, with British support Yudenich launched an offensive against Petrograd, which narrowly failed. Yudenich's aim was to restore the Russian Empire within its former boundaries. (Ed.)

'That the said resolution be rescinded.

'The Congress instructs the Central Committee to draw up and carry out through Party and Soviet channels decisions to improve and develop the structure and activity of the co-operatives in conformity with the programme of the R.C.P. and with a view to substituting the tax in kind for the surplus-grain appropriation system.'

2/7 Explanation of the Change in Economic Policy

LENIN, *Collected Works* [*see* Document 2/6], vol. 32, pp. 286–288.

REPORT ON THE TAX IN KIND DELIVERED AT A MEETING OF
SECRETARIES AND RESPONSIBLE REPRESENTATIVES OF
R.C.P.(B.) CELLS OF MOSCOW AND MOSCOW GUBERNIA
9 APRIL 1921

Comrades, one hears the most varied and highly confusing opinions on the question of the tax in kind and the change in our food policy, and also on the Soviet Government's economic policy. Permit me, by arrangement with Comrade Kamenev,* to share our subjects in such a way that he will give a detailed outline of the laws which have just been issued. This will be all the more appropriate for he chaired the commission which was appointed by the Party's Central Committee and later endorsed by the Council of People's Commissars, and which drew up all the recent laws at a number of conferences with representatives of the departments concerned. The last of these laws was issued yesterday, and we saw it in the newspapers this morning. There is no doubt that each of these laws raises a number of practical questions, and it will take some work to familiarize all the local Party and Soviet workers with them and to devise the proper methods of applying them in the localities.

I should like to draw your attention to their general significance, or the principle behind them. How are we to explain the fact that the Soviet Government and the dictatorship of the proletariat are about to accept some freedom of trade? To what extent can unrestricted trade and individual enterprise be permitted side by side with the socialist economy? To what extent can we permit such a revival of capitalism, which may seem to be inevitable with a free market, however restricted? What has called forth this change? What is its real meaning, character and significance? And how should members of the Communist Party understand it? How is it to be explained, and what are the limits of its practical application? This, approximately, is the task I have set myself.

* Kamenev (1883–1936). One of Lenin's first followers. Shot by Stalin. (Ed.)

The first question is: what has called forth this change, which many think to be too drastic and not sufficiently justified?

The fundamental and principal reason for the change is the extraordinarily acute crisis of peasant farming, and its very difficult condition, which has proved to be much harder by the spring of 1921 than could have been expected. On the other hand, its consequences have affected the restoration of our transport system and of our industry. I should like to point out that most mistakes on the question of substituting the tax in kind for the surplus-grain appropriation system, and on the significance of the change, are made because there is no effort to analyse the nature of the change and its implications. Here is a picture of peasant farming by the spring of 1921: an extremely severe crisis caused by the wartime ruin and aggravated by a disastrous crop failure and the resultant fodder shortage (for the failure also affected the hay crop) and loss of cattle; and the weakening of the productive forces of peasant farming, which in many places was doomed to utter ruin. And here we came to this question: what is the connection between this terribly acute crisis of peasant farming and the Soviet Government's abolition of the surplus-grain appropriation system? I say that if we are to understand this measure we must ask ourselves: what is the transition we are making?

In the event of a workers' revolution in a country with a predominantly peasant population, with the factories, works and railways taken over by the working class, what, in essence, should be the economic relations between the working class and the peasantry? They should obviously be the following: the workers producing in the factories and works, which now belong to them, working class, what, in essence, should be the economic relations between the all that is necessary for the country – and that means also for the peasants, who constitute the majority of the population – should transport all these things on their railroads and river vessels and deliver them to the peasants, in return for the surplus agricultural produce. This is absolutely obvious and hardly requires detailed explanation although it is constantly forgotten in the tax discussions. But it should be borne in mind, because if we are to explain the significance of the tax in kind, which is only a transitional measure, we must have a clear understanding of what we want to achieve. What I have said makes it clear that we do not want the peasants' products to be delivered to the workers' state as appropriations of surplus grain, or a tax. We want them in exchange for all the goods the peasants need delivered to them by our transport system. We must have such an arrangement. It is a basis for the economy of a country which has adopted socialism. If peasant farming is to develop, we must also assure its transition to the next stage which must inevitably be one of gradual amalgamation of the small, isolated peasant farms – the least profitable and most backward – into large-scale collective farms. That is how socialists have always visualized it, and that is exactly how our own Communist Party sees it. I repeat, the greatest source of error and confusion is in appraising the tax in kind without making allowance for the specific features of the transitional measures which we must take, if we are to attain the goals which we can and must reach.

2/8 N.E.P. was a 'Strategic Retreat'

J. STALIN, *Collected Works* (13 vols. Moscow, 1952–1956), vol. 12, p. 124.

A YEAR OF GREAT CHANGE
*On the Occasion of the Twelfth Anniversary of the
October Revolution*

The past year was a year of great *change* on all the fronts of socialist construction. The keynote of this change has been, and continues to be, a determined *offensive* of socialism against the capitalist elements in town and country. The characteristic feature of this offensive is that it has already brought us a number of decisive *successes* in the principal spheres of the socialist reconstruction of our national economy.

We may, therefore, conclude that our Party succeeded in making good use of our retreat during the first stages of the New Economic Policy in order, in the subsequent stages, to organize the *change* and to launch a *successful offensive* against the capitalist elements.

When N.E.P. was introduced Lenin said:

'We are now retreating, going back as it were; but we are doing this in order, by retreating first, afterwards to take a run and make a more powerful leap forward. It was on this condition alone that we retreated in pursuing our New Economic Policy . . . in order to start a most persistent advance after our retreat' (Vol. XXVII, pp. 361–2).

2/9 The Agrarian Problem: Collectivization Foreshadowed, 1928

J. STALIN, *Collected Works* [*see* Document 2/8], vol. 11, pp. 86–101.

ON THE GRAIN FRONT
*From a Talk to Students of the Institute of Red Professors,
the Communist Academy and the Sverdlov University
28 May 1928*

Question: What should be considered as the basic cause of our difficulties in the matter of the grain supply? What is the way out of these difficulties?

What, in connection with these difficulties, are the conclusions that must be drawn as regards the rate of development of our industry, particularly from the point of view of the relation between the light and heavy industries?

Answer: At first sight it may appear that our grain difficulties are an accident, the result of faulty planning, the result merely of a number of mistakes committed in the sphere of economic co-ordination.

But it may appear so only at first sight. Actually the causes of the difficulties lie much deeper. That faulty planning and mistakes in economic coordination have played a considerable part – of that there cannot be any doubt. But to attribute everything to faulty planning and chance mistakes would be a gross error. It would be an error to belittle the role and importance of planning. But it would be a still greater error to exaggerate the part played by the planning principle, in the belief that we have already reached a stage of development when it is possible to plan and regulate everything.

It must not be forgotten that in addition to elements which lend themselves to our planning activities there are also other elements in our national economy which do not as yet lend themselves to planning; and that, lastly, there are classes hostile to us which cannot be overcome simply by the planning of the State Planning Commission.

That is why I think that we must not reduce everything to a mere accident, to mistakes in planning, etc.

And so, what is the basis of our difficulties on the grain front?

The basis of our grain difficulties lies in the fact that the increase in the production of marketable grain is not keeping pace with the increase in the demand for grain.

Industry is growing. The number of workers is growing. Towns are growing. And, lastly, the areas producing industrial crops (cotton, flax, sugar beet, etc.) are growing, creating a demand for grain. All this leads to a rapid increase in the demand for grain – grain available for the market. But the production of marketable grain is increasing at a disastrously slow rate.

It cannot be said that the grain stocks at the disposal of the State have been smaller this year than last, or the year before. On the contrary, we have had far more grain in the hands of the State this year than in previous years. Nevertheless, we are faced with difficulties as regards the grain supply. . . .

This year, by 1 April, the grain supplies available to meet the requirements of the country amounted to 100,000,000 poods* more than last year, and 230,000,000 poods more than the year before last. Nevertheless, we are experiencing difficulties on the grain front this year.

I have already said in one of my reports that the capitalist elements in the countryside, and primarily the kulaks,* took advantage of these difficulties in

* See Glossary.

order to disrupt Soviet economic policy. You know that the Soviet Government adopted a number of measures aimed at putting a stop to the anti-Soviet action of the kulaks. I shall not therefore dwell on this matter here. In the present case it is another question that interests me. I have in mind the reasons for the slow increase in the production of marketable grain, the question why the increase in the production of marketable grain in our country is slower than the increase in the demand for grain, in spite of the fact that our crop area and the gross production of grain have already reached the pre-war level.

Indeed, is it not a fact that our grain crop area has already reached the pre-war mark? Yes, it is a fact. Is it not a fact that already last year the gross production of grain was equal to the pre-war output, i.e. 5,000 million poods? Yes, it is a fact. How, then, is it to be explained that, in spite of these circumstances, the amount of marketable grain we are producing is only one half, and the amount we are exporting is only about one-twentieth, of the pre-war figure.

The reason is primarily and chiefly the change in the structure of our agriculture brought about by the October Revolution, the passing from large-scale landlord and large-scale kulak farming, which provided the largest amount of marketable grain, to small- and middle-peasant farming, which provides the smallest amount of marketable grain. The mere fact that before the war there were 15,000,000 to 16,000,000 individual peasant farms, whereas at present there are 24,000,000 to 25,000,000 peasant farms, shows that now the basis of our agriculture is essentially small-peasant farming, which provides the least amount of marketable grain.

The strength of large-scale farming, irrespective of whether it is landlord, kulak or collective farming, lies in the fact that large farms are able to employ machines, scientific methods, fertilizers, to increase the productivity of labour, and thus to produce the maximum quantity of marketable grain. On the other hand, the weakness of small-peasant farming lies in the fact that it lacks, or almost lacks, these opportunities, and as a result it is semi-consuming farming, yielding little marketable grain.

Take, for instance, the collective farms and the state farms. They market 47·2 per cent of their gross output of grain. In other words, they yield relatively more marketable grain than did landlord farming in pre-war days. But what about the small-and middle-peasant farms? They market only 11·2 per cent of their total output of grain. The difference, as you see, is quite striking. . . .

That is the basis of our difficulties on the grain front.

That is why our difficulties in the sphere of grain procurements must not be regarded as a mere accident.

No doubt the situation has been aggravated to some extent by the fact that our trading organizations took upon themselves the unnecessary task of supplying grain to a number of small and middle-sized towns, and this was bound to reduce to a certain extent the State's grain reserves. But there are no grounds whatever for doubting that the basis of our difficulties on the grain front lies not in this particular circumstance, but in the slow development of the output of our agriculture for the market, accompanied by a rapid increase in the demand for marketable grain.

What is the way out of this situation?

Some people see the way out of this situation in a return to kulak farming, in the development and extension of kulak farming. These people dare not speak of a return to landlord farming, for they realize, evidently, that such talk is dangerous in our times. All the more eagerly, however, do they speak of the necessity of the utmost development of kulak farming in the interests of – the Soviet regime. These people think that the Soviet regime can rely simultaneously on two opposite classes – the class of the kulaks, whose economic principle is the exploitation of the working class, and the class of the workers, whose economic principle is the abolition of all exploitation. A trick worthy of reactionaries.

There is no need to prove that these reactionary 'plans' have nothing in common with the interests of the working class, with the principles of Marxism, with the tasks of Leninism. Talk about the kulak being 'no worse' than the urban capitalist, about the kulak being no more dangerous than the urban Nepman,* and therefore, about there being no reason to 'fear' the kulaks now – such talk is sheer liberal chatter which lulls the vigilance of the working class and of the main mass of the peasantry. It must not be forgotten that in industry we can oppose to the small urban capitalist our large-scale socialist industry, which produces nine-tenths of the total output of manufactured goods, whereas in the countryside we can oppose to large-scale kulak farming only the still weak collective farms and state farms, which produce but one-eighth of the amount of grain produced by the kulak farms. To fail to understand the significance of large-scale kulak farming in the countryside, to fail to understand that the relative importance of the kulaks in the countryside is a hundred times greater than that of the small capitalists in urban industry, is to lose one's senses, to break with Leninism, to desert to the side of the enemies of the working class.

What, then, is the way out of the situation?

1. The way out lies, above all, in passing from small, backward and scattered peasant farms to united, large socially-conducted farms, equipped with machinery, armed with scientific knowledge and capable of producing

* A private trader of the N.E.P. period. (Ed.)

the maximum amount of marketable grain. The way out lies in the transition from individual peasant farming to collective, socially-conducted economy in agriculture. . . .

2. The way out lies, secondly, in expanding and strengthening the old state farms, and in organizing and developing new, large ones. According to the data of the Central Statistical Board, the gross production of grain in the existing state farms amounted in 1927 to no less than 45,000,000 poods with a marketable surplus of 65 per cent. There is no doubt that, given a certain amount of state support, the state farms could considerably increase the production of grain. . . .

. . . There is a decision of the Soviet Government on the strength of which new large state farms (from 10,000 to 30,000 dessiatins* each) are being organized in districts where there are no peasant holdings; and in five or six years these state farms should yield about 100,000,000 poods of marketable grain. The organization of these state farms has already begun. The task is to put this decision of the Soviet Government into effect at all costs. I think that, provided these tasks are fulfilled, within three or four years we shall be able to obtain from the old and new state farms about 80,000,000–100,000,000 poods of grain for the market.

3. Finally, the way out lies in systematically increasing the yield of the individual small- and middle-peasant farms. We cannot and should not lend any support to the individual large kulak farms. But we can and should assist the individual small- and middle-peasant farms, helping them to increase their crop yields and drawing them into the channel of co-operative organization.

All the facts show that the yield of peasant farms can be increased by some 15 to 20 per cent in the course of a few years. At present no less than 5,000,000 wooden ploughs are in use in our our country. This replacement by modern ploughs alone would result in a very considerable increase in grain production in the country. This is apart from supplying the peasant farms with a certain minimum of fertilizers, selected seed, small machines, etc. The contract system, the system of signing contracts with whole villages for supplying them with seed, etc., on condition that in return they unfailingly deliver a certain quantity of grain products – this system is the best method of raising the yield of peasant farms and of drawing the peasants into the co-operatives. I think that if we work persistently in this direction we can, within three or four years, obtain additionally from the small and middle individual peasant farms not less than 100,000,000 poods of marketable grain.

Thus, if all these tasks are fulfilled, the State can in three or four years' time have at its disposal 250,000,000 to 300,000,000 additional poods of

* See Glossary.

marketable grain – a supply more or less sufficient to enable us to manœuvre properly within the country as well as abroad.

Such, in the main, are the measures which must be taken in order to solve the difficulties on the grain front.

Our task at present is to combine these basic measures with current measures to improve planning in the sphere of supplying the countryside with goods, relieving our trading organizations of the duty of supplying grain to a number of small and middle-sized towns.

Should not, in addition to these measures, a number of other measures be adopted – measures, say, to reduce the rate of development of our industry, the growth of which is causing a considerable increase in the demand for grain, which at present is outstripping the increase in the production of marketable grain? No, not under any circumstances! To reduce the rate of development of industry would mean to weaken the working class; for every step forward in the development of industry, every new factory, every new works, is, as Lenin expressed it, 'a new stronghold' of the working class, one which strengthens the latter's position in the fight against the petty-bourgeois elemental forces, in the fight against the capitalist elements in our economy. On the contrary, we must maintain the present rate of development of industry; we must at the first opportunity speed it up in order to pour goods into the rural areas and obtain more grain from them, in order to supply agriculture, and primarily the collective farms and state farms, with machines, in order to industrialize agriculture and to increase the proportion of its output for the market. . . .

2/10 Stalin on Industrialization and the Role of the Agrarian Sector

STALIN, *Collected Works* [see Document 2/8], vol. 11, pp. 255–279.

INDUSTRIALIZATION OF THE COUNTRY
AND THE RIGHT DEVIATION IN THE C.P.S.U.(B.)
Speech Delivered at the Plenum of the C.C., C.P.S.U.(B.)
19 November 1928

I shall deal, comrades, with three main questions raised in the theses of the Political Bureau.

Firstly, the industrialization of the country and the fact that the key factor in industrialization is the development of the production of the means of production, while ensuring the greatest possible speed of this development.

Next, the fact that the rate of development of our agriculture lags extremely behind the rate of development of our industry, and that because of this the most burning question in our home policy today is that of agriculture, and especially the grain problem, the question how to improve, to reconstruct agriculture on a new technical basis.

And, thirdly and lastly, the deviations from the line of the Party, the struggle on two fronts, and the fact that our chief danger at the present moment is the Right danger, the Right deviation.*

I

THE RATE OF DEVELOPMENT OF INDUSTRY

Our theses proceed from the premise that a fast rate of development of industry in general, and of the production of the means of production in particular, is the underlying principle of, and the key to, the industrialization of the country, the underlying principle of, and the key to, the transformation of our entire national economy along the lines of socialist development.

But what does a fast rate of development of industry involve? It involves the maximum capital investment in industry. And that leads to a state of tension in all our plans, budgetary and non-budgetary. And, indeed, the characteristic feature of our control figures in the past three years, in the period of reconstruction, is that they have been compiled and carried out at a high tension. . . .

The question arises: is this state of tension in our plans really necessary for us? Cannot we do without it? Is it not possible to conduct the work at a slower pace, in a more 'restful' atmosphere? Is not the fast rate of industrial development that we have adopted due to the restless character of the members of the Political Bureau and the Council of People's Commissars?

Of course not! The members of the Political Bureau and the Council of People's Commissars are calm and sober people. Abstractly speaking, that is, if we disregarded the external and internal situation, we could, of course, conduct the work at a slower speed. But the point is that, firstly, we cannot disregard the external and internal situation, and, secondly, if we take the surrounding situation as our starting-point, it has to be admitted that it is precisely this situation that dictates a fast rate of development of our industry.

Permit me to pass to an examination of this situation, of these conditions of an external and internal order that dictate a fast rate of industrial development.

External conditions. We have assumed power in a country whose technical equipment is terribly backward. Along with a few big industrial units more or less based upon modern technology, we have hundreds and thousands of mills and factories the technical equipment of which is beneath all criticism from the point of view of modern achievements. At the same time we have

* On this see p. 94 above and Document 2/11. (Ed.)

around us a number of capitalist countries whose industrial technique is far more developed and up to date than that of our country. Look at the capitalist countries and you will see that their technology is not only advancing, but advancing by leaps and bounds, outstripping the old forms of industrial technique. And so we find that, on the one hand, we in our country have the most advanced system, the Soviet system, and the most advanced type of state power in the world, Soviet power, while, on the other hand, our industry, which should be the basis of socialism and of Soviet power, is extremely backward technically. Do you think that we can achieve the final victory of socialism in our country so long as this contradiction exists?

What has to be done to end this contradiction? To end it, we must overtake and outstrip the advanced technology of the developed capitalist countries. We have overtaken and outstripped the advanced capitalist countries in the sense of establishing a new political system, the Soviet system. That is good. But it is not enough. In order to secure the final victory of socialism in our country, we must also overtake and outstrip these countries technically and economically. Either we do this, or we shall be forced to the wall.*

This applies not only to the building of socialism. It applies also to upholding the independence of our country in the circumstances of the capitalist encirclement. The independence of our country cannot be upheld unless we have an adequate industrial basis for defence. And such an industrial basis cannot be created if our industry is not more highly developed technically.

That is why a fast rate of development of our industry is necessary and imperative.

The technical and economic backwardness of our country was not invented by us. This backwardness is age-old and was bequeathed to us by the whole history of our country. . . .

It would be foolish to console ourselves with the thought that, since the backwardness of our country was not invented by us and was bequeathed to us by the whole history of our country, we cannot be, and do not have to be, responsible for it. That is not true, comrades. Since we have come to power and taken upon ourselves the task of transforming the country on the basis of socialism, we are responsible, and have to be responsible, for everything, the bad as well as the good. And just because we are responsible for everything, we must put an end to our technical and economic backwardness. . . .

The question of overtaking and outstripping the advanced capitalist countries technically and economically is for us Bolsheviks neither new nor unexpected. It was raised in our country as early as in 1917, before the

* See Documents 2/21, 2/24. (Ed.)

October Revolution. It was raised by Lenin as early as in September 1917, on the eve of the October Revolution, during the imperialist war, in his pamphlet *The Impending Catastrophe and How to Combat It*.

Here is what Lenin said on this score:

> The result of the revolution has been that the *political* system of Russia has in a few months caught up with that of the advanced countries. But that is not enough. The war is inexorable; it puts the alternative with ruthless severity: either perish, or overtake and outstrip the advanced countries *economically as well*. . . . Perish or drive full-steam ahead. That is the alternative with which history has confronted us (Vol. XXI, p. 191).

You see how bluntly Lenin put the question of ending our technical and economic backwardness. . . .

. . . Today, when we already have something substantial with which to end completely our technical and economic backwardness, we might paraphrase Lenin's words roughly as follows:

'We have overtaken and *outstripped* the advanced capitalist countries *politically* by establishing the dictatorship of the proletariat. But that is not enough. We must utilize the dictatorship of the proletariat, our socialized industry, transport, credit system, etc., the co-operatives, collective farms, state farms, etc., in order to overtake and *outstrip* the advanced capitalist countries *economically* as well.'

Here is what Lenin says on this score:

> As long as we live in a small-peasant country, there is a surer economic basis for capitalism in Russia than for communism. This must be borne in mind. Anyone who has carefully observed life in the countryside, as compared with life in the towns, knows that we have not torn out the roots of capitalism and have not undermined the foundation, the basis of the internal enemy. The latter depends on small-scale production, and there is only one way of undermining it, namely, to place the economy of the country, including agriculture, on a new technical basis, the technical basis of modern large-scale production. And it is only electricity that is such a basis. Communism is Soviet power plus the electrification of the whole country (Vol. XXVI, p. 46).

As you see, when Lenin speaks of the electrification of the country he means not the isolated construction of individual power stations, but the gradual 'placing of the economy of the country, *including agriculture*,* on a new technical basis, the technical basis of modern large-scale production', which in one way or another, directly or indirectly, is connected with electrification.

* My italics – *J. St.* (Footnote in Stalin.)

Lenin delivered this speech at the Eighth Congress of Soviets in December 1920, on the very eve of the introduction of N.E.P., when he was substantiating the so-called plab of electrification, that is, the GOELRO plan. Some comrades argue on these grounds that the views expressed in this quotation have become inapplicable under present conditions. Why, we ask? Because, they say, much water has flown under the bridges since then. It is, of course, true that much water has flown under the bridges since then. [sic.] We now have a developed socialist industry, we have collective farms on a mass scale, we have old and new state farms, we have a wide network of well-developed co-operative organizations, we have machine-hiring stations at the service of the peasant farms, we now practise the contract system as a new form of the bond, and we can put into operation all these and a number of other levers for gradually placing agriculture on a new technical basis. All this is true. But it is also true that, in spite of all this, we are still a small-peasant country where small-scale production predominates. And that is the fundamental thing. And as long as it continues to be the fundamental thing, Lenin's thesis remains valid that 'as long as we live in a small-peasant country, there is a surer economic basis for capitalism in Russia than for communism', and that, consequently, the danger of the restoration of capitalism is no empty phrase.

Lenin says the same thing, but in a sharper form, in the plan of his pamphlet, *The Tax in Kind*, which was written *after* the introduction of N.E.P. (March–April 1921):

> *If* we have electrification in 10–20 years, then the individualism of the small tiller, and freedom *for him* to trade locally are not a whit terrible. *If* we do not have electrification a return to capitalism will be inevitable *anyhow*.

. . . And further on he says:

> . . . Ten or twenty years of correct relations with the peasantry, and victory on a world scale is assured (even if the proletarian revolutions, which are growing, are delayed); otherwise, 20–40 years of the torments of whiteguard terrorism (Vol. XXVI, p. 313).

You see how bluntly Lenin puts the question: either electrification, that is, the 'placing of the economy of the country, including agriculture, on a new technical basis, the technical basis of modern large-scale production', or a return to capitalism.

That is how Lenin understood the question of 'correct relations with the peasantry'.

It is not a matter of coddling the peasant and regarding this as establishing correct relations with him, for coddling will not carry you very far. It is a matter of helping the peasant to place his husbandry 'on a new technical basis, the technical basis of modern large-scale production'; for that is the principal way to rid the peasant of his poverty.

And it is impossible to place the economy of the country on a new technical basis unless our industry and, in the first place, the production of means of production, are developed at a fast rate.

Such are the internal conditions dictating a fast rate of development of our industry.

It is these external and internal conditions which are the cause of the control figures of our national economy being under such tension.

That explains, too, why our economic plans, both budgetary and non-budgetary, are marked by a state of tension, by substantial investments in capital development, the object of which is to maintain a fast rate of industrial development....

II

THE GRAIN PROBLEM

I have spoken so far of the first main question in the theses, the rate of development of industry. Now let us consider the second main question, the grain problem. A characteristic feature of the theses is that they lay stress on the problem of the development of agriculture in general, and of grain farming in particular. Are the theses right in doing so? I think they are....

When, in speaking of our agriculture lagging behind our industry, people complain about it, they are, of course, not talking seriously. Agriculture always has lagged and always will lag behind industry. That is particularly true in our conditions, where industry is concentrated to a maximum degree, while agriculture is scattered to a maximum degree. Naturally, a united industry will develop faster than a scattered agriculture. That, incidentally, gives rise to the leading position of industry in relation to agriculture. Consequently, the customary lag of agriculture behind industry does not give sufficient grounds for raising the grain problem.

The problem of agriculture, and of grain farming in particular, makes its appearance only when the customary lag of agriculture behind industry turns into an *excessive* lag in the rate of its development. The characteristic feature of the present state of our national economy is that we are faced by the fact of an *excessive* lag in the rate of development of grain farming behind the rate of development of industry, while at the same time the demand for marketable grain on the part of the growing towns and industrial areas is increasing by leaps and bounds. The task then is not to *lower* the rate of development of industry to the level of the development of grain farming (which would upset everything and reverse the course of development), but to bring the rate of development of grain farming into line with the rate of development of industry and to *raise* the rate of development of grain farming to a level that will guarantee rapid progress of the entire national economy, both industry and agriculture.

Either we accomplish this task, and thereby solve the grain problem, or we do not accomplish it, and then a rupture between the socialist town and the small-peasant countryside will be inevitable.

That is how the matter stands, comrades. That is the essence of the grain problem.

Does this not mean that what we have now is 'stagnation' in the development of agriculture or even its 'retrogression'?

. . . We, the members of the Political Bureau, absolutely disagree with this assertion, and the Political Bureau theses are totally at variance with such an opinion of the state of grain farming.

In point of fact, what is retrogression, and how would it manifest itself in agriculture? It would obviously be bound to manifest itself in a backward, downward movement of agriculture, a movement away from the new forms of farming to the old, medieval forms. It would be bound to manifest itself by the peasants abandoning, for instance, the three-field system for the long-fallow system, the steel plough and machines for the wooden plough, clean and selected seed for unsifted and low-grade seed, modern methods of farming for inferior methods, and so on and so forth. But do we observe anything of the kind? Does not everyone know that tens and hundreds of thousands of peasant farms are annually abandoning the three-field for the four-field and multi-field system, low-grade seed for selected seed, the wooden plough for the steel plough and machines, inferior methods of farming for superior methods? Is this retrogression. . . . ?

It would be a fine Soviet Government indeed, if in the eleventh year of its existence, it had brought agriculture into a state of retrogression! Why, a government like that would deserve not to be supported, but to be sent packing. And the workers would have sent such a government packing long ago, if it had reduced agriculture to a state of retrogression. . . .

On what does Frumkin* base his assertion about retrogression? First of all, on the fact that the grain crop area this year is less than it was last year. What is this fact due to? To the policy of the Soviet Government, perhaps? Of course not. It is due to the perishing of the winter crops in the steppe area of the Ukraine and partially in the North Caucasus, and to the drought in the summer of this year in the same area of the Ukraine. Had it not been for these unfavourable weather conditions, upon which agriculture is wholly and

* One time Commissar of Finance. A lieutenant of Nikolai Bukharin. (Ed.)

entirely dependent, our grain crop area this year would have been at least 1,000,000 dessiatins* larger than it was last year.

He bases his assertion, further, on the fact that our gross production of grain this year is only slightly (70,000,000 poods)* greater, and that of wheat and rye 200,000,000 poods less, than last year. And what is all this due to? Again to the drought and to the frosts which killed the winter crops. Had it not been for these unfavourable weather conditions, our gross production of grain this year would have exceeded last year's by 300,000,000 poods. How can one ignore such factors as drought, frost, etc., which are of decisive significance for the harvest in this or that region?

We are now making it our task to enlarge the crop area by 7 per cent, to raise crop yields by 3 per cent, and to increase the gross production of grain by, I think, 10 per cent. There need be no doubt that we shall do everything in our power to accomplish these tasks. But in spite of all our measures, it is not out of the question that we may again come up against a partial crop failure, frosts or droughts in this or that region, in which case it is possible that these circumstances may cause the gross grain output to fall short of our plans or even of this year's gross output. Will that mean that agriculture is 'retrogressing', that the policy of the Soviet Government is to blame for this 'retrogression', that we have 'robbed' the peasant of economic incentive, that we have 'deprived' him of economic prospects?

Several years ago Trotsky fell into the same error, declaring that 'a little rain' was of no significance to agriculture. Rykov† controverted him, and had the support of the overwhelming majority of the members of the C.C. Now Frumkin is falling into the same error, ignoring weather conditions, which are of decisive importance for agriculture, and trying to make the policy of our Party responsible for everything.

What ways and means are necessary to accelerate the rate of development of agriculture in general, and of grain farming in particular?

There are three such ways, or channels:

(a) By increasing crop yields and enlarging the area sown by the individual poor and middle peasants.
(b) By further development of collective farms.
(c) By enlarging the old and establishing new state farms.

All this was already mentioned in the resolution of the July plenum. The theses repeat what was said at the July plenum, but put the matter more concretely, and state it in terms of figures in the shape of definite investments. Here, too, Frumkin finds something to cavil at. He thinks that, since indivi-

---

* See Glossary.　　　† Rykor (1881–1938). Active in the Revolution. Expelled from the Party in 1937 and shot in 1938. (Ed.)

dual farming is put in the first place and the collective farms and state farms in the second and third, this can only mean that his viewpoint has triumphed. That is ridiculous, comrades. It is clear that if we approach the matter from the point of view of the relative importance of each form of agriculture, individual farming must be put in the first place, because it provides nearly six times as much marketable grain as the collective farms and state farms. But if we approach the matter from the point of view of the type of farming, of which form of economy is most akin to our purpose, first place must be given to the collective farms and state farms, which represent a higher type of agriculture than individual peasant farming. Is it really necessary to show that both points of view are equally acceptable to us?

What is required in order that our work should proceed along all these three channels, in order that the rate of development of agriculture, and primarily of grain farming, should be raised in practice?

It is necessary, first of all, to direct the attention of our Party cadres to agriculture and focus it on concrete aspects of the grain problem. We must put aside abstract phrases and talking about agriculture *in general* and get down at last, to working out *practical* measures for the furtherance of grain farming adapted to the diverse conditions in the different areas. It is time to pass from words to deeds and to tackle at last the concrete question *how* to raise crop yields and to enlarge the crop areas of the individual poor-and middle-peasant farms, *how* to improve and develop further the collective farms and state farms, *how* to organize the rendering of assistance by the collective farms and state farms to the peasants by way of supplying them with better seed and better breeds of cattle, *how* to organize assistance for the peasants in the shape of machines and other implements through machine-hiring stations, *how* to extend and improve the contract system and agricultural co-operation in general, and so on and so forth. (*A voice:* 'That is empiricism.') Such empiricism is absolutely essential, for otherwise we run the risk of drowning the very serious matter of solving the grain problem in empty talk about agriculture in general.

The Central Committee has set itself the task of arranging for concrete reports on agricultural development by our principal workers in the Council of People's Commissars and the Political Bureau who are responsible for the chief grain regions. At this plenum you are to hear a report . . . on the ways of solving the grain problem in the North Caucasus. I think that we shall next have to hear similar reports in succession from the Ukraine, the Central Black Earth region, the Volga region, Sibera, etc. This is absolutely necessary in order to turn the Party's attention to the grain problem and to get our Party workers at last to formulate concretely the questions connected with the grain problem.

It is necessary, in the second place, to ensure that our Party workers in the countryside make a strict distinction in their practical work between the middle peasant and the kulak, do not lump them together and do not hit the middle peasant when it is the kulak that has to be struck at. It is high time to put a stop to these errors, if they may be called such. Take, for instance, the question of the individual tax. We have the decision of the Political Bureau, and the corresponding law, about levying an individual tax on not more than 2–3 per cent of the households, that is, on the wealthiest section of the kulaks. But what actually happens? There are a number of districts where 10, 12 and even more per cent of the households are taxed, with the result that the middle section of the peasantry is affected. Is it not time to put a stop to this crime?

Yet, instead of indicating concrete measures for putting a stop to these and similar outrages, our dear 'critics' indulge in word play, proposing that the words 'the wealthiest section of the kulaks' be replaced by the words 'the most powerful section of the kulaks' or 'the uppermost section of the kulaks'. As if it were not one and the same thing! It has been shown that the kulaks constitute about 5 per cent of the peasantry. It has been shown that the law requires the individual tax to be levied on only 2–3 per cent of the households, that is, on the wealthiest section of the kulaks. It has been shown that in practice this law is being violated in a number of areas. Yet, instead of indicating concrete measures for putting a stop to this, the 'critics' indulge in verbal criticism and refuse to understand that this does not alter things one iota. Sheer hair-splitters! (*A voice*: 'They propose that the individual tax should be levied on all kulaks.') Well then, they should demand the repeal of the law imposing an individual tax on 2–3 per cent. Yet I have not heard that anybody has demanded the repeal of the individual tax law. It is said that individual taxation is arbitrarily extended in order to supplement the local budget. But you must not supplement the local budget by breaking the law, by infringing Party directives. Our Party exists, it has not been liquidated yet. The Soviet Government exists, it has not been liquidated yet. And if you have not enough funds for your local budget, then you must ask to have your local budget reconsidered, and not break the law or disregard Party instructions.

It is necessary, next, to give further incentives to individual poor- and middle-peasant farming. Undoubtedly, the increase in grain prices already introduced, practical enforcement of revolutionary law, practical assistance to the poor- and middle-peasant farms in the shape of the contract system, and so on, will considerably increase the peasant's economic incentive. Frumkin thinks that we have killed or nearly killed the peasant's incentive by robbing him of economic prospects. That, of course, is nonsense. If it were true, it would be incomprehensible what the bond, the alliance between the working class and the main mass of the peasantry, actually rests on. It cannot be thought, surely, that this alliance rests on sentiment. It must be realized, after all, that the alliance between the working class and the peasantry is an alliance on a business basis, an alliance of the interests of two classes, a class alliance of the workers and the main mass of the peasantry aiming at mutual advantage. It is obvious that if we had killed or nearly killed the peasant's economic incentive by depriving him of economic prospects, there would be no bond, no alliance between the working class and the peasantry. Clearly, what is at issue here is not the 'creation' or 'release' of the economic incentive of the poor- and middle-peasant masses, but the strengthening and further development of this incentive, to the mutual advantage of the working class and the main mass of the peasantry. And that is precisely what the theses on the control figures of the national economy indicate.

It is necessary, lastly, to increase the supply of goods to the countryside. I have in mind both consumer goods and, especially, production goods (machines, fertilizers, etc.) capable of increasing the output of agricultural produce. It cannot be said that everything in this respect is as it should be. You know that symptoms of a goods shortage are still far from having been eliminated, and will probably not be eliminated so soon. The illusion exists in certain Party circles that we can put an end to the goods shortage at once. That, unfortunately, is not true. It should be borne in mind that the symptoms of a goods shortage are connected, firstly, with the growing prosperity of the workers and peasants and the gigantic increase of effective demand for goods, production of which is growing year by year but which are not enough to satisfy the whole demand, and, secondly, with the present period of the reconstruction of industry.

The reconstruction of industry involves the transfer of funds from the sphere of producing means of consumption to the sphere of producing means of production. Without this there can be no serious reconstruction of industry, especially in our, Soviet conditions. But what does this mean? It means that money is being invested in the building of new plants, and that the number of towns and new consumers is growing, while the new plants can put out additional commodities in quantity only after three or four years. It is easy to realize that this is not conducive to putting an end to the goods shortage.

Does this mean that we must fold our arms and acknowledge that we are impotent to cope with the symptoms of a goods shortage? No, it does not. The fact is that we can and should adopt concrete measures to mitigate, to moderate the goods shortage. That is something we can and should do at once. For this, we must speed up the expansion of those branches of industry which directly contribute to the promotion of agricultural production (the Stalingrad Tractor Works, the Rostov Agricultural Machinery Works, the

Voronezh Seed Sorter Factory, etc. etc.). For this, further, we must as far as possible expand those branches of industry which contribute to an increase in output of goods in short supply (cloth, glass, nails, etc.). And so on and so forth.

Kubyak* said that the control figures of the national economy propose to assign less funds this year to individual peasant farming than last year. That, I think, is untrue. Kubyak apparently loses sight of the fact that this year we are giving the peasants credit under the contract system to the sum of about 300,000,000 roubles (nearly 100,000,000 more than last year). If this is taken into account, and it must be taken into account, it will be seen that this year we are assigning more for the development of individual peasant farming than last year. As to the old and new state farms and collective farms, we are investing in them this year about 300,000,000 roubles (some 150,000,000 more than last year).

Special attention needs to be paid to the collective farms, the state farms and the contract system. These things should not be regarded only as means of increasing our stocks of marketable grain. They are at the same time *a new form of bond* between the working class and the main mass of the peasantry.

Enough has already been said about the contract system and I shall not dwell upon it any further. Everyone realizes that the application of this system on a mass scale makes it easier to unite the efforts of the individual peasant farms, introduces an element of permanency in the relations between the State and the peasantry, and so strengthens the bond between town and country.

I should like to draw your attention to the collective farms, and especially to the state farms, as levers which facilitate the reconstruction of agriculture on a new technical basis, causing a revolution in the minds of the peasants and helping them to shake off conservatism, routine. The appearance of tractors, large agricultural machines and tractor columns in our grain regions cannot but have its effect on the surrounding peasant farms. Assistance rendered the surrounding peasants in the way of seed, machines and tractors will undoubtedly be appreciated by the peasants and taken as a sign of the power and strength of the Soviet State, which is trying to lead them on to the high road of a substantial improvement of agriculture. We have not taken this circumstance into account until now and, perhaps, still do not sufficiently do so. But I think that this is the chief thing that the collective farms and state farms are contributing and could contribute at the present moment towards solving the grain problem and the strengthening of the bond in its new forms.

Such, in general, are the ways and means that we must adopt in our work of solving the grain problem.

* Kubyak. Appointed to the Secretariat after the 15th Party Congress. In 1928 he became People's Commissar for Agriculture of the RSFSR. (Ed.)

2/11 The Soviet Industrialization Debate: The Right Wing

Some Views of Bukharin, Printed in A. ERLICH, *The Soviet Industrialization Debate, 1924–1928*, (Cambridge, Mass., 1960), pp. 10, 16.

According to our former concepts, we considered it possible to achieve the planned economy almost at once. Our present concepts are different. We occupy the commanding heights, we establish the key positions firmly; and then our state economy by different ways, sometimes even by competition with the remnants of private capital, keeps increasing its strength and gradually absorbs the backward economic units – a process which occurs in the main through the market. . . .

By using the economic initiative of peasants, small producers, and even bourgeois, by tolerating subsequently private accumulation, we are putting them objectively to the service of the socialist state industry and of the economy as a whole: this is what the meaning of the N.E.P. consists of. By developing trade we have restored the operation of the personal incentive of the small-scale producers, we have stimulated the expansion of output, we have put to the service of socialism the individualist strata of the workers, motivated not by communist ideas but by their private interests, through introduction of the old type of wage payments (piece-work, etc.). . . .

It is correct that we must propagandize in all possible ways the merger into collective farms. It is wrong, however, when it is maintained that this is the main road along which the bulk of the peasantry will advance towards socialism. How should we then attract the peasantry to our socialist system? Only by making it economically attractive to the peasants. The co-operative should appeal to the peasant by giving him immediate benefits. If it is a credit co-operative, he will get cheap credit, if it is a marketing co-operative, he will sell his product on better terms. If he wants to buy something, he will get better quality and cheaper goods.

2/12 Collectivization in Full Swing

STALIN, *Collected Works* [see Document 2/8], vol. 12, p. 147.

CONCERNING QUESTIONS OF AGRARIAN POLICY IN THE U.S.S.R.

Speech Delivered at a Conference of Marxist Students of
Agrarian Questions
27, December 1929

Comrades, the main fact of our social and economic life at the present time, a fact which is attracting universal attention, is the tremendous growth of the collective-farm movement.

The characteristic feature of the present collective-farm movement is that not only are the collective farms being joined by individual groups of poor peasants, as has been the case hitherto, but that they are being joined by the mass of the middle peasants as well. This means that the collective-farm movement has been transformed from a movement of individual groups and sections of the labouring peasants into a movement of millions and millions of the main mass of the peasantry. This, by the way, explains the tremendously important fact that the collective-farm movement, which has assumed the character of a mighty and growing anti-kulak avalanche, is sweeping the resistance of the kulak from its path, is shattering the kulak class and paving the way for extensive socialist construction in the countryside. . . .

2/13 Kulak Opposition to Collectivization

a A. A. STAL' *et al.* (Eds). *Kollektivizatsiya sel'skogo khozaistyva v severnom raione, 1922–1937* (Vologda, 1964), pp. 238–240. (R. M. Tr.)

b *Ibid.*, pp. 249–250. (R. M. Tr.)

a An account by a member of the brigade examining the regions of mass collectivization on the expulsion of kulaks* from the kolkhoz *Novaya Derevnya* (New Countryside) formerly of Shepyakovskaya Volost,* Gryazovetskii District, and the reorganization of the kolkhoz.

(Not before 1 November 1929)

The data collected for me by the regional party committee about the kolkhoz,* *Novaya Derevnya*, recently organized in the village of Voznesen's, have been fully confirmed. The following gives a picture of the origin and nature of this kolkhoz: by the time of its reorganization (1 November this year) the kolkhoz had 27 households from various settlements, near the village of Voznesen'e, the latter being the centre. The plots of land set aside for the kolkhoz as the most fertile were in a radius of several kilometres around this village. A good half of the households admitted into the kolkhoz were from the village of Voznesen'e. This same village is made up of well-to-do kulaks. The most active group of kulaks in this village – calculating that the establishment of a kolkhoz will deprive them of the best land and put an end to their prosperous exploitation – enter the kolkhoz masquerading as middle peasants (*serednyak*).* The local party and Komsomol organizations† as well as the

* See Glossary.
† Young Communist organizations. (Ed.)

kolkhoz organizers, not apparently fully understanding the slogans about the class struggle and the construction of collective farms, are allowing the worst elements into the kolkhoz. The kulaks profit from this and are willingly entering the kolkhoz, continuing their exploitation, excluding the poor peasants (*bednyak*)* from the kolkhoz and undermining the collective from within.

A former village policeman and his family have joined the kolkhoz and he is now starting proceedings under Article 58 of the criminal code, against the secret kulaks (4 householders) and former tradesmen (3 householders). One of these — right from his first entering the kolkhoz began agitating amongst the people against the basic line of the party and soviet power – the collectivization of the countryside.

From the outset this kolkhoz was unable to be a centre for the poor- and middle-peasant masses. The kulaks, being in the dominant position, stood firm on their own line of accepting only strong farms into the kolkhoz.

In this way the initiators of the kolkhoz *Novaya Derevnya* are grossly distorting the Party- and Soviet-line of reconstruction in the countryside and blurring the class struggle in general. A form of class struggle is being used by the kulaks to create a pseudo-kolkhoz. In the preliminary discussions with the poor (*Shchekut'evo hamlet*) before the reorganization of the kolkhoz they said that 'this kolkhoz is not for us but only for those with large farms. If we were to apply to enter they would only laugh at us'.†

The poor are not organized. As the kulaks have not been rebuffed they are becoming impudent, spreading absurd rumours about collectivization of the countryside. The party and Komsomol organizations are too weak in numbers to take on this work. The problem of organizing the poor, the work of explaining the basic line of the party and Soviet power, the task of bringing the poor- and middle-peasants into the kolkhoz is urgent.

Work among the women is also necessary. According to the same poor-peasants one of the major obstacles is the unwillingness of their womenfolk to enter the kolkhoz.

At the general meeting of members of the kolkhoz *Novaya Derevnya* I revealed the present character of the kolkhoz. Having put before them concrete facts by which to judge the class struggle around the construction of the kolkhoz, having shown the onslaughts of the kulaks, I put the question of purging the kolkhoz point-blank.

The party member of the kolkhoz, Comrade Tovieva, drew the attention of those present to the mistakes made on the organization of the kolkhoz and offered suggestions to remedy them while it was not too late. The seven

* See Glossary.
† This is given as direct speech in the original but not in quotation marks. (R.M.)

householders shown above were unanimously expelled from the kolkhoz. Their yes-men were not slow to show themselves and spoke against the expulsion of their comrades (the kulaks) from the kolkhoz. These persons, 4 in number, were also expelled from the kolkhoz.

It may be supposed that those excluded from the kolkhoz will increase their criminal agitation. To counteract this it is necessary to organize the poor- and middle-peasants and bring them into the kolkhoz.

At the same meeting the kolkhoz Soviet and revision commission were elected. Candidates and members came from the most active comrades (2 party members and 2 Komsomol members). Comrade Kabanov, Ivan Semenovich, party member, was elected chairman of the kolkhoz Soviet. At the same time, work amongst the poor- and middle-peasants was divided among all Soviet members.

The remaining core of the kolkhoz *Novaya Derevnya* is completely sound, both in terms of class composition and in political attitudes.

With the corresponding work of introducing the poor- and middle-peasant masses into the kolkhoz and with help from the District Executive Committee to the kolkhoz *Novaya Derevnya*, there is in prospect a wide field of activity in the task of the socialist reconstruction of the Soviet countryside.

b A resolution of a fraction of the All-union Communist party (bolshevik), of Chebsarsk District Executive Committee, concerning the attack by kulaks on landless peasants and collective farmers; and measures against the terrorist activity of kulaks.

(22 November 1929)

1. Recently there has been open activity by kulaks, on a mass scale, against the measures of Soviet power and the construction of kolkhozes. There is a number of cases of attacks on social workers, landless peasants and collective farmers. Anti-kolkhoz agitation has increased. The class enemies – the kulaks and their henchmen – have strengthened their activity: the massacre of landless peasants in Vorontsov and Lomtev rural Soviets, the massacre of members of the tax commission in Vorontsov and Ugol rural Soviets, the murder of a poor peasant, komsomol worker in Siz'ma, the slaughter of collective farmers in Leonov kolkhoz, arson in Leonov and 'August the First' kolkhozes, threats and anti-kolkhoz agitation in Nokshino, Cherneevo and Eremeev kolkhozes.

2. The class struggle is being underestimated by judicial and investigatory organs. Investigations are slow to get under way and the attitude of workers in the administrative department of the militia to the question of the class

struggle is unenthusiastic. Such an attitude of the judicial-investigatory organs strengthens the activity of kulak elements in counter revolutionary activity.

3. The rural Soviets have up to now not decidedly repulsed the kulak and have not generated widespread social opinion around these questions.

The faction of the all union Communist Party (bolshevik) of the District Executive Committee, resolves:

1. To order the people's investigator, and the head of the District Administrative Section, comrade Bobylev, under their personal attention, to complete, within two weeks, an investigation into all these questions, to report to the fraction of the District Executive Committee and quickly to carry out exemplary trials.

2. That the leader of the Regional Administration Department, investigates quickly the activity of kulaks against kolkhozes in Nokshino, Cherneevo and Eremeev. All information arising out of this question is to be investigated with the same urgency.

3. To order the peoples judge, comrade Volganov, to examine urgently all class activities and all new matters as they arise, without delay.

4. To charge all rural Soviets to work for the creation of community feeling around collective farms. To expose all kulak statements. To investigate them and in all cases to communicate to the District Executive Committee.

5. To bring to the attention of the *okrug*★ Executive Committee the intolerable delay with analysis of affairs by the procurator and *okrug* court. To ask the *okrug* Executive Committee to dismiss the deputy procurator, Istomin, and bring him to book, for his bureaucratic approach, absence of liaison with the district (*raion*)★ organizations, and for encouraging the kulaks.

6. To charge the commission, in the persons of Uspensky, the commissioner of the Workers and Peasants Inspectorate, Volganov, to conduct an urgent investigation into the work of the administrative department and its investigator; to show up all shortcomings in the work, together with the comrades concerned (the head of the District Administrative Dept. and its investigator); to indicate practical measures for improving the work and to urgently get all affairs on the move.

Chairman: Kipriyanov
Secretary: Dubov

★ See Glossary.

2/14 Collectivization Problems: A Local View

STAL' *et al.* (Eds.) *Kollektivizatsiya* (*see* Document 2/13), pp. 339–341. (R.M. Tr.)

A resolution of the Komi regional conference of groups of the poor, on the report on kolkhoz* construction.

19 May 1930

The regional conference of groups of the poor notes that in the Komi region, the work of kolkhoz construction has been somewhat successful. This is seen in the growth of the percentage of collectivization up to 15 per cent, in the transfer of more than half the kolkhozes to the new statute for agricultural *artels*,* in the actual socialization of working animals and the basic means of production in the majority of kolkhozes, and in the more efficient organization of labour.

At the same time the conference ascertains that in the construction of kolkhozes some distortions of the Party line and the Soviet Government have been allowed. These are expressed in cases of forced collectivization, dispossession of kulaks unconnected with mass collectivization, in the compulsory socialization of livestock, in the organization in a number of places, of communes (*kommuna*)* without necessary preparation, in the closing of churches, in a number of places, without the clearly expressed will of the majority of peasants.

These extremes have given the kulaks good ground for their anti-soviet and anti-kolkhoz work.

In the majority of kolkhozes groups of the poor are not organized and are extremely weak.

There are a number of serious inadequacies in the economic life of the kolkhozes. Particularly bad is the share of forest provisions where they have been given the worst shares. The rural Soviet, as a rule, has not given the necessary help to the kolkhozes and in the majority of cases has not been directing their work.

The conference resolves:

1. The conference considers that the struggle with admitted distortions of party policy in kolkhoz construction has, up to now, not been adequately displayed. The conference demands from all workers the resolute and unconditional recognition of these admitted mistakes and that the struggle with them be brought to the forefront.

The conference warns against confusion, panic and ignorance of the struggle with the kulaks which some local workers are beginning to show. . . .

* See Glossary.

148

He who forgets for a minute the necessity for the struggle with the kulak is an enemy to socialist construction.

2. To consider the basic problem, at the present time, to be the consolidation of kolkhozes and the successful conduct of the spring sowing campaign, on the basis of socialist emulation and shock work.

3. By steady help to the kolkhozes, increasing all the time, to guarantee that the kolkhozes include the majority of poor (*bednyak*)* and middle-peasants (*serednyak*)* in the current five-year-plan period. At the given period of time. to consider it necessary to give every help to the development of agricultural co-operation. It is also necessary to help individual poor-peasant and middle-peasant farms.

4. Where the ground is not prepared for the organization of agricultural *artels*, which are considered to be the basic form of kolkhoz, to encourage the creation of associations (*tovarishchestvo*)* for combined tilling of the soil.

5. To organize groups of the poor among all the kolkhozes, having designated as their constant task that of securing the influence of the poor and landless in the kolkhozes. The rural Soviets must take the lead in kolkhoz construction, not being confined to general resolutions about the necessity for kolkhozes and must impose positive leadership upon the kolkhozes.

6. To insist on the rapid regularization of kolkhoz work in timber cutting and logging. It is necessary, in particular, to secure in the forthcoming timber cutting, the best endowed shares (of the forest) and their complete extraction....

2/15 The Liquidation of the Kulaks: The Webbs' Assessment

S. and B. WEBB, *Soviet Communism. A New Civilization?* (2 vols. Liphook 1935) vol. II, pp. 562–567, 571.

... We have already described how the Communist Party wrestled with the problem of the shortage of foodstuffs. ... Here we need only recall how, unlike the procedure of a dictatorship, the intellectual wrestling with the problem lasted for a couple of years; how it took the form of a long-drawn struggle in endless meetings and debates, rival pamphleteering and newspaper controversy; how it produced the most acute cleavage in the ranks of the Communist Party that had occurred in all its decade of governmental experience; and how, at last, after interminable parleyings in committee among the warring factions, a decision was arrived at, against which a minority intrigued and rebelled in such a way and to such an extent as to lead at last to the expulsion and exile of some of the most prominent personalities among the 'Old Revolutionaries'. The new policy thus adopted amounted to nothing less than a second agrarian revolution, even greater in magnitude than

* See Glossary.

that of 1917–1918. The innumerable scattered strips and tiny holdings through-out the U.S.S.R. were to be summarily amalgamated into several hundred thousand large farms, on which agriculture could be effectively mechanized. Only in this way, it was finally concluded, could the aggregate production of foodstuffs be sufficiently increased, within the ensuing decade, to meet the requirements of the growing population; to rescue from inevitable poverty the mass of the peasants unable to produce even enough for their own families; and to build up a grain reserve adequate to provide against the periodical failure of crops, whilst meeting the needs of defence against the ever-possible foreign invasion.

This momentous Party decision – perhaps the most important since that of 1918 in favour of accepting the terms of peace dictated by the German Army – committed the Soviet Government, in addition to all its other work, to a task of colossal magnitude and difficulty. Here we are concerned only with the fact that it incidentally involved the 'liquidation' of the last remain-ing sector of individual capitalists. Among the twenty-five million peasant families there were . . . three recognized grades, the poor (bedniaki),* the middle (seredniaki)* and the relatively well-to-do (kulaki).* Of these it was assumed that the first could easily be persuaded to unite in the kolkhosi* that would offer them prospects of larger shares than their tiny holdings had ever yielded. The second grade could, it was supposed, for the most part, be won over by demonstration of the success of the kolkhosi. But it was foreseen that an uncertain proportion of these middle peasants, including both the more energetic and ambitious, and the more obstinate and prejudiced, would prove entirely recalcitrant. Finally, the relatively well-to-do peasant, who had managed to enlarge his holding by renting land, often joining with his farming a little trading and a persistent money-lending; and who had de-veloped his cultivation with the aid of the agricultural co-operative societies, by himself acquiring a greater knowledge and through the employment of low-paid wage labour – in short, the much-hated kulak – would have to be 'liquidated as a class'. It can be inferred that it was actually expected that to carry to completion this new agrarian revolution would involve the summary ejection, from their relatively successful holdings, of something like a million families. Strong must have been the faith and resolute the will of the men who, in the interest of what seemed to them the public good, could take so momentous a decision.

It must be recognized that this liquidation of the individual capitalist in agriculture had necessarily to be faced if the required increase of output was to be obtained. To allow of a mechanization of all the agricultural processes, it was indispensable, not only that the scattered strips and tiny holdings

* See Glossary.

should be merged, but also that no separate holdings should be allowed to obstruct the wide area of each collective farm. It was, it is true, not necessary in Russia, as it had been in the analogous statutory enclosure of commons in the England of 1760–1820, to deal always with whole parishes or manors. But at least each collective farm needed a clear run of hundreds of acres, an area which might be irrespective of village or district boundaries, but which inevitably involved the forcible removal of any holder who refused (or was not allowed to) merge his little farm in the new kolkhos. It was, we may say, not on this point that the serious cleavage of opinion in the Communist Party had arisen. None of the factions wished to show any mercy to the universally hated kulak.

It is hard for the Englishman of the present day to appreciate the abhorrence and hatred felt by the Russian for the kulak. Today, in his 'liquidation', he may seem only the exceptionally thrifty and energetic peasant, who had raised himself by his virtues out of the destitution of the thriftless and incapable mass. But all students of Russian rural life have, for the past half-century or more, stigmatized the kulak as a terrible oppressor of his poorer neighbours. Stepniak, in 1895, gave an appalling description of the effects upon his neighbours of the kulak's inveterate usury, and his virtual enslavement of the landless peasant. . . . Dr Dillon, whose testimony is of unimpeachable authority, declared in 1918 that 'this type of man was commonly termed a kulak, or fist, to symbolize his utter callousness to pity or ruth. *And of all the human monsters I have ever met in my travels, I cannot recall any so malignant and odious as the Russian kulak.* In the revolutionary horrors of 1905 and 1917 he was the ruling spirit – a fiend incarnate.' Many illustrative examples of relentless economic oppression by kulaks may be gathered from Russian sources. Yet the kulaks as a class may be said to have done no more than would have been considered 'sound business' by the individualist economists of Victorian England; namely, habitually to take advantage of the economic weakness of those with whom they made their bargains; always to buy in the cheapest and sell in the dearest market; paying the lowest wage at which they could hire the services of those who begged for employment; and extracting the utmost usury from those who voluntarily accepted their loans.

But whether the successful peasant was a good or a bad member of rural society, the Communist Party was determined that the U.S.S.R. should not follow the example of France in permanently establishing a class of peasant proprietors. The experience of the preceding seven years, during which only 1 or 2 per cent of the peasants in the whole U.S.S.R. had voluntarily joined the various kolkhosi, in spite of these having been expressly favoured in grants of credit and remissions of taxation, showed that a much more determined effort was required. Within the first year after Stalin's enunciation of the new policy, the second agrarian revolution was already in full swing, with summary expulsion from house and home of those objectors whose holdings stood in the way; coupled with confiscation of their property, and forcible removal of themselves and families to new localities. At the same time, taxation was differentiated in such a way as severely to penalize the individual peasant holding, even when it did not stand in the way of a kolkhoz, merely in order to convince its owner that his position would soon become unendurable.

At first the new agrarian revolution went ahead at a rate surpassing all expectation. The First Five-Year Plan had provided for the amalgamation, each year, of 20 per cent of the peasant holdings. But within a year no less than 55 per cent of them had merged their holdings in collective farms. There were nothing like enough tractors and other agricultural machines ready for such a rapid development, and great discontent arose. The Central Executive Committee (T.S.I.K.) reported that something must be done to allay the unrest; and the Central Committee of the Communist Party instructed Stalin to deliver the speech which was circulated all over the U.S.S.R. under the title 'Dizzy with Success'.* In this he sharply rebuked the local committees and officials for their excess of zeal. He insisted that joining a collective farm was to be an entirely voluntary decision of each individual peasant; and that, far from depriving such voluntary recruits of the advantage of the property that they brought in, the kolkhos authorities ought to allow a reasonable equivalent for this addition to the common stock. He declared that any member who wished to withdraw must be allowed to do so upon reasonable terms. The result was that the aggregate membership of the kolkhosi at once fell off by nearly one-half. Collectivization thereafter proceeded with less precipitancy and more discretion. But it continued without a break until, by the end of 1933, about 65 per cent of the peasant holdings had become merged in over two hundred thousand collective farms, which yielded more than three-quarters of the aggregate harvest of the whole U.S.S.R. for the year. In those provinces in which the formation of kolkhosi had been specially pushed forward, comprising nearly the whole of the area on which more wheat is normally produced than is required for local consumption, it could be reported, at the end of 1933, that the liquidation of the kulak had been substantially completed.

It is, we think, to be regretted that no statistics are accessible, and not even a descriptive report had been published, as to the manner in which this enforced *diaspora* of probably some hundreds of thousands of persons was effected. We can form no estimate of the numer of cases in which practically the whole property of these families was confiscated, or was simply taken over by the kolkhosi, which, as kulaks, they were not allowed to join, or membership in which they stubbornly refused. We can form no idea as to how many of them could accurately be described as kulaks, or persons guilty of economic oppression of their less successful neighbours; and how many were merely obstinate individualists who, whether or not their separate cultivation of their little holdings had been successful, resolutely declined to merge these in the collective farms. We do not know to what extent or by what means their cases were investigated, before they were forcibly ejected from their homes. We have been unable to learn how many of these peasants were removed to prison, or (as is specifically alleged) deported to the lumber camps in the northern forest areas, or employed on public works of railway or canal construction, or taken on as labourers at such gigantic industrial enterprises perpetually hungry for men as Magnitogorsk* or Chelyabinsk, or sent to the Donets Basin to work in the coal mines, which have been equally suffering from shortage of labour force. Nor is there any account known to us of the conditions under which these hundreds of thousands of men, women and children have had to live in this process of arbitrary removal and resettlement, nor any estimate of the mortality involved in their displacement. So far as we are aware the Soviet Government has not deigned to reply to the numerous denunciations of the cruelty on a gigantic scale alleged to have been perpetrated by its agents; nor published any explanatory account of its proceedings in this summary 'liquidation' of so large a proportion of its citizens. In fact, almost the only thing publicly known is that travellers throughout the southern parts of the U.S.S.R. have, during the past few years, repeatedly witnessed in the railway stations groups of weary and disconsolate men, women and children, with no more belongings than they could carry, being shepherded by armed guards into trains carrying them to unknown destinations. The sum of human suffering involved is beyond all computation. . . .

We have no wish to minimize, still less to seek to justify, this ruthless expropriation and removal of the occupiers and cultivators who were stigmatized as kulaks, any more than we do the equally ruthless expulsion, little over a century ago, of the crofters from so much of the Scottish Highlands, or the economic ruin of so many smallholders that accompanied the statutory enclosure of the English commons. The policy of compulsorily substituting sheep-runs and large farms for tiny holdings may have been economically sound in the one case as in the other. The Soviet Government may well have been right in concluding that only by a widespread amalgamation of the independent peasant holdings could any general mechanization of agriculture be made practicable; and that only by such mechanization could the aggregate production of foodstuffs be made equal to the nation's

* See Documents 2/22, 2/24. (Ed.)

requirements. In fact, the partial failure of crops in 1931 and 1932 (though, far removed from anything to be properly called a famine) brought many thousands of small peasants within reach of actual starvation; and it may well have seemed that, in these cases at any rate, nothing but removal could save them from death at the next failure of crops, or even before the next harvest. It is, indeed, not so much the policy of removal that is open to criticism, as the manner in which it appears to have been carried out, and the unsatisfactory conditions of life into which the victims seem to have been, without judicial trial or any effective investigation, arbitrarily deported.

2/16 'Dizzy with Success'

STALIN, *Collected Works* [*see* Document 2/8], vol. 12, pp. 197–205.

DIZZY WITH SUCCESS*

Concerning Questions of the Collective-Farm Movement

The Soviet Government's successes in the sphere of the collective-farm movement are now being spoken of by everyone. Even our enemies are forced to admit that the successes are substantial. And they really are very great.

It is a fact that by 20 February of this year 50 per cent of the peasant farms throughout the U.S.S.R. had been collectivized. That means that by 20 February 1930, we had *overfulfilled* the five-year plan of collectivization by more than 100 per cent.

It is a fact that on 28 February of this year the collective farms had *already succeeded* in stocking upwards of 36,000,000 centners, i.e. about 220,000,000 poods,† of seed for the spring sowing, which is more than 90 per cent of the plan. It must be admitted that the accumulation of 220,000,000 poods of seed by the collective farms alone – after the successful fulfilment of the grain-procurement plan – is a tremendous achievement.

What does all this show?

That a *radical turn of the countryside towards socialism may be considered as already achieved.*

There is no need to prove that these successes are of supreme importance for the fate of our country, for the whole working class, which is the directing force of our country, and, lastly, for the Party itself. To say nothing of the direct practical results, these successes are of immense value for the internal life of the Party itself, for the education of our Party. They imbue our Party with a spirit of cheerfulness and confidence in its strength. They arm

---

* The original appears in a letter of 2 March 1930 to *Pravda*, the Party newspaper. (Ed.)
† See Glossary.

the working class with confidence in the victory of our cause. They bring forward additional millions of reserves for our Party.

Hence the Party's task is: to *consolidate* the successes achieved and to *utilize* them systematically for our further advancement.

But successes have their seamy side, especially when they are attained with comparative 'ease' – 'unexpectedly', so to speak. Such successes sometimes induce a spirit of vanity and conceit: 'We can achieve anything!', 'There's nothing we can't do!' People not infrequently become intoxicated by such successes; they become dizzy with success, lose all sense of proportion and the capacity to understand realities; they show a tendency to overrate their own strength and to underrate the strength of the enemy; adventurist attempts are made to solve all questions of socialist construction 'in a trice'. In such a case, there is no room for concern to *consolidate* the successes achieved and to *utilize* them systematically for further advancement. Why should we consolidate the successes achieved when, as it is, we can dash to the full victory of socialism 'in a trice': 'We can achieve anything!', 'There's nothing we can't do!'

Hence the Party's task is: to wage a determined struggle against these sentiments, which are dangerous and harmful to our cause, and to drive them out of the Party.

It cannot be said that these dangerous and harmful sentiments are at all widespread in the ranks of our Party. But they do exist in our Party, and there are no grounds for asserting that they will not become stronger. And if they should be allowed free scope, then there can be no doubt that the collective-farm movement will be considerably weakened and the danger of its breaking down may become a reality.

Hence the task of our press is: systematically to denounce these and similar anti-Leninist sentiments.

A few facts.

1. The successes of our collective-farm policy are due, among other things, to the fact that it rests on the *voluntary character* of the collective-farm movement and on *taking into account the diversity of conditions* in the various regions of the U.S.S.R. Collective farms must not be established by force. That would be foolish and reactionary. The collective-farm movement must rest on the active support of the main mass of the peasantry. Examples of the formation of collective farms in the developed areas must not be mechanically transplanted to underdeveloped areas. That would be foolish and reactionary. Such a 'policy' would discredit the collectivization idea at one stroke. In determining the speed and methods of collective-farm development, careful consideration must be given to the diversity of conditions in the various regions of the U.S.S.R.

Our grain-growing areas are ahead of all others in the collective-farm movement. Why is this?

Firstly, because in these areas we have the largest number of already firmly-established state farms and collective farms, thanks to which the peasants have had the opportunity to convince themselves of the power and importance of the new technical equipment, of the power and importance of the new, collective organization of farming.

Secondly, because these areas have had a two-years' schooling in the fight against the kulaks during the grain-procurement campaigns, and this could not but facilitate the development of the collective-farm movement.

Lastly, because these areas in recent years have been extensively supplied with the best cadres from the industrial centres.

Can it be said that these especially favourable conditions also exist in other areas, the consuming areas, for example, such as our northern regions, or in areas where there are still backward nationalities, such as Turkestan, say?

No, it cannot be said.

Clearly, the principle of taking into account the diversity of conditions in the various regions of the U.S.S.R. is, together with the voluntary principle, one of the most important prerequisites for a sound collective-farm movement.

But what actually happens sometimes? Can it be said that the voluntary principle and the principle of taking local peculiarities into account are not violated in a number of areas? No, that cannot be said, unfortunately. We know, for example, that in a number of the northern areas of the consuming zone, where conditions for the immediate organization of collective farms are comparatively less favourable than in the grain-growing areas, attempts are not infrequently made to *replace* preparatory work for the organization of collective farms by bureaucratic decreeing of the collective-farm movement, paper resolutions on the growth of collective farms, organization of collective farms on paper – collective farms which have as yet no reality, but whose 'existence' is proclaimed in a heap of boastful resolutions.

Or take certain areas of Turkestan, where conditions for the immediate organization of collective farms are even less favourable than in the northern regions of the consuming zone. We know that in a number of areas of Turkestan there have already been attempts to 'overtake and outstrip' the advanced areas of the U.S.S.R. by threatening to use armed force, by threatening that peasants who are not yet ready to join the collective farms will be deprived of irrigation water and manufactured goods. . . .

Who benefits by these distortions, this bureaucratic decreeing of the collective-farm movement, these unworthy threats against the peasants? Nobody, except our enemies!

What may these distortions lead to? To strengthening our enemies and to discrediting the idea of the collective-farm movement.

Is it not clear that the authors of these distortions, who imagine themselves to be 'Lefts', are in reality bringing grist to the mill of Right opportunism?

2. One of the greatest merits of our Party's political strategy is that it is able at any given moment to pick out the *main link* in the movement, by grasping which the Party draws the whole chain towards one common goal in order to achieve the solution of the problem. Can it be said that the Party has already picked out the main link of the collective-farm movement in the system of collective-farm development? Yes, this can and should be said.

What is this chief link? . . .

The main link of the collective-farm movement, its *predominant* form at the present moment, the link which has to be grasped now, is the *agricultural artel*.

In the *agricultural artel*, the basic means of production, primarily for grain-farming – labour, use of the land, machines and other implements, draught animals and farm buildings – are socialized. In the artel, the household plots (small vegetable gardens, small orchards), the dwelling houses, a part of the dairy cattle, small livestock, poultry, etc., are *not socialized*.

The artel is the *main link of the collective-farm movement* because it is the form best adapted for solving the grain problem. And the grain problem is the *main link in the whole system of agriculture* because, if it is not solved, it will be impossible to solve either the problem of stock-breeding (small and large), or the problem of the industrial and special crops that provide the principal raw materials for industry. That is why the agricultural artel is the main link in the system of the collective-farm movement at the present moment.

That is the point of departure of the 'Model Rules' for collective farms, the final text of which is published today.★

And that should be the point of departure of our Party and Soviet workers, one of whose duties it is to make a thorough study of these Rules and to carry them out down to the last detail.

Such is the line of the Party at the present moment.

Can it be said that this line of the Party is being carried out without violation or distortion? No, it cannot, unfortunately. We know that in a number of areas of the U.S.S.R., where the struggle for the existence of the collective farms is still far from over, and where artels are not yet consolidated, attempts are being made to skip the artel framework and to leap straight away into the agricultural commune. The artel is still not consolidated, but they are already 'socializing' dwelling houses, small livestock and poultry; moreover, this 'socialization is degenerating into bureaucratic decreeing on

★ *Pravda*, 2 March 1930. (Footnote in original.)

paper, because the conditions which would make such socialization necessary do not yet exist. One might think that the grain problem has already been solved in the collective farms, that it is already a past stage, that the principal task at the present moment is not solution of the grain problem, but solution of the problem of livestock- and poultry-breeding. [sic.] Who, we may ask benefits from this blockheaded 'work' of lumping together different forms of the collective-farm movement? Who benefits from this running too far ahead, which is stupid and harmful to our cause? . . . Is it not obvious that such a 'policy' can be to the satisfaction and advantage only of our sworn enemies?

One such overzealous 'socializer' even goes so far as to issue an order to an artel containing the following instructions: 'Within three days, register all the poultry of every household', establish posts of special 'commanders' for registration and supervision; 'occupy the key positions in the artel'; 'command the socialist battle without quitting your posts' and – of course – get a tight grip on the whole life of the artel.

What is this – a policy of directing the collective farms, or a policy of *disrupting* and *discrediting* them? . . .

How could there have arisen in our midst such block-headed exercises in 'socialization', such ludicrous attempts to overleap oneself, attempts which aim at by-passing classes and the class struggle, and which in fact bring grist to the mill of our class enemies?

They could have arisen only in the atmosphere of our 'easy' and 'unexpected' successes on the front of collective-farm development.

They could have arisen only as a result of the block-headed belief of a section of our Party: 'We can achieve anything!', 'There's nothing we can't do!'

They could have arisen only because some of our comrades have become dizzy with success and for the moment have lost clearness of mind and sobriety of vision.

To correct the line of our work in the sphere of collective-farm development, *we must put an end to these sentiments.*

That is now one of the immediate tasks of the Party. . . .

2/17 The Development of Productivity

N. BUKHARIN and E. PREOBRAZHENSKY, *The A.B.C. of Communism* (Harmondsworth, 1969. First published in England in 1922.) pp. 315–317, 346–347.

§94. OUR GOAL, THE DEVELOPMENT OF PRODUCTIVITY

The foundation of our whole policy must be the widest possible development of productivity. The disorganization of production has been so extensive, the post-war scarcity of all products is so conspicuous, that every-thing else must be subordinated to this one task. More products! More boots, scythes, barrels, textiles, salt, clothing, corn, etc. – these are our primary need. How can the desired end be secured? Only by increasing the productive forces of the country, by increased productivity. There is no other way.

But here we encounter a formidable difficulty, arising out of the onslaught made upon us by the world-wide forces of the counter-revolution. We are blockaded and put upon our defence, so that we are simultaneously deprived of labour power and cut off from the material means of production. We have to wrest by force of arms, petroleum and coal from the landlords and capitalists. Here is our first great task. We have to set the work of production upon a proper footing. Here is our second great task. We are hard put to it, indeed!

Before the working class had become master of the whole country, this was not our affair. But now the working class is in power. Everything is at its disposal. It is responsible for the destiny of the country. Upon its shoulders rests the whole burden of saving the Soviet Republic from the miseries of famine, cold, and disorder. Before the working class rose to power, its main task was to destroy the old order. Now its main task is to construct the new order. Formerly it was the business of the bourgeoisie to organize production; now it is the business of the proletariat. Evidently, therefore, in the days of the most widespread disorganization, all the thoughts of the proletariat, as far as this matter is concerned, must be concentrated upon the organization of industry and the increase of production. To increase production means to increase the output of labour, to produce more goods, to work better in every possible way, and day by day to achieve better results. The time for fine phrases is past, and the time for hard work has come. No longer does it devolve upon us to fight for our rights in Moscow or in Petrograd; the work-ing class has secured its rights, and is defending them at the front. What we have to do now is to increase the number of nails, horseshoes, ploughs, locks, machines, greatcoats. These things have become absolutely vital if we are to avoid dying of hunger amid the ruin resulting from the war, if we are to be clothed, if we are to regain our strength, if we are to advance by rapid strides along the road to the new life.

The problem of increased production comprises a number of problems. How can we increase the quantity of the material means of production (machinery, coal, and raw materials); and how can we increase the amount of labour power? How can we best organize production (what is the best way of planning our economic life as a whole, how should one branch of produc-tion be linked up with another, how should production be administered, what is the best and most economical way of allotting the reserves of raw material, how can we best dispose of the available labour power)? How can we secure better work, in so far as this depends upon the workers themselves? (the question of a comradely labour discipline; that of the struggle against slovenliness, slackness, idleness, etc.). Last of all comes the question of applying science to production, the question of the work of skilled experts.

All these questions are of immense importance. We have to solve them practically, to solve them in action. We have to solve them, not in a single factory or for a single factory, but for the whole of a huge country, where the working class and the semi-proletariat are numbered by millions. It is evident that in this matter we must stick to one point of view, must drive the nail home, must increase the productivity of the whole country which is building its economic life upon the new foundation of communist labour. . . .

§102. THE UNION OF PRODUCTION AND SCIENCE

For the proper development of productivity, it is essential that science should be wedded to production. Under capitalism, large-scale production was already making extensive calls upon science. In the United States and in Germany, the great manufacturing institutions had special laboratories in which, by prolonged research, new methods and new apparatus were discovered. All this was done in the interest of profits upon privately-owned capital. We, in our turn, must now organize in like manner for the sake of the whole of working society. The investigators of those days kept their discoveries secret. The valuable results of their researches went to fill the pockets and the strong boxes of the entrepreneurs. In contemporary Russia, no undertaking hides its discoveries from other undertakings; whatever is learned becomes the common property of all.

In this matter the Soviet power has instituted a whole series of measures. It has established a number of scientific institutions of a technical and economic character, and has organized various laboratories and experimental stations. Scientific expeditions have been sent out, and among the fruitful results of these may be mentioned the discovery of petroleum wells and of deposits of schist. A means for manufacturing sugar out of sawdust has been discovered. In general, the scientific resources of the republic have been tabulated and have been turned to account.

We still lack many things, and some of these are things urgently necessary, beginning with fuel and ending with delicate scientific instruments. We must clearly realize the extreme importance of such work, and we must do our utmost to promote the union of science with technique and with the organization of production. COMMUNISM SIGNIFIES INTELLIGENT, PURPOSIVE, AND,

CONSEQUENTLY, SCIENTIFIC PRODUCTION. WE SHALL, THEREFORE, DO EVERY-
THING IN OUR POWER TO SOLVE THE PROBLEM OF THE SCIENTIFIC ORGANIZATION
OF PRODUCTION.

2/18 Planning in Soviet Russia

Speech of G. M. Krzhizhanovsky to the Fifteenth Party Congress. Printed in
CLOUGH. *et al. Economic History* [*see* Document 1/4a], pp. 196–198.

Whenever we hear of attempts at planned economics in the capitalist
countries, we must remember that although there have been critical
moments, during wars for instance, in which capitalist countries have been
forced to resort to a systematic conduct of economic life in order to utilize all
forces for war purposes, in reality it is still money that rules in these countries,
and any socialism based on the reign of this yellow metal will be yellow
socialism, a transitory period of what might be named 'yellow planned
economics'. These plans, as they are set up in the capitalist world, collapse as
soon as they encounter a stronger capitalist group. We, however, are dependent solely on ourselves, and if unity of will is our highest trump card, you
may well imagine what a high degree of unanimity and agreement of will is
required if we are to commit ourselves to a programme lasting five years
from motives of actual conviction, and not merely because we are obliged
to.

What has been the actual course of our planned development? As early as
1920 a rough outline of the ground plan of our economy was drawn up. Then
the struggle against economic decline began. Comrade Lenin advised us –
those comrades engaged on the elaboration of the plans – to set aside for the
moment our general ground plan, and to tackle the most urgent questions of
our economic life in this emergency. The State Planning Commission,
organized in 1921, was at once engaged in a struggle against the crises in the
food, fuel, and transport services. It took some time before we were gradually able to return from these questions to the actual lines being laid down for
planned economy.

Let us take for instance state industry. At first glance it would seem as if it
must be possible to introduce a planned régime here with special rapidity.
But in reality it was not until 1925 that we had a comprehensive plan for all
industry, including the techniques of production, the economic analysis, and
the financial programme.

The year 1925 terminated a certain stage of re-organization in our economic structure. Building activity increased, and industry made more rapid
progress. A period began in which it became necessary to embrace in one

comprehensive plan not only the plans for the various branches of industry, but at the same time the whole of the plans for the most important sectors of the national economy. Since 1925–6 we have been working out control figures for the national economy, furnishing the basis for the fulfilment of this task.

The first control figures of the State Planning Commission (1925/6) were compiled exclusively by the collaborators of the State Planning Commission itself. The Government could not make use of these figures for working out a plan of economic operations. In the following year (1926/7) a certain uniformity of system developed. For the first time the control figures contained general paragraphs referring to industrialization, etc.

Finally, the control figures for the economic year 1928 are at last the result of extensive collective compilation. These figures have not been worked out solely by the staff in the State Planning Commission and the corresponding commissions in the separate Soviet republics. They are the final result of the research of many thousands of economists all over our country. A number of congresses were called. At these congresses the general methods of dealing with the material have been laid down, and it may now be stated that, as a result of the work already accomplished, we have now material at our disposal comprising the budget, the financial plan for our industry, and our import and export plans, as constituents of a uniform and consistent plan of economy. This combination has been given a form enabling the Government to make immediate use of the control figures for 1927/8, since these already offer firm bases on which to set up all operative economic plans.

It is obvious that the Five-Year Perspective Plan must not constitute any limit beyond which we must not go. The extent of our development is so great that we cannot come to a standstill at this stage. When we remember that our re-examination of the prospects of the coming five years confronted us at once with a series of burning questions – the question of unemployment, of the possibility of improving the prosperity of the working masses, and of the comparative strength of such huge branches of our economy as industry and agriculture – we see clearly that we must pass as speedily as possible from the five-year plan to the ten-year and fifteen-year plan, that is, to the general plan. The imperative necessity of special activity in the interests of the transport service urges us especially in this direction....

What figures are proposed by us for the Five-Year Plan? The congress of economists collaborating in the plan came to the conclusion that it was impossible to advance only one set of figures for the Five-Year Plan. A plan extending several years into the future is a distant aim. We must proceed like the artillery man. He examines his mark through his glass and then adjusts his aim to two possibilities. The first adjustment is a careful and cautious estimate, taking as the basis the minimum of economic possibilities, guaranteeing the economy against unforeseen accidents. This is the *preliminary* adjustment. The second series of figures deals with more favourable chances, which may in certain circumstances offer the possibility of reaching our goal more rapidly. If this optimal estimate is not quite reached, it is no great misfortune. In spite of all difficulties, and in spite of our only breaking occasionally through the front of the elementary anarchy opposing us, we are advancing in the desired direction. The summing up of our economic possibilities under these two variations facilitates our economic manœuvres. . . .

2/19 The Control Figures and the First Five-Year Plan

Printed in A. NOVE, *An Economic History of the U.S.S.R.* (London, 1969), pp. 145–146.

FIRST FIVE-YEAR PLAN

	1927–8 actual	1932–3 first version	(per cent inc.)	1932–3 'optimal version'	(per cent inc.)
Aggregates					
Employed labour force (million)	11·3	14·8	(30·2)	15·8	(38·9)
Investments (all) (1926–7 prices milliard roubles)	8·2	20·8	(151)	27·7	(228)
National income (milliard roubles)	8·2	44·4	(82)	49·7	(103)
Industrial production (milliard roubles)	18·3	38·1	(130)	43·2	(180)
of which:					
Producers' goods (milliard roubles)	6·0	15·5	(161)	18·1	(204)
Consumers' goods (milliard roubles)	12·3	22·6	(83)	25·1	(103)
Agricultural production (milliard roubles)	16·6	23·9	(44)	25·8	(55)
Consumption:					
Non-agricultural (index)	100	152·0		171·4	
Agricultural population (index)	100	151·6		167·4	

Industrial output targets	1917–8 actual	1932–3 first version	(per cent inc.)	1923–3 'optimal version'	(per cent inc.)
Electricity (milliard Kwhs)	5·05	17·0	(236)	22·0	(335)
Hard coal (million tons)	35·4	68·0	(92)	75·0	(111)
Oil (million tons)	11·7	19·0	(62)	22·0	(88)
Iron ore (million tons)	5·7	15·0	(163)	19·0	(233)
Pig iron (million tons)	3·3	8·0	(142)	10·0	(203)
Steel (million tons)	4·0	8·3	(107)	10·4	(160)
Machinery (million roubles)	1822	?	—	4688	(157)
Superphosphates (million tons)	0·15	2·6	(16·3)	3·4	(21·7)
Wool cloth (million metres)	97	192	(98)	270	(178)

2/20 An Official View of the Success of the First Five-Year Plan

V. M. MOLOTOV, *The Success of the Five-Year Plan* (London, 1931), pp. 40–43, 48–50, 52.

(a) The Progress of the Five-Year Plan in the First Two Years

To discuss questions of internal politics means above all to discuss the struggle for the carrying out of the Five-Year Plan. The Five-Year Plan, the programme of Socialist construction adopted by the last Soviet Congress, has become the basis of our work. The political line of the Communist Party is expressed practically in the Five-Year Plan. The Five-Year Plan is the directing centre for all branches of our activity. The Five-Year Plan has become the central landmark for the working class.

Let us begin with the concrete results of the first two years of the Five-Year Plan. Before dealing with the figures, I will mention the political results of the period under review.

The first and most fundamental result is that during the past two years the Five-Year Plan for the building up of Socialism has not only been carried out according to plan, but that, when all the decisive economic factors are taken into consideration, the achievements can be seen to exceed the level fixed by the plan. The Five-Year Plan had many enemies. Our enemies based their hopes on the assumed inevitable collapse of the Five-Year Plan. They connected the fate of the Soviet power with this collapse. The Bolsheviks have robbed them of these hopes. The Soviet power not only carried out the first two years of the Five-Year Plan, but even exceeded its programme. That is the most important result.

The second result in the period under review is connected directly with the situation of the working class, namely, during this period we have succeeded in practically abolishing unemployment. The political significance of this fact is very striking, particularly in view of the fact that, as a result of the world economic crisis, there is an unparalleled amount of unemployment in the capitalist countries.

The third result is the solution of the grain problem. The solution of the grain problem was not only an economic question. It was one of the greatest political questions with which we were faced. Our success in this matter is connected with the successes of our work as a whole in the first period of the Five-Year Plan. We solved the grain problem in connection with the fundamental turning point in the development of the Soviet village.

The fourth result is the most important of all the various results of the two-year period under review, and is the final turn of the peasant masses towards collectivization. For years our successes in the building up of Socialism were limited chiefly to industry, commodity circulation, etc., whilst agriculture remained almost entirely in its old state, dominated by the small, isolated and ineffective individual farm. The definite turn of the masses of the middle peasants towards Socialism showed itself only in the twelfth year of the October Revolution. During the last two years this historical development has been consolidated.

And finally, the last result, which is directly connected with the change in the development of the village, is that since the masses of the poor and middle peasants have begun to interest themselves seriously in the collective farm, this movement has developed up to the point of the complete collectivization of whole districts and then of whole areas. The result was that the question of our attitude towards the capitalist elements in the village, the kulaks, was raised afresh and under new conditions. The Soviet power has been able to proceed from the policy of hindering and ousting the capitalist elements, to the policy of liquidating the kulaks as a class. This was the fifth political result achieved in the period under review.

Let us now deal with the concrete figures concerning the growth of the economic system in the two years in question. The most important figures, according to the statistics of the State Planning Commission of the Soviet Union are as follows:

RESULTS OF THE FIRST TWO YEARS (1928/9 AND 1929/30) OF THE FIVE-YEAR PLAN

(In milliard roubles)	Proposed Increase for the first 2 years	Absolute Increase	Percentage of set Tasks achieved
National Income	58·3	59·5	102
State Budget	17·0	21·0	124

(In milliard roubles)	Proposed Increase for the first 2 years	Absolute Increase	Percentage of set Tasks achieved
Capital Investments in the basic capital of the Socialist sector	12·7	13·8	124
Total Production of the Socialist sector of industry, including the food and drink trades (on a 1926/7 price basis)	29·3	30·5	104
Area under seed (in million hectares)*	239·0	245·8	103
Production of market Grain (in millions of double cwts)	221·2	267·3	121
Goods Traffic (in millions of tons)	350·9	409·2	117

This table shows that in such decisive matters as the increase of the national income, of the State budget, of the capital investments in the socialized sector of industry, of the production of Socialist industry, of the area under seed, of the production of grain for the market, of the goods traffic, we have not only carried out the estimates of the Five-Year Plan, but have even exceeded them. It is true that as far as the total production of grain cultures is concerned, we have carried out the task set by the Five-Year Plan to the extent of 94 per cent only; however, to set against that, we have considerably exceeded the figure set for the production of grain for the market. . . .

The growth of the production of those industries under the control of the Supreme Economic Council has increased the value of production in the period under review from a total of 9,500 million roubles to a total of 15,600 million roubles, or by 64 per cent as compared with the 41 per cent which was the original estimate of the Five-Year Plan, whereby the production of heavy industry increased by 193 per cent, almost doubling its production. Our engineering industry has increased with particular rapidity. Its production in this period more than doubled, whilst the production of agricultural machinery was increased by 150 per cent.

With regard to the generation of electrical power, we have already completely carried out the Goelro Plan.† This year we shall make tremendous progress in this connection. We intend to double practically the capacities of our overland power centres. When the Five-Year Plan has been carried out completely, the Soviet Union will be the largest producer of electrical energy in Europe and second only to the United States in the world.

Let us now deal briefly with the tasks set by the Five-Year Plan with regard to the question of lowering the costs of production.

* See Glossary.   † The State Commission for the carrying out of the electrification plan worked out by Lenin. (Footnote in Molotov.)

According to the Five-Year Plan, the costs of production were to be lowered by 14·5 per cent in those industries controlled by the Supreme Economic Council. In fact, however, according to the statistics of the Supreme Economic Council, the decrease was only 11·4 per cent. As far as the lowering of the costs of production is concerned, we have not carried out the task set by the plan. The difference, however, was not very great and represents a proof that the task set was not impossible of accomplishment. This must be a lesson to us for the future.

The alteration in the relation between industry and agriculture can be seen best of all from the figures given for total production. These figures show that the share of industrial production in the total production of industry and agriculture in the two years (1928/9 and 1929/30) under review increased from 57 per cent to 67 per cent. In other words, in these two years industrial production accounted for two-thirds of the total production of our economic system. This fact shows the rapid progress made by our country on the path to industrialization. It also demonstrates the rapid growth of the Socialist share in the total production of the economic system.

There is no necessity for me to give any figures concerning the liquidation of unemployment. The situation is perfectly clear.

The solution of the grain problem can be seen from the following basic figures:

Last year, our grain purchase campaign produced 1,000 million poods, a figure which formerly seemed quite illusory to us. This year the total was 1,313 million poods,* although the campaign is not yet at an end. In order to demonstrate the significance of this figure I must inform you that the total amount of market grain (i.e. excluding the grain needed by the peasants themselves) produced in 1913 was 1,300 million pood or, in other words, a little less than the total produced by us for the market by the 1930 harvest. Whereby it must be remembered that the 1,300 million pood produced in 1913 included 281 million pood produced by the landowners and 650 million pood produced by the kulaks. A total of 931 million pood, or 75 per cent of the total market grain produced in 1913 was produced by the landowners and kulaks.*

Particularly important is the way in which the grain problem is solved in the Soviet Union. The solution is achieved by the Socialist transformation of agriculture, by increasing the role of the Soviet and collective farms.

In this connection one cannot refrain from mentioning the prophecies made by the right-wingers only two years ago. They declared: 'The Soviet and collective farms will produce the necessary quantities of grain only in from five to ten years' time, but we must find a solution of the problem at once.' Or they calculated: 'One may assume that in five years the area held

* See Glossary.

under seed by the collective farms will have increased more than five fold.' This was representative of the attitude of all elements suffering from the Right-wing deviation. With these prophecies the Right-wingers tried to cloak their own policy which was one of retreat before the enemy, one of abandoning the decisive positions of the Soviet power in face of the class enemy, instead of pursuing the Party policy of an offensive all along the line against the kulak elements. . . .

(b) *The Current Year and the Fulfilment of the Five-Year Plan*
The tasks set by the Five-Year Plan for the current year are of decisive importance for the success of the whole Five-Year Plan.

As far as agriculture is concerned, we are faced with the task of completing the collectivization of 50 per cent of all individual farms during the present year. The new stream of peasants into the collective undertakings which began last autumn and which is accelerating, shows that this task can be carried out. Much will depend on the carrying out of the spring sowings campaign. The appeal of the Council of People's Commissars and of the Central Committee of the Communist Party of the Soviet Union in connection with the sowing contracts for summer crops, contains the practical programme of the spring sowings campaign. It contains everything necessary concerning both the duties of the State in the support of the collective farms, and the duties of the peasants towards the State. This programme must be carried out under all circumstances.

The collectivization successes which we have already achieved have tremendously extended and consolidated the basis of the Soviet power in the villages. In connection with these successes, [it has been declared that];

From now on, the peasants in the collective agricultural undertakings represent the decisive, the chief support of the Soviet power in the villages.

But we must go still further, we must raise the question: 'For or against the collective undertakings' before all poor and middle peasants. . . . 'For or against collectivization,' this is now the question for the masses of the poor and middle peasants. For the collectivization, for the support of the collective farms, means the support of the Soviet power and a decisive struggle against the kulaks. Against collectivization, against the support of the collective farms, means support for the kulaks in their struggle against the Soviet power. This year each poor- and middle-peasant is faced directly with the question of his attitude towards collectivization. He must make his choice. This fact alone means that 1931 is the decisive year for the whole collective agricultural movement, the decisive year for the whole work of socialist construction. (Interjection, 'Very true!' Applause.)

I shall not deal with the economic plan for the current year. It has been dealt with in the reports at the last session of the Central Executive Committee. I shall mention merely a few figures.

This year an increase of the national income by 39 per cent is planned, a figure which is typical for the tremendous progress made by the whole economic system. Further, the plan provides for an increase of the total production of the Socialist sector of industry (the industry under the control of the Supreme Economic Council and of the Commissariat for Supplies) by 45 per cent. And then the task must be mentioned of lowering the costs of production in the industries under the control of the Supreme Economic Council by 10 per cent, and in the industries under the control of the Commissariat for Supplies by 11 per cent. I shall limit myself to mentioning these decisive figures of the whole economic plan. When these tasks have been carried out we shall be able to judge the results of our struggle to secure a Bolshevist tempo of development. . . .

Bolshevist tempo has been expressed in the slogan: 'Five-Year Plan in Four Years!' Shall we be able to put this slogan into execution? The facts give us the answer. In such branches of industry as the production of pig-iron, steel, milling works and also the production of cotton fabric, the Five-Year Plan will be carried out in four years on the whole. If the time needed for the production of cotton-fabric is a little longer than four years, certainly the time necessary for the production of pig-iron will be less than four years. With regard to the production of cement, the Five-Year Plan will be realized in three years and six months. In the electrical industry, coal mining, peat production and the sugar industry the period will be three years. In the petroleum industry, copper production, engineering, tractor and agricultural machinery production, shipbuilding and locomotive building, the period will be two years and six months. With regard to the industries under the control of the Supreme Economic Council as a whole, the Five-Year Plan will be carried out in about three years and six months. As can be seen, the slogan: 'Five-Year Plan in Four Years!' is actually being put into execution, and there is even a possibility that the period may be still shorter.

It is particularly important that in the heavy industry as a whole the Five-Year Plan will be carried out in less than three years. [Molotov then indicates the kind of increase which would be required and reiterates that 'our present plan is based on the carrying out of the Five-Year Plan in three years in the key industries.]

The Bolshevist policy is winning. This year the struggle for a Bolshevist tempo of development must be intensified. Unless we succeed in this respect our gigantic plan for the current year will be hindered in its execution. Let us draw the Bolshevist conclusions from this.

After the carrying out of the programme of production the Bolsheviks must judge the attitude of our organizations to the carrying out of the general policy of the Party. The struggle to secure the tempo of development laid down by the Soviet power is not only the duty of every Bolshevist, but of every worker and of every honest supporter of the Soviet State.

The Communist Party has defeated the Right-wing opportunists, but in practice Right-wing tendencies are still strong. These tendencies make a serious struggle necessary. Without this struggle we shall not be able to carry out the tasks of this, the third and decisive year of the Five-Year Plan. The Right-wing deviating tendencies in the practice of our organs come at a favourable moment for our enemies. Let us strengthen the struggle against this chief danger in our practical work.

At the same time we must aim a blow against the boastful carelessness, the ostrich policy, which is concealed under the cloak of left-wing phrases. We need less boasting and more preparedness for a real struggle to achieve the tempo laid down for the development of the economic system.

The Communist Party has pointed out the way. The programme is fixed. Let us approach the tasks before us in the correct fashion. The success of our cause depends on us. Each of us, whether he is a member of the Communist Party or not, must do his duty in the struggle for Bolshevist tempo in the struggle for the carrying out of the Five-Year Plan. . . .

2/21 Capitalist Encirclement and the Five-Year Plan

J. STALIN, *Problems of Leninism* (Moscow, 1947), pp. 355–356.

It is sometimes asked whether it is not possible to slow down the tempo a bit, to put a check on the movement.* No, comrades, it is not possible! The tempo must not be reduced! On the contrary, we must increase it as much as is within our powers and possibilities. This is dictated to us by our obligations to the workers and peasants of the U.S.S.R. This is dictated to us by our obligations to the working class of the whole world.

To slacken the tempo would mean falling behind. And those who fall behind get beaten. But we do not want to be beaten. No, we refuse to be beaten! One feature of the history of old Russia was the continual beatings she suffered for falling behind, for her backwardness. She was beaten by the Mongol khans. She was beaten by the Turkish beys. She was beaten by the Swedish feudal lords. She was beaten by the Polish and Lithuanian gentry. She was beaten by the British and French capitalists. She was beaten by the Japanese barons. All beat her – for her backwardness: for military backward-

* This extract is from a speech by Stalin on 4 February 1931 to the First All-Union Conference of Managers of Socialist Industry. (Ed.)

ness, for cultural backwardness, for political backwardness, for industrial backwardness, for agricultural backwardness. She was beaten because to do so was profitable and could be done with impunity. Do you remember the words of the pre-revolutionary poet: 'You are poor and abundant, mighty and impotent, Mother Russia.' These words of the old poet were well learned by those gentlemen. They beat her, saying: 'You are abundant,' so one can enrich oneself at your expense. They beat her, saying: 'You are poor and impotent,' so you can be beaten and plundered with impunity. Such is the law of the exploiters – to beat the backward and the weak. It is the jungle law of capitalism. You are backward, you are weak – therefore you are wrong; hence, you can be beaten and enslaved. You are mighty – therefore you are right; hence, we must be wary of you.

That is why we must no longer lag behind.

In the past we had no fatherland, nor could we have one. But now that we have overthrown capitalism and power is in the hands of the working class, we have a fatherland, and we will defend its independence. Do you want our Socialist fatherland to be beaten and to lose its independence? If you do not want this you must put an end to its backwardness in the shortest possible time and develop genuine Bolshevik tempo in building up its Socialist system of economy. There is no other way. That is why Lenin said during the October Revolution: 'Either perish, or overtake and outstrip the advanced capitalist countries.'

We are fifty or a hundred years behind the advanced countries. We must make good this distance in ten years. Either we do it, or they crush us.

2/22 Stakhanovism

J. SCOTT, *Behind the Urals. An American Worker in Russia's City of Steel* (London, 1942), pp. 128–132.

During 1936 the Stakhanov movement was much talked of, not only throughout the Soviet Union, but in other countries as well. It was an interesting and important development in Soviet economy.

The Stakhanov movement took its name from a Donbas coal-miner and became very important after Stalin addressed the first Stakhanovite conference and pointed out that improved living conditions and technical training of industrial personnel had created the basis for drastic increases in productivity, which should be realized without delay.

It was true. Life had become 'better and more joyful' as Stalin put it. There was more to eat, more to wear, and every indication that the improvement would continue.

The Stakhanov movement hit Magnitogorsk in the autumn of 1935 and was immediately made the subject of various meetings, press notices, administrative orders, and endless conversions, private and public. Brigade and shop competition was intensified. Banners were awarded to the brigades who worked best, and monetary remuneration accompanied the banners. Everyone went nosing around his department, trying to uncover 'reserves of new productivity'. Wages rose. Production rose. Magnitogorsk was animated by a boom.

The Stakhanov movement in Magnitogorsk produced very marked results during the latter half of 1935 and almost all of 1936. The coefficient of blast-furnace work, furnace volume divided by daily production, improved from 1·13 to 1·03; the production of steel per square metre of hearth increased on every single hearth, the average improvement being by 10·5 per cent, from 4·2 tons to 4·65 tons. On the rolling mills productivity rose and costs fell. ...

While this improvement was going on, negative forces were being created. In the first place, the norms were raised in the autumn of 1936 after a publicity campaign and a speech by Stalin himself. This created a restlessness among many workers who had received the impression that all improvements in production would reflect themselves in direct wage increases, and that the norms would never be changed. ...

In March 1936, a conference of leaders of metallurgical industries from the whole Union met in Moscow to redefine the project capacities of various aggregates in the light of the achievements of the Stakhanov movement. On the basis of these new project capacities, new norms and plans were worked our for every unit of each combinat in the Union, including, of course, Magnitogorsk.

In the coke and chemical plant, the Stakhanov movement brought about sweeping changes in some technical processes and was often unquestionably instrumental in raising efficiency in production. Suggestions of improvements of all kinds were made by workers and technicians alike and were often acted on and aided in bringing up production. Regular production meetings were held in all the shops and departments. Here the workers could and did speak up with the utmost freedom, criticize the director, complain about the wages, bad living conditions, lack of things to buy in the store – in short, swear about anything except the general line of the Party and a half-dozen of its sacrosanct leaders. These meetings discussed the plan, passed the list of Stakhanovites for the month, and decided local shop issues. ...

The Stakhanov movement produced striking results on the iron mine. ... The productivity of labour had risen from 2,017 tons per average worker per year in 1935 to 3,361 tons per average worker per year in 1937. This increase in productivity was the best indication of increased efficiency. . . .

2/23 The Soviet Industrial Manager

C. B. HOOVER, *The Economic Life of Soviet Russia* (London, 1931), pp. 4–7.

. . . The responsible manager is probably a Communist, and even if he is not, he knows that his success as a director will be measured in other ways than by the yard-stick of profits. He has a plan to carry out which includes many items other than profits. He is supposed to produce a given amount, of a given quality, in a given time. If he produces this amount or a greater amount in the given time or in a less time, or at the standard of quality or of better quality, these factors are given a greater weight than the amount of profits, in estimating the successfulness of the management. Besides this, there is the matter of the extent to which labour conditions have been improved, which is also taken as a measure of the success of management. One very important measure of successful management does approach the capitalistic method. It is considered highly desirable in Soviet Russia to reduce costs of production. Reducing cost of production is, of course, one way in which the capitalistic manager also increases profits. The Soviet executive cannot, however, use all the devices to lower cost which are available to the capitalistic executive. He cannot reduce wages, at least ostensibly. He cannot reduce time wages at all. Instead he must increase them, at least a little every year. Like his capitalistic brother he may cut piece wages as the productivity of labour increases, but the limitations on lowering costs by this method are somewhat sharper than in the capitalistic world. Speeding up of workers is, however, carried on as forcefully if not as effectively as under the capitalistic system.

In one great field where the profits of a capitalistic concern are largely determined, the directors of Soviet enterprises are little interested. This is in the field of price and of buying and selling. The Soviet manager does not have to concern himself with the effort to buy cheap and to sell dear. Neither does he have any selling problems. There is always a greater demand for his product than he can meet.

The motives for efficiency in production upon the part of the Soviet director are very strong. The rewards for success are great and the penalty for failure is severe. Most responsible directors are now Party members. Success means advancement and advancement means power. . . . The energy in the capitalistic world which finds expression in the struggle for wealth, for social position, for the comforts of life, in Soviet Russia is canalized in the struggle for power.

The responsibility of the Soviet industrial manager is just as great as in the capitalistic world, and if he is a Communist his authority is also just as great. The chance for promotion is infinitely greater in the Soviet economic system than in the capitalistic world. The few old bourgeois managers who are left are rapidly being replaced. A tremendous programme of capital construction and of industrial expansion is under way. The new collectivized agriculture demands the services of thousands of executives. The old classes which furnished the major and minor executives have been swept away. Landlords, bourgeoisie, kulaki,* the old intelligentsia, have been exiled, crushed, or killed. The opportunity for the conquest of power by a man of any force or ability who is a Party member is limitless.

The career of a director of a Soviet enterprise does not entirely depend upon the success with which he carries out his production programme. He can be pretty well assured that if he is an active Party member, and takes care always to be orthodox, he will be taken care of, regardless of what happens. If he is not successful at one kind of work he will be shifted to another. His activity and orthodoxy will be accepted as proof of his good intentions, so that there will be little likelihood of his actual punishment in case he is not successful in production. He may be returned to trade-union work, if he came to his directorship through that channel, or he may be given some political post which does not require the same kind of executive ability as that of production manager. Furthermore, it must be said that an enormous proportion of the time of the average communist director, as is the case with all prominent Party members, must be given to Party work.

In addition to this purely Party work he has to expend a great part of his energy in endless committee meetings, with the workers of his own plant, with representatives of all the workers of the Trust, with directors of the Trust and Syndicate, with representatives of the oblast Executive Committee, with members of the shock brigades in his factory and so on. During the present period of transition from direct worker control to the system now in use of single responsibility and authority, these endless committee meetings have not been lessened. For while the substance of direct control by the workers was being taken from them, it was essential that the workers should be soothed and comforted by at least the temporary retention of all the outward signs, symbols, and manifestations of control. . . .

The reward of the successful executive is not alone the satisfaction of his lust for power. If a Soviet Trust shows a profit, the administrative personnel shares in the distribution of a fund made up of $\frac{1}{4}$ of 1 per cent of the profits of the Trust. On the other hand, if the director is a Communist his salary is limited to two hundred and twenty-five roubles per month (nominally about

* See Glossary.

one hundred and sixteen dollars). But the prerequisites of an executive position are even more important than the monetary rewards.

On the side of material and fleshy rewards for efficiency in production, must be placed the fact that the director of an enterprise of any importance will have a motor-car at his disposal, and of course a chauffeur to drive it. He will have an excellent opportunity to get the best choice of living quarters. These will not be luxurious, and indeed no better than the minimum which is probably necessary for the director to keep up his personal efficiency. But in a country where living quarters are exceedingly restricted in quality and in quantity, this is important. He will have the opportunity to travel to conferences with his expenses paid. He will have every access to the limited opportunities to improvement within his field, such as technical magazines. He may even be sent abroad to study production methods in capitalistic countries. If so, all his expenses will be paid.

He will get better and prompter attention if he or his family is ill. He will get better accommodations at the resort at which he spends his vacations. If his job enables him to live in one of the few large cities, he may even belong to one of the 'business clubs', which are often located in the house of some former rich merchant, and whose membership is confined principally to Soviet directors and engineers.

The sum total of all these material advantages is absolutely very small, no doubt. They may appeal negligible as compared with those of executives in the capitalistic world. Most of these men, however, are former proletarians who have known poverty for the greater part of their lives. These perquisites are, therefore, infinitely sweet.

It must not be forgotten that these material advantages are better than those which accrue to the mass of the population, and are the best which can be obtained under the circumstances. This is of the greatest importance, since it is probable that rewards are of more importance relatively than absolutely. Furthermore, the limitation of salary of the Communist director is not such a great handicap as might be thought. Where the process of rationing is carried to the extent which it is in the Soviet Union, money rapidly loses its importance. Membership in a trade union enables one to get theatre tickets at half rates; if one is listed as a worker his ration of bread and meat is doubled. The co-operative stores situated near factories, and to which the workers of the factory belong, are usually assured of a better supply of the available foodstuffs than are those catering to office workers and the general public. The successful executive has all these advantages which belong to the workers as a class. In short, in spite of his restricted wage or salary, he fares as well materially as it is possible to fare in the Soviet land.

2/24 Magnitogorsk. The Soviet Ruhr

SCOTT, *Behiud the Urals* [see Document 2/22], pp. 5–6, 62–65, 70–71, 91–92 as printed in G. MOSSE, R. CAMERON, *et al.*, *Europe in Review* (Chicago, 1964), pp. 438–442.

In 1940, Winston Churchill told the British people that they could expect nothing but blood, sweat and tears. The country was at war. The British people did not like it, but most of them accepted it.

Ever since 1931 or thereabouts the Soviet Union has been at war, and the people have been sweating, shedding blood and tears. People were wounded and killed, women and children froze to death, millions starved, thousands were court-martialled and shot in the campaigns of collectivization and industrialization. I would wager that Russia's battle of ferrous metallurgy alone involved more casualties than the battle of the Marne.* All during the thirties the Russian people were at war.

It did not take me long to realize that they ate black bread principally because there was no other to be had, wore rags because they could not be replaced.

In Magnitogorsk I was precipitated into a battle. I was deployed on the iron and steel front. Tens of thousands of people were enduring the most intense hardships in order to build blast furnaces, and many of them did it willingly, with boundless enthusiasm, which infected me from the day of my arrival. . . .

The 'Magnetic Mountain', iron heart of Magnitogorsk, is situated on the eastern slopes of the Ural Mountains, some seventy miles east of the watershed which separates Europe from Asia. The surrounding countryside is barren steppe – rolling hills so smooth they remind one of a desert. The summers are hot and dusty, and only about three months long. The winters are long, cold, and windy. There is very little rainfall. . . .

In 1924 the general industrial production of Russia was between 10 and 15 per cent of the level of 1913. For the next four years the country struggled back to its feet with the help of the New Economic Policy. Foreign concessions and the partial development of private enterprise in industry and commerce facilitated this recovery.

During this period, while old capitalist forms were successfully utilized to strengthen Soviet economy, a bitter struggle was in progress between various factions among the leading groups of the Soviet Union. Stalin emerged victorious, annihilated his enemies, and proceeded to force the realization of those measures which he considered necessary.

Stalin's programme was essentially nationalistic. It was dedicated to the proposition that Socialism could and would be constructed in one country in the Soviet Union. Whereas Lenin had counted on revolutions in Central

* Fought between the Allies and the Germans, September 1914. (Ed.)

Europe to aid backward Russia on its difficult road to Socialism, Stalin counted on the ability of the Soviet Union to equip and defend itself.

In order to construct Socialism and defend it against the attacks which Stalin felt sure were coming, it was necessary to build Russian heavy industry, to collectivize and mechanize agriculture. These monumental tasks were undertaken in the late twenties. The first Five-Year Plan provided for the reconstruction of the national economy and the creation of whole new industries, new industrial bases. One of its most important projects was the creation of a heavy industry base in the Urals and Siberia out of reach of any invader, and capable of supplying the country with arms and machines in immense quantities.

This project had several very outstanding advantages. In the first place, the iron deposit of Magnitogorsk had been known for years as one of the richest in the world. The ore was right on the surface and tested up to 60 per cent iron. The coal deposits in the Kuzbas in Central Siberia were almost unique. In some places the coal lay in strata three hundred feet thick. By connecting these two great untouched sources of raw materials into one immense metallurgical combine, the country would be ensured of an iron and steel base, not inferior to that of the United States, to supply the growing needs of the country for decades to come. In the second place, both Magnitogorsk and Kuznetsk were in the centre of the country, some two thousand miles from any frontier, so that new interventionists, which, Stalin felt, were bound to come sooner or later, would be unable to reach them, even with their best airplane.

So great were the expenses and so enormous the technical difficulties that no one in the pre-revolutionary days had ever undertaken to project a Ural–Kuznetsk metallurgical base. The capital investment necessary was much more than any firm, or even the Czarist Government itself, could afford. 'Too large and difficult for the capitalists, the task was left to the workers', as the doctor said.

It was necessary to start from scratch. There were no supply bases, no railroads, no other mills in or near Magnitogorsk or Kuznetsk. But Stalin and his Political Bureau decided that the job must be done, and so in 1928 the first serious attempt was made to project the Ural–Kuznetsk Combine and a powerful, modern metallurgical plant in Magnitogorsk.

Stalin was probably one of the few men in the Soviet Union who realized how catastrophically expensive it was going to be. But he was convinced that it was just a matter of time until the Soviet Union would again be invaded by hostile capitalist powers seeking to dismember and destroy the first Socialist State.* Stalin considered it his sacred obligation to see to it that when the time

* See Document 2/21 above. (Ed.)

came the attackers would not be able to accomplish this. The fulfilment of this task justified all means.

As the doctor told me, there had been many discussions among scientists and economists about the desirability of going headlong into the construction of the Ural–Kuznetsk Combinat with its galaxy of machine-building and armament plants. Initial costs stood twice as high as those in similar units built in the Ukrainian or Donbass industrial regions already equipped with railroads and power lines, and near bases of industrial and agricultural supplies. The regions around Magnitogorsk and Kuznetsk were as yet little known, geological surveys had been superficial. Would it not be better to build in the Ukraine, and wait with the Ural-Kuznetsk Combine until more thorough surveys had been made?

At many times during the late twenties and the early thirties such objections were raised. The tempo of construction was such that millions of men and women starved, froze, and were brutalized by inhuman labour and incredible living conditions. Many individuals questioned whether or not it was worth it.

Stalin suppressed such ideas with his usual vigour. The Ukraine had been invaded by the Germans in 1918. It might be invaded again. The Soviet Union must have an uninvadable heavy industry base, and must have it immediately, said the Georgian Bolshevik. His word was law.

In January 1931, Stalin made an historic speech to a conference of business managers. In his inimitable, simple vernacular Stalin insisted on the necessity of increasing the tempo of industrialization. He warned the Russian people that they must make their country as strong as the surrounding capitalist states within ten years or Russia would be invaded and annihilated. . . .*

The history of the actual construction of Magnitogorsk was fascinating. Within several years, half a billion cubic feet of excavation work was done, forty-two million cubic feet of reinforced concrete poured, five million cubic feet of fire bricks laid, a quarter of a million tons of structural steel erected.

This was done without sufficient labour, without necessary quantities of the most elementary supplies and materials. Brigades of young enthusiasts from every corner of the Soviet Union arrived in the summer of 1930 and did the ground work of railroad and dam construction necessary before work could be begun on the plant itself. Later, groups of local peasants and herdsmen came to Magnitogorsk because of bad conditions in the villages, due to collectivization. Many of these peasants were completely unfamiliar with industrial tools and processes. They had to start at the very beginning and learn how to work in groups. Nevertheless they learned so well that the first dam across the Ural River was finished on 6 April 1931, and the lake began to

* See *Ibid.* for this speech. (Ed.)

fill up. Within two years it was five miles long and assured an adequate water supply to the city and plant for the first half of the construction work.

The first quarter of 1931 saw the ground broken for excavation and foundation work for the basic departments of the plant, while the iron mine went into production. A colony of several hundred foreign engineers and specialists, some of whom made as high as one hundred dollars a day and expenses, arrived to advise and direct the work. Money was spent by the millions (170,000,000 roubles in 1931).

Despite difficulties the work went on much faster than the most optimistic foreigners anticipated, although much more slowly than the chimeric plans of the Soviet Government demanded. By the end of 1931 the first battery of coke ovens and Blast Furnace No 1 were ready to be put into operation. The 1st of February 1932, saw the first melting of Magnitogorsk pig iron. . . .

This was the Magnitogorsk of 1933. A quarter of a million souls – communists, kulaks,* foreigners, Tartars, convicted saboteurs and a mass of blue-eyed Russian peasants – making the biggest steel combinat in Europe in the middle of the barren Ural steppe. Money was spent like water, men froze, hungered, and suffered, but the construction work went on with a disregard for individuals and a mass heroism seldom paralleled in history.

2/25 The Congress of Victors

STALIN, *Collected Works* [*see* Document 2/8], vol. 13, pp. 312–316.

II

THE CONTINUING PROGRESS OF THE NATIONAL ECONOMY
AND THE INTERNAL SITUATION IN THE U.S.S.R.†

I pass to the question of the internal situation in the U.S.S.R.

From the point of view of the internal situation in the U.S.S.R. the period under review presents a picture of ever-increasing progress, both in the sphere of the national economy and in the sphere of culture.

This progress has not been merely a simple quantitative accumulation of strength. This progress is remarkable in that it has introduced fundamental changes into the structure of the U.S.S.R., and has radically changed the face of the country.

During this period, the U.S.S.R. has become radically transformed and has cast off the aspect of backwardness and medievalism. From an agrarian country it has become an industrial country. From a country of small individual agriculture it has become a country of collective, large-scale

*See Glossary.
† This and what follows is taken from Stalin's report to the Seventeenth Party Congress on the work of the Central Committee of the C.P.S.U.(B), 26 January 1934. (Ed.)

mechanized agriculture. From an ignorant, illiterate and uncultured country it has become – or rather it is becoming – a literate and cultured country covered by a vast network of higher, secondary and elementary schools functioning in the languages of the nationalities of the U.S.S.R.

New industries have been created: the production of machine tools, automobiles, tractors, chemicals, motors, aircraft, harvester combines, powerful turbines and generators, high-grade steel, ferro-alloys, synthetic rubber, nitrates, artificial fibre, etc. etc. (*Prolonged applause.*)

During this period thousands of new, fully up-to-date industrial plants have been built and put into operation. Giants like the Dnieprostroi, Magnitostroi, Kuznetskstroi, Chelyabstroi, Bobriki, Uralmashstroi and Krammashstroi have been built. Thousands of old plants have been reconstructed and provided with modern technical equipment. New plants have been built, and industrial centres created, in the national republics and in the border regions of the U.S.S.R.: in Byelorussia, in the Ukraine, in the North Caucasus, in Transcaucasia, in Central Asia, in Kazakhstan, in Buryat-Mongolia, in Tataria, in Bashkiria, in the Urals, in Eastern and Western Siberia, in the Far East, etc.

More than 200,000 collective farms and 5,000 State farms have been organized, with new district centres and industrial centres serving them.

New large towns, with large populations, have sprung up in what were almost uninhabited places. The old towns and industrial centres have grown enormously.

The foundations have been laid for the Urals–Kuznetsk Combine, which unites the coking coal of Kuznetsk with the iron ore of the Urals. Thus, we may consider that the dream of a new metallurgical base in the East has become a reality.

The foundations for a powerful new oil base have been laid in areas of the western and southern slopes of the Urals range – in the Urals region, Bashkiria and Kazakhstan.

It is obvious that the huge capital investments of the State in all branches of the national economy, amounting in the period under review to over 60,000 million roubles, have not been spent in vain, and are already beginning to bear fruit.

As a result of these achievements the national income of the U.S.S.R. has increased from 29,000 million roubles in 1929 to 50,000 million in 1933; whereas during the same period there has been an enormous decline in the national income of all the capitalist countries without exception.

Naturally, all these achievements and all this progress were bound to lead – and actually have led – to the further consolidation of the internal situation in the U.S.S.R.

How was it possible for these colossal changes to take place in a matter of three or four years on the territory of a vast state with a backward technique and a backward culture? Was it not a miracle? It would have been a miracle if this development had taken place on the basis of capitalism and individual small farming. But it cannot be described as a miracle if we bear in mind that this development took place on the basis of expanding socialist construction.

Naturally, this enormous progress could take place only on the basis of the successful building of socialism; on the basis of the socially organized work of scores of millions of peoples; on the basis of the advantages which the socialist system of economy has over the capitalist and individual peasant system.

It is not surprising, therefore, that the colossal progress in the economy and culture of the U.S.S.R. during the period under review has at the same time meant the elimination of the capitalist elements and the relegation of individual peasant economy to the background. It is a fact that the socialist system of economy in the sphere of industry now constitutes 99 per cent of the total; and in agriculture, according to the area sown to grain crops, it constitutes 84·5 per cent of the total, whereas individual peasant economy accounts for only 15·5 per cent.

It follows, then, that capitalist economy in the U.S.S.R. has already been eliminated and that the individual peasant sector in the countryside has been relegated to a secondary position.

At the time when the New Economic Policy was being introduced, Lenin said that there were elements of five forms of social and economic structure in our country: (1) patriarchal economy (largely natural economy); (2) small-commodity production (the majority of the peasants who sell grain); (3) private capitalism; (4) state capitalism; (5) socialism. Lenin considered that, of all these forms, the socialist form must in the end gain the upper hand. We can now say that the first, the third and the fourth forms of social and economic structure no longer exist; the second form has been forced into a secondary position, while the fifth form – the socialist form of social and economic structure – now holds undivided sway and is the sole commanding force in the whole national economy. (*Stormy and prolonged applause.*)

Such is the result.

In this result is contained the basis of the stability of the internal situation in the U.S.S.R., the basis of the firmness of its front and rear positions in the circumstances of the capitalist encirclement.

Let us pass to an examination of the concrete material relating to various questions of the economic and political situation in the Soviet Union. . . .

2/26 Foreign Opinions on Soviet Development

a HEWLETT JOHNSON, *The Socialist Sixth of the World* (London, 1939), pp. 224–229.

b WALTER CITRINE, *I Search for Truth in Russia* (London 1938), pp. 209–214.

c C. B. HOOVER, *The Economic Life of Soviet Russia* (New York 1931), pp. 334–343. Adapted and abridged by S. W. PAGE. *Russia in Revolution. Selected Readings in Russian Domestic History since 1855* (Princeton, 1965), pp. 211–214.

a 1. The Plan* lifts the emphasis of life from personal acquisition to socialist accumulation. Unhealthy and unsocial development of the acquisitive instincts has long exercised the mind of thinkers and moralists. Its dangers became increasingly apparent in the nineteenth century and reached a climax in the twentieth. . . . Soviet planned production with one masterly stroke severed the taproot of selfish acquisition.

True, hard work increases wages, and hard study the rate of wage; but the all-absorbing master principle of acquisition which inspires – and debases – capitalism, has gone for ever in the Soviet Union; the profit motive shrivels through lack of opportunity.

2. The Plan provides profitable employment for all. None is deprived of the opportunity of work. Booms and slumps are gone, and unemployment with them. Unemployment ceased in 1931, never to return. In the nature of things, and given a scientific plan, none need be unemployed so long as any human wants are still unsatisfied.

3. The Plan provides personal security for all. In capitalist countries, personal security is achieved by means of personal and private savings. The individual dare not trust himself to 'the whole'. The whole has never guaranteed his safety, or such guarantee, in the shape of dole or old age pension, is so inadequate and hedged around with so many humiliating restrictions, that wise men supplement it by personal saving. In the drive for security the master instinct for acquisition forms its strongest ally.

The Soviet citizen depends upon the whole community. It guarantees his safety. He stands secure. If he is sick, he receives sick pay, ungrudging in amount, and subject to no time-limit. When old, he draws an ample and honourable pension, with no more shame attached to it than is attached to the pensions of retired Cabinet Ministers.

4. The Plan, on its negative side, removes fear and worry. Fear depresses and devitalizes. Christian moralists are right in their attack on fear. To remove fear is to release energy. . . .

The vast moral achievements of the Soviet Union are in no small measure

* The reference is to Soviet Planning in general. (Ed.)

due to the removal of fear. Fear haunts workers in a capitalist land. Fear of dismissal, fear that a thousand workless men stand outside the gate eager to get his job, breaks the spirit of a man and breeds servility. Fear of unemployment, fear of slump, fear of trade depression, fear of sickness, fear of an impoverished old age lie with crushing weight on the mind of the worker. A few weeks' wages only lies between him and disaster. He lacks reserves.

Fear binds and devitalizes the middle class as well. They perhaps fear more, for they have more to lose, though in a different way. Buttressing themselves around with safeguards on every side, they tremble at the breath of change. Fascism is built on fear: the fear of the possessor in face of the dispossessed. Fear kills initiative and adventure; it makes some servile and others brutal.

Nothing strikes the visitor to the Soviet Union more forcibly than the absence of fear. The Plan removes at one stroke many of the most obvious fears. No fear for maintenance at the birth of a child cripples the Soviet parents. No fear for doctors' fees, school fees, or university fees. No fear of under-work, no fear of over-work. No fear of wage reduction, in a land where none are unemployed.

5. The Plan discourages lies, deceit and sabotage. The premium placed on lies, deceit, and sabotage by capitalistic industry has been a prime cause of distress to those whose moral conscience is normal and sensitive. It is not easy to speak strict and generous truth in most branches of competitive industry and commerce The atmosphere differs so widely from school and church that many avoid the latter lest they add the vice of hypocrisy which they can avoid to the subtle deceits which they cannot. They despise men who commit the deeds on Monday for which they crave pardon on Sunday....

The Soviet Plan discourages lies. There is no need in Soviet Russia to sell paper boots as leather. Nor is one man's speed at work another man's undoing. Speed, skill, and invention increase the pool of goods in which all share. By paving the way to higher technical achievement, skill opens the door of higher wages to all who will learn it. Trade Unions in U.S.S.R. encourage all means of labour-saving that augment production.

In Russia it is wholly social for a good comrade to do good and abundant work. It is social to speak the truth and possible to do so, without risk of unemployment. It is social to augment invention and encourage discovery in a land where technological unemployment ceases to exist.

6. The Plan resolves the struggle between the egoistic and altruistic motives. Disunited, these motives tear our personality in two. United in a common all-absorbing purpose, they lift the personality to unsuspected heights, like waves combining to achieve a higher crest in place of sinking through simultaneous clash. It is a happy order in which my more strenuous

and profitable employment enriches others as well as, or even more than, myself.

Here, the motives are frequently at variance and man is internally torn asunder. In the Soviet Union they combine, and the interior tension is relaxed. The Soviet workers eagerly fit themselves for skilled or higher tasks, commanding higher salaries and satisfying their egoistic urge. But they are aware, even while they do it, that the higher skill adds more amply to the pool; that satisfies the social urge. The altruistic and egoistic motives run hand in hand in Soviet industry....

7. The Plan creates a new sense of ownership and responsibility. The knowledge that every man, woman, and child has a place in the Plan and a share in its product creates a sense of ownership. Peasants, artisans, students, and children speak of 'our' country, 'our' factory, 'our' store, 'our' metro....

A sense of ownership carries with it a sense of responsibility. It is this sense of ownership and responsibility which makes trade unionism in the Soviet Union so perplexing to English trade unionists. In capitalist countries men work on other men's property: in the Soviet Union they work on their own. Sedulously from the first Lenin cultivated this sense of corporate ownership and responsibility: every cook, he said, must be trained to run the country: it is *her* country.

8. Planned production creates a new attitude to work. For the Soviet Union is a land where all must work. No idle classes are tolerated. We talk much cant about the dignity of work, especially those of us who strive all our lives to escape it. Lenin combated from the first the idea that a working class is lower than a leisured class and manual work lower than directive class. The plan needs help from all and ministers service to all. Work must be embraced. The school-child is taught the pride of working in a workers' society. He is to know from his earliest years what he is doing and why he does it. Seeing his own tiny work as essential to the whole, he puts conscience behind it and acts in the comradely way. A leisured *class* is a social impossibility in the Soviet Union, though leisure *for all* is a right, and an increase in leisure an aim.

9. The Plan reduces crime. Crimes are largely, though by no means wholly, committed by the very poor and committed through the fact of poverty. Such crimes lessen as poverty departs.

Another fruitful source of crime is the hurry to be rich. Remove that impetus; remove, too, the ennui and monotony due to overwork and work at tasks which lack social inspiration and drive men to gambling, drink, and sex perversions, and at one stroke you clear half your courts and half your jails. The decline of crime in the Soviet Union is a fact.

10. The Plan adds zest to life by providing creative tasks for all. 'Building socialism' is the fashionable phrase. It is a task to which all are called. Each

has his or her niche in the whole. Each feels he or she is wanted. And the tasks at which they work are of social value. No tasks are futile, or unsocial, or performed simply as a means for gaining access to the money-stream. What this means for childhood and youth we may learn on a later page. Perhaps it is the highest gift of all.

11. The Plan brings its benefits and its challenge to every race or colour or people in the Soviet Union. The plan is comprehensive. It has regard of the whole industrial and agricultural field and of every native race. Neither for military reasons alone, nor for economic reasons alone, were industry and agriculture re-distributed afresh. Humanity demanded it. Men are brothers. There is work for all and benefit for all, and though the highly developed sections under the Union move at a quicker pace than formerly, the backward elements move quicker still, and the day of their equality draws near. That for the scattered races and backward peoples is the message and the good news of the Plan.

b   Then we proceeded to the barracks. . . . Such barracks were a common feature of pre-Revolutionary Russia. From outside they looked quite neat, being long sheds with whitewashed mud walls, and quite symmetrical. Once we got near to them, however, I could see signs of dilapidation. The first thing I noticed was a young woman, trying, like a gypsy, to boil a pan on a small fire on the ground. Another was washing clothes at a pump in the open courtyard. I visited the communal lavatories, there being no indoor lavatories. Their condition was horrible in the extreme. I cannot describe the men's beyond saying that it was not fit for human beings.

Then we went inside the barracks. Needless to say, there was no floor-covering anywhere. The first dormitory was about 50 feet long by 25 feet wide. Twelve beds were ranged round the walls with a pair of lockers between each. There were three bicycles standing alongside some of the beds and on inquiry from a young fellow who was dressing he said one belonged to him and he paid 250 roubles for it, without the accessories. He still had no lamp. He paid 2·60 roubles a year in tax.

There were only single men in this place, and I asked where they washed. I could not see any bowls or provision, and I was told that they washed at the pump in the yard.

'But what about the winter?' I inquired, knowing something of the severity of the climate.

'They wash in the passage.' I looked at this passage, and found it a square hall, very dark, and, of course, like the rest of the rooms, unpainted or relieved with anything except a picture of the Communist leaders.

The second room we went to was likewise for single men. There was a slovenly female supposed to be tidying up the room, and on the bare table there were stains of tea and a loaf of bread. Two young children were clattering about and remembering the women I had seen I inquired what they were doing. I was told they had just dropped in, but I was doubtful about the truth of this.

At the end of the room there were two curtains. They were made out of bed sheets, and strangely enough, one was black and the other was white! I was informed that two young fellows here had married a little time previously, and that they and their wives lived behind these curtains. What had happened was that the space taken by a single bed had been railed off in this inadequate fashion. The couple lived in the confident knowledge that all they said and did was heard by the men in the neighbouring beds.

There were twelve beds in this room, all the covers being dirty, brown blankets. I drew a sketch of the room. There were no chairs that I could see, and I supposed that the men sat on their own beds for meals, until I saw a wooden form under the table.

The men paid a low rent of 2 roubles a month for these beds. The room was far from clean, and there was no attempt whatever to make it look like 'home'. There was none of those flowers or plants which are so conspicuous in the factories for visitors to see. No pictures were visible, except those of Communist celebrities, whose continual presence in factories, public halls and barracks, cannot give exactly the sort of tranquillity one would like at 'home'.

Then we saw another room. This was about 10 feet square. A woman, husband and child lived in this one room. She received 120 roubles and the husband 350 roubles. Although the woman herself was very pleasant-looking, the room was like a pig-sty. Things were scattered everywhere and there was no attempt at order.

I was about sick of this squalor, and I asked how many people were living in these conditions. I was told 40,000. I expressed great surprise at this, as I had read that the number was 6,000. My Trade Union colleagues, however, pointed out that this applied to 'workers', and that we must add to this the number for dependants. I pointed out that even then this would not make 40,000, but they insisted that this was the correct number.

Not even my Moscow friend could shake them in this statement.

I rallied my forces once more.

'Have you shown me the worst?' I demanded.

'Yes, these are the worst,' said my friend.

'How do you know?'

'The Comrades say they are.'

'But I know there are some down by the dam which we have not yet seen, and I am going there,' I retorted.

'All right, we shall go to the dam,' was the reply, and off we went.

'What are those places there?' I inquired a few seconds after we had been travelling in the car. 'They look like houses.'

'Let us see,' said he, and we got out.

It proved to be a collective market where the peasants brought their produce, and what I thought were houses was in reality a dingy restaurant. I couldn't see much produce to tempt anyone to buy in this place. But it was houses I was concerned with at the moment, and off we went again.

Once more I stopped the car. This time there was a row of about six shacks built together under one roof. Out we got, and my guide interrogated some women who were standing about at the back of these sheds. I observed several window-panes, broken and stuffed up with paper or covered with cloth. I peered through the doorway into one.

We were invited into this room by a plump, healthy-looking young woman, whom the dirt and wretchedness of the place didn't seem to disconcert. We looked inside. It was really like one of the Cruikshank sketches of the thieves' den in *Oliver Twist*. A wretched, miserable hovel. Five people were living in one room in two beds, covered with rags for blankets. A young woman was trying desperately hard to straighten her hair before we got into the room, with a child sucking away at her breast.

I wouldn't condemn my worst enemy to such a place. 'Be it ever so humble, there's no place like home.' [The writer] should have seen this place before he wrote those lines. Then he mightn't. There was no water, of course, in this horrible apartment, and I don't know how they cooked or how they lived in the winter. I couldn't ask. I was too indignant to think that they were being left to live like this.

Poor guide! I told him that I really didn't believe that any British sanitary authority would permit the existence of such a rabbit hutch. We had slums in England which made me blush with shame when I thought of them, but I had never seen anything comparable with this.

'Not in England perhaps,' he remonstrated. 'But what about the Klondyke and what about other places where they have to deal with large numbers of people? We couldn't build houses for them all in a day.'

'That is true, but you could at least secure them the elementary means of sanitation, couldn't you?' I argued. 'You say you are a Socialist State, remember that.'

He argued that they must take first things first. If they had not built large-scale industries to make Russia independent of other countries, they would be in the position of China, an easy prey to any capitalist power. They had not enough houses to go round, but in time they would rectify this.

I felt the justice of this, and I remembered the slums of London, Edinburgh and Dublin. Infinitely worse as the Russian hovels were, I felt no pride in our own. I also recollected seeing houses as bad as any I have seen here whilst I was in Spain in the year 1931. Those 'houses' were simply mud huts in many cases.

If we make a comparison with those conditions, I think the Russians can claim that its worst is not the worst in the world.

But is that the real claim which is being asserted? It is not so much what the Russians themselves claim, as what their insistent propagandists claim for them. They give the impression that Russia is rapidly becoming a workers' paradise, with better conditions than exist anywhere else. It is only when they are brought face to face with actualities that they admit conditions are not as they should be. It is extravagant assertions you are up against all the time. That brings out the truth of the remark in the visitors' book in Kharkov; 'Truth is ever desirable; exaggerations are nauseating.'

I inquired whether delegations were shown these conditions. I doubted it. My guide claimed that delegations knew perfectly well what the bad conditions were like in Russia. What they required to know was what the Russians were aiming at. That was the purpose of the delegations; to see what the Socialist State was really doing.

I said that even this argument did not carry them very far. If we compared the Russian best in housing with the best in other countries, it lagged a good deal behind. Countries like Holland, Sweden, France, Germany, not to speak of Britain, were far ahead of the Russian best in that respect.

As I repeatedly remarked, many of these hastily built houses will be slums in ten years' time. The architecture is not unpleasing but the workmanship is execrable. All that is unquestionable. But when we remember that they were constructed with half-trained building workers, the Soviet have done relatively well. We must always, I insist, remember the difficulties which Russia has experienced when we are estimating the results. Judged by that standard she has done well, but not so well that she can claim to be an example for the world to follow.

c Has Soviet Russia actually contributed . . . to the sum total of human experience in an economic and social sense? Everyone knows that there has never been an economic and social experiment on a scale to compare with it.

In terms of present human well-being it would, no doubt, have been better for the generation of the Russian people who witnessed the Revolution if the experiment with Socialism had been abandoned at the time of the New Economic Policy. The benefits which will accrue to the Russian people during the next decade, even if the grandiose plans of the Party are realized, can hardly compensate for the years since the Revolution.

Living conditions in Russia have been worse during the present year than at any time since [1921]. Millions are seriously undernourished and in some parts of the Soviet Union actual famine conditions have been approximated. Faced by this situation, the Government has not hesitated to safeguard the standard of living of the workers in the largest cities at the expense of [the rest] of the population. The supply of almost all commodities is better in Moscow than in any other part of the country. Every available pound of foodstuffs is swept up from the countryside. A nominal subsistence minimum is supposedly left to the peasants, but in many cases they are left practically without grain or flour. The Party is determined that the Revolution shall not perish, even if a few peasants starve. Some foreign observer who was in the Soviet Union in 1925 visits the country now and is shocked to find food conditions much worse. It appears that the Soviet regime is about to collapse.

On the other hand, American engineers and capitalists are shown the great new factories and plants which are being built. They report that Soviet Russia is making gigantic [progress]. The capitalistic world is puzzled. Certainly both types of story cannot be true.

The extraordinary thing is that both are true. The hard conditions of life are due to the unsatisfactory agricultural situation during the past several years, and to the determination to industrialize the country at the earliest possible moment. These conditions, however, must not be taken to prove that the Soviet economic system has been a failure. On the industrial front impressive successes have been scored.

At present the standard of living of the labourer is in some respects worse than during Tsarist times in terms of food, clothing and shelter. But when the advantages of the shorter working day, vacations and social insurance are considered, it must be recognized that the labourer has gained from the Revolution. The standard of living of the individual peasant is distinctly worse than before, and this is true to an even greater extent of the old intelligentsia, office workers, schoolteachers, and the 'white collar' workers in general. Certainly if the *average* standard of living of Tsarist times be compared with [that of] the present, conditions must be said to be much inferior. The income which was taken from the 'exploiting classes' has not as yet fully accrued to the exploited classes who despoiled them.

Nevertheless, the standard of life is so low now, largely because of the determination of the Party to make it much higher in the future.

It is probable that the standard of living in Russia will never reach a level of comparative luxury such as that attained by the bourgeoisie in capitalistic countries. Simple food, communal housing, proletarian club houses, plain clothing, motor transport, short hours of labour, vacations at State recreation houses may be taken to represent the final goal of Communist effort. Such a goal is, no doubt, wholly unacceptable to the bourgeoisie, the intelligentsia, the greater part of the agricultural population and even the upper strata of the working classes of the capitalistic world. It is probable, however, that it would have a wonderful appeal to the most poorly paid and most unintelligent 50 per cent of the population of the capitalistic world.

If the Soviet system has greater possibilities in respect to productivity than is usually realized, in respect to the psychological and intangible possibilities of the system the record is not an encouraging one. In Utopia, meanness, pettiness, greed, envy, and bitterness were to disappear. But Soviet Russia is further removed from Utopia than is capitalistic civilization. In Soviet Russia there is not less bitterness but more. The struggle for power has replaced the struggle for wealth. . . .

Has the new order of life in Russia resulted in a new brotherliness of man to man? The attitude of those in power towards their subordinates is [no] improvement over the attitude of persons similarly placed in the capitalistic world. True, workers themselves are pampered *as a class*. But 'white collar' workers are only one degree better off than the 'deprived' classes who are branded as enemies of Soviet Power. . . .

Nor [is] there evidence of increased brotherliness among the industrial workers. The form of address 'Comrade', has [no] real significance. One [is] struck by the general air of irritation and ill-feeling. One rarely sees a smile or hears a laugh. Partly this is due to the food shortage. But the sense of repressed anger seems due to other causes also.

Never in history have the mind and spirit been so robbed of freedom and dignity. It is not merely that academic freedom, freedom of speech, press, thought, are forbidden. The Party is not content with mere abstention from unauthorized action. Men must publicly deny their real thoughts and feelings. . . .

An engineer is arrested, charged with [sabotage] and is shot. His son is a Party member. He is ordered to sign a statement that he approves of the execution of his father. He refuses, and is expelled from the Party. Never has the human soul been so placed in bondage.

The Soviet regime is founded upon force and fear. The Communist declares that the present policy of violence has been necessary to preserve the socialistic character of the Revolution. Without the activities of the G.P.U.,* the former bourgeoisie, with the aid of foreign capitalists, might have re-established the old regime. Unrelenting warfare on economic heresy has been necessary to preserve the Revolution from internal decay.

Russian Communism has attacked head-on some of the most difficult problems of modern economic and social life. It has had the courage to try

* The Secret Police. (Ed.)

out radical solutions for agricultural and unemployment problems and the status of women.

If the desirability of achieving a really socialistic order is taken for granted, then considerable credit must be given to the Russian Communist Party for having preserved the dynamic character of the Revolution and for having developed a truly socialistic system. The contribution to human experience and knowledge for which the Soviet system is responsible cannot be denied. It has been proved that a socialistic state can exist and carry on the functions necessary for survival.

It is possible, then, to find some justification for the violence and force of the Revolution, the Civil War and for a reasonable period thereafter. However, thirteen years since the [November] Revolution [violence] still continues. It appears that violence has come to be inseparable from Communism.

It has been no small triumph of Communism that it has, partially, at least, substituted interest in the success of the Five-Year Plan for interest in the economic success of the individual.

It must be admitted that the foreign observer feels that life has become a dreary thing, indeed, when placed on such a level. The communist retorts that this is bourgeois prejudice. The economic struggle may give zest to life for those who are successful, but it offers no compensation to the vast majority who fail in the struggle to 'get ahead' and who are always confronted by the threat of economic disaster.

The creation of a system of life which has displaced the money standard of measurement for even the moral and subjective values which exist in bourgeois civilization must be registered as a distinct contribution to human welfare. While it is true that the struggle for power has in many ways replaced the struggle for money, this fact does not entirely destroy the value of this element of the Soviet system. In Soviet Russia men do not devote their time to money-making activities in order to ape the standards of a leisure class. The State employee in a retail shop is not particularly interested in whether the customer makes a purchase or not. He does not, therefore, either fawn on [him], or subject him to high-powered salesmanship. He does not address the customer as 'Sir'. The spiritual advance which is registered cannot be gainsaid. Waiters in restaurants [and] household servants, have also lost both the servility and the false 'Happy-to-serve-you-Sir!' attitude so characteristic of similar workers in the capitalistic world.

There is no class which has a special position on account of wealth ownership. Power, influence, and authority are not accorded to fools, incompetents, and mediocrities simply on account of wealth. Toadies, bullies [and particularly fanatics] do attain to power much more frequently than in the capitalistic world. One cannot but hail, therefore, the destruction of wealth as the universal standard of all values, while recognizing that the transfer of power to the dominant group of leaders in the Communist Party from the owners of wealth has not yet been shown to be a change for the better.

What is the attitude of the population as a whole towards the Soviet regime? In spite of the food shortage of the last several years, many of the workers are still positively loyal. . . . Most of the remainder are at least passively loyal. The Soviet Government has always favoured the proletariat. The workman knows that any change would almost certainly make his lot worse. Nevertheless, even among the urban workers there is bitterness. In Moscow, during March 1930, the writer accompanied by two other foreigners was returning home late at night. We were all better dressed than most Russians. A man passed us. He had been drinking. He hurled a curse at us and said, 'You Party people! We will cut you to pieces!' The proletarian assumed that anyone who was warmly dressed must be one of the Party leaders. . . .

On account of the grain requisitions and the enforced nationalization of the land, the peasants are bitterly hostile. Most of the poorest peasants are loyal, for the same reason that the urban proletariat is loyal. They have been favoured at the expense of the other peasants. [Perhaps] 20 per cent of the peasant population are active supporters of the Soviet regime.

If it were possible to put the matter to a free vote the majority would vote [for] a return of the old Tsarist regime in preference to the present one. [But this] is [not] a fair statement of the case. The present moment is critical. Living conditions are worse now than they were two years ago and worse than they probably will be two years from today. Furthermore, the majority against the present system would come from the peasants. The peasant is being torn up by the roots and transplanted into strange soil. In ten years the peasant may have forgotten his present grievances and may be an enthusiastic supporter of collectivized agriculture.

The significance to the capitalistic world of developments in the Soviet Union cannot be exaggerated. If the present crisis is passed, the Soviet Union, within a decade, will be in a position to offer a standard of living [superior to] that of the more poorly paid workers in capitalistic countries. Unless in the meantime capitalism has notably improved its technique of marketing and distribution, so that underconsumption and unemployment can be prevented, and unless the standard of living of such workers in the capitalistic world shall have been materially raised, the World Revolution will begin to make rapid strides.

2/27 Soviet Economic Development, 1913–1940

Printed in M. DOBB, *Soviet Economic Development since 1917* (London, 1966), p. 311.

Product	Unit	1913*	1928	1940
Pig-iron	m. tons	4·2	3·3	15·0
Steel	m. tons	4·2	4·3	18·3
Rolled steel	m. tons	3·5	3·4	—
Coal	m. tons	29·1	35·5	166
Oil	m. tons	9·2	11·7	31
Electricity	md. kwh.	2	5	48
Copper	th. tons	—	19·1	161
Aluminium	th. tons	—	—	74·4
Cement	m. tons	1·5	1·8	5·8
Railway locomotives	conventional units	418	478	928
Goods wagons	thousands	14·8	10·6	31
Tractors	thousands	—	1·2	31
Motor vehicles	thousands	—	0·7	145
Grain	m. tons	80–82	73	95·5
Sugar	th. tons	1290	1283	2150
Paper	th. tons	205	284	812
Cotton cloth	m. linear metres	2227	2678	3954
Woollen cloth	m. linear metres	95	87	120
Leather footwear	m. pairs	60	58	211
Rubber footwear	m. pairs	28	36	70

* 1913 figures are for Russia with the pre-1939 territory of the U.S.S.R. (Footnote in Dobb.)

NOTE: Soviet growth rates are subject to considerable debate. See A. Nave, *An Economic History of the U.S.S.R.* (London, 1969,) pp. 381–8. (Ed.)

Chapter 3   The Modernization of Industry

Introduction

The economic and political upheavals of the war and the years which followed did not halt the technological progress of European industry. On the contrary, it may well be that in respect of technical efficiency, the rate of improvement was faster in the 1920s than in any comparable earlier period. This is seen, for example, in the speed and effectiveness with which the devastated areas of northern France were restored (3/1, and compare 1/24), although these areas had contained some of the most important industrial and mining centres in the country. Rehabilitation here was aided to some extent by German reparations, but there can be no doubt that elsewhere, too, industrial productivity picked up quickly (3/2) and soon overtook pre-war levels. Industries which had been stimulated by war demands, like iron and steelmaking (3/3, 3/4, 3/5) found it easy to raise their efficiency, but mechanization and new techniques assisted by electricity and precision engineering spread even to the smaller consumer-goods industries (3/6) which had resisted innovation most successfully before 1914. The consequent reduction in the real costs of consumer goods led, in turn, to an increase of their sales which permitted more extended mass production techniques to lower costs still further (see also Chapter 7). This was seen perhaps most clearly in the case of the motor industry in which the French were most successful in the 1920s (3/7), and in the development of electric power, the other major growth industry reflecting and stimulating an extension of consumer demand into new areas (3/8).

Many of the industries showing high growth rates had been those affected by a high degree of concentration or cartelization even before the war. There was a tendency then in the Anglo–Saxon world to look on monopolies and mergers as purely economic phenomena, to be discussed in terms of the increase in costs or the reduction of output (3/14). Elsewhere, however, and above all in Germany, they were treated in political-economic terms, as centres of political as well as economic power. The war showed only too clearly that the Anglo–Saxon definitions had been too narrow. The German cartels, for example, supported by German law before 1914 precisely because they added to German power, were seen to have considerable influence on the conduct of the war and even on the formulation of German war aims;

and the negotiations preceding the various peace treaties with the former Central Powers showed how far international concerns and trusts could influence the drawing up of frontiers and, even more clearly, the political alignments of the weaker States in the new Europe.

It therefore became part of the democratization process of the Weimar Republic to curb the power of the cartels, at least for the purpose of protecting the consumer (3/9). Elsewhere, similar efforts were made by the co-operative societies (3/10). The Act and Ordinance passed in Germany in 1923 remained essentially a dead letter and in the slump and crisis of 1926, in particular, cartelization was not only made more rigid in industries which had developed associations before 1914 (3/17), but also extended into new areas. The Industrial Commission of Enquiry found economic experts willing to testify in favour of the so-called 'compulsory' coal cartel (3/11), and was told, blandly and truthfully, by one of them that competition was now out of the question because 'cartelization has become second nature to all the personalities in the mining industry'.

French industry, much less tightly organized than the German before the war, showed a remarkable tendency to combination and monopolistic practices after it (3/12). What was of particular significance among several of the large concerns, including the powerful armaments combine of Schneider (Le Creusot) (3/13) was the penetration by their branches or associated works into the successor-states in Eastern-Central Europe, a movement which, supported as it was by the banking system, had obvious political and diplomatic implications.

It would be misleading to suggest, however, that the majority of the international links forged by large companies in those years had political objectives. On the contrary, these giant economic units frequently attempted to overcome the artificial barriers of frontiers in their own interests as producers and as profit maximizers, with scant regard to political needs (3/14). In some ways, the world of international capital was attempting in the 1920s to restore to Europe the economic unity it had had before 1914. Even more powerful than individual firms, with their branches, were the greatly extended international cartels, such as those for steel and for potash (3/15, 3/16). In these, victor and vanquished soon took an equal share, but there was little in their growth to please the consumer, who now faced even more powerful groupings which raised prices and restricted output.

Among the criticisms that were levelled against the European cartels was that they raised the relative prices of manufactures and thus aggravated the problems of the food and raw material producing countries, that they created over-capacity, called into being an inactive 'rentier' class, aggravated instability and slowed down the necessary modernization of plant (3/17).

'Rationalization', a concept originating in Germany and spreading to other countries in Europe by the late 1920s, could mean many things. Concentration on the most efficient plant with closure of the rest, a desirable move by itself, might or might not be furthered by the existence of a cartel (**3/17**, also **3/3**); meanwhile, in the absence of boom conditions, it was bound to portend an extension of unemployment. Whether, as the Soviet delegate to the League of Nations alleged in a discussion on rationalization in 1927 (**3/18**), this enlarged unemployment tended in turn to depress the wages of those still at work, or, as was more generally believed in the West, it permitted higher wages to be paid because of the increase in output, remained a moot point. The growth of other new techniques of management to raise output by various incentive schemes is illustrated by the 'Workshop Autonomy' of the Czech Bata shoe factory (**3/19**). A final consequence of the concentration of economic power and the trustification of finance and industrial capital, was the growing inability of the smaller firm to obtain any bank credit and thus to survive at all (**3/20**): there was a 'MacMillan gap' in Germany as well as in Britain, whereas in France attempts were made to bridge it by means of Government-sponsored credit (**3/21**). The long-established tradition of Government intervention in economic affairs in France was also indicated by the formation of the *Conseil National Economique* (**3/22**).

3/1 Reconstruction of the Devastated Areas in France

Department of Overseas Trade, J. R. CAHILL, *Report on the Economic Conditions in France, revised to June 1924* (London, 1924), pp. 24–28, 31–32.

By the middle of 1925 it is highly probable that the reconstruction of the ten *Départements** officially comprised within the war areas, will, for all practical economic purposes, be terminated. The principal work unfinished from a social point of view will be the restoration of adequate housing accommodation of a permanent nature, but the accomplishment of the formidable task of replacing several hundred thousand dwellings can only be gradually achieved.

The remarkable progress made up to the beginning of 1924 may be illustrated by reference not only to the figures of increase in population, but also to those relating to public organization, and to economic activity in the numerous and important branches manifested in these areas. The population then was 4,254,000, as against 3,288,000 three years earlier, and 2,075,000 at the armistice; it was in fact only 430,000 less than in 1914. Ordered local administration had been re-established in 3,239 out of 3,255 communes wherein it had been suspended; of the public schools of all grades there were then

* See Glossary.

7,846 with 15,969 teachers, against 7,400 with 15,920 teachers in 1914, of the private schools, 849 with 3,792 teachers, as against 1,060 with 4,240 teachers in 1914 (but the combined number of pupils in both groups was 213,000 less – 585,000 against 799,000); and the number of post offices being operated was 1,353 as against 1,259 in 1914 and 1,313 at the armistice. . . . The principal public utility services had been restored in their essentials; out of 59,000 kilometres of damaged routes, 42,300 had been repaired; 3,242 out of 6,120 bridges have been definitely rebuilt and 1,550 provisionally repaired; the main railway lines had been restored in their entirety, 2,200 out of 2,409 kilometres of damaged light railways or branch lines had been restored, and 1,040 out of 1,137 kilometres of damaged navigable waterways had likewise been fully repaired.

Agriculture, mining, and the many important manufacturing industries, have all reached very advanced stages towards recovery. Of the 3,306,300 hectares* of devastated land, 2,941,500 had been cleared of projectiles, trenches and barbed wire, and of 1,923,500 hectares of devastated agricultural land, 1,788,800 had been brought under the plough; 120,000 farm buildings had been entirely rebuilt, in addition to 21,000 made serviceable provisionally and 29,300 temporary wooden buildings. Livestock, of which this area possessed in November 1918 only 173,800, or 7 per cent of the 1914 number, amounted at the beginning of 1924 to 1,442,400, or an eight-fold increase; in this total were 529,900 head of cattle (in 1914, 892,500), 420,000 sheep and goats (949,800), and 183,700 pigs (356,600). . . .

Extremely rapid progress has been made in the last eighteen months in the salvaging and the speeding up of production in the devastated coal-mines in the Nord and Pas-de-Calais Departments. These mines which yielded in January 1919 a total of only 1,535 tons, produced in January last 1,222,000 tons, and in May last over 1,260,000 tons; and by 1925, given sufficient labour, will doubtlessly exceed their pre-war output. The coke output of these mines has likewise made immense progress, and is expected by the end of 1924 to exceed that of 1914; in Lens, Anzin, Vicoigne-Noeux-Drocourt, Béthune, Aniche, and other important mines, new modern batteries of coke ovens have been installed. In the course of reconstruction improved by-product and patent fuel plants have also been built, electrical coal-getting appliances have been introduced, electric power stations have been erected, and gas production improvements and enlargements have been provided. The considerable damage done to the thirty-four iron ore mines in the Lorraine, Briey, and Longwy areas, has been made good to a very great extent in all except one mine. The underground galleries of 1,000 kilometres in 1914 have been repaired for 350 kilometres, 337 kilometres out of 711 of

* See Glossary.

underground rail have been replaced, as well as 113 out of 169 surface railway. The number of workers is still, however, less by almost 50 per cent than in 1914 (8,100 against 12,900).

Industrial reconstruction has likewise proceeded apace. On the 1st of January last, 7,963 out of 9,352 damaged industrial establishments occupying at least ten persons had resumed operation and were employing 74·7 per cent (556,600 persons) of the number of workers in 1914; in January 1922, the number of restored establishments was 5,695. It is probable that industrial reconstruction may be considered completed so far as factory establishments are concerned; for all masters having the intention of resuming their activity in these regions and of employing their compensation payments to that end, have by this date rebuilt their works. . . . The balance would be practically made up by the removal to other parts of France, abandonment of business, or war or post-war death of former masters. The considerable discrepancy of 25 per cent in the numbers employed is due to the withdrawal of numbers of male workers from the factories for reconstruction work, which has tended to offer larger reward, to the migration of workers (*e.g.* textile) to other centres which afforded better housing accommodation and other comforts in excess of what was possible in the smaller places of the devastated regions, and to the actual losses in the war. Foreign labour has been and is being introduced – in 1923 nearly 102,000 foreign immigrant workers were distributed among these Departments, but they were allocated to agricultural and reconstructional occupations. In any event, marked progress has taken place within a year; in January 1923, industrial establishments in these areas were employing only 55 per cent of their pre-war labour force. The position is bound to improve further with the progress of reconstruction when the reflux into the factory from the field will ensue.

The completion of this industrial reconstruction, and the establishment of several entirely new undertakings in the same region, will reinforce the industrial power of post-war Northern France, which already shared with the Lyons and Paris regions the bulk of the French staple and exporting industries. The pre-war industrial force of these ten Departments will be realized when it is recalled that their percentage of the national output was 70 per cent for coal, 83 per cent for ore, 64 per cent for pig iron, 63 per cent for steel, 78 per cent for sugar and 93 per cent for linen yarns, and that they held about 60 per cent of the cotton spindles, nearly all the wool combing mills, about 80 per cent of French woollen yarn and cloth capacity, about 80 per cent of French linen weaving capacity, as well as a high proportion of its jute, chemical, engineering and other industrial production. The textile (woollen, cotton, linen and hosiery) industries have in particular been greatly strengthened by improvement in the lay-out and enlargement of factories, and by the replacement or installation of the latest machinery, but the metallurgical, engineering and chemical works have also reinforced their pre-war position; and the progress in the coal-mining industry in the same area has already been noted. . . .

But much work has still to be accomplished before the formidable housing problem created by war destruction shall have received its complete solution. The number of dwellings and of farm buildings destroyed or damaged totalled 866,844 of which 340,799 were destroyed; on the 1 January 1924, 423,145 had been definitely rebuilt or made habitable or utilizable (a year earlier this figure had been 326,252). As regards dwellings only, 303,181 had been definitely rebuilt or restored; 182,844 had been provisionally repaired; 42,400 temporary brick houses had been built as well as 109,000 wooden structures. These figures indicate that the number of regular dwellings of a permanent character in these areas must still be far from reaching either reasonable requirements of a stable population only less by about 400,000 persons to that of 1914. It may be observed, however, that the new dwellings erected, especially by the State, the Northern Railway and the mining companies, show a marked advance on the pre-war type of dwelling, and the influence of their example will result, when the housing reconstruction is completed, in the existence for the working classes of far superior housing conditions especially in the smaller places (mining centres, small textile towns, etc.) of these regions than in pre-war times. . . .

The French State, whilst bearing the responsibility for the financing of reconstruction, has thus distributed a considerable portion of the direct burden of cash payments among various agencies with special functions or with special sources of appeal. Up to the end of 1923 the Treasury had itself found, out of the total of 66,584 million francs expended (namely, 62,081 on private property compensation and 4,503 on reconstruction of railways, etc.), the sum of 21,993 millions, including its payments in National Defence Bonds; the Crédit National* provided 21,566 millions; 8,100 millions represented annuity certificates in respect of decided claims, and 915 millions were French consols. By the end of April, when the Crédit National had further increased its cash payments by 2,597 millions to a total of 24,163 millions, 56 out of the 82 milliards estimated as due had been paid.

During 1923 the total paid in compensation was 10,721 millions, but the Finance Act of March 1922 has reduced the borrowing powers of the Treasury through short-term Treasury Bonds for the devastated regions to three milliards for 1924. No restriction has been placed, however, on the issues of the Crédit National. The separate budget for the Recoverable Expenses for 1924 has not yet been passed. If payments are maintained on the

* See Document **3/21** below. (Ed.)

same scale as during the first four months, when nearly four milliards were paid, those for the whole year bid fair to exceed the figure for 1923. In the event of their like maintenance in 1925 and 1926, it may be anticipated that the capital expenditure for reconstruction purposes will be terminated at the close of the latter year. This consummation would, of course, be hastened, much to the relief both of those who have still to wait for compensation payments for damages of, perhaps, ten years' standing, and of the French State, were substantial reparation payments received from Germany either directly or through the medium of international loans. Up to the end of 1923 France had received from Germany 1,804 millions of gold marks, but after deductions of 1,614 millions as expenses of occupation and as advances to Germany under Spa arrangements,* there only remained a balance of 189 million gold marks as the contribution to reconstruction, to set against an expenditure up to that date of 66,584 millions of French francs.

3/2 The Rise in Industrial Productivity in the 1920s

B. OHLIN, *The Course and Phases of the World Economic Depression* (League of Nations, Geneva, 1931), pp. 66–68.

The rapid technical development during this period and the deep-going changes in organization, commonly called 'rationalization', were factors which increased the need for adaptability. There would seem to be reason to believe that this rationalization movement proceeded at a more rapid rate than before the war, although the evidence is chiefly circumstantial. New machinery was introduced on a larger scale than before, as shown by the enormous expansion of the machine-producing industries. The growth in output of manufactured goods took place in many countries with no, or only a small, rise of the number of workers. Unfortunately, very little material is available to illustrate directly the increased productivity in manufacturing industries. In the United States, the annual increase in output per man was 3·5 per cent in the period 1922–1927, while the figures for 1922 are not much above those for 1905. In Sweden there was little increase from 1915 to 1920, but in the following nine years the annual increment was 3·9 per cent. In Germany, the number of employed workers seems to have been not quite 5 per cent higher in 1929 than in 1925, while the volume of production index was 27·5 per cent higher. This indicates an annual increase of output per man of about 5 per cent. In the United Kingdom, the output per head in manufacturing industries and mining appears to have increased by 10 per cent from 1907 to 1924 and by 11 per cent from 1924 to 1929. . . .

*A reference to the 1920 agreement concerning the distribution of the reparations payments. (Ed.)

It is possible and indeed probable, however, that rationalization increased productive capacity more rapidly than actual output. The effects of this rationalization do not seem to have shown themselves on a large scale until after 1925, when the re-organization had been largely carried through in many industries and countries. Under the influence of continued rationalization, the productive capacity in the years before the depression had greatly increased and its utilization seems in many industries to have been appreciably lower than during earlier boom periods. Failure to recognize this fact and consequently to scrap old machinery and to liquidate less efficient firms contributed to the increase of capacity up to the end of the boom, not only in new industries where demand was growing, but also in old industries with little hope of a greatly increased future demand.

That certain new trades like the motor and the radio industry expanded beyond the limits of possible demand seems indubitable. The former industry in the United States had a capacity of almost eight million cars, but even in boom years, when demand for expensive consumption goods was inflated through speculative gains on the Stock Exchange, it did not produce more than 5·4 millions.

It has already been mentioned that railway construction after the war has been slight, and that its place has been taken by the building of motor roads. Fundamental changes were also taking place in sea transportation, where the effects of the great increase in shipbuilding during and immediately after the war were felt during the whole period. In spite of this large supply of coal-burning tonnage, the building of oil-driven ships was growing rapidly. Many yards which specialize in such ships increased their productive capacity. . . .

3/3 Increases in Productivity in the Iron and Steel Industry

Committee on Industry and Trade (Balfour Committee), vol. IV, *Survey of Metal Industries* (1927), pp. 92–101.

GERMANY

Early in 1926 a company entitled Vereinigte Stahlwerke A.G., of Düsseldorf,* was formed, with a nominal capital of 50,000 M, to prepare the way for the new trust; and the trust itself was formally brought into existence in May 1926, by increasing the capital of the provisional company to 800,000,000 M. In addition bonus shares to the amount of 120,000,000 M have been issued as compensation for the inclusion of such effects and advantages as do not belong directly to the productive plant. The trust has taken over only the mines, blast furnaces, iron and steel works and further processes immediately connected therewith of the different groups, and the latter continue

* Compare Document No. 3/15. (Ed.)

to run by other works independently. Since its formation the trust has absorbed by lease or purchase some outside undertakings, notably the Stumm and Charlottenhütte concerns, and it has thereby increased its quotas in the various syndicates. It holds more than half the participations in the Tube Association, over 40 per cent of the participations in the Pig Iron, Ingot Steel, 'A' Products, Hoop Iron and Thick Plate Associations, about 30 per cent of the participations in the Wire Rod Association, and about 24 per cent of the participations in the Wire Association. Its percentage participation in the Coal Syndicate is about 22.

The primary purpose of the trust was to reduce costs by concentrating production in the most efficient works, and by other methods of so-called 'rationalization'. A considerable measure of success is already claimed to have been achieved. The production of pig iron per blast furnace is stated to have risen from 7,600 tons in September 1925 to 10,100 tons in August 1926, and the daily output per workman from 1·17 tons to 1.60 tons. The production of 96 blast furnaces with 21,000 workmen in the former month was 735,000 tons; and of 84 furnaces with 17,000 workmen in the latter month 850,000 tons. The steel output per man employed is said to have risen in the same time from 1·25 tons to 1·77 tons. Production has been concentrated in the most suitable works, superfluous works have been closed, a considerable amount of extension and re-equipment has been undertaken, and sales have been to a large extent centralized.

Fuel Economy

In connection with the technical progress of the German iron and steel industries since the war, reference must be made to the great improvement in practice in respect of fuel economy. This improvement has been forwarded by a fuel economy institute, known as the Wärmestelle, which was established in 1919 in connection with the Verein Deutscher Eisenhüttenleute. The Wärmestelle does not itself to any great extent undertake research, but acts as a centre for co-ordination and propaganda, in the interests of fuel economy. It was thought that the problems connected with fuel economy could be best attacked by the works themselves, and the Wärmestelle sought to stimulate the creation of fuel economy bureaux at the works. Recording and measuring apparatus is installed at all important points in the works, with a view to a close check being kept on fuel consumption in each process, and the cause of any wastage being detected. Fuel control on these lines is now practically universal in the German iron and steel industry. It is claimed that for the heavy branches of the industry as a whole a reduction of about 15 per cent in fuel consumption has been effected since 1919, while in addition considerable developments have resulted in technique and methods of costing....

FRANCE

Increase in Productive Capacity

The productive capacity of the French iron and steel industry has been greatly increased as the result of the war. In the first place, the restoration of Alsace-Lorraine to France meant the addition to the French industry of well-organized works which produced in 1913 3,870,000 metric tons of pig iron and 2,286,000 metric tons of steel ingots and castings. In the second place, since the industrial regions of north and east France were overrun and their establishments destroyed during the war, it became necessary to develop other districts. Thus, the Normandy iron field was exploited and new factories for wire, tubes and pipes were set up in the neighbourhood of Rouen and Paris. Thirdly, the reconstruction of the factories which were destroyed in the war areas gave opportunity for a partial re-organization of the industry in the northern district. The reconstructed works have an increased capacity and in their operation attention is paid to the newest technical improvements, though the different stages in production are still carried on to a considerable extent in separate establishments, in contra-distinction to the close organization which is found in Lorraine. In the latter area, since the war, there has been considerable 'vertical' organization of production, together with a good deal of coalition among group interests in the same line of manufacture. In the north of France there has also been a growing movement both since and before the war to link metallurgical and coal interest through the acquisition by the steel industry of shares in coal-mines at home and abroad and in native and foreign ore supplies.

As a result of the changes described above, the productive capacity of the French iron and steel industry has been about doubled since 1914: The output capacity of pig iron is about 11 million tons per annum, and that of steel ingots about $9\frac{3}{4}$ million tons. . . .

Post-war problems

The changes which have taken place since the war have created certain difficulties and problems for the French iron and steel industry. The transfer of Lorraine has separated the ore field there from the coal formerly used to smelt it; and as France has not sufficient supplies of coke to deal with this ore, it is practically essential that she should import coke from the Ruhr, the Saar coal not being very suitable for coke-making. French dependence on foreign coke is thus even more marked than before the war, when the French iron interests were, to a great extent, dependent for their supplies on the Rhenish Westphalian Syndicate. Secondly, the increase in French output capacity is much larger than the consumption, greatly though the latter has expanded, and the problem of disposing of the surplus is a difficult one. . . .

BELGIUM

There were manufactured in Belgium in 1913 some 2,485,000 metric tons of pig iron and 2,467,000 metric tons of steel. Nearly all the iron ore was imported, the Belgian production of ore being only 170,000 tons. Some 4¾ million metric tons came from France and 1½ million from Luxemburg, these being 'minette' ores; and smaller quantities were imported from Spain and Sweden. The greater part of the fuel required also had to be imported – mainly from Great Britain and Germany – as Belgium suffers from a deficiency of coking coal. Thus, Belgium is an example of an important iron and steel manufacturing country which imports the greater part both of its ore requirements and of its coal requirements. This is the more remarkable in that over half the production is exported.

The German occupation of Belgium led to the almost total destruction of the Belgian industry; and, after the war, it was necessary to build up again from the beginning. Advantage was taken of the opportunity to replace the old works by plant of the most modern type. The present capacity of Belgium, without Luxemburg, is estimated at some 3,750,000 tons of pig iron and 4,000,000 tons of steel ingots and castings.

Output

The rapid growth of production of iron and steel since 1921 is shown in the following table. It will be seen that the newly built blast furnaces have a much larger average production than those operated in 1913. . . . (*Table omitted.*)

In 1924 the production of pig iron and of steel for the first time exceeded that of 1913; and in 1926 the figures showed an advance of 37 per cent over the pre-war years in the case of both pig iron and steel.

Post-war developments

Methods of mass production have been adopted, and all stages of the industry have been closely connected. The large companies have tended to absorb ancillary concerns. Owing to the necessity for importing coal, fuel economy has been felt to be a particularly pressing problem, and the reconstructed works have striven to arrange the whole of their processes so that full use is made of the waste gases of the coking ovens and blast furnaces. They were planned, moreover, to enable the product of the blast furnaces to be converted into steel and rolled into finished products without being allowed to get cold. There is a strong tendency for the firms in any district to combine for the supply of electric power to all their works from a common generating station, working on the waste products of the whole area. The result of the re-organization is that the industry as a whole is arranged for production at something like full capacity. Diminution in its output at any stage involves a general reduction, and output on a diminished scale means a sharp rise in costs. Belgium, like France, is thus faced with the necessity of finding a market for a great surplus output. . . .

LUXEMBURG

The ironfield of Luxemburg is a continuation of the Lorraine field. The Grand Duchy has ore, but no coal or coke. It is thus dependent on the coke of the Ruhr, for neither France nor Belgium has any coke to spare. Since the war there has been a constant improvement of plant, and the output capacity has been enlarged in consequence. The capacity of the industry in 1927 was put at 2,800,000 tons of pig iron and 2,750,000 tons of steel ingots and castings. . . .

Almost the whole of the steel produced is basic Bessemer steel.

The fact that the plant is working near to its capacity means that it is working economically. Great attention has been paid to economy, and the products are said to have been put on the market at very little above cost price.

The maintenance of output has necessitated great vigilance in foreign trade; and an outstanding feature since the war has been the formation by the great metallurgical interests of a combined organization for joint selling in the export trade ('Columeta') which has opened branches in all parts of the world.

3/4 Improvements in the French Metallurgical Industry

Department of Overseas Trade, J. R. CAHILL, *Economic Conditions in France* (London, 1934), pp. 214–216.

The French nation financed on a very large scale the post-war resurrection and restoration of the [metallurgical] industry, through the payments of compensation in keeping with the magnitude of the war damages sustained. The national payments were supplemented by collective or individual loan or bond issues made to the public on the guarantee both of approved claims on the State maturing at later dates and of the goodwill and assets of the affiliated concerns.

The national cash contributions, which were inevitably on a large scale, indicate the measure of the financial resources made available since 1919 by the nation itself for the reconstruction and equipment in accordance with the most approved modern practice of approximately two-thirds of the industry. One concern, which between 1919 and 1930 had incurred well over 600 million francs of fresh capital expenditure, had received up to 1931 about 450 millions from the State; another mining and metallurgical company had received up to a recent period 648 millions: a third, whose fresh expenditure reached over 400 millions, obtained 225 millions from the State: three or four more received 200 to 300 millions apiece: two or three more 100 to 120 millions. Many other iron-ore and metallurgical concerns with inferior claims also obtained considerable but less substantial compensation. By collective action war-damaged works also raised a loan of 500 million francs in 1920 (when the sterling exchange value of the franc averaged for the year 51·21 francs). Metallurgical works also benefited, of course, in the matter of plant and equipment and of other supplies, from the German deliveries in kind.

These resources enabled the installation of the most approved methods of lay-out, of plant and of general equipment. Missions of experts were sent abroad, notably to America, to study the best ore-mining, coke oven, blast furnace, and steel mills practices. In pig-iron production many basic improvements were introduced in replacement of the old scheme of things. Thus at certain works may now be seen as many as 7 or 8 furnaces in due order, usually with an individual daily capacity of 200 to 250 tons but many also of 450, 380, 350, 300 tons, all providing the recovery of by-products, equipped with mechanical charging of ore and coke, and with scientific methods for observing and meeting the due needs of the furnaces in fuel, gas, water, and other respects. French ironmasters of set purpose have not adopted the 800, 1,000 or more ton furnaces that have found favour in America and in Germany, but French individual average furnace capacity has been more than doubled in the course of after-war reconstruction. The new coke works connected with the blast furnace undertakings are designed on a far larger scale and comprise full recovery of by-products. In the steelworks may be noticed powerful blooming-mills (including very fast electrical mills), cogging down to 140 to 150 tons an hour, continuous rolling, billet, rail, etc., mills, many of American origin, powerful machines for medium plates, many of German origin, not to forget the most modern open hearth and other furnaces and converters.

Technical improvements have of course been introduced into every branch of the process of iron and steel production. As the ore mines shared the general destruction, they also partook of the general restoration: the most complete mechanization possible has been introduced in ore getting and handling, and in its conveyance to the furnaces. . . . Hoisting and conveying machinery, which form so important an element in metallurgical works, have been greatly developed: the supplies of heavy tools, machine tools and other machinery, have been increased. Scientific analysis of products is now frequently provided by new and highly equipped laboratories at the works themselves.

The persistent prosperity of the French metallurgical industry in the years succeeding the reconstruction of the works damaged in the war led to the continuous betterment of the plants in the pre-war area down to 1930, and even since the depression became severe. Thus Longwy undertook in 1930 and 1931 the building of two new blast furnaces, enlargement of an after-war modern cokery, new electric generating units, plant for metallic sleepers; the Boucau, the Commentry-Fourchambault et Decazeville, the Denain et Anzin, concerns are among others reported as having carried out important improvements in 1930 and 1931, Micheville in 1932, and Montbard-Aulnoye in 1933.

The Lorraine works (i.e. those in the present Moselle county) that came within French territory in 1918 were for the most part already great and modern works, some having been erected later than 1900: many had in 1913 produced 600,000 tons of pig and 500 to 600,000 tons of steel. In many of these works considerable improvements and extensions were undertaken since the war. Thus at Rombas three modern blast furnaces of 320 to 380 tons daily capacity were installed in 1920, 1927, and 1929: in 1930 a new Thomas steel mill with seven converters was being built, a new Martin steel mill with four Welmann tipping furnaces of 60 tons capacity was planned and of its ten trains of rolls six were being radically improved, whilst cement capacity was tripled in 1931. At the de Wendel works new and enlarged furnaces (of 350 tons and of 200 to 250 tons) have been built, and considerable general improvements have been carried out in the various branches of their production: late in 1929 a public issue for £1,600,000 was made for the further overhauling of their Hayange works. Similar improvements and enlargements have been executed at several other Lorraine concerns. The *Société Lorraine Minière et Métallurgique*, which has operated on the largest scale in this respect, installed at Thionville between 1924 and 1928 two batteries of coke ovens, and added in 1925–1930 to existing works a conveyor for taking coke direct from the oven to the blast furnace, a dry gas purifier, two new 6,000-h.p. blowers, two turbo-alternators of 12,000 kw apiece; and in 1930 to 1932 it established large new steelworks with induction, electric Martin and Thomas furnaces, two sets of medium or small rolls for special steels, one of larger rolls for Martin and Thomas furnaces and a forge.

In view therefore of the substantial expansion of the industry in the non-war areas both during and after the war, of the almost universal re-construction and equipment of entire works in the Northern and Eastern war areas and of their persistent improvements since the more specific war restoration period ceased, and of the already modern but further improved and expanded Lorraine industry, it can be claimed that the great bulk of the present French metallurgical industry has been recast in the period from 1914 to 1932.

3/5 Scientific Management in French Industry

International Labour Office, P. DEVINAT, *Scientific Management in Europe. Studies and Reports.* Series B. (Economic Conditions No. 17), (Geneva, 1927), pp. 238–242.

In France, where [the automobile industry] is highly developed, both mass production and the manufacture of multiple types are well known. In both cases the application of scientific organization is frequently extremely far advanced. As an example of mass production, it is only necessary to mention the Berliet works in Lyons, which have frequently been described in the technical reviews. Since the war only two types of chassis have been kept, one corresponding to a lorry, the other to a touring car, and the whole system of construction has been based on the scientific organization of labour. All Taylor's methods★ have been applied in their entirety, especially as regards functional control. Instruction booklets have been drawn up for the shop stewards and foremen and standardization is highly developed. It is very difficult to estimate the results obtained, as these have been somewhat obscured by recent financial and economic conditions. Some aspects of detailed application have, moreover, come in for criticism from the experts. It is certain, however, that scientific methods are applied to those works more rigidly than in the majority of French undertakings.

In another undertaking of similar character but of more recent foundation where Taylor's ideas were introduced from the very beginning, it was observed that with the development of business it was more profitable to reduce to a minimum the number of models built and to effect the gradual standardization of the materials, with a view to reducing the chassis to one standard type. This mass production led to the introduction of methods of rational organization, and nowadays a completely installed planning office directs the whole of the manufacturing services. At present the stores, internal transport services, and the sales branch are being completely re-organized.

In undertakings of the same nature where endeavours are made to adapt

★ F. W. Taylor, 1856–1915. Engineer associated with early scientific management. (Ed.)

the models to the customer's requirements, or where mass production is not so fully carried out, the systematic planning of work is of even more value. Certain firms of excellent repute have made great progress in this connection. A number of motor works desiring to avoid certain commercial difficulties have adopted the plan of installing their own smithies and foundries. The problems to which this step gives rise are then generally settled by means of the scientific organization of the new workshops. At the present time the installation of shops and commercial services is of great concern to the managements of the undertakings, which often call in the service of expert engineers and accountants.

Rational methods of production are also extending to the organization of commercial services. . . .

A special place must be allotted in this study to certain engineering establishments of various kinds which have come under the direct influence of Taylorism, owing to the fact that their re-organization was entrusted to engineers inspired by the teachings or example of Taylor. To the French public, the best known of these is Mr. Bertrand Thompson, who since the war has undertaken the re-organization of factories of the most varied character. . . . Without actually asserting that the factories organized by him are examples of complete Taylorism, we feel safe in saying that in them a great admiration of Taylor's principles is shown, and that therefore they may be taken as good examples as far as France is concerned. In these undertakings the planning office always takes a predominant part and works in close contact with the workshops through the medium of job distribution cards. The staff of the various branches is specialized and all details concerning work in the shops are entered on tables showing the progress of the work. The wage systems are logically deduced from the general organization of the work.

Cases of application made in the mining industry of France, although but of recent date and little developed, are highly significant. They throw a new light on the possibilities of increasing the output and the cost of extraction of coal – two most important questions to all European States. At no period in the pre-war days would consideration have been given to the idea of introducing Taylor's methods in work of so varied a character and so difficult to plan out in advance as the hewing of coal. . . . In 1919 when the mines, or at least those situated in Alsace-Lorraine, were still under military control, the Director of the Mines Department of Metz advised the workers placed under his orders, in view of the low quality of labour and of a scarcity of coal, to try certain experiments calculated to establish the work of the miners on a new basis, but the habits and the conservative characters of the miners rendered all attempts in this direction very difficult to realize.

In addition to these experiments, which were perhaps facilitated by the existence of military control, a number of studies made since the war in the Saar and Moselle mines should be noted. When the mines were taken over by private enterprise, a research bureau was set up to study conditions of labour, improvement of plant, the standardization of machinery, and the training of the workers in the various branches of the industry. . . .

The work of the research bureau, which was not set up without a certain amount of opposition, has continued to develop in importance. The workers have come to understand that the changes introduced are to their advantage, and their confidence has been gained by establishing job rates for a period of six months ahead. Those affected by the new methods were paid at lower rates than those enjoyed by the other gangs, but as a result of improved organization they were able to earn, during the same period, one and a half times, and sometimes twice, the normal wage. Apart from the changes introduced in the work itself, every effort was made to encourage the inventiveness of the workers of all grades. Every worker discovering new means of reducing costs received a bonus in proportion to the savings realized. New apparatus was baptized with the name of its inventor. These detailed innovations did much to gain the collaboration of the workers in the new organization of work.

The research bureau has also exercised great influence on the engineers who, on joining the staff of the mine, were required to put in a probationary period in the bureau in order to familiarize themselves with the new methods.

Railways are an important field of activity for all engineers interested in scientific organization, and in France, at all events, it would appear that the efforts made to introduce new methods have met with great success in two directions. On certain lines efforts have been made by a minute analysis of the work of the station staffs, and particularly the staffs of marshalling yards, to estimate the cost of the various operations carried out, and to diminish, in consequence, the staff employed.

The second branch in which attempts have been made to introduce scientific organization is the railway repair workshop. At the conclusion of the war, the railways found themselves in a very difficult situation, which arose from the worn-out state of the rolling stock and the scarcity of labour, or at least its demands and low quality. To meet this situation, the State railways appointed a committee to study the re-organization of their repair shops. The reporter of this committee, Mr. Marcel Bloch, chief engineer of the Paris–Orleans Company, recommended the application of rational methods in accordance with Taylor's principles. The plans he submitted were an obvious answer to the requirements of the moment, and the work to be executed. There could be no question of an immediate introduction of new methods into such varied work as that of the repair of locomotives and rolling stock....

Gradually, as a result of daily experience, diagrams have been evolved in the various shops which show the standard time necessary for each elementary operation. The times for the various operations have been fixed in agreement with the workers. The diagrams also permit the establishment of time sheets, and the bonuses earned are on an average about 15 per cent of the normal wage. The results obtained have exceeded all anticipation. Formerly, the workshops were the centre of frequent disorders which often culminated in partial or complete strikes. The time the locomotives were immobilized during repairs was never fixed and workers were paid wages based on their seniority. Nowadays, however, the situation is completely changed, not only from the standpoint of material results, but also from the psychological and social point of view. The undertaking is so managed that the locomotive never remains over 60 hours in the shops on any account. The various grades in the undertaking all consider it a matter of pride to reduce the time limits, and this spirit is as prevalent in those engaged in administrative duties as among the workers. Bonuses certainly play a part in encouraging the workers to speed up their work, but there would appear to be little doubt that the best stimulus is the satisfaction which is felt by engineers and workers alike in seeing complicated work like the taking-down, cleaning, and reassembling of a locomotive accomplished in as short a time as possible.

3/6 Mechanization in Small-Scale Industry

Ausschuss zur Untersuchung der Erzeugnis- und Absatzbedingungen der Deutschen Wirtschaft (Enquête-Ausschuss). Gesamtausschuss, vol. III (ed. Bernhard Dernburg, Wendelin Hecht, Kurt Neu). (Berlin, 1931), p. 42. (Ed. Tr.)

In general, the mechanization of finishing industries was promoted by the electric motor. In the branches of industry consisting of small and medium-sized concerns (iron and steel articles, toys, musical instruments industries) as well as in handicraft generally, the machine has gained in the extent and efficiency of its use since the pre-war years, partly by complementing and partly by replacing manual labour. Of the 61,115 enterprises in the bakery trade, which had electric motors in 1929, 60,380 had kneading machines, 11,898 mixing and beating machines, 5,543 flour sieving machines, 5,227 sack cleaning machines, 1,882 moulding machines and 883 automatic dough machines ('iron men') in use. In addition, machines were used for dough cutting (644), flour mixing (610), croissant making (798), bread wrapping (50) and other purposes (2,081). Similarly in the butchery trade, where 53·7 per cent of the enterprises enumerated in 1925 were mechanized in some way, the use of machinery, of refrigerators and of speed balances has increased substantially since before the war. Beside the extended use of machines already common before the war, the use of special machines has also increased in many small-scale industries (chiselling, drilling and slotting machines in joinery, dowel cutting, grinding and fretwork machines in carpentry, doubling and nailing machines in shoemaking, oxy-acetylene cutters and welders as well as drilling machines in plumbing, etc.). The use of machinery in small-scale industry was made easier by using mostly the same type of mechanism, though of lower efficiency and with fewer special attachments, as in large-scale industry. Only recently has a new type of machine, the machine tool, been introduced which is particularly suited to the productive and marketing conditions of small-scale handicraft industry....

3/7 The Motor Industry in France

Department of Overseas Trade, J. R. CAHILL, *Report on the Industrial Conditions in France, revised to July 1925* (London, 1925), pp. 98–100.

France takes second place as a producer of automobiles, although with her output of about 170,000 cars in 1924 she is very far behind the United States with a reputed annual output of over two and a half millions. The French market now absorbs about 70 per cent of French production, but the export trade is very important, and in 1924, having reached the high value of frs. 1,513 million, it took eighth place as a separate class of commodity (after, in order of value, linen drapery, silks, cottons, woollens, pearls, iron and steel and yarns). Its development is seen in the following table:*

	Exports millions of frs.	*Imports millions of frs.*
1913	222	18
1921	666	32
1922	557	46
1923	813	59
1924	1,513	110
1925 (first six months)	1,009	76

* Modified from original. (Ed.)

In 1924 Belgium–Luxemburg was the largest purchaser of ordinary cars (9,164) and Great Britain the second (7,707); then Spain (5,301), Algeria (4,899), Germany (4,391), Switzerland (2,529), the Saar (1,398), and Indo-China (1,225). Of commercial vehicles Switzerland bought 754, Belgium–Luxemburg 633, Spain 487, Algeria 420, the Saar 383, and Great Britain 371 (246 in 1923). The import trade is practically monopolized by the United States and Italy; out of the above totals for ordinary cars in 1923 and 1924 the former supplied 7,264 and 12,832, and the latter 967 and 1,225. Great Britain sent only 32 and 27 ordinary cars and 1 and 58 commercial cars.

As regards the future prospects of the British market, fears are held that that market may well become less receptive, partly as a consequence of the Duty, partly owing to the adoption in recent years of large-scale production for the making of relatively low-priced cars, which enabled the English output to reach nearly 100,000 in 1924, and partly owing to the growing output of the British Ford in Manchester. The Belgian market is being adversely affected for the same reason as the British, namely increased duty and increased home production. . . .

The German market during the first four months of 1925 bought only 936 cars against 3,167 in the same period in 1924; this sudden decline is mainly due to the absence of Customs agreement since 10 January, when Germany resumed her Customs freedom. Production is, however, also advancing in Germany, and the future Customs duties are likely to remain stiff. Spain, however, has never been a better customer . . . and the same is true of Algeria. . . . Other French possessions, such as Indo-China, Morocco, Tunis and Madagascar, will also prove permanent and good customers of the French manufacturers.

The French motor-car industry is mainly carried on in the Paris and Lyons areas, but probably considerably over half the output takes place in the former district, where Citroën, Renault, and a score of other well-known makers have their factories. Its growth has been rapid; from an output of 500 cars by 2,000 workers in 1893 to 45,000 in 1913, and to 170,000 in 1924. About 120,000 workers are estimated to be engaged in the various branches. In the Annex to this Report will be found notes on certain principal enterprises engaged in large-scale production. The daily capacity of the most important was stated about two years ago to be 135 cars, and has possibly been since extended to 200; on the basis of the 300-day working year, the former figure gives an output of 40,500, the latter one of 60,000 cars a year. With this maximum capacity, small in comparison with American figures of over 7,000 a day, French makers were somewhat concerned at the announcement of the establishment at Asnières near Paris of a factory of the Ford concern that would produce at first 300 and eventually 500 cars a day, especially in view of the settlement in Europe of the British Ford, which had already celebrated the issue of its 250,000th car at Manchester, and of the Danish Ford, which already has the capacity of the largest French works. The Ford Company has had for some years at Bordeaux a works, principally for assembling, but the new project is a scheme for manufacturing in France. If the present annual absorbent capacity of France is taken at 140,000 to 160,000, of which 15,000 are imported, and if owing to the strong growth of the motor habit a future capacity of 180,000 to 200,000 is assured, it can be understood that French makers have reason to fear a new recruit whose quota would exceed at the rate of 300 a day more than half the present national consumption. Nor is the Ford scheme alone; for already Morris Motors, the well-known British firm engaged in large-scale production, has also entered the field by the purchase of a large automobile factory at Le Mans as a going concern, and will no doubt apply similar methods in this French works. The number of large-scale motor-car producers in France is thus, including the Ford project, increased to about half a dozen, and an inevitable consequence of the arrival of the important British and American companies will be a further extension of mass production by the native French manufacturers.

3/8 The Growth of Electric Power in France

Department of Overseas Trade, *France, 1934* [*see* Document 3/4], pp. 181–185.

Of the 8,373,000 kilowatts which, at 1 January 1931, represented the total electrical generating capacity of French power stations, thermo-electric stations accounted for 5,593,000 kW, or just over two-thirds, while new thermic stations in course of construction, or additions being made to the capacity of existing stations, represented a further 628,594 kW. It should be observed, however, that these figures relate only to electric generating stations, whose output is delivered, in whole or in part, to a public distribution system, and do not include, for instance, the electrical installations of firms producing current exclusively for consumption in their own factories and workshops. The true thermo-electric capacity, therefore, must be considerably greater than that recorded by the official returns. These figures show an increase of 679,783 kW, or nearly 15 per cent, in comparison with the installed capacity at the beginning of 1929....

New thermic stations constructed since 1928 are few in number, but very considerable additions have been made to the capacity of existing units, the numerous extensions of power stations attached to coal-mines being particularly noticeable. The principal new power stations are: in the suburbs of

Paris the Vitry-Sud, or Arrighi, station (220,000 kW) of the *Union d'Electricité*, described in the following paragraph; the Chalon-sur-Saône station (100,000 kW), which began to operate early in 1931; the Mazingarbe station of the *Mines de Béthune*, designed for a generating capacity of 100,000 kW, the first 40,000 kW of which were put into service late in 1931; and the additional station of the *Mines de Vicoigne, Noeux et Drocourt* at Hénin Liétard (30,000 kW), also inaugurated at the end of 1931. France now has at least 38 thermic power stations of 40,000 kW or over. . . .

Perhaps the most noteworthy addition in recent years to the thermic generating capacity in France is the new power station of the *Union d'Electricité* at Vitry-Sud, on the southern side of Paris, which was inaugurated in July 1931. With the equipment then installed it was capable of generating 220,000 kW from four groups of turbo-alternators each of 55,000 kW maximum capacity (normal output 45,000 kW). Provision is made in the plans for an increase of the capacity, in a few years' time, to 500,000 kW, when the power consumption in the Paris area shall have developed sufficiently to need such an addition. As the station will then be one of the most powerful in Europe, a brief description of its installation may perhaps not be out of place. Coal supplies can be received both from a private siding permitting of the unloading daily of two trainloads of 1,500 tons each, and from barges which can unload directly alongside the works on to a quay 160 metres in length, equipped with grabs capable of handling 200 tons an hour. From the coal yard, which holds a reserve of 80,000 tons, or sufficient to keep the turbines running for 25 days, the fuel is transported by automatic conveyors handling 300 to 350 tons an hour, to 'boulet' crushers (two crushers of 9 tons capacity hourly per boiler), whence it is fed to burners of the turbulent type (5 per boiler) consuming three tons of pulverized coal an hour, their rate of combustion being automatically controlled. Water is pumped up from the Seine by pumps with a total power of 10,000 h.p. (5,500 h.p. already installed), to the nine boilers, each capable of yielding 135 tons of steam per hour. The turbo-generators, working at 1,500 r.p.m., produce three-phase current, 50 periods, at a tension of 13,500 volts. Three 25,000 kW step-up transformers for each group of turbo-alternators convert the tension to 60,000 volts, prior to transmission from the station by eight underground cables each capable of carrying 50,000 kva. In addition to being connected with the other principal power stations of the Paris region at Vitry-Nord, Issy, Puteaux, Gennevilliers, Nanterre, St Ouen, etc., the new station is linked up with the Eguzon power of the Paris–Orleans railway and with hydro-electric stations of the Central Plateau, via Chevilly and Chaingy.

The permanent inability of French coal-mines to meet home requirements became more accentuated in the years following the war, when through war devastation they produced, e.g. in 1919, only half the output of 1913. This deficiency in fuel, even when after the restoration of the mines the national production had mounted from 41 million tons in 1913 to 52½ millions by 1926, provoked, as a consequence of the expansion of the activity of the great coal-consuming industries and of thermo-electric stations, ever greater imports. . . . A great impetus was given shortly after the war to the development of water-power resources by the desire to reduce these foreign payments, which in gold were even greater in 1919–1922 than in 1926–1931. In recent years, thanks to the cheapening of money, to the effective encouragement direct or indirect of the State, to the utilization of German deliveries in kind, the development of water-power resources has made notable progress, the generating capacity of hydro-electric stations have advanced from 2,134,000 kW in 1926 to 3,400,000 in 1933. . . .

The State has contributed substantially to the promotion of water-power schemes. Its contribution takes the form of subsidies or advances for the construction of power stations, for scientific investigation and research, and for preparatory work. In the three financial years 1930/31, 1931/32, 1932 (9 months) the total allocations were 73 millions of which 67 millions were for the construction of works. In addition, the State provided out of German deliveries in kind much expensive plant and machinery as well as a large number of German skilled and unskilled workers (e.g. in the Truyère, Chambon, Verdon, Kembs, etc., undertakings).

Investments in French enterprises for the utilization of water-power, which in 1890 were only Fcs. 600,000, were 161·7 millions in 1900, 677 millions in 1910 and 1,026 millions in 1914. In 1928–1931, the last four years for which figures are yet available, there were additional investments of 733, 1,114, 2,760 and 1,170 millions, making a grand total of 11,232 millions engaged in hydro-electric enterprises at the beginning of 1932.

The possibilities of a profitable development of hydro-electric power were demonstrated by the success attending the efforts of 1895 of a paper maker at Lancey in the Isère county to harness a waterfall of 500 metres. In 1901 was formed at Grenoble the *Chambre des Forces Hydrauliques, de l'Electrométallurgie, de l'Electro-Chimie et des industries qui s'y rattachent*, subsequently transferred to Paris and closely allied with the *Comité des Forges de France*.* The Chamber now has 170 members, whose installations represented at the beginning of 1932 a total generating capacity of 4,321,350 kW (of which, 2,680,373 kW from hydro-electric stations alone), and in the course of 1931 distributed 7,970 million kilowatt-hours, of which 6,540 million were developed from hydraulic sources. Grenoble has always been closely associated with the development of water-power in France, and a

* The great French iron and steel combine. (Ed.)

goodly share of the financing that has rendered this development possible has been borne by bankers of the Lyons–Grenoble region, who early realized the possibilities offered by the waters descending from the Alps. The *Crédit Lyonnais*, two regional banks, the *Banque Charpenay* and the *Banque du Dauphiné*, were largely instrumental in financing (and in some cases sponsored) many of the leading hydro-electric, as well as electro-metallurgical and electro-chemical, enterprises; while other banks, not directly connected with this region, which have given noteworthy support to the hydro-electric industry, include the *Société Générale*, the *Banque de Paris et des Pays-Bas*, and the *Banque Renauld* (of Nancy). In the Pyrenees region, great stability and elasticity have been ensured by the formation of the *Union des Producteurs d'Electricité des Pyrénées Occidentales* which, under the aegis of the *Midi* railway company, the *Alais-Froges-Camargue* electro-metallurgical concern, the *Compagnie d'Electricité Industrielle*, the Penarroya mines and other leading producers, constitutes one large group for the distribution of electric power in the south-western portion of France.

3/9 German Anti-Cartel Legislation

Ordinance Against the Abuse of Positions of Economic Power, of 2 November 1923. Printed in VASO TRIVANOVITCH, *Rationalization of German Industry* (Nat. Ind. Conference Board, New York, 1931), pp. 153–155.

In accordance with the Enabling Act of 13 October 1923 (R. G. B1. S. 943) the Federal Government decrees:

Section 1.

Agreements and conventions involving contracts concerning the conduct of production or sale, the application of business stipulations, the method of price fixing or maintenance of prices (syndicates, cartels, conventions, and similar devices) must be executed in writing. . . .

Section 4.

If an agreement or convention (Section 1), or a certain manner of carrying it out, endangers the economic life of the nation as a whole or the public welfare, the Federal Minister of Economic Affairs can:

1. Apply to the Cartel Court to have the said agreement or convention declared null and void or to have prohibited a certain manner of carrying it out. (Section 7)

2. Order that any party to the said agreement or convention may, without prior notice, terminate its agreement or withdraw from the convention.

3. Order that a copy of all arrangements and resolutions adopted in order to put into effect an agreement or convention be sent to him and that these measures shall not become effective until such a copy has been received by him.

Economic life as a whole or the public welfare shall be held to be especially endangered if production or distribution are restricted in a manner which cannot be economically justified; prices increased or maintained; additions to established prices made to cover risks; or if economic freedom is unduly restricted through imposition of conditions of purchase or sale or through the fixing of discriminatory prices or conditions. . . .

Section 7.

In case an application has been filed pursuant to Section 4, paragraph 1 (1), the Cartel Court shall, if in its opinion the economic life as a whole or the public welfare is endangered, declare null and void the agreement or the convention or shall prohibit the particular manner of its being carried out. If the Court should consider the provision set forth in Section 4, paragraph 2(2), as a sufficient corrective, it can order its application instead of declaring the agreement null and void or prohibiting its being carried out in a certain manner.

Section 8.

Any party to an agreement or convention (Section 1), may withdraw from it without prior notice for a reason of weight.

A reason of weight shall be deemed to exist if such a party is unduly restricted in its economic freedom, particularly as regards production, sale, and fixing of prices. . . .

Section 10.

If any terms of contract or methods of fixing prices by enterprises or associations of enterprises (trusts, communities of interest, syndicates, cartels, conventions, and similar combinations) are held to endanger the economic life as a whole or the public welfare (Section 4, paragraph 2) through the exploitation of a powerful economic position, the Cartel Court may, at the request of the Federal Minister of Economic Affairs, order that all parties may withdraw from all agreements containing the terms objected to. If it is possible that the agreement could be concluded without the said objectionable provisions, the decision of the Cartel Court entitles to withdrawal only from the said objectionable terms or methods of price fixing. . . .

Section 11.

The Cartel Court shall be established by the Federal Economic Court. It shall consist of a President and four associate judges.

The President and his deputies shall be appointed by the President of the Republic. They must have the qualifications of judges.

The remaining members shall be appointed by the President of the Federal Economic Court....

Section 12.

The Cartel Court is a court of last resort.

The decision of the Cartel Court is final and binding upon courts of record and tribunals of arbitration, even in so far as it concerns the determination of questions regarding the jurisdiction of the Cartel Court itself....

3/10 Anti-Cartel Action by the Co-operatives in Sweden

R. W. B. CLARKE, 'Industry' in M. COLE and C. SMITH (eds.), *Democratic Sweden* (London, 1938), pp. 132–134.

Kooperativa Förbundet, the Swedish Co-operative Wholesale Society, plays a much more significant part in manufacturing industry than the C.W.S. does here. The output of its factories is relatively small: in 1936 it was about 120 million kr, or about 2 per cent of the total production of Swedish industry. But its influence is very great. K.F. appears to regard itself less as a wholesaler to the retail societies than as a watchdog of consumers' interests in general. Consequently, when a price-raising monopoly appears in a con-sumers' goods industry, K.F. establishes (or, what is sometimes as effective, threatens to establish) a competing factory. The new factory comes into pro-duction, and cuts the price to what the K.F. considers to be a reasonable level. If the private monopoly then proceeds to cut prices wildly, the K.F. factory stops, the object of its intervention having been achieved – the consumers are getting their supplies cheaply, and that is to the real financial advantage of K.F. (for it releases working-class purchasing power for the purchase of other K.F. goods) besides being a good thing in itself. Then, of course, if the private monopoly, having 'driven out' the invader, boosts prices again, the K.F. factory starts once more.

The salutary effects of this policy can hardly be over-estimated. Half a dozen highly restrictive cartels have been broken in this manner. The K.F. began with the margarine cartel. Even with a small factory in 1909–1911, it had been able to force a free market for margarine, and in 1921, when the cartel had been re-formed and was fixing margarine prices 20 per cent above the price in the free Danish market, K.F. opened a big factory. The cartel price was rapidly reduced from 2·79 kr (roughly 1s. 4d. per lb) to 1·10 kr, and at the end of 1922, after a year's extraordinary fluctuation, the cartel price settled down around 2·10 kr, and the K.F. around 1·70 kr. By 1929 the price had been reduced to pre-war level. This margarine development was followed, naturally enough, in 1932 by the acquisition of a vegetable oil extraction plant – logical vertical integration.

A similar process was carried out in the milling trade, with spectacular effect upon the margin between grain and flour prices. This was followed by factories for rolled oats, macaroni and crisp rye bread. These factories are all rationalized together on the all-co-operative Kvarnholmen, an island in the Stockholm archipelago, complete with houses for the workers and social amenities – a brilliant flash of imaginative development. . . .

In 1926 came the attack on the rubber goloshes cartel, which made profits of 100 per cent. The K.F. intervention brought prices down from 7·50 kr to 3·50 kr, and increased sales by nearly one-half in two years. In 1929, K.F. began to produce superphosphates for the farmers, who were being exploited by a somewhat inefficient cartel. In 1932, K.F. opened even a cash register factory, because cash registers of a type suited to Swedish requirements were neither made in Sweden nor importable – now K.F. exports them.

The most spectacular of all the successes, however, was the success of the K.F. electric lamp factory 'Luma'. Sweden, in common with every other European nation, was suffering under the burden of 'Phoebus', the International Lamp Cartel. In Sweden, the price of a lamp in 1928 was 1·35 kr, which incidentally was cheaper than the price of the same lamp in England even today. The impending entry of 'Luma' was announced, and the price at once began to fall. In 1931, 'Luma' came in with a price of 85 öre, later reduced to 80 öre. This reduction represents a saving of the order of 6,000,000 kr a year to Swedish consumers! Interestingly, 'Luma' is actually controlled by the Scandinavian Co-operative Unions as a whole, it is not just a Swedish affair. And its effects upon prices in the other Scandinavian countries have been very considerable too.

I have dealt with K.F.'s industrial production at some length, for it does represent one of Sweden's peculiar contributions to social and economic policy. Certainly its effect upon the price structure, and indeed upon industrial structure itself, has been far greater than its figures of turnover would suggest. How far the plan is of universal application it is difficult to say. Much obviously depends upon the business acumen of the co-operative directors. K.F. has made a practice of never embarking upon manufacture unless there was a definite case for doing so, unless an opportunity presented itself for obtaining good plan and technical advice, and unless the capital requirements could be met from within K.F.'s own resources. These principles are plainly sound, for it is evident that unless the co-operative factory can produce equally efficiently with the best private factory, the enterprise will fail.

3/11 Cartels in Germany

Minutes of Evidence, *Enquête-Ausschuss* [*see* Document 3/6], Sub-Committee I, Group 3, Part 4, *Kartellpolitik*, Part II, pp. 108–110. (Ed. Tr.)

Chairman: Don't you think that forms of organization like compulsory cartels preserve non-viable enterprises in an unnatural manner?

Expert Witness Dr. Herbig (an official of the compulsory Coal Cartel): That need not be the case. In coal-mining we always try to adapt to circumstances as far as possible. We have never had fixed quotas; in periods in which it was believed that incentives to new sinkings were required, quotas were enlarged, and at the following negotiations possibly cut again.

Chairman: Does not a compulsory syndicate severely limit such possibilities?

Dr. H.: We have not been forced into a compulsory cartel as such, we have always formed voluntary cartels under threat of compulsion and have always regulated our quotas in such a way that a certain freedom of manœuvre remained. This is shown in the quota question. The opportunities of mines to combine either in mergers or in selling associations permitted them, during the currency of a cartel contract, to shut down uneconomic pits and assign the quotas to the most economic units. The compulsory cartel caused certain unintended difficulties. The quotas are based on a certain agreed technical formula. Since no one knew what results a free competitive battle would produce, economic capacity was put in its place. During the most recent cartel negotiations for renewal, we tried to award the quotas in line with the capacities. At the time I also thought of the capacity of the pits, but this gave us completely wrong figures: we needed firm figures and the only firm figures are those of the past. Therefore we went back to the maximum output of the past ten years and obtained a certain balance which approached economic justice more closely. ....

Chairman: Is not the fixing of prices a mere façade. ....?

Dr. H.: At the time of the inflation the wages were fixed on Thursdays and the prices were settled on Fridays by slide rule. Things are quite different now. Then the Ministry of Labour dictated the wages, and the Ministry for Economy based its prices on that. But since we are again in the world market, there has automatically to be a new system. The Ministry of Economy cannot any longer fix the prices. We cannot any longer get away with raising prices at will, the British are dictating the price to us; we don't need to negotiate with the Minister for Economy, since he cannot give us anything and cannot take anything from us. Now it is the Minister of Labour who lays down how much of our revenue may be given to the workers in wages. It is he who is now our limiting authority. The free play of economic forces only works downwards. Economic controls mean, as far as we are concerned, that we cannot benefit from the booms, but suffer from the slumps.

Chairman: As long as the market can bear a price increase, isn't there in the regular correlation between wage and price policy a form of collusion against the consumer?

Dr. H.: The situation is different from what it was at the time of inflation. The consumers mostly share in the price-fixing negotiations. They are at times on one side, at times on the other, and at times they disagree among themselves. Apart from the mine owners and the employees there are represented in the National Coal Council: the coal merchants, the coal-consuming industries, small-scale industry, the co-operative societies, the urban and rural coal consumers, the railways, shipping and science. The consumers' representatives meet before the official sessions and attempt to agree on a common policy.

Expert Witness Dr Cappenberg: The uninitiated easily come to the conclusion that the coal cartel represents a monopoly. But there is British coal being imported into the very coal-producing regions, and brown coal being brought in: there can be no question of a monopoly. Supervision is hardly necessary where there is a confrontation within the free play of opposing forces.

Chairman: Would you think it useful in present-day conditions to abolish the compulsory cartel?

Dr. H.: Yes, if the compulsory cartel is abolished, there will be chaos for a time, but this will have its advantages. One of the less pleasant aspects of the compulsory cartel is its irresponsible demands, since all that is being negotiated is only basic issues. This disadvantage of the compulsory cartel is so great that my own view is: while a voluntary cartel would be best, it would be worse not to have any cartel, but a compulsory cartel would be worst of all. The second of these possibilities is most unlikely in mining. Cartelization has become second nature to all the personalities in the mining industry to such an extent that no one would take the responsibility of preventing the creation of a voluntary cartel. The period of transition would be a period of selection.

3/12 Combination in French Industry

Department of Overseas Trade, *France, July 1925* [*see* Document 3/7], pp. 14–16.

The main features in recent years have been enlargement of the units and the tendency towards combination. Consolidation, whether on vertical or horizontal principles or with a parallel blend of both within widely embracing groups, has been noteworthy in several industries; and regional developments of this nature have tended to become national and even international in scope (extending, for example, into Luxemburg, Czechoslovakia, Poland, Belgium, and Holland). Several metallurgical firms now control, or have large interests in, ore-mines, coal-mines, and in a whole range of works producing raw and semi-finished and finished steel products, as well as a variety of engineering products: some of these firms control directly from 18,000 to 35,000 workers. Between even these great firms . . . mutual interests exist in certain other undertakings in France or in Luxemburg. In the engineering industries several cases of large-scale consolidation exist: in the electrical industry one company runs nine factories, each engaged principally in the manufacture of different series of products, and has large participations in a score of other manufacturing concerns as well as in quite as many electricity distribution schemes; and two or three other electrical concerns also possess numerous factories and participate largely in distribution. Electrical material manufacturing concerns also have in some cases working arrangements with big steel producers. The whole aluminium industry is directed by practically one concern.

As a result of fairly recent absorptions or combinations, two concerns absolutely dominate the heavy chemicals trade: one with 23 works in various parts of France, besides having active interests in other chemical undertakings and working in collaboration for certain purposes with coal-mines, also dominates the French glass industry; and the other by its absorption in 1923 of the concern producing about 80 per cent of the French dyestuffs output, now controls that branch of the chemical industry as well as being only second to the former in the production of fertilizers, sulphates, etc., in about twenty separate works. The textiles (other than silk) dyeing and bleaching industry is dominated by a single concern with about fifteen works in the appropriate areas of Alsace, Normandy, the Vosges, and Lyons, whilst silk dyeing is dominated by one or two other undertakings. The sequestrated potash-mines are still worked mainly by the appointees of the State, pending legislative decision, only one mine being in private working, and the sale of the bulk of potash is in single hands. Other chemical industries, such as those of pharmaceutical products, of soap, oil seeds, and candle-making, have likewise come under the control of a few firms.

The cinema and sugar industries are likewise examples of consolidation. The coal-mining industry is mainly operated by very large companies, whose individual outputs will soon reach in many cases between three and four million tons.

The national extension of manufacturing groups has just been noted as regards the various chemical industries, but some metallurgical and engineering firms own or control works in places as wide apart as Paris, Bordeaux, Cherbourg, Havre, Toulon, Joeuf, Caen, Le Creusot, and elsewhere, others in Lorraine, and in the west of France, others near St. Etienne, in Lorraine, in the north, near Biarritz and elsewhere. International extensions will be found in Luxemburg, Czechoslovakia, Austria, Hungary, Roumania, Holland, Poland, and South America.

Improvement in organization and direction has been exemplified on the largest scale in the transport industries. The seven main railway systems have been obliged, under the State-impelled and State-sanctioned reform of 1921, to pursue a common policy in the unification of their freight rates, to accept a compensatory system of profits indemnification on a basis of better working results, to collaborate for practical working through a committee of their own representatives under the supervision of the superior railways council, whose directives after ministerial approval are binding. The shipping industry is now controlled by a few companies which have closely intertwined connections with each other by having directors common to respective boards; and the connections of the shipping companies with the shipbuilding concerns are close, as are those of the latter with the great metallurgical and engineering concerns.

French progress in industrialization is also evidenced by the developments in the organization of the distributive trades. In Paris and in the larger and smaller provincial towns, departmental stores are assuming greater magnitude and importance, and are multiplying. The store of the multiple type is becoming more numerous and representative of more trades: thus in the food and general grocery trades some provincial concerns have as many as several hundred shops, in the boot trade there are now firms with from 100 to 300 shops, and multiple shops in the dairy and wine trade are numerous. Co-operative distributive societies have made some progress in the mining and industrial centres (e.g. in Paris, the north, and Lyons areas) but their importance is far from that of the English movement with its three or four million adherents.

3/13 The Schneider (Le Creusot) Company

Department of Overseas Trade, *France, July 1925* [*see* Document 3/7], pp. 216–218.

Etablissements Schneider (*Le Creusot*): The Creusot concern, so well known to the world as a maker of armaments, is probably the greatest undertaking in the French iron and steel trade; its interests and ramifications at home and abroad are immense, and its products, whether from its own works or from those of its subsidiaries or co-operators, cover a very wide range of raw materials, semi-finished or finished goods within the metallurgical and engineering trades. . . . The town of Le Creusot (population 38,000), which remains its industrial headquarters, is 240 miles south-east of Paris by rail on a cross-country branch of the Paris–Lyons–Mediterranean railway from Nevers to Chagny (on the Paris–Lyons main line); besides the parent works at Le Creusot, which have been greatly modernized and extended since 1914, there are two large modern plants close by, known as the Henri Paul and the Breuil works, and at Chalon-sur-Saône, 33 miles away, is another large works.

This group occupies about 18,000 persons, and its instruments of production include coke batteries (73 ovens), 5 blast furnaces, 2 acid converters, 17 Martin furnaces, 4 batteries of 34 crucibles apiece, 138 other furnaces; in the forge shops, 4 puddling furnaces, 66 various furnaces, 26 trains of rolls, bronze and casting foundries, and a total of 9 pig-breakers and of 134 presses and hammer frames. The products consist of steel sections, rails, structural steel, special steels, electric steels, gas engines, machinery for sugar, distilling and chemical industries, turbines dynamos, guns, armour plate, cranes, locomotives, multifarious engineering products: the Chalon works specialize in boilers, dredgers, marine engines, submarines, tugs, railway and artillery equipment. The steel capacity of these works is 300,000 tons a year, that of its coke ovens 250 tons a day, that of its locomotive shops 25 heavy locomotives a month.

The company owns seven other works: at Champagne-sur-Seine (electric material, mining machinery, etc.); at Havre, Harfleur and Le Hoc (guns and gun-testing, torpedo tubes, diesel engines, aircraft motors, electric motors, agricultural machinery); at Perreuil (refractory products); at La-Londe-les-Maures in the Var Department* (small electric motors, floating mines, torpedoes); at Bordeaux (cartridge-cases, zinc and aluminium alloys, copper tubes, etc.). As to raw materials, it owns two coal-mines in neighbouring Departments, two iron ore mines in the Briey field, and one in the Indre Department.

Apart from its own undertakings, Schneider controls or holds interests in

* See Glossary.

numerous industrial concerns, both home and foreign, that may be large purchasers of its products for direct utilization or for transformation purposes, or that may be suppliers. As to allied concerns producing mainly raw materials or crude or semi-finished products, Schneider holds interests in several coal- and ore-mines in France, in the *Société Minière des Terres Rouges*, in the *de Wendel & Co.'s. Joeuf* works and ... the *Métallurgie de Normandie* (capital 88 millions, which it controls, and which has absorbed the *Hauts Fourneaux de Caen*, built by Thyssen interests before the war); in the Belgian Campine and Dessaix coalfields, the *Ouenza* mines, the *Veitscher Magnesitwerk* in Styria, the Austrian *Berg-und-Hüttenwerke*, the *Société des Forges et Aciéries de Huta-Bankowa* in Poland, the Czechoslovakian *Skodawerke* (which it controls), and the *Société Tschèque de Ruston-Bromoosky*.

As to transforming works, it holds interests in the *Chantiers et Ateliers de la Gironde* (capital 37½ millions, builds ships or ships' parts in Bordeaux, Cherbourg and Havre), in the *Société Provençale de Constructions Navales* (yard at Marseilles), and the *Ateliers et Chantiers de Bretagne* (at Nantes); it is identified with the *Société des Moteurs à gaz et de l'Industrie Mécanique*, with the Paris *Somua* (capital 44 millions, specializes in machine tools, agricultural and hydraulic machinery, tractors, guns, shells, fuses, etc.), with the Paris *Société d'Optique et de Mécanique de Haute Précision* (optical instruments for civil and military purposes, scientific instruments generally), and the *Société de Précision Mécanique*, the *Moteurs Otto*, *Le Matériel Roulant* (rolling stock), *Société des Moteurs Frigorifiques*, *Etablissements Delaunay-Belleville* (motor engines), *Etablissements de Dion-Bouton* (motor-cars), *Société de Construction de Locomotives* (Batignolles-Châtillon concern); *Société Française de Construction Mécanique (Cail)*, capital 30 millions (sugar, etc., machinery), and with other works.

As to other users of Schneider products: it took a leading part in the formation of the *Aciéries de Chili*, of the *Port de Rosario*, of the *Union Européene Industrielle et Financière* (a holding company, capital 100 millions), which yielded a profit of 24 millions in 1924, and through which it has acquired much influence in central and south-east Europe, e.g. in the Skoda group, the Huta-Bankowa (Polish) group, in Polish and Roumanian oil and other undertakings; and in the *Energie Electrique Rhone et Jura*; *La Compagnie Marocaine*, *Société Espagnole de Constructions Electro-Mécaniques*; and since 1921 by the joint foundation of the *Société d'Etudes pour l'Electrification des Chemins de Fer*, it has an arrangement with two of the most important electrical material concerns, namely, the *Thomson-Houston* (capital 300 millions, for its widespread interests), and the *Jeumont* (capital 80 millions), for work connected with the electrification of the French railway systems. The company holds also the manufacturing rights in France of certain foreign patents, such as that for the *Still* engine or for certain Swiss steam turbines; it holds the lease for the Roumanian railway shops, and until quite recently was interested in the *Société de Danube*, engaged in the construction of a port at Gdnyia in Hungary (owing to certain difficulties its interests amounting to 40 per cent or to 25 million francs have, it is stated, been reimbursed).

As regards foreign representation of the Schneider company, reference has already been made above to the *Union Européenne Industrielle et Financière*, a holding company with a capital of 100 millions, which was formed in 1920, and of which the head of the Schneider company is president. It has important holdings in great industrial and banking establishments in central and eastern Europe (Czechoslovakia, Austria, Poland, Hungary, Roumania), such as *Skoda, Huta-Bankowa, Société Minière et Métallurgique, Spoleenosti Berg und Hüttenwerke Gesellschaft, Banque Générale de Crédit Hongrois, Niederöster-reichische Escompte Gesellschaft*. Th representation of the company for central and eastern Europe can therefore be efficiently carried out by this agency and by its allied concerns in the individual countries. In Spain it controls the *Société Espagnole de Construction Electro-Mécanique*, and in other European countries (Italy, etc.), it is suitably represented. For North America has been constituted the *Framerican Industrial Development Corporation* which is controlled by the Schneider company; for South America its interests can be adequately safeguarded through the *Aciéries de Chili*, and through the *Port de Rosario* company in the Argentine.

The Creusot group of works is just now proceeding to the electrification of their shops; the energy is to be supplied by the affiliated concern *L'Energie Electrique Rhone et Jura*, which has recently put into operation its water-power station on the Rhone, near the Swiss frontier, and will be conducted by a line of 120,000 volts over 87 miles.

The company dominates the town of Le Creusot, where, by means of various welfare schemes, it makes manifold provisions for its workers.

3/14 International Combines and Cartels

R. LIEFMANN, *International Cartels, Combines and Trusts* (London, 1927), pp. 33–36, 58–60, 69–71.

Cartels have extended enormously not only in Germany, but – particularly – in other countries. . . . The post-1918 development has been phenomenal, in both numbers and power – and even so, we have probably not yet arrived at the fruition of this economic movement, whose causes may be enumerated as follows:

1. The arbitrary division of States which formerly were definite economic units, and the construction of new political and economic entities with

frontiers which are senseless industrially and fiscally; together with the increasing tendency of many States towards national self-support or protection.

2. The increasingly keen competition:

(a) caused by the impoverishment of many States, especially of the Central Powers; and the flooding of the world market with the products of various safeguarded industries; and

(b) by the general international *overproduction* of certain goods, made possible by the progress in various branches of technique, and by the fact that *purchasing power* does not keep pace with *productive power*.

3. The Fluctuation of the Exchanges: Competition is made more severe for producers in certain States by the depreciated currencies of other States. Such conditions in many cases made the formation of international cartels more difficult; but today the producers in countries with depreciated exchange are generally met by the threat of *anti-dumping tariffs*, and therefore, being unable to reckon on steady export demands for their goods, they prefer to make defensive arrangements with their neighbours, by means of cartels.

4. A further reason for the rapid increase of international cartels since the war may be that the Governments and Parliaments of many countries were still under the *influence of War Psychology* and disposed to ignore economic needs and considerations so that producers were therefore compelled to take up the work of international understanding themselves, without Government support.

5. As a final factor in the growth of international cartels, we may mention the *tendency to amalgamations and mergers* (in the industrial world), because the concentration of capital in a few concerns naturally facilitates international agreements. Especially where an industry is dominated by a few large-scale Trusts, which work through affiliated ventures in several States, international agreement almost invariably follows.

Before the [First] World War, international cartels were mainly considered from the purely economic standpoint. . . .

It was only after the [First] World War that international cartels and trusts acquired *political* significance and their problem was viewed from an entirely new angle. Formerly, perhaps, they were more feared on *economic* grounds: today – still speaking generally – they are furthered and approved and for *political* reasons they are viewed as a means of reducing the economic inequalities caused or emphasized by the war, and of minimizing the unfavourable effects of post-war conditions, either on individual States or the world as a whole. . . .

An example of the facilitation of international agreements by the existence of one great business whose operations are international, is seen in the manufacture of glue. The Joint Stock Company for Chemical Products (formerly H. Scheidemandel) obtained a predominant position in Germany, and organized a great buying agency for bones, and branches and selling agencies in different countries. It also controlled the Austrian Glue Trust. On the initiative of this one firm practically all the European manufacturers in thirteen countries formed an association in 1926. They are to proceed to construct a shareholding company, registered in Switzerland, and to organize joint purchase of bones and raw materials and sale of the finished products.

The most suitable of all important materials for control by a world monopoly is copper, for both the overwhelmingly greater proportion of its production and of distributive trade therein, are concentrated in a few powerful hands. . . . Recently, a world syndicate in copper has been formed, including most of the leading firms in this line, and controlling about 90 per cent of the world's output. Among the leading American firms represented are the American Smelting and Refining Company, which turned out 25 per cent of the world's total output in 1925; the Kennecott Copper Company, with its affiliated concerns – responsible for about 16 per cent of the world's output; and the Anaconda Copper Mining Company, responsible for about 10 per cent (world total), as well as the great African and South American firms: l'Union Minière du Haut Katanga, and Cerro de Pasco Company respectively. Also the large-scale German business ventures, Mansfeld's Joint Stock Mining Company, the Metallgesellschaft, and Aron Hirsch & Sons, are members of this syndicate. The only first-class firms not represented in it are the American Miami Copper Company, the Spanish-British Rio Tinto Company, and the Australian firms, representing together only 10 per cent of the world's copper. The Central Bureau is the Copper Export Trading Company in Brussels. Six selling agencies have been constituted for Germany, and five apiece for both England and France; all of these are held by large-scale business firms dealing in metals. Pooling of supplies is to be carried out later. The chief immediate aim of this cartel is the *elimination* of *middlemen*, who, in the opinion of the smelters, are chiefly responsible for the violent variations in prices of late years. The consumers are asked to undertake to use the amount of copper supplied them for their own purposes, and not retail it to third parties. This has aroused lively opposition on the part of firms interested in the copper trade, and the cartel's future prospects are uncertain. In fact, the most recent information is to the effect that the British Metal Corporation (controlling Rio Tinto) has left the cartel, because it could not obtain the necessary authorization from the British Government to remain a member. This authorization was withheld because the cartel tended to keep up prices in Europe, when they sank in America. It has therefore been resolved to reduce prices in Europe. This seems to be a clear case of the *export cartels*, deliberately fostered by the Government of the U.S.A., to the detriment of the European consumers.

For another important metal, *zinc*, an international post-war cartel has been recently renewed between German, Belgian and English firms. The Germans have already concluded a national cartel among themselves. Negotiations are still in progress on the crucial question of supply-quotas. . . .

Monopolies by any one combine in several countries are rarities. But there are such; the chief is at the present time the *Swedish Match Trust*. It is based on the organizing ability of its Swedish founders and backed by American capital, which the Swedes have known how to utilize in an original and successful way. Not only did this trust surpass the older match factories in technical efficiency, and beat them or buy them up with its greater finance power, but it has now prepared to take over the manufacture of machinery for turning out matches, and – like the patent cartels – *it has strengthened monopolies by private agreements with monopolies by Government concessions*. By advancing loans or guaranteeing annual payments to Governments, it attempts to secure a guaranteed monopoly in as many countries as possible, and makes full use of the fact that in the case of articles like matches, a very high percentage of sale-price over cost of production is possible, before demand becomes limited. Thus, the Swedish Match Trust has a Government monopoly in Peru, Poland, Portugal and Greece, while it has succeeded – partly by cutting prices and partly by cartel agreements with previous manufacturers – in enjoying effective monopoly in other countries. In Germany it is interested in the selling syndicate of the German Match Selling Limited Liability Company to the extent of 65 per cent distribution quota, but owns 'only' 50 per cent of the subscribed capital of 1,000,000 (one million) marks. The German Government has kept a firm hand over prices here, and the match factories of the Wholesale Company of German firms in this trade are not limited by any quota arrangements with Sweden.

The Swedish Trust's method of securing guaranteed selling concessions by advancing loans has apparently found disciples. The second greatest of all American business concerns, after the Steel Trust, the International Telephone and Telegraph Corporation has a monopoly concession for the erection and construction of automatic telephones in Greece, by means of a loan, which is to be repaid, principal and interest, out of the profits on these telephones! It has also succeeded in obtaining the contract for converting the vast network of the Parisian telephonic system to the automatic system. The head of the greatest private business in the world at present, Henry Ford, is endeavouring to get monopolistic control of motor traffic by building special roads for such traffic. It may be assumed that this method of getting control of output will be extended to other fields, and lead to a great predominance of the largest scale capitalistic concerns over their weaker competitors.

3/15 The International Steel Agreement, 1926

Dated 30 September 1926. League of Nations, *International Economic Conference, Documentation: Memorandum on the Iron and Steel Industry* (Geneva, 1927), Annex VI, pp. 109–113.

Article 1

Each country shall pay 1 dollar monthly into a common fund for each ton of crude steel actually produced.

By the term 'crude steel' is meant all the crude steel manufactured in the several countries by the Thomas, Bessemer, Siemens or Martin processes, by the electric crucible, or any other process. . . .

Article 2

The administration of the common fund shall be provided for by a Managing Committee of four members appointed respectively by each of the countries Parties to the Agreement, i.e. Germany, Belgium, France, and Luxemburg. . . . The number of votes of the Managing Committee shall be allotted in accordance with the quotas.

Article 3

The Managing Committee shall fix the quota of each country for each quarter in accordance with the provisions of Article 4 not later than a fort-night before the beginning of that quarter, by applying coefficients – fixed once for all for each country – to the total tonnage representing the probable demand of the market.

Article 4

The coefficients allotted to the different countries can only be modified by unanimous consent.

The total quarterly tonnage, and accordingly the quotas of each country shall be fixed by a two-thirds majority of the votes, each country command-ing the number of votes proportional to its participation, with the proviso that unanimity of all the countries but one shall constitute a sufficient majority even if this latter country represents more than a quarter of the votes.

The Saar shall never vote individually; its votes shall be divided between France and Germany in their ratios of one-third and two-thirds.

Article 5

Every month each country's actual net production of crude steel during that month shall be ascertained, in relation to the figures indicated by the quotas.

Article 6

If the quarterly production of a country exceeds the quota which was fixed for it, that country shall pay in respect of each ton in excess a fine of 4 dollars, which shall accrue to the common fund, in addition to the payment provided for in Article 1.

Article 7

If the production of any country has been below the quota allotted to it, that country shall receive in compensation from the common fund the sum of 2 dollars per ton short.

The tonnage entitling to compensation may not, however, exceed 10 per cent of the quota fixed for the quarter in question. If a shortage of 10 per cent or more below the quota fixed continues during several successive quarters, the tonnage entitling to compensation shall be reduced by 2 per cent for each successive quarter, so that in the second quarter of such shortage of 10 per cent or more the compensation paid shall not exceed 8 per cent, and in the third quarter it shall not exceed 6 per cent, and so on.

In the event of *force majeure*, the General Meeting of the several groups shall decide by a majority vote the amount of the compensation payable. ....

Article 10

The present Agreement was concluded on the assumption that throughout its duration the tariff rates applicable to iron and steel products imported into Germany would not be increased. If Germany should proceed to increase the said rates, the present Agreement may be denounced at any time by each of the Contracting Parties at three months' notice, and each of the Parties shall then recover full liberty of action in relation to its Government as regards tariffs. ....

Article 13

Any disputes arising between the Parties as to the interpretation and carrying out of the present Agreement shall be compulsorily settled by arbitration.

Article 14

It shall be open to steel manufacturers in the other European countries to oin in the present Agreement. ....

NOTE ON SHARE QUOTAS IN THE
INTERNATIONAL STEEL AGREEMENT (1926)

In fixing the share quotas of the individual countries in the International Steel Agreement, the basis taken was that of an aggregate annual production of raw steel of 25,278,000 tons and the annual quotas were fixed on this basis as follows:

	Per cent
Germany	40·45
France	31·89
Belgium	12·57
Luxemburg	8·55
Saar Territory	6·54

These participation figures are changed if the total output rises by 1, 2, 3 or 4 million tons up to 29,278,000 tons. Above this figure the final quotas are as follows:

	Per cent
Germany	43·18
France	31·18
Belgium	11·56
Luxemburg	8·30
Saar Territory	5·78

In the event of any further increase in output, these percentage quotas will remain unchanged. Belgium, however, on joining the International Steel Cartel, was granted a fixed quota of 295,000 tons per month irrespective of any restrictions which might be imposed on output. As a consequence, the other countries were somewhat reduced. ....

At the beginning of 1927, Czechoslovakia, Austria and Hungary joined in the International Steel Agreement. These three countries together received a share of 7·272 per cent, or 2·14 million tons, annually on the basis of a total output by the International Steel Cartel of 27,278,000 tons. These three Central European countries have joined the Cartel as a single unit, the distribution of their quota between them is a matter to be settled by themselves.

3/16 The Franco-German Potash Agreement, 1926

Dated 29 December 1926. Printed in ALFRED PLUMMER, *International Combines in Modern Industry* (2nd ed. London, 1938), pp. 264–267.

Between the Deutches Kalisyndikat Gesellschaft mit beschränker Haftung, of Berlin, hereinafter called 'the Syndicate', of the first part, and the Société Commerciale des Potasses d'Alsace, Les Mines Domaniales de Potasse d'Alsace, and the Société Anonyme des Mines de Kali Sainte-Thérèse, hereinafter called 'the Société', of the second part, the following agreement has been concluded following the Lugano Agreement of 10 April 1926.

Article 1. To the Syndicate is reserved exclusive rights to sell in Germany, as well as in possible German colonies, protectorates and mandated territories. To the Société is reserved exclusive rights to sell in France, and in French colonies, protectorates and mandated territories. The two parties agree to take all necessary measures to prevent any exportations or re-exportations from these territories by a third party without special authorization. In the case where the reserved territories are used as countries of transit, the final destination of the goods will be placed under a rigorous supervision. The measures taken for this control will be communicated to the other party. . . .

The two parties shall come to an agreement, as soon as possible, with regard to the prices and conditions to be established for potash used in the manufacture of different preparations for export, outside of territories reserved to both parties, as well as the form and method of control to be adopted. The exclusive sales rights conceded to France and Germany in the territories under their control carry with them for each party the prohibition to make deliveries of potash salts for export, in no matter what form, into the territory of the other. . . .

Article 2. . . . In Germany, all of the potash mines or plants are obliged to adhere to the Syndicate from the beginning of their production. In France the owners of the mines adhering to the Société agree to bring about the adhesion to the Société of all new exploiters of potash mines or plants. . . . In case of the creation, in the countries reserved to the two parties, of new potash mines or new plants for the transformation of potash originating from the mines, their exports shall be included in the respective foreign sales quotas of the Syndicate and the Société. The signatories undertake to take all necessary measures to effect the reporting and control of the quantities of such potash salts and manufactured products which may be exported by new producers not parties to the present contract.

Article 3. The two parties will jointly take the necessary measures for maintaining the regularity of the market.

Article 4. As from 1 May 1926, the annual sale, outside of France, Germany, their colonies, mandated territories and protectorates, will be divided until an annual sale of 840,000 metric tons of K_2O is reached, in such manner that the Syndicate will receive 70 per cent and the Société 30 per cent. For any tonnage over an annual sale of 840,000 tons, the Syndicate will receive 50 per cent and the Société 50 per cent. It is, however, agreed that when the sale of 825,000 metric tons K_2O shall have been attained, the Société shall receive 3,000 tons of K_2O by right of priority above its fixed quota. If in the fourth year of the contract an annual sale of 840,000 of K_2O has not been reached, the Société shall receive for the fifth year of the contract a priority for the delivery of 8,000 tons of K_2O. . . . Should the sale of 840,000 tons of K_2O not be attained during the course of the fifth year, it is agreed that, in any case, from the beginning of the sixth year, the quantities over the highest annual tonnage reached during the first five years shall be divided in the proportion of 50:50.

Article 5. The two parties have agreed to set up as rapidly as possible, for each country, joint organizations for the development of sales.

Article 6. The two parties shall mutually communicate within the three days following each of the ten-day periods of each month the amount of the orders received and of deliveries made, either by rail or water, within each ten-day period. In case one of the parties exceeds its quota of orders in a country, at the end of one of these ten-day periods a readjustment shall be made, except by agreement to the contrary, immediately if possible, or at most not later than two months, by the transfer of a corresponding number of orders to the other party. In every case an exact readjustment of the quotas must be reached before the end of the season and contract year (30 April of each year). Only in the case where an exact compensation cannot be effected, due to forces beyond control, a readjustment of the quotas shall be made either by a complementary delivery to be made within a maximum delay-period of four months, or by payment by the party in excess to the party in deficit of a bonus of 15 per cent of the gross sale price obtained in the country under discussion.

Article 7. The selling price for each country shall be fixed by a common agreement between the directing boards of the two parties on the basis of the proposals presented by the managing boards of the sales organization, which should take into account the actual conditions prevailing in each country at the time. These prices shall be established by taking into consideration cost prices on the one hand, and, on the other hand, in such a manner as to allow the development of the use of potash for agriculture and industry in each country.

Article 8. The collaboration of the Syndicate and the Société has as its aim the development of the sale of potash according to the needs of the various countries, the realization of economies in general expenses, and the avoidance of unnecessary increases of prices for the consumer. . . .

Article 12. In case of differences which may arise either directly or indirectly from the execution of the present contact, no recourse may be made to the jurisdiction of any ordinary tribunals. These differences shall be settled by arbitration. . . .

3/17 A Trade-Union Critique of German Cartel and Rationalization Policies

Report by OTTO VOSS on 'Concentration, Rationalization and Planned Economy', in *Protokoll der 11. Konferenz des Reichsbeirats der Betriebsräte und Konzernvertreter der Metallindustrie, 28 und 29 Dezember 1931* (Deutscher Metallarbeiterverband, Berlin, n.d.), pp. 87–95. (Ed. Tr.)

In the case of national cartels, the control is tighter within the borders of one country, because all tendencies to national self-sufficiency work in their favour. Home prices are higher than the selling prices of exported goods because of the tariff walls. Thus tariff duties and cartels co-operate in raising home prices. In Germany cartels have been particularly successful. As a comparison of British and German wholesale prices shows, the German prices followed the British index in showing the price tendency of the world market only belatedly and slowly. Between 1928 and September 1931 the British index fell by 34 per cent, while the German yielded only by 24 per cent. Many prices fell far more even in Germany. It is only the average which is less, because of the cartel restraint, since the controlled prices are down by only 10 per cent at the end of November compared with the high point of the boom.

The cartels are resisting the price reductions as far as their power permits. During the boom they provided an incentive for an unwarranted extension of productive facilities. In the slump they now attempt to preserve the surplus investments. This is all the more dangerous, since in many branches of industry the fixed equipment will not be usable in full in the near future. This is true, at least, of the heavy iron and steel industry. . . . The annual capacity of the German works amounts, according to the Society of German Steelmakers, to 18 million tons of crude steel. Compared with this capacity, the highest annual output still fell short by 10 per cent. . . .

Nearly all the firms have kept up their capacity at great cost, or have even enlarged it. . . . The employers will not admit in so many words that the steel industry is suffering from over-investment. But their economic actions confirm this continuously. They attempt to limit capacity by buying up quotas. But this is, in turn, a bad economic mistake. The misdirected rationalization must be wiped out in the slump, or else there will be no upswing of the economy. . . .

But this cleansing effect of the slump will be lost if the over-capitalization is wiped out by dearly paid quotas rather than by losses of capital. But such purchases have occurred in nearly all branches of the steel and metallurgical industries. They have been financed either by the cartels themselves, by the largest units inside the cartel, or by consortia of cartel members. On the occasion of the renewal of the steel agreements, the consortium formed in the heavy steel industry had bought up the steelworks Becker, the Saxon Cast Steel Works Döhlen & Co., the Storch and Schöneberg & Co., the Rhenish-Westphalian Steel and Rolling Mills Co. and the Friedrichshütte. Shares were paid for well above par. Altogether, expenditure of these purchases has been estimated at 70 million RM. At the present rate of employment, this sum amounts to about a third of the annual wages bill of the German iron and steel furnaces. Besides this, the firms buying up quotas have to make a payment when they use these quotas. For rods, bars and plates this rental amounts to 5 RM per ton per annum. This system ensures that the costs of the existing capacity are maintained even while the firms who originally owned the quotas are closed down themselves. Production quotas, once obtained, are relinquished in the cartellized industries only for compensation. Often a fixed price tends to develop for quotas. The price paid for 1 per cent of the Reich railway quota in the locomotive cartel, bought by Henschel from the Hanomag, for example, was 450,000 RM. . . .

The employers are therefore engaged full steam at reducing their over-capacity, and thereby admit that it exists. It is only that they do not want to bear the losses associated with the cleaning up of the errors of misdirected rationalization. They burden the sharply reduced production by large compensation payments and attempt to get over the crisis by high prices and reduced wages, without any cost to themselves. They thereby set themselves in opposition to the market and thus prolong the depression.

Price fixing, which formerly went on automatically under the pressure of the market, depends in the monopoly industries on decisions of economic policy. While it was once the price which determined the extent of a branch of industry, today it is the costs which are a function of the size of the industry which determine prices. Therefore the attention of the entrepreneurs, who are upsetting the economic laws of capitalism themselves, is fixed one-sidedly on the costs of production. But since wages are the most variable costs, the reduction of wages has become the indicator for the reduction of prices. In June 1930 the industrialists of the Rhenish-Westphalian steel industry calculated that the wage reduction of $7\frac{1}{2}$ per cent corresponded to a price reduction of 2–3 per cent. The price was therefore reduced by that amount. Recently this idea of a simultaneous wage and price reduction, with the idea also of a corresponding rate of reduction, has again been strongly advocated. This is done with the motto: 'loosening of economic ties'. In fact, it would create a new, and impossible tie, that between wages and prices. . . .

While the cartels, with their tendency of preserving all the associated firms, have the effect of obstructing rationalization, mergers and trusts tend to work in favour of economy. In most cases they are able to achieve savings by a better division of labour and a better organization of all branches. The same result may be achieved by a redistribution of production among the works having the best equipment or the most favourable location. It has been widely recognized that such a concentration and re-orientation, after the years of artificial expansion to the point of inflation, would represent an important precondition of their restoration.

Let us first cast a glance on the main steps of the concentration process and its accompanying features. Wagon and locomotive building have trodden the inevitable path of concentration and there are few opportunities left for further mergers, while the automobile industry, after much-re-organization, is today once more on the eve of new combinations. In the heavy steel industry, three large combines arose in the three chief geographic regions during the slump of 1926. All other products of the heavy industries were far behind in significance compared with those huge concentrations. If we look at the limited reduction of output and at the stable prices of that year of slump, the term 'rationalization slump' is most apt. In the West hardly a single works remained unaffected by the re-organization. The Vereinigte Stahlwerke was founded as the most powerful bloc in the heavy industries of Europe. In the East . . . the Vereinigte Oberschlesische Hüttenwerke A.G. were formed by merger. Finally, in central Germany, after the manufacturing units were hived off, the remaining heavy sections of Linke-Hofmann-Lauchhammer were united as the Mitteldeutsche Stahlwerke. The Commission of Inquiry has characterized these processes in its report on the iron and steel industries, as negative rationalization.

This type of rationalization was indeed negative in two respects. In the first place, it differs from measures designed to increase efficiency by new investment in that it tries to achieve the same objective by the re-organization of existing works, or even by closing down existing capacity. But the aim was achieved only in as far as costs of production could be reduced. The economic effect of a higher rate of return was missing or diminished, because the newly formed combines had put burdens on themselves by the amalgamations, which neutralized the advantages derived from organizational or technical changes. To a large extent these burdens are still pressing on these enterprises, for they were frequently incurred for many years. In their first years, these concerns were benefited by a boom which covered up these faults. But today everyone can see that these burdens are inhibiting economic success. The concentration movement was therefore in this sense also a form of negative rationalization.

The former owners were compensated in various ways either with a once and for all gratuity or by long-term payments. In the merging of the capital, the combined capital was in several cases entered at far too high a book value. Often the share capital of two unprofitable enterprises was combined by addition in the hope that the removal of competition or the combined powers of production alone would make them profitable. In particular, they failed to take the opportunity of the merger to adjust the over-valued capital in gold mark terms to the possibilities of earning a return on it.

This again applies strongly to the heavy industry. The bankers Jakob Goldschmidt and Luis Hagen confirmed this error as expert witnesses before the Inquiry Commission. Jakob Goldschmidt said: 'In drawing up balance sheets in gold marks, the idea of the rate of return has, in my view, not been sufficiently taken into account, because of the wrong attitude both of practice and of theory. With a view to obtaining credit, the mistake was made always to value capital assets too high rather than too low, particularly in the steel industry.' Luis Hagen agreed in the following words: 'By far the largest part of the gold mark valuation of assets has been undertaken with a false view of the situation. Then great pressure was exerted everywhere not to create over-large combinations. But in the steel industry in particular it transpired in the course of the years that there ought to have been far greater combinations than in fact took place. For in the steel industry, more than in most, it is the case that after a certain period of time there must be renovations, and even complete re-equipment, of plant.'

If the valuation of capital assets in the case of the newly formed combines was guided by the desire to let the entrepreneur continue to participate in the returns by means of a greatly inflated balance sheet figure, the principle of risk of the entrepreneur was often totally neglected in the absorption of further firms.

This became most clear in the guarantee of dividends, often undertaken for decades. Thus the Vereinigte Stahlwerke have guaranteed to the shareholders of the Kraft Co., of Menden & Schwerte Co. and of the Westfälische Eisen- und Drahtindustrie A.G., a dividend of 5 per cent for 30 years. Krupp guaranteed a dividend at the same rate to the Westphalian Wire Industries Co., Hamm. But there are higher rates of obligation. The Luxembourg holding company of the Arbed concern was obliged to provide a dividend of

14 per cent to the Eschweiler Mining Co., and in the Stumm Combine, the ordinary shareholders of the Essen Mining Co. König Wilhelm have a right to a dividend of 12 per cent, and the preference shareholders to 17 per cent. These payments have to be made irrespective of whether the combine, or the branch of the privileged shareholders themselves, make losses or profits. . . .

In these cases the cashing-in capitalists have become rentiers, whose income from capital is secure. There is no risk-taking left for them. A symbol of the negative rationalization of monopoly capitalism, which is in strong contrast to the treatment of the worker set free by rationalization!

Other compensation on the occasion of mergers is paid on similar lines. As a rule, shares are paid for well above market values during the take-over. Purchases in the market raise the value of the shares by only a little. But if the shares are held by people who have no intention of selling, they can be obtained only by gross overpayment. The take-over consortium of the West German heavy industry occasionally pays double the market valuation. In the electrical industry, the Bergmann Electricity-Works Co. acquired a large block of shares of the Frister Co. at a price of 200 per cent.

3/18 The Objectives of Rationalization

a *Report and Proceedings of the World Economic Conference, held at Geneva 4-23 May 1927* (League of Nations, Economic and Financial Section, Geneva, 1927), vol. I, pp. 48–49.

b Minutes of Proceedings, *Ibid.*, vol. II, pp. 136–137, 156.

a The Conference has unanimously recognized the benefits of rationalization and of scientific management, and it asserts the urgent need of greater, more far-reaching and better co-ordinated efforts in this field.

While conscious of the advantages of rationalization, both in the lowering of costs of production and of prices and in expanding markets, the Conference has not been blind to the temporary unfavourable consequences which its application may involve in the case of certain categories of workers. Though, both directly and as consumers, the latter should in due course obtain their share of the advantages of a better organization of production, they may be adversely affected for a time by temporary unemployment while readjustments are being made. In the following resolutions, special account is taken of the legitimate anxiety which may thus be occasioned. . . .

Resolutions

The Conference considers that one of the principal means of increasing output, improving conditions of labour and reducing costs of production is to be found in the rational organization of production and distribution.

The Conference considers that such rationalization aims simultaneously:

(1) At securing the maximum efficiency of labour with the minimum of effort.

(2) At facilitating by a reduction in the variety of patterns (where such variety offers no obvious advantage) the design, manufacture, use and replacement of standardized parts.

(3) At avoiding waste of raw materials and power.

(4) At simplifying the distribution of goods.

(5) At avoiding in distribution unnecessary transport, burdensome financial charges and the useless interposition of middlemen.

Its judicious and constant application is calculated to secure:

(1) To the community greater stability and a higher standard in the conditions of life.

(2) To the consumer lower prices and goods more carefully adapted to general requirements.

(3) To the various classes of producers higher and steadier remuneration to be equitably distributed among them. . . .

The Conference accordingly recommends that Governments, public institutions, trade and industrial organizations or public opinion as the case may be:

(1) Should lead producers to direct their endeavours along the lines indicated above, and, in particular:

    (a) To encourage and promote in every way the investigation and comparison of the most adequate methods and most practical processes of rationalization and of scientific management, and of the economic and social results obtained thereby.

    (b) To apply these endeavours in industry, agriculture, trade and finance, not merely to large but also to medium and small undertakings, and even to individual workers and handicraftsmen, bearing in mind the favourable effects which they may have in household organization and amenities.

    (c) To give special attention to measures of a kind calculated to ensure to the individual the best, the healthiest and the most worthy employment, such as vocational selection, guidance and training, the due allotment of time between work and leisure, methods of remuneration giving the workers a fair share in the increase of output, and, generally, conditions of work and life favourable to the development and preservation of his personality. . . .

    (4) Should spread in all quarters a clear realization of the advantages and

the obligations involved in rationalization and scientific management as well as of the possibility of their gradual achievement.

b *M. Lammers* (Germany) . . . As regards rationalization, he would confine himself to some general observations. The success of rationalization in Germany was due to the hard necessity which had compelled the German people to do everything to overcome their extraordinary difficulties. The sincere collaboration of the workers, which had involved great sacrifices, with the object of setting up the proposed organization was one of the most remarkable phenomena of this period. Rationalization could only be effected if the nations succeeded in establishing in one way or another a division of labour in Europe, but the Conference should emphasize the necessity of rationalization in spite of the difficulties which it entailed. . . .

M. Lepsé (U.S.S.R.) said that more than half the population in the industrial countries of Europe were composed of wage earners and it appeared that, in order to settle the questions, it was indispensable to consider first the problem of wages and the problem of unemployment, which in Europe affected nearly twenty million persons, including the families of the unemployed. Hitherto, however, no reference had been made to these matters, by the representatives of industry. On the other hand, the workers were being asked to make further sacrifices and were being urged to show patience and to collaborate in order to rescue the capitalist system from the dilemma with which it was faced. . . .

He would point out that the Washington Convention had not been ratified and that the eight-hour day had been abolished at a time when wages were lowered for various reasons. This double tendency could only diminish the purchasing power of the working classes.

Certain countries were either suppressing trade unions or curtailing their liberty. The English Government desired to restrict the rights of the trade unions and particularly the right to strike; the Norwegian Parliament was examining a scheme for compulsory arbitration which would limit the right to strike; at Hamburg and at Leipzig, the strike in the textile industry proclaimed by the unions had been prohibited. Such facts could not be removed by idyllic conversations on economic peace and close collaboration. Capitalist rationalization meant only a more intense exploitation of labour for the working classes, i.e. the establishment of production on the basis of a minimum wage per unit of production. This would inevitably increase the number of unemployed. Workers had thus to be on their guard and to demand an extension of production, an increase in salaries and the reduction of the working day to six hours.

Whether the cartels were subjected to supervision or not, they would necessarily lead to a new increase in prices, apart from the difficulties to which they would give rise between the industrial and agrarian countries. He regarded international cartels as a new form of monopolistic capitalism, which would, in the first instance, enable the employer of labour to conduct an offensive against the working classes. . . .

M. *Lavonius* (Finland) said the proposal of the Drafting Committee was quite a conservative one. It said that rationalization should be applied with care in order that the legitimate interests of the workers might not be injured. That was contrary to the first point of the resolution already adopted, namely, that 'the rational organization of production and distribution is the principal factor in increasing output, improving conditions of labour and reducing prices'. The meaning of the expression of the Drafting Committee might be that unemployment should be avoided; but the essential point of rationalization might nearly always be said to save human labour through perfection of the means of production and of distribution, though improved conditions might open new avenues of production and of employment to the workers discharged. The clearer Scandinavian text admitted that rationalization might cause unemployment, but expressed the view that 'unemployment may be avoided by a greater mobility of raw materials, of capital and of labour'. And, further, that if unemployment could not be avoided in that way, its effects ought to be alleviated by measures taken by the community – such measures as would not hinder the adaptation of economic life to the new conditions. . . .

M. *de Peyerimhoff* (France) . . . thought that this (Danish and Swedish) text was inspired by the fear of its authors that the charges resulting from a rapid decrease in labour employed would fall solely upon the employers unless suitable steps were taken. This had never been intended by the Committee or by the Drafting Committee. The words 'suitable steps' had rather referred to unemployment allowances, which did not in any country fall exclusively on the employers, since there were usually allowances paid either by the State or the provinces of the municipality. This was certainly a rather lazy solution, but the interested parties, employers and workers would have to work out the practical solution of the problem.

3/19 The Workshop Autonomy System in the Bata Shoe Factory

International Labour Office, *Studies on Industrial Relations*, Studies and Reports, Series A (Industrial Relations), No. 33 (London, 1930), pp. 229-233.

To describe the motives that in 1924 led Bata to institute his system of workshop autonomy, we cannot do better than quote some passages from Cekota, the best exponent of his ideas:

> Workshop autonomy is Thomas Bata's vital and fundamental achievement. The guiding principle of his organization is the transformation of the worker's mentality – from a man whose wages are his only interest, he becomes a collaborator in the undertaking. . . . To effect this transformation, the worker must be given scope for initiative in the matter of production. His incentive must be the desire for gain, the magnitude of which depends upon the inventive genius of the head of the undertaking. . . . The profits of an undertaking are nothing but the sum of the inventive talents, the labour, the efforts – in a word, the initiative – of everyone employed in it. The aggregate results depend in fact on the comprehension of economic necessities and the co-operative spirit of each worker, however humble his task. . . .
>
> The wage systems which served their purpose in the organization of industry in most European countries during the nineteenth and twentieth centuries do not offer a sound basis for productive and fruitful work; they weaken the worker's sense of personal responsibility far too much.
>
> The effect of piece wages is better, for they make it possible to reward each worker's quickness and zeal at once, and in proportion to the amount of work done. But here again, especially with the modern division of labour, personal responsibility for the work done is abolished, and relations between worker and employer are limited to the number of pieces delivered and the calculation of wages. As to contact between worker and customer, that is now out of of the question. The solitary worker does not in the least concern himself in the interests of the whole group of workshops. Piece wages are too personal and leave the door open to an endless variety of unhealthy consequences of individualism. That the productive methods of the old-time handicraftsman did not give remarkable results is clear, but they did at least foster individual initiative. When a shoemaker made shoes, he knew that the amount of his remuneration would not depend entirely upon his manual skill, but also on his economical use of leather and other material, the care with which he executed his orders, and the quality of his work, which alone could enable him to keep or add to his customers. . . .
>
> Thomas Bata, who started in the humblest way in a handicraftsman's workshop, has never overlooked the value and utility of this kind of responsibility. He has tried to create a similar system of work that would allow everyone, even the operative in a large factory, to work with the same application, the same desire for economy – in time, energy, and

material – and the same responsibility, as the independent head of an undertaking who is paid in proportion to his output. He has tried to perfect a system under which everyone employed in the undertaking would be bound to the others by economic bonds, and could exchange his half-finished or finished products for another's. He solved this problem in 1924 in a novel way, and called his solution workshop autonomy.

It thus seems that Bata in the course of his advance towards large-scale industry has been sorry to see the qualities he had been able to appreciate in his father's workshop dying out in his workers, and has tried to restore to them, together with a sense of their responsibility, a little of that professional conscience and interest in their work that were the pride of the old-time handicraftsmen. There is nothing surprising in such a feeling, but it should not be misunderstood. For Bata, philanthropy is a word devoid of meaning. His driving force is solely the wish to increase profit. He has said as much himself plainly and without hypocrisy. In 1924 he made the following announcement to the workers whom he had selected for his first experiment:

> Our reasons for giving you a share in the profits is not that we think we ought to distribute charity to mankind. Our aim is a different one. We want to raise the level of production. . . . Manufacture can be cheapened and higher wages paid. So far your individual effort has not given good results, because you have had your eyes fixed on your own needs and you have not troubled to work so as to help those who take over from you. Profit-sharing will put an end to this bad practice, by giving you an interest in the speedy and thorough execution of the work of the entire workshop, and by stimulating greater economy of material.

These few words are a lucid expression of Bata's ideas. They show plainly what he wanted, namely, to replace individual effort by collective effort; to establish the worker's responsibility, not only within the limits of his daily job but in the whole scheme of production; to make him observe the results of his own work and help forward that of all his comrades.

Such being Bata's motives, what is his system? At the very outset he drew up a number of precise rules which he has never amended since. Profits should be calculated weekly so as to enable the worker to compare his output as often as possible, and should be set out clearly so that everyone can easily check them himself. The workshops should be divided up into small units so as to give all the beneficiaries of the system an opportunity of contributing personally to the smooth running of the departments. He also declared that he would pay 10 per cent interest on all profits left in the business, and that every worker aged twenty or more with at least one year's service in the workshop could share in the profits. . . .

In making his workshop managers responsible financially, Bata ought logically to have required them to give security; but he has devised another plan. Each week he pays only half the profits earned, and retains the rest as security, crediting it with interest at 10 per cent.

However wide the autonomy thus allowed to the workshops may be, it is, of course, essentially only an autonomy in the keeping of their accounts. A workshop may not use its autonomy except to discharge to the best of its ability the duties assigned to it. It is Bata who, in the last instance, decides as to the allocation of resources and the payment of the different departments.

His system is extremely flexible, but its widely varying forms are always an elaboration of the same rule: to assign to each department its share of costs and profits, with an elastic margin that shall stimulate the managing staff to increase output, not only by the desire for gain, but also by the fear of loss. . . .

The system of workshop autonomy devised by Bata, as has been seen, is much less a social experiment than a measure of industrial organization aiming at securing the maximum output from man and machine. The system bears the clear impress of Bata's realism; as with all others of his achievements, it is circumstances, environment, and business necessities that have forced it upon his mind. Installed at the back of beyond, in a region devoid of industrial traditions, unable to count upon a skilled labour supply, and compelled in consequence to mechanize his manufacture to the last degree, Bata might well fear that his workpeople, however well trained they might be, would not get the utmost out of his plant. To ensure the success of his technical organization, he has called psychological factors to his aid. He has brought his workpeople's sense of responsibility to bear by playing on their desire to increase their earnings.

3/20 Lack of Capital for Small Firms

Enquête-Ausschuss [*see* Document 3/6], Gesamtausschuss, vol. III, pp. 164–166. (Ed. Tr.)

Since every credit business is subject to individual conditions, a general judgment, whether and how far the German banks should give more small-scale credits, particularly in terms of quantity, is hardly possible; nor how far the concentration in banking has made small-scale credit more difficult. This particularly is what the experts among those needing credit have pointed out.

Numerous enterprises in the German finishing industries are indebted for their rise, and in part for their world leadership, to the circumstance that local private bankers would grant the means to extend their businesses to able and industrious small masters, skilled workers or small firms. This collaboration of industrialist and banker, resting not only on personal judgment and often long-standing experience but also on capitalist initiative, was said to have been disrupted by the concentration in banking and the taking over of the most effective banking firms by the large joint-stock banks. The salaried branch managers are neither entitled nor prepared to give risky personal credits or to further the development of new enterprises with novel production problems. What competition there is concentrates first on the old-established businesses.

It may be submitted that the urgency with which nearly all enterprises believed that they needed additional means may have led to unjustified criticism on the part of the expert witnesses in many cases. Nevertheless, the shortage of means among the small- and medium-sized enterprises constitutes, in view of their economic importance, one of the most important tasks of the economy as a whole to which the large-scale banks should also devote themselves energetically. It is highly likely that these branches of industry which are today often limited in the extent of their trade might with additional means help to make the whole of German commodity production and distribution more economic and might develop strong expansionist forces. This would also end the restrictions which today hinder the activities of the banks themselves.

It could hardly be argued against an extension of small-scale credit that it would be inadequately secured. The pressure to meet his commitments is at least no less on the small and medium entrepreneur, who is usually liable with all his personal property for his debts, than on the large joint-stock companies. The spreading of the risk would also be much greater among small- and medium-sized enterprises than among the concentrated vast credit grants for a few firms. Besides, the experts, particularly of the small- and medium-sized enterprises, also complained that since the war personal trust has come to have a far lesser importance for credit than concrete securities. They have designated the lack of independence among bank branch managers as cause for the changed conditions of credit granting. The Report on Bank Credit, based on the evidence of the banking experts, states on this matter:

> The basic trend of granting fewer truly personal credits now than before the war was accentuated by the fact that by the set rules the banks are far less able to meet the personal wishes of the borrowers and have to treat them more or less alike, but above all by the fact that, compared with the pre-war period, a far larger proportion of bank credits is granted by managers who have relatively little independence, and often based on a mechanical estimation of creditworthiness. Before the war it was above all the private banker who, in view of the relatively larger share of his own

capital in the total, was prepared to show greater initiative and could pay more attention to the personal suitability of his borrowers because of his close contacts with the customers. For the branch manager of a joint-stock bank, who has replaced him in many cases and who risks not his own property but the property of the bank, it is only of very limited advantage to take greater risks. . . . The credits granted by the branch office require endorsement by the central office if they exceed a certain, usually rather low, sum, and local managers are therefore eager to submit only those loan proposals which leave nothing to be desired in point of safety.

3/21 State-sponsored Credit for Industry in France

Department of Overseas Trade, *France, 1934* [*see* Document 3/4], pp. 615–620.

In France as in other Continental countries (Germany, Holland, Scandinavia, Austria, Hungary, and elsewhere) the need of special organizations for medium- and long-term as well as for short-term credit, was recognized and met either in the eighteenth or nineteenth century. Numerous special credit institutions have been founded in France: State or semi-State, provincial, county, municipal, mortgage credit companies of semi-State character, companies with special privileges for particular industrial activities, great industrial or 'business' banks: or existing institutions with other principal objects have adapted themselves to serve at least in part the same purposes. . . .

3. *The Crédit National* – In 1919 was created this special organization (capital 100 millions) for the purpose of effecting the vast volume of financial settlements for which the State was liable for the compensation of French war sufferers. In recent years it has been authorized to grant to French manufacturers and merchants loans 'destined to facilitate the creation, development, or starting of industrial and commercial undertakings belonging to French nationals and situated in France, Algeria, Colonies, Protectorates, or countries under French Mandate'. These loans, which may be granted for periods of from 3 to 10 years, must not exceed 5 millions in the case of any one borrower, and must be guaranteed by first mortgage, or joint and several guarantees or securities, and as complementary security, the goodwill of the undertaking. . . . Its business in this respect has reached about 1,400 to 1,500 million francs. The loan committee of 45 members, highly representative of the chief industries and trades, gives monthly decisions which in recent times cover usually 25 millions. It is proposed to develop this branch of the activity

of the *Crédit National* by authorizing higher individual loans than 5 millions and to obtain the remaining resources by public issues under its aegis.

4. *French National Bank for Foreign Trade* – (Banque Nationale Française du Commerce Extérieur). In France, as in some other countries, there had developed both for some years before and during the war a rather widespread and persistent advocacy, somewhat vague, however, as to aims and possibilities of achievement, of the creation of great banking organizations, even of national organizations, that would specialize in some of the financial domains of foreign trade and would render services to the industries of the nations concerned that were working with colonial and foreign markets. This movement assumed considerable importance in France immediately after the war, as it was felt that certain other countries were better provided with their own overseas banking facilities and connections. Under the direct impulsion of the Ministry for Commerce the Bank was founded in 1920, a law of the previous October having approved the contracts regulating its relations with the State. Its capital is 75 millions, of which two-thirds is fully paid: for the first five financial years it received a subvention of 2 millions a year from the State, and it apparently still enjoys from the same source the use, free of interest, of 25 million francs. Its chairman and its managing director must be approved by the State, which also nominates two representatives on its board. About one-twelfth of its share capital was reserved for subscription by the large banks: on its board are representatives of the Bank of France, *Crédit Lyonnais*, *Comptoir d'Escompte*, *Société Générale*, *Banque de Paris et des Pays-Bas*, *Lehideux*, *de Neuflize*, *Compagnie Parisienne de Réescompte* (apart from representatives of various industrial and commercial interests). The Bank is debarred from establishing branches in French towns without first seeking an arrangement with banks already existing therein, and without securing the approval of the two Government directors thereto. At the present time it has offices in Paris, Bordeaux, Havre, Lyons, Marseilles, Mazamet, and Roubaix: it has correspondents in the French colonies and in foreign countries.

It is prepared to do all normal banking business, especially in the Colonies and abroad, but it appears especially to lay stress on the discounting and collection of foreign bills, advances on colonial and foreign commercial bills with medium- and long-term maturities, mobilization of claims on foreign Governments or public authorities which have been insured under the French exports credits guarantee system, and on providing guarantees to foreign public authorities in relation to French firms. Since 1932 it has co-operated with the Paris Chamber of Commerce in the eight clearing-house schemes for commercial credits and debts established between France and Austria, Bulgaria, Chile, Esthonia, Greece, Hungary, Latvia and Yugoslavia, in that it has assisted in securing the mobilization of credits approved by the Paris Clearing House. It has also co-operated as regards the 'payment' agreements signed by France with Germany, Brazil, Colombia and Czechoslovakia. It anticipates further foreign business in connection with the extension of the export credits guarantee system, whereby the French State guarantee will not be confined to orders for French goods for foreign public authorities, but will cover work or services to be effected in the importing country.

The acceptance business of the Bank has not reached the anticipated volume: end of 1932, 110 millions against 184 millions a year earlier. The Bank is generally deemed to have rendered especially considerable services since its foundation by its advances on bills which it extended beyond normal maturity (e.g. to 12 or 18 months).

At the request of the State, the French National Bank for Foreign Commerce established and developed a very important economic intelligence department, which at present possesses and keeps up to date 500,000 files. It publishes a monthly bulletin of special articles and of general information relating to general questions concerning home and foreign trade.

5. *Crédit Maritime* – Special credit facilities have been instituted for the benefit of the French shipping and shipbuilding industry by the Maritime Credit laws of 1928–1931. The *Crédit Foncier* is authorized to grant French shipowners 'short' and long loans for maximum periods of 6 and 20 years respectively, secured on ships built or being built, the total loans in any one year not to exceed 250 millions, and all outstanding loans at any period not to exceed 1,250 millions. The bank is authorized to issue debentures or maritime mortgage bonds up to the value of the loans granted. Loans are limited to 50 per cent of the value of the ship pledged, unless collateral is furnished, when the maximum is 84 per cent; and one-quarter of the building of a ship must be completed before any loan can be considered. Loans on foreign-built ships are authorized only when the ship, clear of all claims, has been registered as French. The interest which is 0·8 per cent higher than that on the bonds issued by the *Crédit Foncier* to cover the loan, is shared between the borrower and the State, with a minimum of 3 per cent and 2 per cent for the borrower in the case respectively of passenger and cargo boats. The basis of this scheme is the utilization both of the long-established prestige for bond issues of the *Crédit Foncier* in the French money market and of the institution by the State of low interest rates for shipping and shipbuilding.

6. *Crédit Hôtelier* – One of the most prominent French industries, by virtue of the capital and of the number of persons employed therein, is the hotel industry. In order to promote the tourist industry, which has been of the highest importance to the French economy, by the modernization of old and

the construction of new hotels, the *Crédit Hôtelier* was constituted by a law in 1923 as a co-operative society with a capital of 5 millions and an endowment of 13 millions for long-term credit purposes. Loans which are not to exceed 12 years, are to be fully guaranteed by mortgage charges and other liens. In the first seven years of its working its loans to hotels totalled 60 millions and enabled the construction or betterment of 18,000 rooms. Funds were obtained by the issue of debentures (*obligations*) by the *Crédit Hôtelier*: the capital and endowment are really destined to serve as guarantee for the interest of the debentures.

7. *Banques Populaires* – In 1917 the State created and endowed a system of co-operative short-term credit societies of merchants, manufacturers, artisans, trading and industrial companies, to be called *Banques populaires*, which were to have as exclusive object the acceptance and endorsement of bills and similar credit instruments, created, signed, or endorsed by members of a *banque populaire* and relating to business operations. The scheme, which aimed at supplying short-term facilities to small and medium merchants and manufacturers, was at first provided with an advance of 18 millions by the State. Each society was eligible to obtain from the State double its paid-up capital for a period of not over 5 years but renewable. The savings banks, normally obliged to invest their funds with the State *Caisse des Dépôts et des Consignations* in Paris, were authorized to lend money to the local *banque populaire*. A somewhat similar organization to that in operation for the 6,000 rural credit societies was then instituted: all *banques populaires* are bound to belong to a central federation in Paris, created by law of July 1929, which controls the operations of the individual banks and acts as distributor of State advances. In 1933 there were 95 banks of this type, usually established in the chief towns of each French county: to these are affiliated in all about 500 branches or an average of about five per *banque populaire*.

8. *Crédit Artisanat* (or for Craft-workers) – Under the definition of the competent committee, those eligible to receive loans under the *Crédit Artisanat* Law of December 1923, are workers of either sex exercising a trade in an independent manner, effecting themselves the manual work of their trade, and employing besides members of their family, at most two persons (or three, if one is an apprentice). Craftsmen as so defined are eligible to obtain loans for a maximum period of 5 years through a co-operative society of manual workers, or through a federation of such societies, or through a *banque populaire*, for the creation, fitting-up or whole or partial refitment of a small undertaking, or for buying machinery or raw materials, within the limits just indicated. Repayment by annuities, and guarantees by a co-operative society of the *banque populaire* type, are required. The societies obtain

their funds for lending at low rates from the central organization which controls the State endowment (in 1923, 2 millions) and the other annual sums varying in amount already accruing to the State, under convention, from the operations of the Bank of France. . . .

3/22 The Conseil national économique, 1925

J. M. JEANNENEY and M. PERROT, *Textes de droit économique et social français, 1789–1957* (Paris, 1957), pp. 356–357. (Ed. Tr.)

Article 1

A *Conseil national économique* is established to study the problems which are of interest to the economic life of the country, to seek solutions to these problems and to recommend the adoption of these solutions by the public authorities. The duties of the *Conseil national économique*, which has autonomous powers over its composition, are administratively of a consultative nature.

Article 2

The *Conseil national économique* is attached to the Prime Minister's Office. Its expenditure shall be financed through credits included in the budget under the expenditure of the *Ministère du Travail*.

Article 3

The *Conseil national économique* is composed of 47 members, representing the various economic and social interests of the nation, in the proportions indicated below:

1. *Population and consumption*
   Cooperatives de consommation and *ligues d' acheteurs*: 3
   Associations of mayors and municipalities: 2
   Users of public services: 2
   Representative heads of households and friendly societies: 2

2. *Work*
   Intellectual work and teaching: 3
   Managerial work: Industry, 3; agriculture, 3; commerce, 2; transport, 1; cooperatives, 1; public services, 1
   Salaried work: Civil servants, 2; technicians, 2; workers: industry, 5; commerce, 2; agriculture, 1; transport, 2
   Urban and rural occupations (artisans), 2

3. *Capital*
   Industrial and commercial capital: 3
   Fixed capital (urban and rural property): 2
   Bank, Bourse, insurance bodies and savings banks: 3

Article 4

The members of the *Conseil national économique* for each category shall be delegated by the most representative organization or organizations.

These organizations shall be appointed by the government on the nomination of the Minister of Labour, after advice from interested ministers. The Prime Minister shall inform the organizations of the number of representatives they must send to the *Conseil*. In cases where decisions taken by the most representative organization or organizations are disputed, the final decision shall lie with the *Conseil national économique*.

Article 5

The duration of the commission of regular members of the *Conseil* is fixed at two years.

Article 6

The members of the *Conseil* must be French subjects, aged at least 25 years and in possession of their civil and political rights. Women shall be admitted under the same conditions regarding age and nationality.

Article 7

The *Conseil national économique* shall hold each year, 4 ordinary sessions of ten days.

If extraordinary sessions are necessary, the *Conseil national économique* may be convoked by the Prime Minister, on the request of the *Conseil national économique*.

Article 12

When a question shall concern an economic or professional category which is not represented on the permanent council, the *Conseil national économique* shall admit, for the study of this question, representatives of this category, who shall participate in its deliberations and who shall be appointed in conformity with the arrangements in Article 4.

Article 14

The *Conseil national économique* may create permanent organs, necessary for documentation and publication.

Article 16

The deliberations of the *Conseil national économique* shall be recorded in the form of reports or recommendations, the conclusions of which shall be published in the *Journal officiel*.

Article 18

For the purpose of information, the Government shall send to the *Conseil national économique* . . . all legislative plans or proposals relating to economic matters.

All economic laws may include a clause requiring consultation with the *Conseil national économique* during the preparation of the rules of public administration which are necessary for its application. The advice of the *Conseil national économique* shall be attached to the papers sent to the *Conseil d' État*. The law shall stipulate the period of time in which the advice of the *Conseil national économique* must be given.

Chapter 4   Inflation, Reparations and the Crisis

Introduction

One of the legacies of the war was an inflation of the currency in the belligerent countries. Everywhere government had spent unprecedented sums for military purposes, exceeding in each case the total available from the revenue raised by taxation and the genuine savings of the people (**1/33**). Among the victorious Western Allies the inflation was relatively mild and could be held in check and even reversed after 1920, minimizing the consequent dislocations. Among the defeated Central Powers, such as Austria (**4/2a**, also **1/25**) and Hungary, and in Soviet Russia, the political revolutions, the uncertain frontiers, the initial breakdown of government and its slow reconstitution, and above all the economic disruption led to post-war inflations much greater than those of wartime.

The highest levels were reached in Germany in 1923. Although less affected by losses of territory than the other two defeated Central Powers, Austria–Hungary and Turkey, or Russia, and recovering industrially much more quickly than they, Germany was in at least two respects much more vulnerable to runaway inflation. First, she had a much larger and more complex industrial sector, and in the years before 1914 she had existed on a balance of payments surplus derived from the returns on huge foreign investments. Secondly, Germany was subjected to much harsher demands for interim reparations, at least some of which were inspired by the hope to see her crushed as an industrial and trade rival. Whatever the actual burden of these reparations in macro-economic terms (to which we return below), they imposed an intolerable strain on the German budget, particularly when they took the form of demands which could not be foreseen at the beginning of the budgetary year, and created government deficits far beyond the capacity of German savers to meet (**4/1**). Default led to the occupation of the Ruhr in 1923 and to the total collapse of confidence in the Reichsmark.

The resultant level of inflation of prices, coupled with a similar inflation of the note issue (**4/2b**) was unprecedented in world history, greatly exceeding even the fantastic figures of Austria, Hungary and Russia. It strained the resources of mathematics as well as of the paper mills and the printing presses and led, at times, to the absurd pre-occupation of the President of the Reichsbank and part of his staff with the sheer physical problem of getting the notes distributed fast enough (**4/2c, 4/3**) instead of considering economic policy. Although the Reichsbank, like the Austrian National Bank, had been made a technically independent institution on pressure from the victors and creditors (**4/8a, 4/8b**), it was unable to stand up to the government demands, which ultimately derived in large measure from the reparation demands of the Allies (**4/3**).

The galloping stages of the inflation in the second half of 1923 became a classic example of the collapse of the monetary standard. Velocity of circulation increased enormously as consumers rushed to spend, since delay would make their cash worthless. Wages were paid daily and prices rose almost hourly (**4/2c, 4/2d, 4/2e**). Those who had the means, rushed into commodities or titles, or into foreign currencies, and speculators could make (or lose) fortunes by the skill with which they anticipated the runaway inflation. Others sustained heavy losses, relatively and absolutely (**4/2e, 4/4a, 4/4b, 4/4c**).

The speed and success of the stabilization were almost equally striking. Basically, the economy was sound, even in the midst of the inflationary fever; German exports were acceptable abroad, and as soon as the extraordinary reparations demands on the budget ceased, a temporarily savage level of taxation restored the balance between revenue and expenditure by the spring of 1924. The main point was the restoration of confidence, in itself as irrational a development as its loss some months earlier. It was achieved in the middle of November 1923, by the creation of the so-called Rentenbank and the issue of 'Rentenmark', secured by a purely notional mortgage on all land, industrial and commercial property (**4/5a, b**). The mark was stabilized at 4·2 billion* to the dollar and the Rentenmark at one billion* depreciated paper Marks, and the rate was kept there by a skilful policy of limitation and restriction of issue.

The immediate consequences of the stabilization were two-fold. On the one hand, commodities were dishoarded at once and again entered into circulation, permitting a fall in prices and a general rise in consumption from the dangerous starvation levels to which many strata of the population had been reduced in the feverish phases of the inflation. But the other side of the medal was a serious rise in unemployment of those who lost their jobs in the inevitable decline of many industries during the period of stern deflation (**4/6a, 4/6b**).

The long-term effects of the inflation and the restoration of the German Mark (and to a lesser extent, of other European currencies) were far more serious. The savings and the capital on which the existence of many members

* This is the German, not the American billion, i.e. one million million, or in American terms, one thousand billion. (Ed.)

of the middle classes was based were almost totally wiped out. This destruction of the livelihood of people who had possibly spent a lifetime of careful economy and hard work acquiring it, or of people too weak economically to look for other income, left them with a bitter sense of grievance, and turned them from being among the strongest defenders of the rule of law and the Constitution towards bitter and resentful hostility. Thus the Weimar Republic, already suffering the disloyalty of those on the Right who alleged that it had lost the peace at Versailles, found some of its other social foundations undermined, and it could not be denied that in the general collapse of all accepted standards in the traumatic experience of 1923–1924 there were grave injustices in the relative experiences of town and country, speculative versus invested capital, or salaried versus wage workers (**4/4c, 4/7a, 4/7b**).

It has also been argued widely that the badly bungled issue of German reparations contributed further to the collapse of the fabric of the Liberal State and the victory of National Socialism in Germany. Whereas many, perhaps most, Germans accepted after 1918 the obligation to make reparation payments to civilians in countries invaded by the German Army, and there was, after all, the precedent of the reparations exacted from France after the Franco–Prussian War of 1870, paid without undue hardship by the French and used effectively by the Germans to advance their economic prosperity, yet the reparations clauses as written into the Treaty of Versailles (**4/10**) and interpreted later by the Allies were not only very dubious morally and in law, having regard to Wilson's Fourteen Points on which both sides had concluded the armistice, but they made no economic sense either. However, neither Keynes, writing from a general analytical point of view (**4/9a**) nor Walther Rathenau, making the best case he could for his country (**4/9b**) managed to persuade the Allies that a realistic assessment of the level of reparations must depend not so much on the total losses and war expenditure of the victors, nor even on the possible excess of German production over German consumption, but on the 'transfer problem', i.e. on the maximum value of goods and services that might be transferred from Germany to other nations without upsetting trade relations and exchange rates. Instead, politicians in the victor countries gained cheap popularity by making demands at a level which satisfied the greed and lust for revenge of their hearers, but had no basis in economic reality. At the same time the United States, by insisting that the wartime loans must be serviced and repaid in full by her allies, added further pressure on those allies to exact large reparations from Germany in order to be able to pay off their debts to the U.S.A.

There has been much argument on the matter, and it is entirely possible that in the years 1919–1923 Germany was in a position to pay more than she did in reparations, and that she pretended to poverty and fiscal weakness by dubious statistics, while in fact enjoying greater prosperity and lower taxes than France and Belgium whom she had despoiled in the war and now refused to compensate in the peace. Yet it is clear that the inflated and vague reparation claims of those years, by leaving Germany no hope of any relief or even any reasonable certainty, called forth growing passive resistance which led, in turn, to the French occupation of the Rhur, and to the total collapse of the Reichsmark (see above).

The Dawes plan (4/12a, b) and the report of the parallel 'McKenna Committee' of experts on the problems of the German capital exports which had done so much damage to the efforts of the German Government (4/11), represented the first systematic review of the reparations question, freed, as the Dawes Committee rather self-consciously asserts, from political overtones. The level of annual payments was now to be much lower than before and it was fixed for many years ahead for the first time. Moreover, while the transfer problem was still largely ignored, there was at least some realism in linking payments to Germany's capacity to pay (including a 'prosperity index' to allow for yearly fluctuations).

For some years of rising prosperity, payments made under the 'Dawes plan' appeared to be raised in Germany and transferred without undue friction. Success, however, was apparent rather than real. For the sums, paid over to the European victors as reparations, were largely transferred by them to the U.S.A. as loan repayments and interest, and found their way back into Germany in the form of American investments. Germany exchanged her obligations under the Peace treaty for obligations to American investors. The sums so transferred are exceedingly difficult to estimate and include German payments in kind which have been given widely different values. However, most observers agree that as long as reparation lasted, Germany made no net payments whatever, and indeed received more American capital than she paid out in reparations (4/16b). Foreign capital was used with great care and efficiency to improve and modernize German productive industry (4/17a, b), raising its competitive ability compared with that of other European countries.

When the financial crisis of 1929 brought this circular flow of payments to a halt; another plan, the 'Young plan' (4/13) reduced German annual payments, and for the first time set a total ultimate ceiling on reparations. The cuts were insufficient, and the reparation obligations contributed their share to the general deflation, trade restriction and rising tide of unemployment which engulfed the Western world in the following years. In June 1931, President Hoover, in his 'moratorium' (4/14) waived payment on the Allies' loans for a year, and thereby permitted the Allies, in turn, to forgo German reparations for a year and even to consider extending further aid to Germany

(4/15). As the crisis deepened, it became clear that payments would not be resumed. The Lausanne Conference of 1932 attempted to maintain the fiction of continuing payments by asking Germany, in effect, to pay in post-dated cheques (4/16a, b), but Germany's default was made absolute and permanent by the Hitler Government which took office early in 1933.

It is arguable that given a long period of world economic prosperity and stability, and occasional downward revisions of the German obligations as happened in the 1920s, the world trading and payments system might have absorbed German reparations without ill-effects. In practice, no such breathing space was granted to the European economy. Following the stock exchange crash in New York towards the end of 1929, the world was plunged into a massive and worsening depression.

The crisis of 1929 and the depression which followed had many of the characteristics of the trade cycles made familiar in the nineteenth century. But the depression of the early 1930s was much more severe in extent, and much more destructive in its consequences, than any known before. There were several reasons for this. One was the maladjustments surviving from the war and the peace settlements, which had caused substantial unemployment in such countries as Great Britain and Germany (4/18), even in relatively prosperous years. A second reason was that the depression came in the midst of a long-term shift in the terms of trade between food and raw materials on the one hand and manufacturers on the other, a shift in favour of the latter which left agriculturalists in Europe and the colonial trading partners overseas increasingly badly off. As they were progressively less able to buy the output of the European export industries, the loss of trade and the unemployment in the manufacturing districts of Europe were accelerated and created the characteristic profile of the Great Depression of the 1930s, grinding poverty in the primary industries and unemployment in the secondary industries.

It was, perhaps, ironic that the technical successes of European agriculture after the war, coupled with the inelastic nature of its market, contributed greatly to its adversity. In Germany, as in several other countries, farmers had, as always, profited by the war, and for a time did exceedingly well in the inflation, as well as by the stabilization, at the expense of townspeople. Ultimately, however, German agriculture suffered by the resulting instability and indebtness (4/19, 4/20, see also 4/4, 4/5, 4/6, 4/7). It is clear that much of the German propaganda on this score tended (as the British and the French had done in similar situations) to make the most of its case by concentrating on the one relatively small – if very articulate – sector which was doing particularly badly, the Junker estate, while omitting to put in the balance on the other side the windfall profits of the war and post-war years, the rising subsidies (4/21) and the tax and tariff concessions. Nevertheless, the Prussian

squirearchy considered that it had a grievance and played its part in the sub-
version of the Weimar Republic and the victory of the Nazi Party for that
reason. There is no doubt that the slump hit many other sectors of European
agriculture with equal severity (4/22, also 4/28).

A third cause of the severity of the depression was that there was a
financial and credit crisis superimposed on it, which had at least in part an
exogenous origin in the reparations arrangements. Since Germany's reparations had been financed entirely by foreign lending which had, indeed,
been responsible for much of the heavy German home investment too, her
foreign balance of payments and her home investment were bound to be
thrown into complete confusion when American lending stopped abruptly
(4/16b, 4/23, 4/26). The strain on the German financial system was aggravated
by the fact that much of the borrowing had been short-term, but had been
used for acquiring long-term assets (4/17a, b, 4/24). The accessibility of
foreign capital together with the genuine need for large public investment in
post-war Germany had encouraged substantial Government deficits, so that
the German national debt, wiped out by the inflation, stood again at a
respectable level by 1929 when it was, paradoxically, further increased by the
opposite economic conditions which created a substantial tax shortfall at the
same time as relief payments made heavy new demands on the budget. The
early period of the depression was accordingly marked by a large budget
deficit (4/25a), but when the serious foreign drain set in 1930 and particularly
1931, the Bruning Government, in an honest attempt to preserve Germany's
integrity while preventing another inflation, had resort to severe deflationary
measures (4/25b, 4/26). It was the correct policy from the point of view of
orthodox finance, but it laid the Government open to the accusation of
having engineered heavy unemployment in the interest of Germany's former
enemies and their unjust Versailles exactions – an argument used to great effect
by the rising Nazi Party. Some of these sentiments may be found in the statement by Papen, the conservative Chancellor who ultimately made way for
Hitler, in his address to the Lausanne Conference in the summer of 1932 (4/27).

The depression showed itself in a fall of prices and of profits (4/28), but
above all in massive unemployment and the resulting downward demand
multiplier. German unemployment, already of formidable proportions in the
good years, was among the worst in Europe, and affected not only the working classes (4/29a, b, d) but also, very significantly from the political point of
view, the lower middle classes (4/29c). From Austria, details of the diets of
families in an industrial village in which the only mill closed down (4/30)
show the levels to which relatively advanced countries could sink in the
slump.* Holland offers the example of a country that was less severely hit

* For famine conditions under different circumstances, see Document 7/18. (Ed.)

than the average, partly because she could, like Britain, substitute a relatively stable home market for falling export demand (4/31). But it was France, above all, which escaped the worst of the slump of 1929–1931 – again largely because of a buoyant home market (4/32a) and an earlier devaluation of the franc, making deflation unnecessary – only to be hit by depression, after the devaluation of the pound (1931) and the dollar (1933). The worst years were 1934–1936 when the rest of Europe showed a modest recovery (4/32b, c, e), but the experience of tourism (4/32f) shows graphically that no country could isolate itself totally from the depression of its neighbours. As elsewhere, the actual extent of unemployment was understated by statistics which omitted the heavy incidence of those partially out of work (4/32d, e).

The growing complexity of business organizations and their international financial links, and the growing intervention by governments in the credit mechanism and in economic affairs in general, permitted a certain type of financier to flourish in post-war Europe. Some of these men merely took unwarrantable risks with other people's money, whilst others were downright fraudulent. Among the more notorious swindlers brought down in the crisis were Ivar Kreuger (4/33) and Alexandre Stavisky (4/34). Their crash showed the extent to which hitherto respected figures in government and high finance had been involved in profiteering and in large-scale frauds. Reported in mass-circulation newspapers, read by millions who were starving on the dole, or who felt insecure in their jobs in the slump despite a lifetime of honest hard work, such *affaires* contributed to the general disillusionment with the organization of Western society.

4/1 Causes of the Inflation in Germany

a *Germany's Economy, Currency and Finance.* A Study addressed by order of the German Government to the Committees of Experts, as appointed by the Reparations Commission (Berlin, 1924), pp. 54–55.

b Minutes of the Conference of Financial Experts held in Brussels, 16–22 December 1920, meeting on the afternoon of 16 December. Printed in MICHAELIS and SCHRAEPLER, *Ursachen und Folgen* [see Document 1/3], vol. IV, pp. 303–304. (Ed. Tr.)

a The gold mark, according to the dollar status maintained since 20 November 1923, is worth no less than 1 billion paper marks. The value of German money has therefore decreased to an extent hitherto unknown in the history of the currencies of any country....

The causes for the devaluation of German currency and also its disastrous effects have been repeatedly treated in memoranda and other treatises published by the German Government. ... Their report attributes the devaluation of

Germany's currency to a number of causes seen chiefly in the deterioration of the country's financial status and balance of payment. These two stand in close reciprocal relation to one another. The balance of payment was influenced by the unfortunate result of the war and the financial burdens and difficulties consequently accruing to Germany. On the other hand the expenses and revenues of the Central Government are determined by the movement of the exchange rates due to the character of the balance of payment.

The most important factor in the German balance of payment is the trade balance, which was adverse even before the war, when Germany was in full possession of her industrial forces. It became more unfavourable in consequence of war and post-war conditions, since imports were still further increased and exports reduced. We have only to call to mind the loss of important territories producing foodstuffs and raw materials, the limitations imposed on German foreign trade by the Treaty of Versailles, the protectionist measures adopted by foreign countries, the various deliveries in kind which Germany has to make without receiving consideration, the faulty and hampered frontier control, the exhaustion of the soil, the harassment and overstrain of the population, the wear and tear on plant and installation and the further decline in the total output caused by the general political situation at home and abroad.

With regard to the remaining factors of the balance of payment, Germany before the war, in her income from maritime freights, from foreign securities and other property invested abroad, from international bank transactions, etc. was in possession of large assets as an off-set to the liabilities in her trade balance, and of a considerable surplus with which to further a constant increase in her national wealth. Not only have these compensatory factors partly or entirely disappeared, but the position for Germany as regards invisible items has largely been reversed. To this must be added new permanent or temporary debit items, including payments resulting from the Armistice and the Versailles Treaty; subsidies for the maintenance of the occupying forces and Control Commissions; payments made under the Clearing Procedure and in compliance with the Recovery Act; the payment of interest on and the discharge of German debts to foreign countries. The flight of capital which, in spite of strict control and legal measures, has been effectuated in various ways, has materially contributed to depress the price of the mark.

The deterioration of the balance of payment necessarily led to increasing devaluation of the currency....

In the vicious circle referred to above, the depreciation of the currency aggravates the state* of the country's Budget, while the progressive deficit in

* Original has: 'status'. (Ed.)

the Budget contributes to the deterioration of the currency, as in order to meet the deficit, it becomes necessary to resort again and again to the printing of notes. By taxing to the limit* the deficit in the Budget could not be expunged, the rapid devaluation of the mark making it unfeasible to adapt expenditure to revenue or revenue to expenditure. As the condition of the currency, however, prohibited the Treasury from negotiating loans either at home or abroad, the Government had no choice but to pursue the same path as that followed by other States in a similar situation – they had in fact to resort to the creation of fictitious capital and were thus enabled to obtain the necessary credits and currency from the Central Institution. ... The above has once more demonstrated that it was the occupation of the Ruhr territory, etc., that gave to the movement its catastrophic character. ...

b In this session, Dr Haverstein, President of the Reichsbank, gave a detailed account of the state of the German monetary system and of the German exchange rate.

He described the effects of the progressive increase in the floating debt on the purchasing power of money according to the state of the exchange rate. A further fall of the exchange rate would equalize the purchasing power of our money at home with its purchasing power in the world market. This would lead to the danger of a further decline. Russia, Austria and Poland were the signposts on the downward path, and Austria was in this respect only one and a half years ahead of Germany. Halting the printing press was, as the international financial conference in Brussels had recognized, the first precondition of an improvement. But meanwhile the constant increase in the floating debt was the barometer used abroad, operating as a constant pressure, and it was above all the German balance of payments, which had become adverse in the highest degree having become identical with the peacetime import excess of 700 million marks, owing to the losses of all the support points of foreign trade and of the merchant marine, as well as the confiscation of German property abroad. The trade figures of the months of January to June 1920 show, contrary to the hitherto inadequate trading statistics which had been put before the international financial conference in Brussels some weeks ago, an adverse balance against Germany of no less than 37 milliard marks as of 1 July of this year, which was presumably likely to increase at the rate of a further 6 milliard a month in the following months, and even in the first half of 1920 we ought to have put the total indebtedness of Germany abroad at more than 50 milliard. The German mark had become extremely sensitive on the world market. In May the dollar rate was 33 M, in July it was 42, now it is 75 (on 12 November it had even reached 87 M). This

* Original has: 'completely exploiting taxation'. (Ed.)

depreciation of the mark was largely due to the fact that since August the bad harvest requiring imports of food and meat, and at the same time the paying off of the negative clearing balance, all needed large and growing quantities of means of payment. Moreover, the falling exchange rate served to encourage exports artificially and made Germany subject to the unjust accusation of dumping. But the saddest and most serious consequence was that imports of necessary foodstuffs and raw materials had had to be restricted. It might well come about that imports into Germany could be obtained only by barter. But that would seal the economic fate of Germany.

4/2 The Course of the Inflation

a F. S. NITTI, *The Decadence of Europe. The Paths of Reconstruction* (London, 1923), pp. 207–10.

b Presidential Address of Viscount D'Abernon to the Royal Statistical Society, 16 November 1926, *Journal of the Royal Statistical Society*, XC (1927), pp. 8–10.

c PETER P. REINHOLD, *The Economic, Financial and Political State of Germany since the War* (New Haven, 1928), pp. 21–22, 52–53.

d Diary entry for 20 August 1923, VISCOUNT D'ABERNON, *An Ambassador of Peace. Pages from the Diary of Viscount D'Abernon* (3 vols, 1929–30), vol. II, pp. 256–257.

e MORITZ JULIUS BONN, *Wandering Scholar* (John Day Company, 1948), reprinted in F. K. RINGER, *The German Inflation of 1923* (London, 1969), pp. 100–103.

a The example of Austria alone is sufficient to show how absurd, ludicrous, and immoral the fundamental conception of the treaties is. Austria, in her present confines, has to live on her own resources; but she is surrounded by hostile States, her capacity for making purchases is limited, and there are high customs barriers against her. In order to live, therefore, she must necessarily import more than she exports. . . . The imports are composed almost entirely of those articles which are most indispensable to human life. The Austrian balance had to sink of necessity under the weight of the treaties. In the financial year 1919–1920 an income of 6·2 milliard crowns was budgeted for, and an expenditure of 16·8 milliards. The situation was one of extreme gravity, and one which ought to have been relieved – and perhaps there was still time – by a reduction of the circulation, by foreign loans, and by great economies. On the contrary, Austria has been compelled to pay all her public debts by new issues of paper money; yet every new issue has raised prices still higher, and has made economy still more imperative. In the year 1920–1921 the expenditure was 70·6 milliards, and the income 29·4 milliards. The budget of 1921–1922 provided for an expenditure of 347·5 milliards, and an income of 209·7 milliards. . . . In June 1919 the dollar was worth 33 crowns;

at the end of the same year, after the treaties had been published, it was worth 155 crowns. In April 1920, after the dissolution of the former Empire into its several States, the dollar was worth 200 crowns; at the end of the year it was worth 603 crowns. In 1921, as the result of fresh issues, the rate of exchange reached bewildering figures. In August the dollar was worth 1,127 crowns; in December, 5,340 crowns. In 1922 the rate of exchange fell to 7,500 crowns in January, and to 30,025 crowns by the middle of July.

Prices naturally increased in proportion to the depression of the currency. The continual increases in wages and salaries only made the situation worse. Prices are now more than 5,000 times higher than before the war. Salaries have risen a thousand-fold or two thousand-fold, which means that the standard of life has been reduced by three-fifths or four-fifths. . . . Comparing pre-war prices – the average prices in 1913–1914 – with prices in the middle of August 1922, one finds that the price of cow-beef has risen from 2·27 crowns to 18,000 crowns per kilogramme; pork from 2·12 to 22,000 crowns; bread from ·22 to 4,688 crowns; potatoes from 0·2 to 1,800 crowns; flour from 0·37 to 6,000 crowns; corn from 2·13 to 30,000 crowns; milk from 0·29 to 2,400 crowns per litre; and eggs from 0·7 to 800 crowns each. In order to buy a suit of clothes, one must spend a million and a half crowns. An overcoat costs a million crowns; a pair of boots, 100,000 crowns; a hat, or a shirt, about 50,000 crowns.

b   TABLE OF REICHSBANK NOTES ISSUED AND
             EQUIVALENT STERLING VALUES

Date	Reichsbank notes in circulation	Rate of exchange of day	Equivalent sterling value of notes in circulation
	(Milliards of paper marks)	(Marks for £)	(£ millions)
31 Dec. 1919	35·7	184·8	193·2
31 Dec. 1920	68·8	258·0	255·5
31 Dec. 1921	113·6	771·0	147·3
31 Dec. 1922	1,280·1	34,000·0	34·4
31 Jan. 1923	1,984·5	227,500·0	8·7
28 Feb. 1923	3,512·8	106,750·0	33·0
29 March 1923	5,517·9	98,500·0	56·0
31 May, 1923	8,563·7	320,000·0	26·8
30 June 1923	17,291·1	710,000·0	24·3
7 July 1923	20,341·8	800,000·0	25·4

Date	Reichsbank notes in circulation	Rate of exchange of day	Equivalent sterling value of notes in circulation
	(Milliards of paper marks)	(Marks for £)	
14 July 1923	25,491·7	900,000·0	28·3
23 July 1923	31,824·8	1,600,000·0	20·0
31 July 1923	43,594·7	5,000,000·0	8·7
7 Aug. 1923	62,326·7	15,000,000·0	4·1
15 Aug. 1923	116,402·5	12,400,000·0	8·9
23 Aug. 1923	273,905·4	23,000,000·0	11·9
15 Sept. 1923	3,183,681·2	410,000,000·0	7·8
15 Oct. 1923	123,349,786·7	18,500,000,000·0	6·8
15 Nov. 1923	92,844,720,743·0	11,000,000,000,000·0	8·4
20 Nov. 1923	180,000,000,000·0 (approx.)	18,000,000,000,000·0	10·0

Month	Paper marks in Circulation (in milliards of marks	Day	Course of the Dollar
1913 (av)	2·4	3. I. 1919	8·02
1920 (av)	67·7	3. I. 1920	49·10
1921 (av)	90·4	3. I. 1921	74·50
Jan. 1922	123·9	3. I. 1922	188
July 1922	202·6	I. 7. 1922	402
Dec. 1922	1,295·2	21. 12. 1922	6,750
Jan. 1923	1,999·6	3. I. 1923	7,525
May 1923	8,609·7	I. 5. 1923	31,700
June 1923	17,350·4	I. 6. 1923	74,750
July 1923	43,813·5	I. 7. 1923	160,400
Aug. 1923	668,702·6	I. 8. 1923	1,102,750
Sept. 1923	28,244,405·8	I. 9. 1923	9,724,250
Oct. 1923	2,504,955,717·6	I. 10. 1923	242,000,000
		21. 10. 1923	40,100,000,000
Nov. 1923	400,338,326,370·5	I. 11. 1923	130,225,000,000
		11. 11. 1923	631,575,000,000
		21. 11. 1923	4,210,500,000,000
Dec. 1923	496,585,345,854·8	21. 12. 1923	4,210,500,000,000

c   I would like to explain how rapid the pace of the drop in the mark was by reference to one fact, namely, that even the printing presses were unable to keep pace with the demand for notes, the whole paper-money system being thereby rendered an absurdity. Can there be any more striking proof of the cumulative ridiculousness involved in this printing of worthless paper with senseless figures than the fact that, at that time, all over Germany people were printing their own money – the so-called 'emergency money' – and that over three hundred paper mills were working at the highest pressure to produce paper for the notes of the Reichsbank alone, and further that in one hundred and fifty printing works, approximately two thousand presses were running day and night to print those notes, that is, as people then believed, to convert the paper into money?

It is only natural that this nonsensical process sucked all purchasing power out of the mark. The most terrible thing occurred that can happen to a civilized State, namely, its legal tender ceased to be recognized by its own nationals; the repudiation of the mark began; only those who have experienced it, can appreciate what that means. It means that the agricultural districts refuse to furnish the towns and cities with food supplies, that the retail shops decline to part with their goods against payment in the national currency, that no standard can be found to decide the amount of wages, that those 'living on their means' have ceased to have any means, that they are reduced to the bitterest penury and unable to purchase a morsel of food to stay their hunger.

Once more hunger riots broke out, and, in September, a state of siege had to be declared. . . .

The fact that certain groups of German speculators and whole economic groups – particularly new commercial firms, which had risen during the inflation period, some of which, fortunately for Germany, later disappeared without a trace – were interested in the fall of the mark and contributed to it by their activities, can and should not be denied. . . .

In the year 1923, in spite of the extraordinarily high tax rates prevailing at that time, the needs of public financing were met only to a small degree by taxes and assessments; by far the leading source of income was supplied by the printing press (in the last months more than 90 per cent), so that at the establishment of the Rentenmark, the Government finally owed the Reichsbank the fabulous amount of 189·8 quintillion marks. In order to make clear the fantastic absurdity of this inflation figure, I should like to point out that, were I to write the amount according to the decimal system, I would have to attach eighteen zeros to the 189. To make a comparison, were one to take old German thousand mark bills and put one upon the other, pressing them tightly together, one would have a pillar of such inconceivable height, as to be twenty-five billion times the highest mountain on earth. I cite this example, in order to show to what absurd heights inflation had reached in Germany when the Government decided to put an end to it at one stroke, by stopping the printing of bank notes and by balancing the budget of the Reich.

How was the German Government to survive the transition period, without the possibility of a foreign loan, until the new taxes fixed in gold were received by the Treasury of the Reich?

d The majority of people here, including those at the head of affairs, do not see the financial abyss into which they are falling. . . . It is hardly an exaggeration to say that those responsible for the financial policy of the country are committing suicide in order to avoid the payment of reparation. . . . In England and America it is a commonplace to assert that, the more paper-money is issued, the less the value of each unit of paper-money will be. . . . But here, this commonplace is denied both in word and in practice. A flagrant example has just occurred. Havenstein, the Director of the Reichsbank, stated openly on Friday that the Reichsbank was then printing at the rate of 20 billion of marks per day, the total amount in circulation being 63 billion marks; but he declared with satisfaction that in the next week the Reichsbank would be able to print 46 billion of new paper-money per day. Forty-six billion marks represent a face value of £2,300,000,000,000, and the note circulation £3,150,000,000,000. Havenstein made this declaration before a Council of State, which is supposed to contain financial and economic experts, yet none criticized the policy stated or referred to its insanity. The speech was largely reproduced in the German Press, and provoked neither outcry nor astonishment.

It appears almost impossible to hope for the recovery of a country where such things are possible. It is certainly vain to hope for it unless power is taken entirely away from the lunatics at present in charge, and put into the hands either of foreign experts or of some body with sober and sensible ideas.*

e Shopkeepers were never sure of covering the cost of replenishing their stocks, irrespective of the prices at which they sold the goods; many goods had completely disappeared. Factories were no longer interested in selling to the home market against money, the value of which was rapidly vanishing. Foreign goods were scarcely obtainable. Manufacturers were permitted to acquire foreign exchange in order to buy raw material abroad for keeping their plants and their workers employed; mere consumers were disregarded.

* The remedy came three months later through the Rentenmark, the death of Havenstein and the appointment of Schacht as President of the Reichsbank. Schacht was a man of immense energy and sound views. (Footnote in D'Abernon.)

Shopkeepers treated their customers almost as enemies – they deprived them of stock which could not be replaced. . . .

One day the village authorities approached my wife. A truck of potatoes, the village winter supply, had arrived at the local station. Since ordering the load, prices had risen so rapidly in paper marks that the village had not enough cash to pay for it. Would she lend them a couple of pounds or so and ensure the potatoes' being unloaded? . . .

. . . Big industrial concerns made their own money to pay wages with it; it was accepted by the local business community. Municipalities printed notes, which circulated freely within their confines but were not valid in neighbouring areas. Emergency money to the amount of 200 billion paper marks was in circulation. In July 1923 the cost of living index had risen 39,000 times. An unskilled metal worker, whose weekly wages before the war (1912) had been 24·44 marks (6 dollars) was getting only 73 per cent of his former income's purchasing power: his weekly wage amounted to 531 million marks in September 1923.

Workers were not the chief sufferers. Thanks to strong trade unions, their wages were regularly revised upward, though generally with a lag. In the earlier stages, before the Ruhr invasion,* unemployment was low, as it always is during the inflation upswing. For this reason labour had not strongly insisted upon stabilization. Accounting was becoming a nightmare. . . . Wages were adjusted at least twice a week according to dollar quotations; so were salaries of civil servants. Most of them asked for cash and rushed immediately to the shops to buy such goods as were available. A few hours later the mark might have gone down another 100 per cent, and the purchasing power of their salaries might have been halved. Those who had spare cash or credit gambled in stocks. As shares were supposed to represent stable physical values of a tangible nature, such as factories or stock piles, their quotations followed, and sometimes even outran, prices. A good many members of the middle class made a precarious living by gambling on the exchange. . . .

. . . But for the housing shortage, a large part of the smaller 'idle rich' would have gone to the wall completely. The value of their investments, insurances, and life annuities had been wiped out; apartments and furniture were often enough the only wealth which remained to them. They generally lived by subletting, payment to house owners being purely nominal. . . .

. . . The so-called *rentiers* were almost wiped out – though they got a pitiful compensation later on. By 1925 their real income had fallen from over 2 billion dollars (in 1913) to 300 million. They were not the victims of socialism, for the working class, too, had lost heavily, since their savings and their social

* By the French in 1923, when Germany was unable to meet the reparation demands. (Ed.)

insurance contributions had vanished (the reserves of the social insurance institutions had been invested in government bonds and mortgages). Their destroyers were the producers, the active businessmen. They had successfully expropriated investors; they had secured additional 'tangible values' (they called them values of substance), such as land, houses, stock piles, shares, by systematically making new debts, which they paid back in rapidly deteriorating marks. Many of the huge combinations they had assembled disintegrated rapidly when the Reichsbank, under its new leadership, refused them the credits with which they had been in the habit of exploiting their fellow capitalists.

When it was all over, the social structure of Germany had been profoundly altered. The steady middle class, closely connected, though not identical, with the professions, was proletarianized at a time when the rising working class ceased to consider itself proletarian and was ready for incorporation with the middle class. It was a genuine revolution, far more devastating than the political collapse in the autumn of 1918 had been.

4/3 The Reichsbank and Inflation

Speech by Havenstein, President of the Reichsbank, to the Central Executive Meeting of the Reichsbank 25 August 1923. Printed in MICHAELIS and SCHRAEPLER, *Ursachen und Folgen* [*see* Document 1/3], vol. V, pp. 543–545. (Ed. Tr.)

It is said that the Reichsbank is, at least in part, responsible for the derangement of the currency and the ever-growing inflation. We are unanimously convinced that these accusations are unjustified and that, if we did find ourselves in opposition to certain proposals, this was inevitably so because they were impracticable and could not have been tolerated by the State, the Reichsbank and the economy.

It is the granting of credit by the Reichsbank which is alleged to have been a major cause of the inflation, and the large and rapidly growing holdings of bills by the Reichsbank are pointed to in proof. It is true that these holdings have now risen to 49 million RM, but they consist to the extent of about $\frac{1}{4}$ of cheques and very short-term bills which do not represent a source of credit to the Reichsbank, but a cash item. The remaining bills represent, at the time of their discounting, little more than 100 million pre-war RM compared with a pre-war portfolio of *c*. one milliard. There is no doubt that the granting of credit by a note-issuing bank increases the paper money circulation; but as long as it grants credits which are economically justified and necessary, and which serve production and trade, the bank does not create any new artificial purchasing power. The important thing is to keep bills that have no economic justification away from the Reichsbank. The Reichsbank has hitherto made the most serious efforts to achieve that aim by most exacting scrutiny and by a policy of restriction.

As sources of inflation these Reichsbank credits are insignificant compared with the basic cause of our inflation. This basic cause, inasmuch as it does not rest on the balance of payments ... is the unrestrained growth of the floating debt and its transformation into currency and giro deposits by the discounting of Government bills at the Reichsbank. The causes of this growth, in turn, are well known: the vast reparations burdens on the one hand, and the lack of sufficient sources of revenue for the ordinary budget on the other hand.

Here, too, the Reichsbank is alleged to bear some guilt, since it did not stand up to the Government and the financial authorities and did not refuse to discount the bills of the Government. But this accusation, too, is unjustified and totally misunderstands the position. The Reichsbank has done all it could do with any hope of success. It has pointed out the situation for years, both before and after it became autonomous,* and has demanded redress most earnestly and most urgently, but it was not in a position to stop discounting Government bills as long as the Government had no other possible way of covering the shortfall in its budget, and as long as the compelling conviction that such a way must be found at all costs had not penetrated all the legislative agencies. For the Government must go on, and a real refusal to discount anything relating to the budgetary provisions, which necessarily are the responsibility of the financial administration, would have created chaos. On the other hand, to have merely threatened to refuse to discount Government bills in general would have been a fruitless gesture. It was only in the most recent period when, under the pressure of inescapable necessity, all legislative agencies were permeated by the conviction and agreed in principle that at all costs the budget policy must be founded on adequate revenue, that the Reichsbank has again had the possiblity of considering the reoccupation of its former position as a purely central note issuing bank, and actually to begin to move in that direction. But it must be obvious to us that in view of the huge tasks still facing the Government and the financial authorities, this solution will take some time and that we must meanwhile envisage a further exceptional swelling of the floating debt and the flood of paper. ....

Naturally the quite exceptional depreciation of the mark has caused an enormous rise in the demand for means of payment, which at times the Reichsbank could not fully meet. Now a simplified production of notes of large denomination has made it possible for us to bring ever-larger sums into circulation. These gigantic sums are only just sufficient to meet the vastly increased demand for means of payment which has lately reached

* In 1922. See Document 4/8. (Ed.)

fantastic heights, particularly because of the extraordinary rises in salaries and wages.

The organization of this note-printing enterprise which has grown monstrously makes demands on our staff beyond all measure. Because of the rush, cash must be sent out by private means of transport. There are numerous consignments of money *en route* daily from Berlin to the provinces. A whole series of banks have to be supplied by aeroplane since there are no train connections for early postal deliveries.

4/4 Social Consequences of the Inflation

a Viscount D'ABERNON, *An Ambassador of Peace* [*see* Document 4/2d], vol. II, pp. 265–266.

b Statistisches Reichsamt, *Germany's Economic and Financial Situation. An Exhibit of After-Effects of the World War* (Berlin, 1923), pp. 30–32.

c ALFRED WEBER, 'The Distress of the Intellectuals', printed in RINGER, *German Inflation* [*see* Document 4/2e], pp. 110–111.

a BERLIN, *7 September 1923.* The position is certainly critical. What precisely will occur one cannot tell, but with the mark at 250,000,000 to the £ sterling it is difficult for the most docile and orderly population not to break out. There are considerable queues in the streets here before food-shops, out-of-work prevails, especially in Saxony. The new government have completely failed in their financial policy as far as exchange is concerned. I do not think they have taken the right measures, and such measures as they have taken or have intended to take have not been carried through with adequate decision. As an instance of weakness, there is the dismissal of Havenstein* – they have been a fortnight over it, whereas to produce the desired effect a dramatic change was absolutely necessary.

b The greater part of the population has been forced down far below their old standard of living, even with regard to the most important necessities of life.

Consequently the foreigner, for example, who has visited Germany since the war, would do well to ask himself whether, in the overcrowded first-class railway carriages, he has found many Germans, or whether in the best seats at the theatre Germans are in the majority. He would do well to inquire whether in fashionable places of entertainment the German or the foreign public predominates, and if he does see Germans present spending their money for light entertainment, let him consider whether these are the majority of the

* President of the Reichsbank. See Document 4/3. (Ed.)

German people. He must not forget either that many people today are influenced by the psychological fact that saving is no longer of any use: 100 marks today will perhaps be only 50 marks tomorrow. He who before the war, for example, had saved 5,500 marks could purchase for that amount furniture for a middle-class flat of three rooms as well as clothing, for a married couple with two children. In the middle of February 1923 (with an average dollar rate of 27,819 for February) the same person, for the same articles, would have had to spend 26·3 million marks in paper money. The man who did not spend the 5,500 marks, but preferred to save it together with the interest thereon might have over 7,000 marks today, with which, however, he cannot even buy a shirt! Who would care to 'save' under such conditions? Does the stranger realize, moreover, that such violent changes in the valuation of German money have meant for many thousands of German savers the annihilation of their savings? Does the stranger see the formerly well-to-do men and women of the middle class who today with a heavy heart carry their old family jewellery to the dealer, in order to prolong their physical existence a little longer? He who before the war could spend the interest on 1 million marks was a rich man, even up to 1919 he could still live upon it with reasonable comfort; today he is poor, for with his 50,000 marks interest he can today barely provide his own person with the necessities of life for a week! Does the stranger see the women and girls from the higher circles, even up to the highest, who are compelled to take up some occupation or who help to eke out the family income by working in their homes for a miserable wage? Does the stranger see the 1½ millions of war cripples, who are struggling desperately to earn their living, because the pensions that the State can afford to pay them are utterly inadequate? . . .

The income from capital has decreased in a still greater measure than that derived from work. . . . The income from pure capital has shrunk almost to nothing. While in time of peace the German middle class derived a considerable income from capital invested in bonds, this income has decreased in exactly the same proportion as the money has gone down in value. If towards the end of December 1922 the cost of living has risen to a multiple of 685, this means that also the interest on bonds has decreased to 1½ per thousand of its buying capacity. In a truly terrible plight are all those whose incomes consist of interest-money in marks, the people of small private fortunes who through old age or incapacity for work are unable to increase their income in any way. These people are actually not in a position to provide for the most elementary necessities of life. And the means provided by mutual arrangement between the national government, the individual states and the local communities for relieving the distress of these *Kleinrentners* have had to be cut down so closely in consequence of the financial position of the Empire that, with an aggregate of 400,000 of such *Kleinrentners* a sum of some 12,000 paper-marks per head, including the appropriations made to homes and institutions on their behalf, is all that is available per annum. As the majority of them had an annual income of less than 5,000 marks, a yearly income of 17,000 paper-marks including the relief funds mentioned or of 25 gold-marks would have to be accepted as the average.

Similar is the distress of invalidity and old-age pensioners under the Invalidity Insurance Acts as well as of the widows and orphans of the insured. . . . In the case of the war-invalids and the families of the war-victims, it was likewise not possible to raise the pensions in proportion to the continuous rise in prices.

c 1. The *de facto* income of higher officials:
According to the salary regulation effective 1 April 1922, the average yearly salary (after tax deductions) for a married official with two children is:

in group X.	Councillors of State	65,026 marks
in group XI.	Councillors of State	70,228 marks
in group XII.	Chief Councillors of State	81,085 marks
in group XIII.	Ministerial Councillors	96,745 marks
in group B3.	Ministerial Directors	131,780 marks

Given a thirty-fold increase of living costs (a rate of increase which has in reality been far superseded even now), this income in paper marks is equivalent to a real income (peace-time income):

in group X.	of	2,168 marks
in group XI.	of	2,341 marks
in group XII.	of	2,703 marks
in group XIII.	of	3,225 marks
in group B3.	of	4,393 marks

In 1913, the corresponding average yearly income was:

in group X.	6,108 marks
in group XI.	6,916 marks
in group XII.	7,736 marks
in group XIII.	10,960 marks
in group B3.	16,520 marks

Thus, the higher officials presently earn:

in group X, only 35 per cent of their yearly income [of 1913]
in group XI, only 34 per cent

in group XII, only 35 per cent
in group XIII, only 29 per cent
in group B3, only 27 per cent of their [former *real* income].

For the unmarried official, even greater cuts are involved. His salary in group X is only 31 per cent of his peace-time income, in B3 only 25 per cent of his peace-time income.

Thus, higher officials presently have on the average only a third to a fourth of their pre-war income. In other words, they have had to reduce their living standards by up to 75 per cent. Thus it happens that a Ministerial Councillor, for example, presently does not even earn the salary of an office-assistant or postal clerk before the war. This loss of 65 to 75 per cent of the peace-time income is especially onerous, since, as is well-known, the higher officials were poorly paid even before the war. Add to this the fact that the higher officials are less able today than formerly to rely upon income from their own capital. The officials had generally invested their money in government bonds with fixed interest rates or in other safe ways. These capital investments have shrunken to nothing as a result of the currency devaluation. . . .

2. The incomes of higher officials as compared with those of other officials and workers:
The income reduction for higher officials is not nearly matched by a similarly pronounced income reduction for other officials and workers in the administration and in government enterprises.

(a) The salary of officials in groups II to IX:
The real income (peace-time income) in:

group II   is 1,347 marks or 82 per cent of peace-time income
group IV   is 1,495 marks or 78 per cent of peace-time income
group VII   is 1,744 marks or 48 per cent of peace-time income
group XI   is 2,012 marks or 43 per cent of peace-time income.

Thus, although the full peace-time income has not been maintained for these groups either, their salary increases do not lag nearly so far behind the increase in living costs as those of the higher officials. . . .

(b) The income of workers in government enterprises:
For workers (married, with two children, in Berlin in government enterprises), yearly wages (after taxes) presently are:

for skilled workers, 40,608 paper marks – real income 1,354 marks
for unskilled workers, 30,474 paper marks – real income 1,282 marks

The peace-time wage for skilled workers was 2,212 marks,
for unskilled workers was 1,349 marks.

Thus, compared with pre-war conditions, the skilled workers presently have 38·8 per cent less, the unskilled workers in government enterprises have 4·9 less [income].

(c) The relative ranking of salaries and wages:
The different developments in the salaries and wages of the several groups of officials and workers have resulted in a levelling tendency which greatly exceeds the bearable and even the objectively permissible. . . . *The higher official, who earned 7 times as much as an unskilled worker in 1913, today earns only twice as much: after tax deductions, as little as 1·8 times as much.*

4/5 Stabilization and the Foundation of the Rentenbank

a *Germany's Economy* [*see* Document 4/1a], pp. 51–52.

b Decree on Rentenbank, R. G. Bl. I, pp. 963–966 (1923), printed in CLOUGH, et al. *Economic History* [*see* Document 1/4a], pp. 127–131.

a   In the course of the second half of 1923, the German currency system had become so disordered as to render the Mark unusable as a means of maintaining value; things came to such a pass that its qualification as a payment medium was further and further lost, while, in trade with foreign countries, it was unsaleable. . . .

A rather sudden turn in the course of events resulted from the introduction of the 'Rentenmark'. The history of the depreciation of the mark shows that all measures taken were condemned to failure as long as the banknotes press was used for Government purposes. By the 'Decree on the Erection of the German Rentenbank' of 15 October 1923, the printing of banknotes for the Government was stopped on the date of issue of the Rentenmark and a plan was realized by which, with the help of German national capital as a whole, an incorporated bank was formed for the purpose of redeeming the debt of the Government towards the 'Reichsbank', to relieve the 'Reichsbank' from the duty of financing the Government's requirements and to issue the necessary stable currency. . . . The issue of the 'Renten' banknotes was commenced in 15 November 1923, and since 20 November the dollar exchange rate has been maintained at 4·2 billion marks, the even more unfavourable exchange abroad having meantime attained this level.

The institution of the Rentenmark system is to be regarded as provisional only, inasmuch as the stability of its notes is not guaranteed, as is usual, by gold funds, or by foreign bills, which could not have been provided by German industry and commerce in sufficient quantity. Goods, such as rye, potash, coal, etc., could not possibly be used as covering, as such a procedure would have led to indispensable goods being withdrawn from trade. . . .

A way out of the difficulty was found in the introduction of a payment medium guaranteed by a mortgage on land and by mortgages on German agriculture, industry and commerce, inclusive of the transport* and banking trades. Every guarantor, compulsory or otherwise, becomes a shareholder in the bank.

It is not the State or the property of the State which forms the base of the 'Rentenmark', but an incorporated bank, in whose favour German private property in its entirety is mortgaged, this bank being responsible for the issue of the 'Renten' mark notes. The mortgage is not a general one, but forms a mortgage on the property of every shareholder in the 'Rentenbank'. On every piece of landed property a mortgage is formed, which is registered upon application by the bank. The liabilities of trade and industry, as far as in their case, mortgages on land are impossible, are embodied in bonds. On the mortgages and bonds, the landed proprietors and/or the bond-issuers have to pay an annuity of 6 per cent. The capital value and the annuity are calculated in gold marks, and are, therefore, not dependent upon the exchange rate of the 'Rentenmark' notes. The same is the case with the payment of the interest on the 'Renten' certificates, which form the connecting link between the mortgages and bonds on the one side and the 'Renten' notes on the other.

An important help towards guaranteeing the stability of the 'Rentenmark' forms the obligation of the German 'Rentenbank' to redeem with 'Renten' certificates, the 'Renten' banknotes which it has issued, a 'Renten' certificate for 500 gold marks (bearing interest from the next following maturity date) being given for 500 'Renten' marks. This forms a prevention against a depreciation of the 'Rentenmark', which is best prevented by keeping the amount of marks issued within the limits of the demand of industry and commerce. . . .

The total floating debt of the Reich towards the Reichsbank to an amount of about 191 trillion† paper marks has meanwhile been discharged, for the greater part at the rate of one 'Rentenmark' for 1 billion paper marks.

b On the basis of the Enabling Act of 13 October 1923, the Government decrees:

1. The German Rentenbank shall be established by representatives of agriculture, and of industry, business, and commerce, including the banks. The Rentenbank shall have its seat in Berlin. In civil law it shall have the attributes of a juridical person.

2. The capital and reserve of the Rentenbank shall amount to 3·2 billion

---

* Original has 'forwarding'. (Ed.)
† Trillion in the sense of a million billion. (Footnote in original.)

Rentenmarks, the sum to be subscribed in equal parts by agriculture (paragraph 6) on the one hand, and by industry, business, and commerce, including banks (paragraph 9) on the other. In order to strengthen the resources of the Rentenbank, any properties covered neither by paragraph 6 nor paragraph 9 shall be included by virtue of the appropriate suspension of government economic control.

3. (1) The Charter of the Rentenbank shall be drawn up by the founders. It requires the approval of the government. . . .

4. Unless otherwise specified in this decree or in the Charter, the Rentenbank shall be autonomous in matters of the administration and management of its affairs as well as in the appointment of personnel. The election of the President of the Bank requires the approval of the government. . . .

5. The Rentenbank shall be free from all taxes of the Reich, the States, and the municipalities, upon property or upon income from either real property or business activity. Because the purpose of its establishment is an expansion of capital, the Reich, the states, and the municipalities shall not be permitted to levy any sort of tax or charge on the issue of Renten annuity bonds [*Rentenbriefe*] or on the exchange of Rentenbank notes [*Rentenbankscheine* against such Renten bonds.

6. (1) The Rentenbank shall acquire a mortgage upon all landed property regularly used for agricultural or forestry purposes. This mortgage shall be expressed in gold marks and shall amount to 4 per cent of the value of the property as assessed for the Defence Levy* and on the taxes due from it in accordance with the law of 11 August 1923, on the taxation of enterprises. . . . In so far as it does not conflict with agreements involving other states, the mortgage takes precedence over all other obligations. . . .

(4) The mortgage shall bear interest at 6 per cent annually. The interest from the effective date of this law shall be payable on 1 April and 1 October, beginning 1 April 1924, and shall be due within a week after that date. The Rentenbank shall determine the system of payment.

(5) For the Rentenbank, the capital of the mortgage is non-negotiable. But property owners may redeem [the mortgages] after a period of five years has elapsed.

(6) The interest, section (4), and the capital, section (5), shall be paid in Rentenmarks at their gold value at the time of payment. . . .

(7) The claims arising from the mortgage shall come into legal force immediately upon notice by the Rentenbank. The notice replaces the executable title. At the request of the Rentenbank sequestration must be undertaken by local agricultural banks . . . or, in case these do not exist, by another

* *Wehrbeitragswert*, a 1913 property tax whose proceeds were initially to be devoted to meeting the costs of defence. (Footnote in Clough.)

authority designated by the Government in conjunction with the state government. . . .

9. (1) The industrial, business, and commercial enterprises, including banks, existing at the time this decree comes into force in so far as they are taxed according to the law on the taxation of enterprises of 11 August 1923 . . . shall owe the Rentenbank the same total amount in gold marks as is charged against agricultural land as a whole. This charge shall be apportioned among the individual enterprises according to the determination of the government and shall bear interest. Section (4) of paragraph 6 shall apply.

(2) If the assets of a business include land, the Rentenbank shall acquire a mortgage on that land expressed in gold marks to the amount of 4 per cent of the value as assessed for the Defence Levy, but not above this valuation. In so far as it does not conflict with agreements involving other states, the mortgage takes precedence over all other obligations. The prescriptions of paragraph 6 . . . apply.

(3) In so far as that share of the charge falling to an individual entrepreneur is not met by a mortgage, the entrepreneur must draw up in favour of the Rentenbank a bond expressed in gold marks. The claim arising from the bond takes precedence over all other claims against the assets of the debtor, in so far as agreements involving other states do not exist. If the entrepreneur does not meet his obligation to issue the bond within a period of two weeks after it is demanded, then on the request of the Rentenbank, the government, or a representative designated and empowered to act in its stead, shall make out a bond in favour of the Rentenbank and binding upon the entrepreneur. . . .

12. (1) On the basis of this mortgage and the bonds drawn in its favour, the Rentenbank shall issue Renten annuity bonds [*Rentenbriefe*]. The Renten bonds shall be issued in denominations of 500 gold marks or multiples thereof.

(2) The Renten bonds bear interest at 5 per cent annually, and after five years may be recalled by the Rentenbank, in their entirety or by series, for redemption at face value. They may be recalled earlier only in the case of liquidation.

(3) As to demands against the bonds drawn in favour of the Rentenbank, the claims of holders of Renten bonds take precedence over the claims of all other creditors of the Rentenbank.

(4) If assets of the Rentenbank should diminish, a corresponding amount in Renten bonds shall be cancelled.

13. (1) The Renten bonds serve as security for Rentenbank notes [*Rentenbankscheine*] issued by the Rentenbank.

(2) The unit of value of these Rentenbank notes is the Rentenmark, which is divided into 100 Renten pennies.

14. (1) Special bills in the amount of 500 Rentenmarks may be issued on the basis of one for every Renten bond of 500 gold marks. These shall be designated Rentenbank notes. The total issue may not exceed the capital and reserve.

(2) In so far as the security provided for in section (1) is not available, no Rentenbank notes may be issued.

(3) The Rentenbank notes are to be accepted as legal tender for all public debts; the detailed regulations shall be issued by the Minister of Finance....

15. The Rentenbank shall be obliged, at any time, upon demand, to redeem the Rentenbank notes against its Renten bonds so that there shall be granted for 500 Rentenmarks a Renten bond of 500 gold marks with current interest from the end of the next interest period.

16. (1) The Rentenbank may operate as a bank only in dealings with the Reich, the Reichsbank, and with private banks of issue.

(2) During the next two years it will grant to the Reich credits payable in Rentenmarks and, except as stipulated in paragraph 17, interest-bearing loans up to the total of 1·2 billion Rentenmarks at the fixed interest rate of 6 per cent. The interest is payable on 1 April and 1 October of every year. The Rentenbank is not permitted to stand security for the Reich.

(3) For the purpose of supplying credit to private enterprise, the Rentenbank is further authorized, in accordance with the Charter, to grant to the Reichsbank and the private banks of issue loans up to the amount of 1·2 billion Rentenmarks. The division of this loan among the Reichsbank and the individual private banks of issue shall be made in accordance with the proportion of notes issued by each on 31 July 1914. The limit on the amount of notes that may be issued by the private banks of issue without special authorizing legislation shall be reduced by the actual value in marks of the loan to which they are entitled.

17. (1) As part of the maximum sum stipulated in paragraph 16, section (2), the Rentenbank shall immediately place at the disposal of the Reich an interest-free loan of 300 million Rentenmarks. The Reich will use this sum for the redemption or partial redemption of its discounted Treasury bills from the Reichsbank.

(2) If the sum of 300 million Rentenmarks is not sufficient to redeem entirely the discounted Treasury bills from the Reichsbank, then, at the request of the Reich, in accordance with paragraph 16, section (2), an interest-bearing supplementary loan shall be applied for and granted. The amount of the supplementary loan is to be negotiated between the Reich and the Rentenbank....

19. As soon as the Rentenbank has begun to issue Rentenbank notes, the Reichsbank shall no longer be permitted to discount Treasury bills. Until

redemption has been completed on Treasury bills previously discounted by the Reichsbank on behalf of the Reich, extensions on such Treasury bills are permissible. . . .

4/6 The Effects of Stabilization

a Viscount D'ABERNON, *An Ambassador of Peace* [*see* Document 4/2d], vol. II, p. 302.

b *Germany's Economy* [*see* Document 4/1a], pp. 42–43.

a   BERLIN, 25 December 1923. The most salient characteristic of the new situation is the astonishing appeasement and relief brought about by a touch of the magical wand of 'Currency Stability'. Not even the most fanatical advocate of stabilization – and this title I yield to no one – could have anticipated more remarkable results from its attainment than those which are now manifest. Food has become abundant in the great towns; potatoes and cereals are brought to market in large quantities; while butter, which was obtainable only in the better quarters, is now offered at stable, if at high prices. Animals crowd the abattoirs and queues have disappeared from before the shops of butchers and provision merchants. The economic *détente* has brought in its train political pacification.*

b   Since the end of November, the exchange rate of the mark on foreign markets has been steadied by the adoption of various currency measures, and, in particular, the introduction of the Rentenmark and the change in the credit policy.

Real wages, too, have, in consequence of the stabilization, been gradually raised although their face value is not very much higher. The real wages of a skilled Berlin metal-worker rose from 43 per cent in the middle of November to 65 per cent in the middle of December of a skilled labourer in the building trade during the same period from 33 per cent to 67 per cent.

On the other hand all the disadvantages attendant on any stabilization also made themselves felt. A large number of persons have lost their former employment through the disappearance of speculation and the disintegration of the whole apparatus necessary for coping with the progressive currency

* The severity of the economic crisis in 1923 may be found in the fact that in that year consumption of beer fell to 33 per cent below the normal figure – on an average two glasses were drunk instead of three. The consumption of meat fell in like measure; the only increase in animals slaughtered for food occurred in dogs – these were to some extent used to supply a deficiency of pork. The consumption of coffee, of sugar, and of tobacco were also sub-normal throughout the inflation period. Since stabilization, the consumption of all the above-mentioned articles of human sustenance – except dogs – has increased from year to year. But it still remains notably below the 1913 level. (Footnote in Original.)

depreciation, thus increasing unemployment. Public and private concerns, moreover, have systematically reduced their staffs, a fact which again adds to unemployment. People no longer hurry to exchange their paper marks for goods, and thus this artificial stimulation of industrial production has collapsed together with the apparent boom in German industries. Instead of spending any small surplus which it is possible to retain after meeting daily needs, the public are now inclined to invest the money in savings. Finally, the people, now that their wages are expressed in terms of stable currency, are just beginning to realize how very much their real incomes have gone down. . . .

The fiscal situation of the Reich also prevents it from comprehensively dealing with unemployment. For the greater part, the unemployed cannot be put to productive emergency work, but have to be supported by a minimum benefit which does not even suffice for the physiological minimum of existence; and this in spite of the fact that relief is only granted on condition that the recipients bind themselves to work. . . .

Under pressure of the general stagnation of the market, a general decrease of prices set in by the end of November as a result of the stabilization. The wholesale prices of the most important goods have, up to the middle of January 1924, decreased by an average of 15 to 20 per cent; meat and iron semi-manufactures even more. . . . The total level of wholesale prices has slowly approached the world-market level. . . .

The retail prices have continued to follow the decrease of the wholesale prices. Those for the most important articles of consumption have dropped by about 20 to 40 per cent since the middle of November, those for meat by even more than 60 per cent. . . .

4/7 The Long-term Effects of the Inflation

a ADOLF GÜNTHER, 'Die Folgen des Krieges für Einkommen und Lebenshaltung der mittleren Volksschichten Deutschlands', in MEERWARTH, GÜNTHER and ZIMMERMANN, *Die Einwirkung des Krieges* [see Document 1/10], pp. 161–162, 172–173, 241. (Ed. Tr.)

b *Enquête-Ausschuss* [see Document 3/6], Sub-Committee II, vol. XII: *Die Verschuldungs – und Kreditlage der deutschen Landwirtschaft* (1930), pp. 86–88. (Ed. Tr.)

a It has been shown that fixed-interest securities suffered particularly, but such securities were mainly held by medium and small property owners. This is related in part to the legislation on trustee and executor investment and is also a consequence of the tendency towards concentration which has affected the German economy and in particular German industry for some decades: it has reduced the opportunities of production for the smaller and medium-sized firms and forced the smaller owners of capital, instead of undertaking production on their own, to share in the production of others who had more capital, by means of shares, stocks, debentures, loans and mortgages, etc. For these and other reasons it was the middle and small capital owners who were the worst hit by the destruction of the sources of income.

It is well known that the legislation on the revaluation created new and apparently permanent norms regarding the debtor-creditor relationship. Obligations which the inflation had reduced to nothing – an effect resisted both by public opinion and legal practice – were given an 'appreciation' (opponents say: 'depreciation') of 15 to 25 per cent of their nominal value at most. . . . It is estimated that the sums which as a result of this legislation have to be paid by debtors to creditors will amount in total to about $1\frac{1}{2}$ to 2 milliard RM. Creditors and debtors are the same people in many cases, but by no means in all; there are far fewer debtors, they belong overwhelmingly to the productive classes, while among the creditors there are many members of the middle classes, including many non-producers. The result was a certain recuperation of income among the middle classes, but it remained well below the amount hoped for by their protagonists. . . .

According to the War Levy* statistics, of the 2·78 million Germany property owners (owning over 10,000 RM each), 1·5–1·6 million owned medium-sized estates of between 10,000 and 100,000 RM each: they formed the core of the comfortably off middle classes. . . . Only to a small extent was this pre-war capital in the hands of category F of the occupational census, i.e. the category of the so-called 'unoccupied', including owners of small properties, pensioners and widows of salaried persons, who between them accounted for only very little capital; a much larger share of middle-class capital belonged to the professional classes, higher grade salaried personnel and independent or self-employed people. . . .

We estimate the total capital in existence within the territory of the present Germany before the war at 140 milliard gold marks and assume that an eighth or a tenth is still in the hands of the original owners; if we now assume that the stratum of *declassé* citizens owned an average of only 3,000 RM a head (also a moderate assumption) its total annihilation could explain the disappearance of 15 milliard RM in capital. This sum is indeed only the minimum estimate of the loss of property of those who, being unable to rebuild their lives on the old basis, had finally to drop out of the middle class. Besides this, the same classes also lost a large part of their goods and chattels, such as furniture, jewellery, family heirlooms, etc. In many places the disposal of such property was made a condition for receiving welfare payments. In the later war years and in the years of the inflation the sale of these things

* The *Wehrbeitrag*, levied in 1913. (Ed.)

allowed them to survive. The revaluation will not allow most of these *declassé* people to rise again; whatever they are due to receive will largely have to be consumed at once.

b The inflation benefited agriculture as a whole at least to the extent that from the middle of 1921 until the beginning of 1923, the prices for agricultural machinery and stores lagged behind the selling prices of agricultural products. Anyone aware of these price relationships could, with the help of the freely available credits which would be paid back in depreciated currency, make good the ravages of the war years by replenishing the living and dead inventory, by intensive manuring, and by repairs and new building. But the economic knowledge and skill of playing the market needed for such operations were not available to everyone. Up to then, speculation and arbitrage operations had been considered shady and immoral in the eyes of the farming community. Some of the farmers, particularly in the more distant regions of the East, lacked the opportunity, by reason of distance alone, to escape the depreciation by the flight into commodities (Flucht in die Sachwerte). . . .

In certain conditions fixed capital could be replenished with the help of the monetary depreciation, but not so circulating capital. Its diminution was hidden at first by the fact that depreciation permitted the taking up of short-term loans at next to no cost, and that the high prices of agricultural produce made it possible to keep a farming enterprise liquid by relatively small quantities of sales. Some farmers also made an effort to maintain liquid capital in the form of easily saleable agricultural produce. They postponed as far as possible the sale of the harvest, stored up the harvest produce and meanwhile financed their enterprise by short-term credits. . . .

The opportunity of using the monetary depreciation to supply the farming enterprises with new real capital disappeared in the summer of 1923, when the industrial associations and commerce went over to a gold currency of account while this path was closed to agriculture, so that the purchasing power of agricultural produce fell below that of industrial goods. Some limited opportunities, however, remained open by means of taking up rye value credits. The purchasing power of the rye rent certificate was still above that of the industrial products. . . .

When taxes began to be levied in gold values, and shortly thereafter, with the stabilization of the mark (November 1923) the taxation screw was tightened further, any enterprise without saleable reserves was bound to be particularly hard hit. It had no option but to sell the harvest of 1923 – mostly for worthless paper money. . . . At the time of the galloping inflation this represented a severe loss amounting to about 40 per cent of the harvest yield.

The sums lost in this way were then badly missed by the enterprises in later years.

4/8 Central Bank Reform in Austria and Germany

a 'The Austrian National Bank during the Period of Reconstruction', Memorandum prepared by the Austrian National Bank. Printed in Sir ARTHUR SALTER, *League of Nations: The Financial Reconstruction of Austria* (Geneva, 1926), pp. 90, 96–97.

b *Act on the Autonomy of the Reichsbank,* of 26 May 1922. R. G. Bl. II, pp. 135–136 Ed. Tr.)

a One of the most important features of the League of Nations scheme for the restoration of Austria, as set forth in the Protocols of 4 October 1922, was the founding of the Austrian National Bank. The principle adopted – and its practical value became clear when the scheme was put into application – was that the stabilization of the Austrian currency and the stoppage of inflation were essential preliminaries to any reorganization of the budget or of Austrian economic life. . . . *The Bank succeeded in stabilizing the Austrian crown,* first on the basis of the Swiss franc, and afterwards, when the latter currency itself began to waver, *on the basis of the American Dollar,* at a fixed rate of, in round figures, 71,000 Austrian crowns to a dollar. . . .

At the outset of its activities, the Bank was unable to pursue a vigorous Bank-rate policy, chiefly because it had had to take over from the Austro-Hungarian Bank a comparatively low rate which was in part a legacy from the period of inflation, when it had been impossible to pursue any real bank-rate policy. At the first signs of the banking and financial crisis in Austria, however, the National Bank boldly raised the Bank rate, in order, on the one hand, to check speculation and, on the other, to make the rate commensurate with the tightness of capital in the country. Then, as the crisis showed signs of passing, the Bank proceeded to reduce the high rate, which had un-doubtedly proved a severe handicap to production . . . in view of the steady economic recovery of the country, there is a likelihood of a further reduction of the rate fairly soon. . . .

It has already been found necessary to *amend the Statutes* of the Bank in various directions. At the extraordinary general meeting held on 17 April 1923, when *a foreign Adviser was appointed,* a new chapter (Chapter XV), defining the position and powers of the Adviser, had to be added to the Statutes and was duly passed into law. Recently, at the extraordinary general meeting of 4 November 1925, an amendment to this chapter had to be intro-duced, as originally the Adviser's period of office was intended simultaneously to end with that of the Commissioner-General of the League; this period of office was *extended for a further three years.* The first Adviser was the Vice-President of the National Swiss Bank, M. Charles Schnyder von Wartensee. He was succeeded by Dr. Anton van Gyn, formerly Netherlands Financial Minister. On the latter's departure the office of Adviser was taken over by Mr. Charles Robert Kay. . . .

b The Banking Act of 14 March 1875* is altered as follows: . . . .

26. The management of the Reichsbank is exclusively the function of the directorate according to the provisions of the Act.

27. The Reichsbank directorate is the administrative, executive and out-wardly representative authority. It consists of the President and an appropriate number of members and its decisions are taken by majority vote.

The President is appointed for life by the President of the Reich on the proposal by the Reichsrat after an expression of opinion by the Reichsbank directorate and the Central Committee. The members are appointed for life by the President of the Reich on the proposal of the Reichsbank directorate and with the consent of the Reichsrat.

28. Officials of the Reichsbank have the rights and duties of the Reich civil service. . . .

4/9 Reparations: The Transfer Problem

a J. M. KEYNES, *The Economic Consequences of the Peace* (New York, 1920), pp. 188, 198–200, 202.

b WALTER RATHENAU, *Gesammelte Reden* (Berlin, 1924): Speech before the Supreme Allied Council at Cannes, 12 January 1922, pp. 362–364. (Ed. Tr.)

a We shall lose ourselves in mere hypothesis unless we return in some degree to first principles, and, whenever we can, to such statistics as there are. It is certain that an annual payment can only be made by Germany over a series of years by diminishing her imports and increasing her exports, thus enlarging the balance in her favour which is available for effecting payments abroad. Germany can pay in the long-run in goods, and in goods only, whether these goods are furnished direct to the Allies, or whether they are sold to neutrals and the neutral credits so arising are then made over to the Allies. The most solid basis for estimating the extent to which this process can be carried is to be found, therefore, in an analysis of her trade returns before the war. Only on the basis of such an analysis, supplemented by some general data as to the aggregate wealth-producing capacity of the country, can a

* See Document 4/1 in Pollard and Holmes, vol. 2. (Ed.)

rational guess be made as to the maximum degree to which the exports of Germany could be brought to exceed her imports. . . .

Let us run over the chief items: (1) Iron goods. In view of Germany's loss of resources, an increased net export seems impossible and a large decrease probable. (2) Machinery. Some increase is possible. (3) Coal and coke. The value of Germany's net export before the war was $110,000,000; the Allies have agreed that for the time being 10,000,000 tons is the maximum possible export with a problematic (and in fact) impossible increase to 40,000,000 tons at some future time; even on the basis of 20,000,000 tons we have virtually no increase of value, measured in pre-war prices; whilst, if this amount is exacted, there must be a decrease of far greater value in the export of manufactured articles requiring coal for their production. (4) Woollen goods. An increase is impossible without the raw wool, and, having regard to the other claims on supplies of raw wool, a decrease is likely. (5) Cotton goods. The same considerations apply as to wool. (6) Cereals. There never was and never can be a net export. (7) Leather goods. The same considerations apply as to wool.

We have now covered nearly half of German's pre-war exports, and there is no other commodity which formerly represented as much as 3 per cent of her exports. In what commodity is she to pay? Dyes? – their total value in 1913 was $50,000,000. Toys? Potash? – 1913 exports were worth $15,000,000. And even if the commodities could be specified, in what markets are they to be sold? – remembering that we have in mind goods to the value not of tens of millions annually, but of hundreds of millions.

On the side of imports, rather more is possible. By lowering the standard of life, an appreciable reduction of expenditure on imported commodities may be possible. But, as we have already seen, many large items are incapable of reduction without reacting on the volume of exports.

Let us put our guess as high as we can without being foolish, and suppose that after a time Germany will be able, in spite of the reduction of her resources, her facilities, her markets, and her productive power, to increase her exports and diminish her imports so as to improve her trade balance altogether by $500,000,000 annually, measured in pre-war prices. This adjustment is first required to liquidate the adverse trade balance, which in the five years before the war averaged $370,000,000; but we will assume that after allowing for this, she is left with a favourable trade balance of $250,000,000 a year. Doubling this to allow for the rise in pre-war prices, we have a figure of $500,000,000. Having regard to the political, social, and human factors, as well as to the purely economic, I doubt if Germany could be made to pay this sum annually over a period of 30 years; but it would not be foolish to assert or to hope that she could.

Such a figure, allowing 5 per cent for interest, and 1 per cent for repayment of capital, represents a capital sum having a present value of about $8,500,000,000.

I reach, therefore, the final conclusion that, including all methods of payment – immediately transferable wealth, ceded property, and an annual tribute – $10,000,000,000 is a safe maximum figure of Germany's capacity to pay. . . . A capacity of $40,000,000,000 or even of $25,000,000,000 is, therefore, not within the limits of reasonable possibility. It is for those who believe that Germany can make an annual payment amounting to hundreds of millions sterling to say *in what specific commodities* they intend this payment to be made and *in what markets* the goods are to be sold. Until they proceed to some degree of detail, and are able to produce some tangible argument in favour of their conclusions, they do not deserve to be believed.

b Germany is a country of wage labour. It obtains raw materials, works them up and sells the manufactured articles. With the exception of potash, the raw materials to be found in Germany itself are insignificant. The potash, which has been mentioned a great deal, is not very significant either. There are also very small quantities of copper and zinc. All other items needed by Germany for clothing, housing and food, have to be largely bought abroad.

Germany, therefore, has to pay cash for all it buys. It is consequently necessary for Germany to have a positive balance of trade and of payments. But our balance starts with food import needs of $2\frac{1}{2}$ milliards and raw material import needs of $2\frac{1}{2}$ milliards, not counting manufactured goods and luxury goods which do not come to much and which Germany buys not so much for herself as for the maintenance of existing trade relationships.

Moreover, in contrast with the former position in which we had an inflow of $1\frac{1}{2}$ milliard a year in returns on our foreign investments, we now have to pay $\frac{3}{4}$ milliard gold marks a year to foreign owners of capital within Germany.

The negative payments thus amount to $5\frac{3}{4}$ milliard gold marks, balanced by exports of only $3\frac{1}{2}$ to 4 milliards. There is therefore an overall negative balance of payments of 2 milliards before we begin to pay reparations.

(Replying to a question by Lloyd George): It is quite correct that in view of the present world index of 1·5, German exports should now amount to 14 to 15 milliard gold marks if they had kept their pre-war position. They have thus fallen to about one quarter.

There are only three possibilities of covering the deficit:

Sale of the substance of the country; large foreign loans; or sale of the German currency.

Unfortunately we were unable to prevent the sale of the substance of the country. It proceeded on a large scale. Land, enterprises, shares, debentures, even furniture have been acquired by foreigners below their true value.

We have tried the foreign loan. It failed, for according to the City the burdens placed on Germany were too heavy.

In these circumstances it was impossible to prevent the sale of German currency, although our money became in this way a subject of international speculation.

Until the middle of 1921 the process of selling German money went on without any disastrous consequences. It was not encouraged by Germany, but begun from abroad, where the internal value of the mark was judged quite correctly to be higher than the foreign exchange rate. About the middle of 1921 something happened which was wholly predictable: a strike of the buyers of the mark. The moment it was seen that we were forced to find one milliard gold marks in a short space of time, and thus would have to sell 30 milliard paper marks, the buyers of marks kept their hands in their pockets and waited. Thus the mark fell catastrophically, and the dollar rate fell from 55 at times up to 300.....

One possible remedy would be a reduction in consumption. But this is hardly feasible, since the middle classes and the workers live already far below their pre-war standards. We are therefore left only with a raising of output and an increase in exports. But such an increase is difficult, because other nations are opposed to the increase of imports from Germany.

4/10 The Treaty of Versailles: The Reparation Clauses

Printed in CLOUGH, *et. al., Economic History* [*see* Document 1/4a], pp. 70–72.

PART VIII: REPARATION

Section I: General Provisions

Article 231. The Allied and Associated Governments affirm and Germany accepts the responsibility of Germany and her allies for causing all the loss and damage to which the Allied and Associated Governments and their nationals have been subjected as a consequence of the war imposed upon them by the aggression of Germany and her allies.

Article 232. The Allied and Associated Governments recognize that the resources of Germany are not adequate, after taking into account permanent diminutions of such resources which will result from other provisions of the present Treaty, to make complete reparation for all such loss and damage.

The Allied and Associated Governments, however, require, and Germany undertakes, that she will make compensation for all damage done to the civilian population of the Allied and Associated Powers and to their property during the period of the belligerency of each as an Allied or Associated Power against Germany by such aggression by land, by sea and from the air, and in general all damage as defined in Annex I hereto.

In accordance with Germany's pledges, already given, as to complete restoration for Belgium, Germany undertakes, in addition to the compensation for damage elsewhere in this Part provided for, as a consequence of the violation of the Treaty of 1839,* to make reimbursement of all sums which Belgium has borrowed from the Allied and Associated Governments up to 11 November 1918, together with interest at the rate of five per cent (5%) per annum on such sums. This amount shall be determined by the Reparation Commission, and the German Government undertakes thereupon forthwith to make a special issue of bearer bonds to an equivalent amount payable in marks gold, on 1 May 1926, or, at the option of the German Government, on 1 May in any year up to 1926. Subject to the foregoing, the form of such bonds shall be determined by the Reparation Commission. . . .

Article 233. The amount of the above damage for which compensation is to be made by Germany shall be determined by an Inter-Allied Commission, to be called the *Reparation Commission* and constituted in the form and with the powers set forth hereunder and in Annexes II to VII inclusive hereto.

This Commission shall consider the claims and give to the German Government a just opportunity to be heard.

The findings of the Commission as to the amount of damage defined as above shall be concluded and notified to the German Government on or before 1 May 1921, as representing the extent of that Government's obligations. . . .

Article 235. In order to enable the Allied and Associated Powers to proceed at once to the restoration of their industrial and economic life, pending the full determination of their claims, Germany shall pay in such instalments and in such manner (whether in gold, commodities, ships, securities or otherwise) as the Reparation Commission may fix, during 1919, 1920 and the first four months of 1921, the equivalent of 20,000,000,000 gold marks.† Out of this sum the expenses of the armies of occupation subsequent to the Armistice of 11 November 1918, shall first be met, and such supplies of food and raw materials as may be judged by the Governments of the Principal Allied and Associated Powers to be essential to enable Germany to meet her obligations for reparation may also, with the approval of the said Governments, be paid

* The general European treaty, which guaranteed Belgian independence and neutrality. (Ed.)

† The gold mark, the pre-war currency of Germany, had a dollar value at pre-war exchange rates of roughly 25 cents. (Footnote in Clough.)

for out of the above sum. The balance shall be reckoned towards liquidation of the amounts due for reparation. . . .

Article 236. Germany further agrees to the direct application of her economic resources to reparation as specified in Annexes III, IV, V and VI, relating respectively to merchant shipping, to physical restoration, to coal and derivatives of coal, and to dye-stuffs and other chemical products; provided always that the value of the property transferred and any services rendered by her under these Annexes, assessed in the manner therein prescribed, shall be credited to her towards liquidation of her obligations under the above Articles. . . .

4/11 The Flight of Capital from Germany

Report of the Second Committee of Experts (McKenna Committee), Reparations Commission, vol. 14, *Official Documents* (1927), pp. 118–120.

The chief method by which Germans have acquired foreign assets since the Armistice has been by the sale of mark bank balances. . . . It is interesting to note that the foreign assets acquired in this way amounted to between seven and eight milliards of gold marks, the whole of which in consequence of the final devaluation of the mark was lost by more than one million foreigners who at one time or another were buyers of the mark credits. . . .

Other principal sources of German foreign assets have been the sale of goods, securities, real estate, precious metals and mark banknotes, interest accumulations, tourist expenditure in Germany. German holdings in ceded territories in Poland, Dantzig, etc., foreign money expended by the Allied Armies of Occupation, remittances from Germans abroad, earnings of shipping, railway and canal freights for foreign goods in transit through Germany, insurance profits, etc.

On the other hand, German foreign assets have been expended on the purchase of goods imported, cash payments to the Allies, interest paid on German securities held abroad, German tourist expenditure, etc. . . .

We are of opinion that German capital abroad of every kind, including capital of varying degrees of liquidity and capital invested in participations in foreign companies and firms, and after taking into account all credit and debit items was at the end of the year 1923 not less than 5·7 milliard gold marks and not more than 7·8 milliard gold marks, and we think that the middle figure of 6¾ milliard gold marks is the approximate total. . . .

The foreign currency in Germany . . . not included in our valuation of capital held abroad . . . we estimate at not less than 1 milliard two hundred million gold marks. . . .

On the other hand, on a broad view of German financial capacity, the value of the property in Germany held by foreigners should not be left out of account. . . . We estimate that the real estate and securities owned in Germany by foreigners represent a value of from 1 to 1½ milliard gold marks. . . .

The so-called flight of capital (from Germany) was in the main the result of the usual factors. It arose principally from the failure of the Government to bring its budget into proper relation, and, as a corollary of such failure, from the raising of large loans and the direct issue of paper money. Secondly, it was due to the action of speculators and timid investors who sold their marks against the currency of other countries, while the exporters of goods retained abroad all that was possible of the proceeds of their sales. In the particular case under inquiry, however, the flight of capital was accentuated by the attitude of the people of Germany towards payments to her war creditors, and was marked by new and ingenious devices and schemes for evading restrictive legislation and for cloaking the real ownership of foreign balances.

The failure of the methods employed, both old and new, demonstrates the final ineffectiveness of restrictive legislation when successful evasion is so richly rewarded. . . .

In our opinion the only way to prevent the exodus of capital from Germany and to encourage its return is to eradicate the cause of the outward movement. Inflation must be permanently stopped. . . .

The method of securing a currency in Germany capable of maintaining a sufficiently stable international value covers the whole question of budgetary equilibrium and the establishment of a bank of issue on a sound basis.

4/12 The Dawes Committee, 1924

a Report, (Parl. Papers, 1924. XXII. Cmd. 2105), pp. 12–15, 24–35.

b German Acceptance, Law of 30 August 1924, R. G. Bl. II, p. 289. Printed in Reparations Commission, vol. 14 [*see* Document 4/11], p. 160.

a We have approached our task as business men anxious to obtain effective results. We have been concerned with the technical, and not the political, aspects of the problem presented to us. We have recognized indeed that political considerations necessarily set certain limits within which a solution must be found if it is to have any chance of acceptance. To this extent, and to this extent only, we have borne them in mind. . . .

Questions of military occupation are also not within our terms of reference. It is however our duty to point out clearly that our forecasts are based on the assumption that economic activity will be unhampered and unaffected by any foreign organization other than the controls herein provided. Consequently, our plan is based upon the assumption that existing measures, in so far as they hamper that activity,* will be withdrawn or sufficiently modified so soon as Germany has put into execution the plan recommended, and that they will not be re-imposed except in the case of flagrant failure to fulfil the conditions accepted by common agreement. . . .

In order that the restoration of Germany may be definitive, the other nations must also return to the conditions requisite for their financial and economic existence and must likewise be enabled to carry on the normal exchange of goods on which the general prosperity depends.

The task would be hopeless if the present situation of Germany accurately reflected her potential capacity; the proceeds from Germany's national production could not in that case enable her both to meet the national needs and to ensure the payment of her foreign debts.

But Germany's growing and industrious population; her great technical skill; the wealth of her material resources; the development of her agriculture on progressive lines; her eminence in industrial science; all these factors enable us to be hopeful with regard to her future production.

Further, ever since 1919 the country has been improving its plant and equipment; the experts specially appointed to examine the railways have shown in their report that expense has not been spared in improving the German railway system; telephone and telegraph communications have been assured with the help of the most modern appliances; harbours and canals have likewise been developed; lastly, the industrialists have been enabled further to increase an entirely modern plant which is now adapted in many industries to produce a greater output than before the war.

Germany is therefore well equipped with resources; she possesses the means for exploiting them on a large scale; when the present credit shortage has been overcome, she will be able to resume a favoured position in the activity of a world where normal conditions of exchange are gradually being restored.

Without undue optimism, it may be anticipated that Germany's production will enable her to satisfy her own requirements and raise the amounts contemplated in this plan for reparation obligations. . . .

We recommend that Germany should make payment from the following sources:

(a) From her ordinary budget
(b) From Railway Bonds and Transport Tax
(c) From Industrial Debentures. . . .

* Refers particularly to the occupation of the Ruhr. (Ed.)

The Committee have noted the important fact that Germany is not in a position to ascertain her liabilities out of the Peace Treaty as demands are made upon her from time to time during the year, which cannot be calculated beforehand. It appears to us a matter of impossibility for any budget to be scientifically compiled and satisfactorily balanced under such an arrangement, and that therefore means should be found to bring this system to an end. The difficulty will be satisfactorily met if Germany's liabilities for any particular year are absolutely limited according to our plan and, as suggested above, made inclusive of all possible charges, whether in or outside Germany, including the costs of the administrative controls which are set up by our plan. . . .

All payments for the account of Reparations (whether from interest and sinking fund on railways or industrial debentures, the transport tax, or from the budget contribution) will be paid in gold marks or their equivalent in German currency into the Bank of Issue to the credit of the 'Agent for Reparation Payments'. This payment is the definite act of the German Government in meeting its financial obligations under the Plan. It is easier to estimate the burden that Germany's economic and fiscal resources can bear than the amount of her wealth that can be safely transferred abroad, and it is the former and not the latter that has formed the first objective of the Committee.

§ 1.

b The agreements contained in the Annexes to the Final Protocol of the London Conference of 16 August 1924, in so far as they have already been signed by Germany or are to be signed under the terms of the Final Protocol on 30 August 1924, are accepted. . . .

§ 2.

The Finance Minister of the Reich is empowered to raise a loan of 800 million gold marks.

§ 3.

The Government of the Reich is empowered to take the necessary measures in order that the certificates specified in Annex III § 1 figure A 1d of the Final Protocol for

(a) 11 milliard gold marks of bonds of the German Railway Company,
(b) 5 milliard gold marks of bonds in accordance with the Industrial Charges Law

may be handed over as from this day. . . .

4/13 The Young Plan, 1930

Summary by Philip Snowden, dated 3 February 1930. *Agreements Concluded at the Hague Conference January 1930. (Parl. Papers, 1929–1930, XXXII, Cmd. 3484), pp. 4–8.*

The *Agreement with Germany* provides for the putting into force of the 'New Plan' (by which term is designated the Experts' Plan of 7 June 1929, together with The Hague Agreements of 31 August 1929, and 20 January 1930) as a complete and final settlement of the financial liabilities of Germany relating to the War. The New Plan fixes for the first time the reparation liabilities of Germany in the form of certain specified annuities payable in each of the years 1929 to 1987. These annuities are those fixed in the Young Plan which the Experts stated that they had 'every reason to believe can in fact be both paid and transferred by Germany', but the amounts due to the United States of America have been omitted as being covered by a separate arrangement. These annuities constitute a definite and fixed obligations of Germany, linked up with her commercial credit, except that Germany will have the right, in case of need, to postpone transfer or payment of a part of the annuities for a period not exceeding two years. The German Government by a clause in the Agreement declares that they are determined to make every possible effort to avoid having recourse to such postponement.

The payments of Germany are in future to be made to and distributed by the Bank for International Settlements, and the Reparation Commission and all other existing organs of foreign control over Germany are to be disbanded....

The share in the German annuities assigned to the United States Government in the Experts' Report is not covered by The Hague Agreements, but is dealt with in a separate agreement between Germany and the United States. In order that no discrimination should result from this separate agreement, the German Government have undertaken that they will not exercise their rights of postponement in regard to the creditor Governments which are parties to The Hague Agreements, without at the same time exercising their rights of postponement under the separate German-American Agreement.

'Arrangement as to the financial mobilization of the German Annuities:'

This records the intention of certain Creditor Governments to issue reparation bonds for 300 million dollars before 1 October 1930.

The German Government undertake not to issue any fresh foreign long-term loan before this issue.

The German Government are to have the option of receiving one-third of the proceeds of the issue, in which case they will meet one-third of the service of the loan (outside the reparation annuities)....

The Bank for International Settlements

The Convention with Switzerland consists of a Treaty between Belgium, France, Germany, Great Britain, Italy, and Japan, on the one hand, and Switzerland on the other hand, for the establishment of the Bank for International Settlements at Basle. The Swiss Government undertake to grant a Charter for fifteen years as soon as the necessary law has been passed, and further to obtain the assent of the Swiss people (which may involve a referendum) to the grant of a Charter for the whole period of the Bank's existence.

4/14 The Hoover Moratorium

Text of President Hoover's Proposal, 20 June 1931. Printed in *Documents on International Affairs* (London, 1931), pp. 115–116.

The American Government proposes the postponement during one year of all payments on inter-governmental debts, reparations, and relief debts, both principal and interest, of course not including the obligations of Governments held by private parties. Subject to confirmation by Congress, the American Government will postpone all payments upon the debts of foreign Governments to the American Government payable during the fiscal year beginning July next, conditional on a like postponement for one year of all payments on inter-governmental debts owing to the important creditor-Powers....

The purpose of this action is to give the forthcoming year to the economic recovery of the world, and to help free the recuperative forces already in motion in the United States from retarding influences from abroad. The world-wide depression has affected the countries of Europe more severely than our own. Some of these countries are feeling to a serious extent the drain of this depression on the national economy. The fabric of inter-governmental debts, supportable in normal times, weighs heavily in the midst of this depression.

From a variety of causes arising out of this depression, such as the fall in the price of foreign commodities and lack of confidence in economic and political stability abroad, there is an abnormal movement of gold into the United States which is lowering the credit stability of many foreign countries. These and other difficulties abroad diminish buying power for our exports, and in a measure are a cause of our continued unemployment and continued lower prices to our farmers.

Wise and timely action should contribute to relieve the pressure of these adverse forces in foreign countries, and should assist in the re-establishment of confidence, thus forwarding political peace and economic stability in the world. ...

I am suggesting to the American people that they be wise creditors in their own interest and be good neighbours. ...

I do not approve in any remote sense of the cancellation of the debts to us. World confidence would not be enhanced by such action. None of our debtor nations has ever suggested it. But as the basis of the settlement of those debts was the capacity, under normal conditions, of the debtor to pay, we should be consistent with our own policies and principles if we take into account the abnormal situation now existing in the world. I am sure the American people have no desire to attempt to extract any sum beyond the capacity of any debtor to pay, and it is our view that broad vision requires that our Government should recognize the situation as it exists.

This course of action is entirely consistent with the policy we have hither-to pursued. We are not involved in the discussion of strictly European problems, of which payment of German reparations is one. It represents our willingness to make a contribution to the early restoration of world prosperity, in which our own people have so deep an interest. ...

4/15 Relief for Germany, 1931

Declaration of London Conference of 20–23 July 1931. Printed in *Documents on British Foreign Policy* [*see* Document **1/26e**], Second Series, vol. 2 (1947), p. 223.

'The recent excessive withdrawals of capital from Germany have created an acute financial crisis. These withdrawals have been caused by a lack of confidence, which is not justified by the economic and budgetary situation of the country.

'In order to ensure the maintenance of the financial stability of Germany, which is essential in the interests of the whole world, the Governments represented at the conference are ready to co-operate, so far as lies within their power, to restore confidence.

'The Governments represented at the conference are ready to recommend for the consideration of the financial institutions in their respective countries the following proposals for relieving the immediate situation:

'(1) That the central bank credit of 100 million dollars recently granted to the Reichsbank under the auspices of the Bank for International Settlements be renewed at maturity for a period of three months.

'(2) That concerted measures should be taken by the financial institutions in the different countries with a view to maintaining the volume of the credits they have already extended to Germany.

'The conference recommend that the Bank for International Settlements should be invited to set up without delay a committee of representatives nominated by the governors of the central banks interested to inquire into the immediate further credit needs of Germany and to study the possibilities of converting a portion of the short-term credits into long-term credits.

'The conference noted with interest a communication from Dr. Brüning relative to the joint guarantee recently placed by German industry at the disposal of the Gold Discount Bank. The conference are of the opinion that a guarantee of this description should make it possible to provide a sound basis for the resumption of the normal operations of international credit.

'The conference consider that, if these measures are carried through, they will form a basis for more permanent action to follow. – J. RAMSAY MAC-DONALD, *President of the Conference.*'

4/16 The Lausanne Conference, 1932

a The Agreement with Germany, 9 July 1932. Printed in *Documents on International Affairs* (London, 1932), pp. 14–16.

b HJALMAR SCHACHT, *My First Seventy-Six Years. The Autobiography of Hjalmar Schacht* (London, 1955), p. 211.

a The Government of His Majesty the King of the Belgians [Here follows a list of the other interested Governments]....

Recognizing that the legal validity of the Agreements signed at The Hague on 20 January 1930,* is not in question'

But concerned by the economic difficulties resulting from the present crisis,

And being desirous to make, so far as they are concerned, the necessary efforts to ensure the confidence which is indispensable to the development of normal economic and financial relations between the nations,

The undersigned, duly authorized to that effect by their respective Government,

Have agreed as follows: ...

Article 1 The German Government shall deliver to the Bank for International Settlements German Government 5 per cent redeemable

* See Document 4/13. (Ed.)

bonds, to the amount of three milliard Reichsmarks gold of the present standard of weight and fineness, to be negotiated under the following arrangements:

(1) The Bank for International Settlements shall hold the bonds as trustee.

(2) The bonds shall not be negotiated by the Bank for International Settlements before the expiry of three years from the signature of the present Agreement. Fifteen years after the date of the said signature the bonds which the Bank for International Settlements has not been able to negotiate shall be cancelled.

(3) After the above period of three years the Bank for International Settlements shall negotiate the bonds by means of public issues on the markets as and when possible, in such amounts as it thinks fit, provided that no issue shall be made at a rate below 90 per cent.

The German Government shall have the right at any time to redeem at par, in whole or in part, the bonds not yet issued by the Bank for International Settlements. In determining the terms of issue of the bonds, the Bank for International Settlements shall take into account the desirability of giving to the German Government the right to redeem the bonds after a reasonable period.

(4) The bonds shall carry interest at 5 per cent and sinking fund at 1 per cent as from the date on which they are negotiated. They shall be free of all German taxes, present and future.

(5) The proceeds of the bonds, as and when issued, shall be placed to a special account, the allocation of which shall be settled by a further agreement in due course between the Governments, other than Germany, signatory to the present Agreement. . . .

Article 2 . . . On its coming into force the present Agreement will put an end to and be substituted for the reparation regime provided for in the Agreement with Germany, signed at The Hague on 20 January 1930, and the Agreements signed at London on 11 August 1931, and at Berlin on 6 June 1932; the obligations resulting from the present Agreement will completely replace the former obligations of Germany comprised in the annuities of the 'New Plan'.

b It took another eight years before the Allied politicians realized that the whole policy of reparations was an economic evil which was bound to inflict the utmost injury not only upon Germany but upon the Allied nations as well. Of the one hundred and twenty milliards which Germany was supposed to pay, between ten and twelve milliards were actually paid during the years

1924 to 1932. And they were not paid out of surplus exports as they should have been. During those eight years Germany never achieved any surplus exports. Rather they were paid out of the proceeds of loans which other countries, acting under a complete misapprehension as to Germany's resources, pressed upon her to such an extent that in 1931 it transpired that she could no longer meet even the interest on them. Finally, in 1932, there followed the Lausanne Conference at which the reparations commitments were practically written off. Of the prescribed one hundred and twenty milliards a clear 10 per cent had been paid. On the other hand each and all of the foreign loans made to Germany, amounting to a clear twenty milliards, remained outstanding. The Allied Governments pocketed the ten to twelve milliard reparations, but foreign private investors lost their money on the loans made to Germany.

4/17 Foreign Loans to Germany

a Memorandum on the Area of Competence and the Activity of the Advisory Council for Foreign Credits, 1 January 1925 to 30 September 1926. Printed in ROBERT R. KUCZYNSKI, *American Loans to Germany* (N.Y., 1927), pp. 92–95.

b Speech by Rudolf Hilferding (S.P.D.) to the Reichstag, 3 December 1927, *Shorthand Report*, vol. 394, pp. 11, 280 ff. (Ed. Tr.)

a   *Public Loans for the Benefit of Industrial Undertakings*

The prohibition upon loans for other than the borrower's own use is based upon the consideration, primarily, of the needs of embarrassed groups of industries. Nevertheless, it has repeatedly occurred that public bodies have made foreign loans or have guaranteed such loans for purposes of investment for the benefit of works wholly or largely owned by them. The Advisory Council has agreed to such loans, barring special reasons to the contrary, because the participation of public bodies having been engaged, not only could more favourable conditions be secured for the companies, but even the procurement of money itself was first made possible thereby. . . .

Application of Loan Proceeds for Productive Purposes

The most desirable application of the proceeds of a loan is expenditure for works which themselves produce values for export or for necessary home consumption, values, in other words, which either provide for foreign currency, or which lessen the need of procuring it. This sort of success is, however, in the case of foreign loans of states or municipalities, definitely demonstrable only in a few instances, as, for example, the harbour projects of Hamburg and Bremen, etc. But the Council has, after all, given preference to such loans as at least indirectly attain the desired aim through the construction or extension of such works as promote manufactures, especially of export goods, and agriculture. On the other hand, those loans have consistently been discouraged, the proceeds of which would benefit primarily local interests. The supply of industry with electric power, gas, and water was usually, in compliance with the foregoing point of view, given approval. . . .

Among the projects which the Council eliminated, for example, were dwellings, as being non-productive according to the Rules for the Guidance of the Council. . . . Exceptions are the erection of workers' houses as part of the scheme of great industrial undertakings.

The erection of long-distance heating systems and public baths out of foreign moneys was also eliminated.

The development of industrial areas was excluded, except in cases where the good of the community at large could be proven. A deciding factor in this case was the fact that earnings, if any, would not materialize until some time in the distant future.

The taking over of existing works with foreign money was excluded by the Council on the ground that, in general, the identity of the owner of a given plant was of little moment economically.

In regard to the transportation projects the Council, at first, included the extension of street railways as one of the legitimate recipients of foreign moneys, among the plans submitted for favourable decision. The reflection, however, that this would necessitate heavy demands on the foreign capital market – considering the large sums which the inadequate transportation facilities of many cities would entail – led to an early reversal of this policy. The Council did not, however, refuse every transport project. In special cases, involving exceptional industrial interests, the Council has continued to make exceptions. Conspicuous instances are those in which it could be unequivocally shown that the contemplated means of transport would be an indispensable connection between large factories and workers' dwellings.

In the case of harbour projects it became necessary to distinguish between those serving overseas transport and those serving inland shipping. The Council was prepared to concede to those facilities serving overseas trade, for which Hamburg and Bremen especially borrowed foreign money, the utmost preference on the assumption that thus would our balance of trade and of payments be furthered. On the other hand the Council maintained a conservative attitude towards harbour projects on inland waterways. . . .

Profitableness of the Projected Undertakings

Aside from the urgency for making the investment, the probable profitableness of the enterprises has always been subjected to critical examination, and, on principle, those projects were refused sponsorship, whose encouragement, it was evident, would ultimately mean that sinking and amortization funds would have to come out of general revenues. . . .

b The fact is that of 42 German cities only 21 have obtained foreign loans of a total of 406 million RM, and that is chicken-feed since it means annual interest payments of 4 or 5 millions a year shared among 21 cities. Within these 21 cities, all non-urgent and luxury expenditure together, for such things as sport, theatres, museums, parks, athletic grounds, amounted to 77 million RM, or 19 per cent of the foreign credit. . . .

How are these loans used in fact? These loans have been used exclusively for industry. Of course, it is arguable whether the Klingenberg works ought to have been built, or if, let us say, electricity generating should have been moved into the Central German lignite field. But these are questions that have been decided in long and detailed discussions with the experts, on purely objective grounds. After the decision to build is made, the whole of the credit flows, not to the city of Berlin – Berlin is only a kind of post office – but to A.E.G.*, to Siemens, etc. in payment for their work, and from there, in turn, they are used to pay the workers of A.E.G. etc. who by this means are being found productive employment. For these works had to be built to supply current to the industries of Berlin, so that their growing needs for electric power can be met cheaply. Before the war the same thing was easier. In those days, A.E.G. or Siemens-Schuckert themselves took up the loans and built tramways for towns and parishes. In those days it was ultimately industry which financed the cities. Nowadays industry is unable to do this, and it would harm all industries if we were to take away the possibilities for the local authorities to finance industry. I would like to quote a classic example of this. Düsseldorf wanted to build a Rhine bridge and went to the Advisory Council. The Advisory Council decided that this Rhine bridge was not a productive object. It therefore refused permission to Düsseldorf to raise this foreign loan. What happened then? The United Steel Works Co. stepped in and took up the foreign loan, avoiding tax on the interest payable; it now builds the very same Rhine bridge for the city of Düsseldorf. Thus the bridge is being built after all; and the only difference is that the bridge has now probably become more expensive for the city of Düsseldorf. This is an absurd state of affairs. . . .

* Allgemeine Elektrizitäts Gesellschaft, the major German electrical combine. (Ed.)

4/18 Alleged Causes of German Unemployment

Speech by Herr Andre, a member of the Zentrum party, in the Reichstag on 5 November 1926. Printed in MICHAELIS and SCHRAEPLER, *Ursachen und Folgen* [*see* Document 1/3], vol. VI, pp. 182–183. (Ed. Tr.)

Unemployment is not only a social, but also a political and economic problem. The present slump began as a question of credit and has meanwhile turned into a demand slump of massive proportions. A lack of opportunities for production on the one hand, and a lack of purchasing power on the other hand have brought it about that whole industries are in a state of severe depression. It is our view that it is the most important task of the Government, the Reichstag and the economy to provide work and bread once more for the people. If we calculate that one pair of hands creates in one year on average a value of 2,000 mark, and take into account that we have 2 million unemployed, this represents a loss of 4 milliard mark. And this does not include the loss due to short-time working. Nor do the 2 million unemployed who have been with us for months on end, include those who have exhausted their insurance rights, and those outside the insurance altogether. Taking it all in all, the loss of production in Germany must run into milliards. If we add the dole payments, we can see how unemployment slowly but surely impoverishes our whole economic life. . . .

The deepest cause of our present unemployment, as I see it, lies in the lost war, in the Treaty of Versailles, in the destruction of international economic links during the war and after it, in the vast burdening of Germany by the Dawes Plan* – we have to bear a Dawes burden of 4 million marks a day – in the cutting off of important economic areas in the east and west of our fatherland, in the occupation of the Rhineland, in the separation of the Saar area, and in the unsolved questions of the eastern frontier.

Further, the past years have shown that the dismemberment of German–Austria has been a grave error from the point of view of Europe and of the world economy. If we add the reduced purchasing power of Russia, the special conditions in the soft-currency (*valutaschwach*) countries, the industrialization of the whole world in the post-war period, the immense increase in the financial and economic power of the U.S.A., and add further the consequences of the tearing up of the commercial treaties, the prejudices and the persisting hatred of the world towards Germany, we have plenty of causes to explain the present economic depression. . . .

May I also refer to the inner burdens of our economy. Welfare burdens are today at least twice as high as before the war. I don't want to suggest that we do not think these social burdens to be necessary. We see in social insurance

* See Document 4/12. (Ed.)

the main pillar of national health in Germany, the main pillar preserving labour power and economic power. We know that social insurance has removed the personal liability of the employers and I say openly: the German economy must adapt to this social burden. In view of the widespread impoverishment of wide circles of our nation, social insurance with its compulsory contributions is the only large savings fund to ensure that the working population in Germany does not sink even lower than it is today in case of illness, of accident, of invalidity and of old age. Without social insurance the burdens of poor and welfare schemes would grow enormously. . . .

We think the efforts of large industrial circles to lower wages even further, to be mistaken. Every wage cut reduces the joy and willingness to work, accentuates the differences and in the last resort proves to be adverse to productivity. On the other hand, wage increases raise the willingness to work, strengthen the interest in the firm, increase purchasing power, strengthen the propensity to save, contribute to the formation of capital and tend to increase productivity as a whole. In the end, the best-paid labour has always proved to be the cheapest. Our industry above all should act accordingly; it would itself benefit most from it.

As far as the increase in the hours of labour is concerned, we oppose the present system. We stand in principle by the eight-hour day, without interpreting it in a rigid and dogmatic sense.

4/19 The Crisis in German Agriculture

MAX SERING, *Germany under the Dawes Plan* (London, 1929), pp. 181–188.

Farming outside the immediate environs of the urban and industrial districts is almost everywhere in a very bad way, while in large rural districts absolute distress exists. . . .

Immediately after the war, the problem of increasing the agricultural output was attacked with great ardour and energy. Scientific experts and practical farmers agreed in the conviction that it would, in the course of time, be technically possible to render Germany capable of supplying her own needs in regard to bread, meat and dairy produce. Many turned to the task with great courage, their motto being: 'Let us, so far as our produce is concerned, make the country independent of foreign food supplies.' This optimism has given place to a profound pessimism; for it has turned out that, in only too many cases, the intensification was unremunerative. Indeed, instead of the expected production of new capital out of the soil, there has taken place a very extensive and severe impoverishment of the rural population.

The Committee of Inquiry appointed by the German Government in 1926 examined thousands of farmers' account books and selected the most reliable; the leased farms and all extreme cases were left aside. The results of investigation were as follows: In 38 per cent of 2,568 farms of all sizes in the year 1924–1925 the expenses exceeded the receipts; deducting the real property taxes burdening the farms, it was found that 51 per cent produced no net profits. In 1924–1925 the crops were very poor. Next year's harvest was exceptionally good. Nevertheless, of 2,773 farms, 27 per cent made no gross profits and 41 per cent no net profits. Interest has not been reckoned in any of these cases – not even where the farm is in debt. During the two years which have since passed, 1926–1927, 1927–1928, there has certainly been no improvement, one reason being that, like the year 1924–1925, the crops were, on the whole, unsatisfactory.

The freedom from debt brought about by the inflation soon gave place to fresh burdens. According to the investigations of the *Institut für Konjunkturforschung*, the indebtedness of German agriculture on 31 December 1927, amounted to 10 milliard marks, exclusive of the Rentenbank Land Mortgage Debt*, but including 3 milliards for revaluation. To some slight extent there was a balance on the other side in the form of deposits with the agricultural co-operatives....

Even though the actual indebtedness is now rather less than in 1913 (13 milliard marks), the average burden of interest per hectare of agricultural land (irrespective of Rentenb. Land Mort. Debt) is 25·9 marks as against 21 marks in the pre-war years....

So far as the data extend to farms with more than 100 hectares of agricultural area, they show that, save for the smaller estates in 1925–1926, these farms, on the average, were worked at a loss, so that the very considerable interest charges due could not be paid without contracting fresh debts, unless the owners of the estates had other sources of income, such as forest property.

Things also look very black in other parts of Germany, especially in the poor mountainous and hilly districts which form such a large proportion of Western Germany....

The reasons for the exceptionally bad condition of German agriculture are not to be found in the question of prices, or if so only in a secondary way. True, when, under the influence of capital received from America, the agrico-industrial price ratio (i.e. the ratio of prices as between manufactured goods and farm produce) became beneficial to the latter on the international market at the close of 1924, the prices of farming produce in Germany followed a course of their own, this being due to the pressure exercised upon them by the enormous short-term indebtedness which many farmers had meanwhile incurred. Subsequently, and quite irrespective of the protective

* See Documents 4/5a and b. (Ed.)

tariff introduced in 1925, suitable measures in regard to credit succeeded, on the whole, in coping with the situation, so that since 1926 the German farmer has been no worse off in respect to prices than farmers in other non-tropical countries. On the contrary, German agriculture in recent years has enjoyed a particularly favourable ratio of prices, inasmuch as nitrogen and potash fertilizers have become sensibly cheaper than before the war. Moreover, agricultural implements and machinery are supplied cheaper than formerly, and cheaper than now in most other countries, especially the United States.

The main causes of the calamitous situation in agriculture are the high rates of interest, the heavy taxation and the social contributions. Thus German agriculture is hampered in the same way as German industry generally; its burdens are the same as those which impede the export of German manufactures...

The heavy public burdens and interest have different effects in agriculture and industry. The reasons are these:

1. In agriculture the production takes place in millions of scattered undertakings. Consequently it has few possibilities of forming combines and shifting the burden of augmented taxation and interest on to the shoulders of the national purchaser as is the case with the industrial cartels. With poor home crops, the protective tariff introduced in 1925 made it possible to raise the grain prices noticeably higher than world prices; but where the home production permitted of rapid augmentation, as in the case of pork and beef, the protective tariff failed and prices fell so that a depression now prevails.

2. Agriculture has not at (its) disposal the technical means with which the manufacturing industries, within their own process of production, are able to mitigate or countervail the effects of dear money, namely, the acceleration of their turnover. The rationalization measures of the industrialists are aimed largely at this goal. In agriculture, which is dependent upon biological processes, the output can be accelerated in only very restricted measure.

4/20 The Burden of Agricultural Indebtedness in Germany

a The Level of Indebtedness, *Enquête-Ausschuss*, Sub-Committee II, vol. XII [*see* Document 3/6], pp. 21–22. (Ed. Tr.)

b Description of the Economy of a Large Estate in Eastern Pomerania, *Ibid.*, vol. XI, pp. 51–52. (Ed. Tr.)

c The Consequences of Indebtedness, *Ibid.* vol. XI, pp. 34–39. (Ed. Tr.)

a   According to the information collected by the *Institut für Konjunkturforschung* there existed on 31 December 1928

new debts, as far as they are known	6·8 milliard RM*
debts due to revaluation	2·0 milliard RM
floating credits, *c.*	1·0 milliard RM
Rentenbank debt	2·0 milliard RM
burdens due to sales, inheritance, etc.	1·2 milliard RM†
Grand total	13·0 milliard RM

Excluding the Rentenbank debt, which does not represent a capital obligation ... the capital indebtedness thus amounts to around 11 milliard RM. ... Calculated per hectare† of cultivable soil, the burden (excluding the Rentenbank debt) may be stated as 374 RM compared with 437 marks before the war. According to the calculations of the *Institut für Konjunkturforschung*, agriculture had to find before the war 750 million Mk interest, while at the end of 1928 the sum due was estimated at 1 milliard RM.

The Inquiry conducted by the Land Finance Offices, originated by the Ministry of Finance, reports an average indebtedness on 1 January 1928 of 304 RM per hectare paying tax. This is 29·9 per cent of the average unit value of 1928 and 18·5 per cent of the average sale price. The total indebtedness of the taxable agrarian enterprises amounted at the beginning of 1928 to 7·2 milliard RM. ...

The difference between the two results arises from the fact that the Ministry of Finance included only enterprises that were taxable. But these are in the main only the enterprises of over 5 hectares. The inquiry by the Ministry of Finance is the most detailed and most comprehensive investigation of agricultural indebtedness undertaken since 1902 ... the investigation covered 87 per cent by number and 81 per cent by area.

While the report of the *Institut für Konjunkturforschung* lists only the total indebtedness, the statistics of the Ministry of Finance also permit a view of the regional distribution. ...

Three zones of indebtedness emerge out of the total territory of the Reich. The first zone is formed by the geographically detached province of East Prussia, the second comprises the area between the Polish border and the Elbe, and the third includes the rest of the country west of the Elbe. The average indebtedness, measured per unit value of land, increases from west to east.

b 1. *General*

Total extent 2,400 Morgen,‡ of which 1,810 Morgen cultivable. Distributed at present

* Increased by 31 December 1929 to 7·3 milliard RM.
† Excluding the capital value of the dower and life interests.
‡ See Glossary.

under crops	1,600 Morgen	=	88·5 per cent
meadow	100 Morgen	=	5·5 per cent
permanent pasture	110 Morgen	=	6·0 per cent

The external transport situation is highly unfavourable because of the high freight costs. Freight for potash, phosphates, feeding stuffs and coal averages 1 RM a hundredweight.* Position in relation to railway is favourable: 4 km distant by main road.

The internal transport situation is highly favourable, buildings are central. Farm buildings are along the crossing of two main roads which divide the fields into four fairly equal parts. Longest distance of fields from the farm buildings: 1·5 km. † The cultivable area lies in one piece, the meadows extend also in a single piece from north to south across the village land. Lanes and paths are good.

2. *Soil and climate*

... According to the land tax assessment,

12 per cent of the cultivable land is of soil class 3
45 per cent of the cultivable land is of soil class 4
28 per cent of the cultivable land is of soil class 5
12 per cent of the cultivable land is of soil class 6
2 per cent of the cultivable land is of soil class 7
1 per cent of the cultivable land is of soil class 8

Surface slightly hilly, but mechanical cultivation possible for the most part.

Climate extraordinarily unfavourable, since the estate lies on the northern slope of the Baltic moraine edge. ...

3. *Economic Conditions*

Main emphasis root crops and grain. ...

(b) cultivation of the arable

28 per cent winter crop
31 per cent summer crop
25 per cent root crops
5 per cent workers' potatoes
8 per cent feeding crop
2 per cent experimental crops

* Metric hundredweight, i.e. 50 kilo, or very nearly 1 cwt. N.B. In Austria, a hundredweight (*Zentner*) equalled 100 kilo. (Ed.)
† Just under 1 mile. (Ed.)

(c) Rotation: Main rotation (7 years): rye, potatoes, oats, rye, potatoes, oats, mixed grasses. Subsidiary rotation (3 years): rye, potatoes, oats. – They are in process of transition to a permanent pasture system. . . .

(d) Fertilizers. Fertilizing on scientific basis . . . potassium sufficient, severe shortage of phosphates, nitrogen needed in large quantity. Mineral fertilizers used:

winter crop: 80 pounds* K, 30 pounds P, 20 pounds N per Morgen
summer crop: 20 pounds K, 20 pounds P, 20 pounds N per Morgen
root crops: — pounds   K, 22 pounds P, 22 pounds N per Morgen
permanent pasture: 40 pounds K, 30 pounds P, 32 pounds N per Morgen

Marl is used for all root crops and all winter crops at 6–8 cwt per Morgen. The cost of fertilizers amounts to 16 RM per Morgen. Stable manure is used for all root crops, at *c.* 100 cwt. per Morgen. . . .

(e) Average crops and their uses. Average crops are

rye	8–9	cwt per Morgen
wheat and winter barley	12–15	cwt per Morgen
oats and barley	11–12	cwt per Morgen
potatoes	90–100	cwt per Morgen

Of the average grain crop which amounts to 9–10,000 cwt, *c.* 40 per cent remain on the estate as home consumption, seed and feeding stuffs, 60 per cent are sold, of which about one half as seed grain. Of the potato harvest, which amounts to 30–38,000 cwt, *c.* 25 per cent remain on the estate as home consumption, seed and feeding stuff, 30–40 per cent are distilled in the estate distillery, 10 per cent are used in the co-operative potato flake factory. Distilling licence for 71,000 litres. The rest is sold mainly as seed potatoes.

(f) Animal husbandry. There are

> 28 working horses
> 130 estate cattle, including 50 cows
> 45 cows belonging to the workers
> 120 pigs (porkers)
> — sheep . . .

average yield 4,000 litres per cow.† Individual feeding according to yield. Average artificial feed in stable feeding 4 lb. per cow. . . .

(g) Capital and labour input.

> * Metric pound of 500 grammes, or about 1⅒ lb. avoirdupois. (Ed.)
> † 4,000 litres = *c.* 880 Imperial gallons. (Ed.)

Value of buildings	230,000 RM	=	*c.* 500 RM per hectare
Value of soil improvements	12,000 RM	=	25 RM per hectare
Value of inventories and equipment	115,000 RM	=	250 RM per hectare
Value of draught animals	24,000 RM	=	55 RM per hectare
Value of livestock	45,000 RM	=	95 RM per hectare
Total	426,000 RM	=	*c.* 925 RM per hectare*

Thirty-two workers' families including craftsmen, herdsmen and specialists are being employed. The total number of the permanently employed is 40 male workers, 16 youths and girls, 3 female workers. There are thus 3·2 workers per 100 Morgen cultivable land. In addition about 40 independent workers from neighbouring villages are being employed during the potato harvest. The total wage bill amounts to 30,000 RM = 16·6 RM per Morgen. Payments in kind amount to about 20 RM per Morgen. The social (tax and welfare) burden is about 6,000 RM = 3·33 RM per Morgen.

There is a motor plough, a steam plough as well as a fitters' and repair workshop.

4. *Revenue and Expenditure*

grain crops account for	35 per cent or per Morgen 36–40 RM
root crops account for	35 per cent or per Morgen 36–40 RM
animal husbandry account for	25 per cent or per Morgen 22–24 RM
miscellaneous account for	5 per cent or per Morgen 4–6 RM

Of the total expenditure, which amounts to 70–80 RM per Morgen on average, the shares are of

Money wages, including social burdens	25 per cent, or per Morgen 20 RM
fertilizer	22 per cent, or per Morgen 16 RM
light, power and heat	13 per cent, or per Morgen 8–9 RM
equipment and buildings	10 per cent, or per Morgen 7–8 RM
general administration	9 per cent, or per Morgen 6–7 RM
seed	8 per cent, or per Morgen 5–6 RM
fodder	7 per cent, or per Morgen 4–5 RM
livestock	6 per cent, or per Morgen 4 RM

In normal conditions, and without considering interest, non-deductible taxes and personal expenditure, the estate yields a revenue of 25–30 RM per Morgen.

* 925 RM per hectare equals something under £19 an acre at current exchange rates. (Ed.)

5. *Indebtedness*

Mortgage debt	222,000 RM =	100 RM per Morgen
bills outstanding	70,000 RM =	25 RM per Morgen
accounts outstanding	68,000 RM =	25 RM per Morgen
	360,000 RM =	150 RM per Morgen

The accounts prove that the total indebtedness since 1923–1924 is due to the following causes, in these proportions:

Interest	33 per cent
taxes and social burdens	20 per cent
losses on price fluctuations	16 per cent
new buildings and equipment	13 per cent
commercial losses	10 per cent
debts due to revaluation	8 per cent

c   The consequences of the heavy indebtedness of agriculture in Pomerania are now to a large extent becoming visible to the outsider. In the enterprises working at a loss and heavily in debt they are seen in the first instance in the fact that orderly husbandry gradually comes to a halt and finally, as no new resources can be made available, turns into a state of management which leads to progressive decay of the concerns. Excessive running down of livestock without replacement, neglect of the buildings by failure to undertake even the most necessary repairs, the cutting down of woodlands beyond the planned rotation are among the first typical signs of decay. Lack of resources leads further to insufficient treatment with fertilizer and inadequate feeding of livestock, which in turn causes a reduction in yields and a falling off in the production of manure, and finally leads to inadequate tillage of the fields and ultimately to an absence of tillage over smaller and in the end even larger areas.

Such decay is hard to capture in figure. How numerous the enterprises are all over Pomerania which show signs of decay today, emerges with clarity from the following: . . .*

The Pomeranian Land Co-operative Bank has instituted a special system of credit control to safeguard to credits granted to about 1,500 enterprises, allowing it to intervene in time if conditions should deteriorate to a point which might endanger the security of the creditor. This has shown that at present there are about 250 enterprises with an area of 75,000 to 100,000 hectares which show clear signs of decay as described above. In over 40 enterprises the decay had reached a stage that has made it necessary, for the

* The rest of the Report shows that Pomerania was much the worst affected of all the Provinces investigated. (Ed.)

313

preservation of the still existing equipment and the security of the creditor, to place them *de facto* under the supervision of an advisory or trustee society or under the trustee of the local office of the Land Co-operative Bank. In 1928–1929 about 35 enterprises were compulsorily brought under new management, since their economic condition had reached a stage where total decay would have set in without outside intervention.

These facts, which confirm all that the local experts expressed unanimously, justify the conclusion that all enterprises which are in debt and working at a loss show more or less serious signs of decay.

The question arises why so many creditors have omitted so far to secure their claims by compulsory liquidation. They know that a sale by auction of enterprises in a state of decay would in most cases bring in only enough to satisfy the first priority creditor in the register, but that those of the second, third or fourth priority will receive nothing. But even the first priority creditors decide only in extreme cases to use this last resort for meeting their claims. Since particularly the largest items rarely find bidders with sufficient resources, it is the creditors themselves who often have to take over the going concern, without thereby achieving the true aim of their procedure – the repayment of the loans plus accrued interest – at least on the first instance. On the contrary, the orderly administration of the enterprise and its eventual liquidation is now their responsibility. Added to this, these creditors, who are mostly credit societies, purchasing and sales co-operatives and associations etc. are afraid of serious repercussions on the delicate balance of the whole credit structure maintained so far. . . .

A sign of the direction in which conditions are being driven is the fact that in the beginning of November 1929 the Pomeranian Land Co-operative Bank had to designate a further 55 enterprises against which compulsory action would have to be taken in the near future. Of these 19 are situated in the Kreis Rügen* and 13 in the Kreis Franzburg, the rest being distributed mainly among the Kreise of Eastern Pomerania.

In the Kreis Franzburg and Rügen the general situation is further aggravated by the fact that a large number of leases have become untenable. The Purchasing and Sales Society of Stralsund, the range of which extends over these Kreise, named no fewer than 32 leaseholds in the middle of November 1929, of which 4 were in Kreis Franzburg and 28 in Kreis Rügen, of a total extent of around 6,600 hectares against which compulsory proceedings would have to be instituted in the near future. Meanwhile this Purchasing and Sales Society has itself run into such difficulties owing to the economic conditions in its area that it had to be shored up from outside with the help of the Government.

* Kreis was a unit of rural local government. (Ed.)

A further natural consequence of the large indebtedness is a general falling into arrears in the repayment of loans and credits. The representatives of the Pomeranian institutions concerned here report unanimously that a large part of the loans had become illiquid beyond the harvest year and that in the main, the only bill traffic consists in the repayment of bills after many extensions and only under threat of court proceedings only to be met again a short while after by the drawing of a new bill.

It is clear that in such a situation the payment of interest is also falling into arrears. The debtor will try to meet the interest claims of at least those creditors who threaten court proceedings which might endanger the enterprise as a whole. It was evidently for that reason that the interest arrears of, e.g. the Pomeranian Land Bank were kept within tolerable limits up to 1928. But the creditors with lesser security suffer much hardship from the inability of the enterprises to pay interest out of revenue; in their case official proceedings are only in rare cases likely to lead to any success.

The same applies to the meeting of other current obligations. Nothing is more significant for the dire straits of many enterprises than their inability to pay the relatively small amounts in premiums for fire insurance or other insurance due in the course of the year.

The consequences of the indebtedness of Pomeranian agriculture are already evident beyond the narrow bounds of agriculture itself. The president of the Chamber of Commerce of Stralsund, in his evidence given in his town, showed on the basis of statistics in a most impressive manner how far the industries in the market towns are suffering under the pressure to which agriculture is being subjected. Not only are many urban firms obliged to suffer material loss owing to the collapse of rural enterprises by the non-payment of debts due to them, but because of the falling purchasing power in agriculture they also experience a reduction in business which threatens their survival and makes it increasingly harder for them to stand the losses inflicted on them.

An equally deep impression was created by the evidence of the Councillors (*Landräte*) about the economic conditions in the Kreise under their administration. The statements particularly of the officials in charge of the East and West Pomeranian Kreise showed signs of serious concern for the survival of economic and cultural life. The agricultural distress has already led, in those districts which are without doubt in a state of crisis, to consequences which are endangering orderly communal administration. The inability of a majority of agricultural holdings to pay their local taxes has already made it impossible for some Kreise, e.g. Rügen and Rummelsburg, to balance their Kreis budgets. In the above purely rural Kreise a large part of the local taxes of the previous year was still unpaid in July 1929, and there were arrears even from 1927. The rating for 1929 had therefore not yet taken place and according to the director of the local district union it was being postponed until such time as the agriculturists had had an opportunity of selling their harvest.

In these conditions the means required by the Kreise to meet their legal obligations can scarcely be raised, and any significant expenditure for social, economic or cultural purposes has become wholly impossible.

4/21 Agricultural Support Payments in Germany

Enquête-Ausschuss, Sub-Committee II, vol. XIII [*see* Document 3/6], p. 14. (Ed. Tr.)

Public support payments for agriculture. Changes between
1913 and 1926. Summary table. (Mark or Reichsmark million*)

			1913	1926
(a)	Support for arable cultivation and soil improvement	Arable husbandry	1·8	3·4
		Land improvement	12·2	38·2
		Forest and timber	1·5	3·8
		Plant protection	0·4	2·1
		Fruit, vegetables, market gardening	1·7	4·5
		Viniculture	1·3	7·9
		Tobacco and other cash crops	0·1	0·4
			19·0	60·3
(b)	Support for animal husbandry	Horses	3·1	3·7
		Cattle	7·3	15·0
		Pigs	0·6	1·3
		Sheep	0·1	0·3
		Goats	0·4	1·2
		Rabbits	—	0·1
		Bees	0·1	0·3
		Poultry	0·3	0·6
		Inland fishery	0·5	0·6
		Dairy	0·9	2·5
		Protection against diseases, insurance	8·5	26·8
			22·0	52·5

* Totals do not add up exactly because of rounding. (Ed.)

		1913	1926
(c) General measures:	Experimental stations	2·7	7·6
	Machinery	0·1	0·9
	Education	14·4	45·0
	General agricultural interests	6·4	10·1
	Administration of Chambers of Agriculture	3·2	8·1
		26·8	71·8
	Grand total	67·8	184·6

4/22 The Agricultural Crisis in Europe

League of Nations Report on Agrarian Conditions, 1931. Printed in CLOUGH, *et al. Economic History* [*see* Document 1/4a], pp. 215–217.

All countries report the existence of a more or less accentuated agricultural crisis, even countries hitherto renowned for the prosperous situation ensured to their farmers by specialization and by the diversification of their agricultural undertakings.

What is called the *agricultural crisis* is not, properly speaking, a crisis, that is to say, a fortuitous event rapidly occurring and disappearing as rapidly as it arises. We are confronted with a period of depression dating back a considerable time, and with every month that passes becoming more serious from the mere fact of its continuance.

Immediately after the world war, agriculture experienced a period of prosperity, but in most countries it passed through a crisis in 1920 and 1921; then a very real improvement took place in 1924 and 1925; finally, a marked depression occurred in the cultivation of cereals, and from 1928 spread throughout the entire world, after having also affected other branches of agricultural production, such as wool and cotton. Gradually, the situation became distinctly unfavourable. The year 1930 was a year of disappointment in every way, and it has left in the minds of farmers the memory of something approaching disaster. The stagnation is such that discouragement threatens to spread to every countryside in spite of the agriculturalists' traditional quality of endurance, and the material difficulties are enhanced by the prevailing atmosphere of despondency. The complaints of the farmers are heard in almost every country. The difficulties have assumed a general international character, though there are certain aspects of them which are peculiar to particular countries. It is not merely a question of bad harvests caused by natural or atmospheric disorders, such as continuous rain or drought. The evil is deep-rooted and its progress may be traced throughout the world.

The crisis is universal; it does not merely affect the European market. It affects overseas States as well as the States of Europe. It operates with *unequal* intensity according to the economic development of the countries, their capacity for resistance and the relative advantages which they enjoy as agricultural producers. They do not suffer to the same extent from the same evils. The manifestations of the crisis vary according to the economic structure of States.

In agricultural exporting countries the economic organization is more severely hit if the products of the soil are sold at a loss; and this fact explains the efforts undertaken since 1930 at successive conferences (Bucharest, Warsaw, Belgrade) by the States of Central and Eastern Europe, which are drawing together to establish between themselves positive economic collaboration, to reach an agreement as to a common defence of their interests and to find in common action a remedy for the situation.

It is the lowness of prices that constitutes the agricultural crisis. It is becoming difficult to sell products, and in many cases prices have reached a level at which they are scarcely, if at all, sufficient to cover the cost of production.

The reason for the crisis and for its continuance is to be found in the fact that agricultural prices are low in comparison with the expenditure which the farmer must meet. The profit-earning potentialities of agriculture are weakened. Agricultural products cost a lot to produce and then fetch very little in the market. In spite of the great technical progress achieved, operating costs remain implacably higher than selling prices, farmers obtain no longer a fair return on their labour or on their capital. Frequently the returns of agricultural undertakings are not enough to cover the necessary outlay for the purchase of the material or products necessary for continued operation or for the payment of wages and taxes and so forth.

This disproportion between the income and expenditure of agricultural undertakings, a condition due to a much more drastic fall of agricultural prices than of goods farmers buy for use in production and consumption, appears to constitute the dominant and decisive element of the prevailing agricultural depression.

Until 1929, prices were low as compared with prices of industrial products, but were above pre-war prices. The predominating tendency to a fall which was observed was not altogether general nor was it abnormally rapid. The general character of the price movement completely changed in 1930. A fall, sometimes catastrophic, spread with extreme violence to almost all agricultural produce. It was so rapid that at the end of the year, whilst some products reached the pre-war level of prices, others fell as low as one-quarter or one-half below the 1913 level. In many countries, this fall in agricultural prices was the most abrupt experienced for half a century, and, save for the period 1920–1921, modern economic history gives few instances of such a decline. Farmers throughout the world have suffered from it. This fall was more serious than that which occurred in retail prices or in the cost of living, and the inadequacy of agricultural prices is for the most part responsible for the agricultural depression.

The harm caused to farming by the relatively low level of prices is greatly aggravated by the *instability* of these prices. The fluctuations have pernicious results both for producers and consumers. They are incalculable and unforeseeable and increase the risks of producers and cause the income drawn by them from their harvest to vary greatly. They are particularly harmful during the months after the harvest, since many farmers are obliged to sell at any price to meet their obligations; and these sales *en masse* mean the collapse of prices. The violent fluctuations that have taken place in the prices of certain products completely nonplus consumers. The value of price stability to farmers cannot be over-estimated. . . .

4/23 Germany's Balance of Foreign Payments, 1924–1931

Report of Committee of Central Bankers, 18 August 1931, set up on the recommendation of the London Conference [*see* Document 4/15]. Printed as a supplement to *The Economist*, 22 August 1931, pp. 1–2.

During the seven years 1924–1930 inclusive, Germany's foreign indebtedness grew faster than her foreign assets by RM 18·2 milliards. The total indebtedness increased to RM 25·5 milliards; but this is partly offset by Germany's own investments abroad.

This net influx of capital to the extent of RM 18·2 milliards, together with 3 milliards which she has received for the services of her shipping and other services to foreigners, has enabled her:

(a) to pay interest on her commercial debt amounting during the seven years to RM 2·5 milliards;

(b) to add to her holding of gold and foreign devisen to the extent of RM 2·1 milliards;

(c) to pay reparations amounting to RM 10·3 milliards; and

(d) to pay for a surplus of imports over exports (including deliveries in kind) to the extent of RM 6·3 milliards.

The situation regarding Germany's balance of international payments has not, of course, been the same in each of the seven years. . . .

In 1930 – an exceptional year in which prices of raw materials fell rapidly – a favourable commodity balance was achieved in spite of lower exports, by a considerable reduction in imports due largely to the fall in prices. This, together with the proceeds of invisible exports, provided two-thirds of the amount required to meet Germany's foreign obligations (which had been reduced in consequence of the lower reparation annuity payable under the Young Plan), leaving nearly one-third to be covered by borrowing.

The capital position of Germany *vis-à-vis* foreigners at the end of 1930 appears to have been as follows:

Total foreign investments in Germany	RM 25·5 milliards
Total German investments abroad	RM 9·7 milliards
Net debt to foreigners	RM 15·8 milliards

The weakness of the German financial situation arises from the fact that whereas about RM 5·3 milliards of Germany's investments abroad at the end of 1930 (including the foreign exchange of the Reichsbank, amounting to RM 0·8 milliards) were on short-term, Germany's short-term foreign indebtedness amounted to no less than RM 10·3 milliards, this latter figure having increased from RM 4·1 milliards at the end of 1926. Of these RM 10·3 milliards, RM 1·1 milliards consisted of the short-term debts of the Reich, Federal States and Municipalities, RM 7·2 milliards of obligations of the banks and the balance of other short-term liabilities. . . .

During the first six months of this year [1931] although Germany's exports fell off, her imports fell to a still greater extent and her commodity trade surplus (including deliveries in kind) amounted to RM 1 milliard to which should be added RM 0·1 milliard for invisible exports. This failed to cover her external obligations (interest on commercial debt RM 0·4 milliard and reparations RM 0·9 milliard) by RM 0·2 milliard. There was also a very considerable outflow of capital funds which Germany had to meet.

Figures of the capital position as at the end of June are not available, but investigations have been made into the situation in July. Statistics show that at the end of July the short-term debt of Germany, excluding the credits recently obtained by the Reichsbank, compared as follows with the debt at the end of December 1930:

(*In milliards of RM*)

	31 December 1930	31 July 1931
Short-term debt of Germany		
Short-term debts of the public authorities	1·1	0·8
Short-term debts of the banks:		
(a) Current account and acceptance liabilities	7·0 ⎫	
(b) Other liabilities	0·2 ⎭	5·1
Other short-term liabilities	2·0	1·5
Total short-term indebtedness	10·3	7·4

Thus the withdrawal of short-term funds amounted in the seven months to RM 2·9 milliards. In addition there was a certain amount of selling by foreigners of long-term investments in Germany, mortgage bonds, etc., and purchasing by Germans of long-term or short-term investments abroad. The sum of these movements appears to have amounted in round figures to about, RM 3½ milliards. This outflow has been met approximately as to RM 1 milliard from the foreign assets of the banks, as to RM 2 milliards from the assets of the Reichsbank (including about RM 630 millions placed at the disposal of the Reichsbank by the Bank for International Settlements and Central Banks and by a New York syndicate through the Golddiskontbank), and as to the balance from other German assets abroad.

Whether under more normal conditions it is possible for Germany to provide out of her own savings the whole of the capital she needs for her internal development and, in addition, to meet in whole or in part her commercial and State obligations to foreign countries; or, alternatively, whether she needs a contribution from abroad – as in the last seven years – towards her internal capital requirements and to borrow the sums needed to meet the whole of her foreign obligations, is not a question that we have been asked to decide. We would only emphasize that if the piling of Pelion on Ossa continues, and the obligations of each year are added to the debt, there must be a steadily increasing charge under the heading of interest (including amortization) on the commercial debt; and, further, that if any considerable proportion of the growing debt is borrowed on short-term, it will leave her increasingly vulnerable to crises of the kind which she is now experiencing.

4/24 Background to German Unemployment

Report of a Commission appointed by the German Minister of Labour, 1931. Printed in HEINRICH HAUSER, *Hitler versus Germany* (London, 1940), pp. 57–59.

Since the turn of the year 1927–1928, conditions in the German labour market have been deteriorating on an increasing scale, a fact reflected in unemployment figures:

Year	Average number of unemployed
1928	1,390,987
1929	1,896,938
1930	3,075,580

'At the end of February 1931, 4,971,843 unemployed were on the registers of the Labour Exchanges.

'The average duration of unemployment has been constantly rising in the last years. In addition to total unemployment, there is also a considerable amount of labour employed on part-time work only. Of all workers organized in labour unions at the end of February 1931, 34·5 per cent were totally unemployed, 19·5 per cent worked part time, and only 46·0 per cent were fully employed.

The German crisis within the world crisis is distinguished by special features. More than other countries, Germany suffered through the World War and its aftermath, as well as under ill-conceived and therefore fruitless attempts, protracted over a number of years, at a genuine liquidation of the war, which is, however, still outstanding. In view of the far-reaching destruction of the German productive equipment during the war, the Ruhr campaign, and the breakdown of the currency, reconstruction through German efforts alone was impossible. The aid of foreign capital was required for that purpose. With this aid, however, the existing strong will towards rehabilitation, the adoption of modern technical methods, and efforts to create work for the growing number of employable persons, found their scope within a relatively short time and were not without success. That endeavours of the kind resulted here and there in an inflation of the apparatus of production and in ill-advised investments is understandable. The impulse given to [the] German economy also produced a sham prosperity which was bound to have unfavourable reactions. It dazzled foreign countries as well as ourselves; it led observers abroad to overrate our economic capacity (for example, in the Young Plan)*; in the domestic field it loosened discipline in all sections of public and private economy. The level of prices, the costs of production, especially interest charges and taxes, and to some degree wages and salaries also, increased to an unwarrantable extent.

This development concealed dangerous elements which, with the commencement of a recession, were certain to accelerate and deepen the depression. The influx of foreign capital came to an end and German capital and reserves were still inadequate, although they had been reconstituted on a

* See Document 4/13. (Ed.)

substantial scale; as a result, many enterprises were faced with the prospects of an early breakdown. Internal political tensions also had unfortunate consequences, nipping in the bud many promising developments. Seemingly well-founded hopes of easier conditions on the capital market were disappointed: a tendency towards lower interest rates was reversed: the spirit of enterprise gave way to pessimism, and a despondency amounting almost to utter despair took hold of large sections of the working population . . . at the present time sufficient loanable funds do not exist in Germany. Recourse to foreign capital – presuming that it can be obtained at reasonable rates of interest – is therefore necessary.

4/25 The Fiscal and Financial Position of Germany, July 1931

Reports by Mr. Thelwall of the British Embassy in Berlin:
a Enclosure with letter of B. C. Newton, 9 July 1931. Printed in *Documents on British Foreign Policy*, Second Series, vol. 2 [*see* Document 1/26e], pp. 172–174.

b Enclosure with letter by Horace Rumbold, dated 24 July 1931. Printed in *Ibid.*, pp. 232–233.

a The difficulties which will be met in balancing the German budgets for 1931 and 1932 are not due only to the world crisis. From 1927 to 1929 commitments for new expenditure were entered into without corresponding permanent revenue being in sight. By 1930 it would, in any case, have been necessary to provide additional revenue, even if the yield of existing revenue had been maintained. Meanwhile, practically all reserves had been exhausted, and much short-term debt incurred. At this point, the progress of the world depression began to show itself in a steadily decreasing yield of revenue and a growing increase of the burden of unemployment relief.

The year 1930 was accordingly a series of scrambles to provide cover for the continually growing budget deficit. Indirect taxation was sharply increased, the duty being raised on beer, tobacco and coffee, while new duties were imposed on petrol, mineral waters and beverages sold for immediate consumption. The turnover tax was also increased. Direct taxation was less affected, but small increases were made in the income tax, and a poll tax, graduated according to income, was introduced. During the year the rate of contribution to the Unemployment Insurance Fund was increased from 3 to $6\frac{1}{2}$ per cent of wages.

On each occasion, however, it was assumed that the trade depression would grow no worse; as it progressed, estimates were found to be overoptimistic, and new measures became necessary. Not until the end of the year was any real effort made to reduce expenditure, the principal item then being a reduction of 6 per cent in all official salaries.

These measures were, however, too late to save the budget for 1930, which after repaying 465 million RM of debt, closed with a deficit now ascertained to be 1,030 million RM (£51,500,000). The outstanding deficit on the extraordinary budget was reduced during the year from 772 million RM to 261 million RM (£13,500,000).

Meanwhile, the budget for 1931 had been prepared during the closing months of 1930. Provision was made for a falling off in revenue (as compared with the estimates for 1930) of 1,143 million RM (£57,150,000), and expenditure reduced accordingly, sharp cuts being made all along the line, except in the military estimates. But, by April 1931, it was already clear that the revenue estimates for the year just beginning were too high. Deficits were admitted, not only in the budget of the Reich, but also in those of the Federal States, the municipalities, and the Unemployment Insurance Institute. These were attacked by the Emergency Decree of 5 June, which finds additional resources as follows:

	Million reichsmarks	
For the Reich	574	(£28,700,000)
For the States and communes	302	(£15,100,000)
For the Unemployment Insurance Institute	400	(£20,000,000)

This involves a series of sacrifices. An additional income tax rising to 1s. in the £, and in certain cases even more, is levied. All official salaries (already reduced by 6 per cent in February) are cut by a further 4 per cent to 8 per cent. The War Pensions Budget is cut by 7 per cent, and other economies of £6 million are made in the budget. The sugar tax is doubled and the petrol duty increased by 70 per cent. Unemployment insurance benefits are reduced by 6 per cent to 14 per cent, and certain classes of workers (including married women and juveniles) are penalized.

The decree was accompanied by a German Government manifesto. . . . The pessimistic tone of the manifesto undoubtedly contributed to the loss of confidence which quickly developed into a financial crisis. It is certainly possible to argue that the limits of both direct and indirect taxation have been reached, and that no further major economies in expenditure are possible. The question has, however, become more political than financial. The inevitable result of the mass propaganda, which was spread practically un- checked, of Germany's poverty and the enormity of the reparation burden, has been to make the bulk of the people believe that they are unable to stand further sacrifices. It has, therefore, become impossible for the Government of Dr. Brüning, based as it is on a minority, to impose heavier burdens, lest it be overthrown to make way for a more extremist Government, which would seek relief by action in the reparation sphere sooner rather than later.

Fortunately the problem has been entirely altered by the Hoover proposals*, and Dr. Brüning lost no time in stating very firmly that the relief afforded to Germany thereby would not be dissipated in concessions to those affected by the decree. The policy of the German Government is stated to be that the financial effect of the decree is to be fully maintained, although they will consider modifications reducing particular hardships or injustices. Thus the saving of some £80 million accruing to Germany through the Hoover plan will constitute a reserve to meet any further falling off in budget revenue, and, if it should not be required for this purpose, it can go to reducing short-term debt of the Reich.

b The effect of the acute financial crisis of the past fortnight on German economic life has not as yet reached a stage when it can be expressed in figures. Unemployment is apparently stationary (3,956,000 on 15 July), there is no perceptible movement in wages, there has not been a flood of bankruptcies. The business world is struggling with a mass of emergency decrees which hamper its activities on every side and which nobody is able to interpret adequately. There can, however, be no doubt as to the repercussions of the situation. While there has, particularly in the large towns, been an inclination to convert such ready money as was available into goods, either owing to fear of inflation or in view of the difficulty of obtaining ready money for some time to come, commercial activity as a whole has been severely reduced and stocks are piling up. . . .

Savings and similar banks, who are naturally receiving little and are being drawn on to the full extent which the regulations allow, have difficulty in realizing their investments, largely mortgage bonds, as the stock exchanges are closed; the same applies to all classes who wish to supplement their ready money supply by the sale of shares. Firms who have declared dividends are afraid to pay them out until the situation has become clearer, and so forth.

Probably the true position will not become evident until a return to normal banking becomes possible. For the time being the bank restrictions, with certain alleviations, have been prolonged until 28 July. The continuation of the 100-million-dollar credit granted to the Reichsbank and an effective guarantee that foreign balances will not be withdrawn from Germany during a fixed period should make the complete removal of the regulations possible, but a resumption of commercial activity on the old scale will even then be highly improbable, particularly as the control of foreign exchange transactions will have to be maintained for much longer.

* See Document 4/14, above. (Ed.)

Under these circumstances, the purchasing power of the home market must remain low, imports will be reduced to a minimum, and exports will be forced by every possible means . . . an immediate large-scale dumping on the part of Germany seem(s) unlikely, but, in view of the pressure which subsequent developments have put upon Germany, she will deliberately set herself to overcome her disabilities in this respect. . . . The one concrete proposal which has been published is that the accumulated stocks of German coal, which amounted to 11,600,000 metric tons on 30 June, should be thrown on to the world's markets at cut-throat prices. The moderate elements oppose measures of this kind, which would only lead to reprisals and would offend the very countries to which Germany is looking for help. The political forces behind the movement are, however, too strong to be entirely ignored.

Even though the decisions arrived at in London on 23 July* and the decree for securing the return of German holdings abroad may enable Germany to avert the worst danger which threatens her at the moment, namely, lack of funds to pay wages, it is probable that she may have to resort to some such step as raising her bank rate still further and printing notes to meet the urgent needs of the country, a proceeding which is being strongly advocated by leading democratic journals. Whatever foreign financial assistance Germany may receive, it is not likely to be enough for the maintenance of her economic apparatus on its present scale; accordingly, widespread capital reductions must be looked for, accompanied by a further fall in wages and at least a temporary rise in unemployment, until a lower, but sounder, level is reached.

4/26 Causes of the German Crisis

Report of a Special Advisory Committee, set up under the Young Plan, and reporting from Basel on 23 December 1931. Printed in *Documents on British Foreign Policy*, Second Series, vol. 2 [*see* Document I/26e], pp. 502–504.

Circumstances and Conditions which have led to the Present Situation

The circumstances and conditions which have led to the situation we have been describing are partly international and partly peculiar to Germany.

I. COURSE OF THE CRISIS

Like all other countries, Germany has suffered from the consequences of the extreme fall of prices which is the characteristic trait of international economic life since the end of 1929. The fall of about 30 per cent of wholesale prices in the world as a whole far exceeds in magnitude the fall in prices that has taken place in any period of depression in the last 100 years. . . .

The sharp reduction of purchasing power of large masses of consumers

* Bank rate was raised from $2\frac{1}{2}$ to $3\frac{1}{2}$ per cent to prevent gold draining away from London. (Ed.)

has involved in the last two years the reduction or complete disappearance of industrial profits, serious unemployment and an uninterrupted slump in Stock Exchange securities. It has threatened in consequence the status of a large number of banks; this banking crisis in its turn has provoked a general lack of confidence and involved a withdrawal of foreign capital from countries which hitherto have had the use of it, and, in particular, from Central Europe. It has only been possible to maintain the exchange value of the currencies of some of these countries on a nominal basis by a system of decrees regulating the exchange market and by the suspension of a part of their foreign payments.

This situation has naturally aggravated the 'crise de confiance' in the lending countries themselves. The abandonment of the gold standard by certain of them has created a fresh source of disturbance in international trading relations, and given rise to the universal tendency to hoard which, if it were to continue, would bring to a standstill the whole system of credit.

Finally, to this monetary crisis is now being added a tariff crisis, each country seeking to defend its diminished production against foreign imports by a fresh increase in import duties and other forms of trade restrictions, which in turn result in the still further shrinkage of international trade.

We cannot here attempt to examine all the underlying causes of this profound disturbance to the economic life of the world, but certain of its aspects are intimately linked with the problem with which we are directly concerned.

Among these factors, the Banking Committee which met in Basle in August called attention to the fact that 'in recent years the world has been endeavouring to pursue two contradictory policies, in permitting the development of an international financial system which involves the annual payment of large sums by debtor to creditor countries, while at the same time putting obstacles in the way of the free movement of goods', and that the case of Germany provides a most forcible illustration of this dilemma. So long as the payments to be made were offset by loans to the debtor country this dilemma did not arise, but as soon as such capital movements ceased, as happened in the autumn of 1929, it becomes evident that in the long run, as the Dawes Committee* clearly pointed out, these payments can only be made in the form of goods. The change from a period of excessive expansion of foreign lending by certain creditor countries followed by an abrupt cessation of such lending constitutes one of the chief points of contrast between the period 1924–1929 and 1930–1931, and has been one of the principal features in the credit situation of recent times. If barriers are imposed to the free movement of goods, the world cannot readily adapt itself quickly to important changes in the course of credit and trade. Attempts to maintain

* See Document 4/12. (Ed.)

the international balance of payments by means of larger and abnormal movements of gold has weakened the monetary foundations of many countries. In fact, when the withdrawal of large sums of capital took place the gold reserves of the countries concerned proved quite inadequate to stand the strain. This led in some countries to the strict control of foreign payments and in others to the suspension of the gold standard.

2. CAPITAL AND COMMERCIAL DEBT OF GERMANY

Germany's demand for capital to fill the gap left by the war, the aftermath and the inflation was very great. As a matter of fact, the influx of foreign capital which began as soon as the mark was stabilized and which was estimated by the Bankers' Committee to be about 18 milliard RM has been partly offset by the 10·3 milliard RM of reparation payments.

But in any case, between 1925 and 1930 Germany has invested a very large amount of capital in both private and public enterprises. She has, for example, reconstructed her merchant fleet, she has modernized and rationalized many of her industries and her towns have carried through large programmes for public purposes. The figures furnished to us by the German delegation show for the period 1924–1929 the investment of a sum amounting to 32,845 million RM, of which 22,428 million RM represent investments by public authorities, for public utilities, housing (other than houses financed purely by private means) roads, canals, &c.

These sums have, of course, been forthcoming partly from Germany's own savings, which reached very high figures in the course of recent years. But the foreign holding of so large a proportion of her capital wealth makes her peculiarly vulnerable to financial disturbance, particularly to the extent that this capital is withdrawable at short notice. Moreover, a substantial part of these short-term credits has proved to be immobilized in long-term investments. The withdrawal of these credits must therefore threaten not only the exchange but also the liquidity of the banks themselves.

3. GROWTH OF THE GERMAN BUDGET

Turning to Germany's budgetary situation, the rapid development of Germany's economic activity in recent years has been paralleled by an increase of Government expenditure. The continued increase of expenditure from 1925 to 1930 has absorbed as fast as it came into being the growing taxable capacity of Germany. In spite of a rapid increase in normal receipts, which increased between 1926–1927 and 1929–1930 from 14,719 to 18,054 million RM, the increase of expenses has been equally rapid. Indeed, they have risen from 17,200 to 20,823 million RM and have resulted in an increase of debt. . . .

When stabilization took place, inflation had reduced the public debt to a very small amount. On the other hand, by 1931 this debt reached more than 24 milliard RM, of which 8·4 milliard RM were for public undertakings (water, gas, electricity, transport, roads), for the building of houses and for various public works (hospitals, sanatoria, &c.). In particular, from 1928 to 1931 – in three years, the debts of the States and communes increased from 7·5 to 12·7 milliard RM.

When the crisis came with the inevitable reduction of private incomes and budgetary receipts which it naturally involved, the fact that expenditure had been so high meant that the deficit was correspondingly large.

4/27 Background to the German Crisis

From the speech by von Papen, German Chancellor, to the Lausanne Conference of 16 June–9 July 1932. Printed in *Documents on British Foreign Policy*, Second Series, vol. 3 [*see* Document 1/26e], pp. 197–201.

Nothing can prove more clearly the catastrophic upheaval which has occurred during this period than a comparison between the world as it was, to all appearances at any rate, in 1929 and the situation today.

In those days there existed a system of international credit which appeared to function without friction and an active and fruitful exchange of capital from one country to another. Commercial relations between almost all countries seemed to be regulated on a solid basis by a clear and well-organized system of commercial treaties. Competent authorities, governments, parliaments, economic circles and public opinion were unanimous in recognizing as unreasonable and in condemning any policy of isolation. Every country was ready to welcome the goods of other countries in well-ordered exchanges. Industry worked at a profit. Agriculture, if not in Germany, at any rate in the majority of other countries, could live. The world opened itself wide to commerce. Banks evidenced a spirit of enterprise and granted credits to foreign countries. Investors were disposed to entrust their savings to foreign governments. In the majority of countries unemployment was still at that time an unknown problem. Those were the characteristic features of the period during which the Young Plan was conceived.

What an abyss between the glowing optimism of those days and the pessimism and despair of today! None of the promises of that period have been realized.

The desperate situation which prevails today is evidenced by the number of 25 million unemployed. . . . In Germany this state of things has most strongly shaken the confidence of the masses in the good functioning of the capitalist system.

A certain number of states have already found themselves obliged to suspend their payments abroad. This constitutes a grave warning not to delay taking the necessary measures in order that other great countries may not find themselves in the same position. I need not describe what would be the repercussions, the disastrous results on the world crisis of such further steps. In the present uncertainty there is no need to be surprised that the international circulation of capital and credit is, for the time, almost entirely arrested. The capitalists of wealthy countries, far from collaborating in a reasonable distribution of such capital, think only of withdrawing as rapidly as possible the credits which they have granted, and do so even though in their own countries capital can no longer find remunerative investment. The employer is often obliged, in order to make up his losses, to live on his capital. The capital which is in existence, and is destined to form the basis of fresh prosperity, shrinks steadily.

On the other hand, as a consequence of the increase in the value of gold, or as a result of the fall in prices, debtors are obliged to pay from 40 to 50 per cent more, and in this connection private debtors and debtor States are in exactly the same position. If an improvement of the situation does not speedily occur, we must expect a general adjustment of debts to become inevitable.

There remain two facts of a general character which I would also like to deal with.

The world has had to pass through crises in the past. . . . In one essential point, however, the present crisis is different from earlier ones. Formerly we had to deal with crises resulting from a lack of equilibrium between production and consumption, and a period of two to three years was generally sufficient to re-establish equilibrium. But upon the present crisis of international exchange there has been superimposed a second crisis – an unprecedented crisis of credit. This credit crisis has causes peculiar to itself. The most important are the public international debts and political payments, which are contrary to all sound or reasonable economic principles. The crisis of international exchange will not be surmounted unless the credit crisis is also overcome, and the latter cannot be overcome unless the specific cause from which it results is ruthlessly swept aside. That is the first point.

The second point is this. Under the influence of political debts a complete displacement has taken place between debtor and creditor countries in the repartition of gold on the one hand and the exchange of merchandise on the other. Gold has accumulated in the two national economic systems which are creditors under the system of international debts, whereas Germany is today the only debtor country which is almost entirely lacking in gold. In the creditor countries gold has become sterile, and in Germany the absence of gold is causing a growing paralysis of the economic machinery.

On the other hand, the commercial balance of Germany has become favourable during the last two years, under the pressure of its external debt, which is closely linked with the political debts, whereas in former decades it was always unfavourable. In the same period a development in the contrary direction has taken place in the creditor countries. . . .

The German problem is the central problem of the whole of the world's difficulties.

The German situation is characterized by the following:

1. The high level of interest, which crushes agriculture and also industry;
2. The burden of taxation, which is so oppressive, in the opinion of the Special Advisory Committee, that it cannot be increased, but has yet been increased, in order to assure the very existence of the State, by the imposition of fresh taxes within the last few days;
3. The external debt, the service of which becomes ever more difficult by reason of the progressive diminution of the surplus of exports; and
4. Unemployment, which is relatively more widespread than in any other country whatever, and which constitutes from 20 to 25 per cent of the population a burden on public funds.

What is particularly fatal is that an ever-growing number of young people have no possibility and no hope of finding employment and earning their livelihood. Despair and the political radicalization of the youthful section of the population are the consequences of this state of things. . . .

The former reserves of the Reichsbank are exhausted. The reserves in gold and foreign currency of which the Reichsbank can freely dispose are no more than 390 million marks for a fiduciary circulation of 3,800 million marks, which means that the legal cover for the currency circulating in the country, which should be 40 per cent, is now no more than about 10 per cent. If in the next few weeks we are to fulfil our obligations, this small cover will become even more insufficient.

The foreign trade of Germany closed in 1931 with an excess of some 3 milliards of marks. . . . The forced development of this favourable balance has led in all countries to protective measures against German imports, with the consequence that the excess of exports rapidly diminished in 1932.

In view of the fact that the prices of all goods have fallen by 50 per cent as compared with the prices of 1928–1929, the loan charges on private German debts abroad have alone reached almost to the level of the normal annuity contemplated by the Dawes Plan.★

Germany could not by herself arrest this development. No international decision has been taken up to now by the responsible statesmen to arrest this

★ See Document 4/12. (Ed.)

development. The very wise initiative of President Hoover in June 1931* was inspired by the idea of giving the world a respite destined to produce a solution of the most urgent economic problems. This goal, nevertheless, has not been reached. Sufficient account has not been taken of the reality of economic laws. . . .

The external debt of Germany, with its very heavy interest charges, is, for the most part, attributable to the transfers of capital and the withdrawals of credits which have been the consequences of the execution of the Treaty of Versailles and of the reparations agreements. Thus, the Special Advisory Committee finds that the 18 milliard marks which were borrowed by Germany from other countries after the stabilization of her currency have been counterbalanced by an exodus of more than 10 milliard marks under the heading of reparation payments alone. At the present time, when we are beginning to convert into goods the value of money obligations, it is almost impossible to form an idea of the importance of the payments which have been made by Germany. I do not want to enter into a discussion of the question of what may have been the real value of those payments to the creditor countries which received them. It is natural that when goods to the value of several milliards are thrown on the market, there is not only a fall in prices, but there is also a non-economic utilization of those goods in the countries which receive them. Therefore, the profit realized by those who receive the goods is considerably inferior to the loss suffered by those who provide them. . . .

It is often said that Germany would become a formidable competitor with other countries if she were freed from her political debts. I am firmly convinced that those fears are based on absolutely erroneous considerations. The lightening of the budget charges produced by inflation, through the reduction of the service of internal debts, only constitutes an apparent alleviation of the burden. Inflation has also destroyed private fortunes and savings; indeed, the whole of the resources in capital which the German economic system had at its disposal. The lightening of the budgetary burden was therefore illusory. A comparison between the fiscal charges in Germany and in other countries is problematical, because such a complete confiscation of fortunes as has taken place in Germany has not occurred elsewhere.

Inflation has, therefore, lessened the capacity for competition of the entire German economic system. The State and private economy have lost their reserves. The destruction of those reserves of capital was followed by the contracting of fresh debts too rapidly and on too large a scale. The consesequences became intolerable to the national economy. Agriculture and industry found themselves faced with the impossible task of meeting interest

* See Document 4/**14**, above. (Ed.)

rates of 10 per cent and more for short-term credits, and only very little less for long-term credits. In addition, they are both crushed under the burden of taxation and fiscal charges. The present high level of public expenditure is to a large extent made necessary by social service obligations. On the other hand, the economic depression has automatically confronted the State with obligations which formerly fell upon private shoulders. The State has only assumed those obligations in view of its duty to prevent social distress and violent disturbances of public order which such distress threatens to bring about. For all these reasons, the German Government has gone to the very limit in the utilization of its resources and reserves. Public and private economy are today once more at the point where they found themselves after the inflation, that is to say they are devoid of any reserves and find themselves faced with an unemployment problem unprecedented in history. It is obvious that an industrial debtor country devoid of reserves, as Germany is now, could not constitute for a long time to come a menace to its competitors.

4/28 Extent and Causes of the Depression

International Labour Office, Studies and Reports, Series C (Employment and Unemployment), No. 16, *Unemployment Problems in 1931* (London, 1931), pp. 13–17.

Extent of the Economic Depression

Economic phenomena, the effects on unemployment of which have often been pointed out, also indicate the extent of the depression and the gravity of the crisis.

Of the 35 countries which prepare index numbers of wholesale prices there are only three which from August 1929 to November 1930 show increases. These are Spain, with 2·9 per cent (owing to the depreciated exchanges), Russia, with 3·3 per cent (the result of its independent monetary policy, adapted to the Five-Year Plan), and China, with 7·9 per cent (on account of the internal unrest and the depreciation of silver). In all the other countries the figures dropped: from 4 to 10 per cent in five countries, from 10 to 15 per cent in five others, from 15 to 20 per cent in 17 countries, and from 20 to 25 per cent in five others. The decrease in individual countries was as follows: Germany, 13 per cent; Poland, 17 per cent; France, 17·3 per cent; Italy, 17·5 per cent; the United Kingdom, 17·6 per cent; the United States of America, 17·7 per cent; Australia, 21·3 per cent; the Netherlands, 22·5 per cent; India, 24·5 per cent; Japan, 24·7 per cent.

In spite, however, of their magnitude, these falls in general index figures, which represent averages of movements in individual prices of a large number of products, do not bring out the economic disturbances caused by the collapse of prices of certain products of essential importance.

In the case of many such products, in fact, the collapse was so great that they are below pre-war prices, and in some instances are even considerably below that level.

The fall in prices has been reflected in a decline in profits. The index figures of industrial shares as compared with the peak figures reached in the period 1928–1930 showed the following decreases in September to December 1930: 5 per cent in Chile; 11 per cent in Norway; 14 per cent in Denmark; 29 per cent in Sweden; 29 per cent in Czechoslovakia; 31 per cent in Switzerland; 31 per cent in the United Kingdom; 34·5 per cent in Austria; 44 per cent in Germany; 46 per cent in the Netherlands; 53 per cent in the United States; 59 per cent in Canada; 59·7 per cent in Belgium; 60 per cent in Poland. The number of bankruptcies has been increasing rapidly.

Official discount rates, which during the last months of 1929, prior to the crash on the stock exchange, had been considerably raised, have been falling almost continually and universally. In New York, the rate dropped from 6 per cent to 5 per cent in October 1929, 4·5 per cent in November, 4 per cent in March 1930, 3·5 per cent in April, 3 per cent in June, 2·5 per cent in July, and 2 per cent in December. In Great Britain the rate has fallen gradually from 6·5 per cent in September 1929 to 3 per cent. In France it was reduced in January 1930 from $3\frac{1}{2}$ per cent to 3 per cent and in May from 3 per cent to $2\frac{1}{2}$ per cent, this last figure being one which had not been fixed since 1898.

The general index figures for the volume of production which are prepared in certain countries give a similarly striking picture of the depression. Taking 1928 as a basis ($=$ 100), the index reached its maximum of 113·5 in the United States in June 1929. By October 1930 it fell to 80. For other countries the figures are: for Germany, 109·8 in January 1929, and 80·5 in October 1930; for Poland, 105·8 in January 1929 and 82 in November 1930; for the United Kingdom, 108·1 in December 1929 and 94·3 in September 1930; for France, 113·4 in May 1920 and 106·3 in November 1930; for Sweden, 137·3 in January 1930 and 110 in November.

It will thus be seen that the depression is of an unprecedented nature and that hardly any country seems able to escape it. All are gradually involved in it. The first duty is to endeavour to ascertain its causes.

Causes of the Depression

At the time of the depression of 1921 or again in 1926 there was considerable discussion amongst experts. Some maintained that the depression was of a 'cyclical' nature, that it bore all the symptoms of this, and that the old law of the fat years and the lean years, to which the industrial world was as much subject as the Egypt of Pharaoh's time, was once more taking effect. Others maintained that, in spite of the apparent grounds for the periodicity theory, the real causes of the depression were the upheavals of the war and post-war periods.

No such discussion took place in 1930. This time the general opinion has been that, in the words of the Governing Body's resolution, there has been an 'accumulation of economic and financial disturbances'. There has been a combination of 'cyclical depression' and 'endemic depression'. They have reacted on and aggravated each other.

There has been a noticeable concatenation of circumstances which have played a decisive and principal part in the general movement and which seem to indicate definitely that this movement has had all the features of a cyclical evolution. For some years past world economy, despite difficulties peculiar to certain industries and certain countries, had been carried forward on a great wave of industrial activity. As has been noted in the Reports of previous years, Europe, thanks to a more or less regular resumption of international relations, and in particular to the re-establishment of currencies and exchanges, had set itself vigorously to work once more in order to recuperate its past losses.

In America, as in Europe, the spirit of enterprise found free expansion in the renewal or transformation of existing industries – manufacture of machinery, countless kinds of chemical industries, including artificial silk, electricity and electrical equipment, motor-cars – as well as in the development of new industries such as aviation, wireless telegraphy, gramophones, various labour-saving devices for the home, etc.

In the new industries, as in the old ones, there was a systematic application of new methods designed to secure the maximum output and based on the application of science to all phases of production. In the United States, under the stimulus of the depression of 1920–1921, a campaign against waste in industry was begun, and in order to carry it out thoroughly [the] American economy definitely adopted as a permanent policy the technical reorganization and transformation of production. In a number of European countries, too, and particularly in Germany, the pressure of international competition and also of international obligations hastened on considerably the process of industrial concentration: industrial methods and equipment were overhauled, and rationalization became the order of the day.

Hence, as in the nineteenth century or at the beginning of the twentieth, the same phenomena and the same effects as have been noted in every ascending phase of the industrial cycle: increased production, rising profits, and bigger dividends. These results were particularly noticeable in the United

335

States: industrial investments in the country expanded, United States credits abroad diminished, and there was an influx of foreign capital into the country. Then suddenly, after the stock exchange crisis, the situation changed: collapse in shares and securities held by private individuals, business undertakings and banks, falls in prices, systematic restriction of buying, decline in all branches of production from the transforming industries to those supplying them with raw material or partly made-up products. Things went from bad to worse; the fact that large classes of the population were obliged to cut down expenditure curtailed production still further.

But what has made the present depression exceptionally serious, especially since the middle of 1930, and has prevented the recovery which experts felt would occur about that date, was the intervention of other disturbing factors – the agricultural depression, certain monetary and financial factors, the consequences of post-war political, financial and industrial settlements, and also the lack of confidence and the anxiety as to the future which gripped public opinion generally.

So far as the cyclical part of the depression is concerned, the view may still be taken, in accordance with the traditional theory, that the evils thus produced will correct themselves in the usual way after a certain time, by a sort of spontaneous reaction of the economic body, only to appear later, however, with an inevitable counter-reaction. On the other hand, there are all the exceptional causes referred to above, which are not part of the cycle, which have been the causes for some years of endemic unemployment, but the real seriousness of which has been suddenly revealed by the new depression....

4/29 The Effects of Unemployment in Germany

a Speech by Wilhelm Eggert, Secretary of the German Trades Union Congress (A.D.G.) at the Extraordinary (15th) Congress, held on 13 April 1932 in Berlin. Printed in MICHAELIS and SCHRAEPLER, *Ursachen und Folgen* [*see* Document 1/3], vol. VIII, pp. 10–11. (Ed. Tr.)

b H. H. TILTMAN, *Slump! A Study of Stricken Europe Today* (London, 1932), pp. 39–41.

c *Ibid.*, pp. 30–33.

d An account by HEINRICH HAUSER, originally published in *Die Tat*, a National Socialist monthly of Jena, printed in CLOUGH, *et. al. Economic History* [*see* Document 1,4a], pp. 247–249.

a What is the fate of the unemployed in Germany? On 1 March 1932 there were 6,128,000 unemployed registered. The number of those actually unemployed may be estimated at about 600,000 more. Of the registered unemployed, *c.* 30·2 per cent were supported by insurance payments, 27·3 per cent by the crisis welfare scheme, 29·9 per cent were on public assistance, and 12·6 per cent received no support whatever. According to statistics of 15 February 1932, 3·5 million were being supported by the insurance and crisis welfare schemes. Of those, 1·4 million had been unemployed up to 13 weeks, 474,000 over 14 and up to 20 weeks, 631,000 over 20 and up to 33 weeks, the same number, 631,000 over 33 and up to 46 weeks, and 381,000 over 46 and up to 59 weeks. Those supported by public assistance numbered 1,833,000. These, apart from some insignificant exceptions, have been out of work more than 59 weeks. Unfortunately there are no detailed statistics about the duration of their unemployment. But a substantial proportion of them must have been out of work for two years or more.

I believe that there is no need to enlarge on these figures in order to recognize the enormous misery lying behind them. In our headquarters office, messages are piling up to the effect that those on assistance are not being paid by local authorities which are themselves in poverty, local authorities which are not in a position to give a single penny to their out-of-work citizens, and whose unemployed are literally begging in the environs of these authorities. We have information from the Westerwald for example, where the out-of-work have had to go begging in large numbers for the past weeks and months for their most limited means of survival. In Baden, an emergency association has turned to the whole of the Baden population with an appeal for help. In their appeal, the committee of the association states, without exaggeration, that there are families who have not had any bread for weeks. Potatoes have disappeared because of a bad harvest. Children arrive hungry at school. In addition, the inhabitants of various communities in Murgtal, in Wiesetal, on the Hardt, around Mannheim and elsewhere are in the most dire distress. . . . A report from the Murgtal reads: 'I have found that in our communities too there are people who survive on potatoes and salt, and weeks may pass before they obtain bread again.' Similar reports are arriving with increasing frequency from all districts. We must not lose any more time in fighting this distress with all our might.

It is often said that the young out-of-work do not suffer as much from unemployment as the older ones. Our experience shows the contrary to be the case. Our disordered economy is today no longer capable of preparing the new generation for its occupational tasks in an orderly manner. Hundreds of thousands of young human beings become unemployed as soon as they have finished their apprenticeship or training, stay in that position for long periods and thus lose again whatever skills they have acquired in training but never used in practice. What is to become of the German economy, I ask, if there is no new generation growing up to preserve the world-famous German skills?

b In another home a family of seven – man, wife and five children – were living in two rooms. The man, workless since the beginning of 1931, had formerly been employed, first as a clerk, and later as a salesman in a store, his wage in the latter occupation being 42s. a week.

The total income of the family, from the 'secondary category' dole, had amounted to about 30s. a week, but this sum was subject to a cut of 20 per cent on 27 June 1932. On the same date the rent of 10s. a week was raised to 12s. 6d., or nearly half their total income, by the reimposition of a rent tax formerly waived in the case of the workless. Thus the relentless march of the crisis forces the living standards of its victims down and down.

Sitting on the only sound chair in that home, in which a sewing machine was the sole article of furniture which would have sold for more than a few pence, I listened while the wife, a woman of twenty-five whose face bore clear marks of strain, explained to me how they managed to feed seven people on 15s. a week.

A loaf of bread a day cost 6d. A pound of dripping a week cost the same sum. They bought one litre (pint and a quarter) of milk a day for the two youngest children, and ¼ lb. of butter a week for the youngest child. Three lbs. of sugar a week, two tins of condensed milk for the baby, aged nine months, and five cigarettes a day for the man, costing one penny a packet, completed the list of 'luxuries'. For the rest, they had 8 lbs. of potatoes a day and, twice a week, 3 lbs. of cabbage costing 3d., boiled into a soup to which, on Sundays, was added a pennyworth of bones. Occasionally – not more frequently than once a month – they bought half a pound of pork at the specially reduced prices charged, under government supervision, to those in receipt of 'doles'.

'The meat cards make a difference, of course,' said the wife, 'but not as much as one might imagine. We are allowed 2 lbs. of meat every two weeks at a special reduction of 2d. a pound. A pound of pork costs us 6½d. instead of 8½d. But we rarely use the cards. You see we cannot afford meat at any price.'

That was all. After inspecting that larder, and a few more in the same district, I was not surprised to learn, on the authority of the medical officer of health of a district of Berlin where dwell 300,000 workers, that he is confronted with the effects of chronic under-nourishment among both children and adults.

From that home I went to another near by – two rooms occupied by a builders' labourer, unemployed for over two years. The rooms were in a cellar below the level of the street, and approached through quarters occupied by another family. The income for a family of three was 16s. a week, 'a little higher than the average', as the man explained to me. The rent, including the new tax, was 6s. a month. The wife produced the rent book, showing

338

that they owed two months' rent, and in view of the new law, already mentioned, which rendered them liable to eviction at any time upon twelve hours' notice, it worried them. If that happened, they explained, there would be no alternative to a shed somewhere on the outskirts of the city, which would mean living like pigs, and necessitate a long walk for the man every time he had to report to the relief officer.

The husband had just drawn 32s., two weeks' relief payment, and I went out with the wife to spend it.

The first 9s. went to pay a debt at the grocer's. A cwt. of coal cost another 1s. 6½d.; 12s. went to pay the fortnight's rent; 2s. 6d. liquidated a debt for potatoes eaten during the previous week. Seven shillings were left, and the wife spent this on eggs, dripping, bread, potatoes and cabbage – which may be described as the universal diet of the German workless. On that menu, they had to exist for another week at least.

When we returned, the husband was sitting on a box, his head in his hands – gazing fixedly into space. Looking for what? As a trade unionist, he had been a member of the Social Democratic Party, the bulwark of the German Republic. Now he was nothing – too broken in spirit to care. Sitting there, a picture of dejection, he might have been looking back to the pre-war days, when the Junkers thundered forth claims to a 'place in the sun', and at least found work for their people. If he was, who will blame him? . . .

c And what of the middle class, which in all countries has endured a proportionately greater contraction of income than any other class of the community? What has been their fate in a city* which today has nearly a third of its office accommodation empty and deserted?

Let the family budget of a typical clerk with a family of four and an income of 240 RM or £12 a month, tell the story.

From that gross income of £12 a month must first be deducted 20s. a month for unemployment insurance contribution, 27s. for monthly contribution to public health insurance for the whole family, and 4s., for citizen tax imposed in the last emergency budget. Formerly a further 1s. a month was required to pay compulsory 'church tax', but this impost is now optional, with the not surprising result, in view of the prevailing conditions, that 85 per cent of all the inhabitants of Hamburg, in order to escape liability, have made declarations that they belong to no religious community.

The net income of the family is therefore 190 RM, or about £9 10s. a month. The home I visited, spotlessly clean and showing evidence of a housewife determined that the slump should not leave its marks upon her

* The reference is to Hamburg. (Ed.)

kingdom, consisted of 3 rooms and kitchen, for which the rent was £3 a month. Electric light cost 6s. and gas (for cooking) the same sum.

Good food for four people, including meat once a day, and such items as household cleaning materials, would have cost that family £7 10s. a month. But the balance available after paying rent, electric light and gas was only 30s. a week. Bridging that gap without permitting her husband and two children to notice any shortage of quantity or absence of variety in the menu, was the task which the housewife is today sharing with thousands of similar middle-class families in Hamburg – and millions in Germany. And, as she was careful to emphasize, that housewife is one of the lucky ones. Her husband has not had one day's unemployment in the past five years. His salary had been reduced, but only by the general average of about 20 per cent. Therefore that family budget may be taken as representative of the standard of living which both the Brüning Government and the present administration consider is what Germany can afford at the present time.

The standard has declined in other respects. That budget allowed nothing for amusements. Although at Hamburg the price of a cinema seat is 7d. up to six o'clock and 8d. after that hour, those I entered were half-empty. The beer-halls of the city were well patronized, but they represent not only a national habit, but also the cheapest form of passing the time available, for a glass of beer costing 3d. or 4d. can, with care, be made to last throughout an entire musical programme of three hours' duration.

More ambitious forms of recreation are beyond the reach of the mass of the people. Germany has no counterpart of the streams of small family cars which can be seen leaving any English industrial city on a fine Saturday afternoon. For the Hamburger, a day's outing for a family of four, including rail tickets to some beauty spot and refreshments, means an expenditure of 10s. And the governments which reduced Germany's income by decree forgot to allow for that item in the household budget. Therefore the 'once-a-month' holiday for the hardworking housewife has gone, although the younger generation escape that particular hardship by participating in the hiking vogue. It costs no more to eat in the open air than at home, providing one keeps away from restaurants and hotels.

Food is the great topic of conversation in Germany today. Since Lausanne* it has replaced even reparations as the burning question of the hour. Where two Englishmen will, in nine cases out of ten, begin discussing sport, two Germans will ask each other why they and their families should go hungry in a world stuffed with food. Why German children should be suffering from rickets for the first time since the Allied blockade? And especially

* See Documents 4/16 and 4/27. (Ed.)

why Germany should be drinking a coffee substitute made from rye while in Brazil they are using unsaleable coffee as fuel for locomotives?

These problems worry other people besides the financiers and economists. Which explains the avid interest which all classes in Germany are taking in politics. In no country I know, not even excepting Soviet Russia, are there so many people listening to political speeches every night of the week.

When men and women, in their tens of thousands, will sit for four hours listening to impassioned oratory from National Socialists, Centre Party men, Socialists, Communists – or anyone else with anything to say – and cheerfully fight in defence of their opinions on the way home, it means that politics have ceased to be a subject for academic debate, and have become a matter of bread and butter.

On my last day at Hamburg, before setting out for my second glimpse of Germany's hungry millions in the homes of Berlin's workless, I ate lunch with some three hundred of the city's unemployed. The meal was provided for workless trade unionists at a social institute where single workers lodged, and the three hundred who were my companions were all lucky enough to possess fourpence apiece – the price of the meal consisting of soup and potatoes *ad libitum* and one-fifth of a pound of sausage per person, with bread.

Sitting with me at that long table was the editor of the local Socialist newspaper. At the end of the meal he epitomized Germany's greatest internal problem – in a single sentence.

'Our problem,' he said, 'is to provide sufficient fourpences for every German man, woman and child to have a meal as good as that once a day.'

d An almost unbroken chain of homeless men extends the whole length of the great Hamburg–Berlin highway.

There are so many of them moving in both directions, impelled by the wind or making their way against it, that they could shout a message from Hamburg to Berlin by word of mouth.

It is the same scene for the entire two hundred miles, and the same scene repeats itself between Hamburg and Bremen, between Bremen and Kassel, between Kassel and Würzburg, between Würzburg and Munich. All the highways in Germany over which I travelled this year presented the same aspect.

The only people who shouted and waved at me and ran along beside my automobile hoping for a ride during their journey were the newcomers, the youngsters. They were still recognizable at once. They still had shoes on their feet and carried knapsacks, like the *Wandervögel*. . . .

But most of the hikers paid no attention to me. They walked separately or in small groups, with their eyes on the ground. And they had the queer

341

stumbling gait of barefooted people, for their shoes were slung over their shoulders. Some of them were guild members – carpenters with embroidered wallets, knee breeches, and broad felt hats; milkmen with striped red shirts, and bricklayers with tall black hats – but they were in a minority. Far more numerous were those whom one could assign to no special profession or craft – unskilled young people, for the most part, who had been unable to find a place for themselves in any city or town in Germany, and who had never had a job and never expected to have one. There was something else that had never been seen before – whole families that had piled all their goods into baby carriages and wheelbarrows that they were pushing along as they plodded forward in dumb despair. It was a whole nation on the march.

I saw them – and this was the strongest impression that the year 1932 left with me – I saw them, gathered into groups of fifty or a hundred men, attacking fields of potatoes. I saw them digging up the potatoes and throwing them into sacks while the farmer who owned the field watched them in despair and the local policeman looked on gloomily from the distance. I saw them staggering towards the lights of the city as night fell, with their sacks on their backs. What did it remind me of? Of the War, of the worst period of starvation in 1917 and 1918, but even then people paid for the potatoes. . . .

I entered the huge Berlin municipal lodging house in a northern quarter of the city. . . . Dreary barracks extended to the edge of the sidewalk and under their dripping roofs long lines of men were leaning against the wooden walls, waiting in silence and staring at a brick structure across the street.

This wall was the side of the lodging house and it seemed to blot out the entire sky. . . . There was an entrance arched by a brick vaulting, and a watchman sat in a little wooden sentry box. His white coat made him look like a doctor. We stood waiting in the corridor. Heavy steam rose from the men's clothes. Some of them sat down on the floor, pulled off their shoes, and unwound the rags that were bound around their feet. More people were constantly pouring in the door, and we stood closely packed together. Then another door opened. The crowd pushed forward, and people began forcing their way almost eagerly through this door, for it was warm in there. Without knowing it I had already caught the rhythm of the municipal lodging house. It means waiting, waiting, standing around, and then suddenly jumping up.

We now stand in a long hall. . . . There under yellow lamps that hang from the ceiling on long wires sit men in white smocks. We arrange ourselves in long lines, each leading up to one of those men, and the mill begins to grind. . . .

What does the man in the white smock want to know? All these fellows in white smocks belong to a very special type of official. The way they let the line flow by while they work so smoothly together is facile, lazy, almost elegant. The way they say 'Mr.' to the down-and-outers from the street is full of ironic politeness. . . . The whole impersonal manner of the officials makes them as incomprehensible as a cash register. . . .

Then come the questions. When and where were you born, and where have you come from? Name of your parents? Ever been in a municipal lodging house before? Where have you spent the last three nights? Where did you work last? Have you begged? The first impression that these questions and answers make on me is that it is just like the army. . . .

My second impression is the helplessness of the men on my side of the bar and the shocking ruthlessness with which the men on the other side of the bar insult this helplessness. Eight out of each ten men on my side of the bar are young fellows and about a third of these are mere boys. . . .

The official presses a white card into my hand and tells me to go to the desk of another clerk that has the sign, 'adjuster', over it. While waiting in line I look at my white card. It is divided into squares and has my name at the top and all kinds of mysterious symbols underneath. . . . I do not remember what the 'adjuster' said to me – there was some inconsistency in my papers, I believe. . . . [He was sent on to a police examiner, but eventually was cleared.]

When I come out I am holding a check that has been given me for a night's sleep and food in the lodging house. . . . The bare walls of the room that we have entered are lined with iron bedsteads. There are no windows, but a sloping roof with skylights that reminds me of a factory. We sit down on the bedsteads along the middle of the room, closely packed together. A voice near me whispers, 'What was the matter with you, buddy?'

'My papers.'

'Say, you had luck to get out again. They kept the fellow that went in with you. He spent his dole of eighteen marks* in two days. Oh, boy, think of it! Eighteen marks! . . . '

I look at the clock again. Our reception ceremony lasted an hour and a half, and we now sit here another half hour, which makes two hours. They do not make it easy for you to get supper and a bed in a municipal lodging house. . . .

4/30 Some Effects of Unemployment in Austria

MARIE LAZARSFELD-JAHODA and HANS ZEISL, *Die Arbeitslosen von Marienthal. Ein soziographischer Versuch über die Wirkungen langandauernder Arbeitslosigkeit* (Leipzig, 1933), pp. 22–27. (Ed. Tr.)

* A little under £1. (Ed.)

From diet notes, kept by 41 families over one week, from conversations in the doctor's visiting hours – which formed partly a good control for the diet notes – and from some household accounts which were kept by several families, we derived a series of data which we now present.

If we organize the 287 days covered by the diet notes according to the number of daily meals, we get the following summary:

Number of daily meals	on days	%
2	6	2
3	210	73
4	71	25
(7 × 41 =)	287	100

Three meals a day – morning, noon and evening – are thus the rule. In exceptional cases food is taken only twice a day; occasionally there is tea in addition to the three main meals. Of the 41 families, meat was eaten per week:

Meat meals per week	Number of families	%
0	6	15
1	22	54
2	8	19
3	2	5
4	3	7
	41	100

All the 22 families who had meat once a week had it on Sunday. All those who had meat more than once, also had it on Sunday. Of the 56 meals containing meat, 34 contained horsemeat, 18 rabbit, 2 beef, one minced meat and one pork. One unemployed man states that cat is also being eaten:

> Again and again cats disappear. The cat belonging to Mr. H. disappeared only a few days ago. Cat's meat is very good. Dogs are also being eaten. But that happened even in the years of good employment. For example, they roasted a dog at JT's. Only a few days ago, a farmer gave a dog to a man, on condition that he killed him painlessly. He ran around everywhere for a bowl to catch the blood and in the end got one, in return for a piece of the dog. The bowl belonged to family A.

The butcher's cutter up reports:

> As long as the mill was at work, we killed 12 pigs and 6 cattle a week. Now only 6–8 pigs and one ox, and even that is not being bought by the people of Marienthal, but by people from the vicinity who used not to

shop here at all. The people of Marienthal have switched from beef and pork to horsemeat. While Marienthal had formerly only one horse butcher, a second one set up last year. At the beginning of unemployment both did a good trade; but after the first few months two horse butchers proved to be too many for this village. The latecomer survived, the first one is going out of business.

The 287 evening meals consisted of:

		%
coffee (mostly black) and bread	132	45
left-overs from midday	114	40
freshly prepared dishes	41	15
(7 × 41 =)	287	100

Some families report that they have not had a lump of sugar in the house for the past two years; to save money, only saccharine is being used, which replaces the taste, but, as is well known, has no nutritional value. In some cases they alternate sugar and saccharine. Usually they start on saccharine in the second week of the fortnightly payments period.

Now follow the diet notes of two families:

Family 81	*Family 167*
(Minimum standard family, 57 Groschen per day and consumption unit)	(Average family, 98 Groschen per day and consumption unit)

Monday
Breakfast: coffee and dry bread
Lunch: peas, sausage soup, groats
Tea: —
Supper: coffee, bread and dripping
Tuesday
B: coffee and dry bread
L: cabbage and potatoes
T: —
S: cabbage
Wednesday
B: coffee and dry bread
L: potato soup and cabbage ravioli
T: —
S: coffee, dry bread
Thursday
B: Coffee and dry bread

Monday
Breakfast: cocoa, rolls
Lunch: split peas and dumplings
Tea: coffee, bread and dripping
Supper: split peas and dumplings
Tuesday
B: coffee and dry bread
L: Maggi soup, cabbage ravioli
T: —
S: cabbage ravioli, coffee
Wednesday
B: coffee and dry bread
L: soup, cabbage and potatoes
T: —
S: coffee, dry bread
Thursday
B: cocoa and dry bread

345

L: potato goulash
T: —
S: potato goulash
Friday
B: coffee and dry bread
L: soup and potato noodles

T: —
S: coffee and dry bread

Saturday
B: coffee and dry bread
L: potato soup and beans
T: —
S: coffee and dry bread
Sunday
B: coffee and white bread
L: soup and poppy seed noodles

T: —
S: coffee and white bread

L: soup, cabbage and potatoes
T: bread and dripping
S: coffee, bread and butter
Friday
B: coffee and dry bread
L: soup and 'ham' ravioli (or horsemeat)
T: —
S: coffee, dry bread, horsemeat sausage

Saturday
B: cocoa and rolls
L: horse goulash and bread
T: bread and dripping
S: horse goulash and potatoes
Sunday
B: tea and rolls
L: beef broth and liver dumplings, mincemeat and lettuce
T: tea
S: mince meat, lettuce, coffee

. . . to complete the picture, we present the fortnightly expenditure of an average family. . . . This is a family of 7 persons (2 adults, 5 children under 14 = 4·8 consumption units). The family draws a dole of 49 shillings a fortnight, and is thus at 73 Groschen *per diem* and consumption unit, i.e. 44 Groschen per child, still well above the level of the minimum standard family.

5½ kg	(12 lb)	flour	3·58
1¼ kg	(2¾ lb)	rice	0·80
12	loaves	bread	8·00
20		rolls	1·40
28 l	(6 gallons)	milk	10·64
3 kg	(6¼ lb)	lard	7·20
5 dk	(2 oz)	oil	0·18
30 dk	(11 oz)	beef and bones	0·95
		beef bones	0·30
1½ kg	(3⅓ lb)	sugar	1·78
1 box		saccharine	0·30
6		eggs	0·72
2 kg	(4⅔ lb)	green vegetables (pickled cabbage, cabbage, spinach)	1·56

8 kg	(17½ lb)	potatoes	1·44
2½ kg	(5½ lb)	legumes (beans, split peas)	1·74
1 kg	(2⅕ lb)	salt	0·70
1 l	(under 1 qt.)	vinegar	0·30
½ kg	(1 lb 2 oz)	malt coffee	0·48
½ kg	(9 oz)	fig coffee	0·48
		cocoa	0·20
		pepper	0·10
45		cigarettes	0·45
		washing soda, soap	1·70
50 kg	(1 cwt)	coal	4·00
			49·00

The high consumption of flour is noteworthy: 5½ kg (*c.* 12 lb) is a fair amount for a fortnight. Against this, the consumption of vegetables is extremely low, and is evidently connected with the high prices of the time of the year (the fortnight covered ran from 14 to 27 May). The little piece of beef with bones was bought for the first Sunday of the period under consideration; the bones for making soup on the second Sunday, since there was evidently not enough left to have meat again. The regular and relatively expensive consumption of milk is also noteworthy, and represents the children's share mainly. The care lavished by the parents on their children, at the cost of even the most urgent of their own needs, was noted by the investigators again and again in the case of this family.

4/31 The Depression in Holland

TILTMAN, *Slump!* [*see* Document 4/29b], pp. 264–268.

. . . Extremes of wealth and poverty have always been absent from the Dutch scene. In normal times one might motor for hundreds of miles through the agricultural districts without seeing either a shabby peasant or a high-powered car. No discernible change has taken place today. The neat well-kept little houses are just as neat as in former years. The same number of bicycles are in evidence to remind the visitor that Holland is the flattest country on earth. The same modest restaurants and cinemas are patronized by the same unostentatious people.

The explanation of that paradox is to be found in the fact that the average Dutch family always lived a little below its income. That wasn't difficult, for if the cost of living were high, so were wages. And a stream of money flowed into Dutch pockets from investments in the overseas territories and in foreign lands. Now that wages are coming down and investments thought to be 'gilt edged' are assuming a very speculative guise, it is the margin that has disappeared. In many homes savings are melting slowly. But rarely has there been, up-to-date, any positive decline in the standard of comfort.

The phases which denote the intensity of industrial depression in Europe are three. First, falling exports and rising unemployment. Secondly, demands for wage reductions, and economy in the public services. Finally, realization that there is no money left for anything but absolute essentials, and that every item of expenditure, public, private and social, must be pared to the bone.

The Netherlands reached the first stage in December 1930, when unemployment shot up from 54,000 to 81,000 representing 15 per cent of all registered workers without jobs. The second stage has been reached this year, when it was realized by the government that the crisis could only be surmounted by a reduction in the cost of production and all-round 'cuts' in wages. The third stage is just round the corner, but Holland has not reached it yet. At present . . . the cost of relieving distress has not swamped the resources of the country, private building of new homes rented at 20s. a week is still proceeding briskly, and private budgets, though they have suffered, have not reached the stage of attrition when 'belt-tightening' becomes a necessity.

That is in the cities. Rural Holland is not so well off by any means, though here again one has to dip beneath the surface to discover that fact.

'Conditions in all branches of agriculture and horticulture have deteriorated to such an extent that a general disaster is feared for the 600,000 persons directly dependent on them' states the latest report on Economic Conditions in the Netherlands issued by the Department of Overseas Trade, and having talked with agriculturists in many parts of Holland I can confirm that statement. Agricultural Holland, whether it be dairy-farmers, market-gardening, flower and bulb growing or poultry-keeping, has thrived on its export trade. And today that export trade is as near dead as makes no difference. One large wholesaler assured me that no one in Holland had made one penny profit on any vegetables, flowers or bulbs exported to Britain since this country adopted tariffs. The choice was between selling at prices which were below the actual cost of production or not selling at all. And the Dutch producer in the absence of alternative markets chose the lesser evil. But unless there is a rapid improvement in conditions he cannot go on being so philanthrophic.

What the slump has meant to the farmers is shown by the fact that the average value of farmland has fallen in one year by 40 per cent! . . .

The quota system applied by the Dutch Government to food imports from other countries has afforded some protection for the smallholder at the expense of Belgium and Denmark. But any decline in the standard of living will nullify this advantage.

If the plight of agricultural Holland, representing nearly half the working population, and indirectly affecting more than half, is more desperate than the cities, industrial Holland has problems of its own which keep it from brooding too long about the woes of others.

In considering the effects of the depression upon industry, the factories may conveniently be divided into two groups – those manufacturing mainly for the internal market or for the Dutch colonial possessions, and those producing mainly for export. The former, which include the margarine, soap, chocolate, biscuit, cycles and leather industries, have suffered less than the second group.

Shipbuilding, and ship repairing, one of the most important national industries, has been especially severely hit by the prevailing conditions. In the two years ending 1 October 1931, the number of workers employed in the Dutch yards fell from 37,209 to 17,238. Since that date a further decline has taken place. The tonnage of ships under construction has fallen from 187,000 at the end of 1930 to 108,000 a year later, while the tonnage building on 30 June 1932, has sunk to 49,000 – a record low level. Fully 50 per cent of all shipyard workers were unemployed in August 1932.

Talking with Dr. Van der Valk of the *Instituut Voor Economische Geschriften*, at Rotterdam, I learnt more concerning the ravages of the slump upon Dutch industry.

'The crisis reached us in 1931,' said Dr. Van der Valk, 'and its effects are shown only too clearly in our unemployment statistics covering registered members of the unemployment funds subsidized by the government. In the metal industries, for instance, there has been a decline of nearly 40 per cent in the number of workers employed, and the number of workless rose from 1,233 in June 1929, to 28,369 on 25 June 1932 – the highest figure for any industry in the country.

'In the textile industries, unemployment rose during the same period from 185 to 7,645; in transportation and navigation from 578 to 13,028; and in miscellaneous factory industry from 266 to 13,475.

'In the textile industry production is down by 25 per cent. On the other hand the output of our coal mines had actually increased from 11,581,000 tons in 1929 to 12,901,000 tons in 1931. At the end of June 1932, only 419 miners were unemployed, but over 14,000 were working short time.

'Our tables of imports and exports tell the same tale of declining prosperity. Comparing the first six months of 1929 with the same period of 1932, imports are down by 50 per cent in value and exports by 60 per cent. This decline has been especially rapid during the last six months, exports for the first half of 1932 amounting in value to only 418,054,000 florins, compared with 1,311,814,000 florins for the whole of 1931.

'This dramatic decline in our overseas trade is due to the growth of tariffs. The effects of the new British protective duties were severely felt in the Netherlands, especially by the dairying and horticultural industries. Our butter exports to Germany have also been considerably reduced by the German import restrictions.'

One might continue through the whole range of Dutch economic life without materially altering the picture presented by these facts. The export trades have been hard hit in the Netherlands, as everywhere else, but with the exception of shipbuilding, not as severely as the same industries in other countries. The industries manufacturing for home consumption have withstood the slump without difficulty and some of them, such as flour and the tobacco industry, have increased the number of hands employed.

One of the largest exporting firms, manufacturing electric bulbs, has reduced its staff by 50 per cent – from 20,000 to 10,000 – in the past two years, showing that where the necessity to compete with world conditions exists, the Netherlands have discovered no sovereign remedy for existing conditions.

4/32 France in the Years of the Depression

a TILTMAN, *Slump!* [*see* Document 4/29b], pp. 218–223.

b 'France in the Depression' *The Economist*, 11 August 1934, p. 260.

c GABRIELLE LETELLIER, *Enquête sur le chômage*. Tome premier: Le chômage en France de 1930 à 1936 (Paris, 1938), pp. 39–42. (Ed. Tr.)

d 'La France économique en 1931' in *Revue d'économie politique* XLVI (Paris, 1932), pp. 1102–1105. (Ed. Tr.)

e Conseil national économique, *Le chômage dans les industries Textiles* (Paris, 1936), pp. 6–9. (Ed. Tr.)

f 'Les industries touristiques et l'hôtellerie' in *Revue d'économie politique* XLVIII (Paris, 1934), p. 857. (Ed. Tr.)

a The slump has hit France, but it did not hit her at all until 1931, and then not as hard as other nations. When I sought the reasons for this satisfactory fact, the answers that I received were many and varied. Some, in answer to my question, pointed out that France is more self-contained than most nations – that her peasants grow food for the cities, and the cities manufacture for the peasants. That 'natural equilibrium' between town and countryside is responsible for much.* Others stressed the fact that exports had never figured as prominently in France's trade budget as, for instance, was the case in Britain. Again, my attention was directed to the high consuming power of

* See Document 5/12 for views on this equilibrium. (Ed.)

the internal market, reduced very little, if at all, up to August 1932. As evidence of the importance of this factor in maintaining prosperity, it was pointed out to me that the so-called 'Paris trades', the manufacture of luxury articles like bijouterie, perfumes, and so on, have been badly hit by the tourist slump, whereas those trades dependent upon the purchases of the ordinary French housewife and her husband have suffered hardly at all. One business man to whom I put the same question saw the answer in that mountain of gold that reposes in the vaults of the Banque de France, but he was a foreigner. Others, Frenchmen, were content to make an expressive gesture in reply, and point out that – well, France is France.

Probably all these different factors have played their part in helping to keep France 'slump proof'. For, despite declining production and increasing unemployment, it remains true that that nation has suffered less from the great 'slow down' than any other country.

France is today the richest nation in Europe. Her workers are the most fortunate and the most thrifty. Her peasants may be grumbling and her wine industry badly hit, but there is no real privation in her countryside. Her organized co-operative movement, a sure index of working-class prosperity, reports that the turnover in the co-operative shops is still rising. I could find no single shred of evidence that revealed any decline in the purchasing power of the French people. One or two trades are suffering badly. But others are hardly touched by the depression. If anyone in France is apprehensive about the future, the reason lies not in the mounting unemployment figure, but in the fact, recently announced by a French statistician, that by 1935 the number of Frenchmen attaining military age will decline by one hundred thousand, due to the sterility of the war years, and there will be an annual shortage of that number until 1940. Hence, perhaps, the feverish interest which the French public is taking in disarmament – and the German demand for 'equality' in the military sphere.

The facts support the optimism of the average Frenchman and justify what I have written.

The volume of industrial production in France for the years 1929 and 1930 was 10 per cent above the 1928 figure. For 1931 – a year of acute and deepening depression all over Europe – production was only 2 per cent below the figure for 1928. Up to 31 December 1931, France could claim that for her there was no slump. For the first three months of 1932, production was 80 per cent of the monthly average for 1928. For April 1932, it had dropped to 70 per cent – a total decline up to that month of 30 per cent. And that contraction had been confined to the opening months of 1932!

To secure detailed figures showing the decline in production for individual industries in France, one is dependent upon figures published in the

351

Bulletin du Marche du Travail, the official organ of the French Ministry of Labour, which record the decrease in activity measured by the reduction in workers employed and decline in hours worked.

The latest figures available from this source show that the output of the French mines for the month of December 1931, was 16·3 per cent below the corresponding figure for December 1930. Textiles were 26 per cent down, the paper industry had suffered a decline of 16.4 per cent. Transport was recorded as having suffered a decline in volume of 9·5 per cent in the year, but building trades had dropped only 5 per cent.

During 1932 a further contraction in exports has taken place. The official Bulletin of the Ministry of Commerce and Industry reports that for the first seven months of 1932 compared with the same period of 1931, imports are down by nine billions of francs and exports by seven billions of francs, exports showing a fall in the year equivalent to about 40 per cent in value.

What may well prove the lowest ebb of French trade was reached in August 1932. During that month imports were 2,274,000,000 francs, against 3,188,000,000 francs in August, 1931, and 4,051,000,000 in the same month of 1930. Exports were 1,426,000,000, compared with 2,310,000,000 francs in August 1931, and 3,127,000,000 francs in August 1930. Thus although industrial production in France had decreased by only 30 per cent, exports were 'down' by more than half in two years, further proof of the remarkable stability of the internal market.

During July 1932, revenue returns showed that the yield of taxation from all sources – another barometer of prosperity – was 33 per cent less than in the corresponding month of 1931.

Traffic receipts of the French railways similarly reflect this slowing down in the economic activity of the country, the total receipts for the first half of 1932 being $17\frac{1}{2}$ per cent below the same period of 1931, for the whole of France, and 20 per cent in the industrial north. The daily average of goods trucks loaded was 65,100 in 1929, 65,400 in 1930, 54,900 in June 1931, 47,200 in June 1932.

In the light of these figures, it may be estimated that the decline in industrial activity in France, due to the depression, amounts to from 25 to 30 per cent.

The number of unemployed workers in receipt of relief on 31 August 1932, was 263,000, of whom 140,000 were in the Paris area. But this figure covers only that fraction of the workless who have exhausted their savings, for the Frenchman still looks upon the 'dole' as a charity, to be accepted only as a last resort, after the last centime accumulated during the good years – and 1930 was a 'good year' in France – has been exhausted.

No official figure exists of the total volume of unemployment in France, but according to an estimate given to me by the Secretary of the General Confederation of Labour, there are one million workless and a similar number partially unemployed, the industries most depressed being iron and steel, textiles and the luxury trades. That idle million were all in jobs in 1929, when France had no unemployment at all. Most of them were working twelve months ago. And there is evidence that the number of unemployed has declined during the past six months, which perhaps explains the confident belief of three unemployed men out of every four that the chance of work will come along before they have exhausted their 'nest eggs', and are driven to apply to the municipalities for relief.

The scale of relief afforded to the citizens of France who overcome their scruples and apply for aid, varies according to whether the applicant resides in Paris, the suburbs or the provinces, being highest in the capital.

Official figures of the French Ministry of Labour show that a single man receives 70 francs (12s. at normal rate of exchange) if living in Paris, and 49 francs (8s.) in the provinces. The corresponding rates for a married man without children are 101·50 francs (17s. 9d.) and 77 francs (12s. 10d.). Payments for families with children are proportionately higher, a family of four receiving 157·50 francs (26s. 3d.) in Paris and 126 francs (21s.) in the provinces.

'This 'dole' is subject to a means test, which perhaps explains its unpopularity with the French workers. For a means test necessitates inquiries and official visits to the home, and every Frenchman resents anyone 'prying' into his private affairs.

In cases where the total income of a family of four, one member of which is unemployed, exceeds 47 francs (7s. 10d.) a day, or 25 francs (4s. 2d.) a day for a family of two, no benefit is allowed.

This means test, and the fact that the Frenchman is loath to apply for aid until no other course is open to him, is responsible for the fact that during 1932 the French Government does not expect to spend more than one milliard of francs, or about £8,750,000 in English currency at normal rate of exchange, upon unemployment. And this despite the fact that no contribution to the unemployment fund is made by either employers or workers! That figure is striking evidence of how the ingrained habit which causes every Frenchman, however small his income, to put aside 25 per cent of his earnings is helping the country to escape one of the major dangers of the trade crisis.

b The most contradictory statements are being made concerning the situation in France. It is indeed equally true to speak of increasing difficulties, of stability, or of improvement, provided these terms are applied to different elements in the nation's activity.

The general business trend is beyond doubt downwards. The real improvement registered in 1933 in the world situation helped to bring about a temporary pick-up in France; but when the recovery abroad seemed to halt for a time – during the first months of 1934 – French industry experienced a serious setback. This was due in part to internal political troubles – perhaps also to the deflation policy, although it is difficult to believe that the modest budgetary measures taken in April have had much more than a psychological effect. In the main, however, it is due to persistent price discrepancies and to the commercial policy of all nations – including France herself. The difficulties of the tulle industry in Calais and Caudry and of the wool combers in Roubaix-Tourcoing are typical. Equally clear are the indications given by statistics of failures, railroad traffic, production figures, etc. Retail trade – as far as can be ascertained from partial data – is not more satisfactory. Official unemployment figures (315,000 persons) remain higher than a year ago by about 60,000 and the seasonal decline at the beginning of the summer period seems to have been less than normal. The actual number of unemployed is generally estimated at around one million, about the 1932 level. Imports are 16 per cent under last year – the bulk of the decline being represented by foodstuffs which were directly affected by the new quotas. On this point, however, the trend may change, in view of the recent settlement of trade disputes with Great Britain, Germany and Denmark.

Some encouraging factors are, however, worth noting. French prices have not lost all their elasticity, and their decline since January has been important. French national goods falling more than imported commodities. While retail prices only experienced slight reductions, the unweighted general wholesale index fell by 10 per cent during the first seven months of 1934. This has allowed exports to stand at the same level as last year in value, and even to *increase* in volume by over 10 per cent.

For agriculture, the term 'stability' seems best to define its position. Quotas have done their part, but so has Nature. At least one element of fear – and a very serious one – has been greatly allayed, namely the wheat situation. The sums involved in the financing of the carry-over at the end of the season will amount to over 3,000 million francs, which have been advanced directly or indirectly by the State, the Bank of France, the Caisse des Dépôts, etc. All forecasts concerning the yield of this year's crop indicate that it will be insufficient for consumption needs. In other words, no additional financing should be necessary, and some of the money thus frozen will possibly be released in the course of next winter. This, of course, does not imply that the present disorganization of the wheat market will soon be remedied. The price-fixing policy meets with growing opposition from the millers and even from some producers, and the official price – 108 francs per quintal –

remains distinctly above the black market quotations, which hardly reach 100 francs at present. At any rate, this year's crop will certainly contribute to the balancing of the market.

The wine-growing districts have also been depressed by heavy stocks, but there are indications that the vine crops also may be well under normal. Should this prove true, the balance of the market would be easier to restore.

In contrast to the general economic situation, the financial position of France has distinctly improved since the beginning of the year. The Budget for the current year has, it is true, not been fully balanced. Economies – which did not cover the total estimated deficit – have been introduced during April only, and their result can only be felt progressively. Furthermore, a part of the work achieved in April is likely to be undone by the latest fiscal measures. These entail the loss of 2,000 million francs of annual revenue, while only 600 millions are expected from new taxes, the balance to be met by the more active prosecution of fraud. Although the new taxes apply to 1934, while some of the important reductions (e.g., those relating to income tax) will only come into force in 1935, the new deficit envisaged for the current year may be said to amount to about 3,000 or 4,000 million francs. But this is an improvement if compared with the 1933 deficit (6,832 million francs). Moreover, disappointing budgetary receipts had been taken into account by M. Germain-Martin when he drafted his decree-laws,* and therefore do not aggravate the situation.

The Treasury also seems to be in a better position. The storm of the month of March has been weathered. Treasury bills and National Defence bonds are being freely renewed, while the funds withdrawn from the savings banks at a rapid pace until late April are slowly flowing back to them. This does not mean that the task of the Treasury is easy. Its charges for 1934 – in addition to the Budget deficit – total 17,000 million francs, of which over 8,000 millions are refunding operations, the bulk of which should be carried out by 1 November 5,000 millions of advances to railroads, the Post Office, etc., to be reimbursed out of funds borrowed by these departments; and 3,500 millions of direct Treasury expenses, to be financed by its own issues. The way for the refunding operations has been prepared by the issue of 4 per cent. Treasury bonds in July, and, provided the market is not shaken by new internal or external political events, there is little doubt that the necessary issues can be placed without undue strain. The Treasury issue floated in July met at first with a fairly favourable reception – thanks to the strong tone of the rente market. A serious lowering of the interest rate is not, however, within sight as long as the Budget is not fully balanced.

* Germain-Martin was Finance Minister. Some of the decree laws were concerned with public works schemes, others with Fiscal reform. (Ed.)

In fact, the Budget question threatens to arise again soon. The Minister of Finance has announced that total credits for the general Budget will not exceed 47,000 million francs in 1935 (about the present figure, allowing for the April economies). This involves a new and serious contraction of expenditure, since the automatic increases of public expenditure should raise it by another 2,500 million next year and since tax receipts are affected by the business recession. A favourable factor, however, is that the Treasury has no important maturities falling due in 1935.

Thus the French situation – in spite of the inherent solidarity of all branches of the nation's economy – may perhaps be summarized as follows: aggravated depression in industry, trade and, probably, consumption; decline in prices; stability in agriculture; and a real, but not final, improvement in public finance. If it be recalled that in France anxiety about monetary stability has, up to the present, been mainly due to the threat of inflation for the purpose of covering the Budget deficit, it is easy to understand why the deflation policy has as yet met with so few obstacles, in spite of illogical protection measures, which make price adjustments so much more painful. Surprising as it may appear, the decline in prices – as long as industrial prices only are concerned – is not considered a national calamity, but an advantage.

c In order to follow the development of unemployment in the course of the six years of the crisis, it is no longer essential to know the exact number of the unemployed. It is sufficient to follow the variations of the unemployed relieved from public funds, and the number of registered job seekers unable to find work. These two curves show recognizably the same shape. They may be taken as reliable representations of the true movement of unemployment. . . .

In the first half of 1930, unemployment was almost non-existent. Its upward move only began in September. The number of unemployed relieved, which averaged 1,566 in the first quarter, 1,027 in the second and 936 in the third quarter, rose to 1,660 in October, 4,892 in November and 11,951 in December; the number of those unable to obtain work, which had remained around the latter figure for some time, rose towards the year's end to 14,963, 18,498 and 22,746. These are very modest figures, and they are . . . certainly lower than the true unemployment figures.

By March 1931, the movement accelerated, with 50,815 on unemployment relief; there followed a seasonal fall, reducing the figure to 35,836 in July. But then the curve rose sharply, reaching 92,157 in November and 147,009 in December. The number of those workers unsuccessfully seeking jobs runs parallel to that of the unemployed: a rise to March, an accentuated seasonal fall in July, followed by a new increase bringing the number of those looking for work to 175,940 in December.

From that moment on, the increase was sharp. In March 1932, the number of unemployed relieved reached 302,473, that of registered persons officially looking for jobs, 349,198. It had doubled since December 1931. Then there followed an improvement which was not entirely seasonal, for by the end of the years the figures were 277,109 and 306,952 respectively.

In the following year (1933) a new increase which brought the numbers of unemployed relieved to 330,874 and those of job seekers to 369,020, was followed by a clear improvement. From February to December, the wave of unemployment showed not merely a halt, but a tendency to recede. It even seemed as though conditions would revert to normal as fast as they had departed from it. In eight months, the figure of unemployed relieved had declined by about 73,000. The hope was that the depression was coming to an end. This was the case in Britain, in America and elsewhere. In France, on the other hand, the year 1934 saw a relapse. It opened with 332,266 unemployed relieved, and 367,212 workers unsuccessfully seeking work. The peak of the first quarter, in March, exceeded that of the preceding year; the seasonal reduction was less marked; it did not last as long; the rise was resumed in June; slow at first, it accelerated after October; the year ended with 419,129 unemployed relieved, and 454,915 job seekers unprovided for. This was a rise as sharp as that seen at the beginning of 1932. It continued in the same rhythm: in January 1935, there were 479,000 unemployed on relief, in February 503,502; in the labour exchange offices, the numbers of those unsuccessfully seeking work were 532,127 and 544,567.

This was the peak of the curve. The numbers of February 1935 were never to be reached again. But the depression was by no means over. The usual seasonal reduction was felt in March, but the lowest figures of the year, those of September, were still higher by 50,000 than those of September 1934. In December, there were 439,782 on unemployment relief and 481,099 unsuccessful applications for work, lower figures than in February, but still well above those of the same period in the previous year.

In February 1936, there were still 487,374 unemployed on relief (only 16,000 less than at the worst point in the crisis) and in July 1936, the end date of our inquiry, 420,000, i.e. 19,000 more than in July 1935. In the labour exchange offices, there were in February 528,624 workers unable to find employment, and in July more than 460,000. . . .

It is also as important to know the proportion of unemployed to the active population, as it is to know their absolute number.

Here again, in the absence of established correct figures of total unemployment, we take as a base, official figures of the numbers of unemployed on relief. . . . (Our) calculation takes as its base the census of 1931 (the results of the census of 1936 still being unknown), deducting owners and independent workers from the totals. The numbers against which our calculations are set are 7,843,694 men, 3,683,640 women, or a total of 11,527,334 wage earners. . . .

Up to November 1931, the proportion of unemployed on relief in the active population varied from 0·02 per cent in October 1930 to 0·03 per cent in October 1931. It rose sharply to 2·2 per cent, 2·6 per cent and 2·7 per cent during the first months of 1932; it fell then to a low of 2·2 per cent in October 1932, rose again to 3·1 per cent in February 1933, fell again to 2 per cent in September, to rise to 3·2 per cent in February 1934, 3·8 per cent in December, 4·6 per cent in February 1935. It returned to 4·4 per cent in February 1936 and 3·8 per cent in July.

Let us not forget that the true figures of total unemployment would be higher than those calculated here. . . . At its highest point, in February 1935, the true proportion of unemployed must have represented about 9 per cent of the active population. In other words, something under one wage earner in ten of those in employment in 1931 was out of work.

Of the active working population against which the proportion of the unemploymet have been measured here, only those employed on the railways and in the fisheries have been excluded.

d . . . The number of workers whom the *offices* have been unable to place in employment enables us to trace and measure, in some approximate way, the development of the unemployment crisis. The appearance of an excess of unsatisfied job demands over *placements* becomes noticeable from November 1930. At the end of January 1931, there were 44,919 workers seeking employment but unable to find it, as against 12,662 *placements*; the gap has increased except for the period when agricultural work was available during the summer, and there were 187,000 workers looking for work but unable to find it at the end of the year (against 26,000 in December 1930).

The comparative trend in unfilled vacancies, which is determined by slightly different factors, complements the evidence provided by trends on the demand side. The number of unfilled vacancies has continued to decrease, fluctuating between 10,000 and 8,000 during the first half year, then falling to 2,900 in December. The proportion of workers placed in employment vacancies – which amounted to approximately 60 per cent each month in 1930 (until October), decreased, in 1931 to 22 per cent in January and 4·5 per cent in December.

The number of unemployed workers in receipt of assistance, which barely exceeded 28,000 in January (1931) increased to 50,815 in March, diminished in the summer . . . and increased to 161,773 in December (1931). The majority of those in receipt of relief lived in the Seine, the Nord, the Rhône, the Seine-et-Oise, the Loire and the Bouches-du-Rhône. The assistance has been progressively increased in amount and duration. . . .

A later estimate of unemployment is provided for us by the monthly inquiry which the *Inspecteurs Du Travail* and the *Ingénieurs des Mines* have made since January 1931 in the concerns which come under their supervision and which employ more than 100 people. These inquiries provide figures relating to the normal work force complement, the number of workers employed and the number of hours worked each week for each concern. This last figure is of particular importance, since it constitutes the only certain figure we have available to assess partial unemployment. As regards the mines, the statistics provide the maximum amount of documentation, since the pits which fall within the inquiry constitute 90 per cent of the mines currently in operation; as for other industries, the inquiries relate to 36 per cent of the working population of the categories within the scope of the inquiry.

[The report goes on to discuss the employment situation in the light of these reports. Based on figures for December 1931, the leading trades affected by the reduction in employment included storekeeping, and work in precious stones.]

The inquiries provide us with exact details regarding the phenomenon of partial employment . . . the proportion of workers not working a full week of 48 hours, kept at about 3 per cent until the last quarter of 1930. From December to January 1931 it increased from 6·4 per cent to 16·7 per cent and at the end of the year it reached 30·3 per cent. This system of working a short week, which offers the double advantage of spreading the burden of unemployment among the workers and of providing the employers with a labour force and trained reserves, all ready for the time when the economy recovers, has been widely used.

The importance of partial unemployment varies a great deal between professional categories, and within each category according to the time of the year. . . . The percentage of partially unemployed in various professions, in relation to their usual strength, was 73·6 per cent in the mines, 71·6 per cent in the fine metal trades, 68·4 per cent in textiles, 49 per cent in the ordinary metal trades, 45 per cent in the skin and leather trade, 43 per cent in rubber, paper and upholstery, etc.

This concept of partial unemployment, however, requires some explanation. For some workers the weekly reduction amounts to only a few hours; for others it involves a period of several days. Thus a scientific statistical analysis must convert the real number of partially unemployed into an estimated number of totally unemployed. All that needs to be done, is to multiply the number of partially unemployed by the number of hours lost by each of them; dividing this figure by 48, which represents the normal working week, a figure is obtained which gives the number of completely unemployed to which the figure for the partially unemployed relates. This calculation enables us to state that partial unemployment in December 1931 amounted to 8 per cent of the total work force in the industries which have been the subject of inquiries, as against 0·8 per cent in December 1930. Altogether, unemployment in 1931 has deprived 20 per cent of the work force employed in 1930 of their jobs.

e For an accurate appreciation of the work situation of an industry, we should need to obtain a figure which would take account both of the reduction in the labour force and the partial unemployment of those who remain at work.

If, with this in mind, partial unemployment were translated into complete unemployment – i.e. if the number of hours lost were divided by 48 – and if one added to the number thereby obtained that of the workers who are out of work, one would obtain a number which, to some extent, measured the total reduction in activity in the industry under consideration.

The following tables, compiled according to this method of calculation, provide an estimate of partial unemployment translated into complete unemployment and the percentage of the total reduction in activity, in the textile industry in relation to the corresponding month of the previous year.

ESTIMATE OF PARTIAL UNEMPLOYMENT TRANSLATED
INTO COMPLETE UNEMPLOYMENT
(Percentage in absolute terms)

	1930	1931	1932	1933	1934	1935	1936
January	0·4	3·0	18·8	6·9	6·1	15·5	10·7
February	0·4	6·5	20·1	7·1	7·7	17·0	10·5
March	0·3	7·5	19·9	7·2	7·4	16·7	9·4
April	0·4	7·7	17·3	7·3	8·5	16·1	9·1
May	0·4	7·6	17·1	7·5	9·5	15·9	9·1
June	2·1	7·2	15·9	6·8	10·8	14·5	9·1
July	0·4	8·0	15·3	5·8	12·2	13·2	9·1
August	0·4	7·2	15·0	5·5	14·3	13·2	9·1
September	0·5	9·8	14·0	5·5	15·5	12·6	9·1
October	0·7	9·4	12·1	5·6	16·2	12·2	9·1
November	0·8	11·3	9·2	5·3	16·4	11·8	9·1
December	1·1	14·9	7·4	5·4	16·2	11·2	9·1

PERCENTAGE OF THE TOTAL DECREASE IN EMPLOYMENT IN RELATION TO
THE CORRESPONDING MONTH OF THE PREVIOUS YEAR, MEASURED BY THE
DECREASE IN NUMBERS EMPLOYED AND THE DECREASE IN THE HOURS OF
WORK, CONVERTED INTO COMPLETE UNEMPLOYMENT

	1931	1932	1933	1934	1935	1936
January	6·6	30·4	+5·9	+2·2	18·7	+4·3
February	10·2	31·1	+9·9	+0·4	19·0	+4·6
March	12·0	29·7	+10·9	+0·2	19·1	+1·9
April	12·2	28·4	+11·5	1·5	17·7	+6·6
May	12·4	26·7	+9·4	3·6	17·2	+6·6
June	11·1	25·0	+9·3	5·5	13·6	6·6
July	14·3	23·1	+9·9	8·6	9·9	6·6
August	14·5	21·9	+10·8	12·2	7·2	6·6
September	15·9	19·2	+10·9	14·9	4·4	6·6
October	18·2	23·8	+7·8	16·8	2·8	6·6
November	21·0	9·8	+3·8	18·2	0·9	6·6
December	26·4	1·7	+4·2	19·4	+1·8	6·6

Figures preceded by a + sign indicate an increase in the number employed.

Taking the situation in 1930 as a base, it is possible to indicate the monthly fall in employment for 1935 and 1936 viewed in relation to the 1930 position.

	1935 %	1936 %		1935 %	1936 %
In January	43·2	40·4	In July	42·5	—
In February	45·5	40·8	In August	41.1	—
In March	45·8	39·5	In September	40·3	—
In April	45·4	38·7	In October	40·3	—
In May	45·3	—	In November	38·6	—
In June	42·3	—	In December	38·3	—

The lowest point was reached in March 1935 with, in relation to 1930, a fall in activity of 45·8 per cent, out of which complete unemployment accounted for 29·2 per cent and hours lost for 16·6 per cent. Since this date a slight improvement has been in evidence, which translated itself up to the end of 1935, into an increase in activity each succeeding month. After a break at the beginning of 1936 . . . the movement continued its upward path in March and in April 1936 a fall in activity of 38·7 per cent was registered, as compared with April 1930, of which 30 per cent related to complete un-employment and 8·7 per cent under the heading of hours lost.

The table we have just presented would not be complete if it did not indicate that, according to the employers' organizations, unemployment in the textile trades is accompanied by a shortage of skilled labour. This concerns those jobs for which a long apprenticeship is necessary, in which trade traditions and skills are transmitted from generation to generation and which quite often require hereditary skills. Now, excessively low wages are dissuading an increasing number of sons from following their fathers' occupation. On the other hand, this family and traditional character of the work also gives it a regional character; consequently one cannot think of bringing into the region labour which is hereditarily unaccustomed and ill-equipped to work in another area, where moreover, quite often, manufacturing processes are quite different. This is a further proof that we are not always able to overcome a certain amount of shortage of skilled labour by enlisting the help of the unemployed. . . .

The situation which we have just described is due, in the first place, to general causes which affect all branches of production. We shall not dwell on these, since it is not our task here to study the present crisis in its entirety, of which unemployment in the textile industry constitutes only a particular part. We shall note only two points: firstly, the dispersed nature of the firms, which in other respects constitutes an advantage, makes the textile industry less resistant to the crisis than an industry in which production is concentrated; on the other hand, the textile industry is affected perhaps more than any other industry by the reduction in purchasing power which the economic depression has brought, since its ultimate market is the individual consumer and when spending power is curtailed, one of the first severely curbed items is expenditure on clothes.

As to the special causes of the crisis in the textile industry, it has been frequently indicated that there are difficulties which relate to the fact that the industry is dependent essentially upon fashion. This fact is not peculiar to our age and if the consequences may be a cause of trouble, for some branches of the textile trade, it so happens that they work to the advantage of others. There is no doubt that present fashion has led to a reduction in the amount of cloth needed for clothes and undergarments, especially in the case of women, but it has led to an increase in activity in the hat trade. Fashion, by making people feel obliged to buy new clothes even when it is not really necessary, acts in a general way as a stimulant in the field of consumption, to an extent, in fact, which is out of proportion to the increase in purchasing power. . . . Fashion enforces sudden variations and changes on production and this does not allow the industry to develop a steady rhythm. But these are factors which are not new and the textile industry, in general, has been well able to adapt to these changing conditions. It can still do so today, but the difficulties of the present crisis make this adaptation a much more painful process.

Among the present causes of the crisis, which are special to the textile industry, the most important, without doubt, is the fall in exports. To a greater or lesser degree all branches are, in normal times, heavily engaged in exporting. . . . From 13 milliard francs in 1929, exports have fallen to fewer than 3 milliards in 1935. . . . There is a less accentuated, but still profound fall, if one considers the quantity of exports rather than the value.

We shall not enter into the reasons which have led various countries to introduce customs barriers, sometimes placing an insurmountable obstacle to imports through prohibitive duties or tightly controlling them through quota limits. . . .

But a special aspect of the problem which concerns us is that as a result of protection of all kinds, textile industries have developed in the countries which were formally markets for French goods, and which can henceforth supply wholly or in great part, the needs of their own market. The new producers extend their activities into foreign markets and compete with our exporters, and this is a competition which, particularly in the case of the Japanese, is proving an extremely dangerous threat.

The depreciation of currencies provides certain of our competitors with a bounty on their exports and monetary instability, exchange agreements, the always difficult and sometimes defective mechanism of the *caisses de compensation,* make it difficult for us to recover our faith in foreign markets. . . .

. . . The employers' organizations . . . complain about the fiscal and social charges with which French industry is burdened and which, without being perhaps always heavier than those which effect producers in other countries, because of the special conditions prevailing in French industry, result in the charges weighing more heavily on the employers. The employers allege, moreover, that the cost of living in France results in wages being higher than, for example, they are in Ireland or Belgium. The workers' organizations deny this. In fact . . . it would appear . . . that in general, wages in the French textile trades are lower on average than wages in French industry.

f Retrospective analysis of tourist activity in France during 1933 unfortunately confirms the pessimistic note which was sounded in our analysis of the economic situation in France in 1932.

The *Office National du Tourisme* in its *Bulletin d'informations,* which appeared in March 1934, gives the following statistics of the number of foreigners who came to France in the course of the last few years.*

	1929	1930	1931	1932	1933
England	881,000	850,000	870,000	522,000	584,705
U.S.A.	296,174	276,344	205,320	143,203	101,200
Spain	350,213	250,123	200,114	120,000	95,000
Other countries:					
Belgium	38,000	25,320	52,430	41,350	42,000
Switzerland	45,230	41,218	46,380	35,200	35,800
Holland	55,000	53,215	51,210	30,300	21,000
S. America	150,000	88,123	50,321	20,250	11,000
Varians	30,155	23,122	20,150	15,300	10,500
Germany	35,215	38,210	28,252	10,250	25,200
Austria	30,120	23,152	18,150	6,500	5,100
	1,911,107	1,667,831	1,542,285	944,358	931,505

4/33 The Kreuger Swindle

OTTO WALTER, (ed.), *Ivar Kreuger, die Katastrophe* (Olten & Konstanz, 1932), pp. 143–152, 209–210. (Ed. Tr.)

A. B. Kreuger & Toll obtained a starting capital of one million Kronor. Certainly a modest enterprise. Neither was the match firm at the beginning large, at 45 million Kronor. . . .

The share capital of A. B. Kreuger & Toll has grown in the following manner:

1911	1 million Kronor	1921	28 million Kronor
1914	2 million Kronor	1927	50 million Kronor
1917	6 million Kronor	1928	65 million Kronor
1918	16 million Kronor	1929	76 million Kronor

The larger the capital, the larger the circle of investors needed for its provision, but the greater, at the same time, the care to be taken that they obtain no influence over the concern. Kreuger proved to be a past master in both directions. . . .

Kreuger's intention (in using the 'participating debenture') was the preservation of his own undisputed control.

* A footnote in the original indicates that the figures do not provide an entirely accurate picture of tourist activity. Many tourists included in the figures were only passing through France. For example, only 222,184 English tourists, out of 584,705 in 1933 spent one week or more in France. (Ed.)

A deluge of these issues descended on the capital markets.

In May 1928 the first 20 million Kronor were offered to the shareholders of A. B. Kreuger & Toll at their face value of 20 Kronor.

In September 1928 a further 45 million Kronor followed. Maatschappij Kreuger & Toll takes over the whole, exchanging 18 million Kronor for preference shares of the Swedish American Investment Corp. and hands over the rest to the American–European banking group which issues it at 525 per cent.

In March 1929 another 16,250,000 Kronor go to the Amsterdam Kreuger & Toll, and from them to the banks and thence to the investing public. The price was 600 per cent. In October 1929 the last 37,961,000 Kronor are released to the capital market. A round milliard Kronor flowed into the coffers of A. B. Kreuger & Toll in the three years 1927–1929 by the sale of shares, debentures and participating debentures. The need was by no means covered by this. . . .

International Match Corporation (of America) was also put into action to provide capital for the trust. Three times in 1924, 1925, and 1926 respectively it issued 450,000 preference shares at $35 and brought in, at rising issue prices, $60 million. Besides this, two issues of debentures for $50 million each were made.

Thus a total of 600 million Kronor was gained for the trust. . . .

Svnska Tändsticks A. B. contributed no less to the financing. In 1922 its share capital is doubled to 90 million Kronor. In 1924 another doubling brings it up to 180 million Kronor; issue price: 110 per cent. In 1927 90 million Kronor at 230 per cent are issued. Half goes to the Dutch associated company Administratie Maatschappij vor Algemeene Nyverheids Vaarden in exchange for founder's shares of Intermatch and of the Cia. Chilena.

The capital needs rise to their highest point in 1931. In Sweden, 60 million Kronor of debentures are issued at the same time as 90 million Kronor of new shares at 150 per cent.

If we add it all up we reach, ignoring the 90 million Kronor 'A' shares, more than another half milliard Kronor.

There were other central units of the trust at Kreuger's disposal, and he did not disdain their aid. . . . But these examples may suffice. . . .

Capital investment and the right to decision making were almost totally separated. The participating debentures . . . formed a means of finance of unparalleled fruitfulness, without giving the purchaser any power. They were shares as far as their return was concerned, but they gave the holder none of the voting power which had been usual hitherto at least in continental Europe.

Even so, Kreuger's own means were too small in relation to the total need for capital for him to have kept all power in his own hands by means of gold debentures and participating debentures alone. Another instrument was put into action and played with consummate skill: The control share. . . . Those splendid 'B' shares were created whose voting power was limited to one-thousandth. It was introduced into Svenska Tändsticks A. B. in 1924. Since then no more fully privileged shares were created. Only the existing 90 million Kronor kept their full voting rights as 'A' shares, 90 million dominated 270 million, or rather, since half was enough for control, 45 million could dominate 315 million, plus 80 million in loans and with it the whole worldwide match business of a total of 700 million Kronor. . . . Of course, Kreuger did not invest anything like 45 million Kronor to dominate the match trust.

The experiment, which succeeded so brilliantly, was repeated in A. B. Kreuger & Toll and further extended. In 1926 the shareholders were offered, in exchange for voting shares, shares of the 'B' series. Since then, the 10 million Kronor in the form of 'A' shares have become the instruments of control.

> 60,000,000 Kronor in 'B' shares
> 139,166,660 Kronor in participating debentures
> 182,238,806 Kronor in gold debentures
> 387,405,466 Kronor faced these 10 million Kronor by
> the end of 1930.

Matters were similar in the telephone combine, and again in the Bolinden mining combine. The non-voting preference shares of the International Match Corporation had the same purpose.

The result is overwhelming. A few million Kronor in shares of A. B. Kreuger and Toll dominate an economic world empire without compare. . . .

The first clear documentary proof of Ivar Kreuger as swindler and forger occurs in 1923. He met Bredberg in the summer of 1923. Bredberg was manager of the newly founded Union financière pour l'Industrie, registered in Zurich. Its share capital was registered at 18 million Kronor. Of this the match company held 6 million, and Bryant & May Limited, London, Nitedals match factories, Oslo and Union Allumettière, Brussels, together held 12 million. Ivar Kreuger informed Bredberg that the American Kreuger & Toll Corporation had bought property to the value of 7,750,000 Swiss francs; and he was to enter this sum in the books of his firm. Bredberg did as he was told, although he never saw a contract. He credited the American branch company with 7,750,000 fr and believed himself to have become an owner of land.

A few days later, on 1 July, Kreuger informed Bredberg that the property in question had been sold to a 'Mr. Lehmann' for 21,200,000 francs. This sum was to be debited to Lehmann. On the other side, Lehmann had already paid 3·2 million fr. in cash, and this was to be credited to him. Kreuger needed that cash personally, and his account was to be debited with that amount in turn. Bredberg followed all these instructions; it was all quite clear. After deducting expenses, the profits were exactly 13,449,920 fr.

The 18 million unpaid by Lehmann were covered by an I.O.U. from him, at an interest rate of 12 per cent. This paper was signed 'E. B. Lehmann'. Bredberg took charge of this obligation and asked for Lehmann's address. He also wanted to know whether he should get in touch with him in order to settle the method of interest payments. But Kreuger replied that he wanted to settle these details himself with Lehmann, since the latter preferred confidentiality and solitude.

Nine years later the police report stated sadly and laconically: 'Mr. Lehmann' never gave any signs of life. Bredberg said in evidence that he never got to know the standing or address of that personage. Nor did he ever pay any interest, but was annually debited with it so that the book debt grew year by year and amounted by the end of 1931 to 33,120,000 Swiss francs. This sum was carried as an asset in the balance sheet made out by Bredberg. It was reported to Stockholm and entered as an asset there. The net profit of the trust has risen by 33 million Swiss francs!

Yet Mr. Lehmann never existed. Ivar Kreuger never, at any time, anywhere sold him any land, any more than the American Kreuger and Toll ever bought any land. The whole story had simply been invented by the head of Kreuger and Toll and of the match trust, in order to pretend to profits which had not been made.

4/34 The Stavisky Affair, 1934

a *The Times* 5, 8, 10, 11 January 1934.

b Proclamation of the *Camelots du Roi* 7 January 1934, in A. WERTH, *France in Ferment* (London, 1934), pp. 90–91.
Both printed in KERTESZ, *Documents* [*see* Document 1/15a], pp. 328–331.

a [5 January 1934.]
Although the total value of the fraudulent bonds issued on behalf of the Bayonne Municipal Pawnbroking Establishment is not yet known, reports now set the figure at about 500,000,000 francs (£4,000,000 gold). The magnitude of the swindle and the possibilities of political repercussions are causing the Government some concern.

This morning M. Chautemps, the Prime Minister, summoned the

Law Officers of the Republic and of the Seine Department* and the Chiefs of the Police and gave orders that no effort was to be spared to apprehend Alexandre Stavisky, who is wanted in connection with the affair, and added that whatever the position of those implicated they must be brought to justice. . . .

Meanwhile two letters written in June and September 1932, by M. Dalimier, the Minister of Labour and now Minister of the Colonies, have been published. The first, addressed to M. Hermant, president of the General Insurance Committee declares that the writer, in accordance with a request from the Minister of Commerce, wishes to point out the desirability of facilitating the placing of municipal bonds. The second, addressed to M. Tissier, the director of the Crédit Municipal of Bayonne, . . . suggests that he should approach the insurance companies for the disposal of the municipal bonds, adding that, in view of the security they offered, the bonds would in all probability be taken up without difficulty. . . .

[8 January 1934.]
. . . An official report issued yesterday says that Stavisky was born in 1886, near Kieff. His father, a dentist, came to France in 1900 and was naturalized. In 1912 Stavisky was sentenced to 15 days' imprisonment and a fine of 25 francs for fraud. He joined the French Army as a volunteer in August 1914. 'Then' – laconically says the report – 'he founded a bank and was sentenced on 15 July 1915, to six months' imprisonment and a fine of 100 francs.'

In July 1926, Stavisky was again arrested on a charge of fraud. In December 1927 he was released on bail of 50,000 francs on grounds of ill health. A police doctor certified that he could be treated at the prison infirmary, but the prison doctor disagreed. On the plea that he was suffering from paraplegia, Stavisky's case was adjourned on successive occasions until last October. It stands on the list for hearing on 26 January. Stavisky was known at various times by the names of Serge Alexandre, Sacha Alex, Doing de Monti, and Victor Boitel. . . .

[10 January 1934.]
Alexandre Stavisky, the financier who, according to the statements of the police shot himself in a villa at Chamonix yesterday afternoon when about to be arrested, died early this morning. . . . It is . . . presumed officially [on the basis of a post-mortem examination] that Stavisky committed suicide. . . .

This evening several hundred demonstrators, mainly composed of *camelots du roi*,† came into collision with the public force who guarded all approaches to the neighbourhood [of the Chamber] . . . Mounted guards charged repeatedly and more than two hundred arrests were made before calm was restored. . . .

* See Glossary.   † A Royalist group associated with semi-Fascist factions. (Ed.)

[11 January 1934.]

Tomorrow's debate in the Chamber on the six interpellations handed in on the subject of the Stavisky affair is likely to be stormy. The interpellations seek to fix the responsibility for the political and administrative errors which the case has revealed, to protect public savings . . . and to impugn Courts and officials who have manifestly failed to do their duty. . . .

The air of the lobbies has reeked for days with the miasma of distrust, suspicion of political profiteering in Stavisky's ill-gotten gains, of shares in the plunder, of collusion and interference in the course of justice. . . .

b Proclamation of the *Camelots du Roi*, 7 January 1934.
To the People of Paris.

At a time when the Government and the Parliament of the Republic declare themselves incapable of balancing our budget, and continue to defend the topsy-turvy foundations of their regime; while they refuse to reduce the burden of taxation and are actually inflicting more taxes on the French people, a scandal breaks out. This scandal shows that, far from protecting the savings of the people, the Republican Authorities have given free course to the colossal rackets of an alien crook. A Minister, M. Dalimier, by his letters of 25 June and 23 September 1932, deliberately* provided an instrument which enabled the thief Stavisky to rob the insurance companies and the Social Insurance Fund of over half a milliard francs. He has been urged to resign; but he has refused to do so.† He should be in prison together with his pals Stavisky and Dubarry; instead of which, he continues to be a member of the Government whose duty it is to inquire into this affair. Dalimier is not alone; we can see behind him a crowd of other ministers and influential members of Parliament, all of whom have, in one way or another, favoured the adventurer's rackets, especially by instructing the police to leave him alone, and by suspending during many years the legal proceedings that should have been taken against him. There is no law and no justice in a country where magistrates and the police are the accomplices of criminals. The honest people of France who want to protect their own interests, and who care for the cleanliness of public life, are forced to take the law into their own hands.

At the beginning of this week, Parliament will reassemble and we urge the people of Paris to come in large numbers before the Chamber of Deputies, to cry 'Down with the Thieves' and to clamour for honesty and justice.

Maurice Pujo.

P.S. Instructions will be sent to our friends in due course.

* The official Commission of Enquiry did not establish deliberate intention to deceive on the part of Delimier. (Footnote in Kertesz.)
    † Dalimier later resigned his ministerial post. (Footnote in Kertesz.)

Chapter 5   The Response to the World Economic Crisis and Depression

Introduction

How did the various West European countries and Scandinavia, excluding the Fascist regimes, respond to the world economic crisis and depression? A major initial reaction following the onset of the depression in 1929 was to increase the barriers to trade through tariffs and quotas (5/1). Countries withdrew into themselves. Restrictions were applied particularly to food and manufactured goods, with the consequence that 'Tariffs moved up sharply from 1930; [and] by 1932 world trade was well tied up.'*

Following the 1929 collapse in America and the widespread consequences which followed from the event and the reactions it provoked, world economic conditions deteriorated through 1929 and 1930 and problems were compounded in 1931 by the international monetary crisis, which originated in Austria. The projected Customs Union between Germany and Austria (5/2) was opposed by the French (5/3), and it was the withdrawal of French funds which exposed the weakness of Austria and particularly that of the major banking institution, the Credit Anstalt, which had become heavily reliant on foreign funds. In May 1931, as a result of the French action, which exacerbated domestic and technical problems, the Credit Anstalt was faced with threatened collapse. Such a situation exposed the financial weakness of virtually the whole of central Europe. After the crisis had been temporarily shored up by an international agreement in August 1931, attention shifted to Britain, and in September 1931 the withdrawal of funds from London was sufficiently heavy to force the British Government to suspend gold payments. There could be no clearer evidence of the destruction of the stable economic network which had previously dominated Europe's commercial relations.

The principal international attempt to resolve the problems of trade and international finance came in London in 1933. The agenda of the London conference was wide ranging: the stabilization of currencies and exchange rates, the raising of commodity prices and the reduction of tariffs, were all to be considered in the light of the attempt to reconstruct world trade.

The attempt by the conference to tackle the problem of commodity prices was reflected in the International Wheat Agreement (5/4). The principal exporting countries agreed to a limitation of wheat exports in 1933–1934 and

* W. A. Lewis, *op. cit.*, p. 58.

in 1934–1935, while the major importing countries promised not to increase the area sown to wheat and to adopt all possible means of increasing wheat consumption. The results of the agreement, however, were limited, with the result that the vicissitudes of nature had a greater impact upon prices than the agreement, which failed to persuade European importing countries to remove barriers and increase imports, which lay at the centre of the world wheat problem.

The efforts of the conference to deal with the world's monetary problem also resulted in failure and were wrecked principally by American attitudes. A powerful group of conference representatives, from major gold bloc countries, Belgium, France, Italy, Netherlands, Poland and Switzerland – and also Great Britain, put forward for American approval a declaration on the international stabilization of currencies (5/5). The declaration of 30 June 1933 was to the effect that 'stability in the international monetary field' should be attained as quickly as possible and that 'gold should be re-established as the international measure of exchange value, it being recognized that the parity and time at which each of the countries now off gold could undertake to stabilize must be decided by the respective governments concerned' (5/5). President Roosevelt, who had abandoned the gold standard in April 1933, rejected this idea of restoring the gold standard because it would hinder American recovery policies. Roosevelt was committed to eliminating the American slump by raising prices and any attempt to do this on the gold standard, he was advised, would have put American prices out of line with world prices. His policy, therefore, was to leave the dollar to fluctuate on the foreign exchanges. 'The sound internal economic system of a nation,' the Americans affirmed, 'is a greater factor in its well being than the price of its currency in changing terms of the currencies of other nations' (5/6). The failure of the conference to achieve a general monetary agreement was not entirely the responsibility of America. Britain's abandonment of the gold standard in 1931 and her monetary and tariff policy were also important factors which influenced America to insist upon 'a free hand to devalue the dollar',* and so upset 'the summit of the international efforts to cope with the depression'.†

By the end of 1931, the first year of the international monetary crisis, countries were divided into three currency categories: those still on gold, those depreciating freely, and those linked to sterling. The London conference failed to bridge the differences between them. After its adjournment, the delegates of all the British countries, except the Irish Free State, reiterated their faith in the monetary and economic policy of the sterling countries, on the

---

* S. Pollard, *The Development of the British Economy, 1914–1950* (London, 1962), p. 230.

† W. A. Lewis, *op. cit.*, p. 67.

grounds that this would not only facilitate Empire trade, but would also stimulate and increase the trade of the world (5/7). America, as already mentioned, maintained its right to depreciate freely (5/6) and during 1934 pressure upon the gold bloc (France, Italy, Belgium, Luxemburg, the Netherlands and Switzerland) from the depreciated pound sterling and the dollar became increasingly acute. This problem for the Gold Countries was discussed at Geneva in September, where they reaffirmed their declaration of 3 July 1933 made at the London conference (5/8, see footnote in 5/8 for their 1933 declaration. In October 1934, a further gold bloc meeting was held in Brussels. At this conference a protocol was signed, which created a General Commission to examine the possibility of increasing trade between the participating states and two sub-committees were also established, to deal with transport and tourism (5/9). It is clear that at this stage international currency divisions had still not been resolved.

It has been suggested that the failure of the 1933 world economic conference in London marked 'in a minor sense, the end of an era'. According to this opinion, 'from 1933 countries abandon hopes of international revival and concentrate on stimulating domestic demand, if necessary at the expense of still greater restrictions on international trade. From 1933 the divergent domestic problems of nations become more important than the international economy, to the extent that even the world market disintegrates into many different markets, with different price levels and restricted interchange.'*

If we examine national policies, between 1928 and 1936 the response in France to the international crisis and depression was to follow a deflationary policy, which was 'perhaps the last sustained attempt to impose deflation as a remedy for depression'.† Policies intended 'to avoid the devaluation of the currency' (5/10), were doggedly pursued. A reduction in State expenditure, a fall in industrial production, falling prices, particularly in agriculture, and increased unemployment all bore witness to the policy, intended to defend the *franc poincaré*. So, too, did the increase in French tariffs and the imposition of quotas (5/11).

French economic policy changed in 1936, with the advent of the Blum Government, which adopted a new and distinctive approach to the country's economic problems. Blum engaged in a wide ranging reform experiment, which came to mark 'a process of far-reaching change' (5/12). 'The restoration of purchasing power destroyed or reduced by the crisis', an attack on 'unemployment and the crisis in industry', the 'rapid execution of a public works programme', the establishment of National Grain Board, the nationalization

---

* *Ibid.*, p.68.

† Tom Kemp, 'The French Economy under the Franc Poincaré', *Economic History Review*. Second series, volume XXIV. No. 1, Feburary 1971, p. 82.

of the Bank of France and measures of 'financial purification' were important aspects of the Popular Front election programme (**5/13a**). The election programme and the Ministerial Declaration of the Popular Front made it clear that the Government's schemes were particularly designed to protect the interests of Labour (**5/13b**), and it was emphasized from the first that the administration was committed to a 'rejection of retrenchment' which had hitherto dominated economic policy during the crisis (**5/13c**).

Blum came into power on a wave of sit-down strikes which paralysed the country, and provided an early test of the seriousness of the pledges which the Popular Front had made to Labour. On 6–7 June 1936, after lengthy discussions between the employers, the Unions and the Government at the Hôtel Matignon, an agreement which ended the strikes was signed, by which wages were increased by about 12 per cent (**5/14**). Legislation followed which provided holidays with pay, and a forty-hour week, with the pay previously granted for forty-eight. The policy of protecting French workers by regulating the immigration of foreign labour (**5/15**), which had developed during the crisis years was continued and the election promise that the Bank of France 'must cease to be a private concern' led to the democratization of the structure of the Bank, although the share capital was not in fact nationalized (**5/16**). A further redemption of election pledges came with the nationalization of the war industries. With the fall of the Blum Government in 1938, however, and the restoration of the forty-eight-hour week, which the national strike called by the *Confédération Général du Travail* could not prevent (**5/17**), the concessions to Labour effectively came to an end, and attempts were made to revive the confidence of capital.

The farmers were a second group which received favourable treatment from the Blum Government's attempt to bring about the recovery of the French economy. In its policy towards agriculture the Government was, in a sense, continuing the national policy which was 'directed towards maintaining a just balance between the urban and rural population' (**5/18a**). France, it was argued in certain quarters, would only maintain her national wealth by remaining 'an essentially agricultural country' (**5/18b**). With half the population living in communes of fewer than 2,000 persons, there were, in addition, other substantial reasons why no government could afford to ignore agriculture, particularly during the period of rapidly falling prices and movement from the land. The significant innovation of Blum's policy was the establishment in August 1936 of a wheat board, the *Office du Blé*, which was concerned with fixing a minimum price for wheat. Its main function was to regulate the quantity of wheat which could be put on the market (**5/19**). The end results, according to certain estimates, was an increase in the price of wheat of between 40–50 per cent during the period of the Popular Front Government.

There was a third aspect to the Blum Government's policy. French prices had become increasingly out of line with world prices despite the savage deflation in the early 1930s and it was commented in 1935 that 'the root cause (of France's economic problem) was ... the disequilibrium between French costs and world costs due to the over-valuation of the franc' (5/20).

By 1935, in fact, before the advent of the Popular Front, the extent of the decline in production and employment had forced the Government of the day to infringe its own deflationary policy. As *The Economist* noted, 'the Government and the Bank of France despite their orthodox canons, have been driven by the exigencies of the situation in the direction of credit expansion' (5/21); an Extraordinary Loan Budget of the summer of 1935, for example, provided for an annual expenditure of 600,000,000 francs on public works and armaments. Such action, while it could not solve the problem of unemployment, was sufficient to arrest the decline in prices and thus made the maintenance of the old gold parity untenable (5/21). The policy of the Blum Government hastened events. The increase in costs which derived from the policy adopted towards labour and agriculture, affected all manufacturers who could not easily adjust their selling prices. French prices became even more out of line in relation to those of other countries. Exports began to fall off and unemployment started to increase. The French dilemma was solved by the International Monetary Agreement of 25 September 1936 between the U.S.A., Britain and France. The French Government, for its part, decided that since that 'the desired stability of the principal currencies cannot be ensured on a solid basis except after the re-establishment of a lasting equilibrium between the various economic systems ... to propose to their Parliament the readjustment of their currency' (5/22), and thus the way was open for the French devaluation. The three parties agreed not to alter exchange rates without consultation (5/22), and if the gold standard had not been restored, a new type of international monetary mechanism had been created.

On 1 October 1936, after a week of intense activity, the French devaluation Bill became law (5/23a). 'The third decisive stage in a process of currency adjustment which began when the pound sterling with a number of other currencies cut loose from gold in September 1931 and continued when the dollar was depreciated in 1933' was completed (5/23b). With the French devaluation the gold bloc collapsed. Contemporaries were aware that this did not solve the world's economic problem. More positively, what it did offer was 'a better prospect ... of true exchange stability, corresponding to a genuine equilibrium between the different national economies' and 'an excellent prospect of the movement of domestic recovery spreading to the countries which had hitherto experienced nothing but a steady restriction of employment' (5/23b). As far as France was concerned, prices were now below world prices, and 'exports, employment and production increased rapidly',* although a variety of reasons – the continued insecurity of the franc, the export of capital, the low level of home investment, the slow natural increase of the population, the return of workers to the countryside, the restrictions upon labour immigration, and, until 1938, the existence of the forty-hour week, reduced the degree of recovery in productivity.

The improvement in the French economy after 1936 was related more to the 1936 devaluation than to the central core of the Blum experiment. The latter, through its concessions to the workers lost the Government the support of the business community, while the raising of agricultural prices and the passing on to the consumers of the rising costs of industrial production alienated the French middle classes 'who held the political balance'.† In view of such factors the amount of co-operation and support the experiment achieved was short-lived and insufficient to permit a major economic break-through.

In approaching the problem of unemployment created by the depression, the introduction of public works policies eventually came to overshadow schemes of unemployment assistance, which became faced with increasing demands as unemployment rose. Unemployment insurance schemes such as that promulgated in Germany in 1927 (5/24), for instance, had not built up sufficient reserves 'before the hard times came',‡ with the result that the government virtually abandoned the insurance aspects of the scheme. The increasing emphasis on public works activity intended to create work for the unemployed, was an important fourth dimension incorporated into the Blum Government experiment (5/25) and in the various schemes which were advocated and adopted in Germany before Hitler's accession to power (5/26). After 1933, of course, under the National Socialists, similar schemes became an integral part of the official economic policy (see 6/3, 6/4, 6/5, 6/6, 6/7).

Outside the totalitarian states, probably the most interesting and successful experiment in the use of public investment and 'well devised monetary control' as a response to the depression, took place in Sweden (5/27). The assumption of power by the Social Democratic Party in 1932 led to a reversal of previous relief activities for the unemployed. The 'reserve projects' which had developed before 1933 were intended only to supply bare necessities to the unemployed to sustain them until private enterprise managed to effect a recovery from the depression. In their policies the Social Democrats favoured

* W. A. Lewis, op. cit., p. 101.
† Tom Kemp, Econ. Hist. Rev., p. 97.
‡ H. Heaton, Economic History of Europe, rev. ed. (London, 1964), p. 736.

the institution of extensive public works schemes financed by borrowed public money. This, it was stressed, would create work and increase purchasing power, which would stimulate consumption and production (5/28). After 1933 such ideas provided the basis for official social policy (5/28, 5/29) and in the opinion of a minister closely associated with the new policy, the result was that between 1933 and 1936 Sweden witnessed a successful and instructive social experiment, which not only contributed to a recovery of the Swedish economy but also increased the country's ability to deal with future depressions (5/30, see also 5/27, 5/28). By the end of the inter-war period, as the I.L.O. recommendation on the national planning of public works indicates, there was official recognition of the major role which such schemes could play in counteracting economic depression and stimulating the economy (5/31).

The need for a state policy to overcome economic problems and the growing acceptance of Keynesian techniques of approaching these problems, (but *see below* pp. 458–9), were major characteristics associated with the various European responses to the depression. A second major lesson, although it took longer to learn, was the need for international economic co-operation. In other words, the dis-equilibrium of the inter-war years and the later effects of the Second World War helped to produce a situation conducive to greater Continental and international co-operation.

5/1 Tariffs in Europe

Royal Institute of International Affairs, *World Agriculture. An International Survey* (Oxford, 1932), pp. 179–184.

In considering tariffs and other protective measures it is possible to make a distinction between permanent protective policies, based on a considered policy arising out of the special national conditions of individual States, and the emergency measures applied by many governments in the past two years in the hope of averting the bankruptcy of their producers in a period of rapidly falling prices. The distinction, though real, must not be pushed too far. There is necessarily much overlapping in this division, since intensification of existing protective measures has been one of the principal resources of importing countries in the present emergency.

But though an importing country may protect her domestic agriculture by the imposition of a tariff on foodstuffs, or by more drastic measures of fixing a quota for foreign imports or even by prohibition, an exporting country cannot assist her farmers in this way, and other methods have been devised, such as valorization schemes, bounties on export, etc.

Continental European countries have imposed duties on almost all agricultural products; the highest duties have been imposed on cereals and sugar.

(a) *Wheat.* The only three countries in Europe offering an unrestricted market for wheat are Great Britain, the Irish Free State, and Denmark. After Great Britain the three largest European importers are Italy (average annual imports 1924–1929, 83·7 million bushels), Germany (average annual net imports 1924–1929, 79·2 million bushels), and France (average annual net imports 1924–1929, 46·5 million bushels). All of them have adopted high protection measures for grain, while almost all other European countries impose serious restrictions.

The International Institute of Agriculture provides the following comparison of Customs Duties on cereals in three great European importing countries (gold francs per quintal):

	France			Germany			Italy		
	1913	1930 July	1932 Jan	1913	1930 July	1932 Jan	1913	1930 July	1932 Jan
Wheat	7·00	16·24	16·24	6·79	18·52	30·86	7·50	16·50	20·46
Rye	3·00	4·26	7·11	6·17	18·52	24·69	4·50	4·50	9·96
Barley	3·00	3·05	3·05*	1·60	14·81†	24·69	4·00	4·00	4·01
Oats	3·00	6·09	6·09	6·17	14·81	19·75	4·00	3·25	3·26
Maize	3·00	2·03	3·41	3·70	3·09	§	1·15‡	1·15‡	1·36‡
Wheat flour	13·50¶	32·49¶	25·99	12·59	38·89	53·29	11·50	23·70	30·65
Rye	5·00¶	7·11	14·21	12·59	31·50	53·29	6·50	6·50	13·88

* Barley other than Malting barley.   † Feed barley, under Customs control.
‡ Except white maize, on which the duty is the same as on wheat.
¶ With milling extraction from 70 to 60 per cent.   § Import monopoly.

The effect of the protection extended to wheat is shown by the fact that between 1924 and 1931, when prices had fallen at Liverpool by 52 per cent, France, Germany, and Italy showed rises in price of 39, 60, and 2 per cent. In February 1931 prices converted for purposes of comparison stood as follows (per cwt.):

England	5s. 2d.	Germany	13s. 7½d.
France	14s. 5½d.	Italy	11s. 10d.

The retail price of bread per kilogramme in the countries listed above was as follows at the same date:

	White	Rye
England	4·0d.	—
France	4·61d.	—
Germany	9·63d.	4·44d.
Italy	4·92d.	—

Figures for January 1931, except for France which are for February 1931. From I.L.O. Report.

It will be seen that there is less difference in the price of bread than in the price of wheat. The reason for this is that the 'margins' for the various processes of manufacture and marketing differ.

As a result of German protective policy the total acreage under wheat rose in 1931–1932 to 5·4 million acres, an increase of more than a million acres over the average of 1925–1929. Only part of this increase was at the expense of the rye acreage.

The German system of grain protection was already in force before the war, but in recent years new devices have been adopted. After the war the immediate need was to feed the people as cheaply as possible and to make good the long years of the blockade, and cereals were imported free of duty. But in 1925 the prewar system in essentials was restored; the 'middle' rates of the 1902 tariff were put into action. The Government of the Reich renewed the right laid down in 1922 to change the duties without reference to the Reichstag; that is, they held the right to impose sliding-scale duties.

In 1926 and 1927 these 'middle' rates on grain were raised and their operation extended to the end of 1929. But in 1929 drastic changes in the law were made. The Müller Government (in July 1929) set aside the 'middle' rates of the tariff and imposed the rates fixed in the Swedish treaty of 1926 for countries enjoying Most-Favoured-Nation treatment, imposing the autonomous rates of the 1902 tariff on countries with no special treaty arrangements (Canada and Australia). Subsequently the treaty with Sweden was denounced, thus permitting the application of the autonomous rates on imports from other sources. At the end of the year sliding-scale duties were imposed for wheat, rye, and pigs. The Government set out the internal prices which tariff policy should aim at securing – the so-called 'right prices'. With the slump in world prices in 1930 these measures were insufficient, and drastic changes were made in the law passed in March of the year. Then came the fall of the Müller Cabinet, and the law was replaced by a more thoroughgoing instrument in April. Under this law the duties were raised on all agricultural imports. For rye, wheat, barley, oats, and peas the Government was empowered arbitrarily to fix the duty on the basis of the 'right' price.

German agrarian policy is designed partly for bargaining purposes. In so far as food imports other than tropical produce are concerned, it aims at establishing reciprocal arrangements with those European countries which offer a market for German goods. Even so, the desire is to be as nearly self-supporting as possible. It is argued that Germany could easily meet her requirements in non-tropical foodstuffs from European sources, and it is certain that in any negotiation for a regular preference system for grain and other produce of the Danubian States Germany would be the most important market.

(*b*) *Sugar.* The European beet-sugar producers are protected by excessively high tariff duties, directed against each other, and against the cane-sugar producers in Java and Cuba, who produce at comparatively low costs and export the greater part of their output. The European industry owes its origin, growth, and present existence to State encouragement by export bounties, subsidies, and protective tariffs. Most European countries have to reckon with a large excess of productive capacity in sugar, and, in order to reserve the home market for the home factories, have imposed high tariffs round their industries. The result of these measures is that only about one-quarter of the world's sugar production comes on the world market. The European industries reckon on selling the greater part of their output in the home market, except in the case of Czechoslovakia, which exports two-thirds of her total output; Germany exports only a very small percentage; Hungary exports 40 per cent, Roumania, Poland, and Bulgaria about one-third. All these countries are obliged to export to maintain the level of home prices, and in order to do this producers are concentrated in cartels which fix high prices in the home market in order to be able to export at low prices. In Germany, Czechoslovakia, and Poland, these cartels are compulsory organizations, with legally enforced membership. Sugar which comes on the world market from European countries is 'dumped', that is, sold below the cost of production in the country of origin.

The general level of tariff duties on sugar imports in 1930 amounted to 75–100 per cent of the wholesale price of sugar. A protective measure adopted by one government is immediately followed by other countries. For example, in April 1928, the British Government reduced the duties on raw sugar and maintained those on refined sugar, thus benefiting the British refiner; immediately Czechoslovakia granted its sugar factories a refund on trade taxes, to enable them to face the world with enhanced competitive power; the German and Austrian Governments followed suit by increasing the duties on imported sugar, and in January 1929 were joined by Italy. With the fall of prices the burden has become heavier.

Tariff Rates on Sugar, 1930

	Custom duties (per cwt.)
France	11s. 5d.
Great Britain	11s. 8d.
U.S.A.	12s. 2d.
Italy	14s. 5d.
Hungary	15s. 3d.
Germany	15s. 11d.
Russia	19s. 6d.
Czechoslovakia	21s. 2d.
Poland	23s. 4d.

Since this time the duties have been raised by several countries and various substitutes for higher rates have been attempted. The difference in the price of refined sugar in Germany and in Great Britain in 1930 corresponded to the difference in tariff protection in the two countries.

Retail Prices per lb. of Refined Granulated Sugar, including Duties in various Countries in 1930

	Pence per lb.
Italy	6$\frac{1}{2}$
Czechoslovakia	4$\frac{1}{2}$
Holland	4
Poland France	3$\frac{3}{4}$
Germany	3$\frac{1}{4}$
U.S.A.	3$\frac{3}{4}$
Belgium	2$\frac{1}{2}$
Great Britain	2$\frac{1}{2}$

Any considerable reduction in the tariff duties on sugar seems unlikely in the near future. European states impose these tariffs, primarily because in continental Europe beet sugar culture is regarded, whether rightly or wrongly, as the necessary condition of all intensive agriculture. The production of beet sugar determines the social conditions of large sections of the rural population. 'The sugar factories enable many field labourers to earn good wages during the winter months when otherwise owing to the climatic conditions they would be unemployed.'

General considerations of this kind, rather than the profit directly derived from the industry, have induced European states to maintain their apparently exorbitant rates on sugar. If it were practicable to change over to other crops providing similar advantages, it would be possible to advocate the abolition of the duties. Expert opinion on the continent of Europe is divided on the advantages of beet over other root crops.

The tariff policy of Germany weighs heavily on Poland and the wheat exporters of south-eastern Europe. For four years Germany and Poland conducted a tariff war in pigs and in rye, terminated in 1930 by the Polish–German agreement of that year. The new agreement of 1932 effected a reduction in the German rates on Polish butter and eggs. The division of the Austro-Hungarian monarchy among six independent states and the erection of tariffs in Austria and Czechoslovakia has seriously affected the Hungarian export of wheat and livestock, which relied principally on these markets before the war. [The Report then refers to the attempts of the Succession States to make common policy for the disposal of their surpluses in Europe by means of the preferential arrangements with the western importing countries.]

The more or less permanent considerations which secure the maintenance of duties on farm produce have been strengthened by the present crisis. In times of falling prices governments feel driven to protect producers' interests, and to attempt to ward off from their nationals the effect of the sudden drop in the price level. In a situation in which the trade balance cannot be restored by normal methods, governments turn to the restriction of imports, and, since the imports of raw materials are essential, they are driven to take action to reduce imports of food and to intensify cultivation at home to make good the deficiency from outside sources.

5/2 The Proposed Austro-German Customs Union

Heads of Agreement, enclosed in a letter from the Foreign Secretary, Henderson, to Sir H. Rumbold at the British Embassy in Berlin, 25 March 1931. Printed in *Documents on British Foreign Policy* [*see* Document 1/26e]. Second Series, vol. 2, pp. 7–9.

In the course of the conversations which took place in Vienna at the beginning of March 1931 the German Government and the Austrian Government agreed to enter forthwith into negotiations for a treaty to assimilate the tariff and economic policies of their respective countries on the basis and within the limits of the following principles:

I

1. The treaty is destined to mark the beginning of a new order of European economic conditions on lines of regional agreements, the independence

of the two countries being fully maintained and due respect being paid to the obligations undertaken by them towards third states.

2. More especially, both parties will in the treaty declare their willingness to enter into negotiations for a similar agreement with any other country expressing such a desire.

II

1. Germany and Austria will agree on a tariff law and a customs tariff which shall be put into force in both customs territories concurrently with the treaty and for the period of its validity.

2. During the validity of the treaty amendments to the tariff law and the customs tariff may only be effected in virtue of an agreement of both parties.

III

1. As long as the treaty remains in force the exchange of goods between the two countries shall not be subject to any import or export duties. . . .

IV

The two Governments shall agree to stipulations in the treaty concerning a provisional arrangement regarding interchange in respect of the turnover tax and as to such goods for which, at the present time, monopolies or excise duties are in existence in either of the two countries.

V

1. The Customs Administration of each of the two countries shall be independent of that of the other and shall remain under the exclusive control of the Government of its respective country. Furthermore, each country shall bear the expenses of its own Customs Administration.

2. Both Governments, whilst fully respecting the above principle, will assure by special measures of a technical character the uniform execution of the tariff law, the customs tariff and the other tariff regulations. . . .

VII

1. No import, export or transit prohibitions shall exist between Germany and Austria. . . .

IX

1. Each of the two Governments, even after the entry into force of the treaty, shall retain in principle the right to conclude commercial treaties with third States on their own behalf.

2. In such negotiations with third States, the German and the Austrian Governments will take heed that the interests of the other contracting party are not infringed by the text and object of the treaty to be concluded. . . .

x

The two Governments will take the necessary steps in due time to bring into accord with one another and with the contents and object of the treaty, the existing commercial treaties concluded by Germany and Austria with third States so far as they contain obligations respecting customs tariff rates or so far as they might impair the execution of the existing import and export prohibitions and other regulations on the exchange of goods. . . .

5/3 French Memorandum on the Special Situation in Austria, 16 May 1931

Printed in *Documents 1931* [*see* Document 4/14], pp. 6–8.

Extract from French Constructive Memorandum dealing with the special situation of Austria, 16 May 1931

It would be desirable that the general programme of European economic restoration should be completed by exceptional measures enabling immediate and effective aid to be given to Austria.

Austria, situated as she is in a pivotal position in central Europe, is bound to live mainly on her foreign trade with European countries. In normal years she sells 49 per cent of her exports to European industrial countries – in other words, 6 per cent, 10 per cent, and 12 per cent more than Belgium, France, and Germany respectively. She also markets 28 per cent of her exports in the agricultural countries of Europe, of which she is one of the principal sources of supply.

Austria is thus bound to suffer more than any other country from the slump in trade between European states, which are forced by the economic crisis to withdraw into themselves, and it may justifiably be feared that, as a result the difficulties she has experienced hitherto are being aggravated.

The Europe community* can no more rest indifferent to this position than can the Government of Austria itself.

It is an imperative duty for the Austrian Government to remedy the evil in so far as the causes of that evil are due to its own action.

But the Powers to which Austria gave a solemn undertaking not to alienate her independence without the approval of the Council of the League, and which must see that nothing is done to jeopardize that independence, are also in duty bound to assist Austria to economic prosperity, at all events in so far as her free existence is at stake. . . .

The French Government proposes that, under the auspices of the League of Nations, the European states which are Austria's principal customers

* The original has this construction. (Ed.)

should examine together the situation of that country and endeavour in concert with it to find solutions which, while compatible with their own interests, are at the same time calculated to improve Austria's trade balance by extending her markets.

The facilities which the states concerned would be asked to grant may vary in each individual case; one country might grant tariff reductions on certain articles, another advantages in respect of transport, and so on. . . .

Convinced as it is that Austria's difficulties are only temporary and are due to the period of economic adaptation through which that country is passing and that Austria will in the near future find sufficient opportunities for economic expansion by exploiting her natural resources and more particularly her water power, the French Government considers that the special régime contemplated should also be of a provisional character.

Any departure from the most-favoured-nation clause which may result in respect of Austrian goods would thus be strictly limited both as regards the time for which it would be applicable and the articles to which it would apply; and, in view of its exceptional character, it should be welcomed by other countries. . . .

5/4 The International Wheat Agreement, 1933

Printed in PLUMMER, *International Combines* [*see* Document 3/16], pp. 260–262.

The Governments of Germany, Austria, Belgium, Bulgaria, France, the United Kingdom of Great Britain and Northern Ireland, Greece, Hungary, Irish Free State, Italy, Poland, Roumania, Spain, Sweden, Czechoslovakia, Switzerland, the Union of Socialist Soviet Republics, and Yugoslavia, having accepted the invitation extended to them by the Secretary-General of the Monetary and Economic Conference on behalf of the governments of Argentina, Australia, Canada, and the United States of America, to take part in a conference to consider the measures which might be taken in concert to adjust the supply of wheat to effective world demand and eliminate the abnormal surpluses which have been depressing the wheat market and to bring about a rise and stabilization of prices at a level remunerative to the farmers and fair to the consumers of breadstuffs have agreed as follows:

Article 1 The governments of Argentina, Australia, Canada, and the United States of America agree that the exports of wheat from their several countries during the crop year, 1 August 1933, to 31 July 1934, shall be adjusted, taking into consideration the exports of other countries by the acceptance of export maxima fixed on the assumption that world import demand for wheat will amount during this period to 560,000,000 bushels.

Article 2 They further agree to limit their exports of wheat during the crop year, 1 August 1934 to 31 July 1935, to maximum figures 15 per cent less in the case of each country than the average out-turn on the average acreage sown during this period, 1931–1933 inclusive, after deducting normal domestic requirements. The difference between the effective world demand for wheat in the crop year 1934–1935 and the quantity of new wheat from the 1934 crop available for export will be shared between Canada and the United States of America as a supplementary export allocation with a view to the proportionate reduction of their respective carry-overs.

Article 3 The governments of Bulgaria, Hungary, Roumania, and Yugoslavia agree that their combined exports of wheat during the crop year, 1 August 1933, to 31 July 1934, will not exceed 50,000,000 bushels. This undertaking is made on the understanding that the aggregate may be increased to a maximum of 54,000,000 bushels if the Danubian countries find that such a supplementary quota is required for the movement of the exportable surplus of the 1933 crop.

Article 4 They further agree that their combined exports of wheat during the crop year 1934–1935 will not exceed a total of 50,000,000 bushels, and recognize that the acceptance of this export allocation will not allow of an extension of the acreage sown to wheat.

Article 5 The Government of the Union of Socialist Soviet Republics, while unable to give any undertaking in regard to production of wheat, agree to limit their exports for the crop year 1933–1934 to a figure which will be arrived at upon the completion of negotiations with the Government of the overseas wheat-exporting countries. They also agree that the question of their export of wheat during the crop year 1934–1935 shall be the subject of further negotiations with the wheat-exporting countries represented upon the Advisory Committee.

Article 6 (Abridged) The governments of the wheat-importing countries in signing this instrument:
    (i) Agree henceforth not to encourage any extension of the area sown to wheat, and not to take any governmental measures which would result in increased domestic wheat production.
    (ii) Agree to adopt every possible measure to increase wheat consumption and raise the quality of bread.
    (iii) Agree that a substantial improvement in the price of wheat should have as its consequence a lowering of Customs tariffs [the clause then indicates the circumstances under which this would occur]. 'It is understood that the rate of duty necessary to assure remunerative

prices may vary for different countries, but will not be sufficiently high to encourage their farmers to expand wheat acreage.'

(iv) Agree that in order to restore more normal conditions in world trade in wheat the reduction of Customs tariffs would have to be accompanied by modification of the general régime of quantitative restriction of wheat imports and accept in principle the desirability of such a modification. . . . The intention of this agreement is that the importing countries will not take advantage of a voluntary reduction of exports on the part of the exporting countries, by developing their domestic policies in such a way as to frustrate the efforts which the exporting countries are making in the common interest, to restore the price of wheat to a remunerative level.

5/5 London Monetary and Economic Conference Declaration, 30 June 1933

Printed in Documents on International Affairs (London, 1933), p. 43.

I. The undersigned governments★ agree that:

(a) it is in the interests of all concerned that stability in the international monetary field be attained as quickly as practicable;

(b) that gold should be re-established as the international measure of exchange value, it being recognized that the parity and time at which each of the countries now off gold could undertake to stabilize must be decided by the respective governments concerned.

II. The signatory Governments whose currencies are on the gold standard reassert that it is their determination to maintain the free working of that standard at the existing gold parities within the framework of their respective monetary laws.

III. The signatory governments whose currencies are not on the gold standard, without in any way prejudicing their own future ratios to gold, take note of the above declaration and recognize its importance. They reaffirm as indicated in Paragraph I above that the ultimate objective of their monetary policy is to restore, under proper conditions, an international monetary standard based on gold.

IV. Each of the signatory governments whose currencies are not on the gold standard undertakes to adopt the measures which it may deem most

★ This compromise draft was prepared at a meeting attended by the representatives of the 'Gold' countries (Belgium, France, Italy, the Netherlands, Poland, and Switzerland) and of Great Britain. (Footnote in D. I. A.)

appropriate to limit exchange speculation, and each of the other signatory Governments undertakes to co-operate to the same end.

V. Each of the undersigned governments agrees to ask its Central Bank to co-operate with the Central Banks of the other signatory governments in limiting speculation in the exchange and, when the time comes, in re-establishing a general international standard.

VI. The present declaration is open to signature by other governments whether their currencies are on the gold standard or not.

5/6 American Reaction to the London Declaration

President Roosevelt's reply of 3 July 1933. Printed in *Documents, 1933* [*see* Document 5/5], pp. 43–45.

I would regard it as a catastrophe amounting to a world tragedy if the great Conference of nations, called to bring about a more real and permanent financial stability and a greater prosperity to the masses of all nations, should, in advance of any serious effort to consider these broader problems, allow itself to be diverted by the proposal of a purely artificial and temporary experiment affecting the monetary exchange of a few nations only. Such action, such diversion, shows a singular lack of proportion and a failure to remember the larger purposes for which the Economic Conference originally was called together.

I do not relish the thought that insistence on such action should be made an excuse for the continuance of the basic economic errors that underlie so much of the present world-wide depression.

The world will not long be lulled by the specious fallacy of achieving a temporary and probably an artificial stability in foreign exchange on the part of a few large countries only.

The sound internal economic system of a nation is a greater factor in its well-being than the price of its currency in changing terms of the currencies of other nations.

It is for this reason that reduced cost of government, adequate government income, and ability to service government debts are all so important to ultimate stability. So, too, old fetishes of so-called international bankers are being replaced by efforts to plan national currencies with the objective of giving to those currencies a continuing purchasing power which does not greatly vary in terms of the commodities and need of modern civilization. Let me be frank in saying that the United States seeks the kind of dollar which a generation hence will have the same purchasing and debt-paying power as the dollar value we hope to attain in the near future. That objective means more to the good of other nations than a fixed ratio for a month or two in terms of the pound or franc.

Our broad purpose is the permanent stabilization of every nation's currency. Gold or gold and silver can well continue to be a metallic reserve behind currencies, but this is not the time to dissipate gold reserves. When the world works out concerted policies in the majority of nations to produce balanced budgets and living within their means, then we can properly discuss a better distribution of the world's gold and silver supply to act as a reserve base of national currencies.

Restoration of world trade is an important partner both in the means and in the result. Here also temporary exchange fixing is not the true answer. We must rather mitigate existing embargoes to make easier the exchange of products which one nation has and the other nation has not.

The Conference was called to better and perhaps to cure fundamental economic ills. It must not be diverted from that effort.

5/7 Declaration of Empire Monetary and Economic Policy, 27 July 1933

Printed in *Documents, 1933* [*see* Document **5/5**], pp. 115–118.

1. Now that the World Economic and Monetary Conference has adjourned, the undersigned delegations of the British Commonwealth consider it appropriate to put on record their views on some of the more important matters of financial and monetary policy which were raised but not decided at the Conference. . . . During the course of the Conference they have had the opportunity of consulting together and reviewing, in the light of present-day conditions, the conclusions arrived at at their meeting at Ottawa a year ago,* in so far as they had reference to the issues before the Conference.

ECONOMIC POLICY

2. The undersigned delegations are satisfied that the Ottawa Agreements have already had beneficial effects on many branches of inter-Imperial trade and that this process is likely to continue as the purchasing power of the various countries concerned increases. While there has not yet been sufficient time to give full effect to the various agreements made, they are convinced

* Ottawa Conference July 21–August 20 1932, the Imperial Economic Conference. The aim was to obtain mutually advantageous means for increasing trade between the British Empire. (Ed.)

that the general principles agreed upon are sound. The undersigned delegations reaffirm their conviction that the lowering or removal of barriers between the countries of the Empire provided for in the Ottawa Agreements will not only facilitate the flow of goods between them, but will stimulate and increase the trade of the world.

3. The delegations now desire to draw attention to the principles of monetary and financial policy which have emerged from the work of both the Ottawa and World Conferences, and which are of the utmost importance for the countries within the British Commonwealth. The following paragraphs embody their views as to the principles of policy which they consider desirable for their countries.

MONETARY AND FINANCIAL

Price Levels

4. At the Ottawa Conference the governments represented declared their view that a rise throughout the world in the general level of wholesale prices was in the highest degree desirable, and stated that they were anxious to co-operate with other nations in any practicable measures for raising wholesale prices. . . .

In the monetary sphere the primary line of action towards a rise in prices was stated to be the creation and maintenance within the limits of sound finance of such conditions as would assist in the revival of enterprise and trade, including low rates of interest and an abundance of short-term money. The inflationary creation of additional means of payment to finance public expenditure was deprecated, and an orderly monetary policy was demanded with safeguards to limit the scope of violent speculative movements of commodities and securities.

5. Since then the policy of the British Commonwealth has been directed to raising prices. The undersigned delegations note with satisfaction that this policy has been attended with an encouraging measure of success. For some months, indeed, it had to encounter obstacles arising from the continuance of a downward trend of gold prices, and during that period the results achieved were in the main limited to raising prices in Empire currencies relatively to gold prices. In the last few months the persistent adherence of the United Kingdom to the policy of cheap and plentiful money has been increasingly effective under the more favourable conditions that have been created, for the time being, by the change of policy of the United States, and by the halt in the fall of gold prices. . . .

6. The undersigned delegations are of opinion that the views they expressed at Ottawa as to the necessity of a rise in the price level still hold good, and that it is of the greatest importance that this rise which has begun should

continue. As to the ultimate level to be aimed at, they do not consider it practicable to state this in precise terms. Any price level would be satisfactory which restores the normal activity of industry and employment, which ensures an economic return to the producer of primary commodities, and which harmonizes the burden of debts and fixed charges with economic capacity. It is important that the rise in prices should not be carried to such a pitch as to produce an inflated scale of profits and threaten a disturbance of equilibrium in the opposite direction. They, therefore, consider that the governments of the British Commonwealth should persist by all means in their power, whether monetary or economic, within the limits of sound finance, in the policy of furthering the rise in wholesale prices until there is evidence that equilibrium has been re-established, and that thereupon they should take whatever measures are possible to stabilize the position thus attained.

7. With reference to the proposal which has been made from time to time for the expansion of government programmes of capital outlay, the British Commonwealth delegations consider that this is a matter which must be dealt with by each government in the light of its own experience and of its own conditions.

8. The Ottawa Conference declared that the ultimate aim of monetary policy must be the restoration of a satisfactory international monetary standard, having in mind, not merely stable exchange rates between all countries, but the deliberate management of the international standard, in such a manner as to ensure the smooth and efficient working of international trade and finance. The principal conditions precedent to the re-establishment of any international monetary standard were stated, particularly a rise in the general level of commodity prices in the various countries to a height more in keeping with the level of costs, including the burden of debt and other fixed and semi-fixed charges, and the Conference expressed its sense of the importance of securing and maintaining international co-operation with a view to avoiding, so far as may be found practicable, wide fluctuations in the purchasing power of the standard of value.

9. The undersigned delegations now reaffirm their view that the ultimate aim of monetary policy should be the restoration of a satisfactory international gold standard under which international co-operation would be secured and maintained with a view to avoiding, so far as may be found practicable, undue fluctuations in the purchasing power of gold. The problem with which the world is faced is to reconcile the stability of exchange rates with a reasonable measure of stability, not merely in the price level of a particular country, but in world prices.

5/8 Gold Bloc Communiqué, 25 September 1934

Printed in *Documents on International Affairs* (London, 1934), pp. 234–235. (Ed. Tr.)

The delegates of Belgium, France, Italy, Luxembourg, the Netherlands and Switzerland, met on 24 and 25 September at Geneva for the purpose of examining jointly how their respective governments might help most effectively to restore international economic and financial co-operation, the necessity of which is unanimously affirmed.

In the first place, they have stated that the countries which have maintained the free functioning of the gold standard remain more determined than ever, as was affirmed in the declaration signed in London under 3 July 1933, to maintain it fully at the present gold parity, this maintenance appearing to them as one of the essential conditions for the economic and financial recovery of the world.* However, they have recognized that in order to contribute fully to the task of general economic recovery, they must adopt as a principal aim an increase in international trade. . . .

Anxious to produce positive results quickly, they have recognized the desirability of entrusting to a commission, composed of delegates of the respective governments, the task of examining the principal problems posed by the development of economic and financial relations between the six nations, without losing sight of the interests of third parties and the need for a wider co-operation on the international plan.

In the first place, this commission will be empowered to concentrate its attention on two essential issues: the increase in international trade, and the development of tourism and transport, the monetary question having already been the subject of an agreement signed in Paris on 8 July 1933 by the Governors of the Central Banks of the states involved. . . .

5/9 Gold Bloc Protocol, 20 October 1934

*Printed in *Documents, 1934* [see Document 5/8], pp. 235–236. (Ed. Tr.)

* Declaration by the representatives of Belgium, France, Italy, the Netherlands, Poland, and Switzerland, 3 July 1933.
The undersigned governments, convinced that the maintenance of their currencies is essential for the economic and financial recovery of the world of credit and for the safeguarding of social progress in their respective countries, confirm their intention to maintain the free functioning of the gold standard in their respective countries at the existing gold parities and within the framework of existing monetary laws. They ask their Central Banks to keep in close touch to give the maximum efficacy to this declaration. *The Economist*, 8 July 1933, p. 64. (Ed. footnote.)

The governments undersigned,*

Convinced, as they affirmed in London on 3 July 1933, that monetary stability is one of the essential conditions of a return to a normal economic situation;

Being of the opinion that by ensuring the stability of their currencies, they contribute to the restoration of the world economy;

Confirming their wish to maintain the present gold parities of their respective currencies;

Recognizing that their common monetary policy implies a development of international trade, which should favour the similarity of monetary conditions existing in their respective countries;

Agree:

I.   To establish a General Commission composed of their respective delegates.

II.   As regards trade:

1. To inquire how it is possible at present to increase trade between their countries. They consider as desirable an increase of 10 per cent in the volume of world trade, over that effected between 1 July 1933 and 30 June 1934;

2. To this end to begin bilateral negotiations without delay, with the object of completing them in the maximum period of one year;

3. To submit a draft international convention on commercial propaganda, to which they give their approval in principle, to the scrutiny of a sub-committee composed of each of the undersigned governments, charged with drawing up in final form the text of the Agreement, in a manner which shall enable it to be signed as soon as possible.

III.   As regards tourism and transport:

To constitute two sub-committees, composed of representatives of each of the undersigned governments, with the task of making a report to the General Commission on the proposals which are already laid before the latter or which subsequently may be submitted to it.

V.   To convene without delay the sub-committees provided for above and to summon a meeting within three months of the General Commission in Brussels, to take account of the progress which has been made and to arrange the rest of its programme, without losing sight of the interests of third parties and the need for a more extensive collaboration in the international field.

* Belgium, France, Italy, Luxemburg, the Netherlands, Poland and Switzerland. (Footnote in D. I. A.)

5/10 Deflation in France

International Labour Office, International Labour Conference, 17th Session, Geneva 1936, *Report of the Director* (Geneva, 1936), pp. 30–31.

In France the year 1935 was characterized by the determined opposition of the Government to any tendency towards devaluation, which took the form of a clear and strong deflationary policy. As a result of Parliamentary discussions on 3 December 1934 and 7 June 1935, which attained a very high level and in which the opposing theses as regards the maintenance of the gold standard and deflation were vigorously debated, the Laval Government, which had been formed on 7 June, decided to give immediate effect to the vote in favour of the existing system. The next day a law was passed giving the Government full powers in financial matters 'in order to avoid the devaluation of the currency'. Thus armed, the Government proceeded to issue a series of Decree-Laws, which embodied an organic system of deflation. It comprised the reduction of State expenditure by a uniform and general cut of 10 per cent on all government payments for whatever purpose – salaries, pensions, bearer bonds, government contracts, etc. – and a reduction of the cost of living by diminishing the cost of bread, coal, electricity, gas, rent, etc. On 17 July, twenty-eight Decree-Laws were promulgated, of which twenty dealt with budgetary reductions and eight aimed at reviving economic activity or affording relief from various charges. On 30 October three hundred further Decree-Laws were adopted in continuation of the same policy.

The energetic and comprehensive action of the French Government represents a systematic attempt to meet the depression by a thorough-going policy of deflation. Sufficient time has not yet elapsed to enable a final judgment of its success to be formed. All that can be said is that as yet there has been no general revival of industry or trade. Unemployment continued to increase during 1935. The index of building activity, continuing the steady downward movement which has been in progress since 1930, reached a figure approximately one-half of what it was in that year. Steel and textile production, while abnormally low, showed a slight improvement; but the output of coal, iron, and automobiles declined further. The indices of the cost of living recorded an appreciable fall, as a consequence of the Decree-Laws, in contrast to the very slight decline in previous years. The index of wholesale prices, on the other hand, which dropped as low as 51·4 in the middle of 1935, had risen to 60 in March 1936. The value of imports and of exports alike attained new low levels and now stand at 36 per cent and 31 per cent respectively of the 1929 figure. In the course of the year the gold reserve was reduced some 20 per cent, but nevertheless remains exceedingly strong. The discount rate of the Bank of France fluctuated widely, being put up to 6 per cent on two occasions during the year. Savings bank deposits increased slightly, but commercial bank deposits fell still further.

5/11 French Tariffs

Department of Overseas Trade, *France, 1934* [see Document 3/4], pp. 670–673.

France remains resolutely and indissolubly wedded to a strong and comprehensive protective policy for her agriculture and her industries. Although greater moderation may find its advocates, yet all visible traces of effective support for free-trade or for mere revenue duties have ceased to emerge in the written or spoken word, in press, platform or parliament. The national policy is sustained with equal vigour by masters and workers in industry, and with even more pronounced and unanimous determination by the millions of peasant proprietors. In principle and in form, French measures relative to foreign imports have undergone marked changes since the close of the war, and not least in the years 1927–1934. Her tariff rates as a whole have moved persistently upwards since 1919. From its introduction in the summer of 1931, the new system of import quotas for agricultural, mineral and industrial products had so progressed by the early part of 1934 that no fewer than 3,000 out of 7,000 articles or classes of goods in the customs tariff were asserted to be importable only in limited fixed quantities over short fixed periods under due licence.

In 1918, France formally denounced all treaties containing the most-favoured-nation clause, and instituted by law in July 1919, the principle of reciprocity for future commercial treaties. Intermediate tariff rates, which were to be percentage reductions of the margin between the maximum and minimum rates, were to be accorded in return for equivalent concessions. Up to the end of 1924 the new principle had been applied, but not absolutely rigorously, in sixteen cases (Canada, United States, Spain, Portugal, Austria, Czechoslovakia, etc.). In the long commercial treaty negotiations (1924–1927) with Germany, the latter claimed from the outset most-favoured-nation treatment [for all products of interest in her trade with France], which, in fact, covered the vast bulk of French industrial imports, and obtained it effectively in the treaty of August 1927, and formally in the following April. Subsequent agreements in 1928 accorded it to Switzerland, Belgium-Luxemburg, Italy, Czechoslovakia. French policy therefore reverted to that principle and to the double-column tariff – maximum and minimum – instituted in 1892, practically every country in commercial treaty relations with France receiving the minimum rates and intermediary rates still subsisting only for a few countries (United States, Canada, Finland and two others). In principle, the French general or maximum tariff is that normally applicable to all countries in the absence of agreements to the contrary effect.

Most significant results of the 1927–1929 treaties arose from the wholesale adoption therein of consolidated duties: in other words, of duties which the contracting parties had undertaken not to raise without mutual consent during the validity of the treaty. In 1931, the Minister of Commerce asserted that between August 1927 and July 1928, duties on 5,064 out of 7,028 tariff headings (72 per cent) had been so consolidated. Under the most-favoured-nation principle these consolidations were also applicable to other countries. When the world depression set in and exchange and other 'dumping' became rife, France found herself deprived of her liberty of action in tariff matters and unable to vary duties on most industrial products except at the cost either of lengthy negotiations or of the denunciation of her major treaties. She did, in fact, negotiate the deconsolidation of a few duties, in exchange for concessions, with Czechoslovakia (1930), Italy (1931), Germany (1931), Belgium-Luxemburg (1931).

As regards most agricultural duties, she was finally able to give reinforced protection by decrees under extensions of the law of 1897, known as the padlock act (*loi de cadenas*), which empowered the Government on the introduction of measures for increased duties on cereals and their derivatives, wines, cattle and fresh meat, to put the proposed modifications into immediate effect by decrees pending parliamentary decision. From 1897 to December 1929 this law had been applied only to the four classes of commodities just mentioned: by a law of December 1929, dairy produce, potatoes and biscuits were brought within its scope, 35 additional tariff items being affected. In March 1931, 44 more animal products were added, and in the following month a further addition of 37 articles brought in sugar and many foodstuffs with sugar content. By the middle of 1933, duties on articles under more than 200 headings could be raised by simple decree under the Padlock Act. The Act has the curious feature of only permitting the increase but not the reduction of duties, even of those raised under its sanction.

The agitation of the industrial and agricultural classes eventually became so powerful that the Government finally decided to introduce the quantitative limitation of imports. It was concluded that the mere raising of duties, even to very high levels, could provide no effective hindrance to excessive importation in face of the heavy fall in prices, of the general disarray or even collapse of many foreign exchanges, of the severe restrictions in the provision of exchange for foreign goods by many others, of the especial attractiveness of the French market, as one of the few remaining solvent markets not having limited external payments, for the sale not only of agricultural products but also of raw materials, minerals, manufactures. It was contended that many imports were offered at prices bearing no genuine relation to their cost of production, and far less to the French level of costs, and that in consequence the French producers were menaced with a general and unduly rapid break in home prices that might fatally upset their businesses. The first quotas were applied in 1931 – to nitrates in May, coal and flax in July, timber and wines in August. As regards manufactures, the primary aim was to reduce German, and to a less extent Belgian and Czechoslovakian products, whose imports had been unduly increasing in 1930 and 1931; but later, after the pound sterling and the dollar had depreciated, no doubt the competition of the United Kingdom and U.S.A., was also taken into the reckoning.

In September 1931 the methodical extension of the system was inaugurated by the proposal of the French Government to Berlin that French and German national associations in certain important industries should mutually agree upon reductions of imports into France by a given approximate percentage of the amounts imported in a previous basic period (year or series of years), and that such quota agreements, if acceptable to the French Government, should be officially promulgated. In cases of non-agreement, quotas would be *ex officio* determined. Similar negotiations for industrial quotas also took place with representatives of trade groups from the United Kingdom, Belgium, Czechoslovakia, U.S.A., and other countries, when these countries were substantial exporters to France of specific categories of goods. On the other hand, agricultural quotas were established by the Government, after consultation of intervocational committees, without previous negotiations of this kind with foreign bodies. By July 1932 the Ministry for Commerce controlled 64 quotas embracing commodities under 1,225 items in the tariff, and the Ministries of Agriculture and of Mercantile Marine controlled the quotas respecting many more hundreds.

In the summer of 1932, the Government indicated that it regarded the system as purely transitional, that existing quotas would, when possible, be enlarged or replaced gradually by higher customs duties, and that, save in extreme cases, no new quotas would be instituted: in the following March it claimed that in the interval it had rejected requests for 33 new quotas. The industrial organizations, in response to the official inquiry respecting the replacement of quotas by higher duties, subsequently insisted in most cases that mere duties could not suffice for their protection. The Government announced a change of policy, at the beginning of September 1933, and even a marked tightening-up of the existing quotas in relation to all importing countries, unless concessions were accorded to French exports to their respective territories: as from 1 October all existing quotas were to be reduced to 25 per cent, but the balance of 75 per cent could be partially or wholly redeemed by countries concerned by the grant of corresponding advantages.

The new policy did not eventually take effect until 1 January 1934, when this reduction was not only applied to the then existing quotas but also about 600 new items were brought under quota and were allocated one-quarter of their total imports in 1932 (which was taken as common basic period for all these new quotas). Allotments of quotas being fixed only for quarterly periods, textile, chemical, agricultural machinery, fish, agricultural products (whose imports being seasonal tend to fall largely in one or two quarters), were among imports likely to be seriously affected by restriction to quarterly quantities. The management of the old quotas was left in the same hands, but the French Government entrusted the working of the 600 new quotas to vocational committees in France representative of the manufacturers of and the dealers in the particular commodities. Applications for import licences, to be sent in in five copies, after examination by the particular committee were, if passed, forwarded to the Customs Department for approval, and then returned to the applicant for presentation at the point of importation.

Additional commodities were subsequently brought under the system. It has been estimated that about 3,000 items have thus been quota-ed, of which two-thirds are manufactures. The Government informed the Chamber of Deputies at the end of February 1934 that there was no question of renouncing the quota policy, which had rendered the most signal services to France in the economic crisis.

5/12 National Economic Life and the French Experiment

International Labour Office, *Report* [*see* Document 5/10], pp. 77–79.

Because the French 'experiment' has not followed any preconceived plan or been inspired by any proclaimed theory, its extent and importance are apt to be overlooked. It presents a composite picture made up of a series of individual measures rather than a symmetrical and logical pattern. But it responds to a profound stirring of national sentiment, which has generated the momentum necessary to carry through a process of far-reaching change in a few months. Between May and December of last year a legislative programme was voted by Parliament, which finds few parallels in French parliamentary annals. Space does not permit even a catalogue of the measures taken to restore financial balance, to reform the constitution of the Bank of France, to institute public works, to provide temporary credit for agriculturists, exporters, small industrialists and traders; to organize the study and adoption of scientific management in industry, to institute a national wheat department, to regulate the coal market, to check unwarranted increase of prices, to reduce the cost of living by common action between the producing and consuming branches of the co-operative movement. On the social side reference has already been made to the introduction of the 40-hour week and paid holidays, the latter of 15 days' duration (of which at least 12 are working days) and applying to all industrial, commercial and agricultural employees. The school age has been raised to 14. Collective agreements have been given legal status and a system of compulsory conciliation and arbitration established. Lastly, the Government is actively engaged in improving the social and labour conditions throughout the French colonial empire by a series of energetic legislative and administrative measures. That this immense programme should have been adopted and put into execution in so short a time is an interesting proof that neither the legislative nor the administrative procedures of democracy are incompatible with swift and decisive action when occasion requires.

Hardly less important than the volume of new legislation are the changes in social organization which accompanied it. A tremendous expansion of trade unionism has taken place, as a further expression of the great popular movement which gave birth to the social programme. The membership of the *Confédération Générale du Travail*, which stood at 1,165,265 in April 1936 had reached the imposing figure of 4,314,170 in December. Every union belonging to the Confederation showed a great rise, but it was particularly rapid and significant in the case of those industries which had hitherto only possessed a skeleton organization. Thus in the building trades membership increased sevenfold, in the textile and clerical trades eightfold, in the clothing trade tenfold, in the metal and cardboard-box trades elevenfold, in the food and woodworking trades twelvefold, in agriculture thirteenfold and in the chemical trade twenty-fivefold. On the employers' side a corresponding movement occurred. The *Confédération Générale du Patronat français*, which had mainly consisted of the highly concentrated basic industries such as coal, steel and textiles, has thrown its net widely over the whole industrial field and has enrolled large numbers of medium and small employers. One result of this growth of organization has been the rapid extension of collective bargaining and the systematic consultation of employers' and workers' organizations by the Government in framing the regulations necessary for putting reforms such as the 40-hour week into operation. As a consequence, the National Economic Council has been entirely reorganized in order to make it an industrial parliament really representative of every trade and profession. It is now composed of twenty sections corresponding to the main branches of economic life, but these are held together and brought to a focus upon national problems by a general assembly of 173 persons and a permanent committee of 40 persons. The Council thus reformed is being frequently consulted by the Government upon industrial problems of all kinds and particularly upon the measures for bringing industrial legislation into force. As the Minister of National Economy expressed it, 'By creating the National Economic Council, Parliament . . . wished to make the State more responsive to the pulsations of modern life and to regulate the relations which should be established henceforth between the political organization and the economic forces of the country . . . If employers' associations and trade unions should remain distinct, it is nevertheless necessary that a common organization should bring them together and impose its law upon them. Otherwise the right of the stronger will settle disputes unjustly and therefore only for the moment, whereby a state of war is maintained in the individual trade and unrest in the whole social organism.'* Together with the introduction of compulsory arbitration and the rapid growth of organization both among employers and workers, the extension of the functions of the Economic Council makes an important advance in the integration of French economic life, which deserves to be followed with close attention.

5/13 Programme of the Popular Front in France, 1936

a The Election Programme. Printed in D. THOMSON, *France, Empire and Republic, 1850–1940: historical documents* (London, 1968), pp. 293–296.

b Ministerial Declaration after the Election, made in June 1936. Printed in CLOUGH, *et. al. Economic History* [*see* Document 1/4a], pp. 256–257.

c Resolution of the Chamber of 6 June 1936, proposing the annulment of the 'decree laws' which attempted to carry through deflation by savage cuts in Government spending. *Ibid.*, pp. 257–258.

a   I. DEFENCE OF FREEDOM

. . . 5. Trade Union Liberties:
(a) Application and observance of trade-union freedom for all.
(b) Recognition of women's labour rights . . .

III. ECONOMIC DEMANDS

1. Restoration of purchasing power destroyed or reduced by the crisis. Against unemployment and the crisis in industry:

* Speech at the inaugural session of the National Economic Council. (Footnote in Original.)

Establishment of a national unemployment fund.

Reduction of the working week without reduction of the weekly wage.

Bringing young workers into employment by establishing a system of adequate pensions for aged workers.

Rapid execution of a public-works programme, both urban and rural, linking local investments with schemes financed by the State and local authorities.

Against the agricultural and commercial crisis:

Revaluation of agricultural produce, combined with measures against speculation and high prices, in order to reduce the gap between wholesale and retail prices.

Establishment of a National Grain Board [*Office du Blé*] to abolish the tribute levied by speculators against both the producer and the consumer.

Strengthening of agricultural co-operatives, and supply of fertilizers at cost prices by the National Boards for Nitrogen and Potash, control and certification of sales of superphosphates and other fertilizers, extension of agricultural credits, reduction of farming leases.

Suspension of distraints and regulation of debt repayments. Completion of the revision of bills of credit.

Pending the complete and earliest possible removal of all unjust measures imposed by the economy decrees, immediate abolition of measures affecting those groups whose conditions of life have been most severely endangered by these decrees.

2. Against the robbery of investors and for the better organization of credit:

Regulation of banking business. Regulation of balance sheets issued by banks and joint-stock companies. Further regulation of the powers of directors of joint-stock companies.

State officials who have retired or are on the reserve list to be prohibited from joining the board of directors of a joint-stock company.

In order to remove credit and investment from the control of the economic oligarchy, the Bank of France must cease to be a private concern, and 'The Bank of France' must become 'France's Bank'. The Council of Regents of the Bank of France must be abolished; the powers of the Governor of the Bank of France must be increased, under the permanent control of a council composed of representatives of Parliament, of the executive authority, and of the main organized forces of labour and of industrial, commercial, and agricultural activity. The capital of the Bank must be converted into debentures, with measures to safeguard the interests of small shareholders.

IV. FINANCIAL PURIFICATION

Control of the trade in armaments, in conjunction with the nationalization of armaments industries. Prevention of waste in the civil and military departments.

Establishment of a War Pensions Fund.

Democratic reform of the system of taxation so as to relax the fiscal burden blocking economic recovery, and raising revenue by measures against large fortunes. Rapid steepening of income tax on incomes above 75,000 francs a year. Re-organization of death duties. Special taxes on monopoly profits, but in such a way as to have no effects on retail prices. Suppression of fraud in connection with transferable securities by bringing into force the fiscal identity card which has been voted by parliament, together with an amnesty on past tax evasions.

Control of export of capital, and punishment of evasion by rigorous measures, including confiscation of property concealed abroad or of its equivalent value in France.

b Gentlemen, the Government comes before you following general elections in which universal suffrage, the judge and master of us all, delivered its judgment with greater force and clarity than at any other moment in the history of the Republic. . . .

From the beginning of the next week, we shall bring before the Chamber a group of bills which we shall ask the two Houses to act upon before adjournment. These bills will deal with:

A political amnesty; the forty-hour week; collective bargaining contracts; holidays with pay; a public works programme to provide facilities for public health, science, sports and tourism; the nationalization of armament production; a wheat office which will serve as a model price support system for other agricultural products such as wine, meat and milk; the extension of the years of [compulsory] schooling; a reform in the organization of the Bank of France that will guarantee the predominance of national interests in its management; a first revision of the decree laws in favour of the most severely affected categories of public service employees and veterans.

As soon as these measures are disposed of, we shall present to parliament a second series of bills dealing with national unemployment insurance, insurance against agricultural disasters, the regulation of agricultural debts, and a pension system guaranteeing the aged workers in the city and on the land protection against misery.

In a short time we shall present a comprehensive system of fiscal simplification and relief in order to ease the condition of industry and commerce, and, above all, to permit general recovery. The measures will require no new revenues, except out of wealth acquired through repression and fraud.

While we shall strive, with your full co-operation, thus to revitalize the French economy, to absorb the unemployed, to increase disposable income in general, and to provide well-being and security for those whose labour creates true riches, we must govern the country. We shall govern as republicans; we shall assure the republican order. We shall apply the laws of republican defence with quiet firmness. We shall show that we intend to instil the republican spirit throughout the entire administration and public services. If democratic institutions are attacked, we shall assure their integrity with the means appropriate to the danger or the resistance.

c Gentlemen, an examination of the consequences of the decree laws of the Doumergue and Laval governments* regarding veterans, war victims, and public servants shows that the laws have worsened the living conditions of an important segment of the population. Disabled veterans whose injuries were minor and therefore did not entitle them to full disability benefits, have been particularly affected, and there are many unemployed among them. Lesser officials, whose previously inadequate salaries were reduced by the decree laws, find themselves in a very difficult situation. Moreover, private industry, emulating the example of the State, has taken advantage of this situation by imposing on their employees new and important wage reductions.

This reduction of the purchasing power of wage earners has had disastrous consequences for small and medium merchants. Businesses fail more and more frequently, and farmers find the market price for agricultural products considerably reduced. As a result, the sale of government bonds has diminished, making budget estimates less reliable and thus putting the Treasury in difficulties.

In view of the fact that justice demands the restoration of the salaries of state and public service employees, and that to do so would be in the best interests of the entire country, we have the honour to propose the following resolution:

The Chamber requests the Government immediately to formulate a bill providing for:

1. Restoration of full rights to veterans and war victims by the suspension of the reductions adopted after 1 June 1932;

2. Annulment of the reductions made after 1 June 1932, in payments for public health and child care, as well as in welfare and social security payments;

3. Immediate suspension of all reductions in pension payments resulting

* A reference to the February–November 1934 administration of Doumergue and the June 1935–January 1936 government of Laval. (Ed.)

from measures taken after 1 June 1932, and complete reorganization of the pension system so as to allow all the retired, both civilian and military, treatment that is equitable and that accords all categories satisfaction of their legitimate claims;

4. For all employees of the State, the departments, municipalities, public services, of Algeria, the colonies, protectorates and mandated territories, abolition of the salary reductions effected after 1 June 1932;

5. Restoration of the 10 per cent cut in interest imposed on government bonds held by small investors by the decree law of 16 July 1935.

5/14 The Matignon Agreement, 1936

Printed in THOMSON, *France* [*see* Document 5/13a], pp. 177–179.

Article 1. The employers' delegation agrees to the immediate establishment of collective agreements of labour.

Article 2. These agreements must include especially the following Articles 3 to 5.

Article 3. As all citizens are under obligation to observe the law the employers recognize the freedom of opinion and the right of workers to join freely and belong to an occupational *syndicate** constituted in accordance with Book 3 of the Labour Code.

The employers undertake not to take into account whether or not a worker belongs to a *syndicate* in making their decisions about taking him on, or organizing or distributing work, or measures of discipline or dismissal.

If one of the contracting parties challenges the grounds for the dismissal of a worker as being in violation of the above-mentioned right, both parties will endeavour to establish the facts and to find an equitable solution for all disputes.

This intervention does not limit the right of the parties to obtain before the courts damages for injury to their interests. Exercise of the right to have a *syndicate* must not lead to contravention of the law.

Article 4. Actual wages paid to all workers on the date of 25 May 1936 will, from the day when work is resumed, be readjusted according to a diminishing scale, starting with a rise of 15 per cent for the lowest paid and amounting to a rise of 7 per cent for the highest-paid workers.

The total wages bill for any company must in no case be increased by more than 12 per cent; the increases already given since the above-mentioned date will be counted towards the readjustments defined above. But

* See Glossary.

increases in excess of these readjustments will remain the right of the beneficiaries.

Negotiations for determining minimum wages by collective agreements, according to regions and by categories, which shall be begun at once, must deal in particular with the necessary readjustment of abnormally low wages.

The employers' delegation undertakes to proceed with any necessary readjustments to maintain a normal relationship between salaries and wages.

Article 5. Except in special cases already provided for by law, every factory employing more than ten workers, after agreement with the *syndicate* organizations or, in their absence, with the interested parties, will have two (titular) or several (titular and deputy) shop stewards, according to the importance of the factory. These shop stewards are entitled to lay before the management any individual claims that have not been satisfied directly and which have to do with application of the laws, decrees and regulations of the Labour Code, wage scales and measures of hygiene and safety.

All working men and women over eighteen shall have a vote, provided that they have at the time of the election been in the factory for more than three months and have not been deprived of their civil rights.

Those eligible for election shall be electors as defined above, of French nationality and aged at least twenty-five, who have worked in the factory for at least one year, but this time must be shortened if the number of candidates would be reduced to five.

Workers who themselves or whose wives keep a retail store, no matter of what kind, cannot be candidates.

Article 6. The employers' delegation undertakes that no sanctions will be taken against strike actions.

Article 7. The confederal workers' delegation will ask workers on strike to decide to resume work as soon as the managements have accepted the general agreement now made, and as soon as negotiations for its application have been begun between the managements and the staffs of the factories.

Paris, 7 June 1936

President of the Council (Prime Minister): Léon Blum.

For the C.G.T.:   Léon Jouhaux, René Belin, B. Frachon,
                  Semat, H. Cordier, Milan.

For the C.G.P.F.: Duchemin, Dalbouze, Richemont, Lambert-Ribot.

5/15 French Policy on Immigrant Labour

Department of Overseas Trade, *France, 1934* [*see* Document 3/4], pp. 30, 31.

Till the close of 1930, when the world economic crisis first began to be felt in France, labour supplies were inadequate for the needs of French industry, and an elaborate organization was then employed to recruit foreign workers and to direct them towards the centres where they were needed. There was a preliminary selection in the workers' country of origin, with medical examination and tests of capacity. Upon arrival at the frontier control station (of which there were seven, at Toul, Marseilles, Perpignan, Hendaye, Modane, Mentone and Basle) a further medical examination was conducted and the accepted workers were set *en route* for the scene of their labours. As the available supply of workers tended in 1928–1930 to fall short of French requirements (for instance, the flow of Italian workers had been greatly affected by recent legislative enactments in Italy), negotiations were undertaken with Poland, Czechoslovakia, Italy and Roumania to ensure larger supplies of workers. An arrangement with Romania was signed at Bucharest on 28 January 1930, and similar arrangements were concluded with Yugoslavia, Italy, Poland, Czechoslovakia and Austria. Agreements also exist between France and Spain for the introduction into France of seasonal workers.

At the present time* the French frontiers are practically closed to foreign workers seeking employment in industrial occupations, though considerable numbers still come in, at the appropriate seasons, for the requirements of agriculture. (In the last eight weeks of 1931 the average number of recorded arrivals for industry was about 400 weekly, and in 1932 the number was often below 200; as compared with several thousand weekly for some preceding years.) No foreign worker may enter the country without being in possession of a definite labour contract with an employer in France, approved by the Ministry of Labour or Agriculture, as the case may be; and there is so much unemployment among French workers that the requisite Ministerial approval, as far as industrial workers are concerned, is accorded only in rare instances, where the applicant possesses some special knowledge or aptitude not to be found among the available French applicants for the vacancy. Every foreign worker already in France must be in possession of an identity card upon which the nature of his occupation is indicated, and he is not allowed to transfer to any other class of work. Infraction of the regulations involves a fine for the employer and expulsion for the worker. Should a foreign worker become unemployed, every facility is offered for his return to his native

* 1934. (Ed.)

land, rather than that he should seek another post; and employers are forbidden to engage a foreign worker if the vacancy can possibly be filled by a Frenchman. As regards workers in agriculture the position is different. The continual stream of migration from the rural areas to the urban has left the countryside without a sufficient labour force for the needs of agriculture, and each year large numbers of foreigners (chiefly Poles, Italians, Spaniards and Belgians) have to be introduced, a large proportion of whom return home at the end of the season. In 1930, out of a total of 221,619 foreign immigrant workers, 92,828 were for agriculture; in 1931 out of a total of 102,267, agriculture claimed 76,463; in 1932 56,675 out of a total of 69,482, and in 1933 48,092 out of 60,302.

5/16 Law on the Bank of France, 24 July 1936

Law of 24 July 1936 modifying and completing the laws and statutes governing the Bank of France. Printed in THOMSON, *France* [*see* Document **5/13a**], pp. 161–163.

Article 1. The General Assembly is composed of all the shareholders of French nationality. Each member is entitled to one vote, however many shares he owns.

Article 2. The General Assembly nominates three auditors. It receives a yearly report on all operations of the Bank.

Article 3. The Governor and the two Deputy-Governors will not have to account for ownership of Bank shares.

Article 4. The Governor will take an oath, in the presence of the President of the Republic, to direct the affairs of the Bank well and faithfully, in conformity with the laws and statutes.

Article 5. The Governor shall receive from the Bank an annual salary equivalent to that of a Vice-President of the Council of State; the two Deputy-Governors shall each receive a salary equivalent to that of a president of a division of the Council of State.

Article 6. The General Council shall decide the terms by which the Governor and two Deputy-Governors shall receive an entertainment allowance and reimbursement of exceptional expenses.

Article 7. During their term of office the Governor and Deputy-Governors are prohibited from holding or receiving any share or interest whatever for services or consultation in any private enterprise, industrial, commercial or financial.

Article 8. The Governor and Deputy Governors who retire from office continue to receive their salaries for three years, on condition that they do not accept any public appointment during this period. Furthermore, they are prohibited for the same period from lending their support to any private enterprises and from receiving from them any remuneration for consultation or services.

Article 9. The Bank is administered by twenty councillors and supervised by three auditors. The Governor, Deputy-Governors, councillors and auditors form the General Council. The auditors have a consultative role on it.

Two councillors are to be drawn from the shareholders, nine represent economic and social interests, and nine represent the collective interests of the nation.

The councillors are designated as follows:

I. Two are elected by the General Assembly from among mill owners, manufacturers, or tradespeople, other than persons assisting with services or consultation or as administrators in a banking house.

II. One is nominated by the National Economic Council from its Vice Presidents.

One is nominated by the Higher Committee of the Savings Banks from its members.

One is elected by secret ballot by the personnel of the Bank of France.

Six are chosen by the Minister of Finance from lists of three names presented by each of the following organizations:

National Federation of Cooperative Supply Stores, General Confederation of French Artisans, Assembly of the Presidents of the Chambers of Commerce of France, General Confederation of Labour (C.G.T.), Permanent Assembly of the Presidents of Chambers of Agriculture, and commercial vocational sections of the National Economic Council.

The latter shall be provisionally chosen by the Minister of Commerce from the best qualified representatives of small tradesmen.

III. Three represent the Ministers of Finance, National Economy and the Colonies.

Six are members *ex officio*: viz.

The President of the Finance Division of the Council of State;

The Director of the general movement of Stocks [*mouvement général des Fonds*];

The Director-General of the Deposit and Consignment Office [*Caisse des Dépôts et Consignations*];

The Governor of the Loan Bank [*Crédit Foncier*];

The Director-General of the National Loan [*Crédit national*];

The Director-General of the National Bank for Agricultural Credit. No Member of Parliament may be a member of the General Council.

Article 10. Councillors elected or chosen by the Ministers upon presentation by interested parties may not sit for more than three consecutive years. One-third are replaced annually. The outgoing councillors may not be chosen or elected again within three years of leaving the Council.

Article 11. The General Council of the Bank may delegate all or part of its powers to a permanent committee comprising the Governor, the Deputy-Governors, and four councillors, one chosen by the Minister of Finance and three nominated by the General Council.

Article 12. The decrees issued before 15 December 1936 by the Council of Ministers, in conformity with the proposals of the General Council of the Bank of France, may modify the texts which control the internal administration of the Bank and decide the regulations for drawing up the balance sheet. . . .

5/17 The 1938 Strikes

a 'La France economique en 1938' in *Revue d'économie politique LIII* (Paris, 1939), pp. 1360–1361. (Ed. Tr.)

b 'M. Daladier's Chance' in *The Economist*, CXXXIII, 3 December 1938, pp. 465–466.

a On 26 November the administrative Committee of the C.G.T. made known, in a long communiqué, the unanimous decisions it had taken regarding the strike of 30 November; it was to be general, was not to involve the occupation of any factory and was to be a peaceful demonstration. The C.G.T. decided to act against the *decrets-lois* which had affected the forty-hour week and claimed to be the interpreter of unanimous public opinion. Orders were immediately given by the federations, at the very same time as the Government, with the full support of the press, apart from the C.G.T. and extremist papers, organized the resistance, concentrating in particular on requisitioning the railways and those concerns involved in national defence.

All those who were not blinded by political passion saw the inevitable failure of the strike, which was completely unjustified and for which the workers showed no enthusiasm, and which assumed an insurrectionary character, not only because it was a rebellion against the operation of legally constituted authorities, but because civil servants were also called out on strike. This feeling of unpopularity for the proposed strike, and the presentiment that it was likely to be unsuccessful, was such that in the days before 30 November there were increasing attempts at mediation with the Government by official representatives of the C.G.T. . . .

All told, the strike was an incontestable and obvious failure. There will be quibbles in the future about the percentage of strikers in any particular corporation; in fact, in Paris particularly, it can be shown quite clearly that all public services carried on as usual and that neither les Halles* nor the large retail establishments nor commercial life in general was seriously disturbed. Proceedings were immediately instituted against those who had tried to bring about the disruption of the public services; action was actually taken or intimated against those civil servants who had judged it preferable, at their own risk, to listen to their union leaders rather than the heads of their departments. In private firms, most of the workers were regarded as having broken their contract without any professional justification and were therefore dismissed.

M. DALADIER'S CHANCE

b If the organized representatives of the French workers have suffered a complete and humiliating defeat they have only themselves to blame. The Confédération Générale du Travail deliberately chose to use the weapon of the general strike against M. Paul Reynaud's decrees;† and it has broken in their hands. According to reports, there were no industries on Wednesday where more than half the workers went on strike, and all the essential public services were functioning as usual. The reasons for the failure are not far to seek. In the first place, the unions had a bad case. It is widely realized, even among the workers, that the forty-hour week has been not only a failure so far as any enhancement of the welfare of the workers is concerned, but also a danger to the economic structure of the nation. The general strike is a weapon that has no chance of success unless it is used in a cause that is generally acknowledged to be just; for since it is general, it can be aimed only at the community itself, and the public has difficulty in seeing itself as beneficiary and victim at once. On Wednesday, the leaders of the C.G.T. seem to have shared the general belief that they were fighting in an impossible cause. The strike was called for one day only, which put it more into the class of a political demonstration than of a serious attempt to force the issue; and, even so, the union leaders were at some pains to apologize for it, and they would have been glad to have been presented with an opportunity for calling it off. As it is, the moderation of their real views and intentions was betrayed by the violence of their language. The Government refused to treat; the C.G.T. was forced to go on with the strike and to accept the humiliation of its outcome.

The C.G.T. has been defeated; but it does not in the least follow that the French workers have also suffered defeat. Indeed, it was their failure to iden-

* The Central Market in Paris. (Ed.)
† Reynaud '1878–1966) was Daladier's Finance Minister. His measures were designed to obtain the freer working of Capitalist Enterprise. (Ed.)

tify the cause of the C.G.T. with their own which, fully as much as the Government's resolute measures of military requisitioning, led to the fiasco. The abrogation of the forty-hour week is as much to the worker's advantage as its institution has been proved to be to his disadvantage. This fact was expressed, with customary pithiness, in one of Low's cartoons* during the past week, in which the French worker was shown butting his head against a stone wall labelled 'Economic Facts of Life (under Free Exchange Capitalism)'. The facts are, indeed, inescapable and one can disagree only with Low's parenthesis, which seems to imply that there is some other form of miraculous economic organization under which a given labour force could produce as much in forty hours a week as in fifty. The point is worth stressing; for there is far too much readiness, on both sides of the French economic controversy, to ignore half the truth. Labour and Capital both have a contribution to make to French salvation; and it is not in Labour's interest that Capital alone should be called upon to contribute any more than it is in Capital's interest that a solution should be sought solely at the expense of Labour. Labour advocates restraints on Capital, which would be useless without an increase in working hours. And Capital advocates the reversal of the social laws of 1936,† which will have no effect unless French capital is once more poured into French industry.

Wednesday's events thus constitute a defeat for the peculiarly mistaken tactics of the C.G.T., but not for the French worker, whose standard of life is more likely to be raised than lowered as a result. Who was the victor? M. Daladier,‡ doubtless; but what does M. Daladier stand for in these days? If he allows himself to convert his victory into a heresy hunt against 'Reds', into an offensive against the workers, or into an invitation to explore the paths of undemocratic government, he will be justifying retrospectively the action of the C.G.T. in calling the strike. Indeed, it is true to say that the outcome of the strike gives him a mandate to put pressure now on the Right. It has been shown beyond doubt that no demagogy of the Left is going to be allowed to interfere with the working of the Reynaud Plan.§ But the real threat to the Plan was never to be expected from the Left. There was not very much dispute about the forty-hour week or much doubt (despite the fulminations of the Socialists and the C.G.T.) about what should be done. But on the methods of securing the co-operation of Capital fierce controversy has raged. This controversy, and the doubts about the Plan's chances of success, still remain. The Government still faces its most difficult task, that of resolving the controversies and removing the doubts that prevail about the proper treatment of

* David Alexander Low, 1891–1963. Famous cartoonist. (Ed.)
† i.e. the social legislation of the Popular Front Government. (Ed.)
‡ The French Premier. (Ed.)   § See footnote to this on p. 410 above. (Ed.)

Capital. The defeat of the strike does not ensure the success of the Plan. It merely gives it a chance.

Capital can be either cozened or compelled. MM. Daladier and Reynaud have chosen cozening. But they are fully entitled – indeed, they are morally bound – to apply the same tactics towards the Right as the Left. If the co-operation of Capital can be secured by consent, that will be by far the best solution, just as an alteration of the social laws by consent, as can now be seen, would have been far better for all parties than the method of the decree and the strike. But to the capitalist as to the worker it must be clearly said that the interests of the community must in the last resort be paramount. France needs her savings fully as much as she needs her workers' right arms. M. Blum's policy was weakened in 1936 because he was unwilling to use force against even the most clearly anti-social activities of the workers. If M. Daladier is unwilling to take any attitude towards the taxpayer, the rentier, the employer and the capitalist than that of gentle persuasion, he will make himself the prisoner of the extremists of the Right, just as M. Blum was hampered by the extremists of the Left. Wednesday's events have made the real issue clearer than ever: will the moneyed classes of the Republic risk their substance for its salvation? If not, then some French Government will sooner or later send the Garde Mobile out requisitioning once again.

5/18 Agriculture and Society in France

a Royal Institute of International Affairs, *World Agriculture* [*see* Document **5/1**], pp. 138–140.

b 'Les répercussions des nouvelles lois sociales' in *Revue des deux mondes*, XXXIV, 15 August 1936, pp. 756–757. (Ed. Tr.)

a The great western European countries, with the exception of Great Britain, aim at being as nearly self-sufficing as possible in food requirements, and the basis of the policy pursued by France, Germany, and Italy requires closer examination.

French national policy has always been directed towards maintaining a just balance between agricultural and industrial production and between the urban and the rural population. Ever since the eighties there has been pro-gressive protection of agriculture. The aim is the nicely balanced economic unit, self-sufficing in essentials – almost completely so if the rich French areas of Northern Africa and Indo-China are taken into account. But even these outer areas (Algeria is an integral part of France and is represented in the Chamber) are not sufficient for all essentials – not, for instance, for cotton and wool. There is, of course, no question of complete isolation, for France wishes to maintain and extend her export of certain agricultural products, notably wines. Drastic steps for the reorganization of the wine-growing industry were taken in 1931.

Tradition is very deeply rooted in the French countryside, and there is little interest in new ways, though, even within the tariff wall, economic pressure has made some change. Shortage of labour since the war has made some labour-saving essential. The character of the peasant varies, north and south, east and west. But two characteristics seem to be universal: a capacity for endless toil in the service of the farm, and a strong individualism.

One of the reasons for the preoccupation of the French Chamber with agriculture may be explained by the fact that half the population still lives in communes* of under 2,000 inhabitants, and parliament has a predominant representation of rural industries. Nearly 9 million persons out of a total occupied population of $21\frac{3}{4}$ million persons in 1921 were engaged in forestry and agriculture. At that date there were 5,219,000 independent farmers, and 2,834,000 agricultural labourers. Agriculture is still mainly a family business, and in 1921 85 per cent of French holdings were of less than 25 acres.

By tradition and policy the most important crop is wheat. There is no tolerance by the French Government of the proposition that wheat might be more cheaply imported and the land at present under wheat devoted in part to other purposes. Every reduction of the wheat area is regarded as a national disaster. Nevertheless, the wheat area declined during the war and the post-war years from an average of $16\frac{1}{2}$ million acres in the pre-war quinquennium to an average of $13\frac{1}{2}$ millions in the five years 1921–1922 to 1925–1926. The acreage in 1930–1931 was slightly less than the last-named figure, but in 1931–1932 the harvest was so great that it was even suggested there might be a surplus for export. A further addition of three-quarters of a million acres was made to the wheat acreage in that year.

Peasant life is the basis of French civilization. Industry and finance remain merely a superstructure, even since the return of Lorraine. [It is said that the French social system still rests upon the peasant.] The economic autonomy of France, based on peasant production, determines French mentality – its individuality, its distrust, its desire for security. The whole conception of the objective of production is different; it is production for its own sake, not for the sake of profit. The conception of wealth is a static conception. [In his eyes, the Report continues, wealth was not something dynamic bound up with general prosperity, but a clearly and legally defined asset such as a piece of land or a house etc.] Ownership of the smallest piece of land is a real satisfaction in itself.

The aims of French policy are an all-round production to supply French

* See Glossary.

needs, and a steady peasant population maintaining the hard-working, frugal tradition of country life. M. Augé-Laribé* writes:

'We may set down one first principle; industrial development ought not with us to be pursued at the expense of agriculture. We have always been essentially an agricultural country. We ought not to attempt to become a country essentially industrial. All the productive forces, all the natural dispositions, so numerous and varied, of France, would be difficult to use if accidental and temporary circumstances were allowed to lead us into one profession to the exclusion of others. Our future and our tradition alike demand that we furnish to the world the example of a wise and harmonious balance. To ruin the culture of the soil for the purpose of making France into an industrial nation – that would be folly.'

The aid given to agriculture by the Government includes: protection by means of a tariff, and, in the case of wheat, by a quota system which requires a high percentage of French wheat in milling; the provision of good roads and communications, and the provision of electric light and power on the farm (the advantage of electricity is very great – there are no dark mornings in a French farmyard in those departments† where the electricity scheme has been carried through); the expenditure of care and money on vocational education of farmers, on seed-testing, veterinary services, propaganda for the use of fertilizers, on the recruitment of labour, and the establishment (in 1929) of excellently equipped departmental offices; support of co-operative societies and grants of credits for rural development. In spite of all this, State expenditure on agriculture forms a smaller percentage of the Budget than in many other countries. [The contrast has been put] between the meagre sums spent by the Government on agriculture and the national love of the soil.

'If there is in France . . . a desire to improve agriculture, if there is talk of bettering rural life and rationalizing cultivation there is also no suggestion for planning and working on any such scale as will save the situation. There is goodwill, but it is not of the heroic sort. There is a love for farming, but it is a love of the technique of the fine act of individual persuasion of nature, of immediate contact with the earth and its fruits. . . .'

b   Indeed, France, it should not be forgotten, will preserve her wealth only if she remains an essentially agricultural country. . . . The leaders of the country who have had a tendency to forget this have always, throughout time, bitterly regretted it.

Now, the increase in the cost of industrial goods is certainly going to result in some grave economic and social repercussions for those engaged in

* A noted writer on French agrarian matters. (Ed.)   † See Glossary.

agriculture, which the founding of the *Offices Nationaux agricôles*, charged with placing high taxes on agricultural goods, will hardly counterbalance. Quite apart from the fact that such a general tax is to be absolutely condemned in terms of its effects, and has failed to work wherever there has been an attempt to apply it, it would not in any case be sufficient to solve the problem.

The distress of the peasants is truly terrible; what will it be like when they have to pay 20 to 30 per cent more for their manure, implements, and agricultural machinery and, for the minority among them who employ labour from outside their own family, when they have to pay 10 or 15 per cent more for their workers? Selling prices cannot be raised as they can in industry; in industrial concerns it is necessary to raise new prices automatically [in such circumstances] as otherwise closure would result and all would be lost; in agriculture, nothing is ever lost, for the peasant goes on for ever, and can live a long time eating bread and dressing in rags; agricultural prices, then, can go down for a long time, almost without any lower limit, in fact. . . . But, in these circumstances, what happens to the normal and healthy conditions of life which are necessary not only for every worker but for every decent and respectable man? And if the State wishes to take some special action over this, too, it will mean increasing the budget deficit still more and that cannot go on for ever. . . .

The sons and daughters of the unfortunate peasants, attracted by the artificial glamour of the cities, by the easier life, and by the 2,000-hour year which is worked there, will hurry their steps in this direction. This is the real reason, as we shall presently indicate, why the forty-hour week will not reduce unemployment as much as had been hoped, if in fact it diminishes it noticeably at all. . . . These young people, more than any other group, because they are young, healthy and easy to please, will sign on to work in the factories, and will aggravate working-class overcrowding in the cities while at the same time contributing to the further de-population of the countryside in a country which, to stay prosperous, must above all else remain agricultural.

5/19 The Office du Blé

'La France economique en 1936' in *Revue d'économie politique* (Paris, 1937), LI, pp. 732–735. (Ed. Tr.)

The year 1936, therefore, is remarkable for a noticeable increase, which raised the price of wheat from 86 to 143 francs (an increase of 66 per cent). But the history of this increase falls into two distinct periods. During the first half of the year, from January to July, the price increased from 86 to 114 francs (32 per cent) in a very irregular movement, which was actually

The Paris Bourse
Per quintal

		In French francs	In gold francs
1914	July	28,62	,,
1933	January	79,62	15,78
	June	79,62	16,34
	December	78,62	16,16
1936	January	86,62	17,17
	February	94,62	18,95
	March	99,62	20,60
	April	97,62	20,21
	May	92,62	19,13
	June	97,62	19,95
	July	114,62	21,40
	August	139,62	22,56
	September	140,62	29,23
	October	141,62	20,67
	November	142,62	20,81
	December	143,62	20,95
1937	March	147,62	21,13

reversed in the month of May. . . . In August a sharp movement took the price from 114 to 139 francs (an increase of 21 per cent) and from this point, it remains practically stable, increasing by a small amount each month. In the meantime a new regulating force had appeared in the market, of which the agent and symbol was a new organization: the *Office du Blé.*

For a long time the Socialist party advocated a tight control over the wheat market; the party had, by turns, criticized the policy followed from 1929 to 1934 (a policy which guaranteed minimum prices, massive exports, and the conversion of wheat to animal foodstuff), which it did not regard as sufficient and had also condemned the policy followed from the beginning of December of 1934 (some lifting of restrictions in the wheat market, milling bounties and output guarantees to millers and bakers), which it regarded as leading in a wrong direction. Swept to power by the May elections in 1936, the Socialist party tried to carry out its own programme; the law of 15 August 1936 creating an *Office national interprofessionnel du Blé,* is the practical expression of such a programme.

At present this law is much more closely allied to Hitlerite policies than those pursued by Roosevelt; it is less concerned with acting directly on production (by regulating sowings, for example) than with regulating the quantity of wheat which may be put on the market. It also neglects the problem of consumption (increasing or restricting it, according to the situation) and concentrates only upon one aspect of the problem; exchange. By mastering exchange, it is thought, the entire problem is solved.

The trade in wheat is no longer free. It is placed entirely in the hands of the *Office du Blé* which controls all transactions. Sales from producer to miller take place, according to preference, either through the intermediary of *Cooperatives de Blé*, which can use tax exemptions and, if necessary, *office national* subsidies to enable them to meet their operating costs (article 5), or through the medium of *négociants en grain français et patentés* who cannot 'claim any fiscal benefits or subsidies' (article 6). In both cases the essential rules are the same: the quantities which each producer 'having sold more than 100 quintals of wheat during the previous year' may offer for sale are fixed by the *Office du Blé* (article 8). . . . These deliveries are made according to a scale which is also determined by the *Office* (article 15). They are paid for at a fixed price during the second fortnight of August by the *Office*; this price is the same for the whole country; it is merely 'increased from September each year by means of a monthly bounty to take account of storage, management and administrative costs' (article 9). Wheat purchased by the *négociants en grain* must be paid for through the agency of the *Caisse regionale de crédit agricole* (article 6); the co-operatives remain free to make payments themselves or to make use of the same intermediary. All these transactions are compulsorily controlled: 'the co-operatives and the *négociants en grain* will send regular monthly bulletins giving details and the total amount of all buying and selling transactions and information regarding the buyers and sellers to the *Comité départmental* (article 6).

Two items complete this machinery; the monopoly of the import and export of wheat and flour conferred on the *Office* by article 16, and the fixing of a differential price at which supplies intended for export, or for keeping in storage, are bought when there is an abundant harvest (article 14). . . .

All of these measures have been applied from the month of August; it is too soon to pass judgment on such a complex mechanism, which will really require several years to perfect. . . .

5/20 France's Economic Problem

'France's Economic Problem', *The Economist*, CCX, 27 April 1935, pp. 943–945.

France embarked upon the crisis with an undervalued currency; and it was consequently not until sterling left gold in 1931 that her economy began to feel the international blizzard. It is true that French wholesale prices began to fall, and so to diverge from the cost of living, as early as 1929. But industrial production continued to rise throughout 1929 and 1930; and though it fell in 1931, it was only 2·4 per cent lower in that year than in 1928. Unemployment increased only slightly in 1930 and 1931. Exports fell from 43,000 million francs in 1930 to 30,000 millions in 1931, and imports from 53,000 millions to 42,000 millions. But the import surplus of 12,000 million francs is estimated to have been offset by invisible exports to the extent of 11,500 millions. So far the generally reduced demand in the outside world had led to a reduction in France's exports and a consequent slight reduction in general economic activity, but it had not yet succeeded in seriously reducing the amount of internal purchasing power available. As a result there was only a small Budget deficit in 1931–1932, partially due to the cessation of Reparation payments.

In 1932 France began to feel the effect of the depreciation of sterling. Under the influence first of falling prices in the outside world, and secondly of the shrinkage in internal purchasing power which resulted from the consequent attempt to reduce costs, the average wholesale price index for the year 1932 fell 15 per cent below the level of 1931, while the cost of living fell by only 8 per cent. Industrial production, which had stood (1928 = 100) at 110·2 in 1930 and 97·6 in 1931, fell to 75·6 in 1932. Exports fell from 30,000 millions to 20,000 millions and imports from 42,000 millions to 30,000 millions; a 30 per cent shrinkage in foreign trade, which still left the import surplus at about 10,000 millions. By this time, however, invisible receipts had dwindled to 4,100 millions, owing to an estimated falling off in tourist receipts from 6,000 millions to 3,000 millions. There was actually an increase in the Bank's gold reserve during the year. But the Bank's holdings of foreign assets fell heavily; and the note circulation and volume of bank deposits both fell off slightly. The deflation of the French economy, occasioned by the fall in sterling, had now begun. The official figure of unemployment, which should probably be multiplied two or three times to give a figure corresponding to the English, rose to 273,000 for 1932. The Budget problem became acute; and, despite economy cuts in the summer, the year ended with a deficit of 10,500 million francs. By May 1933 this deficit had been reduced by further cuts to about 3,000 millions.

During the first half of 1933 the depreciation of the dollar resulted in a rise in American prices more than proportionate to the fall in the exchange; and a reflationary pull was consequently exerted on the rest of the world. France shared in the general recovery. The wholesale price-index rose steadily from February to June. Industrial production expanded about 15 per cent between January and July; and unemployment diminished throughout the spring and summer. The relapse in American recovery in July was followed by the 'gold-buying' policy of October, which deliberately undervalued the dollar, and by the return of the dollar to gold at an undervalued level in February 1934. This series of events set in motion a new deflation of the French economy, and from the summer of 1933 onwards depression steadily deepened. Industrial production fell continuously, and unemployment increased, until the advent of M. Doumergue's Government in February 1934. Foreign trade for the year 1933, however, as a result of the recovery between January and June, only showed a slight reduction. Imports fell from 30,000 million francs to 28,000 millions, and exports from 20,000 millions to 18,000 millions. The import surplus still stood at about 10,000 millions. Invisible exports are estimated to have risen slightly during the year; and a debit balance of only about 3,000 millions remained on all current transactions in goods and services.

In February 1934 the Doumergue Government came into power, and was faced with a large Budget deficit and a deeply depressed industrial and commercial system. It set itself to try the deflationary cure. The Budget deficit was met by drastic cuts in civil servants' wages and in social expenditure; though at the same time direct taxes were reduced. The Government justified this inequitable procedure on the ground that a simultaneous cutting of costs and fostering of the 'confidence' of the rentier classes would lead to industrial and commercial revival. The expected renascence of rentier confidence duly transpired. Gilt-edged prices rose steadily throughout the spring, and the Bank rate, which had been raised to 3 per cent during the February troubles, was again reduced to 2½ per cent.

But the effect on economic activity was precisely the opposite of that which the Government professed to expect. Wholesale prices, under the influence of dwindling internal purchasing power on the one hand, and of the devalued dollar and pound on the other, fell for the rest of the year. But the fall in costs entirely failed to catch up with the fall in prices; and the divergence between wholesale prices and the cost of living steadily increased. As a result, industrial production fell continuously, from (1928 = 100) 82·7 in February to 73·2 in December. The official figure of unemployment fell seasonally between February and June, but had risen by December to 419,129, compared with 312,894 in December 1933. Meanwhile the Government set in motion a reduction of imports far more drastic than any hitherto undertaken by France during the crisis. In consequence imports in 1934 were 20 per cent below 1933, while exports only fell by 3½ per cent. The resulting fall in the import surplus was about 5,000 millions, or 50 per cent; a fall which, being due almost entirely to smaller imports, must have not only reduced consumption in France, but contributed to the slackening of recovery in the rest of the world.

Partly owing to the manifest failure of its economic policy the Doumergue

Government fell in November and was succeeded by that of M. Flandin.*
M. Flandin found the country in the grip of depression. Production and
foreign trade were lower, and unemployment higher, than at any time in
the last five years. As a result the Budget problem had once more become
acute; and the fiscal year closed with a net deficit of 5,620 million francs. The
'economies' of the Doumergue Government had been followed by so great a
shrinkage in economic activity that the Budget itself had become once more
unbalanced. By December even gilt-edged prices had again fallen, and the
rate of interest had risen.

The root cause was still, of course, the disequilibrium between French
costs and world costs due to the overvaluation of the franc. . . . [If the divergence between wholesale prices and the cost of living] may be taken as
measuring the disequilibrium between selling prices and costs of production,
that disequilibrium was greater in France in September 1934 than it had ever
been. And by the end of the year it had grown even greater. Such indices as
are available suggest that there has been no substantial reduction in French
money wages since 1931. This means that wage costs in the sterling countries
have been reduced by 30 per cent to 40 per cent in comparison with French
wage costs since 1931; but it does not, of course, imply that the real income of
the British worker has been reduced, or that it is now lower than that of the
French worker. The effect of French agricultural protection has been to keep
the manufacturer's costs high and the worker's real income low.

In October we tentatively estimated that the equilibrium rate between
the franc and the pound for August 1934 lay between 80 and 90 francs. The
actual rate was then about 75; which suggested a 12 per cent to 15 per cent
overvaluation. Since August British wholesale prices and the cost of living
have been about stable; while by December the French cost of living had
fallen about 1 per cent and wholesale prices by nearly 10 per cent. As the exchange rate still stood at about 75 in December, the overvaluation may have
been slightly reduced by then. But the fall of the pound to 70 six weeks ago
must have entirely wiped out the progress towards adjustment made in
France in the previous five months. Its subsequent rise to 73 has somewhat
eased the pressure on France, but not before Belgium had been forced to
devalue, and so to weaken the position of the franc once again.

M. Flandin's problem, like the problem which induced the new Belgian
Government to devalue, is primarily neither a Budgetary one nor, in the
technical sense, a monetary one. The recurrent Budgetary deficit is merely the
fruit of industrial and commercial depression; and M. Flandin has found it
possible, by a combination of further cuts and of increased short-term borrowing, to hold the Budgetary position. The estimated deficit on the 1935

* The Flandin Government held office between November 1934 and May 1938. (Ed.)

Budget is actually a small one. Nor is the monetary situation technically weak. The gold reserve of the Bank of France doubled between 1929 and 1932 and after a slight decrease in 1933 has now risen again to an almost record level. Meanwhile, the note circulation has actually decreased since 1931; and the volume of deposits in the commercial banks has fallen heavily.

Recognizing that the problem was fundamentally one of comparative price and cost levels, M. Flandin announced in January that the gold reserve was to be used, credit expanded, and prices raised. This policy implied either a considerable outflow of gold or an insulation of the French price level from the outside world by exchange restrictions. But M. Flandin never made it clear which path he intended to take. In the event the credit expansion policy has been whittled down to little more than an expedient to assist Treasury borrowing; and the rise in commodity prices which greeted the first announcement of the policy has vanished away. As a result unemployment and depression remain acute, though there has been no further relapse since February; and the Budget deficit is almost bound to reappear before long. M. Flandin's supplementary efforts to reduce the cost of living have had no sweeping results; and his policy of compulsorily cartelizing industry is at best a counsel of despair. Since deflation has failed, therefore, and devaluation is regarded as politically impossible, the only practical courses before M. Flandin would seem to be either to wait for a rise in sterling and dollar prices, or to allow an outflow of gold calculated to stimulate such a rise, or to insulate the French economy by exchange restrictions in the German and Italian fashion.

5/21 The Monetary Dilemma in France

'France's Dilemma', *The Economist*, CXXI, 30 November 1935, pp. 1058–1059.

The gold bloc volcano is again in eruption. Spasmodically during the past year, the underlying crisis of overvaluation, or, as M. Rist has called it, the 'maladjustment between the internal and external purchasing power' of the gold currencies, has broken out first through one crater and then another. This time the disturbance has taken the form of renewed crisis in France, and gold is once more flowing freely down the mountainside. The present crisis is more confused, however, than that of last June, whose political aspect, the fall of M. Flandin's Government, was simply the consequence of a flight from the franc due in its turn to the fall in Budget revenues. But this week the flight from the franc has been in itself largely caused by political anxieties about the meeting of the Chamber and the future of the Fascist Leagues. Nevertheless, it is the economic crisis which really remains fundamental. For the threat of extremist political pressure only becomes menacing, as the last five years in Europe have repeatedly shown, when public opinion is itself driven to extremity by depression, unemployment and insoluble Budget problems.

There are signs that a far-reaching change has taken place in France's economic situation during the last few months. Up to the early autumn of this year, the crisis was of an easily recognizable nature. Deflation and persistently high interest rates, caused by overvaluation of the currency, inevitably resulted in lower production and falling Budget revenues. Successive instalments of Budget economies merely deepened the depression and curtailed the revenue still further. The Budget was 'balanced' by cuts in the summer of 1932, in May 1933, in February 1934, in December 1934, and finally by M. Laval's drastic surgery of last July. Meanwhile, the Bank rate was being periodically raised – apart from an interlude of 'cheap money' policy under M. Flandin – to stem gold losses; and the industrial production index (1928 = 100) fell from 88·2 in July 1933, to 72·2 in July 1935. The official figure of unemployment rose in the same period from 239,692 to 380,559.

Despite the high Bank rate and Budget cuts of June and July, however, a change seems to have come over the situation in the early autumn. The index of industrial production, which had fallen uninterruptedly for two years, remained stagnant after July and actually rose a point in October. The figures of unemployment and prices also began to suggest stagnation rather than further decline. Were these developments purely fortuitous, or was there some reflationary factor strong enough to offset the deflationary measures of July? This question at once directs attention to the volume of loan expenditure in which the French Government has been indulging in the last few months. An 'Extraordinary Loan Budget', providing for an annual expenditure of 6,000 million francs, to finance public works and re-armament, was passed in the summer, almost simultaneously with the cuts. Meanwhile, owing to the persistent fall in revenues, the Ordinary Budget continued to show a deficit amounting in October to over 500 millions. Total Government expenditure out of loans, therefore, not including the railway deficit, the Algeria deficit and the Post Office, is at the moment running at the rate of 12,000 million francs, or well over £150 millions a year.

Since the recoveries now proceeding in the United States, Japan, Germany and Italy are largely the effect of Government expenditure financed by credit inflation, it is not surprising to find that the fall in industrial production and employment in France has at last been arrested by loan expenditure on this scale. Incidentally, the total deposits in the French big four banks, which had long been declining, began to rise in September. There has also been a marked increase in Government borrowings from the Bank of France since the spring. Indeed, the figure of 'bills discounted' in the Bank of France returns, which as recently as 10 May stood at only 3,949 million francs, rose at the end of June to over 8,000 millions and stood on 15 November at 8,304 millions. Nobody would claim that this increase is wholly composed of commercial bills resulting from a sudden and spectacular recovery in French trade. [It was stated] recently stated that only 2,500 millions of these bills were Government or Railway debts; but [it was not stated] how many of the remaining 5,500 millions of 'commercial bills' were indirectly Government obligations. The fact is that the Government and the Bank of France, despite their orthodox canons, have been driven by the exigencies of the situation in the direction of credit expansion.

Unfortunately, however, this expansion cannot of itself bring recovery, for two reasons. In the first place, public expenditure out of loans, if it is large enough to avert industrial decline but not to reverse it and so increase revenues, merely alleviates the pain without curing the disease. In the second place, precisely as credit expansion arrests or reverses the fall in prices and production, the gold parity becomes more untenable and devaluation the more inevitable.

Such is the inescapable dilemma facing the French Government and Opposition alike; and such is the underlying crisis which has dissipated the fragile 'confidence' inspired by the deflation of July, inflamed public feeling, swollen the strength of the extremist factions, and invested this week's meeting of the Chamber with a sense of painful insecurity. In this embittered atmosphere an 'incident' between the Front Populaire and the Fascist Leagues was almost inevitable. And it duly happened at Limoges ten days ago, when several persons were killed in an interfactional riot. As a result, the Front Populaire, with the reluctant support of the Radical-Socialists, are to call upon the Government to take strong repressive measures against the Fascist Leagues. The intentions of M. Laval,* whose incessant manœuvres on the national and international stage have sorely perplexed foreign opinion during the last six months, are still extremely obscure. His anonymous friends and advisers of the Right, popularly associated with the Comité des Forges† and the Bank of France, are understood to be averse to any determined repression of the Leagues; while M. Herriot‡ on his Left is demanding measures of at least reasonable vigour. In this political tangle, however, M. Laval's remarkable talent for eloquent inactivity may stand him in good stead. He has already, as we write, obtained a preliminary vote of confidence; and the meeting of the Chamber, now proceeding, may very possibly result in a compromise which will ensure the survival of the Government and the

* Pierre Laval (1883–1945), who was later to become a Vichy collaborationist. (Ed.)
† The powerful iron and steel twist. (Ed.)
‡ Edouard Herriot (1872–1957), Radical politician. (Ed.)

consequent temporary cessation of the outflow of gold. A compromise by which finance is discussed first, and the Leagues afterwards, and the Leagues are curbed, but not suppressed, as at the moment appears likely, may secure M. Laval a majority on both crucial issues.

In such an event, however, the fundamental problem of devaluation will remain unsolved. The attitude of the Bank of France, which originally helped M. Laval to office, is still, whatever the Bank return may reveal, 'No devaluation without stabilization.' And even the parties of the Front Populaire, including the Daladier Radical-Socialists and the Blum Socialists, are themselves in part afraid and in part sincerely opposed to any devaluation. They still believe, despite the evidence of the Belgian experiment, and despite the growing support which M. Reynaud has won since June, that a 25 per cent devaluation would mean a considerable rise in the cost of living, a continued Budget deficit, a flight of capital, and a multitude of nameless disasters. Here, in the view of many sincere friends of France, is the real tragedy of her situation. For there is little chance of establishing a strong Left-Centre Government on the Belgian model which would at once carry through an ordered devaluation and pursue at Geneva a policy of willing and active co-operation with the League Powers.

In the circumstances the Front Populaire may be unwilling to force M. Laval's resignation. They may calculate instead that the gold outflow will sooner or later necessitate an embargo, and that devaluation will in this way become an accomplished fact before the elections of next spring. And this now seems by no means an improbable outcome. Already some anti-devaluationist organs in the Paris press are arguing that an embargo on gold exports would not amount to devaluation. Responsibility for such an embargo, reluctantly imposed, could be laid at the foreigner's door; but it would be none the less effective in removing the present over-valuation of the franc. In that case we most fervently hope that when the final choice can no longer be evaded, its difficulties will be overcome without any violence being done to the democratic institutions of France.

5/22 The International Monetary Agreement, 25 September 1936

Official Statement by the British Treasury, printed in *Documents on International Affairs* (London, 1936),. pp. 668–669.

1. His Majesty's Government, after consultation with the United States

* *The Times*, 26 September 1936. Identical official statements (*mutatis mutandis*) were issued by the French Ministry of Finance and the Secretary of the U.S. Treasury. See *Survey* for 1936, Part II(i)(d). (Footnote in *D.I.A.*)

Government and the French Government, join with them in affirming a common desire to foster those conditions which will safeguard peace and will best contribute to the restoration of order in international economic relations, and to pursue a policy which will tend to promote prosperity in the world and to improve the standard of living.

2. His Majesty's Government must, of course, in its policy towards international monetary relations, take into full account the requirements of internal prosperity of the countries of the Empire, as corresponding considerations will be taken into account by the governments of France and of the United States of America. They welcome this opportunity to reaffirm their purpose to continue the policy which they have pursued in the course of recent years, one constant object of which is to maintain the greatest possible equilibrium in the system of international exchanges and to avoid to the utmost extent the creation of any disturbance of that system by British monetary action. . . .

3. The French Government inform his Majesty's Government that, judging that the desired stability of the principal currencies cannot be ensured on a solid basis except after the re-establishment of a lasting equilibrium between the various economic systems, they have decided with this object to propose to their parliament the readjustment of their currency. His Majesty's Government have, as also the United States Government, welcomed this decision in the hope that it will establish more solid foundations for the stability of international economic relations. His Majesty's Government, as also the governments of France and of the United States of America, declare their intention to continue to use the appropriate available resources so as to avoid as far as possible any disturbance of the basis of international exchanges resulting from the proposed readjustment. They will arrange for such consultation for this purpose as may prove necessary with the other two governments and the authorized agencies.

4. His Majesty's Government are moreover convinced, as are also the governments of France and the United States of America, that the success of the policy set forth above is linked with the development of international trade. In particular, they attach the greatest importance to action being taken without delay to relax progressively the present system of quotas and exchange controls with a view to their abolition.

5. His Majesty's Government, in common with the governments of France and the United States of America, desire and invite the co-operation of the other nations to realize the policy laid down in the present Declaration. They trust that no country will attempt to obtain an unreasonable competitive exchange advantage and thereby hamper the effort to restore more stable economic relations which it is the aim of the three governments to promote.

5/23 The 1936 Devaluation

a 'Europe's Currency Crisis. The Story of the Week.' *The Economist*, CXXV, 3 October 1936, pp. 3–5.

b 'The Gold Bloc Falls', *Ibid.*, pp. 1–3.

a *Europe's Currency Crisis – The story of the week*

SATURDAY, 26 SEPTEMBER

A 1.10 a.m. M. Vincent Auriol, the French Finance Minister, announced at the Ministry of Finance that the Government had decided to devalue the franc. He stated that its new value would be between the limits of 49 and 43 milligrammes of gold, 0·900 fine (compared with the previous rate of 65·5 milligrammes), and that an exchange stabilization fund of 10,000 million francs would be set up. Parliament would be convened on the following Monday to ratify devaluation, and meanwhile the Bourse would be closed. At the same time, M. Vincent Auriol revealed the terms of a monetary agreement reached between the French, British and United States governments. He added that devaluation had been made dependent on this agreement.

The agreement was also announced in statements made by the British and United States Treasuries in the early hours of the morning. . . .*

A similar statement was issued by the United States Treasury which undertook to 'use appropriate available resources' to prevent undue exchange disturbances.

Later in the morning decrees temporarily suspending the payment of commercial claims in gold or foreign currencies, and closing the Paris exchanges until further notice, appeared in the *Journal Officiel*. Exports of gold were suspended in fact by the action of the Bank of France in raising the minimum quantity of gold obtainable to an extremely high level.

All foreign exchange dealings were suspended after a short time in the London market. In the few transactions which took place the pound fluctuated between £4·90 and £4·95.

The Swiss Federal Council held a meeting in the morning at which it was decided that the existing gold parity of the Swiss franc would be maintained. At a further meeting of the Council in the late afternoon, however, a decision was taken in favour of devaluation.

In Holland it was announced in the morning that no change would be made in the Government's monetary policy. After an exodus of gold of nearly £2,000,000 during the day, however, the Cabinet, meeting at midnight,

* For the British Treasury statement which follows, see Document 5/22. (Ed.)

decided that the Swiss decision had compelled the Dutch Government to reconsider its attitude, and that since Holland was the only country on the world gold standard, at the pre-1931 parity, the existing monetary policy could not be maintained.

In a statement to the Press in the evening M. Blum said that it was the first time in history that three Great Powers had announced their determination to re-establish normal monetary and economic relations between one another. The French Government would never have devalued 'unilaterally'; but they were prepared to do so as the first step to a new era in economic relations.

SUNDAY, 27 SEPTEMBER

The French Devaluation Bill as submitted to the Finance Committee of the Chamber, and adopted with minor amendments by 20 votes to 12, with 7 abstentions. The Bill contained the following provisions:

(1) The provisional fixing of the full value of the franc between the limits of 43 and 49 milligrammes 0·900 fine.

(2) The institution of an Exchange Equalization Fund of 10,000 million francs.

(3) The approval of a new Convention with the Bank of France by which the profit on the gold reserve should accrue to the Treasury.

(4) The extension of the Bill to colonies and dependencies using French francs as their currency; and a stipulation that it should not apply to foreign payments regularly made in gold before its application.

(5) The forbidding of all imports and exports of gold in bars or coin and all dealings in them at home, except with the authorization of the Bank of France. French holders of gold coin or bullion, whether at home or abroad, to be compelled to declare their holdings to their local tax collector before 20 October; and foreign companies whose capital is mainly French to be subject to the same rule. Holders of less than 60 grammes of gold to be excepted. The excess value of such gold holdings due to devaluation to be sequestrated by the Government; and failure to declare holdings to involve a fine equal to the value concealed. All exchange operations by Frenchmen between 20 September and 26 September to be declared within 15 days, under penalty of a fine equal to three times the amount involved.

(6) The institution of a sliding scale, varying with the cost of living, for all wages specified in the collective wage agreements recently signed or to be signed, and for 'manual' wages and salaries in professions which have no such contracts. Power also to be taken to adjust civil servants' salaries to the cost of living, and to abolish the last of the 'Laval cuts' in ex-soldiers' pensions.

It was later announced in Paris that special privileges would be granted to holders of the recently issued 'Baby Bonds'. The Director of the Sinking

Fund had been authorized to issue reversionary annuities in exchange for *rentes*, Treasury Bonds of a currency of more than six months, and National Defence Bonds, held by persons who had acquired these securities before 26 September 1934, who are more than 55 years of age, and whose 1930 incomes are below the taxable limit. The bonds to be taken back at their par value, and the *rentes* at the average daily rates ruling during the preceding fortnight.

In the course of the evening the Swiss Federal Council requested the National Bank of Switzerland to fix the gold value of the franc between 190 and 215 milligrammes of fine gold, corresponding to a devaluation of about 30 per cent.

MONDAY, 28 SEPTEMBER

The debate in the French Chamber on the Devaluation Bill began in the morning and continued throughout the day. In the main the Right attacked the Government and the Popular Front parties supported it; but both the Radicals and Communists showed themselves restive. M. Bonnet argued that the Government had been forced to devalue by circumstances and had not chosen their own time. M. Paul Reynaud said* the devaluation would have had much better effect if it had come long before. M. Vincent Auriol, in reply, said the currency problem was international and that the monetary agreement between the United States, Great Britain and France was of 'historic importance'. The debate continued throughout the night.

In London there were no dealings in French francs, Swiss francs or Dutch guilders. The price of gold, however, rose to 140s. 9d. an ounce, and sterling depreciated in terms of dollars to about 4·95, compared with $5·03⅛ on Friday. On the Stock Exchange there was some weakness in gilt-edged securities. The French, Dutch, Swiss and Italian bourses were closed throughout the day.

Dr. Colijn,† in a statement broadcast in the morning, said that outside forces had compelled Holland to leave the gold standard. For the present Holland would have a managed currency, and an Equalization Fund of 300 million guilders would be formed. The Government were prepared to abolish trade barriers and work for international stabilization.

The news of the abandonment of gold was received quietly in Holland, and private transactions indicated a depreciation in the guilder of 15 to 20 per cent.

The following statement was issued the same morning by the Bank of Greece:

Consequent on the new international monetary situation the Bank of

---

* Reynaud was later to take charge of French finances. See above p. 410. (Ed.)
† Dutch Prime Minister. (Ed.)

Greece, in agreement with the Government, has decided to base the drachma on the pound sterling. The buying price will be fixed by the Governor of the Bank within the limits of 540 and 550 to the pound. The price of other currencies will be fixed on the basis of their parity to sterling on the London Stock Exchange. After this decision the buying rate of sterling was today fixed at 546 drachmas, and the selling rate at 550. Since the London and Paris Exchanges are closed the Bank is unable to quote a rate for the franc.

The drachma was previously based on the Swiss franc, and on Friday, 25 September, it was quoted at 531–2 to the pound sterling.

Later in the day the Latvian Government announced that the currency would be devalued and attached to sterling. Previously the lat had been attached to the French franc, and had been quoted at 15·50 lats to the pound sterling. The new rate will be 25·22 lats.

In the evening the Turkish Government announced that it had adopted the pound sterling as the basis for its currency instead of the French franc. The new rate would be £T6·35–£T6·38 to the pound, compared with a rate of £T6·34 quoted on Friday, 25 September.

TUESDAY, 29 SEPTEMBER

The debate in the French Chamber on the Devaluation Bill continued during the early hours of the morning. M. Blum, replying to the Government's critics, said that no government could have refrained from devaluing the franc in the existing circumstances. The Bill was finally adopted by 350 votes to 221 at 10.30 a.m. The provision for a compulsory adjustment of wages according to a cost-of-living scale was abandoned in favour of a clause granting general powers to the Government to prevent a rise in prices. In its amended form the Bill also contained provisions permitting the Government to modify import quotas and tariffs, and to arrange a Convention with the Crédit Foncier enabling it to reduce interest rates in return for an advance by the Treasury.

The Dutch Chamber passed in the course of the evening the Bill providing for devaluation, including measures (1) against increases in prices; (2) for the establishment of an Equalization Fund; (3) for the prohibition of gold exports.

Dealings in guilders and Swiss francs were resumed on the London market. Guilders opened at 9–9·20 to the pound, compared with 7·46½ on Friday, 25 September. Swiss francs were at 21¼–21¾, compared with 15·48 on 25 September.

WEDNESDAY, 30 SEPTEMBER

After the approval of the First Chamber had been obtained a few hours previously, the Swiss Lower Chamber adopted the Government's devaluation proposals soon after midnight.

In the French Senate the Government's Bill was debated throughout the day. Finally, despite an appeal by M. Blum, the 'social' provisions were removed, and a single clause empowering the Government to prevent price-raising was adopted. In this form the Bill was voted by a small majority. The Chamber met at 11 p.m. to receive the Bill in its amended form.

In the afternoon Dr. Schacht* read a declaration to the Central Committee of the Reichsbank. He said that Germany did not intend to devalue her currency, but was prepared to join in international negotiations designed to free the channels of international trade and payments. Should an international agreement of a more far-reaching kind than the three-Power monetary agreement prove possible, Germany would consider changing her currency policy.

THURSDAY, I OCTOBER

The French Chamber re-passed the Devaluation Bill in its original form soon after midnight, and added a clause providing for a tax of 50 per cent on all profits made by speculation on Friday, 25 September. The Senate, on receiving back the Bill, adjourned in order to allow its Finance Committee an opportunity to reach a compromise. A plan was eventually adopted which, instead of granting arbitrary power over prices to the Government, provided for the institution of special tribunals to examine dispute questions connected with wages and prices. A new Bill will also be drafted, providing for measures, not included in the Devaluation Bill, to protect ex-Servicemen. This compromise was accepted by the Senate, and later by the Chamber. The Devaluation Bill thus became law.

b The expected has happened. The gold *bloc* has fallen. For five years the garrison had held the citadel with a dogged pertinacity worthy of Verdun's defenders,† though at heavy cost. It was evident, however, that the end was near last week, when the suspension of M. Vincent Auriol's‡ 'Baby Bond' issue and the raising of the discount rate of the Banque de France revealed that M. Blum had abandoned all hope of recovery by a policy of internal expansion within the bounds of the 'Poincaré franc'. In the early hours of last Saturday the outside world learned that the French Government had determined to risk devaluation. Within the next twenty-four hours Switzerland decided also on devaluation, and Holland, swearing she would ne'er consent, consented-though with obvious reluctance. On Monday, finally, it was announced that Greece, Turkey and Latvia were 'aligning' their currencies with sterling.

* President of the Reichsbank. (Ed.)
† Verdun was the scene of the famous French defensive action in 1916. (Ed.)
‡ Auriol was the French Finance Minister. (Ed.)

Thus the past week marks the third decisive stage in a process of currency adjustment which began when the pound sterling, with a number of other currencies, cut loose from gold in September 1931, and continued when the dollar was depreciated in 1933. It is not a final stage of stabilization uniting all the currencies on a new swing of gold parities. But it has been made possible by an act of international co-operation: for the French Government only took the plunge on receiving assurances from Britain and the United States – in terms closely akin to those repeatedly suggested in these columns – that British and American resources would be used to prevent undue exchange disturbances.

One may anticipate with some confidence that in the present case there will be no such period of widespread uncertainty as followed the earlier episodes. The world has learned that uncontrolled inflation is not a necessary corollary of devaluation; that the new franc, like the new pound and the new dollar, need not go the way of the German paper mark. France's present action has, indeed, for a long time been widely regarded as bound to come sooner or later; and the advent to power of M. Blum with his expansive and expensive New Deal has done nothing more than set the seal on the final failure of the policy of deflation. There has been ample time for the most nervous to accustom themselves to the idea of a further change, and to make actual preparations for it. Both foreign centres and the French public itself have certainly done so.

This long notice has enabled an unusually large body of capital to seek refuge in flight from France. But, by the same token, the authorities have had ample time in which to prepare to meet the situation that might be created by its repatriation. And in any case it is unlikely to return to France in its entirety – partly because of the political uncertainty that still persists in France and partly because French economic recovery, though it may be confidentially predicted, will come gradually and not with a sudden boom.

What, in general terms, are likely to be the consequences of the gold *bloc's* action when once the period of immediate readjustment is over? The French franc has never been an *international* currency in the same sense as sterling or the dollar, and its devaluation is likely to have a smaller disturbing effect than the fall of either of its distinguished predecessors. It is to be hoped, therefore, that the stimulus to French internal activity and external trade will be helpful to the world as a whole and will outweigh the effect of France's increased export competition. Certain of her industries – especially her wool textile industry – may be enabled to regain part of their lost markets. But, as we show in a later Note, the 'luxury articles', and many other commodities which figure largely in French exports, are largely non-competitive with the characteristic products of countries like Great Britain and the United States;

and a recrudescence in tourist traffic should help France and Switzerland without seriously hurting anyone else. The devaluation of the Dutch guilder, on the other hand, may have some deflationary effect on the general price level; for a significant share of the world's supplies of such essential raw materials as rubber, tin and oil is produced in the Dutch East Indies. The extent of devaluation in Holland, however, is likely to be less than in the other gold *bloc* countries; and any declining tendency in prices will be checked by the restriction schemes which apply to most of these commodities.

Any adjustments that may have to be made in these directions are, however, of minor importance compared with the fact that an indispensable step has been taken towards the reconstruction of the edifice of world trade which collapsed after 1929. The countries whose currencies have been devalued within the past five years were responsible for more than four-fifths of the world's international trade before the depression set in. In the interim the value placed upon the world's monetary gold reserves (allowing for the effect of devaluation) has increased by approximately one hundred per cent. The latest developments have come at a moment when there is in many countries a psychological reaction against extreme economic nationalism and trade restriction. In many states, further, a definitely expansive economic philosophy is common to Government and people. There is little doubt that a World Economic Conference today would hold out far better prospects of achieving a modicum of sanity in international trade relations than its ill-fated predecessor of 1933.

It would be unwise, nevertheless, to look for a rapid and spectacular transformation of the international scene. In the first place, industries have been fostered and vested interests created by the prevailing system of high tariffs, exchange controls, quotas and prohibitions. Such interests are notoriously prone to outlive the emergencies which call them into being. In the second place, political relationships have changed greatly for the worse since 1931. Industries have been concentrated on armament production, and in more than one country self-sufficiency based on the alleged needs of defence has become an obsession.

These difficulties are formidable; but they should not be allowed to stand in the way of a determined effort by the countries which have adjusted their currencies to secure every practicable amelioration of trade restrictions among themselves. Without a reasonably free apparatus of payment and of valuation, trade cannot flow freely. These countries have an opportunity of demonstrating this truth to the world, and of showing that facilities for trade bring a handsome dividend in increased prosperity.

It is appropriate also that these countries should take the lead. For they are precisely the nations who believe in an increasingly international world as the condition of the advance of civilization, who look upon narrow nationalism as a 'throw-back' towards barbarism.

These, however, are considerations of the longer run. For the moment the task of the world's statesmen is to make the most of the opportunities which the events of the past week have placed before them. Devaluation of the franc, even when it is coupled with an agreement between the three Western democracies, does not automatically solve the problems that are still plaguing the world. But it does present manifold opportunities of moving forward along paths that were blocked so long as a group of the world's most important currencies were still stubbornly deflating. There is now a better prospect than at any time in the past seven years of true exchange stability, corresponding to a genuine equilibrium between the different national economies, and not merely to the rigid imposition of an arbitrarily 'stabilized' rate of exchange. There is now an excellent prospect of the movement of domestic recovery spreading to the countries which have hitherto experienced nothing but a steady restriction of employment. Finally, there is the possibility of a real beginning being made at long last with the task of removing the barbed-wire entanglements which still cumber international trade.

These are great prizes. But they will not ripen and drop from the living tree of events without some exertion on the part of governments. It will exercise all the talents and employ all the experience of the authorities of the three covenanting nations to preserve a genuine stability of the exchanges, a moving equilibrium between disparate national economies. It will need constant watchfulness to ensure that the movement of expansion which can be expected in every country of the world does not degenerate into mere inflation.

The measure of last week's achievement will not be fully revealed until time has been given for all these opportunities to be seized or let slip. If the tide of chance is now taken at the flood, it will indeed lead on to fortune.

5/24 German Law on Labour Exchanges

Law on Labour Exchanges (*Vermittlung*) and Unemployment Insurance of 16 July 1927. R.G. Bl.,* I, p. 187. (Ed. Tr.)

1. (i) The agency for public labour exchange and unemployment insurance. in Germany shall be the Reich Office for Labour Exchange and Unemployment Insurance.

(ii) The Office shall also have responsibility for public employment counselling and apprenticeship. . . .

* The German Statutes of the Realm. (Ed.)

58. (i) The objective of the Labour Exchange is to fill vacancies with the most suitable labour. In this, any special conditions of the vacancies on the one hand, and the professional and physical suitability as well as personal and family conditions, together with the duration of unemployment of the applicant on the other hand, are to be taken into account as far as the state of the labour market permits.

(ii) Employment counselling must take into appropriate consideration on the one hand the physical and mental suitability, the preferences and the economic and family state of those seeking advice, and on the other the state of the labour market and the occupational prospects. It must subordinate the interests of any single occupation to the general economic and social viewpoint.

59. (i) Employment exchange and counselling are to be carried out neutrally, and in particular without consideration of the membership of any association. Questions as to the membership of any association are prohibited. . . .

(iii) There shall be no adverse marking of an employee for the purpose of depriving him of employment, and employment cards may not be used to put in action measures against employees, or corresponding measures against employers. . . .

65. (i) The Reich Minister of Labour may order, on representation by the Reich Office, that employers must register any vacancy available with them with the local Labour Exchange. This obligation may be laid down only for those employees who are subject to the sickness or the clerical workers' insurance; it must not include vacancies in agriculture or domestic employment or in concerns employing fewer than five employees. This compulsory registration may be limited to certain occupations or districts.

(ii) Paragraph (i) does not apply to vacancies arising out of strikes or lock-outs. . . .

69. Insured against unemployment are:

(i) Those who are liable to be included in the Reich sickness scheme or in the Reich mining industry scheme;

(ii) Those who are liable to be included in the clerical workers' insurance and are excluded from the obligatory sickness insurance scheme only because their income exceeds the limit laid down;

(iii) Those who are members of the crew of a German ocean vessel, unless they are exempt by §§70–76, 208 and 209. . . .

87. Entitled to unemployment insurance are:

(i) those who are able and willing to work, but are involuntarily unemployed;

(ii) have fulfilled the time condition of eligibility, and

(iii) have not yet exhausted their claim to unemployment insurance.

88. 'Able to work' under §87 means to be capable of earning, by an activity appropriate to one's powers and abilities, and which may be reasonably expected of one, having regard to one's training and occupation hitherto, at least one-third of the income generally earned by mentally and physically fit persons of a similar kind with similar training by work in the same district. . . .

90. (i) Whoever refuses to accept or to commence work without justifiable cause and after being informed of the legal consequences; even if such work has to be performed outside his place of residence, will forfeit his unemployment relief payment for the duration of four weeks following such refusal.

(ii) Justifiable cause exists only if:

1. the agreed wage, or in its absence the locally current wage for the occupation is not being paid, or

2. the work cannot reasonably be expected of the unemployed person having due regard to his training, his former occupation, his physical condition or the consideration of his future progress, or

3. the work has become available owing to a strike or a lock-out, for the duration of such strike or lock-out, or

4. the situation may endanger health or morals, or

5. the maintenance of dependents (§**103** (ii)) is not adequately assured.

(iii) After the passage of nine weeks from the beginning of his relief or during unemployment common to his occupation, the unemployed person may no longer turn down work on the grounds that it could not reasonably be expected of him having regard to his training or former occupation, except if its performance would lead to substantial disadvantages in his future progress. . . .

94. (i) jobless whose unemployment is caused by a strike or lock-out in Germany will not receive unemployment relief during such strike or lock-out.

(ii) In cases in which unemployment has been caused indirectly by a strike or lock-out, viz. by a strike or lock-out outside the concern, the occupation or the place of work or residence of the unemployed person, he is to receive relief if a denial of relief would constitute unreasonable severity.

(iii) The Administrative Council of the Office shall lay down general guidance lines about cases constituting unreasonable severity. In this it shall take care not to allow unemployment relief to affect economic struggles. . . .

95. (i) The time condition of eligibility is met if the unemployed has been in employment carrying compulsory insurance for 26 weeks in the course of the preceding year. . . .

99. (i) The claim to relief is exhausted when relief has been granted for 26 weeks in all. It may be renewed only when the time condition of eligibility has been fulfilled again. . . .

104. The level of relief payment is determined by the wage.

[Summary of Scales]

Class	Weekly Wage Range (RM)	'Assumed Unit Wage' (RM)	Relief Payment for Single Man, % of 'Assumed Unit Wage'	Plus % for Each Dependent	Up to Maximum Relief Payment, % of 'Assumed Unit Wage'	i.e. allows no. of children	i.e. RM
I	Up to 10	8	75	5	} 80	1	6·40
II	Over 10–14	12	65	5		3	9·60
III	Over 14–18	16	55	5	75	4	12·00
IV	Over 18–24	21	47	5	72	5	15·12
V	Over 24–30	27	} 40	5	65	5	17·55
VI	Over 30–36	33				5	21·45
VII	Over 36–42	39	37·5	5	62·5	5	24·37
VIII	Over 42–48	45				5	27·00
IX	Over 48–54	51	} 35	5	60	5	30·60
X	Over 54–60	57				5	34·20
XI	Over 60	63				5	37·80

5/25 Public Works in France

'La France economique in 1934' in *Révue d'économie politique* (Paris, 1935), XLIX, p. 1125. (Ed. Tr.)

Unemployment assistance is tending to make room for the struggle against unemployment through the creation of work. Towards this end great public works schemes are everywhere advocated or organized. The law of 1 July 1934 authorizes the expenditure in France of 2 milliards 187 millions on behalf of the State and the major railway companies. The funds are supplied primarily by the large public banks and in particular by the social insurance funds, the interest and amortization of the advance being secured by an annual government payment of 637 million provided for in the budget. The implementation of this measure, the path for which was prepared by the decree of 13 May 1934, would be guaranteed by a *Commission nationale des grandes travaux contre le chômage* which was itself created by a decree of the same date. These public works schemes must be carried out according to the conditions laid down in the decree of 9 July 1934, as modified by that of 26 July which repeated almost exactly the terms of the decree of 10 August 1899. . . .

5/26 German Views on the Creation of Employment

From *The Unemployment Problem*, a translation issued by the Ministry of Labour, of the Report of an Advisory Commission appointed by the Federal Government (London, 1931), Part II, 29 April 1931, pp. 50–55.

The Commission enumerate in this section of their Report a number of measures for the creation of employment which they consider to be of major importance.

I. POWER PRODUCTION

From the date of the stabilization of the currency up to 1929, the consumption of electric power expanded in a quite extraordinary measure. . . .

Notwithstanding this fact, however, the electrical power industry, in view of the development of electric power consumption, still offers plenty of opportunities for profitable investment, not only as regards the further necessary expansion of generating stations, but also as regards the extension of transmission lines, which, in the estimation of experts, should effect economies in production costs. . . .

2. TRANSPORT AND COMMUNICATIONS

New investments in the field of transport should only be made after careful investigation to determine whether they will meet any real national requirement. It would be wrong policy to depreciate existing heavily capitalized undertakings by providing additional facilities, so long as the existing facilities suffice for the economic needs of the nation and the further course of production cannot be foreseen. The Commission are, therefore, unable to recommend the construction of great arterial roads for long-distance traffic with the aid of public monies, as such roads would compete with the railways. Canal construction, except when it is a case of canals which are essential for other purposes, e.g., land cultivation, or which have already been begun at great capital outlay and which would deteriorate if work upon them were stopped, is likewise not to be recommended. Even the further extension of the railway system can only be justified at present under special conditions. . . .

Among measures to be encouraged, the Commission would like to include the improvement of the existing road system. The present main roads, from the point of view of direction (passing through thickly populated residential districts, curves, etc.), width and surface, are to a large extent no longer suited to modern traffic conditions, with the result that the speed and safety of traffic suffer. The improvement of these conditions by the levelling, widening and resurfacing of roads and by the construction of by-passes round residential districts is, therefore, urgently recommended. This would have the further advantage of reducing maintenance costs. Another important improvement would be the extension of the rural road system and, in particular, the provision of convenient transport communications for agricultural settlement areas which would facilitate the marketing of their produce. On the whole, greatest stress should be laid upon the construction of tributary, connecting and by-pass roads. . . .

In view of the present acute state of unemployment, an intensification of road-building activity within the limits specified is desirable. The necessary funds could be obtained by raising a loan and using part of the Motor Vehicles Tax. . . . In view of the experience of other countries, the question should be investigated whether the financing of road projects cannot also be promoted with the aid of loans from both home and foreign industries supplying road-making materials.

3. AGRICULTURAL IMPROVEMENTS

The Commission regard agricultural improvement works as a particularly suitable field for the creation of employment, for the reason that, during the execution of the works, great and permanent benefits from the national economic point of view, advantages for private individuals and, in certain circumstances, rapid returns on public capital can be combined with a favourable influence on the labour market. The carrying out of improvement works requires a large amount of labour, a comparatively small amount of capital and, individually, short periods of time. . . .

4. AGRICULTURAL SETTLEMENT

The Commission further advocate effective encouragement of agricultural settlement. Weighty considerations of labour market policy can be adduced in favour of such encouragement, in addition to the well-known reasons arising out of national policy and population problems. Labour conditions in agriculture will be made more secure by settlement, and, since small-scale undertakings employ considerably more workers to the acre than large-scale undertakings, opportunities of employment will be permanently increased. Settlements provide opportunities of employment in the preliminary work (such as road-making and improvements) as well as in the erection of the farm buildings, and the increased demand for building material and implements is of benefit to industry. . . .

5. HOUSING . . . .

The Commission recommend that the inevitable reduction of the public

438

funds available for house-building should be carried out in the way that will cause least hardship, and that efforts should be made to make these funds go as far as possible (grants in aid of interest instead of the granting of mortgages from the house-rent tax, preference to small dwellings, greater encouragement to persons building their own houses by means of their own labour, etc.). . . .

It is to be recommended that where land can be acquired on advantageous terms, dwelling houses should be provided with as large gardens as possible, since this provides the inhabitants of the houses with something to fall back on in periods of unemployment.

5/27 Swedish Recovery

International Labour Office *Report* [*see* Document **5/10**], pp. 24–25.

The case of Sweden affords a remarkable illustration of the result which a bold policy of public investment combined with a well-devised monetary control can attain. The fact of recovery may be seen succinctly from a few figures. The index of production of capital goods which was already 100·9 in January 1935 (1929 = 100) had risen by a further 12 per cent by November. The activity, which in 1934 had depended largely on the export industries, spread to the trades relying on the home market, particularly building, which exceeded all previous records, thanks to a combination of low rates of interest, State encouragement of house construction and the demand for housing springing from the general dissemination of purchasing power. Unemployment continued to decline steadily. Whereas in 1933 the average number of applicants for relief was 165,000 per month, it fell from 93,000 in January 1935 to 61,000 in January 1936, having touched a low point of 41,000 in the summer. It is particularly interesting to note that, thanks to the energetic measures taken by the Government, the number of youthful unemployed (16–25 years), which was 57,000 in November 1933, had dropped to 10,000 in July 1935. In achieving these gratifying results the public works programme played an important part, in 1935 some 55 million crowns being appropriated for this purpose. Moreover, it is clear that public investment on a large scale stimulated rather than checked the process of general recovery. Its financial justification is strikingly demonstrated by the budget position. In 1936 all non-revenue-producing works are to be financed out of income, the budget will be once more balanced and all the short-term loans raised in 1933 and 1934 for emergency public works are to be redeemed. It is even proposed to reduce the income-tax, good presumptive evidence of the soundness of the policy adopted of balancing the budget over a series of years instead of annually. But the Swedish Government is not content to rest on its oars. The King's Speech at the opening of the Riksdag in 1936 significantly pointed out that the unemployment problem was not yet solved: 'in spite of the fact that Swedish trade and industry seem not only to have passed the stage of recovery and consolidated their position, but in some respects to be really expanding', the 'hard core' 'is still considerably higher than during the economic prosperity periods of the decade following the end of the war'. To meet the problem a further programme of improved housing, internal colonization and other measures is being pressed forward; but in addition an inquiry has been set on foot with a view to drawing up an inventory of public works, which can be put in hand should a recession take place.

5/28 Swedish Policy on Unemployment

GUSTAV MÖLLER, 'The Unemployment Policy', in BERTIL OHLIN (ed.) *Social Problems and Policies in Sweden* (Annals of the American Academy of Political and Social Sciences, vol. 197, May 1938), pp. 47–54.

Before 1933 a central organization directing relief activities for the unemployed had existed in Sweden for about eighteen years, that is, since the outbreak of the World War. This central body was the State Unemployment Commission. As the years passed, an ingeniously elaborated state unemployment policy had been created which the Unemployment Commission, according to a decision of the Riksdag, was to apply. According to this system, the unemployed could be aided either by doles or by assignment to some public works project. These projects were generally called relief projects – in later years renamed *reserve projects*. The reserve projects were divided into two groups: State projects and State-communal* projects.

The State reserve projects were paid for almost entirely by the State and were carried out directly by the State Unemployment Commission. In the State-communal reserve projects, State subsidies were given for wages, varying between 30 and 90 per cent, depending upon the tax pressure and the extent of unemployment in the commune involved. If a commune wished to set in motion one or more State-communal reserve projects it had to make application to the State Unemployment Commission, whose approval was required before the project could be carried out. The Commission further determined the number of unemployed to be utilized on the project, and the amount of the State subsidy to be given to the commune. If a commune wished to engage in relief activity it also had to apply for permission to the Commission, which, in such cases as well, determined the amount of the State subsidy and the number of unemployed who could receive assistance.

* See Glossary.

Furthermore, the Commission fixed the amount of the daily wage in both types of reserve project as well as the amount of the daily allowance when cash assistance was given. Finally, the Commission decided how many unemployed each commune would be permitted to send to State reserve projects. It is clear, therefore, that a very strong and firm direction of all unemployment relief policies carried out by State aid lay within the power of the central agency.

Some communes organized reserve projects of their own for which no State aid was requested, and with which the State Unemployment Commission therefore had nothing to do. On the other hand, according to present legislation, no commune can organize assistance for the unemployed, except in the form of poor relief, unless such assistance has been approved by the State Unemployment Commission. During the first year of the depression a relatively large number of unemployed were either engaged in communal reserve projects or supported through poor relief. This number gradually fell, however, because the communes could not, in the long run, carry alone the financial burdens entailed by unemployment within their borders. As soon as they applied for State aid they were compelled to subject their unemployment policies to the rigid control of the State Unemployment Commission.

The basic principle of the old system was that the so-called labour rule was to dominate the unemployment policy, but that projects were to be carried out under such conditions that no worker would quite voluntarily remain with them.

The projects were not to be allowed to diminish the amount of labour which might normally be expected to be required in the immediate future. Neither was the unemployment policy during a depression period to give workers increased power of resistance against wage reductions regarded as necessary in order to adjust the costs of production to the new economic situation which might be created by the depression. For the trade skills of unemployed skilled workers, there was no place in the system. . . .

It has just been said that the central idea of the system was that the labour rule should dominate. In practice, this principle could not be carried through during a period of rapidly increasing unemployment. In March 1933, when unemployment culminated with 186,000 registered unemployed, 17,933 were engaged in *State* reserve projects and 10,945 in *State-communal* reserve projects, or 28,878 in all. In purely communal reserve projects, outside the control of the State Unemployment Commission, there were 17,037 engaged. Altogether, therefore, fewer than 46,000 were employed in different types of reserve projects. About 77,000 unemployed received cash assistance without any returns in the form of work. The emphasis on the labour rule was limited to what was called the testing of the willingness of the unemployed to work, by sending them out on a road project for a brief period, no real attempts being made to have them earn their living by work or to create possibilities for permanent employment. Workers who refused to go to assigned tasks were excluded from all social unemployment assistance. . . .

The starting of reserve projects was not meant to invalidate the principle of the State's passivity in the face of economic change, for the system was meant only to supply the bare necessities to the unemployed, and did not have the purpose of counteracting the depression. This was based on a point of view which held that society cannot successfully influence economic trends by its unemployment policies. . . .

Those opposed to this point of view maintained that a government policy which aimed at the reduction of expenditures had a deflationary tendency and in reality helped to aggravate the depression. A depression is characterized by restricted investment activity and a resultant loss in purchasing power. The right way to fight a depression would therefore be to institute extensive public works financed by borrowed money. This would not only create work directly, but, thanks to increased purchasing power, would stimulate consumption and production in general. In other words, the State should adopt an active crisis policy.

This opinion won such strong support at the Riksdag elections in the fall of 1932 that a Cabinet change became necessary. A Social Democratic government came into power. The new Government did not, it is true, have a party majority in either house of the Riksdag,* but it nevertheless placed before the 1933 Riksdag a proposal for a new unemployment policy completely based on its own conception of the proper means for combating unemployment and overcoming the crisis.

There was included in this proposal a programme for providing work, aiming both to bring assistance to the unemployed and to stimulate economic activity to the greatest degree possible. The public works which were proposed and which were to be carried out under the general conditions of the open labour market, that is, without wages fixed by public authorities, were called *emergency projects* (*beredskapsarbeten*), in contrast with relief projects or *reserve projects*. The proposal was preceded by an inventory of projects the carrying out of which would seem desirable from the social point of view. No special importance was attached to the fact that funds appropriated by the State would be utilized for the direct employment of the unemployed at specific places of work. It was assumed that projects which required a great deal of material and therefore provided industry with orders would be at least as important in combating unemployment as projects which would directly engage a large number of workers. The greater the variation in the

* Swedish Parliament. (Ed.)

kinds of projects in the programme, the more effective their results could be expected to be. Through orders placed with industries, the number of employed would be increased in most trades. Private initiative would be roused from its pessimism and people would receive employment in jobs which were suitable for them, and not merely of an unskilled nature.

The proposal provoked sharp battles between the adherents of the new and the old unemployment policies. Finally a compromise was reached, especially between the Social Democratic Government and the Farmers' Union (*bondeförbundet*), and this compromise was supported by a group of Liberals.

In the compromise the old system was retained in a somewhat polished-up form, while at the same time large sums were set aside for projects in the open market in accordance with the proposal of the Social Democratic Government. Sixty million kronor were appropriated to carry out projects according to the State Unemployment Commission's system, while for projects in accordance with the Government's plan 108,000,000 kr. were appropriated. At the Riksdag of 1934 a similar programme was adopted, but in a somewhat reduced form in view of the decline in unemployment.

In agreement with the point of view on which the Government's proposal was based, the battle against unemployment was organized in such a manner that most aspects of economic activity were to benefit from it directly or indirectly.

Above all, attention was paid to the creation of possibilities for an expansion of the building industry, which is, together with iron and steel, the most important industry from an employment point of view, and which furthermore indirectly provides employment within a series of other industries such as cement factories, lime works, brick works, window glass factories, iron works, woodworking factories, plumbing supply works, heating supply factories, and, by encouraging housekeeping, also in furniture factories and household supply industries. As a dominant capital goods industry, the building industry occupies a place as the perhaps most important key industry from the point of view of economic fluctuations. To stimulate the building industry is to stimulate all economic activity. . . .

For the improvement of communications, large amounts were granted for the building of bridges over the wide rivers in the northern and central sections of the country. Orders for ships, primarily warships, were placed with the larger Swedish shipyards. State grants were made for drainage purposes and for other measures of land improvement and forest protection. Finally, loans were granted, although rather sparingly, to private industrial enterprises (as a rule, small enterprises which during the depression had got into difficulties and could not secure credit through ordinary channels) in

443

TABLE I. NUMBER OF UNEMPLOYED

	Maximum Number		Minimum Number	
	Month	Number	Month	Number
1930	December	31,901	July	5,824
1931	December	88,761	July	30,520
1932	December	161,156	July	94,687
1933	March	186,561	July	138,855
1934	January	171,065	September	78,918
1935	January	93,419	September	41,190
1936	January	61,400	August	20,783
1937	January	33,509	August	9,577

order to prevent bankruptcies and the closing of factories. This completes the list of the most important, if not all, of the projects contained in the programme.

In order to illustrate the movement of unemployment from the preceding boom period through the depression and to the present time, Table 1 [above] is presented, showing the highest and the lowest monthly totals during the years involved.

In order to throw further light on the situation during these years, the average monthly figures for 1930–1937 are presented in Table 2.

TABLE 2

Year	Number
1930	14,000
1931	47,000
1932	114,000
1933	164,000
1934	115,000
1935	62,000
1936	36,000
1937	18,000

These totals must be regarded as minimum figures; there is always a considerable amount of unemployment which does not reach the attention of the authorities. Completely exact figures on the scope of unemployment are never available. A conservative estimate of the actual number of unemployed at the bottom of the depression would probably place that figure at 250,000; while during the summer of 1937 at least 35,000 must have been

444

unemployed, even though the number of applicants for aid was but one-fourth of that number. . . .

In an attempt to take up the battle against unemployment through a state public works programme (hereafter referred to as 'emergency projects'), the extent of the programme must, of course, be definitely proportioned to the amount of unemployment to be overcome. To avoid misunderstanding, the following observations should be kept in mind. . . .

During two depression years, 1933–1934 and 1934–1935, the Swedish budget included altogether 702,000,000 kr. for work appropriations, of which 340,000,000 kr. were directly earmarked as means of relieving unemployment. (Of this amount, State Unemployment Commission projects received 145,500,000 kr.) The *increase* in the works appropriation amounts, as may be noticed, to 437,000,000 kr., to which should be added 130,000,000 kr. invested by communes and private persons as a result of the Government's unemployment policy, or altogether 567,500,000 kr. Of this increase, 136,500,000 kr. fell to the share of State Unemployment Commission projects.

During the two most severe unemployment years, then, capital investments made or stimulated by the State amounted to 832,000,000 kr., or three times the corresponding amount during the two fiscal years of the preceding boom period.

Already in 1931–1932 and 1932–1933 there occurred, compared with the two preceding years, a considerable expansion of the State's capital investments. This expansion was not, however, prompted by a belief that the State *should* meet a depression by means of an expanded activity of its own. On the whole, the increase was conditioned by the needs of the so-called business departments of the Government, of road construction works paid for by automatically growing motor vehicle tax funds, and by an increase of 19,000,000 kr. in the appropriation to combat unemployment.

The *increase* from the fiscal years 1931–1933 to those of 1933–1935 is, however, so very great (451,500,000 kr.) that it furnishes clear evidence of a radically new expansionistic policy. As a further example of the political change which occurred in 1933, one may mention that the Riksdag of that year appropriated 215,000,000 kr. expressly designed to combat unemployment, while the Riksdag of 1932 limited the corresponding appropriation to 28,000,000 kr., although the depression had been in full swing since the fall of 1931 and unemployment figures were rapidly climbing.

We have just compared the sums of all works appropriations regardless of whether they have been made directly or indirectly for the purpose of combating unemployment. This has been done because the budgets of 1933 and 1934, in addition to unemployment appropriations, included large sums for projects which, if the earlier and traditional demand for thrift had been applied, would have been deferred to 'better times'. This expansion of the 'regular' State investments was expressly defended as an integral part of an expansionistic depression policy. It is therefore impossible to secure an adequate concept of the size of the Government's contributions in this field if the unemployment appropriations proper are alone taken into account. . . .

In 1933 the total investment (in buildings and other establishments and in permanent means of production) was estimated at about 550,000,000 kr. below that of 1930. The increase in State investments during the two depression years is therefore about as great as the decline in the total investment during the bottom year of the depression. It is therefore impossible to describe the expansion of the State's investment activity as insignificant in comparison with the vacancy left by the reduction of private investments. As a matter of fact, considerably over one hundred thousand persons were employed directly or indirectly on reserve and emergency projects during the second half of 1934 – a rather impressive achievement when it is recalled that the registered and reported unemployment never exceeded 190,000 and during 1934 amounted on the average to 115,000, seasonal unemployment included. It may be assumed that during this period work was provided through emergency projects for about 70,000, and through reserve projects for about 50,000 persons.

5/29 The New Deal in Sweden

MAXINE DAVIS, *They Shall Not Want* (New York, 1937), pp. 272–279.

. . . Sweden's permanent, continuing work relief programme was set up, as was unemployment insurance in Great Britain, as a cushion against cyclical unemployment and the unemployment incidental to industrial changes in normal times.

It was inadequate for a great depression which this nation in common with the rest of the world endured. During that period Sweden suffered seriously, although her depression came a little later than England's, even after our own. She is abnormally dependent on world trade. Her exports of lumber, machinery, etc., are always heavy. As the world decline came, Sweden felt it acutely. With world recovery, she participated. Her general situation is not affected by any special problems. Although she does have a couple of tiny depressed areas, similar to those in Great Britain, regions which existed by reason of stone-quarrying, an obsolescent industry, they are tiny and not significant in her whole economy.

When the Social-Democratic party came into power, the country was in distress. The reserve works . . . were able to care for only a portion of the needy; direct relief was being given, and the resources of the local communities were being heavily taxed. They were carrying a heavy burden without any State subsidy. In spite of the principles laid down by the unemployment commission, far too many of the unemployed were being given direct relief instead of work relief. Moreover, from the point of view of the destitute, one was as inadequate as the other.

As the depression deepened, these defects were accentuated. After intensive investigation during the autumn of 1932, the Government proposed a vast and comprehensive programme, based on new concepts, to the 1933 session of the Riksdag.*

. . . It proposed that reserve work should be replaced with large-scale public works . . . The new Swedish plan was intended both to give employment and to stimulate recovery. It proposed more important and larger operations which required skilled as well as unskilled labour, and for which wages were to be those prevailing generally for each type of skill required. Thus the Government had the dual objective of providing more work for the unemployed and stimulating private industry indirectly by extensive purchases of materials and supplies from the heavy industries and by the increase of consumer purchasing power. This all sounds very like the New Deal. And it is.

Under this new and enlarged policy, the Government planned State financial aid to industry, agriculture, forestry, and handicrafts, in addition to the regular credits for unemployment relief.

The Riksdag approved this programme for the most part. It retained the Swedish system of reserve works, merely amending the rate of wages payable on them in order to bring them more closely into line with the income of unskilled labour in the open market.

In 1934, the Riksdag made extensive provisions for great public works to be operated under open market conditions, but kept its reserve works and further limited the granting of direct relief.

At the same time, Sweden embarked on a new monetary experiment. She 'went off gold' and adopted a managed currency. This was not an original enterprise. Great Britain is Sweden's best customer. Therefore, when England embarked on her new monetary policy, Sweden followed almost immediately.

Like the Roosevelt administration, the Socialist Government in Sweden made a radical departure in fiscal policy. Sweden planned to spend her way to prosperity.

This was most interesting to me. The new Swedish financial policy represented not only a new departure in her own fiscal methods, but also a very

* Swedish Parliament. (Ed.)

new and modern experiment in national financing. Moreover, it closely resembles the Roosevelt policy which has terrified so many of us, and which the majority of us still fail to understand. Ours was an opportunist policy; the Swedish experiment was reasoned and understood and supported by a majority of the people.

Financial tradition in Sweden has always been strict and orthodox. Loans were floated only for productive purposes expected to yield sufficient profit to cover interest charges. All other expenses were financed by means of taxation.

Professor Bertil Ohlin, one of the most distinguished of the European economists – not, however, affiliated with the Social-Democratic regime – has described the Swedish experiment in the *International Labour Review* of May 1935. In it he says:

'With the advent of the severe depression in 1931 the situation changed. The budget for the financial year 1931 to June 1932 was balanced in less orthodox fashion; the year ended with a deficit, and not less than 70 million crowns in all had to be financed otherwise than out of current revenue. For the sake of simplicity such operations will be described below as "financed borrowing". In addition to this 70 million a similar sum was borrowed for productive investments, which in Sweden are entered under the heading "expenditure for the increase of capital".'

The next year, the borrowing for total real expenditure was about 160 million, somewhat higher than the preceding year.

'The budget for 1933–1934 was based by the new Socialist Government on new principles,' Dr. Ohlin continues. 'To finance unemployment relief during a period of depression by means of loans was declared to be sound, as this would help to maintain purchasing power, provided that the borrowing was so effected as not to restrict the credit given to private industry. Only through such a policy would it be possible to escape not only the cutting down of desirable expenditure but also an increase in taxation that would weigh heavily on industry and trade. It would however be prudent to provide for the amortization of such temporary borrowing over a short period of years by setting aside the income from certain taxation – an increased inheritance tax – for this purpose. In the long run, the financial position of the State would not be weakened; the heavy financial burden of the depression would merely be spread over a certain number of years.

'According to this new budget, borrowing for productive public works – which had always been financed in this way – would be increased to 100 million crowns. Owing to delay in starting these works only 65 million was actually spent before the financial year ended in June 1934, to which sum should be added about 15 million remaining from the previous budget. As regards expenditure which would normally have been financed out of current revenue, it was proposed to borrow 168 million for unemployment relief – relief works, cash allowances, etc. – and for certain building purposes. Furthermore, certain kinds of "savings" which meant a hidden deficit were made; these, however, were covered by the surplus which the budget ultimately gave owing to an under-estimate of certain items of revenue. Of the proposed extraordinary loan expenditure of 168 million, which was accepted by the Riksdag, only 98 million was actually spent. In addition, extraordinary amortization amounted to 24 million so that the sum total of expenditure financed by borrowing must have amounted to about 155 million. This sum was about the same as the corresponding sum for the preceding year, 1932– 1933. . . .

'Some defendants of the new policy have claimed too much for it. It is, however, equally unjustifiable to conclude that it had no influence in the business recovery, as the large amount of borrowing must have exercised a favourable influence on the volume of income all through the depression – both in the decline and in the revival – in the way indicated above. During 1931–1932, other tendencies were stronger, so that economic conditions grew worse, while in the following year some of these other factors tended to promote recovery. Not until 1934 was the stimulating influence of loan expenditure substantially strengthened, and only then did it help to quicken the pace of the revival. In judging this last influence, it should be borne in mind that the general improvement in the economic situation led to so large an increase in the State revenue that if the budget had been handled in the same way as in earlier years when orthodox principles played a greater part – although the deficit figures above show that it was largely lip service that was paid to these principles – the deficit and hence the amount of loan expenditure during 1934 would have been smaller than in 1933. Owing to the change in policy it was instead about twice as large.

'The budget proposals for the year 1935–1936, which were before the Riksdag in January of this year, do not ask for any borrowing for unemployment relief or non-productive public works, although certain sums from the previous budget are still available. As Sweden is no longer in a depression the time for such temporary borrowing has passed. But this does not mean a return to the old principles, and it is in complete accord with the theory that the public finances should exercise a certain stabilizing influence on the business cycle. When good business conditions return, the exceptional loans are to be repaid. In the present budget the sums set aside for repayment are offset by certain hidden deficit items, so that taken as a whole the budget is not more than balanced.

'It should be added that Sweden's financial position has not been seriously damaged by the borrowings of the last four years. This is perhaps most clearly seen from a comparison of the interest payments on the State debt, which will be less than 100 million during the next budget year, with the expected revenue from productive investments and funds, which amounts to over 130 million. Thus no taxation is required for the interest service.

'While it seems to be beyond dispute that the policy of budget surpluses during good years and deficits during the depression had a stabilizing influence on economic conditions, it is also evident that the concentration of the loan expenditure in 1934, when industry and trade were well on their way out of the depression, was unfortunate. The new policy should have been begun two years earlier and preparations made for it in advance. In 1934 the time was ripe for a gradual reduction in public works rather than for an increase.

'The amount of employment given by public works is of course partly dependent on the level of the wages paid. Before 1933 the practice in Sweden was that wages paid for relief work – road construction, forest clearing, etc. – were about 15 per cent lower than the open-market wages of unskilled labour in the district concerned. No unemployed worker, skilled or unskilled, obtained help of any kind unless he was willing to accept work on that condition. In 1933 two fundamental changes were made in this policy. A large part of the public works that were started to reduce unemployment was to be handled in the same way as ordinary productive works, and thus naturally paid at regular tariff wage rates; on relief works proper, on the other hand, the wage was to be equal to the open-market wage of unskilled labour in the district. Some people feared that this would cause a flow of labour from agriculture, where wages are lower than the lowest unskilled wage in many manufacturing regions. Up to the end of 1934, however, these tendencies seem to have been insignificant, and agriculture has on the whole not had serious difficulties in getting sufficient labour. . . .

'Nothing in Swedish experience – either with regard to production or with regard to interest rates – contradicts the opinion that in financially strong countries it is sound and practicable to resort to large-scale borrowing during periods of depression. The idea that the budget must be balanced *each year*, and that otherwise inflation is bound to ensue, is one of those popular maxims which are true in certain circumstances but not in others. The fact that they have been preached as a general gospel without qualifications, especially by bankers, has done much harm. For if an economic policy is believed to be unsound the practice of it cannot fail to call forth certain unfavourable "confidence reactions". In Sweden, fortunately, influences of this kind have been very slight. It is time to learn the lesson of recent experience that intelligent and sound public finance does not require the budget to be balanced each year but only over a number of years, including both good and bad business conditions.'

The end of the story came in 1936.

The increase in revenues from taxation paid the costs of the public-works-recovery programme. The normal taxes, in addition to the special taxes – extraordinary income and property taxes – were sufficient to pay the bill. The Swedish issues were short-term loans. The taxes were more than sufficient to pay them off.

The difference between the Swedish and the American programmes is obvious. The Swedes stopped extraordinary borrowing and expenditures with the coming of recovery and liquidated their depression indebtedness. In the United States we are still borrowing.

5/30 Sweden's Anti-Crisis Policy: an Evaluation

MÖLLER, *The Unemployment Policy* [see Document 5/28], pp. 69–71.

If one desires to evaluate comprehensively the results of the Swedish anti-crisis policy, it is necessary to inquire into the extent to which the goals fixed for the policy were reached. It might appear as if the purpose of the monetary policy, designed not to increase living costs to any large degree, were contrary to that of the agricultural policy, which aimed to increase prices of foodstuffs.

The modest increase in the price of food products which was recommended when the assistance measures for agriculture were introduced did not prevent the monetary policy from becoming rather successful, because the price of other consumers' goods which influenced living costs continued to drop.

The changes in wages and costs of living appear from the Table [below], in which the 1929 figures equal 100.

It appears from these figures that the pressure of the economic decline brought a (compared with most countries, relatively modest) fall in the level of money wages, while the level of real wages to a large extent remained at the pre-crisis level even during the most difficult depression period. During the years of recovery living costs have indeed been slowly rising, but they remained in 1936 considerably below the 1929 level; by 1934 real wages exceeded their highest earlier level and have since been rising somewhat. Without going into detail concerning the various factors influencing this development, it may be stated that the goals which were fixed for both the monetary policy and the agricultural policy have been reached.

451

INDEX CHANGES IN WAGES AND LIVING COSTS

	1929	1930	1931	1932	1933	1934	1935	1936
Wage income per year	100	101	97	92	92	96	98	100
Cost of living	100	97	94	92	91	91	92	93
Real wage per year	100	104	103	99	101	105	106	107

So far as the labour market is concerned, developments have not belied the expectations which were entertained concerning the effects of the anti-crisis policies which were carried out. The economic situation is now such that on the whole, normal conditions have been restored. To this result have contributed the measures for the maintenance of purchasing power, the agricultural policy and the emergency projects, the money policy, the foreign-exchange policy, and exports. Within certain trades there is a lack of labour power, but there is still a slight excess of unskilled workers.

The problems which still remain to be solved pertain largely to two provinces; Bohuslän and Västernorrland – our 'depressed areas'. The problem in the case of Bohuslän is associated with the paving-stone industry. Before the depression, 90 per cent of this industry depended upon exports, which cannot be expected to rise to their former level in any near future. The problem for Västernorrland is bound up with the fact that the main industries of that area are built on forest products. Within these industries the determined rationalization process has deprived some thousands of workers of employment in their old trades since the depression. This does not mean that unemployment in these provinces is as serious as during the crisis. On the contrary, a strong decline has taken place even there: in Bohuslän, from 9,600 in December 1933 to 2,200 in December 1937; and in Västernorrland, from 16,300 to 2,700 during the same period.

At present the efforts of the Government are mainly directed to improving conditions in these areas, especially by guiding new enterprises into them, thereby endeavouring to bring about a greater variation in their industrial life; and, furthermore, by training and transferring into other trades the youth from the homes of stonecutters and sawmill workers who are now in the 15–25-year age group.

Aside from the unsolved problems just mentioned, unemployment in Sweden is lower than it has ever been before. To a large extent it may be said that the goal of the unemployment policy has been reached. From the point of view of results, it makes little difference whether one cause or another of this fortunate outcome is given chief credit.

As to the goals which otherwise were set for the anti-crisis policies, it may suffice to refer to a matter already stated, namely, that the general economic revival permitted the repayment of the extraordinary depression loans within four years, and that the state finances are at present the object of revision which, so far as it can be judged, will give the Swedish Government greater resources than ever to meet difficulties which may eventually arise. The special crisis loans never exerted much pressure on the Swedish money market. The supply of free capital was always great and the interest situation has not been materially changed during the last two boom years.

The conclusion is inescapable that the Swedish anti-crisis policies have done well, considering the goals which they aimed to reach.

During the past years certain experiences have, however, been acquired which can serve as guides if again there should come a period of mass unemployment to be combated by emergency projects on a large scale. In the Swedish programme for securing work in 1933 and 1934 there were included both large projects, such as gigantic hospitals and bridges, the completion of which required a long time, and small projects, which individually required only from one to (at the very most) six months. Of these latter there were nearly a hundred thousand. Experience has taught us that a great number of small projects is more valuable in a crisis period than large projects, even if the latter cannot be completely avoided. The advantage of the small projects is partly that they can be rapidly liquidated in response to possible improvements in economic conditions, and partly that they can be scattered to all corners of the community. To the extent that unemployment strikes all parts of a country, it can therefore be dealt with wherever it exists. Large projects may have to be completed even when the passage of the crisis makes them no longer defensible as unemployment works, and they do not afford a sufficient distribution of employment opportunities. Furthermore, our experience shows us that a very important share of emergency projects should require materials.

Another experience refers to preparations. In 1932 Sweden was completely unprepared. When projects are set in motion by the community, a large number of formalities must often be observed, plans and drawings must be prepared, different authorities must make reports on whether the project in question is needed, whether the plans are acceptable, and so forth. If land is to be bought before the project can be started, it is necessary to negotiate with owners. When communal projects are involved, a waiting period must be observed before a decision takes legal effect* and so forth. Such troubles of different kinds may frequently require many months and may considerably delay the starting of work.

* Every person who lives in a commune has a right to appeal to state authorities from a decision of the commune to which he objects. (Footnote in original.)

In a society which desires to be well armed against a crisis, such obstacles to quick action must be removed beforehand. Plans, drawings, and the necessary negotiations for a large number of projects should be constantly on file to be brought out and begun without delay when the emergency arises. New emergency projects are now being planned in Sweden, and unless a depression were to strike us unawares within the very near future, this should enable us to take immediate and powerful counter-actions should we have the misfortune to be again exposed to a period of crisis of an economic nature.

5/31 I.L.O. Recommendation concerning Public Works

Recommendation No. 51, in International Labour Office, *Official Bulletin*, vol. 22, No. 3 (1937), pp. 86–89.

The General Conference of the International Labour Organization . . . adopts, this twenty-second day of June of the year one thousand nine hundred and thirty-seven, the following Recommendation which may be cited as the Public Works (National Planning) Recommendation, 1937:

Whereas in the absence of advance planning expenditure on public works tends to increase in years of prosperity and to diminish in years of depression;

Whereas fluctuations in the volume of employment of workers engaged on public works are thereby superimposed on the fluctuations in the volume of employment arising out of commercial demand, thus aggravating successively the shortage of certain classes of workers in periods of prosperity and the extent of unemployment in periods of depression;

Whereas it is desirable to time public works in such a way as to reduce industrial fluctuations as far as possible; . . .

The Conference recommends that each Member should apply the following principles:

PART I. TIMING OF PUBLIC WORKS

1. (1) Appropriate measures should be adopted for the purpose of achieving a suitable timing of all works undertaken or financed by public authorities.

(2) This timing should involve an increase in the volume of such works in periods of depression and for this purpose it is desirable to provide for the preparation in advance, during periods of prosperity, of works capable of being held in reserve or exceeding ordinary requirements and which should be ready for execution as soon as the need is felt.

(3) Special attention should be paid to public works which stimulate heavy industries or public works which create a more direct demand for consumers' goods, as changing economic conditions may require. . . .

PART II. FINANCING OF PUBLIC WORKS

4. Among the financial measures necessitated by the policy embodied in the present Recommendation the following should receive special consideration:

(a) the placing to reserve in periods of prosperity of the resources necessary for carrying out works prepared for periods of depression;

(b) the carrying forward of unexpended balances from one year to another;

(c) restricted borrowing by public authorities in periods of prosperity and accelerated repayment of loans previously contracted;

(d) the financing by loan in periods of depression of public works likely to stimulate economic recovery, and, generally speaking, the application of a monetary policy which will make possible the expansion of credit required at such a time for the speeding up of the public works and which will ensure the lowest possible rate of interest on the loans. . . .

PART III. EMPLOYMENT OF CERTAIN CLASSES OF WORKERS

6. In applying the policy of timing provided for in this Recommendation, consideration should be given to the possibility of including works which will give employment to special classes of workers such as young workers, women and non-manual workers.

PART IV. CONDITIONS OF RECRUITMENT AND EMPLOYMENT

. . . 9. The rates of wages of workers on public works should be not less favourable than those commonly recognized workers' organizations and employers for work of the same character in the district where the work is carried out; where there are no such rates recognized or prevailing in the district, those recognized or prevailing in the nearest district in which the general industrial circumstances are similar should be adopted, subject to the condition that the rates should in any case be such as to ensure to the workers a reasonable standard of life as this is understood in their time and country.

Chapter 6 The Totalitarian Economies: Germany and Italy

Introduction

Of all the major European economies, Germany's probably suffered most in the slump beginning in 1929. Following the disturbances of the war economy, the political revolution and inflation, the hopelessness of her six million registered unemployed in the winter of 1932–1933 did irreparable damage to her social fabric. While the years from 1924 to 1929 had seen great industrial expansion and a successful export drive, Germany's balance of payments was still dominated by reparations payments flowing one way (Chapter 3), matched by foreign investments flowing in the opposite direction. The drying up of the inward stream of long-term capital in 1928–1929 and its eventual reversal left Germany high and dry: there seemed to be no way of balancing her payments if reparations were to continue. The devaluation of the pound sterling in 1931 caused further difficulties to German exporters who had hitherto benefited by its overvaluation. To deal with the resulting deficit, the German Government was forced to give up nearly all its gold and foreign exchange reserves as well as resorting to sternly restrictive policies which led to the most serious unemployment problem anywhere in Europe. In fact, reparations payments were soon reduced and payments ultimately stopped altogether, but in a country torn more bitterly by social and political strife than almost any other and with few traditions of political compromise, the economic disasters, which could in part be blamed on the foreigner and on the 'Diktat' of Versailles, added much to the popular support of the ultra-nationalist National Socialist (Nazi) party which seized power in January 1933, the blackest month of the slump. The unilateral default on reparations was but the first major step in the international lawlessness which the new Hitler Government introduced into Europe.

It was a government of a new kind. It is difficult to fit the rule of the new men – maintained by the terror of uniformed thugs in the streets and prisons, contemptuous of the constitution of their own country, of the rule of law and all Western traditions, with their wild dreams of world domination by the German 'race' and paranoid hatred of Jews, Socialists, Slavs, and coloured races – into any accepted political pattern. But in the economic field they had to maintain some contact with reality.

The Nazi ideology took little interest in economics as such. Such coherent

457

statements as exist (**6/1, 6/5**) stress the fostering of free private capitalist enterprise in a somewhat naïve anachronistic manner which ignored the reality of the powerful monopolies dominating German industry. The Nazis also tended to strengthen the power of the employer over the worker by converting their relationship into a para-military one of 'leader' and 'led' (**6/2a, c**). At the same time, the whole of this economic structure was to be subordinated to the politico-military aim of the Party, and it is in this sense that the much-repeated slogan, common interest before self-interest ('Gemeinnutz geht vor Eigennutz') is to be understood. There was no suggestion that this should have a Socialist connotation, despite the appearance of that word in the Party's name; on the contrary, it was one of the first acts of the new Government to destroy totally the Socialist and Communist parties, to rob them of their property and terrorize their members, and this treatment was quickly extended to the trade unions, not only those of Socialist, but also those of Christian leanings (**6/2b**). In their place were put the tame German Labour Front, controlled by and in the interests of the Party, and the so-called 'Trustees of Labour' with powers of compulsory arbitration in disputes on wages and conditions (**6/2a**).

However, the major economic issue facing the Hitler Government in its early months was not very different from that facing all other Governments in 1932–1933: how to deal with persistent mass unemployment. There can be no doubt that Nazi Germany dealt more successfully with it than any other Western European country with the possible exception of Sweden, and there has been much discussion, then and since, how this was achieved, and to what extent Germany anticipated 'Keynesian' principles.

The German Government set out almost at once to create a very large public works programme. Over one milliard RM had been disbursed on direct works by the Government, the local authorities and such Government agencies as the railways and the Autobahn corporation (**6/4**), by the end of December 1933, and about three and half milliard RM by December 1934. Unemployment as a result fell at once and within four years had virtually disappeared. Much was made of this 'miracle' within Germany and by sources friendly to Fascism outside the country, and this success did more than any other to consolidate the regime among the German masses (**6/3**), but the achievement was anything but miraculous.

When looking in detail at some of the measures taken (**6/4, 6/5, 6/6, 6/7, 6/8**) two features stand out. The first is that many of them had political or military motives in addition to their employment-creating functions, e.g. the financial encouragement of large families or the building of the motor-roads. It is significant that while a large network of motor-roads, with their strategic potential, had been completed by 1939, the Volkswagen cars that were supposed to run on them had hardly begun to roll off the production line. In a similar way, the measures relating to German agriculture (**6/9a, b, c**) were derived at least as much from the political needs of placating the powerful large landowners and the farmers, and from the myth of blood and soil as a source of Germanic strength, as from a purely economic motivation.

Secondly, far from engaging in deficit spending for its own sake, the German authorities were in fact attempting to pursue 'orthodox' and respectable financial policies for as long as possible. Thus part of the 'work provision', the retirement of women from employment, was employment spreading rather than creating; it was stressed that much of the expenditure was clawed back by reduced unemployment payments; and the relief of the parish-debt burdens was at the expense of the creditors rather than at the expense of the Exchequer (**6/7, 6/8**). At the same time, the authorities were well aware of the multiplier effects, e.g. of employment created in the building industry (**6/6**), and understood the concept of pump priming. Perhaps the difference between the Hitler Government and the governments of the other major industrialized states may be summarized in this way: the financial authorities everywhere attempted to maintain the kind of 'orthodox' restrictive and budget-balancing policies which aggravated the unemployment problem; but to the extent that Germany, for political reasons, more frequently overrode them, her employment position benefited. By mobilizing idle balances and mopping up the plentiful savings by short-term loans, including such ingenious devices as the 'Mefo' bills (**6/13**), but above all by using idle labour and capital, the Germans succeeded in increasing output faster than money supply and thus achieving the first three years or so of remarkable recovery with hardly any inflation (**6/12**).

The tensions between the two main features described so far, the need to operate in a relatively normal capitalist home (and foreign trade) economy, while subjecting it to the capricious political demands of the Party, dominated the remainder of the economic history of Nazi Germany. Whatever the initial successes of work provision and reconstruction, it soon became clear that this economic programme was not an end, but a means: a means to wage and win the next major war. But the rate at which rearmament, first in secret and then openly (**6/10**) was pressed forward exceeded the economic capacity of the country, so that after about 1936 the pursuit of respectable financial policies became increasingly difficult, particularly in view of the continued dependence of Germany on imports of food and strategic raw materials.

In part, Germany's foreign exchange problems arose from the failure of the rest of the world to recover at the German rate and provide growing markets for German exports. To some extent, her foreign links were also disrupted by the persecution of the Jews and the damage done to Jewish businesses. It was, however, mainly the rapacious demands of the rearmament programme which made the balance of payments Germany's most vulnerable point. Hitler's confidential memorandum (6/16), the political sections of which (omitted here) are largely concerned with the inevitable German attack on Russia, shows the indifference with which the supreme leadership viewed the economic aims of the much-vaunted Four-Year Plan, except as providing the means for offensive war. Hjalmar Schacht, President of the Reischsbank, and often dubbed Germany's financial 'wizard', and the other experts, managed to sustain the external value of the mark for several years by a series of measures which included the default on reparations and foreign loans, the blocking of foreign Reichsmark earnings and default on part of them (6/10, 6/13, 6/14a, 6/14b), the restriction and control of all foreign transactions together with bilateral barter agreements in which political and economic power was used to impose Germany's will on weaker countries (6/15), and the total and totalitarian mobilization of all German-held foreign assets and of gold. Import substitution by 'ersatz' productions was also pushed forward, with mixed results. Internally, inflation was held off by financing the Government's expenditure both by taxation and by absorbing private savings (6/11). Public indebtedness rose by about 11 milliard RM between 1933 and 1937.

After about 1936 the dykes began to give way. When attempting to spend its earnings the bulk of the population, hard at work all the week, faced a shortage of consumer goods (6/17) such as it had not experienced since the World War. Even apart from the shortages, real wages were held down by the need for forced savings to finance rearmament, and industrial unrest (6/18) was aggravated by the unabashed luxury living among profit earners and Party bosses. Shortages of skilled labour led to wasteful and annoying restrictions and regulations even in peace time (6/19). In spite of the windfalls of the Austrian gold hoard carried off after the *Anschluss* and the raw materials found in Austria and Czechoslovakia, the reckless overstraining of the economy in the interests of rearmament had reached its limits. Responsible opinion, as that expressed by the Reichsbank Directory in January 1939 (6/20), before Schacht's resignation, could see no way out of inflation and national bankruptcy, except by a total reversal of policies. Instead, the leadership plunged into a war which it had prepared, with mixed economic success, ever since it gained power.

The economic policies of Fascist Italy derived not so much for an expansionary militarist drive, as from the determination to preserve the social system against the double onslaught of universal suffrage and widespread grinding poverty. Nevertheless, in spite of this apparent difference of origin, the actual economic policies pursued by the two countries showed remarkable similarities, creating an ideological *rapprochement* between them which cemented ultimately into an alliance in spite of divergent national interests.

The Italian law on Corporations of 1926 (6/21a) which prohibited all trade unions and disallowed strikes, and substituted a single Fascist-oriented organization for each trade or district, bears striking resemblance to the parallel German provisions (6/2a, b). The later development of the so-called corporations (6/21b, 6/22) to form the pillars of a 'corporate' state, though discussed in Germany, was however never driven to its logical conclusion there. The general attitude to labour and to private enterprise, as exemplified by the Labour 'charter' of 1927 (6/22) was, of course, also fundamentally the Nazi attitude. Similarly, such measures as land reclamation and the literature to justify it (6/23) recall the later work provision schemes, but above all the myth of 'blood and soil' of the northern people. As far as measures of this type were concerned, the two leading Fascist states found eager imitators in other parts of Europe, including Spain, Portugal, Poland, Hungary and Romania, where Fascist or quasi-Fascist Governments were in power by the 1930s.

6/1 Nazi Economic Philosophy

OTTO DIETRICH, 'Economic Thinking in the Third Reich', speech of the Reich Press Chief in Essen, 28 January 1936. Printed in SCHRAEPLER, *Quellen* [*see* Document 1/29], pp. 174–176. (Ed. Tr.)

'Common Interest before Self-Interest'

The economic field of application of this principle is not the so-called 'economy', obeying laws of its own and standing above or beside the nation, but it is the economy as the economic organism of the nation, which all its members have to serve, just as it in turn serves all its members. The cell out of which the national economy is built up is the works community, in which all, leaders and followers, are aware that they are dependent on each other, and in which all understand their work to be a service to the national commonwealth which supports and keeps them all. . . .

We must wipe out the error once and for all that the quest for private income is inconsistent with the quest for the common interest as demanded by National Socialism, and might be adversely affected in its natural and successful working.

We National Socialists are not so lunatic as to choke off the healthy personal striving for success and thereby throttle the strongest motor of human economic activity. On the contrary, just as National Socialism is working with all its power to develop the personality within the community and make it operative for the community, so it also demands within the framework of its economy, personal achievement as its strongest and irreplaceable motive power. We know that it is the strongest carrier of economic progress and the indispensable precondition of our civilization. . . .

The idea of the common interest has the same meaning for the follower and worker as it has for the leader and employer . . . (but) world history is not driven forward by duty. It is very difficult to persuade a man who, for example, works day after day in dirt and sweat in a coal mine, of his exalted economic mission by such well-meaning but inadequate arguments. In practice this appears quite different. In the end, man lives to seek happiness and not in order to do his duty. At any rate, this is how they all tend to imagine it. Even the most common labourer wants to get on in life. And it is only the hope for this personal advancement for oneself and one's children and the faith in the possibility of achieving it that enables many to perform their heavy work more easily. To put as their aim in life simply the fulfilment of their duty without the satisfaction of their personal striving, is the chatter of unworldly moralists or of anti-socialist capitalist individuals who speculate on the simplicity of their fellow citizens. . . .

The concept of 'common interest' of National Socialism is no theoretical phrase or empty idea, no cheap slogan; on the contrary, it has for the first time given meaning to the term 'Socialism'.

Our Socialism is no unworldly utopia, but natural, full-blooded life.

It is the Socialism of the readiness to help the poorest of the poor and the Socialism of the achievement for all who work.

It does not promise eternal bliss, pretends no inaccessible illusions to the workers, merely to lead them ever deeper into misery in practice. It does not sermonize on the childish doctrine, flying in the face of all reality, of the equality of men and the equality of their claim to the worldly goods, but it returns the assurance to them of belonging to a great nation, to which they are tied for good or ill, and in which everyone can contribute what he is able in ability and achievement. The sole equal economic demand which it is willing to grant to all members of the nation is the right to work.

This the only true, because the only possible, Socialism sees to it that the conditions for the advancement of each member of the nation are the same so that character, ability and achievement are the sole measure of advancement. . . .

One should not underestimate the deep spiritual effects, the large moral

462

power and the vast practical significance of these opportunities for the broad mass of working fellow nationals.* We have introduced in the German people an economic and social order in which every fellow national, whoever he may be and whence he may come, can arise to the highest positions in economy and state, as long as he possesses the power, the will and the ability for it!

6/2 The Abolition of Free Labour Organizations

a The Law for the Organization of National Labour, January 1934. Printed in CLOUGH, *et al.*, *Economic History* [*see* Document 1/4a], pp. 271–275.

b Decree by the Leader of the German Labour Front of 22 June 1933. Printed in MICHAELIS and SCHRAEPLER, *Ursachen und Folgen* [*see* Document 1/3], vol. IX, pp. 642–643. (Ed. Tr.)

c The Reich Labour Service Act of 26 June 1935. Printed in S. H. ROBERTS, *The House that Hitler Built* (London, 1937), pp. 212–216.

a *1.* In each establishment the owner of the undertaking as the leader (Führer) of the establishment and the salaried and wage-earning employees as his followers shall work together for the furtherance of the purposes of the establishment and for the benefit of the nation and the State in general.

2. (1) The leader of the establishment shall make decisions for his followers in all matters affecting the establishment in so far as they are governed by this Act.

(2) He shall promote the welfare of his followers. The latter shall be loyal to him as fellow members of the works community.

3. (1) In incorporated associations and other bodies the statutory representatives shall be the leaders of the establishment. . . .

5. (1) In establishments which as a rule employ at least twenty persons, confidential men shall be appointed from among the followers to advise the leader. Together with him and under his presidency they shall constitute the confidential council of the establishment. . . .

6. (1) It shall be the duty of the confidential council to strengthen mutual confidence within the works community.

(2) It shall be the task of the confidential council to consider all measures directed towards the increase of efficiency, the formulation and carrying out of the general conditions of employment (especially the establishment rules), the carrying out and promotion of industrial safety

* Volksgenossen. See Glossary.

measures, the strengthening of the ties which bind the various members of the establishment to one another and to the establishment, and the welfare of all members of the community. Further, the said council shall endeavour to settle all disputes within the works community. Its views shall be heard before penalties are imposed under the establishment rules. . . .

8. A person shall not be appointed as a confidential man unless he has completed his 25th year, has belonged to the establishment or undertaking for at least one year and has worked in the same branch or related branches of employment or industry for at least two years. He must be in possession of civic rights, a member of the German Labour Front,* characterized by exemplary human qualities and guaranteed to devote himself unreservedly at all times to the National State.

9. (1) Every year in March the leader of the establishment shall draw up a list of confidential men and their substitutes in agreement with the chairman of the National Socialist establishment cell organization. The followers shall then decide for or against the list by ballot. . . .

18. (1) Labour trustees shall be appointed for large economic areas, the boundaries of which shall be fixed by the Federal† Ministry of Labour in agreement with the Federal Ministry of Economic Affairs and the Federal Minister of the Interior. They shall be Federal officials and shall be under the service supervision of the Federal Ministry of Labour. The Federal Ministry of Labour in agreement with the Federal Ministry of Economic Affairs shall fix their headquarters.

(2) The labour trustees shall be bound to observe the principles and instructions laid down by the Federal Government.

19. (1) The labour trustees shall ensure the maintenance of industrial peace. In order to achieve this task, they shall take the following action:

1. They shall supervise the formation and operations of the confidential councils, and give decisions where disputes occur.
2. They shall appoint confidential men for establishments and remove them from office in accordance with subsection (2) of section *9.*, subsection (2) of section *14.* and section *15.*;
3. They shall decide respecting appeals from confidential councils in accordance with section *16.*; they may quash the decision of the leader of the establishment and themselves issue the necessary ruling.

* The Nazi labour organization that superseded all independent trade union groups. (Footnote in Clough.)

† In this document 'Reich' (untranslated in previous documents) has been translated as 'Federal'. The national government is meant. (Footnote in Clough.)

4. They shall decide respecting proposed dismissals in accordance with section *20*.;
5. They shall supervise the observance of the provisions respecting establishment rules (sections *26. et. seq.*).
6. They shall lay down principles and collective rules under the conditions specified in section *32*.; and supervise their observance.
7. They shall co-operate in the exercise of jurisdiction by the social honour courts under sections *35. et. seq.*
8. They shall keep the Federal Government supplied with information respecting social progress, in accordance with detailed instructions issued by the Federal Ministry of Labour and the Federal Ministry of Economic Affairs. . . .

b It is the intention to oppose the multiplicity of employers' and workers' organizations with the creation of the German Labour Front. This is designed to hit not only the last refuge of Marxism, but also to bring to an end the unhappy splintering of the German working population. Petty and selfish individuals are unwilling to recognize this great revolutionary act and are trying to weaken this work with imitations and self-help organizations.

It is the Führer's will that apart from the German Labour Front not a single organization, neither of workers nor employers, shall henceforth exist. The only exceptions are the *ständische* organizations having as their sole object the promotion of occupational training.

All other associations, including the so-called Roman catholic and pro-testant workers' associations, are to be regarded as enemies of the state, be-cause they obstruct and bar the great rebuilding. That is the reason for our fight against them, and it is high time for them to disappear.

(sgd.) Dr. Robert Ley.

c On 26 June 1935, the Reich Labour Service Law was promulgated. It provided that every German man should serve for six months in a labour service camp at some time between his 18th and 26th birthdays. . . .

The camps are organized on thoroughly military lines. Discipline is rigid; the boys wear uniforms like soldiers; the only difference is that they carry spades instead of rifles and work in the fields. Three aims are sought, physical exercise, intensive drill, and training of the mind; and each day is divided between the three, although, as the Nazi literature on the subject points out, the training in National Socialism principles comes first and 'permeates the service from early morning until bed time'. That is why the army is said to have opposed the scheme from the first – because the boys are too well-trained in the Nazi way before the Army gets hold of them.

Everything goes according to routine. At each of the 1300 camps in Germany, every boy will be doing the same thing at a given time. . . .

The service is organized down to the last button of the last man. There are thirty 'service districts', corresponding to the political districts of the Reich. Each of these is divided in anything up to ten groups, each group has six to ten *Abteilungen*, each of which occupies a camp. In the whole of Germany there are 1,260 camps. Each camp is a duplicate of the other. . . . Everybody is plastered with badges of rank, for the Service has a military hierarchy with no less than fifteen distinct grades. In a word, in time of emergency, the *Arbeitsdienst* could immediately put 200,000 drilled and well-organized infantrymen into the field.

The system of training is equally intricate. . . .

The boys who have graduated through the various Nazi youth organizations now take on the wider responsibilities of adult leadership, and in many ways the training institutions of the labour service – the troop leaders' school, the *Feldmeisterscchule*, the *Bezirksschule* and the *Reichsschule* – are determining the nature of the Nazi State of the future. . . .

Although it is forever being asserted that the main aim of the labour service is to train the mind and bodies of Young Germany, the economic aspects are not lost sight of. Here we have a body of 200,000 lusty young men, who receive twenty-five pfennigs a day as pocket money, and whose keep never costs more than eighty-two pfennigs a day. That is to say, it is a disciplined labour supply for a little over a mark a day, a supply that can be sent anywhere and put to any kind of work.

So far the service has been used mainly to reclaim lands that can be used in the fight to make Germany self-sufficient in her foodstuffs. It is in keeping with the Nazi cult of 'Blut und Erde'* to bring the adolescents into close contact with mother earth, and wrest waste lands away from destruction.

6/3 Early Work Provision Projects

SCHACHT, *My First Seventy-Six Years* [see Document 4/16b], pp. 304–305.

The first work-creation programme to be decided upon by the Cabinet was the so-called Reinhardt Programme, which aimed at the repair and reconstruction of houses, factories and machinery. It was intended especially to benefit the building industry – the hardest hit of all – which, as a key industry, is universally and at all times acknowledged as the employer of

* Blood and Soil. (Ed.)

auxiliary industries. To this programme the Reichsbank contributed the sum of one milliard marks.

The second job to be tackled – and it was tackled very soon – was the construction of national *Autobahnen*. For this I sanctioned an initial credit of six hundred million marks which, however, was to be repaid out of the national Budget. Within a very short time the State Railways Board took over the completion and running of the *Autobahnen*. With the object of making the *Autobahnen* pay, I had stipulated with Hitler at the beginning that road and rail traffic must work in-and-in with each other. Why this purpose should have been lost sight of I am unable to say, since in course of time, and after I had received back the six hundred million marks for the Reichsbank, I had nothing further to do with the *Autobahnen* construction. . . .

Besides these special work-creation tasks, the *Gauleiter* in every district throughout the country endeavoured to carry through all those projects hitherto held up for lack of money or recently asked for. It is necessary to put oneself in the place of rural councils and provincial governors who, dependent solely on a niggardly budget, had been compelled during recent years to postpone or abandon so many undertakings in their districts which they would gladly have carried out in the interests of the population and the business community. These included the construction of roads, dykes and embankments, canalization, land clearance, drainage and irrigation, land-settlement buildings, hospitals, old people's homes and similar enterprises awaiting completion in every part of the country.

After the collapse of Germany, national, provincial and county officials were constantly blamed for having so readily offered their services to that 'criminal' Hitler. But under Hitler they now received a steady supply of funds which enabled them to carry out all the works in which they had long been interested and which previous governments had hitherto refused to sanction. . . .

Reports from individual districts and counties piled up, showing that unemployment had decreased by so and so much or had perhaps even been done away with altogether.

6/4 Setting up the Autobahn Corporation

Act on the Setting up of the Reich Autobahn Corporation, of 27 June 1933, *R.G.Bl.*, II, p. 509. (Ed. Tr.)

(1) The German Railway Company is authorized to set up a branch corporation, to be named *Reichsautobahnen*, for the purpose of building and managing an efficient network of motor roads. . . .

(2) The motor roads shall be public highways destined exclusively for general motor vehicle traffic.

(3) The *Reichsautobahnen* corporation has the exclusive right to build and manage the motor roads and the subsidiary enterprises connected with them.

(4) The Reich government shall supervise the *Reichsautobahnen* corporation.

(5) The Reich Chancellor shall appoint a general inspector of German roads; he shall determine the layout and design of the motor roads. The German Railway Company shall take over the administration and agency of the *Reichsautobahnen* corporation. . . .

(7) The *Reichsautobahnen* corporation is entitled to charge tolls. The rates of charges require the authorization of the Minister of Transport. . . .

(11) In order to ensure uniformity in the planning of the road network, the general inspector of German roads is authorized to require all lands, provinces and other highway authorities to submit to him their plans for the building and extension of roads. He has the right to object to all road building plans which would adversely affect the construction and development of the *Reichsautobahnen* enterprise.

6/5 The Economic Policy of the National Socialist State

Speech by the Minister of Economic Affairs, Dr. Schmitt, to a group of leading economists on 13 July 1933. Printed in PAUL MEIER-BENNECKENSTEIN (ed.), *Dokumente der deutschen Politik* (2 vols., Berlin, 1939), vol. I, pp. 198–199. (Ed. Tr.)

I believe, and so does the Führer, that it could not possibly be the task of the state and the Ministry of Economic Affairs or any other authority, to determine and settle responsibly the economic process in detail. The tasks before the German economy must be solved by the economy itself, i.e. by responsible leaders emerging from within it. The state must govern and lead the economy by its economic policy, but not manage affairs itself.

The basic problem is the return of five million human beings to the process of production. . . . Here we cannot wait until recovery arrives by natural means. To that extent I am wholly in favour of the Government undertaking all in its power to end the depression. Gradually the whole economy must be embraced, revived and set in motion in such a way as to lead to a natural upswing and a natural advance. Therefore it is the intention of the Führer so to design the provision of work in the future as far as it is undertaken by the Government, that there are not only direct orders for public work, but that the private productive sectors are relieved by sums which can be converted into work.

But the decisive point – and here I see the primary task of the Minister of Economic Affairs – is to create the precondition of a firmly anchored belief as quickly as possible, to the effect that we have the greatest imaginable degree of certainty in our economic calculations.

We are aware that without a firm legal framework and without the possibility of economic calculation the entrepreneur is most seriously handicapped in his decision making. . . . The Führer has stated more than once with all clarity that we cannot do without the brains of the private economy and that all attempts to socialize the economy must founder on human nature, for there are no human beings who would want to forgo in advance every opportunity of their economic advancement. What has made us great is the full use of individual talent. If we socialized everything we would take the slowest rate of work as the measure of the national rate. We must never allow domination of the higher ability by the lower. . . .

It is not the task of the Ministry of Economic Affairs to interfere in the individual branches of the economy and order everybody about. But the possibility of intervention must be kept open. The National Socialist State demands the right to withhold complete freedom in economic matters, the freedom to do as one likes, and to damage whole sectors of the economy for reasons of competition. The State, however, will use its power wisely and will consider carefully before intervening in the interest of order. But the power to intervene must be there.

6/6 Early Economic Plans on Employment Provision

Speech by Minister of Economic Affairs, Dr. Schmitt, on 20 September 1933. Printed in MEIER-BENNECKENSTEIN, *Dokumente* [*see* Document 6/5], vol. I, pp. 203–204. (Ed. Tr.)

This January the number of workless amounted to over 6 million. By today it has dropped by 2 million. According to the monthly insurance statistics, the number of employees at work reached its lowest level in January 1933 at 11·5 million. Today there are again 13¾ million people in paid employment.

At the same time the average hours of work have been appreciably increased. The numbers in employment are still rising. In particular, the signs of rising prosperity are unmistakable compared with the corresponding seasons of earlier years.

In August of this year, to make but one comparison, over 1 million more *Volksgenossen** were in employment than in August 1932. This favourable development has arisen because of the economic policy measures taken by the Government.

Of the over 2 million workers who have found employment in the past 8 months, about 300,000 owe their jobs directly to the work provision measures of the Reich, the Reich railways and the Post Office. The majority of the remainder owe their bread to the orders placed by the lands, the parishes and the other public bodies, but above all to the initiative of private firms, powerfully strengthened by measures of the Government.

May I stress here particularly, that in contrast with the former attempts to create work, the struggle of the Reich Government against unemployment is not limited to creating a market for some branches of industry by some direct public orders; even the measures to date have, on the contrary, revived private initiative on a broad basis by the new system of the indirect provision of work, through tax remissions, marriage loans, welfare tickets, subsidies for various purposes, etc. . . .

I would like to stress that the Reich Government has in all its economic policy measures, extended particular care towards agriculture and building. In reviving the building industry it started out with the old experience that the revival of building activity is the decisive precondition for a general economic upswing and that the strongest impetus for the revival of general economic activity derives from the building market.

6/7 Unemployment Policies, 1933

Address by the Secretary of State for Finance, Reinhard, to the German School of Politics, 14 February 1934. Printed in MEIER-BENNECKENSTEIN, *Dokumente* [*see* Document 6/5], vol. 2, pp. 224–230. (Ed. Tr.)

As long as there are any unemployed, the financial and fiscal policy in the Third Reich is geared towards first the reduction, and finally the abolition of unemployment. . . .

The number of unemployed rose from the end of 1929 to the beginning of 1933 by about 4 million, from 2 to over 6 million! It fell in the first year of Hitler by 2·3 million, from 6,013,000 on 31 January 1933 to 3,774,000 on 31 January 1934! There is no question that we shall succeed substantially in further reducing the number of unemployed and in virtually abolishing unemployment in a few years! . . .

* See Glossary.

The recovery is being speeded up and strengthened by financial, fiscal and labour market measures of the Reich Government. . . .

If human needs are to lead to effective demand, and this to work, and this, in turn, to new needs, to new effective demand and to more work, and the fly-wheel of the economy is to be put and kept in motion, there have to be two preconditions. First, the economy and all strata of the people must have unconditional faith in the leadership of the State, and secondly, as long as the economy is still not running at full speed, the State must undertake appropriate measures to induce the meeting of existing needs. Both these premises were lacking in the multi-party State, but both obtain in the Adolf Hitler State. . . .

In particular, the following financial measures may be mentioned: . . .

By the Provision of Work Act of 1 June 1933, 1 milliard RM was made available for the expansion of work provision. Work provided by the lands, parishes, unions of parishes and other public corporations was favoured in particular.

The second important Act, the Act for the Creation of the Reichsauto-bahn Corporation, contains the preconditions for the creation of an efficient network of motor roads. In 5 to 6 years some 4–6,000 km of motor roads will be built, or about 1,000 km a year.

By the Housing Repairs Act of 21 September 1933, 500 million RM have been provided for the support of repair, extension and similar works on buildings. The 500 million are being provided in the form of cash subsidies by the Reich. For repairs and extensions the cash subsidy amounts to 20 per cent, and for the division of flats and the conversion of other rooms into flats it amounts to 50 per cent. . . .

Next, the Parish Debt Conversion Act of 21 September. This is designed to bring relief to parishes that have got into difficulties or are threatened by difficulties because of short-term indebtedness. These parishes may offer their creditors to convert their short-term loans into long-term loans at 4 per cent, and at 3 per cent from 1936. . . .

Now to the fiscal measures.

First there is the Motor Tax Act of 10 April 1933. According to this, all private cars put on the roads for the first time after 31 March 1933 are freed of all motor taxation. . . .

Next, the Motor Tax Redemption Act of 31 May. This permits the owners of older cars to redeem the motor tax to which these vehicles are liable by a single payment. . . .

Next the Act on Tax Remission for Replacement Purchases. That is Section II of the Act for the Reduction of Unemployment of 1 June 1933. . . .

Next, the Act on Tax Reductions of 15 June 1933. Particularly Paragraph

1, still valid, by which the entrepreneur may set off against his tax liability 10 per cent of all expenditure on repairs or extensions of all industrial and commercial buildings. . . .

Next, the Tax Reduction Act of 21 September. Reduction of the agricultural turnover tax from 2 per cent to 1 per cent, reduction of the agricultural land tax by 25 per cent, so that the State tax on agricultural land is almost entirely abolished!

Reduction in land tax on buildings erected between 1924 and 1930 inclusive.

Next, tax remissions for newly built lower-priced flats and houses. . . .

And now we turn to the measures dealing with the labour market.

Here we note particularly the Act for the Removal of Female Labour to Domestic Duties and the Law to Encourage Marriage of 1 June 1933, both being part of my great Act for the Reduction of Unemployment.

By the Act for the Removal of Female Labour to Domestic Duties the employer of female domestic servants will receive income tax-remissions. . . .

Next the Act for the Encouragement of Marriages of 1 June. . . .

By this Act we grant a marriage loan to those of our young Volksgenos-sen* who are getting married, provided that the bride had hitherto been in paid employment and undertakes to leave employment as soon as she is married. . . .

The marriage loans are interest free. They have to be paid back in monthly instalments of 1 per cent of the total loan. . . . On the birth of the first live boy or girl 9 months later, the monthly instalments are reduced by 25 per cent, and the original monthly sum is reduced by a further 25 per cent on the birth of each additional child. . . .

6/8 The Financial Aspects of Unemployment Policies

FRITZ REINHARDT, 'Financial Policy', in *Germany Speaks. By twenty-one leading Members of Party and State* (London, 1938), pp. 138–143.

The principal measure introduced to combat unemployment was the Act passed on 1 June 1933, Section VIII of which provided for the granting of loans to couples intending to marry. This provision has been in force since 1 August 1933. In order to qualify for such a loan, the prospective wife must have been in some sort of paid employment for nine months out of the two years immediately preceding the marriage. Prior to 1 October 1937, the prospective wife was also required to give up her paid employment (if any) but this undertaking is now no longer insisted upon. Women already mar-

* See Glossary.

ried are permitted to take up paid employment for the duration of the second Four-Year Plan.

Between August 1933 and December 1936, we granted 650,000 such loans, the average amount of each being 600 RM. We shall continue to grant from 15,000 to 20,000 similar loans each month until there are no longer any candidates for them.

The effects so far produced by this policy may be summarized as follows:

1. The labour market has been relieved to the extent of 650,000 persons. Assuming that, out of the 650,000 recipients of the grants, about 150,000 young couples would have married in any case, the fact still remains that some 500,000 more marriages were concluded during those three years and 500,000 more households were established than would have been the case without the loans.

2. The labour market has been relieved by at least another 150,000 persons owing to increased employment in the furniture industry, the industries turning out household requisites, and similar ones.

3. An expenditure of about 400,000,000 RM has been saved per annum in respect of unemployment relief.

4. The major part of the sum of about 400,000,000 RM hitherto paid by way of grants has been spent on purchases, thus increasing – directly or indirectly – industrial output, and causing a corresponding increase in the tax yield.

5. The number of marriages has considerably increased and the birth-rate has gone up.

No interest is payable on the loans. They are to be repaid at the rate of 3 per cent per month so long as the wife is in paid employment, and at the rate of 1 per cent per month thereafter, but a reduction of 25 per cent is made from the total amount in respect of each child (excluding still-born children).

The funds required by the Government to grant these loans are obtained by raising the rates of income tax payable by unmarried persons.

The proceeds derived from the repayment of the loans are used in the form of allowances paid to poor persons with a large number of children. . . .

Children's allowances differ from wages and salaries in that they are exempted from taxes and social insurance payments. Thus, in the case just cited, the purchasing capacity of the family concerned has gone up by nearly 20 per cent since August 1936.

At present, recurring allowances are paid in respect of about 400,000 children. . . .

473

Children's allowances are not regarded as charity payments, but as the necessary outcome of a policy whose aim it is to alleviate social inequalities. The justification for granting them lies in the fact that persons with a large number of children have to pay larger amounts in respect of turnover tax, taxes on consumption, and inland revenue than others, and it is these amounts which are refunded to them. . . .

All these measures naturally tend to increase the purchasing capacity and therefore the standard of living of the persons concerned. Thus, certain principles underlying the country's economic, social and population policy have been uniformly applied to serve a practical purpose.

GENERAL TAX EXEMPTIONS, REDUCTIONS AND ADJUSTMENTS

The chief measures here concerned are the following:

1. Exemption from the motor-car tax in respect of all passenger cars licensed subsequent to 31 March 1933. The result has been a considerable rise in the demand for passenger cars.

2. Reduction of the turnover tax and real estate tax (the former by 50 per cent) payable by farmers, the former having become effective as from 1 October 1933, and the latter as from 1 April 1934. The result has been an increase in agricultural production.

3. Lowering of the rate of contributions in respect of unemployment assistance, effective 1 April 1934 and 1 January 1935. The result has been an improvement in the purchasing capacity of wage earners.

4. Lowering of the tax on inhabited house property, effective 1 April 1936. The result has been to make it easier for house-owners to spend money on the upkeep and repair of their property.

6/9 National Socialist Agrarian Policy

a Radio Speech by the Reich Minister of Food and Agriculture on the New Order in Agriculture, 19 September 1933. Printed in MEIER-BENNECKENSTEIN, *Dokumente* [*see* Document 6/5], vol. I, pp. 220–221. (Ed. Tr.)

b Preamble and Definitions of the Reich Hereditary Farmstead (*Erbhof*) Act of 29 September 1933. Printed in MICHAELIS and SCHRAEPLER, *Ursachen und Folgen* [*see* Document 1/3], vol. IX, pp. 709–712. (Ed. Tr.)

c R. WALTHER DARRÉ, Minister of Food and Agriculture, Reich Farmers' Leader, 'The National Food Estate', in *Germany Speaks* [*see* Document 6/8], pp. 148–154.

a On 12 September the German Government has taken decisions which are of momentous consequence for the future of the German farming community and the whole food economy. . . .

The legal opportunities now provided for the building up of the National Food Estate (*Reichsnährstand*) have arisen at the right time. The inadequacies of the market, above all of the grain market, are sufficient proof. We have to be perfectly clear in our minds, that the farmer is not an entrepreneur in the accepted sense. The Food Estate cannot and ought not to participate in the game of free price formation; it must not be exposed to the dangers associated with it, for its tasks are momentously important for the nation. We need the *Bauer** as the blood source of the nation and we need him as the provider of food for the German people.

Therefore it does not matter so much whether the *Bauer* obtains the highest possible price for his produce, so that his enterprise produces the highest possible revenue, but it does matter that the *Bauer* shall be firmly rooted in his soil and receive a fair wage, i.e. fair living prices for his labour.

The *Bauer* must always view his activity as working for the sake of his generation and his people and never merely as a purely economic task, to make money. A true farming policy must be directed towards that aim.

Whoever wants to fit farming enterprise into a system of liberal-capitalist economics, or, following many attempts of recent years, wishes to drive them into adopting liberal methods, sins against the spirit of the German *Bauer* and thus of the German people.

We can only achieve just prices in agriculture for agrarian produce, i.e. close the price scissors between agricultural produce and necessary farm supplies, if the *Bauer* opposes the combines, trusts, cartels, guilds etc. by using his own organization for the distribution and processing of agricultural produce. . . .

The new Act gives me the possibility in principle to go over to a system of fair and firm prices for the *Bauer*. . . .

We are tackling the agrarian sector as the first within the framework of the new fixed price system. Two special Acts will form the basis of this, which are mutually related and complementary. These are the Act on the Combination of Milling, which is already known to the public, and the Law for the Fixing of Grain Prices to be published in a few days.†

b The Reich Government wants to preserve the peasantry (*Bauerntum*) as the blood source of the German people while safeguarding the old German tradition of inheritance.

---

* See Document **6/9b**.

† Law on the Combination of Mills, 15 September 1933 (*R.G.Bl.* I, p. 627) and Law on the Fixing of Grain Prices, 26 September 1933 (*R.G.Bl.* I, p. 667).

Farmsteads are to be protected from indebtedness and fragmentation on inheritance so that they may remain forever in the hands of free *Bauern*★ as the heirloom of the clan.

Measures shall be taken for a healthy size distribution of agrarian holdings, since a large number of viable small and medium-sized farmsteads, as far as possible evenly distributed over the whole country, will form the best guarantee for the continued health of nation and State.

The Reich Government has therefore decided to pass the following Act. The basic ideas behind the Act are:

An agricultural and forest holding of at least the size of a field-subsistence (*Ackernahrung*†) and of 125 hectares★ at most is an *Erbhof*† if it belongs to a person capable of being a *Bauer* (*Bauernfähig*).

The proprietor of an *Erbhof* is called a *Bauer*.★

To be a *Bauer* a man must be a German citizen of German or related (*stammesgleich*) blood and of good legal standing.

The *Erbhof* is to descend to the chief heir without partition.

The rights of the co-heirs are limited to the rest of the *Bauer*'s property. Descendants other than the chief heir are to have an occupational education and inheritance appropriate to the resources of the farmstead; if they are in difficulties through no fault of their own, they may take refuge in the family home.

This right of inheritance may not be over-ridden or limited by testamentary provision.

The *Erbhof* must in principle be neither sold nor burdened by mortgage.

. . .

(Definitions are provided by the Act as follows:)

PART ONE: THE *ERBHOF*

I. CONCEPT

(1) Agricultural or forest real estate is *Erbhof* if it
    1. conforms to the size requirements of secs. 2 and 3, and
    2. is in sole occupation of a *bauernfähig* person.

(2) Farmsteads held by tenants are not *Erbhofe*.

2. MINIMUM SIZE

(1) The *Erbhof* must be at least of the size of one *Ackernahrung*.

(2) *Acknernahrung* is that quantity of land which is necessary to feed and clothe one family independently of the market and the general state of the economy, and preserve the economic running of the *Erbhof*.

★ See Glossary.
† See below.

3. MAXIMUM SIZE

(1) The *Erbhof* must not exceed 125 hectares* in size.

(2) It must be workable from a single farmstead without sub-tenants or cottagers (*Vorwerke*). . . .

PART TWO: THE *BAUER*

11. CONCEPT

(1) Only the proprietor of an *Erbhof* is called a *Bauer*.

(2) The owner or occupier of any other real estate used in agricluture or forestry is called a *Landwirt* (husbandman). . . .

13. REQUIREMENT OF GERMAN OR RELATED BLOOD

(1) To be a *Bauer*, a man must be of German or related (*stammesgleich*) blood.

(2) A man fails to be of German or related blood if he has Jewish or coloured blood among his ancestors on his father's or mother's side.

(3) The operative date for the condition under (1) is 1 January 1800. . . .

15. GOOD STANDING AND CAPABILITY OF THE BAUER

(1) The *Bauer* must be of good standing (*ehrbar*). He must be capable of working his farmstead in good order. Lack of mature years by itself shall not be a bar.

(2) If the conditions of (1) do not apply or if the *Bauer* cannot meet his debts although it ought to have been possible for him to do so with normal husbandry, the Court of Inheritance is empowered, on demand by the Land *Bauer* leader, to transfer the management and beneficial use of the *Erbhof* to the spouse of the *Bauer* or to the prospective heir. . . .

(3) If there is no spouse or heir, or if they in turn are not capable of working the farmstead, the Court of Inheritance is empowered on demand by the Reich *Bauer* leader, to transfer the property to a person proposed by the latter. If properly qualified relatives of the *Bauer* exist, the Reich Bauer leader is to propose one of them. . . .

c When the National Socialist party acquired power on 30 January 1933, German agriculture was on the brink of ruin. Some 12,000,000,000 RM of new debt had been contracted by farmers between 1924 (when the currency was stabilized) and 1932. The area covered by the farmsteads sold by auction during that period was about equal to that of Thuringia. The proceeds derived from the sale of farm produce decreased from some 10,000,000,000 RM

* See Glossary

1928–1929 to 6,400,000,000 RM in 1932–1933 – an amount insufficient to recover the cost of production. On the other hand, farmers had to pay high rates of taxes and interest and heavy social charges. . . .

Under the National Socialist regime some 700,000 hereditary farms (*Erbhofe*) have been created and about 40 per cent of the soil used for agricultural purposes has thus been liberated from the arbitrary interference of professional speculators in real estate. The law enacted to that end has strengthened the farmer's connection with the soil he tills and has secured his rights of possession. Besides, the charges on farm property have been reduced to a reasonable level, partly by lowering the rates of interest and facilitating the repayment of debts and partly by granting tax abatement.

The National Food Estate (*Reichsnährstand*) was set up by the Act passed on 13 September 1933. It is the sole organization in the country embracing all persons associated in some way with farming or with the production and distribution of human food. . . . The highly developed system of co-operative societies was likewise made subject to the administration of the N.F.E. . . .

Organizations have been created for all the markets here concerned, such as those for cereals, cattle, dairy products, sugar, potatoes, eggs, beer, fish, fruit, vegetables, wine, and others. Each of these separate market organizations is composed of all persons connected with its particular trade, thus – for instance – that for cereals consists of all the growers, grain dealers, grain associations, mills, mill-produce dealers, and bakers. . . .

Particular interest – not only in Germany, but also elsewhere – is taken in the market control set up by the N.F.E., which is more consistently carried out than any corresponding system introduced in other parts of the world. The successes achieved prove that the fundamental principles underlying the German system are sound. According to the calculations of the Institute for the Study of the Business Cycle, the proceeds derived from the sale of agricultural produce increased in value from 6,400,000,000 to 8,800,000,000 RM during the three years that have passed since the introduction of the control system, whilst the prices payable by consumers did not undergo a rise in any way comparable to the benefit obtained by the producers. . . .

The introduction of that organization* presented some considerable difficulties. The various markets were in a condition bordering on chaos. In almost all of them the speculative character of the wholesale trade tended to augment the lack of proper organization. The uncontrolled influence of the prices ruling in the world's markets reduced those obtainable at home to a ruinous level and made production unremunerative. The unscrupulous competition among dealers led to widespread insolvency, the consequences of which were most disastrous to the farmer. Unfair business methods and an

*The N.F.E. (Ed.)

excessive number of middlemen helped to aggravate the position still further, more particularly in the 'up-grading' industries. . . .

6/10 Schacht on the Financing of Rearmament

Memorandum by Schacht, President of the Reichsbank and Reich Minister for Economic Affairs, 3 May 1935. Printed in *War Crimes Trials* (Nuremberg, 1948), vol. 27, pp. 50–52. (Ed. Tr.)

The basis of the following remarks is that the task of German politics is the completion of the armaments programme, at its proper speed and extent, and that therefore everything else has to be subordinated to this purpose lest the pursuit of other questions may endanger the main aim itself. Even after 16 March 1935,* the problem is still that we cannot subject the German people properly to the propaganda for supporting armaments without endangering our international position. The financing of the armaments programme, barely feasible as it is, is therefore made even more difficult.

There is another assumption which has to be clarified. The printing press may be used for financing armaments only as far as the maintenance of the value of money permits. Every inflation raises the prices of foreign raw materials and raises internal prices; it is therefore a serpent which bites its own tail. The fact that our rearmament up to 16 March 1935 had to be fully camouflaged, and since then still partially so, has led to the full use of the printing press right at the beginning of the armaments programme, while it would have been natural to use it only as the last resort. In the portfolio of the Reichsbank of 3,775 million + 866 million diverted (*abgezweigte*) bills of exchange = total 4,641 million RM, the armament bills amount to 2,374 million RM (as of 30 April 1935). The Reichsbank has mainly invested those sums in German marks available to it and belonging to foreigners, in armament bills.

Our armaments are therefore being financed in part by the deposits of our political antagonists. In addition the *c.* 500 million RM, created in January 1935 by the Reich loan and deposited with the savings banks have been used for financing the armaments programme. Within the regular budget so far, 1,100 million RM have been set aside for the armed forces in the financial year 1934–1935 and 2,500 million RM in the financial year 1935–1936.

The budgetary deficits created since 1928 will increase, according to the estimate for 1935–1936, to a total of between five and six milliard RM. This aggregate deficit is being financed by short-term loans through the money-market. To that extent, therefore, the possibilities of making use of the public

* The revocation by Germany of the disarmament clauses of the Treaty of Versailles. (Ed.)

money market for armaments have been anticipated. The Reich Minister of Finance put it correctly in his budget statement: 'Since an annual deficit is ... impossible year after year, since one cannot count on a higher tax yield to wipe out fully the deficit and other advance payments, yet since on the other hand a balanced budget is the sole firm basis for the great military policy incumbent upon us, we must have a budgetary policy which in principle and with deliberation solves the problem of the financing of armaments not only on the income side, but on the savings of expenditure side, by the organic and planned reduction of other expenditure.'

The urgency of this requirement is underlined by the fact that an endless range of tasks has been undertaken and is in process of being completed by State and Party, all of which are outside the budget and have to be financed quite separately from the ordinary taxation out of contributions and credits provided by the economy. This existence side by side with the most varied budgets, all of which have more or less public objectives, forms the greatest handicap towards getting a clear view of the financial resources available for armaments. ... Unless there is eventually to be some concentration and some unified central control the worst must be feared for the task of financing armaments, since it is barely possible now even without these difficulties.

We face therefore the following tasks:

1. Someone must be appointed to the task of listing all sources and incomes arising from taxes and contributions to the State, to the Lands and to the Party, including surpluses and other incomes of public and Party enterprises.

2. Following this, a committee has to be charged by the Führer to ascertain how these sums have been used hitherto, and how much may in future be diverted from present purposes towards the financing of armaments.

3. The same committee should check the sums owned and held by all public and party organizations, to see how they are invested and to what extent they may be used for the financing of armaments.

4. The Ministry of Finance is to be charged with an inquiry into the possibilities of raising the level of taxation either by creating new taxes or by increasing the rates on existing ones.

Hitherto under existing political conditions it was necessary for the Reichsbank to finance the armaments programme, and the political success attained is proof of the correctness of this procedure. Now, however, other ways of financing armaments must be found at all costs. In the process all less urgently needed expenses in other fields will have to be stopped, and the whole financial power of Germany, limited as it is, will have to be concentrated on the single objective of financing armaments. Whether the financial problem can be solved along this direction is not at all clear, but without such concentration it is bound to founder.

6/11 Schacht on the Financing of Work Provision

Speech delivered in Konigsberg on 18 August 1935. Printed in MICHAELIS and SCHRAEPLER, *Ursachen und Folgen* [*see* Document 1/3], vol. X, pp. 507–510. (Ed. Tr.)

Finally we come to . . . the home financing of our whole employment policy, including rearmament. Even very influential and expert people at home and abroad are racking their brains over where the money for the provision of employment is to come from. I do not wonder at this question, it employs me daily but I can give the assurance that it is done neither by witchcraft nor by trickery. The secret consists entirely in the unified and disciplined co-ordination of the whole of our economic and financial policy, such as is possible only in an authoritarian political framework. One could not solve this problem under a democratic parliament. It is a fact that the tax revenue has considerably improved with the progress of productive employment. The liquidity of the money market has made it possible for the Reich to borrow substantially on short term at interest and even without. The Reichsbank was able to offer this help, as far as it could be justified from the point of view of monetary policy, since private industry made fewer demands on it. The more liquid position of the bank debtors, arising from their profitable employment, made it possible to divert some part of the credits necessary for the creation of employment to the private sector of the banking industry. The funds that have been injected into the economy by orders placed by the authorities are thus put back by the economy for the use of the Reich in its great tasks. The very limited extension of the note circulation and the scarcely larger extension of the non-monetary means of payment are a natural consequence of the expanded transactions within the economy.

We have thus anticipated future long-term finance by means of short-term funds. This future funding is of course an important and indispensable task, and I will not deny that the main difficulty still lies ahead of us. My German *Volksgenossen,*★ no one must forget that we have to thank the Government employment programme, and especially the armaments programme, for the almost total success in removing the vast army of the unemployed.

★ See Glossary.

The sums required for this are huge, when measured by normal standards, and at some time they will have to be funded by the production and savings of the people. We have to tell the German people again and again that we do not live in Cockayne's land. Unfortunately, there have been many errors committed in this direction, too, by the many theoreticians who have juggled with tax reductions, bank chits, accommodation cheques and the like. . . . The size of the sums which are being spent on the provision of employment may easily lead to the view here or there that a few millions more or less do not matter. At a time when we are unable to increase wages, every penny spent unnecessarily makes the general position more difficult, and we cannot appeal sufficiently often to the sense of responsibility of all spending Departments. There is, you know, a modern theory which claims that one is the richer, the more one spends. This kind of economist is to be judged like the inventor of the *perpetuum mobile* in mechanics.

If we have chosen so far to tread the path of short-term finance in the financing of the employment programme, this was not done irresponsibly, but is a carefully thought-out transitional measure until such time as sufficient savings will have accumulated for a long-term consolidation. In the last resort, it is on the savings potential of our people that we have to rely for the funding. But the savings potential will show itself only where the willingness to save exists. . . . It would be virtual suicide and would make it impossible to carry through the employment and armaments programme, if the Reich Government were to injure the interests of savers. In the end, employment creation has to be financed out of the saved surpluses of the economy and of labour, and it must not and cannot ever be done at the expense of the currency.

6/12 The Economic Aspects of Rearmament

Minutes of the Ministerial Council on the economic aspects of rearmament, 12 May 1936. Present: Göring (Minister President), Blomberg (Minister of War), Schacht (President of the Reichsbank), Count Schwerin von Krosigk (Minister of Finance), Dr. Popitz (Prussian Minister of Finance), with Lt.-Col. of the General Staff, Löb, as Secretary. Printed in MICHAELIS and SCHRAEPLER, *Ursachen und Folgen* [*see* Document 1/3], vol. X, pp. 525–530. (Ed. Tr.)

Schacht: (Describes development so far.) When it was decided two years ago to rearm, it was resolved to raise the necessary finance in the main outside the Ministry of Finance. This meant throwing in the last reserves right from the start. A decision which caused some misgivings. . . . Within the past two years the extent and the speed of the programme have been increased. Thus the demands on the Reichsbank have also been enlarged. . . . Up to now about 11 milliard RM have been raised for work provision and rearmament outside the budget without upsetting the currency or the exchanges; rates of interest have been lowered. In personal conversation and in the Cabinet, the Führer had emphasized that the speed of re-armament was to be sustained until the spring of 1936. This was promised and has been carried out.

Göring: has heard nothing of this limitation in time.

Schacht: The crucial question for the continuation of the programme is, how much money can be abstracted in future from the economy. Perhaps 2 milliard may be funded annually in long-term loans, but 8–9 milliard cannot be demanded; whether as much as that can be delivered depends on the development of the money market. It is necessary to concentrate the money market wholly in the hands of the Reichsbank. If the Reichsbank had to issue more notes than the money market could take, one would have to use other means. (Dr. Schacht will have no part in an inflation; the Führer is also firm on that point.) There is danger of such an outcome. . . . Looking at it from the point of view of commodities, we have to recognize that we are dependent for many commodities on foreign countries. Even small percentages have great effects. In many cases the necessity to import arises from commercial treaty relations; therefore the raw material position cannot be viewed as a purely internal matter. Relations with foreign countries must not be broken off precipitously. The negotiations with Standard and Shell, for instance, have been conducted on this basis.

*Göring:*When the ersatz materials can be produced in sufficient quantities, we won't need the imports which cause us so much trouble.

Schacht: In many cases, German products have been used as payments to make imports possible, e.g. tankers for oil imports. Above all, however, there should be no mention in public of plans and measures in this field, so as not to cause disquiet among foreign importers.

Göring: If the Führer has said anything along these lines, he has done it in order to correct the growing pessimism on this issue at home.

Schacht: In any case, all disturbance must be avoided. . . . At the beginning of the world war, Germany had 7–8 milliard worth of raw materials in stock; the present stocks are under one milliard. . . .

Göring: If war were to break out tomorrow, we should have to make do with ersatz materials. Money will be of no account. If that is so, we must be prepared to create the preconditions in peace time. . . .

von Krosigk: The basic question is whether the printing of notes to this extent would really lead to inflation. (He does not believe it would.) The price rise so far did not arise from the monetary side, but is derived from the price increases of raw materials and agricultural products. One cannot therefore speak of an inflation.

Göring: (does not think there will be an inflation caused by the monetary side.) Measures which might lead to inflation in a country governed by parliament need not necessarily lead to the same effects in an authoritarian state. Of basic importance here is the mobilizing of an appropriate propaganda, so that the assistance of the Ministry of Propaganda promised by the Führer will be of great significance.

Schacht: (provides a summary of the current bill holdings of the Reichsbank: 4,353 million RM bills, of which 3,731 million Mefo*-bills.) There are 2.2 million RM Mefo-bills in process of clearing. There are over 5 milliard in bills placed in such a way that they might, in the event of a disturbance of the market for any cause, be presented at any time. Therefore any sort of disturbance must be avoided at all costs.

Göring: (Is prepared to act as a 'shield' for the financial measures, so that no disturbance may arise.)

6/13 The Creation of Home and Foreign Credits for Rearmament

SCHACHT, *My First Seventy-Six Years* (*see* Document 4/16b), pp. 316–318.

I had no intention of allowing the German debtors to escape their liabilities. With this object in view, and by means of a law dated the 9 June 1933, I created a so-called 'Conversion Fund', into which the German borrowers of foreign loans were to pay the amounts of interest and amortization in German Reichsmarks as they fell due. From time to time the Reichsbank, in conjunction with the Conversion Fund, then undertook the transfer of these sums into foreign currency.

The stopping of interest payments meant, of course, that the foreign creditors suffered considerable loss. True, the amounts were credited to them in marks with the Conversion Fund but they were unable to change these into their own currency. In order that the creditors might not be left entirely unsatisfied, the Reichsbank authorized the Golddiskontbank to purchase these credits at fifty per cent of their nominal value. Dealings in these vouchers for mark credits, known as 'Scripts', soon became very lively. The profit accruing from the fifty per cent saving went to the promotion of export. These measures served to give practical encouragement to what had always been acknowledged in theory, namely, that the only way in which Germany

* See Document 6/13.

would meet her foreign liabilities was through her export trade. Germany's use of the Scrips to pay for additional exports gave the creditor countries an interest in buying as many goods as possible from Germany so as to preserve or increase Germany's ability to transfer payments.

In course of time, the more German marks piled up in the Conversion Fund the more urgently did other countries seek opportunities to spend those marks. Many such opportunities were created in the interests of the creditor countries, such as travel in Germany, relief work in Germany, investments in Germany, the purchase of certain goods in Germany, etc. This system of different mark categories – Travel Marks, Register Marks (*Registermark*), Aski Marks (*Special Foreign Account Marks*) has been much criticized and ridiculed. The fact is that it reacted to the advantage of the foreign creditor, the losses he had originally envisaged being greatly mitigated thereby. Many other countries adopted a similar principle after World War II. Britain, for example, has greater varieties of pounds sterling today than Germany then had in marks.

In addition to the immense and difficult task of regulating the foreign loans, the question of financing the Work Creation projects had to be dealt with. That first milliard which I had sanctioned for the Reinhardt programme was insufficient, as we knew from the first that it would be. Further funds had to be provided, and at the same time a way had to be found to avoid an undue increase in the holding of bills of exchange by the Reichsbank, and a correspondingly undue increase in the issue of bank-notes. To raise the necessary money by a simple process of inflation would have been to bungle the whole business. I reflected that if there were unused factories, unused machinery and unused stocks (as was indeed the case) there must also be unused capital lying fallow in business concerns. To capture this capital by the issue of State loans would have been a hopeless undertaking. Public confidence in the State's ability to pay had been undermined by previous Governments. It would be a matter of years before that confidence was restored. I had therefore to find a way of extracting this fallow capital from the safe deposits and pockets where it now lay, without expecting it to remain absent for long or to lose its value.

From this train of thought there arose the scheme which later became known as *Mefo-Wechsel* (Mefo-bills). The name Mefo derives from *Metall-Forschungs A.G.* (Metal Research Company Limited), a Corporation founded, at the instigation of the Government, by the four big firms Siemens, Gutehoffnungshütte, Krupp and Rheinstahl. The State assumed direct liability and security for all debts incurred by this small company. From now on, all suppliers of State orders tendered bills on Mefo against their requirements.

The Reichsbank declared its willingness to exchange these bills at any time for ready cash over the counter. That is the quite simple and plain idea behind the Mefo-bill system.

Where the working of the system was concerned, the State could use the Mefo-bills to pay for its orders to business firms, orders which, as time went on, were extended especially to cover armaments. The suppliers could immediately exchange their bills for cash at the Reichsbank.

The question remained to what extent the Reichsbank might be compelled to accept Mefo-bills against cash in its portfolio. In this connection, what I had expected came to pass, namely that the money lying idle in the safes and cash boxes of business firms, not intended or able to be used for long-term investments, was immediately used to get possession of these short-term investments. Since the bills carried four per cent interest and could be exchanged for ready money at the Reichsbank at any time, they took the place of ready cash, so to speak, and earned interest into the bargain. In four years the total amount of Mefo-bills had risen to twelve milliard marks, and the above arrangement made it possible for a good six milliard of these to be taken up by the market, which meant that they were never presented at the Reichsbank, thus avoiding any inflationary development in providing funds for Work Creation projects, and any decline in the value of money.

Once production had been set on its feet again – thanks to the accumulation of Mefo-bills – and the money market was improving, the Mefo-bills became a specially favoured security for the short-term investment of bank funds. Any Mefo-bills not absorbed by the market could immediately be included in the Reichsbank portfolio. When one considers that in 1930 the Reichsbank's holding in bills and secured loans had sunk to less than two milliard marks, it is easy to realize how greatly the turnover of goods had declined in German business and how much scope the Reichsbank could offer for the intake of Mefo-bills without thereby endangering the currency.

6/14 The Repudiation of German Foreign Debt Obligations

a Law Concerning Foreign Obligations of 9 June 1933. Printed in C. R. S. HARRIS, *Germany's Foreign Indebtedness* (London, 1935), pp. 105–106.

b Communiqué of the German Debt Conference, 29 May 1934. Printed in *Documents, 1934, [see* Documents **5/8**], pp. 242–243.

a The Government has decreed the following law, which is herewith promulgated:

Article 1. (1) Interest, dividends, and regular amortization payments, also house-rents, ground-rents, and such-like regularly recurring payments on credit balances, credits, loans, mortgages, debts incurred in respect of landed property, shares, and other investments of foreigners and Saarlanders, must be paid in Reichsmarks by the debtor at the agreed date of maturity in favour of the creditor at the *Konversionskasse* for German Foreign Debts. (Article 2.) . . .

(3) So long as a debtor makes his payments to the *Konversionskasse* for German Foreign Debts, he is free from his obligations. The responsibility to creditors of the *Konversionskasse* for German Foreign Debts is determined by the provisions of *Article 3.* . . .

Article 2. (1) A *Konversionskasse* for German Foreign Debts is hereby established. The *Konversionskasse* is a corporation in public law. It is subject to the supervision of the Directorate of the Reichsbank, and keeps its account with the Reichsbank. The Directorate of the Reichsbank appoints the responsible officers. . . .

Article 3. The sums paid in (Article 1, paragraph 1) are credited to the foreign or Saarlander creditors. The claims of the creditors arising out of this crediting are determined according to the principles established in the statutes of the *Konversionskasse*. The Reichsbank decides at what moment payments may be effected in respect of credit balances.

Article 4. The liabilities of the Reichsbank and of the Deutsche Gold-diskontbank, and such liabilities as, with the approval of the Reichsbank, form the subject of an agreement between groups of foreign creditors and domestic debtors (the so-called Standstill Agreement), are not subject to the provisions of this law. . . .

b The Debts Conference, which has since 27 April been engaged in the discussion of Germany's debts transfer problem, has reached the following conclusions. . . .

After a careful study of the present and potential foreign currency situation of Germany, the creditor delegates agree that the problem of Germany's external indebtedness is not one of incapacity of the debtors as a whole to pay, the difficulties being those of transfer only. . . .

The conference decided that the situation would be best met by Germany's making an offer to her creditors.

The following offer is therefore made by the Reichsbank with respect to the transfer of interest on Germany's long and medium-term non-Reich debt:

The offer applies to coupons due during the period commencing 1 July 1934, and ending 30 June 1935.

(1) Against the surrender of his coupon at any time on or after the due date thereon the coupon-holder shall be entitled to receive funding bonds of the Conversion Fund in the same principal amount as the nominal amount of the coupon and in the currency of the coupon. These funding bonds will mature on 1 January 1945, and will bear interest at the rate of 3 per cent per annum from the date thereon. The accrued interest will be payable at regular intervals.

Every year a fund equal to 3 per cent of the outstanding amount of funding bonds will be applied to the purchase of such bonds on the open market for retirement, or the drawing by lot for payment at the principal amount thereof, plus accrued interest.

The payment of principal, interest, and sinking fund will be guaranteed by the German Government, and will not be subject to the operation of any transfer restrictions.

The bonds shall be subject to repayment in whole or in part by lot on any interest payment date at the principal amount thereof, plus accrued interest.

The bonds will be available for purchase under the supplementary export system.

(2) To coupon-holders who prefer cash to the funding bond, the Reichsbank gives an undertaking to purchase the coupons at 40 per cent of their face value.

The coupon-holders shall be entitled to receive payment of the purchase price against surrender of the coupons at any time commencing six months after the due date of the respective coupons. . . .

The payment will not be subject to the operation of any transfer restriction.

However, since the ability of the Reichsbank to make these payments is dependent upon the foreign exchange available to Germany, the Reichsbank reserves the right to withdraw its offer with respect to such cash payments on thirty days' notice published in appropriate newspapers in the various creditor countries. . . .

(4) The creditors who do not desire to accept either of the foregoing alternative offers, and who accordingly determine to keep their coupons, retain all rights under the coupons.

(5) In addition to the coupons, the offer applies to all interest, dividends, and other regularly recurrent payments of a similar nature, whether or not represented by coupons.

6/15 The German Economic Penetration of South-Eastern Europe

Secret dispatch of the German Foreign Ministry to the Embassy in Italy, 21 June 1934, on the German–Yugoslav Commercial Treaty of May 1934. Printed in CLOUGH, *et al. Economic History (see* Document **1/4a**), pp. 289–291.

SUBJECT: The political and economic significance of the Commercial Treaty with Yugoslavia.

The German-Yugoslav Commercial Treaty transmitted in the dispatch under reference, which will apply provisionally as from 1 June next, represents a fundamental remodelling of trade relations between Germany and Yugoslavia.

The object of the negotiations was to place the mutual exchange of goods on a broader basis and to keep opportunities of developing the Yugoslav market open to Germany in future, besides providing us with an economic foothold in Yugoslavia and thus also in the Little Entente,* from which it would be possible to prevent or at least render very difficult Yugoslavia's becoming economically bound up with other countries contrary to our wishes.

The German concessions suffice to make the German market indispensable to Yugoslavia's exports should the Treaty remain in force for a prolonged period, since even under the German system of monopoly management it has proved possible to make substantial allowance for Yugoslavia's export interests in her most important products (plums, eggs, apples, wheat, maize and lard), and under the agreed rebate system, which is tantamount to a disguised preference system, Yugoslavia is assured of far-reaching export possibilities on the German market, which would be virtually non-existent without this system. . . .

Given the economic importance of these concessions, the various possibilities for terminating the agreement place us in the position of being able, if required, to exert adequate pressure on Yugoslavia.

The economic advantages accorded to us by Yugoslavia not only provide an economic counterpart but, in addition, will probably work out to Germany's advantage.

Germany obtains, through the unrestricted most-favoured nation treatment and release from all future quota measures, an open door in Yugoslavia which, taken together with numerous tariff concessions, may be expected to lead to a favourable development for our exports. Moreover, the Yugoslav Government's promise about the promotion of imports from Germany, especially in connection with public works, opens up further opportunities of development for German exports.

* Interwar alliance among Yugoslavia, Czechoslovakia and Roumania. (Footnote in Clough.)

As regards the value of goods to be exchanged, the object was not to try and strike a balance but rather to aim at the largest possible trade surplus in Germany's favour whilst providing adequate transfer facilities. A surplus of this kind would correspond, in Yugoslav opinion also, to the normal proportions of the exchange of commodities between the two countries. Transfer facilities for this surplus are provided by the general clearing agreement, by the agreement on tourist traffic, by the inclusion of the 7·7 million marks secret refund payable by us, and by foreign exchange obtained from the export of wheat to third markets.

The possibilities indicated in the Treaty are to be further developed in future. Responsibility for this will devolve on the Government Committees which are, if only for this purpose, indispensable. Furthermore, they provide a means of ensuring that in allocating quotas and concessions the actions of the Yugoslav authorities shall correspond to Germany's interests. . . .

Should the Embassy consider it appropriate to inform the Italian Government in broad outline of the outcome of the negotiations . . . such explanations should, as far as possible, avoid conveying to the Italian Government the impression that the Treaty also serves political purposes and is not exclusively designed to promote reciprocal trade relations. . . .

6/16 The Objectives of the Four-Year Plan

Secret Memorandum by Hitler of August 1936. The political sections wholly omitted here are largely concerned with proving that war with Russia – i.e. the attack on Russia – was inevitable. Printed in MICHAELIS and SCHRAEPLER, *Ursachen und Folgen* (*see* Document 1/3), vol. X, pp. 536–542. (Ed. Tr.)

. . . The economic position of Germany sketched very briefly in outline, is as follows:

1. We are over-populated and cannot feed ourselves on our own.

2. When our nation has 6 or 7 million unemployed, food supply appears more favourable because of the absence of purchasing power of these people. It does of course make a difference whether 6 million people have 40 marks a month to spend or 100 marks. It should not be forgotten that we are here concerned with one third of the working population, i.e. recalculated on the basis of the total (dependent) population; thanks to the National Socialist economic policy, about 28 million people have received an increase on their previous standard of living from an average of at most 50 marks a month to at least 100–120 marks. This means an enlarged and understandable pressure on the food supplies.

3. If this increase in employment had not taken place, then a large proportion of our nation would have been lost from our body politic as a factor of value because of undernourishment. It is therefore, in spite of the difficult food situation, the supreme commandment of our economic policy to ensure that the preconditions for normal consumption shall be created by incorporating all Germans into the economic process.

4. As far as this consumption consists of articles of general use, it can very largely be satisfied by an increase in production. As far as it turns towards the food supply, it cannot be satisfied from within the German economy. For while there are many goods, the output of which can easily be increased, the product of our agriculture cannot be raised substantially. Similarly, we are unable at present to produce synthetically, or to replace in other ways, certain raw materials which we lack in Germany.

5. But it is totally irrelevant to repeat these facts again and again, i.e. to state that we lack foodstuffs or raw materials; what is decisive is to take such measures as will provide a final solution for the future, and a temporary relief for the transitional period.

6. The final solution lies in an extension of the *Lebensraum*, i.e..of the raw materials and food bases respectively, of our people. It is the task of the political leadership ultimately to solve this problem.

7. The transitional relief must be found within the framework of our present economy. In this regard we have to state:

(a) Since the German people will increasingly be dependent on imports for its food consumption, and similarly must inevitably draw certain raw materials at least in part from abroad, we have to use every available means to enable these imports to be brought in.

(b) The increase of our own exports is a theoretical possibility, but in practice hardly likely. Germany does not export in a political or economic vacuum, but inside a hard-fought arena. Measured against the general international economic decline, our exports not only did not fall more, but actually fell less than those of other nations and countries. However, since food imports in general cannot suffer a major reduction, but rather tend to rise, a balance must be struck in other ways.

(c) It is, however, impossible to divert to food imports foreign currency holdings destined for raw materials, without striking a heavy, even perhaps a destructive blow against the German economy. But it is totally impossible above all to do this at the expense of national re-armament. I must object here most strongly against the view that it is feasible to stockpile raw materials to benefit Germany in times of war, by means of reducing national rearmament, i.e. the production of arms and ammunition. Such a view rests on a total misunderstanding – not to use a stronger term – of the tasks lying before us and of our military needs. For even a successful saving of raw materials by a reduction for example, in the production of ammunition, would merely mean that we stockpile these raw materials in peace time in order to work them up after war has broken out, i.e. we deprive the most critical months of ammunition and hold instead raw copper, lead, or possibly iron. In that case, however, it would still be preferable for the nation to enter the war without a kilo of copper in reserve, but with filled ammunition arsenals, instead of with empty arsenals but 'enriched' raw material depots. . . .

. . . No state is able to stockpile sufficient raw materials before the outbreak of a war, if that war lasts more than, say, one year. But if a nation were really enabled to prepare such masses of raw materials for one year, then its political, economic and military leadership deserves to be strung up. For it piles up its available copper and iron ready for a war instead of turning out shells. Germany entered the world war without any stocks. What appeared to be available as stocks accumulated in peace time, was richly paid for and devalued by the miserably low stocks of ammunition. Besides, the masses of raw material needed for a war are so large, that never, in the history of the world, has there been an effective stockpiling for a longer period! As far as accumulating a reserve of foreign currency is concerned, however, it is quite clear that

    1. the war can always devalue foreign currency or that part of it which is not in the form of gold, and

    2. there is not the slightest guarantee of a transformation even of gold into raw materials in war time. In the world war Germany still possessed very large holdings of foreign assets in very many countries. But our clever economic politicians were unable to use them to bring fuel, rubber, copper, or tin in sufficient quantities into Germany. . . .

I therefore lay down the following programme for the final solution for our pressing need for survival (*Lebensnot*):

I. As in the case of the military and political rearmament or mobilization respectively of our nation, there also has to be an economic one, at the same rapid rate, with the same resolution and also, if need be, with the same ruthlessness. . . . Only one view is possible, and that is that Germany must politically and economically be brought into a state of self-sufficiency.

II. To this end foreign assets have to be saved in all areas in which our demand can be met by German production, in order to channel them to provide for those needs which must in all circumstances be met by imports.

III. In this sense fuel production from German sources has to be pushed forward with all speed and must be totally achieved within 18 months.* This task has to be tackled and carried out with the same determination as the waging of a war; since the conduct of the next war depends on solving it, rather than on the stockpiling of petrol.

IV. Equally obviously, the mass-production of synthetic rubber has to be organized and secured. . . .

V. The question of the cost of these raw materials is also totally irrelevant, for it is always preferable for us to produce expensive tyres in Germany and use them, rather than to buy theoretically cheap tyres, but for which the Ministry of Economics cannot grant foreign currency, and which therefore cannot be used.† If we are being forced to build up what is very largely a self-sufficient and autarchic economy – and we are – . . . then the detailed price of raw materials does not play a decisive part any longer.

It is further necessary to raise the German production of iron to the utmost. The objection that we are unable to produce pig iron as cheaply out of German ore of 26 per cent iron content as out of the Swedish etc. ores of 45 per cent is irrelevant, for the question is not what we would like to do but what we are able to do. The objection that in that case all German blast furnaces will have to be altered is also insignificant, and above all it is not the business of the Ministry of Economics. The task of the Ministry is merely to set the economic targets, and it is the duty of private industry to fulfil them. But if private industry should believe itself unable to do so, the National Socialist State itself will know how to deal with it. . . .

* This impossible request rested on the assertion of a non-expert, Lt.-Col. Löb of the General Staff, taken over by Hitler. V. Wolfgang Birkenfeld, *Der Synthetische Treibstoff 1933–1945* (Gottingen, 1964), p. 87. (Footnote in M. and S.)

† This is a reference to a statement by Schacht at the Cabinet meeting of 27 May 1936. (Footnote in M. and S.)

It is further necessary to prohibit at once the distilling of spirit from potatoes. This fuel must be won from the earth and not from potatoes. Instead, it is our duty to use the acreage thus made available either for human or animal food, or for the planting of fibre plants.

It is further necessary to make our supplies of industrial fats independent of imports with the greatest speed, and to use those derived from coal. This task has been solved chemically and cries out for completion. . . .

It is further necessary to raise the output of German ores without regard to costs, and in particular to raise the output of light metals to the utmost, in order to replace certain other metals with them.

It is finally necessary for our rearmament to use, even today, if at all possible, those materials which will have to replace, and *will* replace, scarce metals (*Edelmetalle*), in case of war. It is better to consider and to solve these problems in peace time, than to wait for the next war before these tasks, in the midst of all other problems, are tackled by economic researches and methodical experiments!

Briefly summarized: I consider it necessary that henceforth we shall with an iron resolution become independent of outside supplies and achieve a 100 per cent self-sufficiency of these important raw materials, and shall also thereby save the foreign currency necessary in peace time for the import of our foodstuffs. . . .

I therefore set the following tasks:

I. The German army must be ready to fight in four years.

II. The Germany economy must be capable of waging war in four years.

6/17 Shortages in the Nazi Economy

Report in *Der Deutsche Volkswirt*, 2 September 1938. Printed in HAUSER, *Hitler versus Germany* (*see* Document 4/24) pp. 118–119.

The coupling of purchases of foodstuffs and fodder has been prohibited, with a view to reducing prices. If a purchaser can get certain merchandise only on condition that he also buys other merchandise, he is compelled to spend more money. If the merchandise he is forced to buy along with what he really wants should remain unused, it raises the price of other goods. But increase of prices is forbidden.

In spite of this prohibition, the following practice is frequently to be observed. Fruit is scarce this year, and the demand for it is large. The people have been willingly following the advice, 'Eat more fruit.' The demand for the scanty supply of fruit is so great, it is so quickly taken out of the hands of dealers, that it is able to carry with it other merchandise with which it may be coupled. No matter how stale and wilted vegetables may be, coupled with fruit they find a ready sale. With good reason, this scanty commodity is known in dealers' jargon as 'gold dust' – it gilds everything.

In the existing market organization, wholesalers and retailers are mere *distributors.*

Now what does the wholesaler do? The merchandise he receives is allotted to him not in accordance with his requirements, but according to the crop yield. He may want red cabbage most urgently, yet he may receive very little of it, and a large amount of white cabbage instead. Is he to lay in a stock of the superabundant white cabbage? He isn't going to do that. Any retailer who wants red cabbage must take white cabbage as well, because the wholesaler himself was supplied with white cabbage against his will.

But there is a prohibition of 'coupling', with severe penalties attached. Consequently, the wholesaler does not say: 'I am prepared to sell you red cabbage if you buy twice as much white cabbage,' – plain speaking of that sort has outlived its usefulness. A finer technique is employed, more veiled but not less effective. The retailer long ago learned the right way to buy. Observing that the wholesaler has much white cabbage and only a little red cabbage, he knows perfectly well that if he asks for red cabbage alone, he won't get any. He asks first for white cabbage, and only then for the scarce red cabbage. Is this 'coupling' or isn't it? . . .

Because of rigorous supervision, the retailer dare not engage openly in coupling – but what is the term 'regular customer' for?

The regular customer who buys abundantly at the retail shop is likely to get more of the scarcer things, and get them quicker. Today, merchandise does not wait for a buyer; the buyer searches out merchandise. The retailer does not distribute his goods indiscriminately. The customer who buys often and profusely gets a higher quota of the scarcer articles. This does not resemble coupling, but it favours the well-to-do bachelor over the housewife with many children.

6/18 Economic Failure and Political Unrest

Quarterly Report of the Reich and Prussian Minister of the Interior (June–August 1935). Printed in MICHAELIS and SCHRAEPLER, *Ursachen und Folgen* [*see* Document 1/3], vol. X, pp. 510–515. (Ed. Tr.)

In order to understand the existing economic situation, we may preface our report by some summary remarks which will allow us to recognize and understand the existing tendencies, tensions and opportunities from the general point of view of the economy.

Rearmament and the importation from abroad of materials needed for armaments have necessarily created a shortage of foreign exchange for the rest of the economy. Therefore there had to be some substantial cuts in the provision of other raw materials and imported commodities.

The consequent shortage of raw materials, and the reduction in orders because of the boycott, had adverse and hampering effects on the export industries.

On the other hand, the measures of work provision and the re-absorption of the unemployed by the process of production led to growing prosperity at home. The correspondingly greater demand would have led to rising prices, had not the State intervened in time and issued orders to regulate prices.

Similarly, wage rises had to be prevented at all costs, since the export industries could not have borne any higher costs, and besides, the point was to distribute the aggregate volume of wage funds over as large a working population as possible and to create further jobs.

The rural population had to be protected socially and financially, and its livelihood had to be fortified as the basis of a healthy German nationhood. Therefore, prices for farm animals and grain were stabilized and aligned to certain basic prices in the interest of the farming community. Thus the laws of supply and demand were suspended as far as agricultural products were concerned.

The German agrarian economy was extensively isolated from foreign trade by appropriate means, and re-directed towards autarchy. In consequence, certain temporary shortages arose in particular products, especially since the harvest did not come up to expectations, and private arbitrary power intervened at times to abuse self-interestedly the monopoly positions which emerged within the regulatory system.

Since wages could not be raised, the problem was to keep food prices correspondingly low also and to counteract effectively the pressure to increase prices. We had to lay down minimum prices in the interests of farmers, and these were matched by maximum prices in the interests of consumers. The result was a squeeze on distributors' profits, arising in the trading sector from the difference between buying and selling prices.

INDUSTRIAL DEVELOPMENT

Political Outlook of the Working Population

All these circumstances are reflected in the outlook of the population and its attitude to the State. Even if the individual might be disposed to subordinate his own desires and interests to the demands of the common good, yet the cares and troubles of daily life obtrude again and again with such insistence that they can easily destroy any objective insight and limit the field of vision to questions of immediate moment. In spite of the goodwill of the individual, it will in the end be the solution of these insistent economic problems which will be decisive for the political destiny of the future.

The Wages Question

It is the wages question, above all, which influences the political outlook of the working population. Wages are everywhere a matter of complaint, since in some industries they hardly exceed the level of the dole, and partly even remain below it. A low level of wages is found not only among factory workers, but also among agricultural labourers, though it must be felt particularly severely in urban industries. Wages are so low that even with the greatest economy they are only just sufficient for the daily bread. If we bear in mind that the weekly income of married fathers of families who may have to keep a family of five or six, is no more than 20 RM on the average and often drops as low as 12 RM or 14 RM, it is not surprising that the outlook of the working population often becomes depressed. Police Headquarters in Münster report that the nurses at the teaching hospital get such low wages, despite their strenuous work, that their incomes have to be supplemented from the welfare agencies. . . . (In the Aachen mining district), the low pay and the high prices of groceries and potatoes have created the impression that the State has ceased to care about the welfare of the workers. . . .

The Price Rise

The evil most needing reform is felt to be the increase in prices, which continues all the time and is discernible everywhere. It is particularly the necessities of life, which one cannot do without in daily consumption, that have shared in this price rise. Compared with 1933, the increases in the case of margarine, oil, lard, meat and dripping amount to 50 per cent and up to double the price. This rise shows itself first of all in the poorer qualities, on which the working population is dependent, while the better qualities have been largely exempt from it. It is not surprising that this is considered an unfair hardship, notably since the return of inflationary conditions has been officially denied in the most definitive manner.

The poorer population in particular believes its economic survival to be once again threatened by these conditions; as far as it is concerned, the worry over the daily bread looms like a huge shadow over the country, but it sees it to be beyond its powers to exorcise this spectre. It need hardly be mentioned, for example, that the prices of fruit and vegetables greatly exceed the purchasing power of large sections of the population who are thus excluded from their consumption. It may be noted in passing that there are working-class families in the Rhenish industrial district who can be proved to have had no vegetables on their table for months, and whose children have not eaten a single fruit all the year. Much more significant are the prices of meat and fats, since these foods are of decisive and predominant interest for the workers who have to perform hard physical labour.

The prices of sausage, margarine etc, are precisely those which are often beyond the reach of the average worker earning 70–80 RM a month. The miner who has to go down the pit in Upper Silesia with a sandwich containing only pickled cabbage, naturally blames the Government for his poor standard of living and says openly that the NSDAP* did not keep its promises, and that formerly he could afford more out of his unemployment benefit than he can today, when he has to work hard. . . .

Even though it is not feasible on economic grounds to return prices to their former levels, every unjustified and selfish price rise must be stopped by means such as fines, the closure of shops, and protective custody. For the economic position must not be used to allow certain individuals to gain undue advantages and profits, if they are unscrupulous enough to exploit a favourable market situation in their own interest. Butchers and slaughterers who think nothing of exceeding the fixed maximum or recommended prices, contribute by their actions to the unrest among the population. . . . The shortage of certain products which goes hand in hand with the price rise, has also created great excitement and uneasiness. There is again talk of a State-controlled economy, of bread and meat rationing, and many arrests had to be made for incitement and the spreading of false rumours about economic conditions. . . .

Salaries in Industry and Party

All this might be tolerable, however, if there were not further circumstances to make the worker fully conscious of his economic hopelessness. These include above all certain high salaries of managing directors and managers of large firms, that is to say, persons who are in the limelight of economic and public life. . . . These high salaries might perhaps be justifiable in a free capitalist economy, not subject to State steering and carrying their own risks. For in that case, the higher salary might have a proper relation to the greater risk and responsibility. But if there is no risk, if the responsibility is largely transferred to the State, and the functioning of the concerns is secured by employment provisions of the State, these relationships are basically altered, and there is no further justification for a very high salary. . . .

Wage Disputes

In spite of the difficult wage conditions, wage disputes have hitherto remained very rare and most of them could be solved quickly by the inter-

* The National Socialist Party. (Ed.)

vention of the Gestapo★ in collaboration with the arbitrators ('Treuhänder der Arbeit')★ of the Labour Front. . . .

6/19 Labour Shortage in Germany

Report in the *Frankfurter Zeitung*, 25 February 1939. Printed in HAUSER, *Hitler versus Germany* (*see* Document 4/24), pp. 83–84.

Before the district judge and jury, the head of an important plumber's business of Darmstadt appeared as defendant. The firm had an order for installing several kilometres of tubes for a gas-pipe line. The installation of the tubes required a special welding technique, not possessed by ordinary welders. The defendant therefore sent ten of his workers to the welding-school at Duisburg. Eight of them passed the examination, and the defendant then thought he could proceed with his work. However, in the course of practical experience the men were found to be inadequately trained. The defendant thereupon inquired from a pipe-line construction company whether they could lend him specialists to teach his men, but the company refused. The defendant therefore advertised in the papers for specialists.

In response a welder came to see him and demanded an hourly wage of 1·15 RM and 6 RM per day to be paid to his present employer as compensation for his releasing a specialist. The defendant at first declined the offer, thinking the demand too high, but pretends to have found out later that other firms, also working on the pipe-line, paid the same wages; he therefore accepted the proposition of the welder. The latter thereupon gave notice to his employer, who refused, however, to release him. Subsequently three other men came forward, demanding similar wages, which the defendant granted, and they were engaged as welders, while the first comer was made a foreman for the assembling work. The latter remained with the defendant for a number of weeks but proved unsatisfactory, being especially incapable of training the workers in the required technique. The other men who had come in response to the advertisement were immediately claimed by their firm and by the labour exchange. All four people had been with the above-mentioned pipe-line construction company, which lodged a complaint with the Reich Trustee of Labour. The defendant, heard in his defence, stated he had had no intention of enticing workers away from their employers through the promise of higher wages and more favourable conditions of work. He had needed specialists to teach his own men, he said.

The Court, after long pleadings, came to the view that the defendant had

★ See Glossary.

infringed the decree, dated 25 June 1938, of the Commissioner for the Four-Year Plan and the instructions of the Reich Trustee of Labour for Hesse. The Court therefore imposed a fine of 6,000 RM. The presiding judge, in the legal argumentation of the sentence, stated that in the opinion of the Court the defendant knew the men were still in employment. For him the completion of the work entrusted to him was a matter of prestige, and he therefore had no compunction about enticing workers away from their employers. The reason why the Court imposed a fine only (the presiding judge said) was that the defendant employed 280 men and was indispensable in his enterprise. If a prison sentence were imposed and he were sent to jail, the enterprise and the employment of the persons on its payroll would have been endangered.

6/20 The Costs of Rearmament: Inflation

Memorandum by Schacht and the Board (Directory) of the Reichsbank to Hitler, 7 January 1939. Preceded Schacht's resignation as President of the Reichsbank. Printed in MICHAELIS and SCHRAEPLER, *Ursachen und Folgen* [*see* Document 1/3], vol. X, pp. 587–588. (Ed. Tr.)

. . . The overall German currency position appears at present as follows:

(1) Outward: there are no more gold or foreign currency reserves. The adverse excess of imports over exports is increasing apace. Exports no longer reach the value of the imports required by us. The reserves formed by the absorption of Austria and the calling up of foreign assets and German gold coins are now dissipated. The *devisen** certificates issued by the control commission to importers are today no longer covered by assured *devisen* earnings and therefore run the risk that one fine day they might no longer be met because of the lack of *devisen*. This would wipe out the last remaining foreign credit for our commodity imports.

(2) Inward: the assets of the Reichsbank consist almost entirely of State papers (mainly Mefo†-bills). The note-issuing bank is replete with them and if it should have renewed demands made on it by the economy it will be unable to grant the required credits. Outside the Reichsbank there are some 6 milliard RM of Mefo-bills outstanding, which may be presented at any time to the Reichsbank with a demand for cash and which therefore represent a permanent threat to the currency.

On 1 January 1933 the note circulation amounted to 3,560 million RM. It rose until 1 March 1938 to 5,278 million RM. This increase of about 1·7

* See Glossary.
† See Document 6/13. (Ed.)

milliard RM in over five years did not necessarily lead to any distrust of the currency, since the output of the German economy almost doubled in the same period, including both production of capital goods and of consumption goods. In the period from 1 March to 31 December 1938, however, the note circulation rose to 8,223 million RM, i.e. without counting the needs of Austria and the Sudetenland, by 2 milliard RM. It thus rose in the past ten months more than in the whole of the previous five years. In the end it is the ratio of monetary circulation to consumption goods output which determines the stability of the value of money. If the monetary circulation increases faster than the production of consumption goods, the consumers dispose of an enlarged purchasing power in the aggregate, which faces a reduced supply of commodities, and this must raise prices. No coverage of the money issued by land, paper assets etc. can preserve the value of the money, as the history of the assignats during the French revolution has shown most clearly, when the notes were wholly devalued in spite of controlled exchanges, rigorous penalties, etc. . . .

It is not our task to prove how far an unrestricted issuing policy is compatible with the output and savings of the German economy or with the social needs of the population. But our responsibility demands that we point out that no further demands on the Reichsbank, either directly or by other requisition measures over the money market, can be justified from the point of view of currency policy, and must lead directly to inflation. . . . It is not possible to raise commodity production by an increase in pieces of paper. An increase in monetary circulation can, in view of the full and even over-full employment in the German economy, lead only to an increase in prices and wages, but not in production.

We are convinced that the ill-effects of the past ten months on the currency may still be repaired and that the danger of inflation may still be removed by the strictest attention to staying within the budget revenue. The Führer himself has repeatedly opposed inflation in public, as stupid and useless. We ask for the following measures:

1. Neither the Reich nor other public authorities may undertake any expenditures, guarantees, or obligations in future that cannot be covered out of taxes or out of such sums that may be raised by loans without disturbance to the long term capital market.

2. For the purpose of effectively carrying out this policy, the Minister of Finance must once again have full control over all public expenditure.

3. There must be effective price and wage control. The current abuses must be removed.

4. The Reichsbank alone must decide on the demands made on the money and capital market.

(Sgd.) Directory of the Reichsbank.
Schacht, Dreyse, Vocke, Eberhard, Puhl, Hülse, Kretzschmann, Blessing.

6/21 Corporations in Fascist Italy

a The Law on Corporations of 3 April 1926. Printed in CLOUGH, *et. al.*, *Economic History* [*see* Document I/4a], pp. 267–270.

b The Law on Corporations of 5 February 1934. Printed in KERTESZ, *Documents* [*see* Document I/15a], pp. 401–402.

a *Article 1.* Associations of employers and of workers, both intellectual and manual, may obtain legal recognition when they can prove that they comply with the following requirements:

(1) in the case of associations of employers, that the employers who have voluntarily registered as members employ not less than one-tenth of the workers in the service of the concerns of the kind for which the association has been formed, existing in the district in which it operates; and in the case of associations of workers that the workers who have voluntarily registered as members number not less than one-tenth of those of the class for which the association has been formed, existing in the district in which it operates;

(2) that besides the protection of the economic and moral interests of its members the association proposes to promote, and does actually promote, the assistance, instruction, and moral and patriotic education of its members;

(3) that the director of the association affords guarantees of ability, morality, and sound national loyalty. . . .

Article 6. The associations may be communal, district, provincial, regional, inter-regional, and national. . . .

Legal recognition can only be granted to one association for each class of employers, workers, artists, or professional men. Similarly, legal recognition can only be given to one federation or confederation of employers or workers or artists or professional men, referred to in the preceding paragraph, for the class or classes of employers or workers represented within the district assigned to each. . . .

In no case can associations be recognized which, without the preliminary consent of the Government, have contracted any ties of discipline or dependance with associations of an international character. . . .

Article 10. Collective labour contracts drawn up by the legally recognized associations of employers, workers, artists, and professional men, are valid in respect of all employers, workers, artists, and professional men belonging to the category to which said contract refers and which the associations represent in accordance with the provisions of Article 5 of this Act. . . .

Article 18. The lock-out and the strike are forbidden.

Employers who without justifiable motive, and for the sole purpose of obtaining from their dependants changes in existing labour agreements, suspend work in their factories, establishments, concerns, or offices render themselves liable to a fine of not less than ten thousand and not to exceed one hundred thousand lire.

Three or more employees or workers who, by preconcerted agreement, leave their work or perform it in such wise as to interfere with its continuity or regularity, with a view to obtaining from their employers different labour conditions render themselves liable to a fine of not less than one hundred and not to exceed one thousand lire. . . .

When the persons guilty of the offences foreseen under the above paragraphs are more [than three], the leaders, promoters, and organizers are liable to detention for not less than one year and not to exceed two years, besides the fine provided for under said paragraphs.

Article 19. Persons in the employ of the State and of other public bodies or bodies performing essential public services who, in the number of three or more, by preconcerted agreement, leave their work or perform it in a manner likely to interfere with its continuity or regularity, render themselves liable to imprisonment for a period of not less than one month and not to exceed six months. . . . The leaders, promoters, and organizers are liable to imprisonment for a period of not less than six months and not to exceed two years, and to interdiction from public office for not less than three years.

Persons carrying on public services, or services essential to the public who suspend, without justifiable motives, work in their establishments, concerns, or offices, are liable to imprisonment for a period of not less than six months and not to exceed one year, and to a fine of from five thousand to one hundred thousand lire, besides temporary interdiction from public office.

b 1. The Corporations mentioned in the sixth clause of the Labour Charter* . . . shall be established by decree of the Head of the Government on proposal of the Minister of Corporations with the approval of the Central Corporative Committee. . . .

* See Document 6/22. (Ed.)

7. The associations combined in a Corporation become autonomous as syndical bodies but continue to belong to their respective Confederations. . . .

8. . . . A Corporation shall make rules for the collective regulation of economic matters and for the unified direction of production. . . .

10. A Corporation, within its own field, shall have the power to fix rates . . . for economic employment and services, as well as prices for goods offered to the public. . . .

12. A Corporation shall pass judgment on all questions that commonly interest the particular branch of economic production for which it is established, whenever it is so requested by the public administration concerned. . . .

6/22 Labour Legislation in Fascist Italy

The Labour Charter (*Carta del lavoro*) 21 April 1927. Printed in S. B. CLOUGH and H. S. SALADINO, *A History of Modern Italy. Documents, Readings and Commentary* (New York, 1968), pp. 466–467.

I. The Italian nation is an organism having ends, life, and means of action superior, by virtue of its power and duration, to those of the separate individuals or groups of individuals which compose it. It is a moral, political, and economic unity that is realized integrally in the Fascist state.

II. Labour in all its forms, intellectual, technical, and manual, is a social duty. By right of this fact, and only by this right, it is safeguarded by the state. The whole of the process of production is unitary from the national point of view; its aims are unitary and are summed up in the welfare of individuals and in the growth of national power.

III. Syndical or occupational association is free, but only those syndicates that are recognized by law and subjected to the control of the state have the right to represent legally the whole category of employers or employees for which they are established. . . .

IV. The solidarity between the various factors of production finds concrete expression in the collective labour contract, by means of the conciliation of the opposed interests of employers and employees and their subordination to the higher interests of production.

V. Labour courts are the organs with which the state intervenes to regulate labour disputes. . . .

VI. The legally recognized occupational associations assure legal equality

504

between employers and employees; they maintain the discipline of production and labour and promote their increasing perfection.

The corporations constitute the unitary organization of the forces of production and integrally represent its interests. By virtue of this integral representation, and inasmuch as the interests of production are national interests, the corporations are recognized by law as organs of the state. Representing the unitary interests of production, the corporations may impose compulsory rules on the conduct of labour relations. . . .

VII. The corporative state considers private enterprise in the field of production as the most effective and useful instrument in the promotion of national interest. Inasmuch as private organization of production is a function of national interest, the organizer of an enterprise is responsible to the state for the direction its production takes. . . .

IX. State intervention in economic production takes place only when private initiative is lacking or insufficient, or when the state's political interests are at stake. Such intervention may take the form of controls, encouragement, or direct management.

6/23 Land Reclamation in Italy

Report on the Progress of Land Reclamation, 1931. Printed in CLOUGH, *et al.*, *Economic History* [*see* Document 1/4a], pp. 285–287.

I. *Integral Land Reclamation*. The integral reclamation of the land is one of the fundamental enterprises of the Regime. It is the outcome of the conditions of Italian economics and of the will of Fascism.

A dense population confined within a circumscribed territory, poor in natural resources; a Nation desirous of growing in power and of spreading Italian ideals throughout the world, must of necessity create new centres of intensified rural life, in order to increase the revenues of the Nation and fortify the healthy and prosperous family life of the country against the destructive forces of the towns.

It is this that the reclamation of the land aims at. . . .

Land reclamation becomes *integral* reclamation when the whole of the enterprises necessary for the new order of land production demanded by the economic, moral and political aims of the Nation, have been carried out.

III. *The Importance of the Mussolini Act.* The most important contribution to the development of the rural policy of the Regime was the Act of 24 December 1928, relating to the integral reclamation of the land, which law represents the greatest effort of the State towards the full development of the land and the greater efficiency of rural life. . . .

VI. *The results obtained in the last four years, taking into special consideration the first year of the enforcement of the Mussolini Act.* Let us give a rapid glance to what has already been accomplished towards the reclamation and improvement of the land.

On a surface of 31 million hectares* Italy has over 2,300,000 liable to drainage.

Over 700,000 hectares have been reclaimed. Half of these, however, still call for the building of roads, houses and water conduits, to guarantee the results of drainage and to permit a more profitable cultivation of the soil.

Some 1,200,000 hectares are being drained, and drainage operations have still to be begun on another 1,485,000 hectares. . . .

The direct execution of reclamation works by the State has been gradually decreasing while, on the contrary, concessions have been steadily increasing: so much so, that in these last years the direct intervention of the State has been restricted to the upkeep of the works and to a few other enterprises. . . .

* See Glossary.

Chapter 7   Social Trends

The years between November 1918 and September 1939 have been described as 'the saddest, the most exciting and the most formative in human history'.* For the economic historian they usually represent the years of the great crash, economic depression and world-wide mass unemployment. More dramatically, they have been described as years when 'a complete re-examination was felt to be necessary: a re-examination of all traditional ideas about reality, all values, all principles.'† Any analysis which ignores such evidence would misrepresent the times. Not everything in these years, however, was tinged with such shadows and it would be a mistake to ignore the fact that between 1919–1939 living standards were increasingly under-pinned by legislative activity and important changes began to occur in European consumption patterns.

The Europe which experienced these changes was growing only slowly in size, as a result of the loss of life in the Great War, the fall in the birth-rate during the war and the epidemics which followed it. This population prob-lem was particularly acute in France (7/1), where the loss of life in the War was compounded by a continuing low birth-rate (7/2). Contemporaries expressed concern at such 'an alarming phenomenon' and some, projecting trends into the future, began to think of France as a desert. During the period of rapid reconstruction which preceded the onset of the depression, labour shortages were overcome by the immigration of foreign labour, particularly from Italy (7/3 see also 5/15), and attempts were made to encourage the French birth-rate through a system of family allowances (7/4). An official population policy was not confined to France. The National Socialist Government in Germany, for example, which was keen to increase the size of the population for military reasons, 'initiated a large number of measures to stimulate marriage and birth-rates'. One of the earliest and most important, was the granting of marriage loans, intended not only to encourage marriage and pro-creation, but also to reduce the level of unemployment through the with-drawal of women from the labour market (7/5 see also 6/8). Elsewhere, in Sweden, following the classic Myrdal report in 1933, which stressed the problem of population decline, marriage loans and attempts to reduce the

---

* W. A. Lewis, op. cit., p. 11.

† K. Mannheim, Essays on the Sociology of Knowledge, edited by Paul Kecskemeti (London, 1952), p. 2.

cost of having children became a major feature of social policy. It was hoped that such policies would increase births and reduce the level of abortions. No distinction was made in the application of these policies between married and unmarried women (7/6).

In brief, the basic population problem of Europe in the inter-war years, was the low birth-rate, which was chiefly related to 'the cost of a large family' (7/7, see also 7/2). It was a problem which played its part in reducing the production and exchange of primary products – the number of mouths to feed grew only slowly – and in restricting France's economic development. It was also a situation which governments in general found difficult to solve, to an extent that just before the Second World War the various attempts to change the situation were categorized by one expert as 'struggling in the dark with small chance of success' (7/7).

The population policies pursued in most of Europe were often part of a general trend to improve the quality of European life. In France, for example, which up to that time had been one of the most backward countries in Europe in regard to compulsory insurance, provision was made in 1928 for the intro-duction of 'a single scheme of insurance for sickness, invalidity and old age' (7/8). Some of the most important changes in population policies and health welfare, however, took place in the Soviet Union. There, official policy was concerned to overcome the expenses of motherhood which, coupled with the cost of infant care, was in capitalist countries 'one of the potent causes of the chronic poverty of large sections of the wage-earning class'. Consequently a universal and complete provision was made for maternity and infancy, which also had the effect of promoting 'equality of conditions between men and women', through the granting of 'functional expenses' to women who engaged in child bearing (7/9). There was also an increasing concern for those who survived infancy and in 1920 rest homes were established for those who, although not technically ill, needed 'a rest under medical supervision' (7/10), with the aim of providing workers with a break from their daily routine and restoring their energies. The expansion of the Soviet medical service under-pinned this health drive. There was a 'fixed determination on the part of the Soviet authorities, without too narrowly counting the cost, to provide the whole country . . . with a medical staff numerically adequate to the need, however great that may prove to be, and however difficult the task of recruit-ing' (7/11a). The recruitment problem was less acute than might at one stage have been supposed. The greater rewards and prestige associated with work in industry, which drew away potential male recruits from the medical profession, was overcome largely by the training of women doctors, with the result that 'the preponderance of women' became 'one of the most striking features of Soviet medicine' (7/11b).

The need for educated and skilled labour, of which doctors were only a part, worked with socialist principles towards a universal and free system of education in the Soviet Union, which exerted another major influence on the quality of Russian life (**7/12a**). The need for free education and educational equality was also increasingly emphasized in the democracies of Western Europe, while in Germany, following their accession to power in 1933, the National Socialists re-orientated the nature of German education, bringing it into line with their own conception of national priorities and values (**7/13**).

Another significant development, also aimed at improving the quality of life, was seen in housing reform. In 'Red Vienna', for example, 'mass housing, hygienic and beautiful living quarters within the reach of the average worker's pocket and in harmony with an intelligent town planning,' became firmly established in the priorities of the Social Democrats. It was, however, a policy that was to be aborted by the advent of the Dollfuss Government (**7/14**). Elsewhere, State and municipal drives to provide cheap housing accommodation were launched in the 1920s by the Swedish authorities (**7/15**), while in France, where legislation to provide State assistance towards the building of working-class dwellings stretched back as far as the 1894 Siegfried Law, a series of legislative enactments were passed, including the 1928 Loucheur Law, which provided for 'a substantial amount of financial assistance from the public authorities'. Some progress was made, but in the depression of the early 1930s the housing associations encountered financial difficulties owing to delays in the payment of rents and the repayment of sums due from individual borrowers (**7/16**). What was firmly established, however, was the wider acceptance of the principle of public intervention into a sensitive area of social policy.

Any attempt to assess living standards and trends must take account of quantitative factors as well as the qualitative changes we have so far outlined. In this respect it is clear that consumption underwent certain periods of sharp reversal, although by 1939 standards were generally higher than in 1914. The immediate post-war period in Germany witnessed a particularly sharp fall in consumption (**7/17**) and the immediate post-revolutionary period in Russia also involved considerable consumer hardship. In 1919, in this latter connection, the accounts of the American Relief Association that – 'Emaciation, deformity from hunger, filth and disease were . . . everywhere' – constituted a powerful reminder that even in the twentieth century famine could not always be avoided (**7/18**). In certain countries, however, standards very quickly surpassed the immediate pre-war period. As an instance of this, the post-war recovery in the boom in France was particularly reflected in higher urban living standards (**7/19a**). There was a demand for more and better meat which was satisfied through increased imports, and one observer noted that the high wage scale since the war had enabled industrial workers in general to establish a higher standard of living than was possible before the war began. The same workers also demanded better clothing and more general luxuries (7/19b). The depression, of course, affected consumption in most countries, with varying degrees of severity (7/20), and impressed itself upon personal and social consciousness to an extent that many believed the inter-war period had produced no significant consumer gains.

Without attempting to deny or ignore the real suffering which resulted from the world economic crisis, it is important to keep in mind the trends and developments, apart from the extension of welfare and related facilities, which reflected an improvement in the quality of life and which were to become established as part of Europe's life style. For example, the shift in incomes towards the German working classes in the late 1920s, led to the emergence of new consumer patterns. In many instances this was 'reflected in the demand for better mass-production goods combined with a reduced demand for the highest quality goods and services' (7/21). Observers also commented on the 'strong standardization of the consumption habits of the population', and the increasing demand for better quality furniture and housing, which had previously been beyond the reach of most workers (7/21).

Certain developments which were to exercise a considerable cultural impact on European society also originated in this period. With the development of the radio, for example, culture came to be transmitted through the spoken as well as the written word. Not that radio ownership showed an effortless expansion. The outlay for a set could be prohibitive, while manufacturers found themselves affected by external tariffs and lack of homogeneity within internal markets (7/22). A more powerful cultural effect, of course, was exerted by the cinema and the image of Hollywood 'stars' began to penetrate into every corner of the world, affecting the psychic lives of millions of fans (7/23a). The cinema, however, had a wider significance and the importance of the medium as a propaganda weapon was quickly realized by the early Fascists (7/23b see also 7/34a, b) and the Bolsheviks. The latter in particular, managed to combine political-revolutionary cinema with aesthetic advancement, especially in the work of Eisenstein (7/23c), while in the early post-revolutionary period, a section of the Russian live theatre, the Proletcult Theatre, with which Eisenstein was also associated, was a further vehicle for a new challenging revolutionary art (7/24). This flowering of the Russian cinema and theatre before the Stalinist restriction was, in fact, only a part of the post-revolutionary cultural explosion in Soviet society. Some observers commented on the pent-up demand for literature which was awakened through education, although some of the evidence, even where meaningful, needs to be treated with reserve (**7/25**). Other observers were equally impressed by the Parks of Culture and Rest, 'centres of recreation and civilized entertainment', intended to restore the spiritual and physical lives of Soviet citizens (**7/26**).

The increase in the number of radio sets and the development of the cinema brought European societies closer together. At the same time, the increase in the number of motor-cars also reduced the tyranny of distance. There was, for instance, a significant expansion of motor-vehicle ownership in France, although it must be stressed that the car was still a luxury and beyond the majority of consumers (**7/27a**). Other countries also witnessed a growth of car ownership and Sweden, which had not been a significant car-owning nation before 1914, saw motor-cars 'predominate on the roads', to an extent that 'in the neighbourhood of the larger towns the number of cars' represented '95 per cent or more of the entire volume of traffic' (**7/27b**). Overall, although punctuated during the depression years, there was a steady growth in car ownership during the inter-war period within the more affluent sections of European Society. The progress of the aeroplane was rather less successful. Plane travel remained expensive, with only a restricted private use and at first, over certain commercial routes, air companies, found it difficult to compete with an efficient railway system (**7/28**).

The improvement in European communications was one factor which lay behind the growth of tourism, which was particularly pronounced in the mid-1920s, and was itself indicative of rising standards and aspirations and a greater opportunity for holiday leisure. Evidence of this growing importance of tourism was indicated in France by the fact that in the peak years of 1927–1930 tourist expenditure amounted to approximately one-quarter of total French invisible exports (**7/29a**). It was in these years that Southern France, particularly Monte Carlo, Nice, and Cannes became the increasingly fashionable haunts of the upper middle-class British. These developments, of course, were severely affected by the onset of the world economic crisis (see **4/32f** and **7/29b**) and in the thirties, until the 1936 devaluation, by the overvaluation of the franc, which made holidays in France relatively expensive for many Europeans (**7/29b**). The tourist boom of the twenties, however, cannot be doubted and further evidence of it was displayed in the extensive hotel-building programme which was carried out in France during these years (**7/30**).

It was not merely the European middle classes who engaged in holiday activity. The potential market for tourism and holidays in general was increased by the growing acceptance of the principle of holidays with pay, which became a feature of European workers' lives in the inter-war years (**7/31**). With the reduction in the number of hours worked, the problem of 'free time', in fact, began to assume a new and growing importance. It was cushioned for some workers, particularly in Germany, by employer paternalism, which, following an established tradition, guaranteed a wide range of welfare provisions and recreational activities for workers employed by these 'enlightened' firms (7/32). As for the specific problem of holidays, a large number of bodies concerned with organizing this aspect of the workers' lives came into being and the workers themselves also founded organizations. For example, in Belgium, the General Confederation of Labour established an association called 'Holidays and Health' and similar bodies were to be found in Denmark, Finland, and Switzerland. Employers, too, involved themselves as did private organizations, such as youth movements, co-operative groups, and Sport and Travel associations. Finally, there were official and semi-official agencies such as the Office of the Under Secretary of State for Recreation and Sport, which in France was charged between 1936–1938 with co-ordinating 'the various facilities for workers' holidays with pay' (7/33).

In the two major Fascist countries of Italy and Germany the State dominated and replaced all other bodies in the attempt to organize the workers' leisure time. In Italy the emphasis was clearly upon using it for the furtherance of Fascism. 'The *Dopolavoro* Organization', recognized from 14 September 1929 as a distinctively Fascist institution, promoted schemes 'for the better employment of the free time of workers of all classes, with the object of raising the intellectual, moral, physical, and social status in accordance with the policy of enhancing national values promoted by Fascism....' (7/34a). In its actual operation it intervened in workers' lives at a variety of levels, from organizing sporting matches, and offering prizes for the 'neatness and order of their homes' to propaganda work through the medium of literature and the film (7/34b). In Germany a similar kind of activity was attempted through the 'Strength through Joy' sub-organization of the German Labour Front (7/35a). In this connection, in line with the National Socialist determination 'to further all good and healthy instincts for the material and personal well-being of the people as a whole', subsidized pleasure cruises and holidays were arranged, as well as theatre visits and sporting activities (7/35b). Official opinion on such activity was concerned to emphasize that in National Socialist Germany the contentment of the day's work vibrated into the leisure hours when fresh strength was gained for the next working day (7/35b). This *Kraft durch Freude* activity was linked with the Beauty of Labour concept, which was concerned with improving working conditions and both policies, and both it should be recognized, had purposes deeper than those which lay on the surface. They were attempts to raise a healthy nation, and to win over a proletariat to National Socialism, while supposedly furthering the Nazi ideal of a 'classless People's Community' (7/35c). In such a situation workers' lives became heavily politicized.

The pre-war years, therefore, were not simply characterized by the existence and emergence of fundamental economic problems, which brought in train a succession of harsh social consequences. They were, in addition, years which saw some underpinning of living standards and the quality of life through State initiated social policies, as well as the movement, albeit in an irregular and uneven manner, towards a society which presaged the post 1945 consumer affluence. This is not to say that the problems which arose out of episodes such as collectivization in Russia and the general West European depression, which followed the 1929 crash in America, were unimportant. They were of central significance and succeeded in significantly impressing themselves on the lives of millions who lived through such difficulties and, furthermore, continued to influence the lives of their children. What it is intended to convey, however, is that the years were richer in their social complexity than has often been supposed.

7/1 The European Population Problem

NITTI, *Decadence of Europe* [*see* Document 4/2a], pp. 193–195.

The war, and the state of want which followed it in many countries, probably cost Europe a number of men exceeding the population of any of the largest belligerent states.

According to the most reliable official figures, the number of officers and men killed in the war exceeded eight millions, in addition to twenty million wounded, and more than seven million taken prisoners or reported missing. The figures concerning Russia are very uncertain. Among all the other countries, Germany, which had been compelled to fight simultaneously on several fronts, had the greatest number of killed. But, to a different degree, the losses of almost all the belligerents were enormous. France, Great Britain, and Italy together had considerably more than two and a half million.

During the war the death-rate was higher, not only in the belligerent countries, but also in neutral countries, and the birth-rate was lower. On account of the decreased birth-rate and the increased death-rate, there is a reduction of at least eight millions in the civil population, excluding Russia, whose figures are not available, but whose losses were undoubtedly very severe.

After the war vast epidemics of typhus, smallpox, cholera, and influenza devastated Eastern Europe; in Central Europe tuberculosis is spreading; in

Southern Europe, in addition to the spread of tuberculosis, there has been an enormous increase in malaria and diphtheria.

The wounded, according to the most reliable official statistics, and excluding Russia, exceeded twenty millions. About a quarter of these are wholly or partially disabled, and their economic power is considerably reduced.

Tuberculosis has developed in a violent and threatening manner in almost all countries, and is spreading rapidly in Germany and Austria, and even in the victorious countries. Inclusive statistics for whole countries are not available; but, if we examine the figures of the large cities (which are, in nearly all countries, the only ones available), we notice an alarming development of tuberculosis. Syphilis, too, in all the countries which took part in the war, is increasing enormously. Malaria has spread throughout all parts of Italy, the Balkans, Greece, and Turkey, and, in some areas, is pandemic. There are a number of cities in Central Europe in which the number of deaths from tuberculosis has doubled, and even trebled, and the whole population is under a perpetual menace.

The physique of all the belligerent peoples also has deteriorated to an extraordinary degree. Those who died were not only the most virile element of the population, but also the superior element from the point of view of morals. They were those who did not shrink from their duty, and who gave proof of the greatest spirit of self-sacrifice. Those who, during the European conflict, cried aloud for war in the streets of the cities of all countries, and who showed the greatest spirit of intransigence, paid but a slight tribute to death. Those who died were, above all others, the most industrious and active members of the community; they were those who accepted the war as a national duty and not as a political weapon.

According to the latest census of each country, women are much more numerous than men in Europe. Leaving out some of the Balkan states, where, in any case, the census figures are very unreliable, there is a surplus of women in every country of Europe. If we classify the various populations according to sex and age, we receive a still worse impression, because there is not only a surplus of females, but males from twenty to thirty-nine years of age have diminished in number.

The vital statistics of some states present an alarming phenomenon. In France, there were 605,000 births in 1913, 594,000 in 1914, 387,000 in 1915, 313,000 in 1916, 342,000 in 1917, 399,000 in 1918, and 404,000 in 1919. As about half the number of children born are females – there were not less than 104 females to 100 males in France in 1911 – France had a birth-rate of 291,000 males in 1914, 189,000 in 1915, 153,000 in 1916, 167,000 in 1917, etc. Part of these will die, or will become incapable of bearing arms, before they are twenty. This means that, if France wishes to keep her army at its present strength or even a little lower, she will be compelled, even with the institution of a long period of military service, to summon to the colours all available males for several years; i.e. she will be compelled to withdraw from productive labour all the most virile members of her population.

7/2 France's Declining Birth-Rate

M. HUBER, *La Population de la France. Son evolution et ses perspectives* (Paris, 1932), pp. 229–231. (Ed. Tr.)

We are faced with a significant demographic revolution in the sense that the tendency for population to increase, which, apart from periods of war, disease or famine, has always been a characteristic of French society, has been succeeded by a tendency for the population to decrease.

Without undertaking a thorough examination of the causes of this revolution, it seems appropriate to assemble the principal factors in this situation, if only to indicate how powerful and many-sided they are. Without doubt, one of the most significant has been the weakening of religious opinion, since the Christian religion has always forbidden as a mortal sin, the use of any means to prevent the transmission of life; the existence in the past of families with ten, twelve, or even more children, which were common even among the wealthy, but which nowadays are quite exceptional, resulted from Christianity more than any other factor.

The expansion of education, which has been one of the principal factors contributing to the progress and improvement in living standards, has played a large part in reducing the number of births; it has developed in young people a perfectly reasonable wish to improve their status and it has not been difficult for them to realize that it was much easier to achieve this if they were not burdened with a large family. At the same time, education has made them aware of contraceptive methods, which allow them voluntarily to limit the size of their family, and this is an immensely important factor, which must not be lost sight of in this discussion: without it the demographic revolution which we are witnessing would never have been possible.

Many other factors have contributed to bring about the fall in the birth-rate; the influx of people into towns, where it is difficult to bring up children, the pressures of an increasingly sterile society in which the only-child and even childless families seem almost the norm, the increasing interest in travel which is a costly and heavy burden for heads of families, the temptations of modern life which have multiplied the number of artificial wants, and the increase in abortions.

These various causes of the reduction in births have all exercised an influence, in some cases with an increasing intensity, and there is another factor which at the present time is more important than these, and which is making itself increasingly felt: the significant difference between the standard of living of those without, and those with, children.

When they observe the striking contrast between the material standards of those who are voluntarily sterile and those families with three or four children, it is inevitable that young people who marry should try, as far as possible, to restrict the size of their family. In the first example, the wife works in addition to the husband; two salaries for two people spells comfort; in the second instance, the demands of the children tie the woman to the home and only the husband works: one salary for five or six people spells poverty and, if the father suffers in the least degree from ill health, it means they become destitute.

The greater the increase in the number of childless families or those with only one child, whose standard of living is high, and the greater the increase in the average material standard of the population, the greater the degree of inferiority in the standard of living endured by large families in relation to the average. Far from being recompensated for the service which it renders the nation, the normal family upon whom the future of the country depends, is at present severely penalized.

The possibility that matrimonial fecundity will continue to decrease, resulting in an accelerated depopulation, cannot be questioned; it is necessary, therefore, to remove the causes which tend to keep down the birth-rate, or to neutralize them, by encouraging fecundity.

7/3 Foreign Labour in France

Department of Overseas Trade, *France, 1924* [*see* Document 3/1], pp. 128–131.

The most striking phenomenon in the social life of France during the last 30 months has been the magnitude of the immigration movement. Recent official returns show that 180,000 alien industrial and agricultural workers were introduced through the State agencies in 1922, 262,877 in 1923, and 68,840 during the first five months of 1924. In May 1924 alien workers were entering the country at the rate of about 6,000 a week, the first three weekly statements having recorded the arrival of 6,300, 5,600 and 5,981 such immigrants. Of those introduced in 1923, 210,478 passed through the offices of the Ministry of Labour and 52,399 through those of the Ministry of Agriculture: in addition to this total of 262,877, these Ministries placed 34,553 aliens previously introduced, and brought the number of aliens for whom they found employment in that year to 297,430. They were distributed over the following occupations:

Coal mines	31,040
Iron mines	4,850
Building trades	40,457
Navvy work, etc.	24,284
Metallurgical and engineering trades	13,348
Unskilled (industrial occupations)	48,376
Agriculture	83,601
Miscellaneous	54,294
	297,430

Italians formed the largest contingent among the 262,900 immigrants in 1923, having numbered 112,500; there were 55,000 Poles, 36,500 Spaniards, 34,000 Belgians, 12,000 Portuguese, 4,300 Czechoslovaks, and 3,350 Russians. Among the minor contingents were included about 2,000 Dutch, and some British and Maltese. In the first four months of 1924 there were introduced 32,000 Italians, 11,000 Poles, 5,000 Spaniards, 7,000 Belgians, and 10,000 Portuguese. As has been often noted in the case of the European immigrants in North America, the various nationalities tend also in France to find their way in large proportions into particular branches of industrial activity: Italians are predominantly employed in the building trades, on road-making and repair, reconstruction and railway work; Poles in the coal- and iron-mines (in some cases Poles represent about half of the underground workers); Belgians in the textile, engineering, and other manufacturing industries in the North and in the Paris area. A great proportion of many nationalities, however, go into agricultural occupations: thus, in 1923, about 80 per cent of the Spaniards (especially in the regions in the South-West within a line drawn from Bordeaux to Nîmes); 42 per cent of the Poles (widely scattered but more especially in the East and North); 30 per cent of the Belgians (especially in flax, sugar-beet, dairy work in the North and East); 70 per cent of the Czechoslovaks (sugar-beet, etc.); and 31 per cent of the Portuguese. It may be noted that 102,000 immigrants in 1923 (of whom 36,000 were Poles, 33,000 Italians, and 26,000 Belgians) took up employment in the devastated areas.

The permanent settlement of these immigrants appears to be on the increase.... A considerable number of Spaniards are gradually settling down in agricultural occupations in the South-West and Pyrenean areas, as are

Belgians in the northern counties, whilst Poles, Italians and other nationalities are settling down permanently in many industrial areas. . . .

The systematic introduction of foreign industrial workers is controlled by the Ministry of Labour, whose Foreign Labour Department, with head-quarters at Paris, has frontier depots on the Belgian frontier, at Toul, Modane, Marseilles, Mentone, Perpignan and Hendaye, as well as offices at important centres such as Nantes, Bordeaux, Toulouse, and Lyons. It directs to their destination the immigrants (who come in response to specific demands of employers), facilitates the re-employment of those previously introduced, and watches the observance of the wages, working conditions, and other points which may have been stipulated in any agreements concluded with foreign governments. Such agreements, which have been made with Poland (7 September 1919), Italy (30 September 1919), with Czecho-slovakia (20 March 1920), Belgium (30 November 1921) and Luxemburg (4 January 1923), in particular the detailed agreements with the three first-named Powers, specifically provide for equality of treatment of the immi-grants with French workers as regards wages, working and living conditions, accidents, insurance, machinery for settlement of disputes, education, etc. The Labour Ministry has at its disposal as agencies the various employment offices of the Departments* and of the urban centres. The Ministry of Agriculture has several frontier stations (through which 52,000 workers were introduced in 1923).

These ministries work, as regards recruitment, in close relation with the authorities of the countries providing immigrants. In the case of industrial workers the demands of the French employers are certified and sent by the French Foreign Labour Department to the corresponding authority in the country from which the workers are sought. Foreign workmen on entry into France must produce a labour contract certified by the Foreign Labour Department or by a French employment office administered by a public authority; the only exceptions are coal-miners and agricultural workers, of which the constant dearth in France is so definitely recognized that their entry is not likely to affect the employment of French citizens. It would appear, therefore, that the number of foreign workers who pass through the govern-ment offices do not necessarily represent the total immigration into France. The labour needs, especially of French agriculture, are so great and so con-stant that probably a large number of unrecorded Spaniards, Italians, and Belgians are therein absorbed respectively in the Pyrenean and south-west areas, in Provence and Dauphiné, and in the north and north-eastern Departments.

France seems destined to receive even greater numbers of Italians and

* See Glossary.

Poles as a consequence of her own mining, metallurgical, and agricultural needs, and of the overflowing population of these countries, which no longer possess as an immigration outlet the United States, which absorbed before the war from each of these races about 250,000 to 300,000 persons a year. The extension and intensification of manifold French relations with her African possessions are also likely to lead to a considerable infiltration of population elements from these territories, although not upon a scale comparable to that resulting from the systematic introduction of the European industrial and agricultural workers.

7/4 French Family Allowances

Department of Overseas Trade, *France, 1934* [*see* Document 3/4], pp. 64–66.

In the recent social history of France probably the most signal innovation in the relations between employers and employed has been the widespread introduction of family allowances. These allowances are payments, additional to wages, made solely on the ground of the family charges of employed persons, without any precise relation to services rendered. The practice, which originated in the great war, was subsequently developed to an ever-increasing extent by most employers in several great industries (e.g. coal, mining, metallurgy, engineering, transport, building, printing, textiles, etc.). The action of the State in this respect rather precipitated its widespread application. The first Act providing unearned benefits solely on the score of family burdens was that of April 1917, under which married permanent State employees (clerical as well as manual workers) with remuneration not exceeding 3,600 francs and with one child, and those with not more than 4,500 francs, in the case of two or more children, were to receive 100 francs per child. In 1918, maximum earning limitations were suppressed, and all State employees became entitled in accordance with the number of their children of eligible age. The actual rates of benefits payable per child have been frequently altered by legislation. In 1928, the annual rates were 604, 806, 1,210, and 1,411 francs for one, two, three, four (and for each above four) children, so that all State employees with five young children were entitled to receive an annual allowance of 5,442 francs. Since that date one alteration (December 1929) has been made, raising the above rates to 660, 960, 1,560 and 1,920 francs, and thus making the annual allowance for five children 7,020 francs. By the Act of 1924 the pension or superannuation allowances of State employees are furthermore raised by 10 per cent if the beneficiaries have reared 3 children up to the age of 16, with 15 per cent for each further child so reared: and if, when pensioned, they are rearing children under 16, they are entitled to the same benefits for family burdens as if they were still in active service.

From the State viewpoint this action was in conformity with the public policy of promoting natality, which has been legislatively manifested in various directions, such as in the measures of general application relating to aid to deserving families, maternity allowances, natality bounties, or in those providing the heads of large families with special benefits under old age pensions and industrial accidents acts, under income-tax, and legacy and succession duties, or for housing, acquisition of property, railway travelling, military service. As the State employees with assimilated persons (county, municipal, railway employees) number over one and a quarter million persons, their example no doubt strongly influenced the rate of extension of the practice, which was favoured in the years 1919–1930 by the intense shortage of industrial labour and by the resultant keen competition therefor, as well as the public employees of all classes. [It was recognized that] that greater stability of staff would be secured by the employment of the large possible number of married persons with children.

The general adoption of the principle was gradually advocated in many quarters; and in March 1932 an Act was passed making compulsory the payment of family allowances by all firms or persons in industry, commerce, agriculture, or in the liberal professions, who regularly employ any staff otherwise than upon commission. Prior to the passing of this Act some 5 million employed persons of all kinds, including the State employees, are stated to have been in receipt of the allowances. Since 1920 the increase had certainly been noteworthy for the non-State or private employees: the central organization, which then grouped 56 benefit funds representing about half a million employed and distributing 65 million francs, reported in July, 1932, that it then grouped 245 funds with 1,850,000 adherents which distributed annually 380 million francs. To this total must be added the numerous firms that paid allowances without being members of an organization for that purpose, as well as the public employees of all classes, so that the approximation of five million beneficiaries would seem not too wide of the mark. It is anticipated that, as a result of the decrees published, or those to be published in 1934, about three million more employed persons will become beneficiaries under the Act of 1932.

The Act was not brought into operation until 1 October 1933, when it was applied by decree to the textile, building, mining, metallurgical, metalworking, and chemical industries in about twenty counties. Decrees relating to most, if not to all of the remaining counties are expected to appear in 1934: in these trades it was already in general application under private action. In

February 1934 the Act was extended to numerous branches of the food, paper, printing, cardboard, rubber, leather, timber, stone-working, ceramic, transport and other industries; and as from 1 April to several branches of the clothing industries, to unskilled workers, packers and warehousemen. Its application to banks and insurance companies is fixed for 25 May; and to cabinet-making, musical instruments of wood, fancy goods, brushware trades and to law-courts employees for 1 October. It was also announced that other decrees were in preparation for applying the Act to a number of wholesale and other trades.

Payment is due in respect of all children supported by the employed person, who have not passed the school-leaving age (normally 13 years), or up to the age of 16 in the case of apprentices or children pursuing their studies, or debarred by illness or infirmity from earning. The Minister of Labour is required to fix by public decree for each county minimum scales, which may be flat rates applicable to all employments therein or specific rates for specific occupations. Numerous decrees promulgated in August 1933 fixed the minimum rates. In the Seine County (Paris), for which they are the highest, they are: one child, Fcs. 1.20 daily, or Fcs. 30 monthly; two, Fcs. 2.80 or Fcs. 70; three, Fcs. 4.80 or Fcs. 120; for each after the third child, Fcs. 3.20 or Fcs. 80. They are lowest in the Cantal County: Fcs. 0.60, 1.20, 2.80 and 1.60 daily, or Fcs. 15, 30, 70, and 40 monthly. These allowances are far lower than the scales already paid by the State, railways, and various groups in the mining, metallurgical, textile and other trades to which they were made statutorily applicable. . . . Certain groups of employers already paying family allowances on a higher scale than the statutory minima, have already taken steps to reduce former rates. Thus the important Association of Textile Manufacturers of the Roubaix-Tourcoing district put into effect as from 1 March 1933 reduced scales as follows (former rates in parenthesis). One child, Fc. 1. (Fc. 1); two. Fcs. 2.40 (Fcs. 3.50 10); three, Fcs. 4.40 (Fcs. four, and each subsequent, Fcs. 3.20 (Fcs. 5); at the same time they introduced a distinction between French and foreign (non-resident in France) staff by basing payments to the latter on the value of Belgian currency, or about 30 per cent lower than the allowances to French workers. Other employers, e.g., in the building, iron and steel, engineering trades, have similarly revised their scales in a downward direction. This action was not solely dictated by the effect of the introduction of the obligatory allowance: it was due to the general trade depression, causing very frequently the reduction of wages proper, and in some cases that of family allowances only, without interference with wages rates.

In contrast with the course adopted for the execution of the Social Insurance Law, the State has not set up any new State organization or separate machinery for the administration of family allowances. The existing funds, set up by employers for controlling and ensuring the regular payment of the due allowances to their employed, are left untouched. Employers not already affiliated to such funds must, however, either join an existing approved organization of this type, or set up a new one, to be approved by the Ministry. Failure to comply is punishable by fine.

7/5 German Population Policy

D. V. GLASS, *The Struggle for Population* (Oxford, 1936), pp. 22–25.

In June 1933, Dr. Frick, Minister of the Interior, gave the opening address to the population and race-policy experts gathered together in Berlin, and emphasized the point that 'in the new Germany, the nation, the towns, and the rural communities must judge the whole field of administration from the point of view of population policy, and, where necessary, remould that administration'. Since that date the German Government has initiated a large number of measures to stimulate marriage- and birth-rates in the country. The earliest of these, and the most important so far as immediate results are concerned, was the Act for the provision of marriage loans which was passed in July 1933, and came into force in August 1933. Under this Act, 150 million marks per year are to be made available for loans to some 275,000 couples who wish to marry, but who cannot themselves afford to furnish a home and buy the necessary household equipment. The grant is obtained from revenue raised by means of the income-tax, and the loans, which at the maximum are 1,000 marks (for the period 1 August 1933 to 28 February 1934, the average loan was 620 marks), are given in the form of coupons of varying denominations which may be exchanged at shops for certain kinds of household goods – furniture, linen, kitchen utensils, wireless sets, and so forth.

It should be remembered, however, that the Act for providing marriage loans was part of the general legislation aimed at reducing unemployment. The Act, therefore, had a twofold purpose – not only to encourage marriage, but also to withdraw women from commerce and industry and so to provide employment for men. It is, in fact, hoped by this means to diminish unemployment by 400,000 in the first year and by 200,000 in each succeeding year, as well as to reduce the monetary requirements of the Unemployment Relief Fund by 200 million marks in the first year, and by an additional 100 million marks in each subsequent year. Herr Reinhardt, Secretary of State in the Ministry of Finance, and the official to whose initiative the scheme is due, believes that the result will also be to stimulate the whole of German industry. Since the Act aims at replacing women in employment by men, loans are given only when the women to be married have been employed for at least nine months in the previous two years, or, if they have been engaged in household tasks at home, only if they are replaced, when married, by domestic servants. In addition, there are, of course, domiciliary, racial, and medical requirements which the applicants must fulfil. In particular, they must not be of 'non-Aryan' extraction, and 'both of the applicants must be free from inheritable mental or physical defects, infectious diseases, or other illnesses threatening their life and appearing to prevent their marriage from being in the interest of the community'. But apart from the 'Aryan' and medical clauses, all these regulations imply that, although no upper income limit is stipulated, the loans are to be granted only to members of the working class and lower middle-class. It is important to bear this fact in mind when analysing the increase in births attributed to the Act. The couples who borrow the money have to repay it at the rate of 1 per cent per month – no interest is charged – and an inducement to have children early is given by the clause that a quarter of the initial loan is cancelled with the birth of each child. It is also to be noted that the loans are to be discontinued at the end of 1938, after which date repayments will be used to provide various child welfare services.

The other measures initiated cover a wide field, ranging from such small aids as the transference of expectant mothers and mothers with young children to better-class railway carriages during the 'rush-hours', to important modifications in the inheritance and income-tax laws in favour of large families. Under the old property tax, for example, there was a maximum exemption limit of 20,000 RM. If the inheritance exceeded this amount, the whole property was subject to the tax. Under the new laws of 16 October 1935, much larger exemptions are allowed to members of the family, 10,000 RM tax-free inheritance being allowed for the head of the family, for his wife, and for each dependent child up to a maximum of three children. And even if the inheritance exceeds the tax-free limit, only the excess is actually taxed. The new income-tax law is a very complicated one, but, briefly, it gives considerable relief to middle-class and working-class families in respect of their dependent children. This relief takes the form of tax-free allowances, and they vary from 15 per cent of the total income when there is one child, to 100 per cent when there are six children, though it should be noted that in terms of actual money the maximum allowance for six children is 9,000 RM. At the same time the new law raised the age-limit for dependent children from 21 to 25 years, provided, of course, that children of that age are still students at a recognized institution.

Among the other methods of encouraging marriage and the bringing up of children is that of giving preference to the heads of large families when allocating places in the local and central government medical services, while labour exchanges distribute vacant jobs on the same basis. Since April 1935 a family allowance system has been set up among the working-men's club doctors (Kassenärzte), so that those with a relatively large number of children receive an additional fifty marks per month for each child. In addition, a number of towns have undertaken to 'sponsor' the subsequent children of already large families. In Berlin, for example, some 2,000 additional allowances are to be given each year, amounting to thirty marks per month during the first year of the child's life, and twenty marks per month from that point until the child has completed his fourteenth year. These allowances, which are tax-free, are only to be given to the third and subsequent children, and the usual 'Aryan' and medical requirements have to be fulfilled. The 'sponsorship' does not consist only in these allowances, for the families and children honoured in this way also receive precedence when applying for jobs, flats, and houses – in fact, in any situation amenable to the influence of the city of Berlin. At the same time, because of the anti-population effects of modern urbanism, attempts are being made to transfer working-class families to semi-rural communities, where houses and allotments are provided for them. But most of these measures did not come into force until late in 1934 and can scarcely have had any effect upon the marriage- and birth-rates up to the present. The Act to which the greatest influence may be attributed is that for the provision of marriage loans.

7/6 The Population Question in Sweden

D. V. GLASS, 'Population Policy' in COLE and SMITH (eds.), *Democratic Sweden* [*see* Document 3/10], pp. 288–292.

An attempt to raise fertility by suppressing birth control and increasing the severity with which abortion is punished would make birth prevention more surreptitious but probably not less effective. There is very little record of success in the countries which have adopted this method of trying to stem the falling birth-rate. The Royal Commission realizes this clearly – in fact, its mandate categorically stated that homes which were economically badly off should not be burdened by too many children – and one of its major proposals is to make contraceptive knowledge available to everyone. It aims at making every maternal and child-welfare clinic a birth-control clinic as well. So far nothing has been done, and there is still in Sweden an obscenity law which can be directed against birth-control propaganda though in fact this has rarely been put into practice for the purpose. Sweden is, then, still behind Denmark, which has a new law, coming into force in October 1939, as a result of which public birth-control clinics will be set up in every county. However, it is hoped to put through new measures during the coming parliamentary session, and a bill for legalizing abortion on eugenic, humanitarian and medico-social grounds was passed on 18 May 1938. The present Government – probably because it is a coalition – does not intend to legalize abortion for purely economic and social reasons, but hopes to reduce the frequency of abortion by removing the causes which make women desperate enough to try any method of preventing the birth of a child. These causes it regards largely as linked up with poverty, so that in 1937 a law was passed giving free maternity care to every woman whose income was below 3,000 kr. (£150) per year, together with a gift of 75 kr for incidental expenses associated with childbirth. In addition, needy mothers are entitled to obtain sums of up to 300 kr from the State besides regular monetary help from the Poor Law authorities. Further, laws have been passed giving women employed by the State and by local authorities the right to leave of absence on pay during childbirth, and to prevent the dismissal of women on the grounds that they have or are about to have children. These changes, together with the spread of birth-control knowledge, should make women less anxious to resort to abortion and more willing to allow their pregnancies to go to term, particularly as the new laws make no distinction between married and unmarried mothers. But whether in fact that will be the result can scarcely be said in advance.

The second section of the Swedish programme consists in an attempt to encourage marriage, particularly to enable marriage to take place at an earlier age than it does now. To this end an Act was passed in 1937 granting marriage loans of up to 1,000 kr (£50) to be repaid within five years after marriage. But notice that the system differs from that in Germany. There are no part-cancellations of the loans on the birth of children, the loans are not free of interest – interest has to be paid at the same rate as that at which the State obtains its own loans, at present about 3¼ per cent – and there is no obligation for the wife to stay out of paid employment. In fact, the main idea of the loans is to enable people to marry young, when their expenses are least and their ability to repay the loans highest, and to keep them out of the difficulties in which they are usually involved by the hire-purchase system. Judging from the effects in Germany, these loans are very likely to increase the amount of marriage, but there are three points to be taken into account in considering their net result. First, the increase of marriage may be due merely to the legalization of unwedded unions, of which there are many in Sweden. Secondly, they do not really increase the ability of the professional classes to marry. In Sweden the University-educated section of the population is in rather a peculiar position. Although primary education is free and secondary education very cheap, little assistance is given to students proceeding to the Universities. At the end of a degree course a student often finds himself owing 10,000 kr or more, and such an amount must be a serious barrier to early marriage. Finally, if the result of the loans is merely to increase the amount of marriage, or to lower the average age at marriage, the Act may defeat the aims of the Royal Commission. For if the age at marriage falls this will probably mean that births occur earlier in the life of the mother. This reduces the length of the reproductive generation, and the population, once it begins to fall, will fall even more rapidly than would have been the case with a higher marriage age.

For the rest, the Swedish programme is based on the thesis enunciated by the Myrdals in their book* – that what is needed to provide an atmosphere encouraging fertility is not so much a general rise of the standard of living – though this, too, is regarded as necessary – as measures aimed at reducing the *extra* costs which having children involves. Only a brief survey of these is required here . . . They include a system of taxation more equitably graded according to the cost of family life, free meals to all schoolchildren, the re-habitation of needy families – for example, by setting them up on farms – and a complete reconstruction of the housing system. Of these measures, only the housing programme has so far been tackled, and even there most of the programme is still to be carried out. The idea is that house and flat construction should be taken over by local authorities and by the non-profit-making bodies set up by the co-operatives. A first mortage of 50 per cent of the cost of building is taken up on the open market, and of the remainder 5 per cent is given free by the local community (in addition to a free gift of the land) and 45 per cent lent by the State at the interest it has to pay for its own loans, plus a small charge for administrative expenses. It is estimated that in this way rents will be reduced by 10 to 15 per cent below the present level. In addition, the State will give subsidies to cover the cost of rent rebates to tenants with families, the rebates being up to 30 per cent for families with three children, 40 per cent for four children and 50 per cent for five children. Where the building takes the form of blocks of flats, special provisions are to be made for families, including collective crèches where for a small charge children can be looked after and fed while their mothers are at work. These provisions apply specially to urban housing, but there are similar measures for rural housing as well.

. . . People who have been impressed by journalistic eulogies of life in Sweden will be disappointed to learn that in the cities not less than 40 per

* A reference to G. and A. Myrdal, *Kris i Befolkningsfrågen.* (Stockholm 1934). (Ed.)

cent of all families with three or more children live in flats consisting of one room and a kitchen, while among the working class this proportion is over 50 per cent. In the rural areas conditions are no better, for although only one-third of rural dwellings consist of one room and a kitchen as compared with one-half in the towns, rural families are considerably larger than urban. So that the fact that there is no 'slum' problem in Sweden does not mean that housing conditions are satisfactory. Nor do the statistics of the distribution of income make a better impression, for it is probable that 200,000 children under 16 years of age (13 per cent of all children in this age group) belong to families with incomes of under 1,000 kroner (£50) per year and having three or more children to provide for. The census of 1935–1936 shows that the proportion of families having incomes of less than 1,000 kroner per year in 1935 was 23 per cent of all families with no children under 16 years of age, 19 per cent of those with one child, 19 per cent with two, 22 per cent with three, 26 per cent with four, 28 per cent with five and 33 per cent of those with six or more children. These figures of income are certainly under-estimates, but the broad fact remains that the families with the largest numbers of dependent children generally have the lowest incomes. Evidently the measures envisaged by the Royal Commission will constitute a real attempt to raise the standard of life of the Swedish family. In such a situation the question that forces itself up is not why has fertility declined, but why, with such incomes, do the people have any children at all?

The account of the growth of public interest in Sweden in the population problem may have given the impression that there is a general acknowledgment of the need for governmental action of the kind described. But this is not the case. Until very recently Professor Myrdal, whose name is most closely associated with the programme, was sneered at, while his name was used almost as an obscenity. Large families were called 'Myrdal's families', and a new verb, 'to Myrdal', meaning 'to copulate', was introduced into the language. More serious than this are the attacks from Left and Right politicians, the Left believing – as was stated in the Social Democrat newspaper *Arbetet* – that the movement was pandering to militarism, while the Right maintained that the whole programme was designed to cloak the entrance of Socialism through the back door. Even the new census of 1935, the first direct census to be taken in Sweden, was hailed with opposed cries of 'Fascism' and 'undue interference with individual liberty'. But the programme gains more adherents with the promulgation of each new measure. For whatever the man-in-the-street may think about the future of the Swedish population, it is obvious that for him the programme means gains in every direction, losses in none.

7/7 Stimulating the European Birth-Rate

D. V. GLASS, *Population* [*see* Document 7/5], pp. 87–91.

... Within the next few years, [we may] see most of the governments of Europe attempting, in their turn, to stimulate the birth-rate. The question that arises is, what kind of action is likely to have such a result?

On the positive side, we cannot learn a great deal from the experiments which have been tried in other countries. In France, Belgium, and Italy the measures applied may, it is true, have prevented an even steeper decline from taking place. But they offer no dependable solution because any possible effects have, up to the present, been imperceptible. Nor can we learn much from German experience. There has been a sharp rise in the birth-rate in that country, but the circumstances in which it occurred were so abnormal that we cannot tell how far it was influenced by external action, and how far it was due merely to the postponement of marriages during the economic depression of 1930 to 1932. On the negative side, however, we can arrive at some important conclusions. In the first place we can see the faults in some of the schemes which have been instituted. If, for example, the economic factor is really influential in keeping down the size of the family, then the family allowances given in France and Belgium cannot by themselves be very effective. Since they rarely cover more than 25 per cent of the cost of bringing up a child, they will only offer a real inducement to those people whose desire for children is relatively urgent. So far as we can tell from the size of the modern family, such people form a small proportion of the population. Nor, to take an Italian example, can we expect a significant change in the amount of marriage to result from a bachelor tax which, at its highest, is still far below the cost of a dog licence in Italy. In Germany, on the other hand, a loan of £50 may well encourage marriage among relatively poor people. But here again, although the cancellation of a quarter of the loan on the birth of a child may tend to discourage abortion to some extent, it is unlikely to effect any profound change in people's desire to have children. Above all, we should remember that the systems adopted abroad have three peculiarities. First, the basic measure in the present population campaign in France and Belgium – the family allowance – was not originally introduced for the purpose of raising the birth-rate. It was undoubtedly designed to ease the burden of the married man who was bringing up a family, but it did not aim at offering any real inducement to raise children, and although the allowances have undergone a number of modifications in the last fifteen years, none of these modifications was for the specific purpose of stimulating births. Secondly, even where, as in Italy and Germany, there have been genuine and concerted attempts by the Governments to increase the rate of population growth, the means used have been *ad hoc* – aimed at particular problems rather than at basic causes. Finally, in none of the countries examined does the Government really understand why there is this continuous fall in the birth-rate, or exactly how that fall is making itself felt. It is with this last question that we must specially be concerned.

If we are to explain why the birth-rate has fallen, and continues to fall, it is useless to stop at the intermediate stage and accept the answer – 'because of the increase in contraception and abortion'. Although that is a perfectly good explanation of how the present situation has come about, what we really need to know is, why people are restricting the size of their families. Apart from medical reasons, the frequency of which we do not know, it is evident that the small family pattern of today has been created largely from economic motives. There are other important influences – personal investigation shows that parents are, for example, affected by the fear of war in the near future – but the main factor is the cost of a large family. This does not, however, mean the simple money cost of bringing up children. What is involved is the whole complex of factors which combine to make it advantageous for people in almost all social classes to have small rather than large families. To take an example, people are not only influenced by the fact that house-rents are generally high, but also by the stereotype which speculative builders have been creating in the last fifteen years.

The whole trend of modern suburban house construction has been the setting-up of two- and three-bedroom houses. That is, private, and even public enterprise has intensified the small family movement, and helped to make conditions more difficult for the large family. Moreover, parents are now much more ambitious for their children than was the case even at the end of the nineteenth century. The prevailing aim is no longer for sons to carry on their fathers' occupations, but to begin where their fathers left off. The cost of bringing up children therefore includes many more items today – not only the mere expense of food, clothing, and housing, but the cost of 'waiting', that is, of the postponement of the earning period while the child is receiving some form of higher education, and parents have to consider, besides their income at the time, the prospects of employment in the future. Add to this the fact that large families generally form a barrier to social inter-course, particularly today when there are so many kinds of attractions out-side the home, and it is evident that very heavy pressure is being brought to bear upon people and helping to decrease their willingness to have children.

These are just a few of the factors at work in the present situation, and our knowledge will need to be supplemented by much more information before we really know all the important forces which must be circumvented if the birth-rate is to rise again. We must know, for example, the precise influence of urban life upon the family. It is obvious that the town is less fertile than the country, and that, in fact, the town depends to a very large extent upon the country for increasing or even maintaining its population. But what we have to discover is, whether the circumstances which keep down fertility in the town are inherent in urban structure, or whether they are merely part of the particular urban civilization which has been developed up to the present. The latter may be the case, for since the Industrial Revolution, at least, there has been scarcely any serious attempt to make towns not only places in which to work, but also communities in which people can satisfactorily live and bring up families. Since our civilization is largely urban this is a problem of supreme urgency.

What, further, we need to know, is the way in which the falling birth-rate is making itself felt. A variety of investigations has shown us that there is a difference in the birth-rate between social and economic classes. Briefly, the wealthier members of society tend to have smaller families than the poorer members, though there is some reason to believe that the gap is closing up because the poorer members are also limiting the size of their families. But we have only a very indistinct picture of what is taking place within each class. Different kinds of people respond in different ways to the social stimuli which present themselves. Occupations may, for example, have an important influence upon people's willingness and ability to have children. Coal-miners, to give an actual instance, generally raise large families, while textile workers have relatively few children. The reason is, apparently, that in the textile districts married women are frequently engaged in the industry, while in the coalfields they have few opportunities of obtaining employment. Also, inside the occupations there may be important differences. We do not know whether all kinds of families are showing a similar tendency to decrease, or, on the other hand, whether the large families are only very slightly affected, so that the fall in the average number of children is due, instead, to a rapid increase in the number of childless marriages. If the latter is the case, a special kind of positive measure would probably be necessary, for a stimulus which would induce already large families to become slightly larger might not have any effect upon the willingness of childless married couples to raise children.

Our conclusion is, then, rather important even though it is not positive. What seems imperative is, first, a series of detailed studies of movements within the population of this country, and, secondly, a careful analysis of the factors which are urging people to keep down the size of their families. Until this is done, attempts to raise the birth-rate will be so much struggling in the dark with small chance of success. There are only two points on which we may be fairly positive at present. First, repressive measures are unlikely to be effective; what appears to be much more necessary is the creation of a general environment conducive to the bringing up of relatively large families. Secondly, if there is to be any significant increase in the birth-rate, the major part must come from the working-class. Consequently, no action is likely to have a permanent influence unless it provides conditions in which the working-class is able to bring up children without thereby suffering from economic and social hardship.

7/8 French Social Insurance Law (1928)

JEANNENEY and PERROT, *Textes de droit* [*see* Document 3/22], pp. 376–378. (Ed. Tr.)

Article 1

Social insurance covers sickness, premature invalidity, old age, death, and allows a participation in family and maternity allowances, and involuntary unemployment benefits, in accordance with the conditions laid down in the present law.

All workers of both sexes whose total annual remuneration, of whatever kind, excluding family allowances, does not exceed 18,000 francs, are compulsorily affiliated to the social insurance scheme.

The *métayers** who usually work on their own, or with the assistance of members of their family, wives, ancestors or descendants and who do not own any part of the livestock are treated as salaried workers.

Article 2

Apart from contributions by the State, the funds for social insurance are derived from a payment equivalent to 10 per cent of all gross wages up to 15,000 francs: a 5 per cent charge on the insured, retained from his pay, [and,] a 5 per cent charge on the employer upon whom . . . (in all circumstances) the payment of this double contribution is incumbent. . . .

Article 4

Sickness insurance covers general and special medical costs, pharmaceutical costs and appliances, costs of hospitalization and treatment in a medical institution and any necessary surgical charges for the insured, his wife and children (who are) below the age of sixteen and not in employment, in accordance with the following conditions:

The insured is free to choose his doctor. . . .

(The next clause is concerned with the contribution of the insured towards treatment received.)

* See Glossary.

531

The allowances commence from the beginning of the date of sickness or treatment, which shall be regarded as the first medical consultation, and shall last for a period of six months.

Article 5

If the sick insured person is unable, after medical treatment, to continue or resume employment, he has the right, from the sixteenth day after the beginning of the illness or accident until cured or, until the expiration of the six months provided for in article 4, to a daily benefit for each working day, equivalent to an average half a day's wage. . . .

Article 9

In the period of pregnancy and the six months which follow delivery, the insured and the wife of the insured, benefit from medical and pharmaceutical allowances in accordance with the conditions and limits fixed by articles 4 and 5.

Six weeks before and after delivery, the insured enjoys by right the daily allowance referred to in article 5, on condition that she ceases all paid work during this period and has subscribed to the scheme regularly for sixty days during the three months which preceded the onset of pregnancy.

Article 10

The insured who, according to medical testimony, is still affected by complaint or injury, resulting in at least two-thirds loss of capacity, at the expiry of the period of 6 months referred to in article 4, or in the case of accident after the healing of the wound, has the right first of all to a provisional, then, if necessary, to a permanent invalidity pension. . . .

Article 12

The invalidity pension is fixed, provisionally for a period of five years. During this period the assured benefits from the provisions of article 4 relating to medical and pharmaceutical attention. . . .

The pension is withdrawn if the capacity to work becomes greater than 50 per cent. This abrogation takes effect from the date of the medical examination.

The pension is consolidated, on the basis of an expert medical opinion, at the expiry of the provisional period of five years.

Article 13

Old age insurance guarantees a retirement pension to wage earners who reach the age of sixty. . . .

Article 19

Death insurance guarantees to beneficiaries of the assured payment on death of a capital sum amounting to 20 per cent of the average annual wage. . . .

Article 21

The guarantee against unemployment is granted according to the conditions hereafter defined, to each obligatory insured person of French nationality in possession of a work contract, who finds himself in a state of involuntary unemployment through lack of work.

It guarantees for a maximum period of three months during each twelve-month period the payment of benefits amounting to 10 per cent of wages, calculated according to the rules established for sickness insurance. . . .

Article 26

The management of social insurance is entrusted in each Department* to a single *caisse départementale*. . . . These organizations, which operate within a departmental framework, are constituted and administered in conformity with the general regulations of the law of 1 April 1898 on mutual aid societies, subject to the arrangements of the present law. . . .

Article 37

On condition that they are of French nationality and that their annual income from work does not exceed 18,000 francs, farmers, cultivators and métayers who are not provided for in article 1 [as well as] artisans, small employers, non-salaried intellectual workers and generally all those who although not drawing a salary, work for their living, may be admitted, at discretion, to social insurance benefits.

7/9 Soviet Motherhood

WEBB, *Soviet Communism* [*see* Document **2/15**], vol. II. pp. 817–819.

It is, however, not enough to set women free from legal and political fetters, and even from the economic disabilities due to ancient prejudices. There is one function exclusively feminine, of supreme public importance, the due performance of which imposes on women, not only a serious strain on health, but also, in capitalist countries, a heavy financial burden. The mere expense of motherhood, coupled with that of infant care, is one of the potent causes of the chronic poverty of large sections of the wage-earning class. For centuries this was succoured only by private philanthropy, and sometimes (especially in England) as part of a system of public Poor Relief to which a

* See Glossary.

stigma of disgrace was attached. Only in the present century have some countries included, in their national systems of social insurance, a scanty and inadequate 'maternity benefit'. In the Bolshevik conception of the Remaking of Man a large place was found, from the outset, for the maintenance of the pregnant woman so that she might fulfil her function as mother, worker and citizen. Just as the man in any office or employment is repaid, as a matter of course, over and above his wage or salary, the various 'functional expenses' which he has to incur in the performance of his duties, so it is held that the woman who fulfils her peculiar function of child-bearing, although it is impossible to enable her altogether to avoid the pain and discomfort, should at least be permitted to escape from the exceptional pecuniary burden that is involved. In the USSR the whole cost of child-bearing is, as far as possible, treated as a functional expense of the woman in the performance of her public duty.

The purpose of Soviet Communism in this matter is not merely to be kind to the sufferers – not even chiefly an improvement of the health of the community, or the reduction of the frightful rate of infant mortality of tsarist Russia – but specifically the promotion of equality of conditions between men and women. It is in order to go as far as possible towards raising women to an equality with men in the performance of work, with equal opportunities in the choice of occupation, that so much more is done collectively for maternity and infancy in the U.S.S.R. than in any other country of the world. What is new in the U.S.S.R. is, of course, not the maternity hospital, nor the crèche, nor any similar service, which were not altogether unknown in tsarist Russia, and are to be seen, in tiny numbers, sporadically and capriciously provided by private philanthropy, in nearly every other country today. What is unique under Soviet Communism is the universality, ubiquity and completeness of the provision made at the public expense for all the mothers in so vast a country, where over six million births take place annually . . . .

For the women about to become a mother (*whether or not her union is legally registered*), who is employed at a wage or salary in any kind of work in town or country, or who is the wife of anyone so employed, the U.S.S.R. offers, entirely free of charge, without any individual contribution, wherever the system is in full operation, medical care during pregnancy; admission for confinement to a maternity hospital; twelve or sixteen weeks' leave of absence from her work on whatever wages she has been earning; constant medical supervision and aid; the right to be reinstated in her job when medically fit, with regular intervals every three and a half hours in which the infant can be breastfed; a grant of money for the infant's clothing, with a monthly grant for the first year towards the infant's food; and the provision of a crèche in which from two months to five years old the infant may be safely cared for during the mother's working hours. This seems, to the foreigner, an astonishing list of maternity benefits. But every one of them is covered by the conception of freeing the woman from her 'functional expenses', and from the 'economic bondage' in which her fulfilment of her exceptional function, so vital to the community, would otherwise tend to place her. The aim is, so far as this is physically possible, to set her as free to work in any occupation, to be as productive in her work, and to make as good an income from it, as if she did not become a mother. In short, in the view of Soviet Communism, maternity is never to be treated (as it sometimes is elsewhere) as if it were a misdemeanour, punishable either by summary dismissal from the job (as in the British and some other government services, and also in some private employments), or at least, in all cases, by a substantial pecuniary fine. It is in fact held that the least that should be done for the mother is to relieve her of all the pecuniary cost involved in the fulfilment of her exceptional function. The whole cost is borne, partly by the commissariat of health of each constituent or autonomous republic, and partly by the service of social insurance, in which there is no individual contribution.

We do not need to describe in any detail the maternity hospitals to be found in every city of the USSR, and, on a smaller scale, to an increasing extent in the rural centres. What is extraordinary is the degree to which this institutional provision for childbirth has already been made throughout the USSR.

7/10 Rest Homes in the Soviet Union

H. E. SIGERIST, *Socialised Medicine in the Soviet Union* (London, 1937), pp. 172–175.

It is not only very important to have vacations guaranteed to everybody, but it is equally important to have provisions made so that the worker can spend them in such a way that they will give him the maximum benefit. Where do the Soviet workers go for their vacations? Many go to *rest-homes*.

The institution of the worker's rest-home was founded in 1920 upon Lenin's initiative, In the beginning, palaces and homes of members of the bourgeoisie in town and country were taken over by the Government and were turned into such rest-homes. New buildings have been erected since then all over the country. As a rule, these rest-homes are operated by the trade unions and are financed from social insurance funds. The number of beds available has increased steadily:

Total number of beds in rest-homes operated by
the All-Union Central Council of Trade Unions

1926	36,000
1929	46,200
1932	72,000
1937 (plan)	113,000

It is obvious that not every worker can spend his vacations in such a place. The facilities although numerous are still limited, and can take care of only a definite number of people. In 1932, 4 per cent of all insured workers went to rest-homes, in 1937, 7 per cent. The physicians and the local committees of the working places select those persons who, although not ill, need a rest under medical supervision more than do other workers. I once asked a physician who was in charge of this special work whether Party members received preferential treatment. His answer was that the percentage of Party members sent to rest-homes was perhaps somewhat larger than that of non-Party members for the reason that Party members do a great deal of extra work and therefore need a rest more urgently. The total number of workers spending their vacations in rest-homes is illustrated by the following figures:

Total number of persons accommodated in rest-homes of the All-Union Central
Council of Trade Unions

1928	437,200
1932	914,000
1933	973,000
1937 (plan)	2,034,000

As an example of the utilization of rest-homes by one particular industry, an article appearing in *Pravda** may be cited. According to this article 100,000 miners from the Donbas coal-mines had special provisions made in 1936 for their vacations. Seventy-three thousand spent their holidays in rest-homes: 11,400 were sent to sanatoria in Sochi, Alupka, Yalta, and other places. A large number of the remaining miners spent their vacations on long-distance excursions.

Rest-homes should not be confused with sanatoria. They do not admit sick people although their guests are under medical control. Of the many rest-homes all over the Union that I visited, I shall describe only one, the Kalinin Rest-Home in Tarasovka near Moscow where I spent a very pleasant free day. The place is large, accommodating about 1,800 adults and 200 children. The workers live in cottages and bungalows with rooms of from two to four beds, that have been built in a wooded area with a diameter of about six miles.

* The Government newspaper. (Ed.)

Meals for the adults are served in three dining-houses, the kitchens of which are entirely mechanized. The children have their own cottages, their own kitchen, and their own personnel. They are the children of the workers who are staying in the rest-home. The mothers may see their children at any time but are free from responsibility and worry.

The principle applied in this rest-home, as elsewhere, is that of active rest or a combination of relaxation and stimulation. The workers sleep under good hygienic conditions, and diet is ample and supervised by physicians. There are play-grounds for all kinds of sport and trainers are available to advise the workers. The rest-home has a club house, a library, and a concert hall. When I arrived a famous singer from the Bolshoi Theatre in Moscow was giving a concert attended by more than a thousand people, most of whom were women, textile workers from Moscow factories. The event of the day, however, was the visit of six girl parachutists who had just set up a world record by jumping from 7,035 metres without oxygen apparatus. We had dinner together and in the afternoon a meeting was held in the open air at which the girls gave most eloquent reports of their experiences in aviation.

The director of this home, Dr. Rakhman, is a physician. He is assisted in his work by eleven other physicians and a personnel of about two hundred people. If the number of physicians seems large, it should be remembered that the children's section has close medical supervision as do nurseries everywhere. The guests of the rest-home, although not sick, also need medical examination occasionally and some general treatment. There are facilities for massage, hydro-therapy, and photo-therapy. It is very wise to utilize the vacation period for remedying minor ailments and for increasing resistance to disease.

7/11 Soviet Doctors

a WEBB, *Soviet Communism* [see Document 2/15], vol. II, pp. 842–845.

b SIGERIST, *Socialised Medicine* [see Document 7/10], pp. 130–131.

a The special point of interest in the health service of the U.S.S.R. is the fixed determination of the soviet authorities, without too narrowly counting the cost, to provide the whole country, and not the cities only, with a medical staff numerically adequate to the need, however great that may prove to be, and however difficult the task of recruiting. Tsarist Russia, within the present frontiers of the U.S.S.R., had fewer than 13,000 qualified doctors, or less than one per 7,000 of the whole population; and this, in the rural areas, meant less than one per 21,000. Soviet Communism has had in mind a standard everywhere of something like one for each thousand. Naturally this has not yet been attained. Since the end of the civil war the number of medical practitioners, nurses and other officers, two-thirds of them women, has been increasing year by year. . . . In 1928 the qualified medical practitioners stood at one to 4,000 of the population. By the middle of 1935, whilst the total staff had risen to three times the figure of 1918, the qualified medical practitioners throughout the whole U.S.S.R. had been multiplied seven times, and had become one to every 2,000 of the population. Unfortunately there is manifested among the doctors the same attraction to the cities as among the population at large, and the annual increase in their numbers was, for some time, not many more than were immediately absorbed in manning the institutions and special services, notably those in connection with the factories and schools, actually started in the rapidly growing urban areas. But each year the number of men and women completing their five years' course for qualification as medical practitioners increases; and this now enables an ever larger contingent to be annually assigned to the villages. As is usual in the U.S.S.R. for all occupations, the maximum number of candidates admitted to each of the medical colleges for training is necessarily decided by the Government, actually by the Council of Labour and Defence (STO), if only because each involves a subvention from public funds. In the absence of parental fortunes there was no way of creating anything like enough additional doctors; and moreover, no other way of making the training effectively open to all suitable persons, than providing every one who was chosen, not only with free tuition, but also with an annual stipend or scholarship varying with his means, so as to ensure at least sufficient for maintenance. Candidates for training, who may be of any age, are nominated by all sorts of bodies, mostly by trade union and school committees, though individual applications are not excluded. 'On these applications,' to take the instance of the medical school of Rostov, 'the local soviet first sits, and their recommendations come before a commission consisting of a representative of (1) the administrative medical faculty; (2) the professorial staff; (3) the trade unions; and (4) the student wokers.' Admittedly, young men and women actually engaged in manual work in industry or agriculture still enjoy some preference, and the more so if they are also of proletarian parentage. But there is now no exclusion of sons and daughters of the intelligentsia, especially if, as is usually the case, they have been temporarily engaged in manual labour. Other things being equal, those more advanced in education stand a better chance of admission than those with only elementary schooling. The mixed commission rejects candidates who are plainly unfitted for the training or for the occupation, but is naturally concerned to enrol the full number permitted.

The training for the medical practitioner in the U.S.S.R. combines, from the first, an unusual amount of practical work with theoretic teaching. 'In his

538

first year he must assist in minor medical and surgical work, including cleaning up after the work is finished. In his second year the medical student has to help in actual nursing; and in his next three years the student likewise engages in practical medical work at various hospitals, polyclinics and ambulatoria, while continuing his scientific training. When qualified, the doctor is offered a post at once. He may have specialized from the end of his third year, though this is a debatable policy. He is required to be fairly competent in all branches of medicine, as he may have to practise alone in a country district. . . . A recent regulation has made the conditions . . . more stringent.' Something like 9,000 new students are now admitted annually to the sixty-two institutions in the U.S.S.R. giving medical training, which have, in the aggregate, nearly 50,000 men and women students. There were only six such institutions in 1912. There were then no medical research institutions, whilst in 1935 there are a couple of hundred. It looks as if it may be nearly another decade before the far-flung millions, from the Baltic to the Pacific, from the Arctic Ocean to the mountains of Central Asia, can be all supplied with a fully qualified doctor for each 250 families. Yet this is the goal at which the Soviet Government steadfastly aims, and for which it persistently plans.

The reader will ask about the quality of the training thus supplied wholesale, and about the efficiency of the gigantic health service so created. Tsarist Russia, whilst it had relatively few doctors, and generally neglected nine-tenths of the population, gave the nobility and the wealthy a medical attendance that was, by contemporary standards, fairly efficient. It produced also a certain number of men of outstanding genius. . . . It is difficult to measure against this a medical profession which, under Soviet Communism, grapples with a different task. It is almost too freely admitted today by the older doctors that the average of medical attainments throughout the profession, and especially the average schooling of the medical student, are below the pre-war level. On the other hand, there is said to be a change for the better in the spirit in which the work is generally done, notably as regards enthusiasm in practice and scientific research, and in the almost universal desire 'to improve one's qualifications'. Every country practitioner now gets six months' 'study leave' on full pay every three years, an opportunity not generally provided in any other country, and one which the soviet doctor eagerly embraces. 'Even now,' in the latest and most authoritative judgment, 'it is indubitable that, although the average individual standard of medical students of today is lower than that of the fewer students in pre-revolution times, the aggregate quantity, as well as the quality, of medical aid available for the mass of the people is being enormously increased and improved.'

b To the foreign visitor one of the most striking features of Soviet medicine is the preponderance of women in the medical profession, just as the visitor to the United States is amazed to find that elementary education is almost entirely in the hands of women. Until 1934 the percentage of women among medical students increased steadily. It amounted to 52·0 per cent in 1928, 58·0 in 1931, 75·1 in 1934. The reasons are obvious. The demands of industry have already been mentioned. Although many women went into engineering, women as a rule make better doctors than engineers. The protection of mother and child requires a large number of physicians and no one is better qualified for this type of work than women. Until 1935, moreover, engineers were paid higher salaries than physicians, and during the heroic years of the first Five-Year Plan they were at the top of society. Because achievements were far more conspicuous than the physicians' work, engineering was infinitely more attractive to intelligent young men than was medicine. Women therefore were encouraged to step into the gap. Today physicians' salaries have been raised considerably. The demands of industry, although still great, are less tempestuous. Medical work finds greater recognition and more men are entering the medical schools. I have no figures available but I was told at the Commissariat in Moscow that there is a marked change in the constitution of the student body.

However, there is no doubt that women will always play a very important part in Soviet medicine. In fascist countries women are kept out of schools of higher education as a matter of policy, the result of a reactionary programme. In the United States medical schools are reluctant to admit women and many hospitals refuse them flatly. This is partly due to the fact that women physicians who marry often give up their profession. Consequently, it seems a waste of money to train them. Such reasons do not exist in the Soviet Union. Women are the equals of men not only in theory but in fact. Marriage does not interrupt a career as provisions are made to take care of the children and to simplify housekeeping. Soviet women have established themselves in the medical field and are holding a large and distinguished position in it. The reader should constantly keep in mind that the achievements described are largely the achievements of women.

7/12 Universal and Free Education

a WEBB, *Soviet Communism* [*see* Document 2/15] vol. II, pp. 890–893.

b L. JAUBERT, *La Gratuité de l'enseignement secondaire.* (Bordeaux, 1938), pp. 131–132. (Ed. Tr.)

a We need waste no words in appraising either the mere magnitude of the increase effected since 1917, or in reciting the particular achievements in 1935 of the soviet service of education. We may note, however, that so great was the social devastation of 1914–1921 that, for years, nearly all the schools and colleges in the U.S.S.R. sank down to the lowest depths, with the teachers on starvation wages; destitute alike of proper accommodation and often even of heating, together with books and writing paper, ink and pencils. So little attention could be given to education by the sorely taxed soviet authorities that it took a whole decade even to get back to the pre-war totals of schools and scholars.

The most important feature today is the extraordinary 'universalism' of the system. In the whole of the U.S.S.R., education, in the full sense of training for life, has now to be provided, as a matter of course, gratuitously and with attendance made compulsory, in every town and village, for every child, irrespective of sex or race or colour or creed or nationality even among the numerous backward races of the U.S.S.R. There is no other fragment of the earth's surface, at all comparable in extent, in which anything like this conception of an educational service prevails.

It is, indeed, firmly held that communism can be effectively established only on the basis of universal participation in the life of the community. Thus, it involves, merely to begin with, universal literacy. 'Without literacy,' said Lenin, 'no politics, but only rumours, small talk and prejudices.' When the Bolsheviks took office something like 70 or 80 per cent of the whole people were illiterate. Today, throughout European Russia at any rate, and also in all the settled parts of Siberia, all but a tiny remnant of the elderly and the aged have left this stage. 'Recently we noticed in the newspapers a news item, modestly put in small type. . . . *Everyone in Moscow who was this year called up for military service was able to read and write.*' It has taken little more than a decade to get schools in practically all the villages of the U.S.S.R., however imperfect may still be the teaching and the accommodation, and to bring, at least in all the settled areas, nearly all the children into school. In 1914, there were only seven millions at school; in 1929 there were over eleven millions. Not until 1931 could school attendance be made universally compulsory by law, and the numbers then rose to nineteen millions. Although it is not to be supposed that schools have yet reached every nook and corner of Soviet Asia, the Caucasian mountains, or the Arctic Circle, by 1935 the aggregate total on the school and college registers for full-time education of all grades had grown to over 26 millions, or one person in six. Meanwhile the number of children under 8 in kindergartens and other institutions of 'pre-schooling' had grown to over six millions, making in all thirty-three millions, or actually one in five of the census population under full-time instruction of one or other kind or grade.

The universalism in education in the U.S.S.R. is, in one respect, in outstanding contrast with the school system of Great Britain and other capitalist countries. In the Soviet Union there are no schools designed specially for the reception of the children of the middle class and the wealthy bourgeoisie or the aristocracy. All infants and children of school age and all adolescents obtaining higher education, classified merely by age or by grade of study, attend the same schools and colleges, whatever the position or the income of their parents. There is, alike in practice and in formal regulation, none of the segregation or grading of pupils according to parental rank or profession, wealth or income, which in other countries has so much influence alike on the schools themselves and on the pupils.

b It is not only an act of justice to allow each child to develop his natural abilities, it is also an act of social foresight.

The more educated a population is, the more prepared it is for the ceaseless competition which exists between countries. Experience shows that a nation which wants to keep its position in the international economic struggle must not lose any of its wealth, but, on the contrary, must utilize all its vital resources.

'Is it,' M. F. Buisson asks, 'the action of a nation which has understood the need to avail itself of its most important capital, (which is) human capital, to grant everything to 200,000 rich children and to grant only to 5 million poor children an education which will stop dead the moment they have a semblance of physical strength, and which will only allow them to be employed as cheap labour in the fields and factories?'

To maintain its position in the world after the agony of the Great War, which reduced its child population, France in particular, must make up the loss by concentrating on quality. To replace the lost *élite*, to enrich it in numbers as well as quality, to develop it to the greatest possible degree, it must make education available to everybody.

M. Zoretti, who has made a study of the whole problem of education has suggested that the solution lies in social reform. 'For us,' he says, 'education has two very different aims. But one cannot be neglected for the other. It is not even possible to separate them. There is first of all the improvement of national production, and then the preservation of the intellectual standards of the country.'

For a long time already, other countries had taken the lead over us in this respect.

At the height of the war, children in Germany who were designated by their teachers as intelligent, were able to pursue a free education in secondary schools and even in higher education, and Germany was itself merely following the example of the United States, Switzerland, and the Scandinavian countries.

Could we afford to remain backward? A nation which is not concerned with the mass of the population has no future. In the opinion of its advocates, free education was intended to be an expression of this concern.

The free *lycée* must provide secondary education with its real aim: 'to produce a democratic *élite*' by ensuring a better distribution of intellectual wealth. Individual interest is consonant with the collective interest.

7/13 National Socialist Educational Philosophy

a ROBERTS, *The House* [*see* Document 6/2c], pp. 254–257.

b B. RUST, 'Education in the Third Reich' in *Germany Speaks* [*see* Document 6/8], pp. 98–101.

a The Nazis have laid a heavy hand on education. They know that the textbooks of today are shaping the political realities of the decades to come, and accordingly have made every part of education – curiously enough, even mathematics – a training ground in Nazi ideology. As soon as the child enters an elementary school (*Grundschule*) at the age of six, his days are given over to the idealizing of the Nazis. He counts up Storm Troopers, he sews crude figures of Black Guards, he is told fairy stories of the Nazi knights who saved the civilized maiden from the bad Russian gnomes, he makes flags and swastikas. After four years of this, he emerges to the *Volkschule* or *Mittelschule*, thinking of Hitler and his cabinet in the way that we regard Christ and His disciples. Their schoolwork is secondary to their activities in the youth organizations, especially when they reach the secondary school stage.

The whole of their education is tendentious. One of the earliest reforms of National Socialism was Dr. Frick's* ban on the older form of education that failed to preach morals. Frick upbraided the teachers for having fallen behind in the national regeneration and warned them that they had to atone for their past faults by intense propaganda for the Nazis in the future. His warning particularly applied to the teaching of history. History was not a matter of objective fact, he told them, but a machine for inculcating German patriotism. All great men of the past were connected with Germany in some way or other, said Frick; all life-giving streams of civilization were due to the penetration of German blood or influence, all German history has been a struggle against encircling enemies, and never more than since brutal Imperialists

* Frick was Reich Minister of the Interior. (Ed.)

forced her into a war of self-defence in 1914 and diabolically ground her to the dust. All world-history since the war has meaning only as bearing on the rise of Adolf Hitler; no other fact in the world counts as much as the new-found regeneration of the nation and the rise of the *Führer*.

This was the pattern to which the facts had to conform. When they could not be made to do so, they omitted whole slabs of them. 'How can you do this?' I asked a noted German historian, and he replied, 'My children must eat'; and, in several other cases, the reply was that the means justified the end. The German nation was being benefited by the false teaching, and, after all, said one historian, what difference was there between propaganda in peace-time and propaganda in wartime, especially nowadays when actual military operations were probably the least important part of war? There is probably nothing more revolting in Germany, not even in the stories of physical atrocities, than the degradation of professional historians.

Rust and Hinkel are the administrative leaders of German education to-day. Bernard Rust was, for over twenty years, a schoolteacher in Hanover, but his experiences as a battalion commander in the war made him chafe at the restrictions to which he was submitted. He sought relief by interfering in provincial politics. At last his extremely pugilistic nationalism lost him his job. A schoolmaster cannot very well conduct a vendetta against the parliament of his province. At this time Rust was approaching his fiftieth year, and he was saved from starvation only because the Nazis elected him to the Reichstag and made him leader of the Hanoverian group of the Party. His promotion was rapid. He became first Commissioner and then Minister of Education in Prussia, and later, in the whole Reich, distinguishing himself at each stage by his efforts to subordinate education to Hitlerite doctrines. He claimed that even scientific subjects could be used as media for instruction in National Socialism. His doctrines naturally reflected his personal experiences, and he approached his task with a bitter feeling against the professional leaders of education in Germany, against those who merely did their jobs without interfering in politics. . . .

At present, then, education is a weapon in the fight for a Nazi *Weltanschauung*. Preference is given at all stages to Nazis. Most of the scholarships are reserved for children who have been members of some Party organization. With a few exceptions, non-Aryans are excluded, and plans are being made for the segregation of such children in special schools of their own. For nine out of ten such unfortunates, education necessarily ends at the high-school stage. The professions are closed to them.

Yet there is another side to the educational question in Germany. The Nazis have introduced order and efficiency in administration. Previously the educational system was cluttered up by too many administrative organizations. Much dead wood existed, and the ruthless pruning of Dr. Rust did much good. Moreover, it would be erroneous to assume that the earlier system was free from political elements. Many German teachers had adopted a defeatist attitude and this penetrated their whole teaching. In some of the larger cities, the children of the poorer districts were being taught Bolshevik ideas; and, throughout Germany, much evidence existed to support Rosenberg's* attacks on *Kultur-Bolschevismus*. This applied particularly to art, music, literary criticism, and history, and was quite as destructive as the super-patriotism of the Nazis – in some ways more so. Despite the good points of the German system under the Republic, it had lost much of its objectivity. Even where it was not openly subversive it suffered from faults of emphasis, such as the discarding of many non-practical subjects as mere frills. It would thus be a great mistake to assume that the Nazis took over an educational system as detached from politics, say, as the British system. Of course, this does not excuse the new Nazi tendentiousness; but it explains why, quite apart from their concept of politicized education, they were so concerned about the 'purification' of teaching. I have seen curricula from working-class schools of Berlin and Hamburg that are grotesque travesties on education; yet these had received the blessing of the Republican authorities. As recent German writers have pointed out, it was not the Nazis who started the idea of making education a field for *Kulturwaffen* – a clash between rival systems of *Kultur*: the communists set the ball rolling, the Hitlerites merely kicked the goal.

b A careful study of the situation shows that the German people are sound to the core and are gifted with just as much national sentiment as any other. Hence, the temporary lowering of their previous high standards could not have been the result of any innate inferiority, but the reason must be sought in a faulty system of education, which – notwithstanding its high intellectual achievements – tended to impair the healthy spirit of the nation, men's energies and their soundness of judgment, and to produce selfishness and a deficient sense of national solidarity. Besides, it was obvious that certain elements intending to secure private advantages for themselves by injuring the healthy forces of the nation had succeeded in achieving undue prominence in public life.

National Socialism was therefore compelled to ascertain and remove the causes that had brought about so unsatisfactory a condition, and to open up new resources capable of being used for a regeneration, the Führer, in his book *Mein Kampf*, having clearly indicated the road that had to be followed.

* Alfred Rosenberg (1893–1946), Nazi ideologist. (Ed.)

Two main causes had contributed towards the unsatisfactory results.

1. Although the intellectual capacities of young persons had been excellently trained and although they were thoroughly qualified for their vocations in after-life, the importance of knowledge for knowledge's sake had been over-estimated, whilst physical education and the training of the character and the will had been neglected. Metaphorically speaking, youth had been offered crystal-clear water to drink, but the health-giving mineral constituents contained in it had first been carefully removed. This interference was bound to do much harm to popular health.

2. Excessive importance had been attached to the individual as such, whilst it was almost forgotten that each individual is at the same time a member of a racial community, that it is only in that capacity that he can perfect his powers to their fullest extent, and that it is his duty to work for the good of that community. Such natural forms of the racial community as the family, the clan, the tribe, and the nation (natural because they are based on the ties of blood) either failed to receive the attention to which they are entitled, or they were disintegrated by an exaggerated individualism or superseded by artificial and super-national sham communities. Such a mental attitude enabled Jews and others animated by selfish motives or by international and anti-racial ideas to obtain a prominent influence upon all spheres of national life and access to high offices of state and to poison the healthy feelings of the nation by means of their educational policy.

It is the purpose of all education to prepare the rising generation for its functions in after-life as the true representatives of the nation and the State, both in a political and a cultural sense. Their training, therefore, must proceed along the lines just indicated. In conformity with the teaching of history and the laws of biological and racial science, it is necessary to train the faculties of the body, the character and the will just as much as the intellectual ones. The lost equilibrium must be restored; or rather, the harmonious co-existence of all these faculties must be maintained and developed instead of being destroyed. To be and to remain strong and healthy, has become the fundamental law governing Germany's youth, and it is the first and foremost duty of educationists to give effect to it. Such strength and health, however, is unthinkable without racial purity and the striving after a perfect racial type.

The attainment of high intellectual standards will certainly continue to be urged upon the young people; but they will be taught at the same time that their achievements must be of benefit to the national community to which they belong. As a consequence of the demand thus clearly formulated by the Nuremberg Laws*, Jewish teachers and Jewish pupils have had to quit German schools, and schools of their own have been provided by and for them as far

* A reference to the anti-semitic laws passed by the Nazis in September 1935. (Ed.)

as possible. In this way, the natural race instincts of German boys and girls are preserved; and the young people are made aware of their duty to maintain their racial purity and to bequeath it to succeeding generations. As the mere teaching of these principles is not enough, it is constantly supplemented, in the National Socialist State, by opportunities for what may be called 'community life'. By this term we mean school journeys, school camps, school 'homes' in rural neighbourhoods, and similar applications of the corporate principle to the life of schools and scholars.

History insists that every biological race deterioration coincides with the growth of big towns, that these latter exercise a paralysing effect upon community life, and that a nation's strength is rooted in its rural elements. Our National Socialist system of education pays due regard to these important considerations, and makes every effort to take the young people from the towns to the country, whilst impressing upon them the inseparable connection between racial strength and a healthy open-air life.

The systematic reform of Germany's educational system was started immediately after the coming-into-power of National Socialism, and received a great stimulus when, on 1 May 1934, a National Department of Education was established.

The steps that had to be taken comprised the internal re-organization of school teaching in accordance with the above principles, new methods for the training of teachers, and a re-modelling of the existing types of schools.

7/14 Housing Progress in Vienna

J. LEHMANN, *Down River* (London, 1939), pp. 30–31.

The main achievement, within the far-reaching general programme of advanced social legislation, which made 'Red Vienna' famous all over the world for so long and changed its appearance almost as much as the two or three great building periods of its long previous history, and in a far more humanist sense, was the slum-clearance and re-housing. Before the World War housing conditions in the city had been among the worst in Europe, overcrowding was normal and sanitation almost non-existent in the decaying hovels and barracks in which a large proportion of the working classes lived. It was natural, therefore, that the first offensive to improve the living conditions of the proletariat should have been aimed at the slums. It was not long before the giant tenement-blocks began to appear in the outer districts of Vienna, which have for years drawn hundreds of visitors to admire them aesthetically and study them scientifically; they continued to rise until the Social-Democrats, who paid for them mainly out of luxury taxes on the rich, were so crippled financially by the Dollfuss Government that all their great unfinished schemes had to be abandoned. I attended the ceremonial opening of the enormous Engels Hof, by the banks of the Danube in the Brigittenau, in July 1933. It seemed difficult then to believe that this white and splendid giant would be the last monument of the workers' own government, of the popular Revolution of 1918. There was great enthusiasm, challenging speeches were made, red flags flew from tier after tier of windows above the swarming crowds and the *tableaux vivants* of amity between manual workers, peasants, and white-collar workers set on the entrance pillars; but my friends told me that the scene was pale compared with former years, and in spite of the size of the undertaking, features were pointed out to me which showed the desperate need for increasing economy. A few years later a Catholic home for impoverished families and a neat little chapel had been built ostentatiously beside its flagless windows; and a year later than that it was a forest of regulation swastikas.

In the course of the fifteen years they were in charge, the Social-Democrats had managed to build over 50,000 new flats and 8,000 individual houses. And the 180,000 people whom they had re-housed paid ridiculously low rents for the most modern living conditions: there was no interest on borrowed money to be paid, and no landlord charges. The Karl Marx Hof, the Matteotti Hof, the Gartenstadt, and the Goethe Hof were historical landmarks in the solution of mass-housing, and a proof that it was possible to establish hygienic and beautiful living quarters within the reach of the average worker's pocket, and in harmony with an intelligent town-planning, even under capitalism.

The Socialist tenement-blocks were not only houses, but complete settlements in themselves. The largest have their own communal baths, laundries, lecture-rooms, playgrounds, and in many cases a kindergarten, a special open bath for children and a workers' library as well. They were not fortresses, as their enemies tried to maintain in February, in order to justify the use of artillery against them.* (The same enemies maintained a few years earlier they had been so scrappily built that they would collapse at any moment.) But they were a proof that the Viennese Social-Democrats laid a very strong emphasis indeed on raising the cultural level of the masses.

7/15 Swedish Housing Programmes

I. BOLTON, 'Social Services' in COLE and SMITH (eds.), *Democratic Sweden* [see Document 3/10], pp. 254–259.

* In February 1934 these tenement blocks became Socialist strongholds and were attacked by the Dollfuss Govt. (Ed.)

Housing standards in Sweden are quite different from those in England. It is true that there are no slum areas but only individual slums in Sweden, and that Swedish town planning is superb; also that the problem of housing is latterly being attacked with the usual generous civic spirit of the Swedes and with great foresight. It still remains true, however, that there is a great deal of overcrowding in Stockholm and Göteborg where housing conditions are relatively good, and that in the north, amongst the mining population and the foresters, the situation is far worse. There is no official standard of over-crowding in Sweden, and flats and houses of one room and a kitchen are more common than any other type. Middle class and working class people alike regard all their rooms, often including even the kitchen, as bed-sitting rooms with divan beds and writing desks, and the standard of a separate bedroom for every person and a common living-room is rare. They show an economy of planning in their sanitary arrangements, and even in the newer flats in Stockholm a combined lavatory and shower bath with flue ventilation is common; but the Swedes are so orderly and clean that nowhere does one find a dirty or untidy apartment, and the flue ventilated lavatories even in the hotels were never objectionable.

The town population even of small towns lives mostly in flats of five or six storeys, and in the country flats are not uncommon. There is a tendency to reduce the height of these blocks; the H.S.B.* (which is the largest co-operative working-class housing concern in Sweden) now restricts them to three or four storeys, and in the suburbs of Stockholm and the working-class flats of Göteborg three storeys is usual.

These flats are usually very well planned and built, of excellent brickwork or concrete, considerable variety of layout and elevation, with sun balconies which rarely cut off any light from the window below, and amenities such as communal well-equipped wash-houses and drying-rooms, lifts, central heating, children's playroom or gymnasium, large planted courtyards, and often a kindergarten.† There is a standard kitchen (which is an economically planned workshop pure and simple) for all new flats and cottages, whether working class or not (at any rate in the Stockholm area): these have standardized pressed steel sink and draining boards and cupboards which would appeal to any housewife but which would be prohibitive in price if they were not made in very large quantities.

* Hyresgästernas Sparkasse Byggnadsförening (the Tenants' Savings Bank and Building Society). (Footnote in Cole and Smith.)

† The H.S.B. usually provides in its large blocks of flats, kindergartens which are sometimes combined gymnasiums and workrooms. The playrooms and crèches are in charge of persons fully competent to look after infants in arms as well as older children, and children can be left for part or the whole of the day for a very small payment by the parent. There are also social rooms for the parents. (Footnote in Cole and Smith.)

Most of the cottages are built of wood with strong brick foundations, and are often sectional buildings.

While it is true that cheap housing accommodation is a serious problem in Sweden, and that conditions are far from satisfactory, the efforts being made to cope with this need are so fine that any English administrator can learn something from them.

Communal efforts to deal with the housing shortage are the usual mixture of State, municipal co-operative and voluntary activity which is characteristic of Swedish life. The policy of the State and municipalities has been to finance loans and facilitate building operations and the acquisition of sites, but to leave the actual building to private and co-operative enterprise. A large proportion of the land is State or municipally owned and is let on lease or provided free for housing purposes.

Recent legislation has been directed into four channels – the construction and improvement of houses for agricultural workers, the construction of cottage estates, the provision of block dwellings in towns and the housing of large families.

The Own Homes Fund was established in 1904 to enable people in rural areas to obtain loans at low rates of interest in order to acquire a freehold house or small holding of their own. It is a State organization with local Boards in every commune and a central Board in Stockholm. The Fund is administered by the local boards, which are subject to certain regulations and supervision of the Central Board, and which carry their own risks for the funds they administer. The amount of the loan is one-half to three-quarters of the value of the dwelling (which must not exceed £500 in value) or one-half to five-sixths of an agricultural holding, the value of which must not normally exceed £750. An additional 'bonus' loan not exceeding £75 is given for improvement of extension of agricultural holdings by increased dwelling accommodation or agricultural improvements. This loan is advanced as the work proceeds and does not have to be repaid. The amount of the loan is at present £12,500,000, and under this loan 20,000 'own homes' have been acquired, 48,000 of which are agricultural holdings. The total advances at the moment amount to £900,000 per annum.

In 1909 the State was partly responsible for the establishment of a credit organization for the purpose of advancing money on first mortgages for building purposes. The central fund, known as the Town Mortgage Fund of the Kingdom of Sweden, operates through local societies of borrowers. Unlike the Own Home Fund, it lends largely on big apartment houses and does not make a speciality of furthering new production. The State is strongly represented on the organization, and is responsible for debentures up to the amount of the original capital.

In 1920 the State Dwellings Loan Fund was established. This fund is administered by the State Buildings Bureau, and it grants credits to builders. In 1930 this work was extended by the setting up of a central fund (the Swedish Residential Credit Fund) for the purpose of granting secondary credits for apartment houses, co-operative dwelling houses and 'own homes'.

In 1933 the Government launched a programme to combat the great depression in the building trade and to reduce the housing shortage. A State fund of two and a half million pounds was established for this. ...

Most of the expenditure under the 1933 programme was on rural housing. Small farmers and crofters could claim from the State 50–80 per cent of the cost of necessary repairs and rebuilding and could borrow the remainder from the State interest free. (In 1937 it was made possible for very poor persons to receive the whole cost of the work from the State as a gift, themselves contributing only their own labour.) Altogether 50,000 houses have been affected by this scheme and have usually been rebuilt entirely. There is need for 50,000 more houses in the countryside; there are still many tied cottages attached to farms, and often these house two families. In cases of need the farmer can get help from the State at $3\frac{1}{2}$ per cent interest; in fact a recent statute enables the municipalities to use compulsion.

At the same time there was an extension of the Own Homes movement to help seasonal workers to augment their incomes. Loans up to £300 can now be obtained from the State for the purchase of a small holding of 5 to 7 acres and some stock, and for the erection of a two-roomed house; the wife usually works on the holding all the year and the man works on it during his period of unemployment. Two-thirds of the loan has to be repaid in 35 years; while the other third is not repayable, although the borrower must find the interest on it.

In 1935 the Government created a fund of £525,000 for the housing of large families. Loans are granted to municipalities and public benefit building societies for the erection of blocks of flats with a minimum of 2 rooms and a kitchen, primarily for families with three or more children. The sites must be provided free by the local authority, and the builder can borrow the whole cost from the State at 3 per cent interest repayable in 40 years: the local authority is the guarantor for 50 per cent of the loan. These buildings must conform to special regulations – there must be a playroom and crèche in charge of experts in or near the houses, a communal wash-house and a bathroom for each family. The rent is fixed by the State and is calculated on building costs only, the cost of the site being ignored. The State further gives rent rebates of 30 per cent for families with 3 children under 16, 40 per cent for 4 children, and 50 per cent for 5 or more children. Up to April 1927 the loans were granted for 2,561 such flats.

Stockholm has itself built under this scheme and has helped to promote two companies for the same purpose, i.e. Family Dwellings Ltd. (A.B.F.) which has been formed in co-operation with H.S.B. and Homes in Stockholm Ltd. (A.B.S.). During 1936–1937 the city built 170 such flats with 509 rooms; A.B.F. 324 flats; and A.B.S., which has only recently started, has planned for 1937–1938 600 flats with 2,000 rooms, half for large families and the rest for other tenants with small means. The ordinary cost of a flat of one room and a kitchen in Stockholm is £60, and the usual workman's wages £150 to £200 per annum. The income limit to qualify for cheap housing for a family of 3 children is £175 (£25 extra is allowed for each additional child). The actual rent paid by a family with 3 children for a flat of 2 rooms and a kitchen is about £25 to £45, and would be £20 where there are 5 children.

Co-operative building societies have long played an important part in the provision of houses in Sweden. In 1916 a new and more democratically constituted type of society was formed on the initiative of the Central Union of Social Labour and with the financial co-operation of the Stockholm County Council – namely, the Stockholm Co-operative Housing Society (S.K.B.). This society builds blocks of flats for its members, who pay a deposit proportional to the rent of the flat: this deposit is refunded when the tenant leaves. Up to the present the S.K.B. has built 30 blocks of dwellings totalling 1,857 flats of 1 or 2 rooms and a kitchen, of a total capital value of over £1,500,000. The City of Stockholm has a minority representation on the Board of the society.

In 1923 a still more important Co-operative Housing Society was formed – the H.S.B. (Tenants' Saving Fund and Building Society). This organization originated in Stockholm but has spread to Göteborg and nine other towns. An H.S.B. consists of a central society and a number of subsidiary societies. The central society buys all sites and finances and builds all the houses, and then sells them to the residents. Each block of flats is owned and controlled by its residents who form a separate subsidiary society, but the central society keeps the books, sells the flats and makes bulk purchases of coal, etc., for each subsidiary society. The H.S.B.s themselves are federated in a State league for arranging loans and extensive bulk purchases of building materials, etc.

In Stockholm, 12,000 people, of whom 60 per cent are working class and 40 per cent 'professional' class, live in H.S.B. flats. Rents are 25–30 per cent less than in the open market. The H.S.B. builds flats of four classes. In 'A' and 'B' types the tenants must pay a deposit of 10 per cent and 5 per cent respectively; 'C' type are let without payment to poor tenants and are subsidized by the municipality; 'D' type are also subsidized by the municipality and are reserved for large families.

H.S.B. flats are well built with central heating, lifts, mechanized wash-houses, rubbish shoots with incinerators, carpet-beating rooms, children's play-grounds, gymnasia, day nurseries and sometimes central kitchens.

The Stockholm Society also supplies good modern furniture and runs clubs, study circles, a journal, and a training school for infant and children's nurses; also a 'summer colony' where 400 members own week-end cottages.

7/16 Cheap Housing Policy in France

League of Nations, *Urban and Rural Housing* (Geneva, 1939), pp. 80–97.

Assistance by public authorities towards the building of working-class dwellings is entirely controlled by the legislation on 'cheap housing'. This legislation goes back to the *Siegfried* Law of 1894 which laid down the principles of financial assistance by the State to public utility societies building working-class dwellings. It was extended on several occasions, notably by the *Ribot* Law of 1908 on housing credit societies, established mainly to assist families of slender means to acquire small properties, and by the 1912 Law, which, because of the comparative failure of earlier provisions which had entrusted the carrying-out of the work to private societies and philanthropic institutions, provided for the setting-up of the Offices publics d'habitations à bon marché (public cheap-housing offices) by the municipal and departmental authorities. After modification by the 1922 Law, all this legislation was further developed by the *Loucheur* Law of 1928, which provided for a substantial amount of financial assistance from the public authorities. The *Bonnevay* Law of 1930 added a number of provisions regarding 'improved' cheap housing. Fresh methods of financing were introduced by a Law of 1934. The Decree of 24 May 1938 practically revives the Loucheur Law and adds certain provisions for the co-ordination of cheap housing with the slum-clearance campaign.

The aim of cheap housing is to provide families in modest circumstances with a healthy dwelling in an apartment or one-family house at a rental not exceeding a certain maximum. This 'ceiling' which, in 1928, was fixed at 1,310 francs for Paris and suburbs and 1,092 francs for the provinces, and subsequently raised by several stages to 1,900 francs for Paris and 1,529 francs for the provinces (Decree of 27 April 1937), represents a dwelling consisting of three rooms having a floor area of nine square metres each, plus kitchen and W.C., and a total habitable area of at least 45 square metres. The Loucheur Law also provided for the erection of 'medium-rent' dwellings for families in comparatively comfortable circumstances, the maximum rental being fixed at

3·6 times that laid down for cheap housing. In 1930, an intermediate type was also provided for – namely, 'improved' cheap housing, with a rental value double that of the ordinary type.

The State's object in lending funds at a rate below the open-market rate is to bring construction, rental and credit sale costs within the means of the working classes. A further contribution to this end is afforded by the tax exemptions applied to cheap housing. Furthermore, the public authorities pay a proportion of the rents of large families.

The *Offices publics d'habitations à bon marché* (Public Offices for Cheap Housing) are set up under a Decree of the *Conseil d'Etat*. They receive endowments in the form of funds or real property from the municipal or departmental authorities and may also accept donations and legacies. Their objects are the building, installation and management of cheap dwellings, the improvement of existing houses, and the creation of garden cities and allotments. The buildings thus constructed are generally intended for simple letting.

The *Sociétiés d'habitations à bon marché* (Cheap Housing Societies) may be either joint-stock companies or co-operative societies with variable capital.

They must obtain ministerial approval. Their regulations must always contain certain clauses concerning the maximum share capital, the restriction of the dividend (6 per cent on paid-up capital) and the distribution of the assets. The erection of buildings is their chief object. The buildings may be intended either for simple letting or for sale on a hire-purchase basis or for sale for cash.

The *Sociétiés de crédit immobilier* (Housing Credit Societies) are purely and simply credit organizations. The only form they may assume is that of a joint-stock company but, in order to receive ministerial approval, their regulations must always contain certain provisions concerning the object of the society, the maximum annual dividend to be distributed to shareholders, etc. Their chief object is the granting of mortgage loans for building purposes or for the purchase of individual cheap dwellings. In addition, they grant loans, to some extent, to cheap housing societies for transactions connected with hire-purchase or mortgage loans.

There are also cheap housing foundations, allotment societies and shower-bath societies which benefit by the cheap housing laws. Some mutual aid societies and regional agricultural credit societies may also serve as intermediaries for action by the public authorities.

On 1 May 1938 there were in France itself and Algeria 297 public offices and 1,090 cheap housing societies, whilst the number of building credit societies was 294.

The cheap housing movement is financed chiefly by means of State loans.

Through loans made to the Treasury by the *Caisse des dêpôts et consignations* (National Deposit and Loans Fund), the Minister of Finance grants an aggregate loan up to the amount of an appropriation which is included each year in the finance law. There is a special committee to determine the amount of the loans to be made to each organization on the basis of the building schemes submitted to it.

The rates of interest charged are, since 1928, as follows: 2 per cent for average cheap dwellings, 3 per cent for improved cheap dwellings, and 4 per cent for 'medium-rent' dwellings. The departments* and communes* may contribute up to not more than 1·5 per cent to the payment of interest and redemption charges. The State, in its turn, pays to the National deposit and loans fund interest which is settled quarterly at the average rate of the income earned from the whole of the investments made by that institution on its own account. The State therefore bears the sacrifice represented by the difference between this rate and the rate which it receives itself from cheap housing organizations.

The loans granted to the public offices and to societies and foundations for the erection of cheap housing or for the reconditioning of existing houses may not exceed 75 per cent (before 1938, 80 per cent) of the cost price. This ratio may be raised to 90 per cent if the repayment of the loan is guaranteed by the department or the commune. For 'medium-rent' dwellings, the maximum is fixed at 70 per cent.

In the case of housing credit societies, the sums remaining due from a society may not exceed five times half the capital not yet called up and the amount of securities guaranteed by the State belonging to the society and deposited by it with the National deposit and loan fund. The granting of the departmental or communal guarantee permits, however, of a considerable increase in this borrowing power.

The period for which loans are granted may not exceed forty years in the case of building organizations or twenty-five years in that of housing-credit societies. . . .

The following table shows that, after the great effort which was made between 1929 and 1932, this activity had, owing to the financial difficulties of the State, to be reduced to very modest proportions. Larger credits have, however, been granted for cheap housing in respect of the years 1938 and 1939.

Cheap housing organizations may obtain funds from loans other than those contracted with the State – e.g. by applying to the savings banks. . . . The bonds are redeemable within a period varying between twenty-five and forty years. The rate of interest must not as a rule exceed 6 per cent. Before

* See Glossary.

Loans granted to Cheap Housing Organizations.

Years	State Loans		Loans granted by savings banks
	to public offices, cheap housing societies, etc.	to housing-credit societies, etc.	
	(In millions of francs)		
1921–1928	868·1		273·9
1929	837·0		52·4
1930	1,199·9	1,188·9	63·8
1931	1,276·7	1,163·8	77·0
1932	1,031·3	1,070·9	72·1
1933	36·5	10·9	79·2
1934	111·0	236·5	88·4
1935	183·5	5·3	102·5
1936	166·6	181·5	115·0
1937	124·4	117·6	

1928 interest charges were borne entirely by the borrowing organization. Since the Loucheur Law, the State makes itself responsible for part of the interest; the organization has to defray only 2 per cent over and above redemption charges and costs. To this contribution may be added that of the department or commune, which is limited to ½ per cent.

Under a law of 1934, the Minister of Finance may request these organizations to procure the funds they need either by issuing loans, the interest on which will be guaranteed by the State, or by issuing loans secured on annual payments made by the State in the form of advances to the organizations concerned. In practice, it has been found difficult to apply this method of financing, owing to the restrictions on the money market. It seems, however, to have made it possible for the savings banks to participate to a fuller extent in the cheap housing movement.

The laws of 1919 and 1922 concerning cheap housing introduced State subsidies in favour of all organizations constructing buildings reserved chiefly for dwellings for families with at least three children under 16 years of age. These subsidies could not exceed one-third of the cost price of the building. The subsidies granted up to 1933 amounted to 550 million francs. Further, the Loucheur Law with a view to facilitating the purchase of small properties by large families, provided for the payment of a lump sum varying between 5,000 and 15,000 francs in the case of families with from three to seven or more children. In this way, nearly 596 million francs were distributed during the period 1928–1933.

Since 1934, parliament has not voted any further appropriations for the above-mentioned subsidies. Certain departments and communes, however, assume responsibility for part of the annual payments due from large families and disabled ex-service men. In this case, the State makes a contribution of half in respect of large families who receive assistance under the Law of 14 July 1913. . . .

In 1928, the number of dwellings constructed during the previous twenty years in application of the laws on cheap housing was estimated at about 60,000. With the credits granted up to 1932 under the Loucheur and Bonnevay Laws there were also built some 180,000 cheap dwellings, 15,000 'medium-rent' flats and 9,000 or 10,000 improved cheap dwellings. In order to complete the construction of the 260,000 dwellings contemplated under the Loucheur Law, there remained to be constructed 20,000 cheap dwellings and 32,000 of the intermediate type. It would seem that this programme has now been practically completed.

The sanitary condition of dwellings erected with the assistance of the public authorities must be verified by the *Comités de patronage locaux des habitations à bon marché* (Local Committees for the Promotion of Cheap Housing). Cheap dwellings comprise, in principle, a living-room-kitchen, one or more bedrooms, a small entrance hall, a lobby or porch in individual houses or a service balcony outside the living-room-kitchen, and a W.C. The minimum floor space between wall and partition is 25 square metres for dwellings consisting of one room and a kitchen, 35, 45 and 54 square metres respectively for dwellings consisting of two, three or four rooms and a kitchen. The two- and three-roomed types would seem to be the most frequent. Cheap dwellings are of good average comfort, sometimes exceeding the minimum requirements. They are not usually provided with a bathroom. To some extent this need is met by collective shower-bath establishments. Dwellings recently constructed, however, fairly frequently contain a shower-bath. 'Medium-rent' dwellings usually have a fully fitted bathroom, and those of the intermediate type are provided with a lavatory large enough to permit of the installation of a bath and geyser.

Whilst the assistance of housing credit societies has led to the creation of numerous small properties around industrial centres, the work of the public offices and cheap housing societies has been concentrated more particularly in the large towns, on the outskirts of which these bodies have erected large collective buildings. Very frequently these buildings have been grouped to form satellite cities which are provided with collective services, social centres, playgrounds, etc.

It is reported to be sometimes difficult to ensure that poor families obtain the benefit of the measures in favour of small property. Many housing credit societies, while willing to lend private individuals the amount required for the building, do not seem prepared to advance the cost of the land. Furthermore, the cost price of a small house (e.g. three rooms and a kitchen) has rarely fallen in the Paris area below 40,000 francs. If account is taken of the life insurance, and if it is supposed that the purchaser has been granted a maximum period of twenty-five years in which to complete his payments, he would have to pay an annual instalment of at least 2,500 to 3,000 francs. A few years ago, such expenditure was thought too high for many working-class families. At present, notwithstanding the increase in wages, the situation is almost the same, for the increase in building costs has raised to 3,750 or 4,500 francs the amount of the annual instalment that has to be paid for the small family houses recently erected.

For similar reasons, it is not easily possible for poor families to acquire dwellings intended to be bought on a hire-purchase system. On the other hand, a great many of the dwellings intended for simple letting are reserved for poor families and, in the first place, for large families. . . .

The *Conseil supérieur des habitations à bon marché* (Central Council for Cheap Housing) points out in its annual reports that in recent years a number of organizations have been faced by serious financial difficulties owing to delays in the payment of rents and in the repayment of sums due from individual borrowers. These delays are said to have been due not only to unemployment but in large measure to a certain agitation amongst the borrowers, who had been led to understand that they were going to obtain large reductions in their annual payments. In view of the arrears caused by this development, the National deposit and loans fund in some cases required that the guarantee of the local authorities should be implemented, with the result that a number of departments and communes were no longer willing to give their guarantee to cheap housing offices and societies. These difficulties, together with the increase in building costs, are said to have compelled many organizations to abandon their building schemes.

7/17 Consumption 1913–1914 and 1923–1924

GÜNTHER, 'Die Folgen des Krieges', in MEERWARTH, GÜNTHER, and ZIMMERMANN, *Die Einwirkung des Krieges* [*see* Document 1/10], pp. 204–209. (Ed. Tr.)

Most of the data appears to derive from upper working-class strata, in a large city: . . .

Consumption per day and full person equivalent

Period	albumen (g)	fats (g)	carbohydrates (g)	calories
July 1921	53·6	40·9	355·5	2011
July 1923	58·3	78·2	381·4	2510
1st quarter 1924	53·5	80·1	316·7	2261
2nd quarter 1924	64·5	92·4	369·8	2635
3rd quarter 1924	71·4	103·7	376·5	2752
4th quarter 1924	70·9	104·8	360·2	2668

. . . making certain adjustments, we may assume the pre-war base to have been 3,000 calories a day, which is the general assumption in nutritional science. This has never been reached again after the war; while the daily consumption of a full person equivalent amounted to two-thirds of normal in July 1923, there was an approximation to the norm in the middle of 1924, but it was nowhere near to being reached. There has been a particularly strongly marked reduction in the consumption of fats and albumen: compared with the peacetime level of 93·4 g of albumen a day, only 53·4 g in 1921 and 70·9 g at the end, in 1925; compared with 121 g of fats only 41, rising to 105 g later: even the consumption of the cheaper carbohydrates fell behind (400 g in peacetime, c. 360 g after the war). . . .

Pre-war data showed the following normal consumption of fats per annum:

	butter	dripping	artificial fats
Incomes of 2,000–3,000 M	31·0 kg	5·6 kg	4·7 kg
Incomes of 3,000–4,000 M	40·6 kg	10·3 kg	8·2 kg
Incomes over 4,000 M	46·5 kg	7·5 kg	4·6 kg

Against this, the consumption of butter for the first six months of 1924 stood, according to Tyszka, at 6·4 kg, and rose in the first six months of 1925 only to 7·8 kg. This amounts to 13 kg and 16 kg respectively for the full year, i.e. at most one half of the consumption of the lowest income group (2–3,000 M) in the pre-war statistics, and only a fraction of the consumption of the better-off. The change-over to the lower quality and the substitute is also evident, and is confirmed from other sources, although in view of the differences in the methods of calculation no exact comparisons can be made. Moreover, the quality of the artificial fat has probably improved since before the war, so that a relative increase in its consumption as against natural fats may not necessarily imply a drop in quality. . . .

We may also use a different kind of material bearing on the extent of the changes in consumption in Germany: this consists of the so-called 'calculations of total consumption', which lack the exactitude of the budget sources, but have the advantage of a much wider coverage. By using both methods together, we may hope to reduce any possible errors. We are basing our-selves on the Statistical Year-book of Germany for 1924–1925. This combines the pre-war and post-war figures in joint tables in a welcome manner. To be sure, the crude *per capita* calculations are less reliable than the calculations used so far, based on full person equivalents; but it may be assumed that the large numbers involved may reduce the error to a tolerable level. Of course, it has been one of the most important consequences of the war and the post-war period that proportions of the sexes and ages have changed appreciably in Germany since 1913, so that any tables using the number of people as divisors will be slightly inaccurate, making comparisons more difficult. Moreover, the territory of the Reich has altered. The official statistics for 1913–1914, 1922–1924 and 1926–1927 are put together in the following tables:

Grain available for consumption in Germany for human and animal food and for industrial purposes/ kg per capita

	Rye	Wheat and Spelt	Oats	Barley	Potatoes
1913–1914	153·1	95·8	128·3	108·0	700·2
1922–1923	89·7	46·5	57·1	29·3	559·6
1923–1924	105·2	57·4	87·3	41·5	433·1
1926–1927	97·2	78·8	95·3	70·5	381·9

(a) *Meat and Animal Fats, based on slaughterings cwt. million*

	Beef	Veal	Pork	Mutton	Horsemeat
1913	8·0	1·5	13·9	0·4	0·4
1923	4·6	1·1	5·1	0·3	0·4
1924	6·4	1·5	9·0	0·4	0·2
1927	7·6	1·8	15·5	0·4	0·3

(b) *Total of meat and animal fats per head, kg*

1913	43·5
1922	26·2
1923	23·2
1924	33·6

Without going into detail, we can observe a tremendous reduction in the consumption of the main grain and meat varieties. It is larger than the reduction observed in the comparison of individual budgets. There is no reason to assume that industrial consumption forms a major explanation of this fall; at any rate, no reduction there could possibly be made responsible for the overwhelming reduction in the figures as a whole.
The fall in consumption amounted to:

Between 1913–1914
and 1923–1924   Between 1913 and 1924

Rye	31%	
Wheat	40%	
Barley *per capita*	62%	
Oats	47%	
Potatoes	38%	
Meat and Animal Fats		23%
Beef		20%
Veal	total	—
Pork	consumption	35%
Mutton		—
Horsemeat		50%

The reduction in the consumption of grain is even greater than in the consumption of meat. This does not seem to tally with other observations, but may possibly be explained by the fact, mentioned above, that larger sections of the population got used to meat consumption during the war, as well as by the increasing industrialization and urbanization of the nation. Such developments tend to raise the consumption of meat. But the emphasis is on the fall in consumption as a whole rather than on the differences in detail.

7/18 The 1919 Famine in Russia

H. H. FISHER, *The Famine in Soviet Russia, 1919–1923* (New York, 1927), pp. 88–91.

The most striking examples of the horrors incident to the famine and social decay, the A.R.A.* men found in the hospitals, the children's homes – particularly the emergency institutions known as collectors – and at the railway stations. Emaciation, deformity from hunger, filth, and disease were, of course, everywhere, but more significant of the state of affairs was the shortage of materials, revealed in these brief notes made by an American on an inspection of government institutions.

Home No. 1. – There are 81 children, of whom 20 have had typhus and of whom 10 are now ill with it. There are 21 beds, 20 blankets, no bed linen or body linen, no warm clothing, no footwear, and some of the children, although they had been a month in the institution, were literally half-naked.

Hospital. – 100 adults sick, and 67 children. For the 167 there are 100 beds, 70 blankets (if rags may be called blankets) and there is no linen.

* American Relief Association. (Ed.)

Evacuation Home. – 290 children from 3 to 14 (years of age). This evacuation home, which is typical of those in the Tartar Republic, is filled with children picked up from the streets. Twenty-five is the average number received daily. Owing to the lack of space in the children's homes in Chistopol, some have to remain in this home for a month, in which accommodation is very elementary. There are no blankets, no linen, and no warm clothing. The children are in a half-naked condition.

Children's Hospital. – 184 children from 1 to 14. About 25 per cent of the cases are due to hunger, the others to disease, including tuberculosis and typhus. There are no blankets, no linen, no footwear, no warm clothing, no medicines, and the doctor has since my last visit died from typhus. The hospital is fairly clean.

Distributing Home. – There are 53 children of whom 36 are ill with typhus. There are no beds, no blankets, no linen, no laundry, and no clothing and the home is very unclean.

In the case of the hospitals, food for patients requiring a special diet was out of the question, since there was not enough of any description to keep the patients alive. Many, because they were too weak to leave, remained in the institutions and ran the double risk of dying from disease or, if they escaped that, from starvation. There were no medicines, no soap, no fuel, no water, but few worn instruments – even beds were lacking. Hunger made attendants apathetic. That these institutions were able to carry on at all was due primarily to the heroism of the doctors, who, hungry, overworked, and unremunerated, fought bravely to save others until they themselves succumbed.

The emergency children's institutions or collectors offered an even more ghastly picture than the hospitals. Usually they were housed in buildings unfit and inadequate. Confusion and disorganization reigned under the mismanagement of persons listless with hunger. The children, their bodies deformed by starvation, covered with the vermin-infested rags, huddled together on the floor like blind kittens, the sick, the starving, and the dead indiscriminately. The buildings invariably lacked even the crudest sanitary equipment, and the rooms in which these helpless creatures were confined gave off the stench of a long neglected latrine. To such places came boys and girls whose parents had died or had deserted them, ghastly caricatures of childhood, with faces emaciated and yellow, or swollen and blue, with eyes burning with the terrible sparkle of hunger, with angular shoulders and arms like flails.

Rivalling the collectors in horrors were the railway stations of the cities and junction points, where the peasants who had left their homes in panic became marooned. Here they waited for trains which never came, or for death which was inevitable.

Imagine a compact mass of sordid rags, among which are visible here and there, lean, naked arms, faces already stamped with the seal of death. Above all one is conscious of a poisonous odour. It is impossible to pass. The waiting-room, the corridor, every foot thickly covered with people, sprawling, seated, crouched in every imaginable position. If one looks closely he sees that these filthy rags are swarming with vermin. The typhus stricken grovel and shiver in their fever, their babies with them. Nursing babies have lost their voices and are no longer able to cry. Every day more than twenty dead are carried away, but it is not possible to remove all of them. Sometimes corpses remain among the living for more than five days.

Once – only once – it was decided to clean the railway station. Old rags, remnants of foodstuffs, dirty bandages, fifteen wagons of every conceivable filth were hauled out.

These inhabitants of the railway stations are refugees, homeless, starving. It has proved to be impossible to clear them out, although *thirty-six decrees* ordering it have been issued. No registration is attempted. Whence they come and whither they are going, no one knows.

A woman tries to sooth a small child lying in her lap. The child cries, asking for food. For some time the mother goes on rocking it in her arms. Then suddenly she strikes it. The child screams anew. This seems to drive the woman mad. She begins to beat it furiously, her face distorted with rage. She rains blows with her fist on its little face, on its head and at last she throws it upon the floor and kicks it with her foot. A murmur of horror arises around her. The child is lifted from the ground, curses are hurled at the mother, who, after her furious excitement has subsided, has again become herself, utterly indifferent to everything around her. Her eyes are fixed, but are apparently sightless.

One attempt was made to establish a rest-house for the refugees, but at the end of the week it became rather a death-house. It was impossible to keep it in order and it was finally closed as a spreader of contagion. It is impossible to close the railway station. *There is no way to stop this great wave of starving peasants who come to the city to die.*

The Soviet authorities tried to stop the wave and were engulfed by it. More and more the refugees came, and fewer were the trains that the demoralized, overburdened railways could deliver to move these dazed people. The stream moving westward from the Trans-Volga, clogged into pools of human misery in the Volga cities, and similar pools formed at Chealiabinsk and Orenburg of those who vainly tried to reach the fabled plenty of Siberia and Turkestan. The situation was so far beyond the resources and abilities of the local officials that they seemed no more able to stem the vast tide of human misery than to stem the current of the Volga. On ruined towns and desolated villages across the bleak, dreary steppes had fallen the heavy pall of black misery, of inert despair. . . .

7/19 French Consumption during the Inter-War Years

a MICHAEL, *Survey of France* [*see* Document 1/23,] pp. 7–10.

b *Ibid*, pp. 177–178.

a . . . the demand for meat in urban and industrial centres has increased. Not only has there been an actual increase in the numbers of city dwellers; but, after the war ex-servicemen who had acquired a taste for beef and mutton in the army have demanded more and better meat in recent years. The high wage scale since the war has enabled industrial workers in general to establish a higher standard of living than was possible before the war.

The pre-war *per capita* consumption of meat was approximately 105·4 pounds; city dwellers consumed about 116·9 and rural inhabitants about 96·1 pounds *per capita*. In the cities the *per capita* consumption was approximately 75·8 pounds of beef and veal, 13·8 pounds of mutton and goat meat, and 27·3 pounds of pork. In rural districts about 27·7 pounds of beef and veal, 6 pounds of mutton and goat meat, and 62·4 pounds of pork were consumed per inhabitant.

In 1925 the general *per capita* disappearance★ of meat was 93·1 pounds. Consumption in the cities had increased to 119·4 pounds, or 2·5 pounds above pre-war, whereas estimated disappearance★ in rural districts was only 70·3 pounds *per capita* or 25·8 pounds below the 1909–1913 average. It is probable that the *per capita* decrease in rural disappearance★ of meat is not as great as the estimates based upon the reported livestock statistics would indicate, since there are probably more cattle, sheep, swine, and goats than the published statistics indicate. But there has been a very materially lessened rural consumption and a very materially increased urban demand during the five-year period ended 1925. It is the urban demand, as modified by the domestic surplus, that quantitatively and qualitatively determines the international trade in a food product.

In 1925 the cities of France consumed approximately 76·2 pounds of beef and veal, 11·1 pounds of mutton and goat meat, and 32·1 pounds of pork per inhabitant, a *per capita* increase in beef and veal of 0·4 pound, an increase of 4·8 pounds of pork, and a small decrease in mutton of 2·7 pounds.

The domestic supply of meat animals has been considerably below the 1909–1913 average, so that the French nation has had recourse to heavy importations of meat since the war. During 1909–1913 the net importations

★ Presumably disappearance means consumption. (Ed.)

of fresh, frozen, and cured meats totalled only 7,836 short tons. During 1925 importations were over sixteen times as great, reaching 127,204 short tons.

One of the features of the meat situation that has been an outstanding development of wartime conditions has been the use of imported frozen meat. At first introduced for the use of the army and government institutions, its use has been extended to private families. At Havre, 25·1 per cent of the beef consumed in 1923 was the imported frozen product, whereas in 1924 frozen beef represented 42·4 per cent of total consumption. Seventy per cent of the mutton consumed at Havre in 1924 was frozen as compared with 60·6 per cent in 1923. The price of frozen meat, which is considerably below that of the fresh product, has extended its use to masses of the population who had previously found it beyond their means.

The consumption of bread is approximately normal, perhaps somewhat higher than before the war. With the trend of cereal production downwards, it is probable that French importation of wheat at least will equal or even exceed what is was before the war. But unless the price relationships between bread and meat are materially changed, it is probable that meat production will continue to be more profitable than the production of cereals and that further expansions in animal industry may be expected. The degree of this expansion will depend upon available supplies of feeding stuffs, and unless greater productivity is forthcoming from her soils, France must import concentrated feeds in order to increase the flocks and herds to the point of meeting the meat requirements of her people.

It is probable that, just as the influx of cheap wheat from overseas increased wheat consumption at the same time that the acreage planted to wheat was being decreased, so now the influx of cheap frozen meat will extend the use of meat to the masses of urban dwellers. At the same time the availability of cheap frozen meat is bound to react upon the price of the native product. History repeating itself indicates that the French farmer will follow the example of Danish and British agriculture and concentrate his efforts upon dairy and other high-priced animal products.

As far as the American farmer is concerned the United States has relatively only a small interest in the French meat situation. . . .

Before the war French meat importations from the United States were limited to a little over 1,112 tons of cured pork, some 470 tons of sausage, and about a half ton of salted beef, which represented about 20·2 per cent of the total French import. Although during and following the war our meat trade was considerable, it has dwindled until in 1925 we exported to France only 552 tons of cured pork, 684 tons of sausage, and minor amounts of fresh pork and beef and cured beef amounting in all to only 1 per cent of the total import.

Our trade with France in cereals has had a higher commercial interest for American agriculture than has that in meats. . . .

Before the war France purchased from the United States 4·3 per cent of her normal cereal import. During the war shipments from the United States to France greatly increased, but by 1924 had returned practically to the pre-war level. During 1925 large shipments of wheat and oats brought our cereal trade with France to almost four times the pre-war normal.

During 1925 French importations of cotton from the United States returned to almost the pre-war average, whereas the trade in tobacco increased 50 per cent.

It is probable that international trade in agricultural products between the United States and France will develop as regards cereals, tobacco, and cotton, but probably very little change is to be expected in our trade in meats unless it takes a downward trend.

b The tremendous losses of manpower, the destruction of property, and the devastation of the soil itself have taxed the recuperative powers of France to the utmost. Yet during the interval of the few years since the armistice France has, unaided, practically completed the restoration of the 10 devastated Departments.* Hundreds of thousands of farms and dwellings have been re-equipped, and since 1923 industrial and commercial activity have given steady employment to all available labourers and hundreds of thousands of workers have been recruited from neighbouring countries.

Employment at good wages has rendered possible the establishment of a higher standard of living in urban and industrial centres than has ever been before enjoyed among the masses of the people. More wheat and more meat are in demand as well as better clothing and more luxuries. This fact is of cardinal interest to the farmers of the United States, as is also the fact that more cereals are being consumed on farms, thus keeping from the markets certain supplies of food that now must be imported from abroad.

The increased urban demands for food and clothing, for which the United States supplies wheat and cotton, are probably permanent developments associated with the progress made by industry and the steady growth of the industrial population, which has been at the expense of rural communities, thus rendering farm labour scarce and expensive. Women are replacing men as tillers of the soil, and the productivity of that soil is decreasing.

Before the World War agriculture was steadily losing its position of predominance in the national economic life. Field-crop production had been on the decline more than two decades and the country lands had been slowly going to grass. Livestock numbers had not increased proportionately to the

* See Glossary.

greater available home-grown and imported forage and fodder supplies, but the live weights and quality of animals and the yield of milk had increased. The sale of livestock and animal products formed more than 70 per cent of the farmer's income. France was practically independent of outside sources of meat supply and had become an exporter of dairy products.

This situation was reached as the result of a series of adjustments to changes that had occurred in world agriculture. The world market had been flooded with American wheat, and French farmers took up animal industry, the world market became flooded with American cotton, and Australian wool and the French farmer abandoned flax, hemp, and wool production and turned his attention to meat. Now the world market is being flooded with frozen meat and the farmers are turning more and more to dairying.

The *per capita* consumption of meat, butter, milk, and wheat is increasing. France cannot meet the demand for increased supplies of animal products without abandoning still further the area under bread cereals which, under the wasteful system of scattered land holdings, cannot be economically produced in competition with the broad acres and power farming of the New World. There will be a future growing market for cereals and animal products, of which the United States can supply wheat and lard and other pork products. The improved industrial situation and the higher standard of living in the cities have created a growing demand for cotton and tobacco and in supplying these commodities the United States will take an important part.

7/20 Consumption and Depression

OHLIN, *World Economic Depression* [*see* Document 3/2], pp. 150–152.

Statistics and other sources of material which throw light on the changes in demand and consumption are exceedingly scarce. Figures for world production probably provide the best basis for an opinion regarding the variations in world consumption. It is true, however, that in many cases stocks have varied considerably from one year to another, and the magnitude of such stocks is never completely known. . . .

Consumption has naturally been affected very differently from one country to another, just as within individual countries the various groups have suffered in different degrees. As might be expected, the industrial countries record a far smaller contraction than those whose economy is largely dependent on the export of cereals or other crude products which have fallen heavily in price. The extent of the contraction has again in part depended on the social and economic organization of the countries concerned, and in part on the length of time during which conditions have been depressed.

Returns of the production and stocks of foodstuffs have shown that the world's food consumption has been well maintained in spite of the impoverishment caused by the depression. Other sources of evidence – e.g. from the retail trade – amply show that, in European countries at all events, food consumption has been but little affected. The depression has in many countries led to less serious physical want than might have been anticipated, although in the last few months conditions appear to have been aggravated in many parts of the world. Wage indices have almost everywhere fallen less rapidly than the cost-of-living indices, and State relief or insurance benefits have done much to maintain the consumption of the unemployed.

Even where incomes have fallen, however, consumption of all but the very poorest classes has on the whole been well maintained, owing to the rigidity of personal habits. It would seem that the habit of eating meat and wheat bread acquired in the past ten years in many parts of Central and Eastern Europe is resisting the recent changes. Thus, although the fall in the retail price of meat, eggs and fats has been relatively small during 1930, the consumption of these commodities was maintained in Germany, Hungary and other European countries which have been not the least affected by the depression. Indeed, so far as foodstuffs are concerned, it would appear that the upward trend of demand for animal foods, vegetables, fruit, etc., noticeable before the depression, continued to assert itself, although less strongly than before. This phenomenon has of course been partly due to the fall in prices.

The maintenance of consumption is of course also in part the result of the inability of the peasant to sell his produce except at prices greatly lower than he had anticipated. Its value to him as a consumer came to exceed its exchange value.

In Germany, the consumption of fish, eggs, groceries, sugar, coffee, tea and exotic fruits was greater in 1930 than in 1929, but for certain of these articles the figures for the first quarter of 1931 showed signs of decline. In Belgium, the rapid expansion in imports of exotic fruits was arrested, but the figures were higher than for any year except 1929. The yield of the various taxes on consumption in France was 6 per cent below the 1929 figure, but the latest monthly figures show no pronounced downward trend. In Austria, more exotic fruits, more wine, more sugar were being consumed *per capita* in 1930 than in the previous year.

The consumption of beer, wines, spirits and tobacco has, in 1931, been very considerably reduced. In Germany, the consumption of cigarettes was lower in the first quarter of 1931 by 46 per cent and that of cigars 49 per cent than in the corresponding period of 1930. The reduction in the United States was 9 per cent for cigars for the period January–May in these years. Consumption of tobacco in Italy in the first five months of 1931 was 11 per cent less than in the corresponding period of 1930. It is uncertain, however, to what extent this has been due to reduced purchasing power. Taxes on such goods have been increased in many countries, and the consequent increase in the price paid by the consumer has naturally reduced demand.

The countries mentioned above are chiefly those with a large manufacturing industry, which have suffered less than many others from the depression. The situation has been somewhat different for countries largely dependent on the production and export of primary products, although, even in their case, the decline in consumption has been mainly confined to goods other than foodstuffs. Some countries, however, whose economy is dependent upon a single raw material or upon a small number of them, have been so much affected by the depression that even their consumption of food has been radically cut down. The Gold Coast may be selected as an example.

Percentage Reduction of Imports into the Gold Coast
(From the first quarter of 1930 to the first quarter of 1931).

Canned fish	66	Milk	28
Rice	58	Gin	98
Flour	64	Sugar	60
Salt beef	42	Tobacco	69
Canned beef	94	Cigarettes	74

7/21 Changing Consumer Patterns in Germany

Ausschuss zur Untersuchung . . . der deutschen Wirtschaft [*see* Document **3/6**], General Report III, pp. 198–206. (Ed. Tr.)

Since 1924 house building and the building market generally have been extended by the investment of public funds, and at the same time the flow of public funds has loosened the ties which formerly existed between the development of house building and the development of other commodity markets, and has broken the former links between building and the trade cycle. The net addition of dwellings amounted to 94,800 in 1924, 281,100 in 1927 and 312,300 in 1929. The consumption demand generated by this building was increased by renewals of household goods and replacement buying to fill the gaps of the war and the inflation, particularly since the legal rent control on old dwellings made further resources available for such spending. Based on this long pent-up demand, the furniture industry, some branches of the iron and steel industry, the china and earthenware industry, the watch and clock industry, the handicraft branches of the wood and ironworking industries, and firms on maintenance work (e.g. painters and paper hangers), could increase their turnover appreciably. The total turnover of handicraft industry rose by about 50 per cent between 1924 and 1929.

The consumption by the German people of consumer goods in the narrower sense had seriously shrunk during the war and the inflation. Thus in the long periods of shortage a huge demand had built up, which – as soon as it had purchasing power behind it – formed the mainspring of economic expansion and was, in turn, expanded by the development of the capital goods industries. . . .

In general, the quantitative changes in the German demand for commodities depend on the changes in taste, in expectations and in quality, and similar considerations, which had a far larger influence on the different productive industries than the development of German commodity turnover as a whole.

These changes have been triggered off in part by the supply of goods which were not on sale before the war, or only on terms which kept them out of reach of large sections of the population, e.g. motor vehicles and electrical goods. The total stock of motor vehicles (excluding small motor-cycles) came to 293,000 in 1924 and 992,000 in 1929, and the number of small motor-cycles was 27,000 in 1926 and 222,000 in 1929.*

The number of radio subscribers rose from 1,580 in 1924 to 1·4 million in 1927 and about 2 million at the beginning of 1930.

The more long-established consumption goods have been transformed by mass consumption. After the stabilization of the currency the income of wage and salary earners rose. In addition, many households acquired more purchasing power by having more members at work, and freed more of it by having to spend less on the education of their children. Against this, demand based on incomes from fixed interest securities did not reach its original level after the destruction of property by inflation. There were also less favourable economic conditions for recipients of independent trading incomes, particularly in agriculture, compared with pre-war years. The shrinkage of agricultural incomes was, however, compensated in part by the granting of credits.

This shift in incomes is reflected in the demand for better mass production goods combined with a reduced demand for the highest quality goods and services. Consumption in Germany is concentrating more than in the pre-war period on products of medium quality. However, the intensity of the demand for quality differs among the various classes of consumer, and it is precisely in this greater differentiation that the development since 1924 differs from the enforced levelling of the years of war and inflation. The

* However, part of this increase is due to changes in the statistical method of enumeration. (Footnote in Original.)

transition to other and superior qualities of commodity was particularly pronounced in foodstuffs. In meat, coffee, tea, rice, grain, and flour products it is the top qualities which are in demand today.

The rising quality demanded in food, as expressed in the increasing switch from grain products to meat products, is however in part due to the changing structure of the population. The average age of the German population is today considerably higher than before the war. The share of consumers with the consumption habits of adults, and above all of urban populations, is considerably greater. . . .

The development of the demand for household goods is almost solely explained by the rising demand for quality. Even in the last pre-war years there was an ever-increasing adaptation to the dwelling standards of the middle classes, particularly among skilled workers. This was taken up again by the demand of the skilled workers after the currency stabilization, but now the rising demand has also spread among the unskilled labourers. Thus in the case of furniture, instead of painted softwood the demand is for real hardwoods. Because of the greater standardization of demand and the consequent increase in factory-made furniture, the price of quality furniture has been relatively reduced compared with pre-war. The demand for china has increased with the smaller price differential as against earthenware; in the case of watches and clocks it is the mantel clock which has shown the most marked increase in sales as an ornament, apart from the wrist watch which has found favour because of sporting activities, and is in increasing demand by women. In spite of these developments, the German demand *per capita* of many consumption goods is still far behind the quantities in demand in important comparable areas abroad.

Among the commodities which were improved in numerous ways after the war, first place is taken by the newly built dwelling. The increasing costs associated with the improved quality have been bridged by government subsidies which reduce the price of the product to the consumer. Here it is not without significance that the demand for the increase in quality came not so much from the tenants as from the Government, for social reasons. It was met above all by the better equipment of the dwelling in various ways, especially in heating, ventilation and sanitary arrangements.

In part, the changed style of life, and the closely linked alteration in concept of large sections of the population as to the necessary standard of life, found expression in the development of housing and furnishing. With a growing demand for greater choice, this development has led to a disregard for ornamentation, which has been commented upon uniformly by the representatives of the building, furniture, pottery, watch and clock, and clothing industries. Linked with this disregard for ornamentation and decoration, which had been characteristic of the last pre-war decades, was a strong standardization of the consumption habits of sections of the population formerly differentiated in this respect. These consumption habits, which foreign products had begun to influence strongly after the war, became dominant without any great differentiation among the younger urban or rural population. The altered style in housing and dress is hidden to some extent in its fundamental development by the vagaries of fashion which are particularly important in textile, footwear and leather goods production.

In clothing, less value is placed today than used to be the case on durability and solid finish, but more emphasis is laid on fashionable appearance and on the availability of a good selection.* The dictates of fashion, which had developed in dress even before the war, have since also influenced shoes, stockings and underwear. Because of the relatively high wages, there has been a strong transition in clothing from made to measure to mass-produced, factory-made goods. Contrary to the trend in outer garments, however, the quality of underwear has, according to the evidence of the experts, decreased appreciably. . . .

The altered total style of life among large sections of the population is expressed in the development of the style of housing, in the consumption patterns in furniture, in dress, and in other fields. Many experts have enumerated, for example, the growing interest in sport among wide sections of the population as an important cause of the changes in demand for their products. The investigations have shown further that among large sections of the population, in part as the consequence of increased political interest, participation in public events and public life in general take up a far larger part of their time. This has had important consequences for the disposal of their incomes. Parts of their income which were formerly used within the private household are now spent outside it, so that the household itself is relieved of expenditure for entertaining. Besides, in the general development it is worthy of note that there is not only a larger share of the employed in the total population, but also an increased employment of women, which presupposes some lightening of household burdens, aided by the technical equipment in the home. Also included here is the transition to food which does not need much preparation, even if it might cost relatively more.

7/22 Early Radios

G. LEHMANN-HORN, *Die Marktbedingungen des Rundfunks* (Berlin, 1934, Ph.D. Dissertation), pp. 16–17, 66–69. (Ed. Tr.)

* The increased demands for selection are expressed in the case of clothing also in the increased demand for post-sale alterations. (Footnote in Original.)

As far as the price of radio sets is concerned, the price of competing goods (gramophones, musical instruments) provides certain pointers. In principle, there has to be a relationship between the costs of production and distribution on the one hand, and the income level of the population on the other hand....

In order to cater for the different income levels, it is necessary to provide sets at different prices, by creating different models as well as by marketing detector, one-valve, two-valve, three-valve, and multiple valve sets.

The demand is subject to seasonal fluctuations. These may be explained in part by technical causes (e.g. better reception in cold seasons), and in part by economic ones. Increases in sales may be observed particularly at Christmas and during harvest periods in the countryside, while sales drop in the summer (travelling season).

Sales also fluctuate with the trade cycle. The published figures do not show this with full clarity, since they consist of additions and losses of subscribers and only reflect the net changes. The sensitivity to the state of prosperity appears to depend on the extent to which the country in question is already provided with radio sets. Where a high density had not yet been achieved, there is a constant growth of numbers of listeners in years of prosperity, above all with the increase in transmitting stations. Even in periods of depression the increase continues for a time, since the population will switch its expenditure from other items, like cinema, entertainments, etc. to broadcasting. The reason for that lies, no doubt, in the greater satisfaction for the same price derived from broadcasting. In addition, in slack times there is also a growth in the do-it-yourself movement, since the greater leisure associated with unemployment permits the building of sets at home which are at the same time also cheaper than those bought in the shops. For these reasons, and in spite of a growing loss of subscribers in depressions, a net increase is still registered because of the faster growth of new subscribers. However, if the general economic recession becomes too severe, there is a reduction in the number of subscribers, and above all in the sales of spare parts, even in countries of low radio density.

In countries of high density the periods of increase and decrease balance. In periods of depression there is an excess of loss, since the increase due to the poorer classes and the home-made sets is absent. These classes are already provided with radio sets. The problem is merely to sell sets to those who have little interest in broadcasting, which has a lower chance of success in hard times.

The differential sensitivity to the trade cycle can be derived in the main from the fact that in countries of low density the structural influences are stronger than the cyclical. It is above all the construction of new transmitters or the increase of power in existing ones which create new developments that are hardly, or not at all, influenced by the state of trade.

The task of the radio industry and the broadcasting company is to keep prices as low as possible and to adapt itself to variations in incomes by changing the periods of payment (e.g. in hire purchase agreements), and in this way to meet the consumer in the matter of prices. . . .

The technical development of radio has achieved a high level in the short period since the introduction of broadcasting as entertainment, and things that appeared impossible in the beginning, have already been developed after rapid laboratory work and have been made marketable. But there has been no corresponding rapid economic development to show itself in a parallel expansion of the market. The causes for this are, that on the one hand a radio receiver is a complex technical apparatus the construction of which involves corresponding costs, and on the other hand broadcasting appeared rapidly and as a wholly new commodity on the market and first had to establish for itself a space in the consumer's budget. The necessary sums were high in the beginning – the first detector-receivers cost 40 RM* – and the willingness to forgo other goods in favour of radio grew only slowly. But the purchase of a radio set remained a major effort which made it necessary for most income groups to trench into savings; they therefore hesitated, even though it is a purchase that will last for years. The expenditure on a radio receiver is less than the current expenditure on theatre, cinema, newspapers, etc., for the same time-span, but the latter are more easily absorbed because they recur in regular small amounts.

The costs of production for radio receivers are high because the market is divided into many smaller separate markets, because each of these has a non-homogeneous character, and because the costs of production as such are high. In part the reason for the absence of a larger market that would extend beyond the borders is to be sought in the patent laws; but the main reason is the desire for self-sufficiency of almost every country. The patent situation in the world radio industry is obscure. But it is clear that patent ownership makes the import of receivers into many countries either more difficult or wholly impossible. Perhaps even more than the patents, it is the customs barriers, the import prohibitions, and the currency regulations of different countries which have contributed to the splitting up of the world market. . . . To what extremes the idea of self-sufficiency is driven in some countries is shown by the Italian case, where the broadcasting company, in association with the State, has organized a prize competition for radio sets, in order to create an Italian radio industry.

If the splitting up of the world market prevents a lowering of the costs of

* C. £2 sterling. (Ed.)

production, and an extension of low costs into all countries, the lack of homogenity within the separate markets may be blamed even more for the high costs of production. Everywhere there is a multitude of types of receiver to cater for the multifarious wishes of the listeners and the different ideas of the radio industry. Moreover, each market is subject to large fluctuations, rooted either in the demand or the supply. The special conditions of the receiving locality may require sets for tropical as well as normal, conditions and the conditions of the grid may require A.C. or D.C., of the most varied voltages, beside battery sets. Again, according to the transmitters, sets must take long, medium or short waves, with higher or lower selectivity. Consumers may demand sets with large speakers, portable or combined sets, and speakers and receivers in highly variable combinations for personal reasons. If we then add the different types which cater for different income groups, the number of models is further multiplied. Price differences may be expressed in the efficiency of the set (3, 4, or 5 valves), in the sound (electro-magnetic and electro-dynamic speakers), in the serviceability (accuracy of calibration), and in appearance (loudspeakers of softwood or pressed casings). Such a variety leads to price increases. . . . But a low rate of production means that the development costs of any given technical achievement are high since sale figures are low – quite apart from the fact that the development of many models itself is very costly. Similarly, the acquisition and securing of each patent becomes more costly, and finally, – and this is the most important point – it is difficult to introduce mass production methods with their cost reducing effects. The higher the number of models, the smaller the production of each, and the more complex the storage problems of producers and retailers.

While the heterogeneity of the demand led to numerous models, the radio industry itself contributed to the increase in their number. There are two main reasons for this. First, every type demanded had numerous technically feasible solutions, and secondly, it was possible – particularly in the early years of radio – for many separate producing firms to be established, because of the low development and starting costs of receiver building, and each marketed its own models. Moreover, the market was flooded not only with numerous complete sets, but also with equally numerous and varied components performing the same functions. Technical innovations were introduced not merely for the sake of lower sales prices, but also to lower costs of production. The sale of so many models was possible, since the patent protected each separately, and in the mass of innovations, no one could judge which would turn out to be the best. Because of the low development and starting costs it was possible to combine many of the numerous innovations to produce receivers or components. Few machines had been invented –

partly because they were difficult to use – and inasmuch as it was the existing electrical engineering industry which turned to the production of receiver sets, it was able to use its existing organization and sales network. This low demand for capital was matched by a low supply of capital, for capital was not immediately available for the construction of radio receivers, or could not be made available because of the high risks. For this reason also, the use of large capital sums was avoided and this made it possible even for entrepreneurs who were without large credits, to commence production. An exception to this was formed by the huge cartel firms of the German electrical engineering industry which did have the resources for the production of receivers.

At a time when thoughts of rationalization were applied in all other fields, the explosion of broadcasting demand led to ever-increasing numbers of models, and instead of a unification of production, new dwarf companies shot up everywhere. There existed in Germany alone 80 different detector sets (autumn 1924), 131 types of valves (autumn 1927) and 40 A.C. receiver models (autumn 1928).

7/23 The Social and Cultural Significance of the Cinema

a *Le cinéma des origines à nos jours*. Préface par Henri Flescourt (Paris n.d.), pp. 281–282. (Ed. Tr.)

b LUCIANO DE FEO, 'The Cinema', in International Labour Office, *Recreation and Education* (Studies and Reports: Series G, Housing and Welfare, No. 4. Geneva, 1936), pp. 45–47.

c *Le cinéma* [*see* Document 7/23a], pp. 241–242. (Ed. Tr.)

a The stars of the cinema are the popular figures who dominate our age. Their fame is universal. Chaplin is better known throughout the world than all the important political figures. On his world tour Douglas Fairbanks was recognized by Japanese children, Chinese students, and Siamese and Hindu fans. Twenty million men dream of Greta Garbo. Tens of thousands of women have wept, wailed and become distraught as they filed past the body of Rudolph Valentino which should have been embalmed. Great theatrical actresses established an influence over cities and regions; indeed, the name of Sarah Bernhardt was known in nearly every country in the world; but had all those who talked about her or thought of her with admiration, actually heard her – or only seen her in some illustrated magazine?

Each day, with greater ease, rapidity and more resources, the cinema penetrates into the most remote corners of the world. The travelling film show which at night puts on a performance in the open air for a few *sous* before a crowd seated on the ground or on light wooden seats, projects the same image of Hollywood's most sensational star, which a few months or years before fascinated the public in Piccadilly, the Champs Elysées, or the New York Roxy. It is not a double, or an imitation, it is the real Gloria Swanson who offers her scintillating smile to the Paraguayan peasants, the small Arab boy or the workers in Lens or Essen. . . .

The stars will grow old, but their films will continue to show them in the best years of their lives; they will stop the course of their lives at the point of a dazzling, perfect and unbelievable youth; they will preserve in a marvellously crystallized form, rare moments of passion: the most noble, generous, and only really moving moments of their lives. It does not matter what the stars would have been without rouge, how they would have appeared without their false eyelashes, without the flattery of artificial lighting. . . it matters little that they are loved for what they are not, that they are taken for what they do not want to be, or cannot become . . . the stars are not real people; in the eyes of their fans they cannot be separated from the roles they play. . . .

b So far, mechanical reproduction has mainly supplied the masses with the output of persons engaged in the industry itself. Vulgarity and vulgarization are two closely connected terms. Is it not legitimate to ask whether the comparative vulgarity of popular literature, popular records and popular films is not essential to any close contact with the masses? Can one be sure that the latter would straightway have appreciated literary works which are exquisite in style and have a profound philosophical content, articles on social subjects the meaning of which eludes their impulsive grasp of life, the music of the best composers, comedies the subtleties of which are only apparent to a penetrating mind, plastic works of art which in their exaggerations and deformations may possibly be a reaction against the cold and exasperating precision of mechanical reproduction itself? Now, in their vain or snobbish anxiety to arrive at these higher forms of what they more or less pretentiously call their 'art', people engaged in the industry have succeeded, if not in making those higher forms more intelligible to the crowd, at any rate in carrying a large proportion of the latter with them; and, whatever one may say, that is a step forward. No doubt many, too many, readers neglect the literary page of their newspaper for the crime and accident columns; many gramophone enthusiasts prefer music-hall songs and tunes played on the accordion to a classical symphony or an aria sung by Caruso; many listeners-in, as soon as a lecture or a good concert is announced, hurriedly switch over to a station which is broadcasting some cheerful and ear-splitting jazz music. Yet there is also an increasing number of people who after perusing the literary and artistic columns of their newspaper proceed to read the book they have seen reviewed or to visit an exhibition; of people who after hearing good music on the radio begin to frequent the Opera and classical concerts and to play on the gramophone the tunes that have pleased them.

The statement that the mechanical reproduction of the means of expression has brought about a considerable progress in the general, intellectual and artistic education of the masses will not be questioned by anyone who can see that, in order to satisfy their customers' requirements, the newspaper, cinema, gramophone and broadcasting industries are to an ever-increasing extent employing authors and artists of excellent standing, and that the latter no longer despise media which they held for a long time to be unworthy of their art.

This tendency which is noticeable in every branch of mechanical reproduction is particularly apparent in the cinema industry, where the recent and sensational success of truly artistic and instructive productions, expressing noble sentiments or significant opinions in social matters, afford evidence that the public is undergoing a salutary evolution.

In spite of this, good and evil still co-exist in reproductive industries, nor is it certain that the former prevails over the latter. Should one wait until the public slowly and steadily eliminates what may prove harmful to it? Is such confidence in the wisdom of the crowd justified? Should one leave the work to organizations which are quite rightly shocked by the excessive triviality, stupidity or immorality of some productions, but will react more or less violently, more or less unilaterally, and will be tempted to go too far? Should one not recognize the fact that, intentionally or otherwise, the reproductive industries have launched a formidable avalanche of ideas and symbols on modern society, have taken that society by surprise and made it lose its bearings by subjecting it to an intensive education for which the various peoples and classes were not all prepared? And when the form of mechanical reproduction which will outstrip all the others, that is television, is already beginning to appear on the horizon, is it not reasonable to ask whether the time has not come to do a little tidying up on this round earth which is the home of all men?

The need for such measures where the introduction of cinemas and television in 'spare time' centres is concerned is all the more urgent in view of the fact that these centres are, as it has already been said, social institutions – that is, institutions which, by definition, aim at educating the masses.

Television and the cinema, like other reproductive industries, raise social problems of the utmost significance.

It seems that in the examination of these problems an initial principle may serve as a starting-point: man should only use a means of expression – whether it be an extremely primitive one or the most highly efficient reproductive apparatus – for his own good and that of his fellows.

This principle may be accompanied by the following comment: the extent of the damage or the good which may be done with any means of expression varies with the range of that means.

The conclusion which follows logically from this principle and comment is that the greater the range and the suggestive force of any means of expression, the more necessary will it be to watch the effects obtained and to introduce some discipline with a view to ensuring that as much good and as little evil as possible is done.

If the justice of these remarks is recognized, there will be no difficulty in admitting that they apply to the cinema and to television in relation to workers' spare time more than to any other means of spreading information and popularizing artistic and intellectual productions.

c The Russian cinema was born out of the revolution, since it is as if the companies which operated before this, even those whose heads have since assumed an important place in the history of the cinema, never really existed. The first films that Soviet Russia brought to our attention; . . . the *Demon of the Steppes, The Tsar Ivan the Terrible* have serious and sincere qualities which should be recognized, but they did not foreshadow the profound originality of the works which were to appear later.

It was Eisenstein's *Battleship Potemkin* which, in 1926, announced the new force which was developing in the Russian studios. A great deal has been written on this film, but everything which has been written can be summarized in these several lines from M. Georges Altmann: 'With Eisenstein and Potemkin, there appeared on the screen for the first time the primordial qualities of the Soviet cinema, which explain its natural position and the influence it exercises; the irresistible dynamism, the maximum use of direct expression, the return to naturalism in the cinema, the voluntary abandonment of the cinema 'star', powerful expression of group and community action and crowd scenes, the attempt to illustrate a collective soul; all these represented a new approach and were to some extent revolutionary. . . . A work which owed nothing to literature or the theatre, a film which was of the cinema and which consequently represents a land-mark in the attempt to create a real language of the cinema.'

It can be seen how far removed these principles are from those which dominate American film production. . . .

7/24 The Proletcult Theatre

H. CARTER, *The New Theatre and Cinema of Soviet Russia* (London, 1924), pp. 81–83.

... I next come to the section of the Left Group theatre under the direction of the workers themselves, who seek self-expression and are excluding professionalism in favour of voluntaryism. At the head of this division is the Proletcult theatre. This theatre is second in importance to the Meierhold theatre, from which it derives a great deal. As its name implies, it belongs to the proletarian culture movement which sprang up after the Revolution. This movement was designed to promote culture among the workers, and to encourage gifted young men and women from the common people, largely factory workers, to express themselves freely in art, drama, poetry, literature, etc. It was the culture of a class striving for self-explanation and self-publication. The founders rightly assumed that the Russian people are naturally gifted, and the common people have a rich store of natural abilities and apparently inexhaustible physical health.

At the head of the Moscow organization is V. F. Pletnev, a gifted working-man author and organizer. He has written plays and essays, and has closely concerned himself with the cultural problems of a class to which he belongs who struggle to free themselves from the tyranny of the monied classes, and seeks to make institutions, including a theatre, for their own use.

The Proletcult theatre was then conceived of as a theatre for the special use of the working-class and for promoting working-class culture. It was organized by representatives of the workers, to be controlled and directed by workers, and to admit certain instructors drawn from the old anarchist intelligentsia and the Right theatre. Its methods were designed to superimpose the modern industrial 'will' upon the traditional 'will' of the theatre, and thus to make the theatre, as far as possible, a party instrument and a State and a national one; to make the workers understand that their destiny was in their own hands, and they must no longer support the ruling and subjecting of their own lives by others; and to develop them as citizens and defenders of their country. According to the latter purpose acting was based on a system of physical drill, and at one time the Proletcult theatre was largely a recruiting ground for the army. This attempt to drill the workers through the theatre into 'cannon fodder' and to use the drilled for every passing war whim of the military governors has died down. Physical drill still forms the basis of the method of acting followed by the workers, because it is necessary to the expression of the spirit of a vital life.

Viewed historically, the Proletcult theatrical movement started in 1918, as a part of a general working-class cultural movement. It attracted the support of many able thinkers and workers, theorists and practitioners, who ever since have continued to speak and write on the ideas, ideals and methods to be pursued. Moreover, they have urged on every possible occasion that the utmost encouragement should be given, and every facility offered to the workers to express themselves, whether in literature, art, drama, or any other high form. The columns of the Press were to be thrown open to them, publication made easy, and paths of communication of all sorts opened up. They recognized the urgent need of self-explanation and self-publication by the working-class. We have only to turn to the Proletcult Bulletins published since 1917 to see the amount of time, trouble and thought expended in this endeavour to express and propagate proletarian cultural ideas. Among the many theorists one notes A. Lunacharsky, with his workers' aesthetic; P. Kergentseff, with his encouraging ideas on the self-expression of the working-class in new forms of theatre and plays, and emphasis on the importance of the Socialist Mass theatre and plays; and V. Smyschlaiev, with his carefully elaborated system for training the worker-actor. The object before all three writers was the common one of the workers themselves in building their theatre. They saw (1) that the workers were conscious of a new life; (2) that a new culture was needed; (3) that new conditions of life were likely to determine its form; and (4) that a new social synthesis must, inevitably follow.

7/25 Reading Habits in Post-Revolutionary Russia

JOHNSON, *Socialist . . . World* [*see* Document 2/26a], pp. 341–343.

The spread of education, the new leisure, the new zest for life, and the new security show themselves in a rising level of national culture. A seven hours' working day – the shortest working day in any industrial country – sends the worker home at an early hour and with a reserve of energy for other occupations. A lengthening annual holiday with pay lays up a store of strength and, through the opportunity it affords for travel, leads often to a wider outlook upon life. Insurance against sickness, infirmity, and old age removes the strain from brain and nerves, whilst the ban upon exploitation and the decreased incentive towards, and opportunity for, the development of the acquisitive instinct set men and women free for higher pursuits.

One immediate result, as we have seen, has been a new passion for reading. This is met by periodical literature and book publications.

Immense progress has been made in the press, both in quantity and quality. The Tsarist Russia of 1913 possessed 859 newspapers with a circulation approaching three million copies. The Soviet Union of 1937 possessed 8521 newspapers with a circulation of thirty-six million copies.

No less remarkable has been the progress in book production and book circulation. At the end of the First Five-Year Plan book production in the U.S.S.R. was greater than that of England, Germany, and Japan taken together.

So great is the quest for new books that one book shop in Moscow sold 1000 copies of a new edition of Leo Tolstoi's *Resurrection* in a single day: 600 copies of Pushkin's works issued in a single volume were sold in under three hours.

Tsarist Russia, in its peak year, 1912, published 133·6 million copies of books: the U.S.S.R. in 1937 published 571 million copies. In 1938 the issue was to be 700 millions.

During the twenty years from 1917 to 1937 Gorky's works have appeared in thirty-two million copies; Pushkin nineteen million; Tolstoi fourteen million; Chekhov over eleven million; Turgenev nearly eight million; and Gogol six million.

Naturally political writers and books reach astronomical figures. Eight thousand classical works of Lenin-Marxism have reached a total of 350 million copies in the past twenty years. Half of these 8,000 titles were in the national languages of the U.S.S.R.

The growth of literature among the national minorities is simply amazing when one compares it with the rigorous repression of all minority self-expression under the Tsarist regime. The Moscow International Book House, one house out of many, publishes books in 85 languages, text-books, novels, fairy tales, technical works, or translations of the classics. Nine million volumes were published in the Ukraine. Tolstoi's work is in great demand amongst the national minorities as well as in Russia proper; 61,000 copies have been published in the last year in the small republic of Armenia.

The abstruse works of Professor Einstein have scanty sale in most lands. Germany banishes the man. The sale of Einstein's books in England would, I imagine, be reckoned more readily in hundreds than in thousands. Yet in the Soviet Union the circulation had reached 55,000 between the years 1927 and 1936.

The value placed on books in the U.S.S.R. is seen in the way it houses them. The new Lenin Library in Moscow, an immense and stately building not far from the Kremlin, contains shelves which, set end to end, would stretch from London to Cambridge, and though the place is so vast, a book can be delivered to a reader in any part of the building in the briefest time. The State Librarians ransacked the world for the most efficient methods, and then improved on all by methods of their own.

The New York Public Library moved 500,000 books and took two months to do it. The twelve million volumes of the Lenin Library were transferred in three months without the interruption of a single day of reading.

In literature, as in music or art, the Soviet people look across the frontiers. They are the heirs of the ages. Shakespeare is theirs, Goethe is theirs; Balzac, Molière, Schiller, all are theirs. In the land of his birth, the 375th anniversary of Shakespeare passed unnoticed. Throughout the Soviet Union his anniversary was recorded in book, journal, and theatre, and his memory honoured by hundreds of thousands of peasants and artisans.

Shakespeare is regarded as a component part of the culture of the Soviet people. He comes into his own in a country where culture has become more truly of the people. Thousands of workers' amateur art circles are working on Shakespeare's plays, producing 'Hamlet', 'Macbeth', or 'Romeo and Juliet'. The performance of 'King Lear' was attended by 200,000 people in Moscow this spring. And the people of Kirghizia, Kazakstan, Bashkiria, and many other national republics besides can see his plays performed and read his books in their own tongue. In the small republic of Armenia 32,000 copies of Shakespeare have been sold in the last five years.

Foreign writers in general are extensively translated and widely read, Upton Sinclair, Maupassant, Victor Hugo, Anatole France, Balzac, Dickens, Darwin, and of the moderns Ernest Hemingway, H. G. Wells, Frank Norris, Lion Feuchtwanger, Heinrich Mann, Justar Regler, and Arnold Zweig.

Writers are not only read, they are created. The Soviet Union gives ample play and great encouragement, both consciously and unconsciously, to self-expression.

7/26 Parks of Culture and Rest

SIGERIST, *Socialised Medicine* [*see* Document **7/10**], pp. 166–167.

The Maxim Gorky Park, beautifully located along the Moscow River and covering an area of about 750 acres, has play-grounds for all sports and every evening you can see thousands of young people in training. Most popular is the parachute-tower. Parachute jumping has become a regular craze in the Soviet Union, and it was embarrassing to me to have to confess repeatedly that I had neither jumped from an aeroplane nor had I ever felt the desire to do so. Dancing and singing are very popular in the park. Young physical-culture and music students lead the groups in such dancing and singing. All kinds of amusements are provided but the atmosphere is totally unlike that of Coney Island or of other Western amusement parks. You will not find the blinding floods of light, nor hear the deafening noises and the shrieking laughter customary in such places. The senses are not lashed by violent means. The light is soft neon light, the crowds move gently. American visitors often report that the Russians cannot possibly be happy because they do not laugh. They do laugh and very heartily, but it is not that raucous laughter that so often scarcely conceals the tears. The Slavs and Anglo-Saxons have very different temperaments. The Russian folk-songs, as a rule, are in minor tune. Besides, there is no alcoholic hilarity in these parks.

A large section of the Maxim Gorky Park provides cultural and educational facilities. Libraries are scattered all over the place and they distribute 2,000 volumes a day. On the shore of the lake is a pavilion with newspapers and magazines that can be read in comfortable armchairs. Lectures are held and exhibitions are displayed. Chess-players can meet their partners in a special pavilion. The foreign workers have their international club. Several theatres and cinemas give performances every night. The Green Theatre, an open air theatre, attracts large numbers of people. I saw Dzerzhinski's opera 'Tikhii Don' (And Quiet Flows the Don) performed there by a cast of one thousand for an audience of twenty thousand. In ten days 200,000 Moscovites had enjoyed the opera.

Concerts are given regularly in all the parks. I cannot hear the stirring bars of Tschaikowsky's Fourth Symphony without recalling the deep shadows of the park in Kharkov, and the crowd of men and women, all dressed in white, listening enraptured to the wild outcry of Tschaikowsky's music. And the Unfinished Symphony will always remind me of a hot summer night in Sochi, on the Black Sea, when Schubert's melodies were intermingled with the music of the waves. These were great evenings and I shared them with thousands of fellow workers.

A special feature of the Maxim Gorky Park is its Children's Village where children not only find playgrounds but also technical, chemical, and photographic laboratories, and art studios in which study and play are combined harmoniously. A great deal is done in the Soviet Union for the rest and recreation of children. . . .

An average of 120,000 people visit the Gorky Park daily. On free days corresponding to our Sundays there may be as many as 250,000. And yet the park is so large, so widely extended that whoever seeks complete rest and solitude will find it. Festivals are held in the park. Students of the Moscow schools meet there at the end of the academic year. Workers of a factory may celebrate the fulfilment of their plan of production in the park. Carnival festivals are held, with fireworks, music, and masques.

Moscow, however, has more than one park. Each of them has a character of its own, as have the parks in the various cities. In the South they are conspicuous for their luxuriant vegetation. In small towns the park may be very modest, but I have spent many pleasant evenings in such small parks where the music consisted of a brass band or only a few accordion and balalaika players. The spirit was the same everywhere. And what impresses the foreign visitor most is the feeling of social security expressed on all the faces. These people are adjusted to their environments. After a day's work they rest and relax. They need not worry about their job. There is no doubt that these Parks of Culture and Rest are institutions of great hygienic significance.

7/27 The Motor-Car in Sweden and France

a M. BLOMSTEDT and F. BÖÖK (eds.), *Sweden of Today. A Survey of its Intellectual and Material Culture* (Stockholm, 1930), pp. 331–333.

b Department of Overseas Trade, *France, 1934* [*see* Document 3/4], pp. 253, 257–258.

a Motor-cars now predominate on the roads. Traffic returns show that in the neighbourhood of the larger towns the number of cars represents 95 per cent or more of the entire volume of traffic. In the prosperous agricultural districts the number of horse-drawn vehicles is still fairly large, and in such districts the percentage of motor-cars may fall to between 70 and 50. The percentage of horse-drawn vehicles on the roads is steadily declining, and the day will perhaps come when a horse-drawn cart will become a rarity.

The rapid growth of motor traffic will be seen from the following figures. In 1916 there were in Sweden no more than 5,800 motor vehicles, 3,000 of which were motor-cars and the rest motor-cycles. By 1920, the year in which the expansion began in earnest, the number of motor vehicles had increased to 52,000, of which 21,000 were cars. In 1929 the figure for motor vehicles amounted to no less than 190,000, including 135,000 motor-cars. This corresponds to one car for every 45th inhabitant. In Europe only England and France and some smaller, densely populated countries have a smaller corresponding figure. In the United States there are barely 6 inhabitants per car. It is clear that the 'saturation point' is far from reached in this country. About 29 per cent of the cars are motor-lorries, the overwhelming majority being light vehicles, 1 ton lorries and less. Cars of Swedish manufacture represent but a small proportion of the total number, American cars dominating the market completely. Indeed, these latter cars, with their powerful engines, are eminently suited to Swedish roads, which are still comparatively hilly and rough, and thanks to mass-production the prices of American cars are low. The cheap Ford car is much used in Sweden, about every fourth car in the country being a Ford. The home production of motor-cars, in which a high standard of quality has been the chief aim, is of more importance in regard to heavy motor-lorries and motor-buses than in regard to private cars. As the volume of motor traffic in the country gradually increases it is to be hoped that there will be a possibility of big-scale production of Swedish cars. It is not only cars and spare parts that are imported into the country on a large scale, but also petrol, lubricating oils, etc. Motor tyres are for the most part imported, as also the rubber for such tyres as are manufactured within the country. This heavy volume of imports, which attains a value of over 100 mill. kronor, of which over 40 mill. kronor refers to cars and spare parts alone, is one of the dark sides of the picture. Imports involve a serious dependence upon foreign countries, and any steps calculated to reduce them are well worth considering. It is possible for spirit distilled as a by-product in the manufacture of sulphite pulp to be used, partially at least, as a substitute for petrol. It remains to be seen, therefore, whether it will ever be possible to dispense with imported petrol.

Motor traffic has brought about a revolutionary change in the conditions of life, particularly out in the country districts. Distances have practically been eliminated. A 30-mile journey in a horse-drawn vehicle was formerly an undertaking that would require a whole day. Nowadays, by car, it would be a comfortable trip, taking little more than an hour. The transport of milk and other supplies to the towns is largely done by motor-lorry, and this fact has considerably widened the area from which the towns can draw their supplies. Goods are also distributed throughout the provinces by car. In every part of the country there has come into existence a network of motorbus-routes over which regular services, approved by the authorities, are maintained for the conveyance of passengers and goods. The buses have rendered it possible to establish regular, rapid, comfortable and cheap passenger and postal services, connecting up the most remote parts of the country, which could never have been made accessible by railway. It is now possible to travel by motorbus, practically without a break in the connection, from Ystad to Haparanda, and even still farther north.

Unfortunately motor traffic has given rise to a heavy toll of accidents, many of them fatal. It is to be hoped that improved roads, including particularly the abolition of railway level-crossings, and a more highly developed traffic sense, will result in a diminution of the number of accidents.

The institutions engaged in the improvement of the road-service are, apart from the Government, primarily the Royal Board of Roads and Waterways, local Road Boards and the District Road Boards, as well as a number of voluntary organizations. The State-supported Swedish Road Association, founded in 1914, has done valuable work in this field. For more than twenty years the Royal Automobile Club has worked hard for the promotion of motor traffic and for the increase of safety on the road. Scientific research in connection with road and traffic problems is being carried on, with State support out of the motor-tax funds, by the Swedish Institute of Roads, founded in 1923 and still vigorously supported by the R.A.C.

b Nearly twelve times as many passenger cars are in use today in France, as there were in 1913, the number of registered or tax-paying passenger cars having grown from 107,857 in that year to 1,279,142 at the end of 1932; since 1928, when the number was 757,668, the increase has been over half a million. Pre-war figures respecting commercial motor vehicles are not available, but since 1920 their number rose from 79,076 to 331,588 in 1928 and to 433,758 in 1932. The proportion of increase between 1931 and 1932 was 2·2 per cent in the case of passenger cars, while commercial vehicles were fewer by 4,109, or 0·9 per cent. At the end of 1932 there was a motor vehicle (exclusive of cycle-cars or motor-cycles) for every 24 inhabitants of France, whereas in 1927 there was only one for every 43 inhabitants. In point of density, therefore, France now lays claim to the highest figure save the United States (1 in 4·7), Canada (1 in 8.6) and Australia (1 in 12). The saturation point appears therefore to be not yet reached. Cycle-cars (814 in 1920) have declined continuously in number since 1926, when they attained a total of 27,541; the last three annual returns have given their numbers as 23,536, 21,550 and 18,977 respectively. By July, 1933, passenger cars had increased to 1,385,146 and commercial vehicles to 449,485.

Motor-cycling has gained favour in a remarkable manner in recent years: the number registered more than quintupled between 1924 and 1933 (96,416 and 523, 695). In 1913 it was 35,141. The boom that made its appearance in 1927, when the number of motor-cycles paying tax increased by 94,000, or 70 per cent, continued more or less during four years, the increases in 1928, 1929 and 1930–1931 being 69,700, 77,400 and 62,200 respectively. Its subsidence coincided with the first appearance of more difficult times, the yearly increment dropping to 46,000 and 12,800 in the two fiscal years 1931–1932 and 1932 (9 months). . . .

In the French motor-car industry noteworthy progress has been made in standardization during the last seven years. The industry is one in which there was particular scope for the introduction of some form of standardization, for owing to the multiplicity of small manufacturers (50 or more of whom produced between them only about 10 per cent of the total output of the country, each seeking to strike a note of individuality), there was an inevitably tendency towards an unduly large variety of designs and dimensions, even of the most ordinary parts. A normalization bureau was set up in 1926 by the association of accessory and spare parts manufacturers, and by 1928 standards had been established for 29 parts, resulting in price reductions, in some cases, of 86 to 95 per cent. For instance, the number of different types of caps for radiators and petrol tanks has been reduced from 88 to five, accumulators from 120 to seven, brake linings from 320 to 28, dynamos from 30 to four. As witness to the beneficent effects of this much-needed weeding-out of superfluous varieties, it may be mentioned that, eight months after the reduction of the number of accumulators to seven models, their price had been reduced by 20 per cent on the average, and it is quite possible that a further reduction of about 10 per cent may be realized when the old-fashioned cars, for which manufacturers still find it necessary to make accumulators of types other than the seven now adopted as standard, disappear from circulation. By January, 1933, the bureau had established standards for no less than 176 parts. Close contact is maintained with the engineering standards associations of other countries, some 18 or 20 of which have combined themselves into an international committee (*Bureau international de normalisation de l'Automobile*), with headquarters in Paris.

Government departments and public utility concerns, such as the Ministry for War and the motor transport concession holders working in collaboration with the railways, are lending useful support to the normalization movement by inserting a clause in their specifications requiring suppliers of vehicles to employ only parts conforming to the accepted standards. Promoted by the Normalization Bureau, the Society of Motor-Car Engineers was formed in 1927: it holds sectional meetings weekly and general meetings monthly, and has 1,200 members.

The tendency towards standardization was further manifested about 1929 by a fairly general decision of leading French motor-car manufacturers, whereby each firm concentrated its energies on two or three types of cars, instead of trying to cater for the whole range of motor-car users, private and industrial; the Citroën and Peugeot firms, in particular, being prominent protagonists of the new policy. The individualistic French temperament, however, proved itself too strong for this policy to be followed for long; and at the motor shows of 1931–1933 a reversion to the former practice of putting on the market as many different types of cars as each producer thought he had a chance of selling, was clearly apparent. Thus, Citroën now offers 4-cylinder cars of 9 and 10 French horse-power (the latter in three sizes for carrying from four to seven passengers), a 6-cylinder 15 h.p. car in two sizes, and is credited with the intention of producing shortly a 5 h.p. car to meet the popular demand for a very small vehicle to cope with congested traffic conditions in Paris and other large towns; Renault has cars of 7, 8, 11, 16, 14, and 41 h.p.; Mathis seven models ranging from 5 to 23 h.p.; Bugatti five (from 9 to 31 h.p.); Donnet and Talbot four each, and so on: to say nothing of the innumerable permutations rendered possible by the choice offered between many varied styles of coachwork.

7/28 Air Transport

C. DOLLFUS and H. BOUCHÉ, *Histoire de l'aeronautique. Texte et documentation* (Paris 1932), pp. 491–493. (Ed. Tr.)

Up to the present time, commercial aviation has established its most extensive network in Europe. At the present level of technique, it is in Europe too that regular air transport experiences the greatest difficulty in providing basic services. Indeed, the railway which can operate a day and night traffic, puts on trains reaching average speeds of sixty to seventy kilometres per hour on the main line systems, against which the aeroplane, capable of staying in the air for eight to twelve hours according to the season, is unable to compete. For air transport to be regarded as equivalent to rail transport, it would not be sufficient merely for air transport to provide services which were proportionate to its return fares, which remain extremely high. The public shows no indication that it is prepared to pay much more to travel by air than by rail; this has led to a policy of massive subsidies which, prevailing in Europe as elsewhere, has resulted more than elsewhere in the shocking multiplication of superfluous airlines. An incredible entanglement and constant duplication have resulted from each country wanting its own lines . . . (For example) on a route such as from Vienna to Budapest, six subsidized companies of different nationalities, share a freight which would hardly suffice to keep one of them in business.

Even in Europe, however, there are some routes where commercial aircraft provide a service and where the service would be even better, if the apparent competition were not totally illusory. For example, Paris to London is a short route, linking two vital world centres and saving travellers the boredom of the channel crossing. The same is true of the Paris–Constantinople link . . . which, in good weather, is only six to fifteen hours' flying time, while the railway takes one to three days.

In 1919 it seemed that Africa, where European activities and interests are so significant, was an area ideally suited to commercial aviation. Yet, with the exception of the Sabena Services to the Belgian Congo, it was not until 1932 that one of the great trans-African routes, from Cairo to the Cape was opened up to regular public air transport. Also, it was not until quite recently that there has been an extension of the service from Egypt to Kenya which, in 1931, opened up the northern section of this British Empire route. This operation has been characterized by major disappointments; the precarious terrain, servicing difficulties in tropical and equatorial territories; the delays incurred in despatching mail and passengers by relief planes, have all affected the local governments to an extent that, however attracted they are to the prospect of rapid subsidized communication, they have come to doubt its value at the present time.

In the light of this experience, it is easier to understand how and why France, which was particularly interested in linking up with Madagascar, . . . has not yet decided to undertake a transport link; the cost is too high and the commercial return uncertain. . . .

. . . The aeroplane and the seaplane have not yet succeeded in establishing themselves on the trans-oceanic routes. . . . Throughout the world, in 1932, no trans-maritime air service operates unbroken flights for more than one thousand kilometres. . . . Apart from the Cairo to Cape journey, the great trans-continental air routes are very few in number and the services are generally weekly. . . .

7/29 France: a Tourist Centre

a Department of Overseas Trade, *France, 1934* [*see* Document 3/4], p. 557.

b *The Times*, 29 July 1936.

a Foreign visitors, who for generations had brought a considerable contribution to the French national income, assumed in the period 1919–1930 an immense economic importance. Before 1914, France, Switzerland and Italy had stood forward as the chief resorts of tourists, but in the after-war years France for various reasons (general international sympathy for a country which had suffered invasion, desire to visit the scene of warfare, attractions of her varied climates and of her monuments, cheaper cost of living, etc.) occupied a predominant place, and reaped a rich harvest. She benefited also from the strong propensity towards travel of the ever-growing sections of modern industrial civilizations, which has been stimulated by the all-round development in the facilities for transport. Competition to share has grown most keen; and the organized efforts carried out in more recent years on an intensive scale by so many countries (Germany, Austria, Italy, Spain, Portugal, Czechoslovakia, Egypt, Belgium, Holland) constitute the signal and universal recognition of the high value to a nation of the foreign tourist traffic. The special importance attached thereto by France has been shown by the fact that she has created a special department of Government, presided over by a parliamentary Under-Secretary of State, to direct and co-ordinate matters connected with the attraction and the handling of foreign visitors. It was fully realized that the traffic provided profits not only for the transport, hotel, food and drink, and amusement industries, but also for an endless variety of trades, luxury and other, in which French achievement was conspicuous, notably in dressmaking, underwear, hosiery, woollens, silks, laces, jewellery, perfumes, fancy goods, and so forth. The annual expenditure of foreign visitors cannot of course be exactly computed. The French estimates for the best years (say 1927–1930) have put it at from 12 to 15 milliards of francs; at the par value of the franc this would represent about 100 to 125 millions sterling. This section of the invisible exports would accordingly represent about a quarter of the value of the total visible exports. The extent to which France benefited by her prosperous foreign tourist traffic is testified by the comparative desolation that has overtaken, since the world depression set in, both the numerous places or areas mainly haunted by the foreigner and the various trades of which he was a bounteous customer.

b The marked decline in the number of foreign visitors to France during the past few years formed the subject of an animated debate in the Chamber today.

Three Deputies had put down questions on this subject, and M. Spinasse, the Minister for National Economy, replied that the Government were fully alive to the position and that they intended to ask for more money to finance an extensive publicity campaign.

The Deputy for the Côte d'Or pointed out that in a good year foreign visitors to France spent up to 15,000,000,000f. (£200,000,000) in the country. In 1927 about 2,125,000 foreigners had visited France, but in 1934 the number was no more than 700,000 – yet other countries were improving their position. Germany, Russia, Italy, and Great Britain were all spending large sums on travel propaganda, and he thought that France ought to follow their example.

King Edward's decision to cancel his Riviera holiday and Mr. Baldwin's intention to spend his holiday in England instead of at Aix-les-Bains were discussed by the Deputy for the Haute Savoie, who said that these cancellations would involve French hotel proprietors in serious losses.

People were not coming to France, he said, because they feared disorder. Moreover, French prices were much too high. He thought they ought to copy the Italian example and to create a special tourist currency which would enable them to offer foreign visitors a holiday in France on moderate terms.

M. Spinasse admitted that the present appropriation for tourist propaganda was inadequate, but remarked that the number of foreign visitors in 1936 was nearly 28 per cent higher than it had been last year. He thought that the root of their difficulties lay in the fact that so many foreign countries placed obstacles in the way of their nationals who wanted to buy francs. In the meantime they were doing all they could to encourage their own people to travel.

While the Minister was speaking in the Chamber the first contingent of workers in the North of France, who are now assured of an annual holiday on full pay, was on its way to Belgium. They said that they could not afford to travel in France, but could do so in Belgium, as the cost of living there was about half of what it was at home.

7/30 The French Hotel Industry

Department of Overseas Trade, J. R. CAHILL, *Report on the Industrial Conditions in France 1925–1926* (London, 1927), pp. 255–257.

It is notorious that in France, as in Switzerland, hotel-keeping especially for foreigners has long ranked as one of the leading national industries. Recent years have enhanced its magnitude and multiplied its profits. The immense influx of strangers immediately after the war, and the still greater influx since 1923 . . . have completely changed the financial position of the whole industry, and have led to radical and general improvements, to considerable extensions, and to much new building. The more modest and backward hotels have been bettered to a surprising extent, general improvements and enlargements have taken place in the ordinary good hotels, and numerous new hotels of various dimensions have been created. Activity in all these respects has been prodigious in Paris. In hundreds of the older and smaller hotels the introduction of improvements, which had been in constant progress before the war, has been accelerated and generalized: such as hot and cold running water in all bedrooms, the installation of bathrooms attached to bedrooms, or the provision in good number of bathrooms for general use, and the heating of all rooms on the central system. Modern entrance halls or lounges have very often been created by ingenious ground-floor transformations, and sitting-rooms – traditionally a frequent lack in smaller French hotels – are more commonly provided.

A considerable number of the existing large hotels have extended their premises either by the building or the acquisition of annexes hard by or in their near neighbourhood, or by raising the height of their buildings. Thus one large hotel in the Champs-Elysées has added 150 more rooms to its complement of 450 by taking over the upper part of an adjoining new building, several hotels in the neighbourhood have raised their height a couple of stories, others have acquired whole adjoining houses or built separate hotels for their overflow.

But the building of new and very modern hotels has been quite astonishing. Within the last 18 months have been opened three hotels with 250 bed and 250 bathrooms; two with 200 bed and with 200 and 160 bathrooms respectively; two with 150 bed and 150 bathrooms; two more hotels with 150 bed and with 100 and 75 bathrooms respectively. Of other hotels recently opened one contains 120 rooms with 80 bathrooms; a second, 100 rooms with 80 bathrooms; a third, 70 rooms and 48 bathrooms; and a fourth, 48 bed and 48 bathrooms. One hotel now in an advanced stage of construction has 600 bedrooms and 600 bathrooms; and three others also under construction will have about 100 bed and 80 bathrooms apiece. Plans have been formed for two more large hotels one of which would have 1,200 bedrooms and 1,000 bathrooms. The enlarged or new hotels here referred to are practically all in or close to the Champs-Elysées, or in or near the Boulevard Haussmann; in other quarters of Paris, both on the right and the left banks of the Seine, quite half a dozen new hotels have opened within the last two or three years, and considerable extensions and transformations have been effected. In the few years preceding the war the building of new hotels or their extension or improvement had not been neglected, and although two large new hotels of that period were acquired by banks after the war, yet the amount of bedroom accommodation of a superior kind provided by Paris hotels probably shows a net increase over 1914 of five thousand units.

Similar improvements have been steadily carried out in provincial hotels, where the movement was stimulated by the exertions of the Touring Club of France, of the French Automobile Club, and of the Official National Touring Office, as well as by the active demand for better accommodation by the ever-growing army of motorists. Provision of running water and central heating is general in all the better hotels, partly to meet the comfort of customers, partly by reason of the acute labour shortage; rooms are found equipped with bathrooms, and sanitary arrangements have been enormously improved. Existing accommodation in places like Nice, Cannes, Monte Carlo, Aix-les-Bains, Vichy, Biarritz, and so forth was of course already of the very first order. New building has been very frequent, e.g. in Grenoble (four new hotels since 1924, one of which has about 200 rooms with baths); Uriage-les-Bains; new first-class hotels in Bordeaux, Lille, Lyons, Avignon, St. Raphael-Valescure, Cannes (one with 550 rooms and 500 baths), Agay, St. Juan-les-Pins (100 rooms with bathrooms), La Baule (200 rooms with bath), Biarritz (two, one with about 250 rooms and 200 baths), Luchon, Strasbourg. In many other places, apart from the great hotel areas of the Mediterranean coast or on the North coast, considerable enlargements have been effected in existing hotels (e.g. Rheims, St. Germain-en-Laye, Chartres, St. Briac, Royan and so forth). It may be recalled that within a quite recent period large modern-equipped hotels had been already built in Lille, Lyons, on the

Riviera and in the Pyrenees, e.g. at Sospel, Cannes, Nice, Beauvallon, St. Raphael, Font-Romeu, Béziers, Toulouse, Luchon-Superbagnères, Carcassonne, Aix-les-Bains, Annecy, Chamonix, La Baule, St. Jean-de-Luz, and in the summer resorts along the Channel. As the net result, the hotel accommodation throughout France has been immensely increased and improved, especially in the smaller towns, where, until the touring and especially the motoring habit became generalized, the hotels tended to languish for lack of custom.

For some years a certain tendency towards the formation of hotel groups or combines has been apparent in this as in other French industries. Before the war an international element with this tendency had obtained a footing in the control and in the management of many larger hotels. German or Austrian interests existed in Paris hotels, in many hotels along the Mediterranean, in the Pyrenees (e.g. at Vernet-les-Bains), and in other much-frequented resorts; Swiss interests were frequent at Paris and in several towns and resorts east of the Rhône, and Italian interests were especially frequent along the Riviera. The sequestration of the Austrian and German interests facilitated to a certain extent the grouping which has developed since 1919. One sequestrated group of Austrian origin consisted of the Astoria with four other considerable hotels at Paris and one at Trouville, and other groups are reported at various places.

Participations are frequent at the present time. The Union Hôtelière Parisienne, which works directly two hotels (Vendôme and Calais), has holdings in the well-known Paris hotels Meurice, Regina, Majestic, and Hôtels de l'Etoile, as well as in others; and some of those mentioned have mutual participations. The Claridge (Paris) group controls the biggest hotel at Nice and others at Nice, the Palace at Lyons, besides the two greatest hotels at Madrid and hotels at San Sebastian, Santander, Brussels and Dinant. The Société Française des Hôtels Modernes controls the Hôtel Continental in Paris as well as the leading hotels at Hyères, Nantes and Poitiers. The Société des Hôtels Réunis, which controls the newly-opened Hôtel Scribe in Paris, controls at Nice the leading hotels Ruhl, Royal, Savoy, Plaza and France; at Cannes the leading hotels Carlton, Majestic and Hôtel de Provence; at Dinard the Hôtels Dinard and Royal; at Cabourg the Grand Hotel.

The close working of the leading hotels at Nice and Cannes is observed. It may be added that the important Hôtel Métropole at Cannes, its namesake at Monte Carlo, and the Bristol at Beaulieu are controlled by one British company, whilst the Riviera Palace at Nice and the Splendid Hotel at Evian are affiliated to another group in London. The Continental at Cannes and the chief hotel at Rheims belong to the same proprietor. At Marseilles the Compagnie Hôtelière is said to control not only two of the leading hotels but also two other large hotels in the same city, the Gold Hotel at Hyères, besides two of those vast cafés on the Cannebière for which Marseilles is famous. At Strasbourg the three leading hotels are under the same control. At Vichy five of the greatest hotels (Parc and Majestic, Carlton, Thermal Palace, Pavillon Sévigné and Radio) are under the same control. At Granville in Normandy the same concern owns the two chief hotels, the Casino, the baths and the golf-links. The list need not be lengthened: in a large number of towns and health or pleasure resorts ownership or control of two or more hotels is frequently found; and it is not unusual to find that owners of hotels in winter resorts are also owners of hotels in summer resorts, so that they are enabled to work at their trade throughout the year and to utilize their staff.

Railway and shipping companies should also be mentioned as owners of important series of hotels. The Southern Railway maintains first-class hotels at Bordeaux, Toulouse, Béziers, Bayonne, Font-Romeu and Luchon-Superbagnères; the Paris-Lyon-Méditerranée owns hotels at Lyons, Marseilles, Briançon, Veynes and St. Maurice-en-Trièves. The greatest French shipping company has established in recent years a series of hotels in Morocco, Algeria and Tunis in connection with its tourist services. The Touring Club of France, the French Alpine Club and the Paris-Lyon-Méditerranée are co-operating in the creation of hotels to attract and to provide for visitors to places in the French Alps, Savoy and Dauphiné, such as Col de l'Iseran, Le Carro.

Another form of combination in the hotel industry which has shown considerable development has been that for centralized purchase of hotel requirements. Formed in 1917, the organization known as Les Hôteliers Français now supplies its members not only with foods and wines, but with all kinds of equipment, including paints, paper, furniture, glassware – in fact, all ordinary requirements. Its membership grew from 180 in 1917 to 981 in 1921 and to 3,110 in February, 1926, and its business from 7·8 million francs in 1921 to 26·6 in 1925.

Large Hotel Profits 1919–1926. Many hotel undertakings do not appear to publish annual balance sheets, and exhaustive details are not readily available for comparative purposes. The best evidence, however, of the profitable character of the hotel industry in France in recent years (after the lean years 1914–1918) is the obvious eagerness to invest money in those improvements, enlargements and new constructions of hotels. . . .

7/31 Holidays with Pay

COLE and SMITH, *Democratic Sweden* [see Document 3/10], pp. 325–326.

Although it has had to refuse to enact a general forty-hour week on the grounds that it would place Sweden at a disadvantage in the world market, the Social Democratic Government has this year* introduced a scheme of holidays with pay for all workers. Previously about three quarters of the workers covered by collective agreements had paid holidays, but only in a very few cases indeed did these amount to as much as the twelve days now accepted as the standard.

The Holidays with Pay law follows closely the lines of a report presented a few months ago by a committee appointed by the Social Board. The main provision is that every worker who has been employed by the same employer for at least six months shall have the right to one day's paid holiday during the summer for each month in which not less than eighteen days' work has been done. Thus normally a worker will get a holiday of fifteen consecutive days between the months of May and September.

There are certain modifications of this principle in particular occupations – for example employers of agricultural labourers are not obliged to give all the days off consecutively. The difficulty of piece-work has been met by enacting that piece-workers shall receive for holidays the average wage they have had in the past year. It is significant of the strength of the Trades Unions that the Government has in practice left the enforcement of the law to them. There is no provision for supervising the carrying out of the Act, and no penalty is prescribed for infringement. An employer who has failed to give a holiday, however, may find himself sued by his employees, acting of course through their Union.

According to calculations made by the Board of Trade, on the basis of 1936 figures, the cost of this scheme will be about 55 million kr. or slightly over 1 per cent of the estimated value of production. Against this, Government spokesmen claim there must be set not only the obvious social advantages of the scheme but the fact that a decrease in industrial accidents can be expected and that therefore holidays with pay may be looked on in rather the same light as a measure of anticipating illness, likely to increase efficiency by improving health and well-being.

7/32 Welfare and the Employers

International Labour Office, *Industrial Relations* [*see* Document 3/19], pp. 53–62.

The firms† have always paid particular attention to the welfare of their staffs. Some of the welfare institutions have a history which goes back for eighty years. The purpose of welfare schemes must always be related to the

* 1936. (Ed.)
† Within the large Siemens combine. (Ed.)

conditions of the particular firm. Conditions at Siemensstadt, where the majority of the workers live a long way from their work and cannot go home at lunch-time, have exercised a considerable influence on the form assumed by some of its welfare institutions. Thus particular attention is devoted to the provision of mess-rooms.

In order to provide a hot midday meal for the workpeople, mess-rooms have been established in all the works. Special rooms are provided for higher officials, salaried employees and wage-earning workers respectively. In these mess-rooms hot midday meals are provided consisting in each case of one main course with other subsidiary courses at the choice of the individual consumer. The main course always consists of meat of some kind, with fish once a week, and potatoes and vegetables. . . . The prices charged to salaried employees and wage-earning workers are not sufficient to cover the costs, and the firm contributes about 45 pf per meal in the case of salaried employees and about 30 pf per meal in the case of wage-earning workers.

The administration of the mess-rooms is, with one exception, entirely in the hands of the firm. In this one exception, the administration is undertaken by a committee of the workers, with the assistance of the firm. The wishes of the workers are expressed either through special mess-room committees or through the Works Council representatives.

The fact that the various mess-rooms are in the particular works makes it possible for the workpeople to reach them without delay during the midday meal hour. In one works the midday meal is brought in mess wagons to the work benches. About 44 per cent of the salaried employees and 18 per cent of the wage-earning workers regularly take their midday meal in the mess-rooms. The main reason for the fact that but a small proportion of the wage-earning workers take advantage of the hot meals provided is to be found in the convention of the Berlin worker to eat at midday a cold meal of bread and sausage. That the explanation is to be found in this convention is suggested by the fact that in the Vienna works of the firm almost 100 per cent of the staff eat in the mess-rooms, although the price of the meal in Vienna bears a slightly higher proportion to the wage than it does in Berlin. The only alcoholic liquor sold in the mess-rooms is beer. If the workpeople prefer to bring their midday meal with them from home, the firm provides hot closets in which the meal may be kept hot.

In addition to the mess-rooms, special shops are maintained by the firm in the works, at which various forms of foodstuffs and household articles may be obtained. The workpeople do not themselves come to buy in these shops, but give their orders to special messengers, one of which is employed for each 200 workers. These messengers are paid by the firm, and their sole duty consists in taking the orders of the workpeople in the particular works, fetching the goods from the shops and delivering them to the workpeople. The foodstuffs chiefly bought in the shops are bread and sausage. About 80–90 per cent of the staff take advantage of the facilities afforded by these shops, where goods are sold at 10 per cent lower prices, on an average, than they can be obtained elsewhere. . . .

It may also be mentioned here that a bureau is maintained for the sale to salaried employees of products of the Siemens firm. Any such products may be obtained at a reduction of 33⅓ per cent of the normal prices.

The firms maintain their own convalescent homes on the shores of the Baltic and in the Harz Mountains. With the assistance of the Works Sick Fund, the workers may go for four weeks, receiving free passage money, free board and lodging, and the payment of pocket money, either, in the case of men, to the convalescent home at Koserow, or, in the case of female workers, to the home at Ahlbeck. . . . In cases where a change of air does not appear to be necessary, convalescent workers, male and female, may be sent to a home in Siemensstadt itself. The Siemens firm also possesses a holiday house, the Siemens-Etterphaus at Bad Harzburg, with accommodation for 60 inmates, to which officials and salaried employees of the firm may go for their holidays at a nominal cost.

For workpeople affected with lung trouble, two medical treatment centres have been set up by the firms; arrangements have also been made with the lung establishment at Belzig, which has accommodation for 180 patients. An agreement has also been made by the firms with the Paulinenhaus Hospital, according to which preferential treatment is accorded to workpeople of the firms and members of their families.

In cases where the wives of workpeople are sick, the firm assumes, in whole or in part, the expense of domestic help in the household concerned. A children's home is maintained in Siemensstadt, to which women working in the firms may bring their children in the morning and leave them during the day until they are ready to take them away in the evening. In some cases fresh clothing is given to the children. With the Children's Home is associated an Infant Welfare Centre, in which free medical advice is given to mothers and expectant mothers.

In the school at Siemensstadt, a school nurse is maintained by the firms. In cases where children require change of air, they are sent, almost exclusively at the expense of the firms, to the Siemens Eleonorenheim, Neuhof, near Häringsdorf on the Baltic. Over 800 children in the course of the summer are sent to this home.

An Apprentices' Institute is also maintained, with gymnasium, reading-room, hobby rooms, etc., for the use of the Siemens apprentices after the hours of work.

The firms maintain a works library of about 33,000 volumes, which is at the free disposal of salaried employees and of wage-earning workers. Most of the volumes are volumes of general literature. . . . in the special technical libraries of the particular works. A remarkable feature of this library is the wide use made of it. In the year 1928–1929, 400,000 books were lent; about half of these were loaned to salaried employees and half to wage-earning workers. The number of books loaned has quintupled since 1914–1915. . . .

A special section of the library, containing some 3,000 volumes, has been established with a special view to the needs and desires of the apprentices in the Siemens Works.

In connection with the works library and under the direction of the division of the Industrial Relations Department devoted to its management, there is a section responsible for the organization of general lectures, film representations, concerts and theatrical performances of special interest to the workpeople.

A Works Magazine, the *Siemens-Mitteilungen*, richly illustrated, gives information with regard to the Siemens firms and also contains articles of a general kind.

The various Clubs of the employees of the firms are associated in the Association of Siemens Employees (*Verband der Siemens-Beamten*). Some 7,000 salaried employees of the firm belong to this association. The firms supply free accommodation, free secretariat, and thus cover nearly 20 per cent of the operation expenses of the Association. The other expenses are covered by membership fees, which vary from 3 RM to 25 RM per annum. The associated clubs include associations for the following activities: wireless, gardening, swimming, tennis, foreign language conversation, rowing, photography, stenography, orchestral and choral music, rhythmic gymnastics, philately, chess, shooting, glee singing. In addition, the Association maintains a welfare branch, providing friendly benefits in case of death. It also possesses a domestic economy branch, which provides for its members certain advantages in lower prices of goods of common consumption. The Association also maintains a shop of its own in which some such goods may be obtained. A magazine, the *Nachrichten des Vereins der Siemens-Beamten*, is also issued. This magazine, which accepts advertisements, contains information with regard to the activities of all the constituent clubs and also a certain number of general articles.

There are also in connection with the firms a Foremen's Club and an Apprentices' Club, the *Werner Siemens Jugendverein*.

With a view to meeting the need for housing at Siemensstadt, the firms undertook in 1922 the construction of a Garden City. In this Garden City some 500 dwellings have now been erected. Some of them are flats, others individual houses. Every house has a large garden attached to it. In the case of the flats there is a communal garden. The number of rooms per flat or house varies from two to five. Two other garden cities have also been constructed at Siemensstadt by independent companies with loans provided by the firms. Each of these two other garden cities contains approximately 500 dwellings. The total number of dwellings in the Siemensstadt garden cities, therefore, amounts to about 1,500. These houses are all of the most modern construction, with electric light and, in many cases, electric heating and cooking installations.

The firms have also been concerned with the provision of churches. . . .

In the immediate neighbourhood of the Works temporary dwelling accommodation has been constructed by the firm for the housing of unmarried workers, usually specialists in some craft who come to Siemensstadt to work in the firm, to accommodate them until they can find permanent quarters.

A part of the grounds in the neighbourhood of the Garden City has been set aside by the firm as allotments, and workers not living at Siemensstadt are granted allotments in this area. The firm also maintains a nursery from which plants and seeds may be obtained at a low cost by the workers, either for planting in their allotments at Siemensstadt or elsewhere. . . .

The working of industrial relations at Siemensstadt is the resultant of the operation of two factors which are often considered to be inconsistent: in the first place, the thorough-going application of the principles of scientific method to all industrial relationships; and in the second place, the development of essentially personal relations between the head of the firm and his workpeople, on the basis of an old tradition of family contacts. The mere framework of industrial relations is, indeed, the same at Siemensstadt as in all other German firms, for it is constituted by legislation and collective agreement. The particular significance of Siemensstadt resides in the fact that it represents the filling in of this framework on the largest scale and in the most complete manner. . . . Siemensstadt is undoubtedly a remarkable example, in a firm of the largest size, of the maintenance of direct personal relations between management and the workers side by side with and in addition to the relations through representation provided for by the works councils and otherwise. It is a striking illustration of the view that the application of legal machinery for ensuring industrial relations is not inconsistent with the retention and even the development of freer and less formal contacts between management and the workers.

7/33 Workers' Leisure Organizations

International Labour Office, *Facilities for the Use of Workers' Leisure during Holidays* (London, 1939), pp. 17–24.

In all countries where holidays with pay are given, there is some combined action, generally taking a number of different forms, to facilitate the use of their holidays by the workers. Its aim is, more exactly, to help them to use the facilities made available by undertakings conducted with a view to profit (hotels, tourist agencies, transport companies, etc.) as well as those offered by non-profit-making institutions. Many of these are indeed established for the express purpose of providing such facilities. This combined action is taken by numerous organizations of widely different sorts, which are grouped below under four main headings. The classification should not be regarded as rigid, however, for the action studied may result from collaboration between bodies belonging to two or more of the four classes, and in that case it has been placed in the class to which it seemed on the whole to belong.

Combined action may be in the hands of bodies set up by workers, by employers, by private associations, or by public authorities, associations and institutions.

§ 1. BODIES SET UP BY WORKERS

These bodies may be divided into two groups – those established for a particular occupation and those which make no distinction between occupations. Although holiday organizations of the former type are always to be found, at the moment the tendency seems to be to develop institutions catering for all workers and their families, whatever the occupation or industry in which they are engaged.

OCCUPATIONAL BODIES

Holiday facilities organized by trade unions or federations of trade unions are to be found in all countries. Generally such action has, in the first instance, been taken by organizations of salaried employees and officials. In some countries, *Argentina* and *Bulgaria* for example, organizations of this type almost exclusively provide holiday facilities.

In a number of countries the trade unions provide holiday facilities: in *Belgium*, the building workers', railway employees' and miners' unions; in *France*, the Christian Union of Needlewomen, the Metal Workers' Union and the Public Transport Workers' Union; in *Poland*, the typographers' and railwaymen's unions; in *Sweden*, the typographers' union; in *Switzerland*, the unions of railway employees, metal workers and watchmakers; and in the *United States*, the Ladies' Garment Workers' Union.

BODIES CATERING FOR ALL OCCASIONS

The aim of these bodies is to provide all workers and their families, whatever the labour organization to which they belong and the occupation or industry in which they are engaged, with facilities for their paid holidays. . . .

Trade Union Institutions

Several federations of trade unions have established institutions for popular travel. . . . In *Belgium* the Workers' Tourist Agency is connected with the General Confederation of Labour. In *Finland* a people's tourist association was established in 1939. In *France* the General Confederation of Labour established a people's tourist office in 1937 and it amalgamated in 1938 with an association established by a group of teachers; at present this body is entitled 'Travel and Holidays for All'. In *Poland* the Workers' Travel Society established by the Central Committee of the Union of Occupational Organizations and the Jewish trade union federation 'Kulturliga' have their own holiday institutions.

Sporting, Educational and Similar Associations

Holiday facilities are often provided by associations for gymnastics or sport (as in *Poland, Switzerland*, etc.). Other holiday organizations depend on institutions for workers' education; in *Norway* the organizations affiliated to the Workers' Education Association established in 1939 a society entitled Norwegian People's Holidays ('Norsk Folke-Ferie'); in the *Netherlands* the Friends of Nature Society is a branch of the Workers' Education Institute.

Independent Bodies

. . . In *Belgium* the General Confederation of Labour has established an association, entitled 'Holidays and Health', and the Confederation of Christian Trade Unions has another, entitled 'Holidays and Recreation'; in doing so each of these confederations has 'set up an independent institution in the form of an association not working for profit, whose governing body includes representatives of the trade unions, the co-operative and provident societies, women's and youth organizations, workers' education centres and the workers' travel associations already in existence. Both institutions carry out studies, collect documentary material, co-ordinate the work of, and issue instructions to, their affiliated associations and local branches, publish information in handy form, open inquiry offices, try to facilitate the organization of holiday homes and see that they are used, and do their best to provide the labour movement with real travel and excursion agencies that are not worked for profit.'

Associations resembling in some respects the two just mentioned have recently appeared in *Denmark, Finland* and *Sweden*...

Although it is not the case in all countries, bodies for joint holiday arrangements are sometimes established by groups with religious or political affiliations. In *Belgium* the trade unions belonging to the General Confederation of Labour, the Christian organizations and the liberal trade unions, each have separate facilities; in *France*, too, there are separate holiday associations for the unions belonging to the General Confederation of Labour and the Christian unions; and in *Poland*, the Jewish trade unions have their own services.

§ 2. BODIES SET UP BY EMPLOYERS

When an employer or an undertaking provides holiday facilities, they are for his or its employees only. It is at present rare for holiday arrangements to be made by groups of undertakings or by employers' associations. In *Germany* some undertakings arrange holidays for their staffs through a special organization, the Association for Holiday Homes in Industry and Commerce. . . . An instance of a somewhat different character is provided by railway companies; in *Argentina* and in *France* the railways have established holiday facilities for all or part of their personnel.

An undertaking which desires to provide its staff with facilities for the use of its holidays may make its own arrangements for the purpose. Instances are the railways in *Argentina*, certain departmental stores in *Belgium*, the 'Sächsische Werke' in *Germany*, and numerous undertakings which organize holiday camps in the *United States*. There are arrangements of the sort in almost every country.

Some undertakings have recourse to special services for this purpose. In the *Netherlands*, for instance, the Philips Works have a separate recreation department. . . .

Undertakings which do not wish to organize their holiday arrangements themselves may proceed in another way, viz. by paying subsidies to special bodies, usually workers' travel societies. Action of this sort is reported in *Belgium* (Association of Metal Works in the Liége Region), *Bulgaria, Germany, Poland, Sweden* and other countries.

§ 3. BODIES SET UP BY PRIVATE ORGANIZATIONS

When holiday facilities are provided by private bodies, the aim is to reach certain sections of the population in particular. This applies, for instance, to the Young Men's and Young Women's Christian Associations, and the same holds good for the activities of certain Catholic organizations, such as the Christian Young Workers' Associations (J.O.C.) in *Belgium*,

France and *Switzerland*. A similar tendency may be observed in the organization of Youth Hostels in some countries. In *France* there is a secular Youth Hostels Association and a League of Youth Hostels, the latter having been established first; in addition to these two groups, a new body has recently been set up by the Catholic organizations, known as 'Travellers' Rests' ('Gîtes d'étapes'). The same applies in *Belgium*, where a further distinction is made between the Walloon and the Flemish youth hostels, though there is a connection between the two central organizations.

The holiday work undertaken by these private bodies is not reserved for workers. In some cases employed persons form the major part of the membership, particularly in the Christian Young Workers' Associations; but this does not apply, for instance, to the co-operative organizations, which draw a large part of their membership from the middle classes. Nor is it true of the youth hostels; in *France* employed persons formed 10 per cent of the membership in 1936, and in *Luxemburg* 30 per cent in 1937.

The private associations which organize holiday facilities may be divided into several groups.

(1) Youth movements – Y.M.C.A., Y.W.C.A., youth hostels, boy scouts, etc., which exist in most countries.

(2) Co-operative groups, as in *Bulgaria*, *France* (National Committee on Recreation), *Great Britain* (Holiday Fellowship), *Poland* and *Switzerland*.

(3) Sport and travel associations, in *Belgium, Bulgaria, Hungary, Netherlands, Sweden, Yugoslavia*, etc. The Friends of Nature Societies in various countries may be said to belong to this group.

(4) Religious bodies: in the *United States* the different Churches organize their holiday facilities; in *Belgium* and *France* the Christian Young Workers' Societies with their many separate sections for boys, girls, farmers, seamen, etc., have numerous holiday homes; in *Poland* and *Yugoslavia* action by religious organizations is also reported.

(5) Social bodies, such as 'settlements' in *Great Britain*, *Sweden* and the *United States*, organizations for social service in *Hungary* and *Sweden*, and adult education movements in a large number of countries.

(6) Bodies set up by political parties, such as the Socialist Women's Groups in *Belgium*, the 'Friends of *Le Populaire*' (a Socialist daily newspaper) in *France*.

§ 4. OFFICIAL AND SEMI-OFFICIAL BODIES

Action taken by public authorities, associations and institutions with a view to facilitating the use of workers' holidays may be of two kinds. In some cases previously existing bodies play an active part in the provision of such facilities, but only as a branch of their regular work; in other cases, owing to the national importance of the problems raised by the rapid extension of holidays with pay, special bodies are created to deal with all these related questions.

BODIES NOT SPECIALIZING IN HOLIDAY PROBLEMS

Frequently official bodies or public services direct holiday schemes for certain groups of workers, this constituting only an accessory part of their activities. Such is often the case with social insurance institutions, which may include provision for workers' holidays in their general preventive measures. Further, certain services or undertakings operated by the authorities or by public institutions provide holiday facilities for their staffs in their capacity of employers.

In *Bulgaria* the labour and social insurance authorities organize convalescent homes which may also be used as holiday centres. In *Germany* the National Post Office has a rest home for its employees. In *Hungary* the Social Insurance Institute has organized holiday homes for apprentices. In *Poland* a large number of public services are concerned with holiday schemes; among these are the National Institute of Physical Education, the Ministry of Education (covering adult education and youth hostels), the Social Insurance Institute, the Labour Fund and the Maritime and Colonial League. In *Yugoslavia* holiday institutions form part of the social insurance system.

BODIES SPECIALIZING IN HOLIDAY PROBLEMS

A growing number of countries have official services for holiday questions. . . .

In *Belgium* the National Office for Workers' Holidays, established in 1937, is assisted by an advisory body – the Committee for Workers' Holidays – on which all the organizations concerned are represented; this National Office is attached to the Ministry of Transport. In *France* the office of the Under-Secretary for Recreation and Sport, which was set up in 1936, functioned until 1938, when it was replaced by a department of the Ministry of Education; one of the main tasks of this service is to co-ordinate the various facilities for workers' holidays with pay. In *Germany* the 'Travel, Excursions and Holidays' section of the National Socialist organization 'Kraft durch Freude' (itself a part of the Labour Front) was instructed in 1934 to provide facilities by which workers with small means might use their paid holidays for travel; this organization not only concludes agreements with transport undertakings and hotels in order to obtain special terms for workers on holiday, but also owns and administers its own establishments and steamers for cruises. . . . In *Luxemburg* a National Committee on Recreation, established early in 1938, has taken the organization of workers' holidays as its main object. In *Norway* an official body, the State Holiday

Council ('Statens Ferieråd') was established on May 1939; its chairman is the Director of Public Health. In *Poland*, after a conference held in the spring of 1938, a Committee on Recreation was established at the Ministry of Social Welfare; this Committee is particularly concerned with the question of workers' holidays. . . . In the *U.S.S.R.* all that relates to workers' holidays is within the competence of the Central Trade Union Council; for travel proper there is a section of the Council, and as regards holiday residence the network of rest homes is administered by the social insurance authority, itself under the direction of the Central Trade Union Council.

7/34 The Italian Dopolavoro

a Views expressed in TOMASO SILLANT (ed.), *What is Fascism and Why* (New York, 1931), pp. 209–214. Printed in CLOUGH, *et al., Economic History* [*see* Document **1/4a**], pp. 280–284.

b *The Times*, 30 April 1928.

The vast organization commonly known under the name of *Dopolavoro* (Leisure time) which promotes schemes for the better employment of the free time of workers of all classes, with the object of raising their intellectual, moral, physical and social status in accordance with the policy of enhancing national values promoted by Fascism, has assumed such proportions, especially recently, under the auspices of the General Secretary of the P.N.F. [National Fascist Party], that it may be considered as one of the most characteristic achievements of the Fascist revolution. The following notes give a brief summary of the history, organization and functioning of this institution, founded by Signor Mussolini.

The Dopolavoro passed through several phases before reaching its present organization. These may be divided into three different periods: in the first phase, it was an attempt due to private initiative; in the second, it was affiliated to the National Confederation of Fascist Syndicates; and in the third it assumed a State-controlled and national character.

The first period dates from 1919 to the end of 1923.

The Dopolavoro Office proposed in the beginning to carry out a work of propaganda, advice and assistance, with the object of encouraging employers' welfare schemes on behalf of their workers and also of promoting the spread of higher general education and of sport among the people.

When the National Confederation of Fascist Syndicates, with a view to the moral uplift of the masses, as understood by Fascism, added educational propaganda to its regular tasks, the Dopolavoro Office became its mouthpiece. It was then that the first lines of the movement began to be laid down, although in very rudimentary form, for it was impossible to attract those who were not connected with the syndicalist federations into the orbit of the institution.

With the creation of the *Opera nazionale Dopolavoro* (National Leisure-time Organization [O.N.D.]) by Act of Parliament on 1 May 1925, and the acceptance of its presidency by H.R.H. the Duke of Aosta, the Dopolavoro organization began to take definite form; its new status entitled it to federate thousands of clubs, societies, sporting, educational and artistic groups, and enabled it to extend its efforts into the ranks of the great State services by means of organizations in aid of railway and postal employees and those of the Tobacco Monopoly, in accordance with the Royal Decrees of 25 October 1925, 9 July 1926 and 19 May 1927.

The Secretary of the National Fascist Party, who took over the supreme direction of the organization after the resignation of the Duke of Aosta, has re-organized the entire administration of the Dopolavoro, as well as its pro-gramme, giving it an organic structure more in accordance with the aims and methods of the National Fascist Party. And on 14 September 1929, the work was officially recognized as a distinctively Fascist institution at the five-yearly Fascist Assembly, and included among the Government schemes.

The Leisure-time movement, as developed during recent years in Italy, has much in common with the welfare work in Anglo-Saxon countries, which embrace all the efforts of the greater firms for the assistance and future provision of their employees; and has also several points of analogy with other great organizations such as the Y.M.C.A., the Playground and Recrea-tion Association of America, the Carnegie United Kingdom Trust, the National Education Association of the United Kingdom, the *Commission centrale des Loisirs des Ouvriers de l'Hainault* of Belgium, and other foreign organizations and associations that promote libraries, culture and artistic education for adults, sport, popular tours, and so on. In addition to these characteristics, however, the Italian movement has intrinsic features of its own which differentiate it from all organizations of the kind.

The Dopolavoro is a public institution which, by its technical, organizing and directive functions is able to deal directly with the problems of welfare, education and recreation of the working classes. Whereas in other countries – including those that have reached the highest degree of material civilization – the solution of the various problems of instruction, physical education, and the various forms of social aid for the working classes is left to private initia-tive, in Italy alone, thanks to the enterprising spirit of Fascism, these tasks have become an integral part of the State's activities, and in this field also the State asserts its position as the controlling force of the nation. ...

The programme of the O.N.D. is divided into four great sections: *Instruction* (culture for the people and the teaching of trades); *Artistic education* (dramatic societies, music and chorus singing, cinematography, wireless, folklore); *Physical education* (Italian Excursion Federation and Central Sporting Commission); *Social welfare and hygiene* (dwellings, hygiene, provision for the future, leisure-time occupation for the various classes of workmen).

It will probably be of more interest to give a brief summary of the more important works, rather than a detailed explanation of the various services that correspond with the several branches of the above programme and with their many ramifications.

Extensive arrangements have been made in all the local Dopolavoro offices and societies federated to the O.N.D. for the higher education of the people; and the same measures have been taken in numberless industrial concerns, in the offices of the Railway Dopolavoro and those of the Postal Service and Tobacco Monopoly: libraries, reading rooms, evening instruction courses, lectures with lantern slides or cinematograph [motion picture] films, people's universities. The general management supports and subsidizes these undertakings, supervising them with a view to their co-ordination and consistent purpose. The Dopolavoro makes considerable use of the educational cinema. . . . It was the first to organize open-air cinemas in Italy. The O.N.D.'s programme of popular instruction has the approval and constant support of the Ministry of National Education. A measure has been passed providing that elementary and intermediary teachers who give their work for the benefit of the Dopolavoro's higher education for the people shall be entitled to a special order of merit, which will have preference over other documents in competitions and examinations for promotion. The National Institute also interests itself in promoting and assisting evening and Sunday vocational schools and courses in technical improvement.

In this important field, which is the index to the civilization of a country, out of 1,437 institutions controlled by the Dopolavoro in 1926, only 87 were promoting sections for higher education, folklore, and trade teaching, the number of such sections being 1,249 altogether. In 1930, the number of institutions controlled had increased to 14,027 and of this number 5,225 had promoted no less than 78,744 sections in the above mentioned branches. The Dopolavoro had 178 libraries open to its members in 1926, while in 1930 the number had increased to 2,388.

The Institution is endeavouring to encourage the revival of the love of drama by every means in its power: propaganda, theatrical schools, dramatic publications, artistic shows, the touring 'Cars of Thespis', tours in the provinces; provincial, regional and national societies, reduced author's rights, and other forms of encouragement.

In the realm of sport a vast, fertile, and original work is being carried on. A truly imposing number of young men and women now go in for athletics and are being trained in all the soundest forms of sporting exercise, from gymnastics to fencing, swimming, rowing, cycling, running, and so on.

The Italian Excursion Federation has grouped together hundreds of sporting, alpine and excursion institutions, promoting very extensive patriotic pilgrimages to the battlefields and cemeteries of the war, joint tours of pleasure and instruction, and Sunday cruises and excursions, in which thousands and thousands of authentic workers have taken part. The institutions affiliated to the Dopolavoro have increased the 2,538 sports and excursion sections that existed in 1926 to the very big number of 115,676 in 1930.

The Institution promotes exhibitions, matches, and competitions for the benefit of the welfare section and carries out an important work of propaganda and organization.

In 1927, the O.N.D., in collaboration with the 'Ente Nazionale delle piccole industrie' (National organization of small industries) got up the exhibition of the 'Three Venetias' for economic house-furnishing. They also arranged two other great competitons, in 1928, for the economic and rational furnishing and fitting out of the home, the competitions being held in every part of Italy. They constitute the biggest and most organic experiment of the kind that has yet been attempted anywhere.

Research and studies, popular campaigns and practical courses are now being organized to encourage the cultivation of allotments and kitchen gardens. After taking part in the International Congress for the organization of kitchen gardens, which was held at Luxembourg in June 1927, the Dopolavoro has been endeavouring to unite together the manifold but disconnected efforts being made in outlying districts and by various local societies into a national organization.

In addition to the O.N.D.'s part in creating new hygienic conditions of life for the working classes: improved dwelling houses, kitchen gardens and flower gardens, factory restaurants, depots for the sale of foodstuffs, small-loan banks, etc.; the institution concerns itself with hygienic propaganda, collaborating, by its publications and lectures, in the campaigns against tuberculosis and cancer and drink, in the anti-malaria crusade, the propaganda for seaside hospices, alpine colonies and sanatoriums.

The progress of the Dopolavoro organization may be realized from the following figures concerning membership cards. In 1926, the O.N.D. controlled 1,497 institutions with a total membership of 280,584; in 1929, the number of institutions controlled was 11,084 and the number of members 1,445,226....

If such satisfactory results have been obtained already in the short existence of the institution – six years – it is mainly due to the fact that the heads of the Dopolavoro have always put into practice the fundamental principle of

Fascist education, which consists in working with purpose, method and order. Before the advent of Fascism, people here were forever talking of social reforms, everyone was posing as apostle of the workers' redemption, but it all ended in words, for nothing practical was ever accomplished. Today, little is said, but much is done. Improved organizations, better equipment, a broadening of functions, the growing number of members are all so many signs of the vitality of this work, which Fascism ranks among its finest achievements.

b A clearer idea of what the Dopolavoro does may be gained when one considers it in relation to a single category of workers. To take, for example, the railwaymen, whose membership, as I have already stated, numbers 152,000; every variety of sport has been organized among them. Three thousand volumes (almost entirely in the nature of Fascist propaganda) have been distributed, and thousands of subscriptions have been paid on their behalf to illustrated magazines and reviews. A sum of 12,500 lire was distributed in prizes to those railwaymen who, while occupying dwellings of the working-class type, have distinguished themselves for the neatness and order of their homes. Among railwaymen whose work is carried out in isolated localities have been distributed some 40,000 copies of a year-book containing various moral, scientific, literary, and practical information. Along the line in Sardinia and the Naples district the Dopolavoro has organized 30 experimental poultry-rearing stations with 60 poultry yards, and it is proposed now to give advice as to the raising of rabbits and bees, as well as to the cultivation of orchards and gardens, particularly for the benefit of those railway employees who live in small rural centres. Various professional classes for railwaymen have been instituted. Several circulating libraries have been established and many wireless sets distributed gratis. A special film, 8,000 metres long, dealing with the State railways, was prepared for the railwaymen, as well as films illustrating the progress and use of 'white coal' (hydro-electric energy), and the new Rome-Naples direct-line railway (the 'Direttissima').

7/35 Strength Through Joy and the Beauty of Labour

a R. LEY, 'Social Policy in the New Germany' in *Germany Speaks* [see Document 6/8], pp. 166–167.

b ROBERTS, *The House* [see Document 6/2c], pp. 224–228.

c A. SPEER, *Inside the Third Reich. Memoirs* (London, 1970), p. 57.

a Special mention should be made of a sub-organization of the G.L.F.*–

★ The German Labour Front. (Ed.)

styled 'Strength through Joy' – which is mainly concerned with holiday and leisure-time arrangements. Thanks to this branch of the G.L.F., Germany's social policy has been extended to the cultural sphere.

The great popularity of the arrangements made by the 'Strength through Joy' organization is proved by the large number of participants in them. The section for travelling and hiking is perhaps the most popular one, its membership having trebled in the course of the past three years. Its pleasure cruises to foreign countries have attracted great attention, both at home and abroad. They have enabled German workers to visit Norway, Finland, Great Britain, Lisbon, Madeira, the Azores and the Baltic countries; and even though personal contact with the inhabitants of those parts has necessarily been but brief and cursory, it has been sufficiently effective in showing up the preposterousness of many an anti-German prejudice.

Equally valuable results have been attained by the tours within Germany. Whatever regional antagonisms may still have divided Germans, they have been dispelled by numerous opportunities thus afforded for obtaining a better knowledge of one another. Ethically and morally too, division into North and South has vanished. In 1934, the number of persons taking part in these travelling and hiking arrangements amounted to some 2,000,000; but by the end of 1936, it had gone up to more than 6,000,000, whilst several more millions will be added during the current year. The ultimate object is to enable 14,000,000 persons of small means to benefit from these arrangements every year. The cost is so low that 16 RM will pay for one week's seaside holiday this year.

b From the human point of view, one of the most interesting experiments in Germany has been the attempt to supplement wages by providing facilities for travel or enjoyment. A most popular section of the Labour Front is the department known as 'Strength through Joy' (*Kraft durch Freude*). This was set up at the end of 1933, and only the lower paid workmen can take advantage of its facilities. The limit is a variable one. A typist cannot enter the organization if she earns more than 150 marks a month, whereas a worker with four children is still eligible even if he earns as much as 500 marks.

The idea is to get the workman away from his everyday surroundings. Any workman who wishes to travel gets into touch with the works member of the 'confidential council' (set up by the Labour Front) and thus with the district office of the movement. He receives a card which is stamped with his weekly contribution and, when he has saved enough money, he goes on one of the trips. In the first year of operations, 3,000,000 workers took such trips, and this year* the number is expected to exceed 6,000,000. When the hotels

* 1938. [Ed.]

were filled, the trippers went on hired boats. Today six vessels go to Madeira or Norway, and the Labour Front is building boats of its own. Last summer 150,000 workers took sea trips, a week's cruise to Norway costing less than thirty marks.

In addition, eighty recreation homes have been built, and at present the Government is constructing a huge spa on the island of Rügen to accommodate 20,000 people. Seaports are being organized along the entire northern coast, and there is barely a region of Germany that is not being opened up by some form of this tourist activity. The motorist in Germany encounters the huge buses with the *K.d.F.* symbol in the most inaccessible spots and frequently finds towns overrun by them, until his zest for the organization almost changes into a feeling of exasperation.

The amazing feature is that, apart from administrative personnel, the scheme is claimed to be self-supporting, because hotel proprietors and railway owners are satisfied with smaller profits in order to get the extra business. The central authorities in Berlin told me that this applied to building ships of their own, but I fail to see how huge liners can be made to pay at a daily rate of six-and-a-half marks per person.

Nevertheless, *Kraft durch Freude* appears to be an excellent device for providing holidays for people who would not otherwise get them. Its varying success in different districts provides a kind of social barometer. At headquarters in Berlin, regional graphs . . . enable the authorities to see at a glance how many people from each town are taking holidays, where they are going, how many more or less are going than at this time last year. They are multicoloured marvels of statistical ingenuity and, if accurate, afford excellent data about the prosperity and loyalty of each region in Germany. I investigated the applications from Silesia and the distressed Rhineland area and was amazed to find no essential difference from elsewhere.

Another department of the organization arranges theatre facilities for the same class of people. A census of the great Siemens factories taken when the Nazis came to power showed that three-quarters of the people never went to theatres. The Government therefore arranged with theatrical managers that blocks of seats should be made available to workers at special rates. Workmen who received good reports thereupon take part in a ballot for these seats, so that for seventy-five pf, a man may find himself in the front row of the stalls or up in the gallery.

The position here is rather complicated, because the Propaganda Ministry frequently intervenes, giving grants in special cases and sometimes taking over whole theatres. Some propagandist plays may be opened to the public for nothing, while, at other times, the Ministry takes over an ordinary commercial theatre when some play or picture with an historical moral is being presented. There may be a direct grant for a given play, or merely indirect aid through a reduction of taxes; and, to complicate matters, such grants may come either from the Labour Front or from the Propaganda Ministry. The upshot of it all is that a worker may go to selected plays for seventy-five pf, to operas for ninety pf, and to ordinary plays in outside theatres for half the ordinary rates. Officially no compulsion is exerted on owners of theatres, only 'persuasion'. The Labour Front argue that the owners welcome their intrusion because empty seats are filled and plays booked in advance; but it is obvious how such a system must work in the direction of making the theatre a subsidiary propagandist body for the Party.

Films, other than moralizing historical presentations, are outside this scheme in the towns. But, in the country districts, film shows and concert parties circulate in parts where otherwise they would not pay. There is a definite move to educate the musical taste of the people, in the direction of chamber music, for instance. Orchestras are sent round to factories, and, for a few pence, workers can hear conductors like Feuchtwangler.

Already 25,000,000 people a year benefit from these facilities, and, once again, it is claimed that the State pays nothing, although obviously the sub-ventions from the Propaganda Ministry and the losses in taxes must be counted on the debit side. If one puts aside the propagandist element, one must admit that this movement is definitely providing facilities that would not otherwise exist, although it is at first a little strange to pay many marks for a seat in a theatre and find a neighbour who has paid only a few pfennigs. The system reaches its height in the *People's Theatre* in Berlin, the former circus in which Max Reinhardt staged his most flamboyant spectacles. The great circular building has now become a People's Theatre, at which two-thirds of the seats are reserved for workers. Last year the productions varied from *Peer Gynt* and *The Merry Wives of Windsor* to operettas of Strauss and Lincke. It must be added, however, that a popular revue, *Let's have a Good Time*, had by far the longest run.

A further department of the 'Strength through Joy' movement is that which provides facilities for cheap sport. This arouses more attention in Germany than it would in a British country, and my mentors could not understand my lack of interest in this phase of their activities, a phase of which they were particularly proud. The idea that sport was not a matter for the Government found no support with them; and I had to listen to accounts of the intricate organization for popularizing sport amongst the German masses. The Labour Front provided funds for endowing this department, and a huge pyramid of committees was set up from factory to the whole Reich. It was all taken very seriously. Lectures are a regular part of the programme, and the aim is to improve the bodies of the Germans, and in no sense to create new records. It was in the academically serious atmosphere of this department that I felt myself most a foreigner in Germany.

No arrangements are made for football and handball, on the ground that these are already too popular, but a workman can obtain an evening's sport by paying twenty pf, or, if he wants instruction in swimming, ten pf more. The accompanying lectures even in central Germany, go as far afield as sailing and ski-ing. From a little over half a million in the first year, the number of people using these facilities has swollen to 6,000,000 a year. This was stressed as one of the greatest achievements of the new regime, and my arguments that British sport needed no such State aid were received with kindly sympathy as still another instance of how we were losing the race. Even my aide from the Foreign Office, a man who had taken a degree in an English University, thought my attitude to Government-organized sport – so palpably one of the most cherished achievements of the Third Reich – a little flippant. For the women, there is a special department called 'Jolly Gymnastics and Games'. It should be added that only 'citizens' may share in this comradeship of sportsmen; in other words, Jews and part-Aryans are excluded.

And so, runs a piece of propaganda, 'the contentment of the day's work vibrates into the leisure hours in which fresh strength is gained for the next working day', and, at the same time, one's pride of nationality and heritage is increased. At first I was inclined to interpret 'Strength through Joy' as a spectacular embellishment of government, but, after further investigation, I realized that it was one of the most striking forms of social service I had yet seen and, at the same time, a most efficient method of propaganda. The Germans rank it with the Labour Service camps as a great instrument of national regeneration and one of their most original contributions to social history. It is an officially organized campaign for *Health, Joy, and Homeland*, and, as such, is a cult peculiarly Teutonic. Nevertheless, propaganda apart, it is a most attractive organization. Beethoven for sixpence, Bavaria for eighteenpence and Norway for six shillings a day, the sea for the mountaineer and the mountains for the sailor – its prospects are most alluring, and I regretted my inability to accept Dr. Ley's invitation to go on a cruise to the Norwegian fjords – eight days for twenty-two marks – if I insisted on paying for myself.

c After 30 January 1934, at the suggestion of Robert Ley, head of the Labour Front, a leisure-time organization was created. I was supposed to take over the section called 'Beauty of Labour'; the name had provoked a good deal of mockery, as had the title 'Strength through Joy' itself. A short while before, on a trip through the Dutch province of Limburg, Ley had seen a number of mines conspicuous for their neatness and cleanliness and surrounded by beautifully tended gardens. By temperament Ley always tended to generalize, and he now wanted to have all of German industry follow this example. The project turned out to be an extremely gratifying one, at least for me personally. First we persuaded factory owners to modernize their offices and to have some flowers about. But we did not stop there. Lawn was to take the place of asphalt. What had been wasteland was to be turned into little parks where the workers could sit during breaks. We urged that window areas within factories be enlarged and workers' canteens set up. What was more, we designed the necessary artifacts for these reforms, from simple, well-shaped flatware to sturdy furniture, all of which we had manufactured in large quantities. We provided educational movies and a counselling service to help businessmen on questions of illumination and ventilation. We were able to draw former union leaders and some members of the dissolved Arts and Crafts Society into this campaign. One and all devoted themselves to the cause of making some improvements in the workers' living conditions and moving closer to the ideal of a classless People's Community. However, it was somewhat dismaying to discover that Hitler took hardly any interest in these ideas. He could lose himself in the details of an architectural project but proved remarkably indifferent when I came to him with reports of my progress in this social area.

Glossary

ARTEL   Russian artisans' or farm co-operative.

BAUER   German farmer or peasant. For the official Nazi definition, *see* Document **6/9b**.

BEDNYAK (pl. BEONIAKI)   Poor peasant, having some land but usually not enough to support a family (*see kulak, serednyak*).

COMMANDITE   A form of company organization in which at least one partner or shareholder bears unlimited liability, while the rest of the partners (shareholders) carry liability only to the extent of the capital invested.

COMMUNE   The smallest French administrative territorial division.

COMMUNE (Sweden)   The basic unit of local government.

DEPARTMENT   Administrative sub-division of France.

DESSIATIN (DESYATIN)   Russian measure of land, 2·7 acres or 1·09 hectares (*q.v.*)·

DEVISEN   Claims, such as bills and cheques, on foreign countries in foreign currency, i.e. a form of foreign exchange holdings.

DUMA   The Russian Parliament in the Tsarist period.

GESTAPO   Geheime Staatspolizei, secret state police, developed as a dreaded instrument for suppressing opposition by the Nazi Government.

GUBERNIA   Russian administrative province.

HECTARE   Metric measure of surface, equals 100 Are or 2·47 acres.

KOLKHOZ (pl. KOLKHOZES, KOLKHOSI)   Collective farm. The most common is the *artel*, but also includes *kommuna* and *toz* (*q.v.*).

KOMMUNA   Commune. The most complete collective farm in which there was no private property; all land was worked collectively and its produce shared. Sometimes included collective eating and living. Although communes were known before collectivization they were few, and were rarely introduced after 1928.

KULAK (pl. KULAKI)   Rich peasant, employing others.

LAND CENTRAL GOVERNMENT   The Government of the individual German states within the *Reich* or empire.

MENSHEVIKS   The 'minority' group within the Russian Social Democratic Workers' Party. The 'majority' were the Bolsheviks.

MÉTAYER   One who farms under the share-cropping system, under which

616

the farmer (*métayer*) pays rent in kind while the owner furnishes stock and seed.

MORGEN   Measure of land, varying slightly in different parts of Germany. In Prussia it equalled 25·5 Are, or just under $\frac{2}{3}$ of an acre.

OBLAST   An administrative area comparable to the pre-revolutionary *Gubernia* (*q.v.*) See also *okrug, raion*.

OBSHCHESTVO   Society or commune, also company, as in joint-stock company (*see tovarishchestvo*).

OKRUG   Administrative area, subdivided into regions (*oblast*) and further into districts (*raion*).

OTRUN   Farm with enclosed fields; where arable land belonging to the peasant household was enclosed into one or more plots but where the peasant dwelling and kitchen garden were separate from the arable.

POODS, POUD, PUD   Russian measure of weight, *c.* 36·1 lb or 16·38 kilogramme.

RAION   District (*see okrug, oblast*).

SEREDNYAK (pl. SEREDNIAKI)   Middle peasant or 'average' peasant Self-sufficient but without hiring labour. Regarded as the majority of the peasantry upon collectivization.

SOCIALIST REVOLUTIONARIES   The traditional party of the peasant revolution. The party split into SR (left) and SR (right). The former moved closer towards the Bolsheviks, before their suppression.

SYNDICATE   Trade Union.

TOVARISHCHESTVO   Association, looser than *artel*, also company or partnership in a business sense (*see obshchestvo*).

TOZ   The loosest form of collective farm, amounting to little more than a marketing co-operative.

TREUHÄNDER DER ARBEIT   Trustees of labour: officials created by the Nazi Government by decree on 19 May 1933 with powers of compulsory arbitration in labour disputes. They were responsible for maintaining industrial peace and had some influence on the drafting of labour and welfare legislation.

UEZD   Former Russian region, comparable to the *okrug*.

VOLKSGENOSSEN   Literally: fellow nationals. A word used by Nazi spokesmen to designate the German people. Both halves of the word have emotive overtones: 'Volk' recalls the common and popular heritage, and 'Genosse', i.e. comrade, the form of address among trade unionists and Socialist parties.

VOLOST   Former Russian district comparable to the *raion*.

ZEMSTVO   Russian district or provincial assembly.

Index

Index